05/07

UNIVERSITY OF WOLVERHAMPTON

Harrison Learning Centre
City Campus
University of Wolverhampton
St Peter's Square
Wolverhampton WV1 1RH
Telephone: 0845 408 1631

2 7 DEC 2013

KT-443-491

Telephone Renewals: 01902 321333 or 0845 408 1631
Please RETURN this item on or before the last date shown above.
Fines will be charged if items are returned late.
See tariff of fines displayed at the Counter. (L2)

WITHDRAWN

Organizational Behavior
A Diagnostic Approach

Seventh Edition

Organizational Behavior
A Diagnostic Approach

Seventh Edition

Judith R. Gordon
Carroll School of Management
Boston College

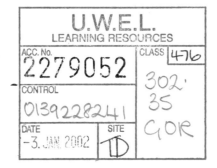

Prentice
Hall

Upper Saddle River, NJ 07458

Library of Congress Cataloging-in-Publication Data

Gordon, Judith R.
   Organizational behavior: a diagnostic approach / Judith R. Gordon.—7th ed.
      p. cm
   Includes bibliographical references.
   ISBN 0-13-032847-2
   1. Organizational behavior. I. Title
   HD58.7 .G67 2001
   658.3—dc21

                                                                    00-069872

Acquisitions Editor: Melissa Steffens
VP/Editor-in-Chief: Jeff Shelstad
Assistant Editor: Jessica Sabloff
Media Project Manager: Michele Faranda
Marketing Manager: Shannon Moore
Managing Editor (Production): Judy Leale
Production Editor: Theresa Festa
Production Assistant: Dianne Falcone
Permissions Coordinator: Suzanne Grappi
Associate Director, Manufacturing: Vincent Scelta
Production Manager: Arnold Vila
Manufacturing Buyer: Diane Peirano
Designer Manager: Patricia Smythe
Designer: Steven Frim
Interior Design: Carlisle Communications, Ltd.
Cover Design: Donna Wickes
Cover Illustration/Photo: Diana Ong
Illustrator (Interior): Carlisle Communications, Ltd.
Associate Director, Multimedia Production: Karen Goldsmith
Manager, Print Production: Christy Mahon
Composition: Carlisle Communications, Ltd.
Full-Service Project Management: Carlisle Communications, Ltd.
Printer/Binder: Courier/Westford

Credits and acknowledgments borrowed from other sources and reproduced, with permission, in this textbook appear on appropriate page within.

Prentice
Hall

10 9 8 7 6 5 4 3 2 1
ISBN 0-13-032847-2

*To Steve, Brian, Laurie, Michael, and our new son-in-law Steve
With much love and appreciation*

Brief Contents

Contents

■ PART III   Groups and Teams
in Organizations   176

Chapter 6   *Creating High-Performing Work Groups
and Teams*   **176**

Chapter 7   *Improving Communication*   **212**

Preface

Managers today face an extremely unpredictable, dynamic environment as they struggle to compete in the global marketplace. Dot-com companies have changed the face of business, giving rise to overnight successes and equally quick failures. Managers must have a repertoire of skills and experiences to help them manage today's workforce in the dot-com, global workplace. The seventh edition of *Organizational Behavior: A Diagnostic Approach* helps managers develop the knowledge and abilities to effectively lead their organizations in the 21st century. This book includes extensive examples of real-world organizational situations in which managers have dealt with the challenges of the new millennium.

▌ CONTENT UPDATES

The seventh edition incorporates the latest thinking about individuals, groups and teams, and organizations. Note particularly expanded or new coverage in the following areas:

- Additional competencies required by managers (chapter 1)
- Organizations of the new millennium (chapter 1)
- Key forces that shape industry (chapter 1)
- Women, minorities, older, and physically-challenged workers (chapter 3)
- Broadbanding and competency based pay systems (chapter 4)
- Electronic group decision making (chapter 5)
- Virtual teams (chapter 6)
- Multinational teams (chapter 6)
- Electronic communication (chapter 7)
- Types of cultures (chapter 11)
- Lattice organization (chapter 12)
- Virtual and networked structures (chapter 12)
- Managing in a dot-com, global workplace (all chapters)

▌ THE DIAGNOSTIC APPROACH

Similar to previous editions, the diagnostic approach provides the conceptual underpinning of this book. This approach encourages managers to describe situations completely, diagnose the organizational behavior found in a situation, prescribe the best practices or most appropriate behavior for given organizational situation, and then act effectively in those situations. Each chapter's introductory scenario describes a situation. Then the theories and concepts that help diagnose the events of the scenario as well as other organizational situations are presented. End-of-chapter activities and end-of-part cases give students the opportunity to practice their diagnostic and action skills.

SPECIAL FEATURES

The seventh edition has a number of special features:

- Current real-world examples integrated throughout the text.
- Learning objectives at the beginning of each chapter.
- A Manager's Preview at the beginning of each chapter that highlights key action areas and topics.
- A Summary at the end of each chapter.
- A Manager's Diagnostic Review at the end of each chapter that helps managers implement the key topics presented in the chapter.
- Thinking Critically about Organizational Behavior discussion questions to prompt critical thinking about chapter topics.
- End-of-chapter activities that allow students to practice the Diagnostic Approach and apply knowledge and skills from the chapter.
- A strong supplemental package.
- A comprehensive Web site.

ORGANIZATION OF THE BOOK

The seventh edition, like previous editions, begins with individuals in organizations, then looks at groups and teams, and finally considers the nature of the organization itself. The book begins in chapter 1 with an overview of issues faced by today's managers. It offers approaches for studying them and also describes the diagnostic approach.

Part two considers individual behavior. Chapter 2 examines perception, attribution, and learning in the workplace. Chapter 3 looks at individual characteristics of managers and workers, as well as workplace diversity, and career and work-life issues. Chapter 4 presents ways to motivate and reward employees. Chapter 5 investigates decision-making by individuals in organizations.

Part three examines group and team behavior. Chapter 6 discusses the nature of high-performing work groups and teams. Chapter 7 presents issues related to effective communication. Chapter 8 identifies the nature of effective leadership. Chapter 9 helps managers diagnose power and manage conflict and stress. Chapter 10 looks at the interactions between groups and ways of negotiating effectively.

Part four considers organizations in action. Chapter 11 talks about ways to build an effective and productive organizational culture. Chapters 12 and 13 explore various structural options. Chapter 14 examines the management of change in organizations.

Acknowledgments

I wish to thank many people for their support in developing the seventh edition of *Organizational Behavior: A Diagnostic Approach*. First, I want to thank the adopters and reviewers of previous editions of this book. I extend my special thanks to the reviewers who helped with this revision: Linda Gibson, Pacific Lutheran University; Pamela Pommerenke, Michigan State University; Hamid Akbari, Northeastern Illinois State University; and Timothy McCartney, NOVA Southeastern University.

Second, I want to thank the people at Prentice Hall who contributed to this book. My greatest appreciation for their help and support goes to Melissa Steffens, the acquisitions editor, and Theresa Festa, the production editor.

Third, I extend my appreciation to my colleagues at the Carroll School of Management of Boston College who have supported my writing efforts and have adopted my book in their class. I thank Helen Frame Peters, Dean of the Carroll School of Management, for her support. I extend special thanks to Jean Passavant, Mary Dunn, and Emily Peckham who have helped handle administrative and other details.

My greatest appreciation goes to my family. As always, I dedicate this book to them.

Judith R. Gordon
Newton, Massachusetts

Chapter 1

Setting the Stage

Learning Objectives

After completing Chapter 1, you will be able to

1. Identify the challenges faced by today's organizations.
2. Comment about the nature of today's workforce.
3. Describe managers' and employees' roles in today's organizations.
4. Define organizational behavior.
5. Discuss ways of collecting data about organizational behavior.
6. Discuss ways of conducting research about organizational behavior.
7. Identify the major historical ways of thinking about organizational behavior.
8. Describe the four steps in the diagnostic approach.

A Manager's Preview

Describe . . . Diagnose . . . Prescribe . . . Act

- Handle the challenges faced by today's organizations.
- Deal with today's workforce.
- Demonstrate the competencies needed by effective managers.
- Understand the importance of effective organizational behavior.
- Systematically describe and study organizational behavior.
- Apply the four-step diagnostic approach.

Web Masters: Managers in Dot-Com Companies

Jeffrey P. Bezos, CEO of Amazon.com, has set the dot-com world on its ear by leading the remarkable start-up and now bellwether venture. Bezos has orchestrated Amazon's high-risk strategy to make it the top e-retailer, with a product line that extends from its original books to videos, toys and games, and even health and beauty products. The company has expanded from a national electronic bookstore to a global electronic retailer. Bezos has built an online customer database that other e-retailers pay big dollars to Amazon to reach. Although Amazon's stock value had climbed steadily since its founding, recent questions about its cash flow and high debt may have contributed to a decline in the company's stock price and concern about its long-term viability.

Meg Whitman, CEO of eBay, has helped pioneer the online auction and has successfully beaten back competitors and kept eBay on top. Although some believe that Whitman was in the right place at the right time when she joined eBay, others attribute her success to her ability to make decisions quickly and her comfort with change. She has also focused on rigorous financial control and has led eBay to profitability while growing aggressively. She also imposed control on eBay's free-form environment and increasingly geared the site to big sellers. Whitman has charmed eBay's customers and welcomed their feedback, keeping them loyal even when a major technical problem shut down the site for 24 hours, a lifetime for an online business. Whitman is now focusing on global expansion, with one site already in Germany. She is trying to increase revenues outside the United States from 10 to 50 percent in the next two years.

Steven M. Case, CEO of America Online (AOL), brought the Internet to more than 25 million consumers through AOL's easy-to-use dial-up online services. Beginning as a small, proprietary service, AOL now services more than 21 million subscribers, making it an Internet heavyweight. Most recently, Case has led his company into a $183 billion takeover of media giant Time Warner, turning AOL into an all-media powerhouse. Case faces the challenge of blending the two corporate cultures so that the combined company can take advantage of its strong media presence. He continues to look for ways to bring consumers what they want, often before they know what they want. Case has partnered with many new start-ups, making AOL one of the biggest stakeholders in the Internet economy.[1]

How do these three Web masters manage their companies in the dot-com, global workplace? Are they effective? In this book, we investigate the way managers such as Bezos, Whitman, and Case handle the challenges they face in today's organizations. In this chapter, we first examine the nature of these twenty-first-century organizations. Then we investigate the key forces that shape industry. Next we look at the workforce in today's organizations. Then we define organizational behavior as the actions and attitudes of people in organizations, and look at ways to systematically study organizations and organizational behavior. We next investigate the ways organizations have evolved over time and consider the implications of this development for understanding organizational behavior today. Finally, we introduce the diagnostic approach and explore how it can help managers understand and handle the challenges they face.

❙ ORGANIZATIONS OF THE NEW MILLENNIUM

Managers such as Bezos, Whitman, and Case work in a dynamic and unpredictable environment. They have led the dot-com revolution, which has resulted in hundreds of thousands of new start-ups, instant successes and instant failures, and whirlwind introductions of new technology. Napster, a company threatened with extinction because of its alleged copyright infringement, typifies some of the new companies that have used the technological revolution to try to attain a competitive advantage. Napster uses a technology called peer-to-peer file sharing that lets people trade computer files, including music files, with each other over the Internet. While the particular service it provides has encountered major legal challenges, the possibility of using such technology for other products and services could further revolutionize e-commerce businesses.[2]

A shift in the nature of modern organizations has occurred. While the more traditional and long-standing industries—such as heavy manufacturing, education, health care, and government—still exist and have a significant impact on employment, new types of organizations, such as high-technology and dot-com companies, have begun to dominate the industrial landscape. For example, Microsoft has replaced General Motors as a focus of attention. Many graduates of major business schools now seek opportunities in dot-com or other high-technology companies rather than in investment or consulting firms, the previous "hot" employers, although the failures of many dot-com companies have tempered this interest.

Dot-Com Companies

The industrial landscape has changed dramatically with the introduction of myriads of start-ups, dubbed "dot-com companies," that typically rely on an e-commerce product and venture capital to support them. Often started by relatively young, technically savvy entrepreneurs, they have begun to transform the global marketplace. Keen.com pays KeenSpeakers, people who sign up as experts on a topic, to give advice to customers. Customers desiring information click on the listing of an expert, who then calls them and provides advice for a per-minute fee.[3] Well-known companies, such as Amazon.com, have prospered, even without making a profit. Others have been less successful and, after an initial burst of success and investor enthusiasm, have entered bankruptcy or been dissolved.

The environment faced by such companies creates challenges in fiscal management, product development, and staffing. Managing employees in dot-com companies requires the ability to deal with highly educated, highly motivated, generally younger employees with little real-world corporate experience. These employees require skilled managers and leaders who can deal with the fast-paced environment they face and help companies find ways to meet employee needs and customer requirements.

Customer Focus

All companies have learned that serving their customers well has important consequences for their profitability and overall performance. Executives encourage managers and employees to carefully determine their customers' needs and find ways to meet them. The success of Werner G. Seifert, CEO of the Deutsche Börse, for example, has been attributed to his understanding that the stock exchange customers want cheap and efficient trading.[4] Senior executives of John Deere participated in customer focus meetings. Once per quarter, these top executives met with customers in various parts of rural North America. The farmers' comments about topics ranging from production agriculture to the weather provided the executives with useful information for new product launches and follow-ups.[5] Mobil Oil responded to its customers' needs by introducing Speedpass, which lets customers get gas and pay without seeing an attendant.[6]

Successful managers also recognize that customers' preferences can change over time. Bezos of Amazon.com expanded the product line offered by the company. Particularly with the introduction of new technology, changing demographics, and changing economic conditions, companies must continuously reassess their customers' preferences and the way they respond to them. Customers' preferences also may vary in different countries, and organizations must respond to these differences. Savvy executives recognize such local differences and respond to them by offering products and services that meet their unique needs. For example, the Coca-Cola Company bottles Diet Coke in the United States but Coke Light in Europe because *diet* has unpleasant connotations for Europeans.

Increasingly, organizations such as Amazon, eBay, and AOL use information technology to help meet customers' needs. Wachovia Bank & Trust, with headquarters in Winston-Salem and Atlanta, uses its Continuous Relationship Management system to support relationship banking, a core feature of its service delivery for three decades. Profitable Relationship Optimization (PRO) software, for example, analyzes information about customers and then specifies a set of potential customers for specific bank products. Bank employees then contact targeted customers for a relationship-based dialogue and hopefully a sale of bank products.[7]

Team-Based Management

To respond quickly to the changing environment, workforce demands, and customer requirements, many companies have instituted team-based management. This approach reduces the traditional hierarchy and gives all employees more responsibility and accountability. Companies create various types of teams to perform work, generally giving workers significant autonomy. For example, at Meadville Medical Center in Meadville, Pennsylvania, surgical unit nurses worked to create a better flow of care for inpatients. They created a team for each to-be-admitted preoperative patient with the goals of providing uninterrupted nursing care, increasing the satisfaction of the patients and their families, and decreasing interruptions and the resulting frustration experienced by the staff. These teams included at least one RN and at least one LPN, each with clearly specified duties. They used beepers and established a code system so that other parts of the surgical unit could contact the team easily but with fewer telephone calls. The success of the team approach was evident in the improved quality of attention received by inpatients, the reduction in staff overtime, and improved communication with patients and their families.[8]

Interdisciplinary teams create the advantages of improved communication across functional areas. They also allow companies to bring diverse skills to complex projects. The Reflect.com team at Procter & Gamble, for example, grew from four to 25 people within a few months as they added employees from functional areas as needed. The team, which is developing custom beauty-care products using a patent-pending system for mass customization, has ultimate authority over its budget and other work activities.[9]

Teams in today's workplace are increasingly temporary, with workers joining for a specific project and then disbanding the team after completing the work. Employees at Eaton Corporation's Aeroquip Global Hose Division typically join a work team and a problem-solving team. One team formed, for example, to reduce the percentage of unusable hose by 52 percent, to 2.5 percent of sales. The division's quality administrator challenged the team to reduce the percentage still further, to 2 percent, offering to let them shave his head if they succeeded. The team reached 1.9 percent after 18 months and gave their supervisor his haircut. The factory held a celebration, including steak cookouts for its employees.[10]

Many companies now reward employees for acquiring new skills that contribute to their ability to work on a team and accomplish their organization's goals, rather than for merely moving up the organization's hierarchy. Members of a materials/purchasing team of the Large Systems Group of Exide Electronics, a North Carolina manufacturer of uninterruptible power systems, have become a close-knit group, learned each others' responsibilities, and covered for and assisted each other as needed. Similar to members of other teams in this and other organizations, the employees share ideas for improvement and challenge themselves to continuously improve.[11]

New Forms for Old Businesses

The changing environment affects not only start-ups and e-commerce businesses, but existing organizations in the profit and not-for-profit sectors. These companies have had to make significant changes to compete effectively. Extensive and rapid communication has become a key to effective organizational functioning. Executives have encouraged managers and employees at all levels of their organizations to better respond to customers' demands. Companies have introduced flexible organization structures to support closer contact with the customers, increase the company's speed in responding to change, and take advantage of technological advances. While the organization of the twentieth century could be characterized as a domestic pyramid with an internal focus and structured management style, the twenty-first century organization is more typically a global network with an external focus and a flexible style.[12] For example, Cisco Systems is a networked organization that uses the Web to conduct almost all administrative functions.[13]

Horizontal organizations, such as those created by Ford Motor Company and General Electric, form groupings around customer needs and work processes rather than functions.[14] Modular organizations outsource nonvital functions while retaining control; they use information systems to bind loosely coupled parts of the organization.[15] Virtual companies include temporary networks of independent companies that share skills, reduce costs, and jointly access markets. They quickly join to exploit rapidly changing opportunities, and then disband equally quickly.[16] Barrier-free structures replace traditional job roles with more fluid and ill-defined tasks and roles.[17]

Companies that fail to respond to changes in the environment and retain their old, stodgy, bureaucratic structures experience competitive difficulties. Matsushita Electric, for example, has resisted the type of corporate restructuring that has typified many U.S. and European firms. With its 282,000 employees in 160 factories, this former superstar company is viewed by many as bloated and demoralized. So far, executives at Matsushita have been unwilling to make the hard decisions that will involve changing their suppliers, reducing the number of middle managers, leaving unprofitable industries and eliminating unprofitable products, and spinning off divisions that can perform better independently.[18]

▌ FORCES THAT SHAPE INDUSTRY

Even well-managed companies can fail as a result of unexpected events or a few bad decisions. Managers must expect that constant change will always impact their jobs. Whitman is moving eBay into the European market, and Case is focusing on the Time Warner merger. Although managing effectively involves taking risks, meeting significant challenges, and even facing professional dangers, excellent managers can increase the likelihood of a company's success by understanding the challenges organizations today face:

- Managers must learn about, implement, and adapt to advances in technology that affect business.
- Managers operate in a global arena and must meet the challenges of global competitiveness.
- Managers must recognize the importance of managing knowledge about products, services, customers, the workforce, and the environment in the new organizational world.
- Managers must behave ethically in organizations that have increased their concern for ethics in business dealings.

Technology and the Dot-Com World

Significant advances in information technology, including both computer software and hardware and particularly the Internet, have reshaped the workplace. For example, Finest-Wine.com provides online customer service. Prior to installing its new customer-service software, Finest-Wine.com had overstuffed voice-mail boxes filled with messages that were never answered, handled letters through a cumbersome manual response process, and took much too long to answer e-mail. The new system, while still not preferable to an immediate personal telephone response from employees, has significantly improved customer service. The Web master uses HumanClick to track shoppers and eliminate customers who seem to be browsing rather than buying the company's products. His ability to identify the most likely customers and use a small, white chat window to begin a conversation and start a sale has contributed to the company's increased sales.[19]

Now people can work from remote locations, allowing them more job flexibility. Organizations have reengineered their work processes, beginning virtually at ground zero and reconstructing tasks and their interactions in the best way. They have automated the sales process, work flow and document management, manufacturing, and design. The virtual corporation, in which individuals or even subsidiaries are connected through computer terminals, has become a reality. General Life Insurance Company of Edwardsville, Illinois, a 15-employee direct insurer, relies on efficient and automated products to service its customers. The company uses the Web to post cases for possible reinsurers who, after examining the cases and related documents, can offer a proposal for servicing them. General Life then chooses the best proposal.[20] AgInfoLink, another virtually run company, tracks beef along the supply chain from the ranch to the refrigerator. The company's employees span a wide geographical area, including Australia, Argentina, Canada, Mexico, and the United States, and so communicate primarily electronically.[21]

Companies that have downsized or rightsized by replacing humans with computers sometimes find that they lack enough employees to do the job well. The remaining employees feel burned out, which results in lowered productivity. Carefully diagnosing the number and types of employees required to accomplish the organization's goals is critical.

Managers must understand technological advances and have the skills to choose appropriate information technology and use it for performing work and accomplishing organizational goals. Zara, a Spanish clothing retailer, relies on technology to support its pioneering quick, customer-made retailing. By integrating its manufacturing and design systems, Zara can offer designer clothing at a moderate price. The company relies on computer information systems to link its stores to corporate headquarters, enabling it to monitor sales and customer requests, as well as to decide what types of clothing to produce. Zara has new designs in stores almost twice a week rather than the typical every six weeks.[22]

Globalization and Organizations of the Twenty-First Century

Managers function in a global marketplace where businesses deal within and across national boundaries. Big Five accounting firms have offices worldwide; Fortune 500 companies often have manufacturing and sales offices worldwide; e-commerce easily uses the Web to deal globally. Charis Gent, the CEO of Britain's Vodafone Air-Touch, notes that the exciting part of his business is creating a global powerhouse through its sales of global telephony.[23] The permeable boundaries of the European Union have made employment in a unified Europe much easier for young workers. Employees have no travel or work restrictions, allowing them to move among countries easily and frequently.[24]

Continuous change in economic circumstances, rapid technological advances, and dramatic upheavals in the political arena present hurdles to conducting business globally. Downsizing has created anxiety among workers that organizations often find difficult to remove. Ongoing changes in the European Union and in the balance of power in Asia have caused companies to develop new strategies for dealing with a changing economy. Managers think more creatively about where to locate operations and who will staff those operations to take greatest advantage of lower labor costs. The availability of lower-cost labor in other countries has caused organizations to close manufacturing facilities in the United States and seek low-cost solutions in Mexico, China, and Indonesia. Even Japanese corporations have been shifting production overseas faster than before in response to the high value of the yen, a maturing economy, and the attraction of the global marketplace.[25] Yet, locating businesses in these and other countries can pose major challenges to managers. Panamerica Beverages, Inc., Latin America's largest Coca-Cola bottler and distributor, has successfully combined access to capital with knowledge of local customs to weather economic crises and political interference and become a successful competitor.[26]

Managers also need to question their old assumptions about how people in different geographical locations work together. For example, the widespread availability of electronic technology has eased communication between employees located at geographically distant sites. A physician in Boston can read an X-ray of a patient in a small rural town in Oklahoma or India. A consultant in London can access information from other consultants in the same firm who are located in Los Angeles, creating a powerful virtual team. Although easy long-distance communication can bridge geographical distance, managers must ensure that their employees can work together effectively and accomplish the organization's goals.

Knowledge Management

Managing the human resources of organizations has posed interesting and important challenges to managers in the new millennium. In particular, the changing demographics have resulted in a new cadre of professional, skilled workers, often known as *knowledge workers*. Intellectual assets have become the source of competitive advantage for many organizations, particularly those providing legal, biotechnological, financial, general consulting, or other services. Knowledge workers have become a mainstay of computer, health care, and communications organizations in the information sector of the economy. These well-educated employees perform nonroutine work and make key decisions in their organizations.

Knowledge management refers to the business practices and technologies that help an organization capture its employees' collective expertise to obtain maximum competitive advantage and generate revenue from its internal knowledge.[27] Knowledge management uses technology to support the collection and sharing of workers' knowledge; it also promotes collaboration and facilitates access to information.[28] For example, Buckman Laboratories International, a chemical manufacturer, introduced knowledge management systems in the 1980s. Now it uses the company's intranet to give employees access to engineering and product data and even creates virtual teams to solve customer problems.[29]

Some companies have chief knowledge officers, who are responsible for overseeing knowledge management systems in their organization. They help locate the knowledge in their companies and create systems to collect, access, and distribute it.[30] Chief knowledge officers design knowledge-based systems, directories of information, and knowledge-intensive management practices. They encourage company executives to invest in information technology to support the sharing of knowledge. They also help create social environments that facilitate the sharing of knowledge by bringing together communities of employees with common interests who may not frequently interact.[31]

Some companies establish centers of excellence as a way of harnessing the expertise in the company. Three types of such centers include:

- **charismatic centers,** where one or more individuals is internationally recognized for her knowledge;
- **focused centers,** where excellence is built around a single area of knowledge, such as direct marketing; and
- **virtual centers,** where the key individuals work in different cities and primarily use electronic communication to interact.

Andersen Consulting, for example, has created a focused center of excellence in Windsor, United Kingdom, around a small group of consultants with the responsibility for building the company's capability in media technology. Such a center was created in areas of strategic importance to the firm. It comprised a small number of people who had leading-edge knowledge in the field. The center's role was to transfer those employees' leading-edge knowledge to other parts of the organization while simultaneously building their knowledge base.[32]

Both blue- and white-collar employees can become knowledge employees and be innovative in their organizations.[33] Shell has established knowledge communities of employees. A group of safety and reliability engineers, for example, shares information on best practices at 11 U.S. refineries.[34] Managing these workers can require different skills from managers. In particular, managers need to focus on coaching and empowering them. Managers also need to understand the changing culture prompted by the increase in knowledge workers: Knowledgeable individuals hold power, leadership becomes critical, shared values replaced a control mentality, and risk management dominates over bureaucracy.[35]

Many organizations rely on computer technology to share knowledge among their global workforce. BT Laboratories, for example, developed a knowledge management network that helps spread information about technology trends and research and development throughout the company. Knowledge management in this case involves collecting, analyzing, and disseminating information using an intranet and groupware (see Chapter 7).[36]

Ethics in Action

Legal requirements mandate certain types of ethical behavior. For example, in 1996, U.S. businesses paid the federal government more than $1.3 billion in fines and assessments.[37] In addition, companies need to avoid conflicts of interest and unlawful competitive activity. Consider the Venture Law Group, a 90-lawyer professional services group. This company takes a financial stake in companies its attorneys have helped to launch. The company has turned small investments of less than $50,000 into multimillion-dollar gains. Are such deals unethical? Although they seem to border on conflict of interest, the former head of the American Bar Association ethics committee noted that such deals are not unethical if the client agrees to them.[38]

Equally important, citizens generally agree that organizations have a social responsibility to help sustain a high quality of life. Valero Energy, a San Antonio company with about 3,000 employees, donated $5,000 cash to each of three Valero employees displaced by torrential floods in Texas and sent teams of workers to clean up flood debris. All employees donate one percent of their income to United Way's Care Share program, and Valero adds 50 cents for every dollar donated.[39]

Yet, the pressures of business today and the lack of clear organizational values may contribute to an increase in unethical behavior in organizations. To combat this, businesses worldwide have established codes of conduct, used ombudspersons to resolve ethical issues, and introduced hotlines to support employee concerns about ethical behavior.[40] Companies and professional organizations have also instituted training programs to help employees act more ethically in the workplace. The Securities Industry Association's Institutional Ethics Program offers case materials for classroom instruction by a firm's in-house training or compliance personnel.[41]

Managers, too, develop a personal approach to making ethical decisions. Often they face two difficult alternatives. Consider the problem faced by Robert Harnett, a product manager in a dot-com company. After learning that a product does not live up to its claims, the company's president has told Harnett that any announcement about the deficiencies will send the company into bankruptcy and, likely, extinction. What should Harnett do?

Managers such as Harnett may make decisions according to criteria such as the following:[42]

- what feels comfortable in this situation;
- balancing the needs of all parties concerned;
- what is morally just or right;
- what has been done in similar situations;
- what is likely to benefit a person's career; or
- the company's written policy.

What would you do if you were Harnett? What rules-of-thumb do you use in making ethical decisions?

Doing business internationally may add a new dimension to situations like Harnett faced and complicate the notion of ethical action. Cultural differences in the meaning of *bribery*, for example, highlight problems in setting ethical standards. In China, *guanxi*, or the tradition of favoring friends in business, is legal, while in the United States some may view it as unethical in certain situations.[43] In addition, Chinese merchants regularly sell counterfeit products, such as Gillette razor blades or pirated CDs, at a fraction of the cost of the original.[44] The variety of standards espoused by international law further reflects the complexity of the ethical arena. For example, General Electric, Motorola, and Levi Strauss give local managers significant responsibility for making ethical decisions that fit with corporate policy.[45]

▍TODAY'S WORKFORCE

Today's organizations employ a more educated, diverse, and empowered workforce. While these characteristics help organizations to better meet the challenges just described, attracting and retaining talented employees can provide further significant

FIGURE 1-1

The percentage of civilian labor force participation has changed over the past 25 years.

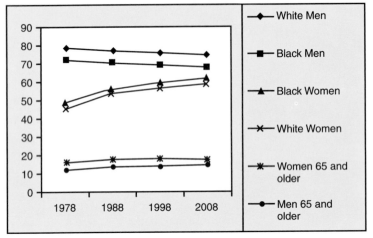

Source: Employment projections stats.bls.gov/emplt981.htm

challenges. Managers need to make sure that the right skills are positioned where needed regardless of the geographical location of employees, that they disseminate state-of-the-art knowledge and practices to all parts of the organization, and that they identify and develop talent globablly.[46] Dot-com companies, in particular, draw from a pool of highly educated, technically savvy workers who have many employment options. Companies such as Etensity, a Web consulting and services firm, offers unusual incentives, such as $400 per month in car payments and $10,000 toward a new home, and has a Fun Stuff event-planning team.[47]

Managers meet the challenges of a global workforce by encouraging people to work in many countries during their work lives. Employees can either move frequently among overseas assignments or travel frequently from a single geographical base. Managers can give them awareness-building assignments in which they develop cross-country sensitivity, create SWAT teams of highly mobile experts who are assigned to solve a specific problem or complete a specific project in a short time frame, or use virtual solutions.[48]

Changing Demographics

The U.S. workforce has become increasingly diverse. Not only do more women and minorities own small businesses,[49] but they also compose a larger percentage of the workforce. Figure 1-1 reflects the changing rates of labor force participation. For example, the percentage of white and African American women has increased significantly since 1978. So has the percentage of older U.S. residents who work. Some corporations see a new role for older workers as customers also age, in spite of a recent reduction in this group due to discrimination in the workplace.[50] Arizona Fast Foods is among those companies that seek older workers because they bring maturity and wisdom to their jobs.[51]

Progressive executives recognize that a diverse workforce creates a larger pool of talent. Diversity brings a wider variety of skills, experiences, and perspectives that enrich the work environment, improve customer service, and increase corporate performance. But managers often experience difficulty in getting members of a diverse workforce to work together in a way that guarantees that minorities feel comfortable and respected on the job. By law, managers have to offer equal opportunities to all individuals. Yet these legal protections have not been sufficient because people bring prejudices to the workplace and need to be made aware of differences and taught to respect them. Although GTE has a strong diversity program, the subtle stereotyping of Asians seems to have kept many Asians in entry-level technical positions, rather than being pushed toward higher-level management ones.[52] Getting minorities into decision-making positions is critical. Shoney's, after settling a class-action lawsuit brought by 20,000 employees in 1992, has made a significant and successful effort to create a multi-ethnic workplace.[53]

Even if a company hires a diverse workforce, managing diversity requires managers to develop a greater awareness of and sensitivity to differences. Unseen forces, such as prejudice or ignorance, can impair the effectiveness of the workers. Managers and nonmanagerial employees may need special training to prepare for the challenges of the multicultural and multinational workforce. The division of US WEST that creates yellow-page directories provides a three-day diversity awareness workshop that extends beyond merely focusing on differences stemming from racial or ethnic backgrounds to understanding differences among all its workers. Addressing the relationship between individual supervisors and subordinates and creating a culture that supports diversity are essential ingredients of such preparation.[54] Organizations may also need to introduce reward systems to show that they value diversity and can use it to successfully accomplish organizational goals.

Even countries other than the United States experience challenges because of a diverse workforce. Quebec, for example, must find ways to successfully employ both English-speaking and French-speaking citizens. Various European countries, such as England, France, and Germany, also have an increasingly diverse workforce as immigration becomes more common.

An Empowered Workforce and Changing Roles

As companies have faced more complex problems, relying mainly or only on managers to solve them has proven inadequate. At the same time, executives have given workers more responsibility and control over their work as a way of increasing their work satisfaction. Worker autonomy has combined with an emphasis on teamwork and collaboration. As a result, workers have become empowered to make decisions. Home Depot, for example, allows all employees to have decision-making authority. The company values what the salesperson on the floor says at least as much as what the district manager says because the salesperson is closest to the customers.[55]

The empowering of the workforce and the increasing use of self-managing teams in the workplace have blurred the distinctions between managers and their employees. Today workers often assume responsibilities typically entrusted solely to managers, such as planning, staffing, and rewarding employees. Managers have become more adept at using technology, often performing word processing, analysis, and communication roles formerly delegated to staff employees. Managers also have moved into a more coaching and counseling role. They create teams of workers, who often differ from the manager in gender, race, culture, language, values, and lifestyle. Managers must then manage this diverse workforce in an uncertain and changing environment.

The Contingent Workforce

Increasingly, the U.S. workforce includes a large number of people who do not have a long-term employment relationship with a single company, but work for a firm that brokers employees to other companies. The contingent workforce includes both contract employees and part-time workers who perform short-term and moderate-length assignments for companies that do not directly employ them.[56] For example, computer programmers may work for a company that places them in short-term assignments with their client companies. The programmers can control the number of hours they work by taking or refusing certain assignments.

Some employees prefer the more flexible work arrangements that part-time and contract employment offers. Even though contingent workers seem to earn less and receive health insurance less often than noncontingent workers,[57] they can pick jobs they like and better control the balance between work and leisure time.

Companies may use these contract employees because they can't find the workers they need through normal hiring processes in a tight labor market. Helmac Products Corp., a Michigan manufacturer of clothing-care household products, uses temporary workers to help meet the need for 20 percent more employees during the company's busy season. The company then hires the best of the temporary employees into the full-time labor force at the end of the season. According to the company's CEO, the policy of hiring temporary workers keeps the company from having to lay off employees during slow periods and reduces the uncertainty associated with recruiting.[58]

Also, with contract employees, companies get the precise skills they need only for the time they need them. Although wage rates may be higher for contract than permanent employees, the company does not have to pay the employees benefits because they do not work full-time for them. Increasingly, companies use suppliers of contingent workers like Manpower, Select Group, and Labor Ready to hire, train, and schedule employees on the company's site. These providers may offer benefits to their long-term employees. Some manufacturing companies even use contract executives. Richards Corporation, a former defense contractor, hired a contract executive when it bought a company that manufactures the appliances in aircraft galleys because he had the expertise their top executives lacked.[59]

Problems can exist when permanent and contingent employees work together. Jealousy over differential pay and benefits can negatively influence performance. In fact, several unions have taken cases to the National Labor Relations Board asking it to relax rules to making it easier for temporary workers to join the same unions permanent employees do.[60]

The increased flexibility that such contingent employees provide has become attractive to today's organizations. Companies believe that using fewer permanent employees gives them a strategic advantage because they can more carefully control labor costs, a large component of corporate performance. Companies can tap into a talented pool of workers as needed and so more readily adapt to fluctuating business cycles while ensuring stable employment for their core workers.[61] A recent Arthur Andersen survey, for example, indicated that 85 percent of firms in North America and Europe now outsource at least part of one essential business function.[62]

COMPETENCIES REQUIRED FOR MANAGERS

Effective managers like Bezos, Case, and Whitman need the following competencies to function effectively in the twenty-first century:

- **Adaptability.** Managers must recognize and respond to ongoing and unexpected changes, to alter plans and activities in a timely fashion, and to respond to new pressures and demands.
- **Knowledge about state-of-the-art practice.** Managers need a repertoire of techniques based on the best practices for handling organizational situations or addressing problems. They need to benchmark competitors to learn what policies, programs, and practices work in various situations.
- **Intercultural competencies.** To function in companies with locations outside the United States, managers need fluency in multiple languages, cross-cultural sensitivity, and the ability to adapt to new settings.
- **Information technology skills.** Managers must have strong technical skills so that they can readily learn new software, demonstrate facility with a range of hardware, diagnose information technology needs, and evaluate potential solutions.
- **Critical thinking skills.** Managers must have the problem-solving skills to allow them to apply the right techniques to a particular situation. The diagnostic approach fosters the development of critical thinking skills.
- **Creativity.** Managers need to demonstrate creativity in inventing new options or reconfiguring already-used approaches. Managerial creativity often involves bringing workers together in new ways to perform their jobs and accomplish their organization's goals.
- **Interpersonal effectiveness.** The increasing emphasis on teamwork and collaboration in organizations heightens the importance of managers possessing strong interpersonal skills. This includes the ability to effectively lead and communicate with a diverse workforce. In addition, managers can serve as mentors to other employees, as well as model the types of behaviors they desire from their subordinates.

WHAT IS ORGANIZATIONAL BEHAVIOR?

As noted earlier, we define *organizational behavior* as the actions and attitudes of people in organizations. The *field of organizational behavior (OB)* is the body of knowledge derived from the study of these actions and attitudes. Knowledge from the field of organizational behavior can help managers identify problems, determine how to correct them, and know whether the changes would make a difference. Such knowledge can help people better understand situations they face in the workplace and find ways to act differently so their performance and the organization's effectiveness increase.

As a field of study, organizational behavior includes a collection of separate theories and models, ways of thinking about particular people and events. It has its roots in the social science disciplines of psychology, sociology, anthropology, economics, and political science. Organizational behavior can help managers understand some of the complexity in organizations. It can also help them recognize that most organizational problems have several causes. Organizational behavior principles play an essential role in assessing and increasing organizational effectiveness, which is a central responsibility and focus for all managers.

▌ THE HISTORICAL BACKDROP

Managers can use the history of organizational behavior to enrich their understanding of organizational situations. In particular, applying the structural, human, and integrated perspectives, as described in the next sections, can help focus current diagnoses of organizational events. In the next section, we briefly recount the history of organizational theory by presenting selected perspectives, as shown in the timeline of Table 1-1. We can then apply these theories to diagnose organizational functioning in situations we currently face.

Structural Perspectives

The earliest theorists focused on the structuring and design of work and organizations. Scientific management, the classical school, and bureaucracy each addressed issues of structure in the organization.

Scientific Management.   Although some early economists, such as Adam Smith, talked about the division of labor,[63] the theorizing of Frederick W. Taylor, a foreman at the Bethlehem Steel Works in Bethlehem, Pennsylvania, helped management emerge as a field of study in the early twentieth century. Taylor's observations about industrial efficiency and *scientific management* offered prescriptions for the effective structure of organizations and the design of management activities in manufacturing organizations, which had become more common after 1900.

Taylor described management as a science, with managers and employees having clearly specified yet different responsibilities. Managers scientifically select and then train, teach, and develop their workers. Workers no longer choose their own work nor train themselves. Instead, managers and workers divide work and responsibility almost equally according to their skills. Managers also ensure that all work is done according to scientific principles.[64]

Taylor's principles applied best to increasing productivity on a relatively simple task. He showed that a pig-iron handler, who formerly loaded 12½ tons per day, loaded 47½ tons after applying scientific management principles.[65] Imagine, if you can, someone shoveling iron ore into a furnace. An observer, the equivalent of a modern-day industrial engineer, times how long it takes a worker to pick up a shovel, move it and the ore into a car, drop off the ore, and then prime the shovel for the next load. At the same time, another observer records the precise physical movements the worker made, such as whether he picked up the shovel with his right hand or his left (no women handled iron ore at the Bethlehem Steel Works), whether he switched hands before moving it, how far apart he placed his feet, and so on. Taylor used these data to help determine the physical positions that led to the fastest time for shoveling ore, and developed the science of shoveling.

Classical School.   Henri Fayol was a French manager whose works were translated into English in 1949. His views typified the *classical* view of administration,

TABLE 1-1

Historical Schools of Thought Incorporate Structural, Human, and Integrative Perspectives.

School	Decade	Perspective	Description
Scientific Management	1910s	Structural	Described management as a science, with employees having specific but different responsibilities; encouraged scientific selection, training and development of workers and the equal division of work between workers and management
Classical School	1920s	Structural	Listed the duties of a manager as planning, organizing, commanding employees, coordinating activities, and controlling performance; basic principles called for specialization of work, unity of command, scalar chain of command, and coordination of activities
Bureaucracy	1920s	Structural	Emphasized order, system, rationality, uniformity, and consistency in management; these attributes led to equitable treatment for all employees by management
Human Relations	1920s	Behavioral	Focused on the importance of the attitudes and feelings of workers; informal roles and norms influence performance
Group Dynamics	1940s	Behavioral	Encouraged individual participation in decision making; noted the impact of the work group on performance
Decision-Making Theory	1950s	Behavioral	Suggested individuals "satisfice" when they make decisions
Leadership	1950s	Behavioral	Stressed the importance of groups having both social and task leaders; differentiated between Theory X and Theory Y management
Systems Theory	1960s	Integrative	Represented an organization as an open system with inputs, transformations, output, and feedback; systems strive for equilibrium and experience equifinality
Contingency Theory	1980s	Integrative	Emphasized the fit between organizational processes and characteristics of the situation; called for fitting the organization's structure to various contingencies

which listed the duties of a manager as planning, organizing, commanding employees, coordinating activities, and controlling performance, as shown in Table 1-2.

Organizational theories used Fayol's principles to identify four features of organizations, which we still examine when diagnosing organizational behavior today:[66]

1. **Specialization.**   Organizations should arrange workers by logical groupings, such as place of work, product, expertise, or functional area.

TABLE 1-2

Fayol's Fourteen Principles of Management Illustrated the Classical Approach.

Principle	Description
Division of work	The specialization of work
Authority	The right to give orders and expect obedience
Discipline	Obedience and the outward marks of respect
Unity of command	Receipt of orders from only one superior
Unity of direction	One superior and one plan for a group of activities with the same objectives
Subordination of individual interests to general interests	A person's or group's interests should not supersede the organization's concerns
Remuneration	Fair payment for services
Centralization	Degree of consolidation of management functions
Scalar chain	Chain of superiors from the top authority to the lower ranks
Order	All materials and people in the appointed place
Equity	Equal (although not necessarily identical) treatment
Stability of tenure of personnel	Limited turnover of personnel
Initiative	Designing a plan and ensuring its success
Esprit de corps	Harmony and union among the employees

2. **Unity of command.**   Each organizational member has exactly one direct supervisor. For example, in most accounting firms, a partner supervises a manager who supervises a senior auditor who supervises other auditors.
3. **Chain of command.**   The chain of command specifies the reporting relationships in an organization and generally begins with the chief executive and extends to the least skilled employee.
4. **Coordination of activities.**   Managers use tools to ensure communication among specialized groups. The tools may range from formal written directives to informal corporate policies to electronic media.

Bureaucracy.   Max Weber was a German sociologist who studied European organizations in the first part of the twentieth century.[67] He described a *bureaucracy,* which he considered to be a basic form of organization. Although today bureaucracy conjures up an image of massive red tape, Weber saw its emphasis on order, system, rationality, and consistency as assets. He believed that these assets helped managers treat employees equitably, rather than arbitrarily.

Weber's principles of bureaucracy outlined the best structure of an organization:

■ Each employee in a bureaucracy has specified and official areas of responsibility that are assigned on the basis of competence and expertise.
■ Employees have only a single boss, and this results in an orderly system of supervision and subordination.

- Managers use written documents extensively in managing employees. Detailed employment manuals include corporate rules and regulations.

- Managers of offices, departments, or other groups of workers receive extensive training in their job responsibilites.

- Managers are expected to use rules that are consistent, complete, and learnable.

Behavioral Perspectives

Managers need to consider the human side of organizations in addition to the structural issues reflected in the scientific management, classical, and bureaucratic perspectives. The human relations, group dynamics, decision making theory, and leadership schools explicitly considered this human side of organizations.

Human Relations School.   The Western Electric Company, in conjunction with the National Academy of Sciences, performed five studies of various work groups at Western Electric's Hawthorne plant beginning in 1924.[68] The first study looked at the effects of lighting on the productivity of workers in different departments of the company. It examined the effects of certain illumination levels on work production. The researchers tested a lighting level of extreme brightness and then decreased the light until the work area was so dim that assembly material could hardly be seen. Do you think employee output increased, decreased, or remained at normal levels? Surprisingly, the workers maintained or even exceeded their normal output whether researchers increased or decreased the illumination.

Later studies tried to explain these results by introducing changes in the workplace, such as rest pauses, shorter working days and weeks, wage incentives, and supervisory change.[69] In observing and interviewing the employees, the researchers discovered that during the experiments the employees felt that someone paid attention to them, so their morale improved and they produced more. This so-called *Hawthorne Effect* offered the first dramatic indication that the attitudes and feelings of workers could significantly influence their productivity. In the final experiments of the Hawthorne series, the researchers noted the significance of the informal groups that workers develop among themselves.

Group Dynamics.   During World War II, Kurt Lewin, a social psychologist at the University of Iowa, studied barriers to change in households. His experiments showed that people who participated in discussions about a particular change, such as housewives reducing the amount of meat consumed in their households, more often made the changes than those who merely listened to others talk about them.[70]

Lewin's associates later applied these results to business settings.[71] For example, employees at the Harwood pajama plant in Marion, Virginia, learned new work methods more readily if they had the opportunity to discuss the methods and could influence how to apply them in their jobs.[72] Studies such as these led to a greatly expanded awareness of the impact of the work group and highlighted the relationship between organizational effectiveness and group formation, development, behavior, and attitudes.[73]

Decision-Making Theory.   Herbert Simon and James March introduced a different decision-making framework for understanding organizational behavior in the 1950s.[74] They emphasized that people work in rational organizations and thus behave rationally, though in a limited way. Individuals examine a subset of possible alternatives rather than all available options when making decisions. They *satisfice;* that is, they accept satisfactory or "good enough" choices, rather than insisting on optimal choices. Managers who understand this limitation can design a decision-making process that should result in effective outcomes.

Leadership.   The 1950s saw the beginning of concentrated research in the area of leadership. One series of studies described groups as having both task and social leaders.[75] The task leader helped the group achieve its goals by clarifying and summarizing member comments and focusing on the group's tasks. The social leader helped the group develop cohesiveness and collaborate better by encouraging member involvement.

Another set of leadership studies distinguished between Theory X and Theory Y managers.[76] Those who believe Theory X assume that workers have an inherent dislike of work, that they must be controlled and threatened with punishment to ensure adequate effort, and that they prefer to avoid responsibility. In contrast, managers who believe Theory Y assume and act as if people feel that work is as natural as play or rest, will work toward their objectives without outside control, and can learn to seek responsibility. Subsequent theories tried to specify what made leaders effective, with limited success.

Integrative Perspectives

Since the 1960s, organizational thought has stressed the integration of structural and behavioral theories and also considered external influences. It looks at the fit between the organization, its managers, its employees, and the situation. What this translates to is that there isn't one correct answer for every OB issue—rather, the best answer depends on many factors. This perspective is the foundation of the diagnostic approach presented in this book.

Systems Theory.   The general systems model, with roots in both the behavioral and natural sciences, incorporates ideas from both the structural and human perspectives. Systems theory represents an organization as an *open system,* which has the following characteristics:[77]

- **Every system is made up of a number of interrelated, interdependent, and interacting subsystems.** For example, production interacts with marketing, and marketing and production both interact with the human resources department.
- **Every system is open and dynamic.** The system continually interacts with the surrounding environment. It constantly receives new energy, called *inputs,* in the form of new resources (people, materials, and money), goals, or information from the environment.
- **Every system transforms inputs into outputs.** How would the system work in manufacturing a DVD player? We'd take metal pieces (inputs) and combine (transform) them to produce a working DVD player (output), as shown in Figure 1-2. Less tangible inputs, such as worker knowledge or information, are similarly transformed through processes such as decision making, leadership, or motivation into outputs such as performance, satisfaction, morale, turnover, or absenteeism.

FIGURE 1-2

Information about outputs can help modify inputs and transformation processes.

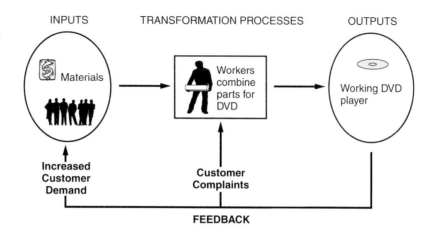

Every system seeks to maintain equilibrium. Organizations that receive new inputs or experience transformations seek stability. When they become unbalanced, such as when changes in the environment or organizational practices make current resources inadequate, the organizations attempt to return to the original or a different steady state. They use information about their outputs, called *feedback,* to modify their inputs or transformations to result in more desirable outcomes and equilibrium, as shown in Figure 1-2.

Every system has multiple purposes, objectives, and functions, some of which are in conflict. Various parts of an organization—for example, different departments, work groups, or even managers—may have different and even conflicting purposes, functions, and objectives. The marketing department might willingly make changes in product specifications to satisfy the customer, whereas production might want more stable specifications so they can ensure high-quality products at an acceptable cost.

Every system demonstrates equifinality. Organizations may employ a variety of means to achieve their desired objectives. No single structure or other transformation process results in a fixed set of inputs, outputs, and transformations. Using laptops at a customer's site might increase profitability for one company but not for another.

If a system does not adapt to changing circumstances, it will entropy. Failing to make appropriate changes in a system in response to new inputs will eventually result in the system's decay and demise.

Contingency Theory.   Like systems theory, contingency theory provides a more complete view of behavior. It also calls for a fit between organizational processes and the characteristics of the situation. Early contingency research looked at the fit between an organization's structure and its environment. One early study prescribed a mechanistic structure—a machinelike bureaucracy with a rigid hierarchy and chain of command—as the best structure for organizations functioning in a stable environment. The same study recommended an organic structure—a more flexible, less bureaucratic, less hierarchical structure—for organizations operating in a dynamic environment.[78]

Other research found that the organization's technology influences the type of structure the organization should develop: whether the technology focuses on producing a one-of-a-kind unit from start to finish, mass-producing products using an assembly line, or creating product from a continuous process, such as oil from a refinery.[79] A mechanistic type of organization fits best with a mass production technology (for example, manufacturing heavy equipment or processing insurance claims). A more organic form of organization responds best to a unit technology (such as manufacturing *objets d'art* or writing novels) or continuous process technology (such as chemical production). The basic premise of fitting behavior to the situation underlies the diagnostic approach described in this book.

▌THE DIAGNOSTIC APPROACH

How can a manager effectively meet tomorrow's challenges? The aim of this book is to develop your ability to *understand* organizational events and then to *act effectively* based on this understanding. The application of such knowledge and skill to a real situation is *diagnosis. Accurate diagnosis forms the basis for effective action.*

Although some managers rely on intuition to attack problems and resolve issues, the diagnostic approach is more effective. Why? It is a systematic approach to understanding complex situations and then changing behavior and attitudes to make organizations function better. Because events, behaviors, and attitudes typically have more than one cause, the more completely we understand the causes, the more appropriately we will act in organizational situations.

In this book, then, we will use a four-step diagnostic approach to help you meet the many managerial challenges awaiting you. The approach involves description, diagnosis, prescription, and action, as shown in Figure 1-3. Although you may find using this approach slow or cumbersome at first, over time you will begin to use it easily and automatically.

Description

Phase 1, *description,* is simply that: a reporting of concrete aspects or events in a specific situation without any attempt to explain the reasons for the events or to make inferences about a person's motives or purposes.

We can describe a number of concrete and observable occurrences at Amazon.com, eBay, and AOL. In analyzing these situations you might then specify any assumptions you are making about the events: For example, you might assume that the workers have a legitimate right to influence the way they are managed, that complaints signal the existence of a problem situation, or that effective managers respond to employees' complaints. As much as possible, you should test these assumptions to identify any that can be added to the list of facts.

People begin to understand organizational behavior by describing events, behaviors, and attitudes. How can they obtain accurate and timely information about situations they face? They might gather data by directly observing the situation, surveying the people involved, asking them questions in interviews, or looking at written documents. Each of these methods helps to accurately describe events, a first step in determining their causes and then acting on them. Together, these methods help validate our perceptions of the events, behaviors, and attitudes.

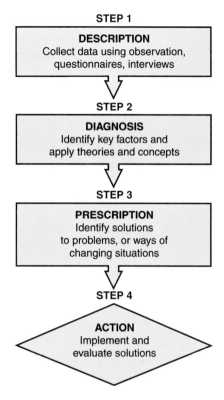

▌ FIGURE 1–3 ▌

The four-step diagnostic approach offers a systematic way of analyzing and then acting in organizational situations.

When people use direct observation, they describe concrete events they have seen. We might, for example, spend some time attending meetings and then describe what we see happening. We can use formal tools, such as checklists, to gather observations. For example, we can check off each time an employee asks his boss a question or gives directions to a subordinate. We can also collect observations informally. For example, we can watch company employees as they wait for an elevator, sit in the company lounge, or meet in the hallways. We can listen to their conversations to learn about their attitudes toward their supervisor, job, or organization.

Rather than relying on our view of events, we can write questions to learn about others' opinions. We might send a questionnaire to employees or customers of the Web companies to understand their attitudes about the company and its services or products. We could also interview organization members—that is, ask them a series of questions in person to explore in depth their attitudes and opinions. Managers often interview employees informally, chatting with them about their views of a particular situation.

Finally, we could gather data about past performance, work team behavior, or other aspects of individual, group, and organizational functioning from the firm's records, including annual reports, departmental evaluations, memoranda, or nonconfidential personnel files. Then we could analyze the content of these documents. A review of records, such as all internal memoranda or performance reviews, might further specify the nature of communication, the quality of supervision, or other possible reasons for the situation at a company.

The process of simple description is much more difficult than it looks. Sometimes it is not easy to separate facts from assumptions. Most of us don't have much practice in doing this. Yet, diagnosing and understanding a situation correctly depends on our having an accurate and relatively complete description of it. The better we can describe situations, the better we will understand them. So, throughout this book, you will be given opportunities to describe what you have read or seen.

Diagnosis

The next phase, *diagnosis,* attempts to explain the reasons for, or causes of, the behaviors and attitudes described. We diagnose when we first describe a situation, behavior, or attitude and then identify its components and causes. In the case of the Web companies described at the start of this chapter, for example, we must first identify the key elements of the situation. Bezos must deal with declining sales. Whitman is facing new global challenges. Case must handle the merger with Time Warner. Each of these situations might suggest problems. Sometimes symptoms, such as employee dissatisfaction, declining revenues, or increased costs, indicate a problem situation.

Second, we can identify several problems or potential causes of these symptomatic behaviors and attitudes. For example, a deficient reward system may affect employee performance. Ineffective communication may influence employee morale. Poor decision making may create inferior customer service.

In sum, the diagnostic stage involves four steps:

1. **Study a number of potentially relevant theories.**   You might, for example, review the various motivation theories presented in Chapter 4 and the communication theories in Chapter 7.
2. **Explain the situation with each theory in turn.**   You might use motivation and communication theory to explain the situation faced at the dot-com companies.
3. **Identify ways different theoretical perspectives might apply to the same situation.**   You might investigate how motivation, communication, and even leadership and organizational design theories complement each other and provide a richer explanation of the events at these companies.
4. **Check to make sure that you have applied all relevant theories.**   You can increase the accuracy of your diagnosis by doing this. Over time, you will learn better which theories to use.

Keep in mind that we can't understand all issues by applying *all* organizational behavior models and theories. An inappropriate reward system may help explain the situation in a company, but unsatisfactory career development may not. Looking at the negotiating process used by a CEO may offer new insights into the situation, but looking at her personality may not.

Diagnosing means being able to critically evaluate different perspectives and theories and determine whether they apply to each specific case. By examining the fit between the theories and the key aspects of each situation, you will identify the most likely causes of specific behaviors and attitudes. You will also determine how well different perspectives apply. Throughout the diagnosis, you should develop your own explanations for the events you describe.

Prescription

Phase 3, *prescription,* is the first part of translating diagnosis—or your understanding of a situation—into action. After identifying, reviewing, and evaluating the diagnosis, you can decide on a course of action. Managers propose one or more ways to correct each problem identified in the diagnosis phase. Action based on a strong diagnosis should be more effective than action based on very little understanding of the problem. Correcting defective communication, for instance, calls for different strategies than improving inefficient job design. Changing perceptions calls for different approaches than improving negotiations.

In the prescription phase, Bezos, Whitman, and Case might look for ways to improve their companies' performance. Prescriptions might include changing the organization's structure, hiring new managers, or changing job responsibilities. Because most problem situations have more than one solution, managers should begin the prescription phase by proposing multiple solutions to diagnosed problems.

You should consider as many reasonable, feasible, and practical alternative solutions to each problem as possible. Evaluate these alternatives and their effectiveness by using the relevant theories to predict the outcomes of various actions. Determine the costs and benefits of each alternative. Then select the alternative with the relatively lowest costs and highest benefits.

Action

In the final phase, *action,* we implement our proposed solutions. We test the solutions to see if they are feasible. Often the correct solution is impractical. We might agree, for example, that Whitman needs to reorganize eBay if it is to compete globally. But how does she actually do that? What pitfalls will she encounter in trying to translate prescriptions into reality?

Action might involve testing the prescription in a limited part of the organization. Or we might simulate the action we propose using facsimiles of the organization. Managers often use pilot programs to implement change in organizations in measured, observable ways. Top management might introduce a bonus program or a new performance evaluation form. They might provide extensive training throughout the organization. Experimentation often precedes a plan of effective action.

The action phase also includes a careful scrutiny of all people and systems in the organization as part of anticipating the impact of any changes. Managers need to assess possible resistance to change and plan ways to overcome it. Implementing staffing or policy changes might require new education programs. These programs might in turn call for new staff or financial resources. Thus, the effects of action may cascade through an organization. Managers then evaluate the actions implemented, starting the cycle once more. They describe the situation and then diagnose the reasons the changes succeeded or failed, offer new prescriptions, and once more act.

In this book, we apply the diagnostic approach to three types of behavior: individual, group, and organizational. We explore individual behavior in Part II of the text, group behavior in Part III, and organizational behavior in Part IV. Figure 1-4 shows the interrelationships among the various levels of organizational behavior, with the environment impinging at each level.

A comprehensive diagnosis of organizational behavior requires assessment of behavior at the individual, group, and organizational levels.

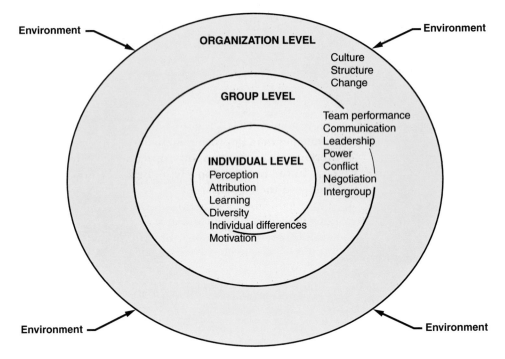

▌ Summary ▌

1. Organizations of the new millennium pose new and interesting challenges for managers and employees: the rise of dot-com companies, an increased focus on customer needs, the institution of team-based management, and the use of new forms for old businesses.

2. Key forces, including the widespread use of information technology, customer focus, globalization, knowledge management, and a concern for ethical behavior, shape industry.

3. Changing demographics, an empowerment of employees and changing roles, and contingent workers characterize today's workforce.

4. Managers require adaptability, knowledge of state-of-the-art practices, intercultural competencies, information-technology skills, critical thinking skills, creativity, and interpersonal effectiveness to function effectively in today's organizations.

5. Organizational behavior refers to the actions and attitudes of people in organizations. The field of organizational behavior is the study of these actions and attitudes and includes a collection of separate theories and models.

6. Structural perspectives, including scientific management, classical theory, and bureaucracy, focused on the structuring and design of work and organizations. Behavioral perspectives, including human relations, group dynamics, decision-making theory, and leadership schools, investigated worker satisfaction, leadership, and interpersonal relations. Integrative perspectives, including systems theory and contingency theory, examined both structural and interpersonal interactions.

7. The diagnostic approach, which includes the phases of description, diagnosis, prescription, and action, helps managers systematically diagnose the causes of events and then act.

8. Description involves specifying the major aspects or events in a specific situation; diagnosis attempts to explain the reasons for the behaviors and attitudes described; prescription involves identifying, reviewing, evaluating, and then deciding on a course of action; action is the implementation of the solutions proposed.

A Manager's Diagnostic Review

☐ Understand the challenges faced by organizations of the new millennium.
   - Is it a dot-com company?
   - How strong is the customer focus in the company?
   - Does the company use team-based management effectively?
   - Has the company successfully adopted new forms of operating?

☐ Respond effectively to the key forces that shape industry.
   - How well does the company utilize state-of-the-art technology?
   - How well does the company operate in the global arena?
   - Does the company manage its knowledge workers effectively?

☐ Deal with today's workforce.
   - How do the changing roles affect performance?
   - How do the changing demographics affect performance?

☐ Practice the competencies required for effective management.
   - What key skills and capabilities should managers have in the twenty-first century?

☐ Understand the importance of effective organizational behavior.
   - What organizational behavior affects individual, group, and organizational performance?

☐ Apply the four-step diagnostic approach.
   - Does the organization have effective mechanisms for collecting data about its functioning?
   - Do managers conduct systematic inquiry into organizational performance?

Visit the Gordon homepage on the Prentice Hall Web site at

http://www.prenhall.com/gordon

for recommended readings, additional activities, Internet exercises, updated information, and links to related Web sites.

▌ Thinking Critically About Organizational Behavior

1. What impact does the globalization of organizations have on managers?
2. How do flexible organizations better respond to customer requirements?
3. How can managers keep pace with changing information technology?
4. What ethical challenges do managers face in the workplace?
5. How do the changing demographics affect today's organizations?
6. What is a contingent workforce and why does it exist?
7. Why have managers empowered their workforce?
8. What competencies do managers need in today's organizations?
9. What is organizational behavior?
10. Why should managers collect data systematically or conduct research in organizations?
11. Why is the history of organizational behavior relevant to managers today?
12. Why does the diagnostic approach increase the effectiveness of organizational behavior?

ACTIVITY 1-1: THE DOT-COM START-UP

STEP 1: Read the following background information.

You have held a variety of positions in marketing, culminating with the vice presidency in a large conglomerate that sells foods and consumer goods. You have decided to take the "plunge" and get involved with the dot-com world. Currently, a small start-up has been interviewing you for the position of vice president of marketing. You think you can do the job in your sleep, but you know that the CEO will need to be convinced that you can make the transition from a Fortune 500 company to a dot-com business. As part of your preparation for the interview, you have decided to list the key issues you believe you will face in moving to the start-up.

STEP 2: Outline the key issues, particularly focusing on the ones you think the CEO will address. Then prepare a set of questions the CEO might ask you and the answers you would give.

STEP 3: Your instructor will direct you to participate in a role-play with the CEO.

STEP 4: Discussion. In small groups or with the entire class, as directed by your instructor, share your list of issues, questions, and answers. Then answer the following questions:

1. What are the challenges of moving into the dot-com environment?
2. What talents translate well into that environment? Which ones do not?

ACTIVITY 1-2: HAVE COMPANIES CHANGED?

STEP 1: Choose two organizations. Secure their most recent annual report and copies of their annual reports from 1980 and 1990.

STEP 2: Review each report and identify the three major issues the company faced in 1980, 1990, and currently.

STEP 3: Individually, in small groups, or with the entire class, compare and contrast the key issues at the three time periods. Then answer the following questions:

1. What were the major issues companies faced in 1980, 1990, and currently?
2. How have these issues changed over time?
3. What issues will they likely face in 2010 and 2020?

ACTIVITY 1–3: SHOULD COMPANIES USE CONTINGENT WORKERS?

STEP 1: Your instructor will assign you to teams that will debate either the pro or con side of the following issue:

Resolved: Companies should use contingent workers instead of hiring permanent workers for open positions.

STEP 2: Prepare your position.

STEP 3: Conduct the debate with the opposing team.

STEP 4: In small groups or with the entire class, discuss and answer the following questions:

1. Which side was more convincing?
2. What should organizations consider before deciding to rely on contingent workers?

ACTIVITY 1–4: THE STAFFING SHORTAGE PROBLEM

STEP 1: Read the following background information.

You are the director of human resources in a dot-com company that markets computer hardware and software products and consulting services using the Web. The company has grown from 50 employees to 200 in the past two years and plans to double its size again in the next two years. You are responsible for recruiting qualified employees for all types of positions in the company. Because of a strong labor market, you have not had success using traditional sources of employees. You need to develop a creative plan for dealing with the staff shortage. Your first task is to identify several new possibilities for recruiting the knowledge workers you need and then to assess their advantages and disadvantages.

STEP 2: List five possible sources of recruits; specify the advantages and disadvantages of each.

STEP 3: In small groups, share your lists. Then prepare a revised list that considers the options proposed by group members.

STEP 4: Discussion. In small groups or with the entire class, as directed by your instructor, share your memoranda. Then answer the following questions:

1. What options did you identify?
2. What are the advantages and disadvantages of each?

ACTIVITY 1–5: PLANNING FOR GOING GLOBAL

STEP 1: Read the following background information.

You are the assistant to the founder of e-resale.com, a start-up that markets used clothing in the United States. The company's sales have grown dramatically since its founding three years ago. Your boss believes it's time to expand the business globally. She has asked you to prepare a memorandum outlining the advantages and disadvantages of going global.

STEP 2: Outline the key points that you want to include in the memorandum.

STEP 3: In small groups, share your outlines. Then prepare a memorandum for the company's owner.

STEP 4: Discussion. In small groups or with the entire class, as directed by your instructor, share your memoranda. Then answer the following questions:

1. What are the advantages and disadvantages of going global?
2. What issues must a company consider before deciding to expand globally?

PART 1 CASES

Peninsular Insurance (A)

Patrick Wale stood in the conference room staring in amazement at the chairman, Tan Sri Ibrahim Nassan. Ibrahim Nassan, the titular head of Peninsular Insurance, had just taken charge of Wale's planning meeting with an interruption that Wale saw as an attempt to subvert his authority with his managers. By the looks on their faces, Wale surmised that his managers were just as surprised as he by such an overt power play. With the 1985 Malaysian economy in recession, and company revenues sliding, now was not the time to play politics. As his adrenalin began to flow, Wale was at a loss as to how to regain control of the meeting and, by implication, of his Malaysian insurance organization. As his mind raced, he thought, "All I know is that, whatever I do next, it's going to have to be played by the Malay rules: respect for elders and 'saving face.' The question is whether I can show one without losing the other."

BACKGROUND

Patrick Wale had arrived in Kuala Lumpur ("KL," capital of Malaysia) almost three years previously to oversee the merger of the wholly owned Malaysian subsidiary of New Zealand Insurance Corporation (NZI) with the Malaysian-majority-owned Peninsular Insurance. He should have been finished within the first 12 months. In fact, however, after the first two years, he had barely scratched the surface of a project that was becoming more Byzantine by the week.

Wale considered himself good at adapting and working with other cultures. His work for NZI had taken him to Nigeria, South Africa, India, and, in his last position as branch manager, to Hong Kong, NZI's largest branch in Asia ($8 million in annual sales). (See Exhibit 1 for a profile of Wale and other key executives.)

Wale had felt at home in the free-wheeling, business-first culture of Hong Kong. The absence of political barriers allowed him to concentrate on "getting on with business" without the worry of government regulations. But when the NZI general manager of International Operations called to offer him the position of chief executive officer of the Malaysian joint venture, Wale jumped at the opportunity.

The combination of NZI's $12 million subsidiary with its 49 percent owned, $4 million Peninsular would be double the size of the Hong Kong division in staff and sales. The task was an unusual one, because Wale would actually be wearing two hats—as the head of the NZI subsidiary reporting to the home office in New Zealand, and as general manager of Peninsular reporting to the local board. That situation would change, however, when the merger went through and the combined ($16 million) entity would be 74% owned by NZI and working under a single management.

NZI, LTD

"New Zealanders pride themselves on their self-reliance . . . it's called kiwi ingenuity."[1]

NZI was a diversified financial-services company based in Auckland, New Zealand. One of the country's largest companies, NZI was formed in 1981 from the merger of New Zealand Insurance (founded 1859) and South British Insurance Company (founded 1872). The result was a multinational corporation operating in 24 countries through hundreds of offices.

Revenues of the merged company had reached $630 million in 1982, with a reported net-income of $28 million. The international divisions of NZI's General Insurance Group contributed 35 percent of divisional income. (See Exhibit 2 on page 32 for organization of NZI.) Each of the seven divisions of the company was run as a profit center.

NZI had concentrated its foreign business in the Pacific Rim and Africa and adopted a strategy of growth through local offices in order to gain a balance in both operations and the product mix offered by the company.

This case was prepared by James M. Berger, Darden '92, under the supervision of Professor L. J. Bourgeois. Copyright © 1992 Darden Graduate Business School Foundation, Charlottesville, VA. Rev. 2/98.

---

[1]Annemarie Orange, Darden 1992, native of New Zealand.

Patrick Wale

Age 42

After dropping out of high school in New Zealand, 16-year-old Patrick Wale began work in 1961 as an office boy with NZI. He studied in night school for three years to complete the insurance exams, and began to move up the corporate hierarchy. In 1966, he was offered a position with the overseas staff.

A self-described "adventurer," Wale accepted transfers to offices around the world, including Nigeria, India, South Africa, and Hong Kong. Each move improved his position within the corporation and finally led to his present appointment as CEO of the NZI joint venture with a Malaysian partner.

Married in 1969, Wale met his wife in Calcutta, where she was working for the British High Commission. Their two children, a 14-year-old son and 13-year-old daughter, had been recently sent to boarding schools in England.

Nigel Fisher

Age 57

Fisher had been employed by NZI since 1942; he was appointed to a senior position with the Home Office in 1960 after a series of international transfers. His progress within the company appeared stalled after the 1981 merger produced a surfeit of middle managers, but he was appointed general manager of the International group in 1985 after its previous two years of results fell well below corporate expectations for the Asian operations. Fisher was due to retire in June of 1986.

Fisher was described by a colleague as possessing strong analytical but weak interpersonal skills and having a "dour" personality.

Tan Sri Haji Ibrahim Nassan

Age 73

Tan Sri Haji Ibrahim Nassan Bin Haji Ibrahim Siddiq[a] (his full name) had had a prominent civil-servant career with the Malaysian government culminating as Secretary General of Internal Affairs, responsible for the Police, Justice, and Immigration. Retired at age 55, he was quickly invited to sit on several company boards and had been Peninsular Insurance's chairman since 1967. He was required to retire from all but Peninsular's board at age 70.

Nassan was known as a man who paid strong attention to detail and required a high level of protocol at all times. He was married with five sons.

[a]A convention in Malaysian names and titles conveyed social and political rank, lineage, and Muslim pilgrimage: "Datuk" was a title conveyed on men of accomplishment. "Tan Sri" was a higher honor, fewer in number. It was given by the Sultan, usually for public servants of high rank. "Tun" was the highest honor possible in Malaysia, short of royalty. "Haji" indicated that the individual had made the pilgrimage to Mecca. "Bin" meant "son of."

NZI had recently been riding a tremendous wave of new business brought about by booming regional economies and an aggressive new corporate style of management that expanded the company's business into previously unconventional areas. NZI had also concentrated on shifting power to the local offices in order to encourage growth, and the new strategy called for equally aggressive management by NZI's field managers, who were afforded a large degree of autonomy by the "Home Office." Within the Pacific and Asian regions' financial-services industry, NZI was considered to be one of the most aggressive in its mix of markets, products, and technologies.

EXHIBIT 2

NZI Organization in 1985

[a]Percent of total NZI revenues.
[b]Percent of total General
Insurance revenues.

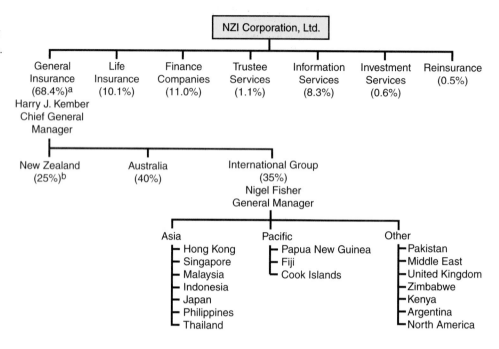

NZI held interests in two key Malaysian operations. NZI Malaysia was a branch network offering the full range of insurance services and accounting for $12 million in revenues. Peninsular Insurance Company, with $4 million in revenues, was 49 percent owned by NZI, with the remainder owned by Malaysian nationals. Peninsular had been formed by NZI in 1967 with the ultimate aim of controlling all its business interests in Malaysia, in line with government policy of local incorporation of foreign branches.

Weak profits in an otherwise growing economy had led to a decision in 1982 to consolidate all Malaysian operations in order to reduce costs and provide for a more coherent strategy. An agreement was reached that Peninsular Insurance would merge with NZI Malaysia in a pooling-of-interests transaction.

MALAYSIA

The Federation of Malaysia was a peninsular country located at the southern tip of Thailand, with two Malaysian states located several hundred miles across the South China Sea on the island of Borneo. Following independence from the United Kingdom in 1957, the federation was established in 1963. Malaysia was a constitutional monarchy with a parliament and prime minister. The king (the Yang di Pertuan Agong) was elected for a five-year period by a council of nine ruling sultans from nine of the 13 federated states. (Federally appointed governors headed the four other states and the federal territory.)

Natural Resources and the Economy

Malaysia had a population of 14.8 million people, with the capital of Kuala Lumpur housing 938,000. The country held a dominant world position in rubber, palm oil, pepper, tin, and tropical hardwoods; these and other abundant natural resources had given Malaysia one of the highest annual growth rates per capita in the world: growth at 4.5% per year since 1965 and per-capita gross national product over $1,555 by 1985.

The government had been aggressively pushing the economy toward a manufacturing base since the 1970s. Emphasis was on building the travel and communication infrastructure necessary for industrial growth, and the government maintained a policy of encouraging rapid population growth in order to stimulate domestic demand. The policy appeared to be working: manufacturing began to overtake agriculture as a percentage of gross domestic product and, by the 1980s, was the main source of economic growth. The unemployment rate was 5.6 percent in 1985 and the inflation rate 3.7 percent.

Political Aspects and the "NEP"

"It's not a law, it's a government policy, and it is really like shadow boxing because you never really know quite where the target is."[2]

Because Malaysia was a multiracial society, friction generated by the different cultures was the most important aspect of Malaysian politics. Political parties were based primarily on racial lines; the United Malays National Organization was the largest, but shared power in a broad-based coalition with the Malaysian Chinese Association, the Malaysian Indian Congress, and several other, smaller parties. Malays made up about 50 percent of the population, Chinese about 35 percent, and Indians about 10 percent. The three ethnic groups spoke different languages and followed different religions. While Malays were the most powerful politically, the Chinese controlled most of the nation's economy and owned a large proportion of Malaysia's businesses.

After a violent race riot in 1969, the Malaysian government established the "mitigation of inequity between races" as the overriding goal for the government. As a response to this goal, the New Economic Policy (NEP) was established in 1970. NEP was established to help the "bumiputra" (Malay for "son of the soil"), which refers to native Malays, who were considered the main beneficiaries of the policies. One way the NEP attempted to reach its goals was through increased spending on education and basic services. Public enterprises such as the Trust Council for Indigenous Peoples were chartered to finance native Malay businesses and to provide advice to prospective Malay businesspeople.

The government had also set a goal of increasing native Malay ownership in the corporate sector to 30 percent by 1990. All other Malaysians were designated 40 percent corporate ownership, and foreign-owned stakes were to have access to the remaining 30 percent. In addition, foreign-owned companies were required to restructure equity so at least 70 percent was held by Malaysian investors.

According to Wale, at the time of his arrival in 1982 the government was putting extra pressure on foreign firms to "domesticate" their firms and to increase their local share holdings. One way of applying this pressure was to grant very limited-term work permits. Government regulations in 1982 required all foreign nationals to apply for a Visitor's Work Visa, usually for 12 months. But when pressure on a company was desired, only 3 or 6 months were given, and the threat was always present that a visa would not be renewed. As Wale described this threat, "I had no idea whether I would be here for the full five years of my assignment or I would be on the plane in a month's time. They were playing the game with all insurance companies here that the best way to make foreign companies take on local partners was to mess around with their work permits."

Another important factor in the Malaysian political structure was the presence of the military. In the early years of the federation, in a period known locally as "the emergency," the country was plagued by civil war. Not until the middle 1970s did the threat from the communist insurgents greatly lessen. The product of the civil war was a virulently anti-communist government that retained full constitutional control of the professional military force.

THE NZI MALAYSIAN STAFF

"Well it's all very much tied into the Asian face thing, that you don't just say what's on your mind to the guy in case you offend him."[3]

Not long after taking over as General Manager of Peninsular, Wale established good working relationships with the management and board. (Wale was appointed to the board in March, 1983, as an alternate for Harry Kember, a board member based in New Zealand.) The foremost figure of the company was the local chairman of the board, Tan Sri Ibrahim Nassan, a prominent citizen in Malaysia who had once served as a high-level government official in the Interior Department (see Exhibit 1).

Wale soon realized that the chairman was remote from any real decision making for Peninsular; he served in mostly a ceremonial role. The chairman would show up at board meetings, start the occasion with a brief speech (usually written for him), and then leave management to discuss the mundane operational issues. Wale found the chairman to be a supportive gentleman; he allowed Wale to go about the business of modernizing the company's operation and organizing the mechanics of the merger,

---

[2]Patrick Wale.

[3]Patrick Wale.

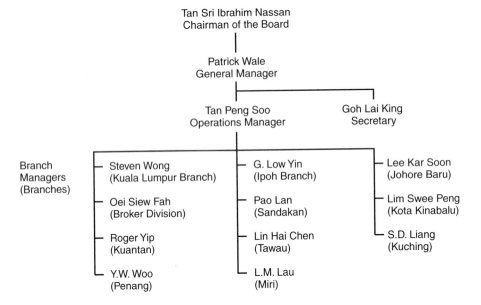

and he was particularly helpful in the area of smoothing over potential problems with the government. Immigration had been one of the departments under the chairman's supervision, and he several times expedited Wale's reapplication for a work permit.

The 73-year-old chairman, at 5′7″, was quite a contrast with Wale who, at 42, was 6′4″ and 250 lbs. Recently, Nassan had been forced to leave most of his other board positions because of the mandatory retirement age written into most public companies' bylaws. Peninsular, as a private company, did not have such a rule. The chairman was thought to be quite well off financially, although Wale had also heard that he had recently been involved in some rather unfortunate investments, probably in the volatile Malaysian stock market.

Since the early, supportive days, Wale had found himself on occasion becoming annoyed by the chairman's tendency to bypass Wale and call the corporate secretary, Goh Lai King, when he wished to check on the business or consult with a manager. King had been with Peninsular for almost 15 years, and the chairman had formed a separate line of communication with him. Wale believed that, as a matter of protocol, the CEO should be the first to be consulted for advice or questions, but he had also recognized how petty it would be to try to cut off this communication. (See Exhibit 3 for Peninsular organization.)

Wale had also quickly formed a close working relationship with the Malaysian operations manager, Tan Peng Soo. Tan was particularly knowledgeable

about the daily workings of Peninsular, and Wale relied on his judgment about how best to implement the new training and computerization programs that would bring Peninsular's operations up with the rest of the NZI organization. Because Wale expected to move on when the merger was consummated, he began grooming Tan Peng for the CEO position. Wale understood that Tan's strong business acumen and Malaysian nationality would make him a natural choice to run the merged company.

MEETING WITH THE CHAIRMAN

The question was whether the merger would ever come to fruition. Wale had become increasingly frustrated by the tortuously slow nature of Malaysian business dealings, particularly those with the vast government bureaucracy. Two years had already passed, and almost nothing had been accomplished. He spent most of his time waiting months for written replies from government officials, replies that would have taken days in Hong Kong.

During this first two years in Malaysia, Wale occasionally visited the chairman at his home in a wealthy KL neighborhood to update him on the progress of the merger and discuss how the business was doing in general. Wale had arranged such a meeting to discuss the slow replies of the government and an upcoming board meeting with the visiting directors from New Zealand.

As a courtesy, Wale had always visited the chairman at home, but he was becoming increasingly uncomfortable with the practice. He had noticed that, while they were seated in the chairman's sitting room discussing business, the chairman's wife would be sitting in the adjacent room apparently listening in on their conversation. She would often make an excuse to come in and interrupt, and would then linger on during the discussion. The chairman's wife was quite a bit younger than he, probably 15 or 20 years. Wale recognized that she was a strong-willed woman, and perhaps this trait, combined with her ability to make her presence felt and known, was what made Wale uncomfortable.

On this humid day in July, 1984, the chairman seemed to have little to offer in regard to the government delays. Wale then asked, "Well, sir, do you have any suggestions on where we may want to host the dinner for our visiting board members? I thought that your club did a superior job on the last occasion."

The chairman leaned forward, "Yes, well, I believe . . ."

"The club? Certainly not the club!" His wife suddenly emerged into the room. "Why don't we try the Rasa Sayang for a change? I think the gentlemen from the home office would much prefer that."

Wale observed the chairman as his wife continued telling them where the meeting should be and what should be on the menu. The chairman was obviously a bit taken aback, and Wale realized that he probably had the same expression on his own face.

Driving back to his office that afternoon, Wale decided to discontinue the practice of going to the chairman's house to talk business. Perhaps he was being silly, but the wife's interference was bothersome.

NIGEL FISHER VISITS

Several months later (February 1985), Wale received a call from Nigel Fisher in the New Zealand office telling him that Fisher would be visiting the Malaysia office in two weeks. Fisher was the newly appointed general manager in charge of International Operations, the third general manager in as many years. Fisher had worked with Wale before, and Wale looked forward to being able to discuss with him the reasons for the merger's slow going. Wale hoped to receive the level of support from the Home Office necessary to accelerate the merger.

A few days before Fisher's arrival, the chairman called Wale to his office. He requested that Wale arrange for King, the company secretary, to be present at Nassan's meeting with Fisher "just in case there is anything that I would like to put on the

record." Wale checked with King later that day to arrange for him to attend the meeting.

The day before the meeting, King approached Wale and asked whether it was really necessary for him to attend. King said, "I am very sorry, but I realized that I have a prior appointment with the Tax Department and think that it oughtn't be broken." Wale readily agreed that the appointment was important and promised that, if necessary, he would take notes. Wale assured King that the chairman would not mind.

"Well, the chairman did bloody well mind," Wale recounted later. Before the meeting with Fisher, Wale went to the chairman's office and asked whether he would like for Wale to sit in and take notes on the meeting. "No, I would prefer this meeting to be one on one," the chairman responded. The meeting lasted almost an hour, and immediately afterward, the chairman called Wale into his office. "Where was Mr. King?" he asked as Wale took a seat. "I instructed you to have him here to take notes."

"Yes, he came to me yesterday and informed me that he had a previous engagement with the Tax Office. I told him to carry on with his meeting and that I would take any notes if you wanted. But obviously you . . ."

"This is very upsetting, Patrick. Why did you countermand my specific instructions for the secretary?"

Wale had never heard this kind of tone from the chairman, who was always scrupulously polite. "I must apologize if it seems that way. It was a genuine misunderstanding on my part. I had thought that under the circumstances he should carry on with his meeting and I could take notes."

"The circumstances were that I gave specific orders and you saw fit to ignore them. If you ever countermand my instructions again, I will call the Home Office to have you removed from Malaysia."

Wale left the office feeling confused and a bit angry at the chairman's behavior. It was becoming apparent that he would have to start keeping his eyes open to what was a changing situation at Peninsular.

Soon thereafter, Wale asked Fisher about what had transpired during the meeting. Although Wale had never particularly got on with Fisher, finding Fisher's style too aloof for his tastes, he was confident that Fisher was sufficiently loyal to him not to discuss things with a local chairman behind Wale's back. Fisher said, "Oh, we mostly discussed the mechanics of the merger, the pricing of the shares, and that sort of thing. I told Tan Sri Nassan that NZI believes in keeping an arms-length relationship with our foreign offices. Said we would act as corporate advisors and assured him that we wouldn't steamroll the minority stockholders." When Wale brought up the timing of the merger and his troubles with the bureaucracy, however, he was frustrated by Fisher's lack of support.

"I'm sure you will get things moving along. You're just going to have to stop spending so much time dealing with the politics," Fisher said, smiling weakly.

Wale understood that his point was not getting through. If he had learned one thing from his two and a half years in Malaysia, it was that business *was* politics here.

THE ANNUAL PLANNING MEETING

"I guess I was fairly stunned."[4]

In the next six months, the two companies made some real progress toward merger. Wale met with the corporate attorneys, who calculated that, at the negotiated pricing, NZI should control 76 percent of the new entity, which would afford the company similar representation on the board. The company planned to keep the present 4-to-4 ratio of NZI representative and local board members, however, to keep up the appearance of a joint venture.

For the moment, Wale was concerned with the annual planning meeting scheduled for the end of September. During the meeting, the managers of each of Peninsular's 12 regional branches would present their individual financial plans and their strategies, staffing, and support needs for the coming year. As Wale described it, "We would put all these into the melting pot at this workshop and then come back about a month later with a finalized plan on a countrywide basis. This was the start of that cycle—asking each territory to stand up for 15 to 20 minutes and give a rundown on their major objectives for the year, their strategies, and where their strengths and weaknesses were. Normally, it would be the practice of two or three of us at the KL office to ask probing questions of the branch manager." The managers were encouraged to try out new ideas and to question each other or Wale about operational practices. Wale saw this open forum as serving two purposes: it encouraged branch managers to think beyond their own office's needs, and it could anticipate many of the questions that would come from the Home Office when budget requests were reviewed.

This year, Wale was particularly concerned about the downturn in the Malaysian economy and wanted to keep the next year's costs to a minimum. (Peninsular was projecting a small loss for the year—see Exhibit 4.) As he always did, Wale asked the chairman if he would like to address the meeting before morning tea. The Chairman agreed and accepted Wale's offer to write a brief speech on the state of the company.

The meeting was held in the boardroom; the large, adjustable table was that day configured in an open square, at which sat the 12 branch managers, the corporate secretary, the technology manager, Operations Manager Tan, and Wale and the chairman (seated next to each other). The morning started normally enough. The chairman offered his welcome to the branch managers and read Wale's

---

[4]Patrick Wale.

New Zealand Insurance, Ltd.

(NZ$millions)

	1982	1983	1984
Revenues	630	752	805
Net Income	28	18	49

Peninsular Insurance

NZ$millions[a]

	1982	1983	1984	1985(e)
Revenues	5.6	4.9	4.8	4.2
Net Income	.3	.6	.4	(.04)

[a]Converted at NZ$1.00 = 1.17 Malaysian Ringitt
In 1985, NZ$1.00 = US$0.468

opening statement. After the morning tea, Wale called the meeting to order. To his surprise, the chairman had not slipped out as he normally did but had come back to his seat next to Wale.

During the second presentation by the Sandakan branch manager, Wale interrupted to question the manager's figures:

Wale: "Mr. Pao, I'm not sure I see the basis for your staffing requirements. What are the growth projections that you are using for your figures?"

Branch Manager: "We are forecasting a 15 percent growth in sales and revenues."

Wale: "From what I have seen of your present operations, I would say that you already have the excess staffing necessary to support even a 15 percent growth, which is certainly aggressive. From a cost basis, I do not see how you can justify that many more people. Do you suppose . . ."

Chairman: "Hold on, Patrick. It is very easy for you managers in the central office to look at numbers and question them. But this man is dealing with the reality of working in the field and seems to have very good reasons for his staffing numbers. You always expect these poor chaps in the branch to meet the targets, but then they never get the proper support from you. Now they cannot even get the staff they require to do their job correctly."

Wale: (After pausing for a moment) "Mr. Chairman, perhaps we should take a look at this situation after the meeting. I'm sure we can discuss this and have it sorted out very quickly."

Chairman: "The issue is certainly an important one. I believe that all of the branch managers would like clarity about the signals they are getting from the central office in Kuala Lumpur. Mr. Pao's projections seem perfectly reasonable, and I know from my long association with Peninsular Insurance that his office is one of the finest in this organization. Mr. Pao, please continue with your excellent presentation. And Patrick, I will be happy to discuss this with yourself and Mr. Tan at the end of these proceedings."

The chairman waved his hand at Mr. Pao as a signal for him to continue. The branch manager stammered to a start and quickly moved on to a new topic.

Wale did not hear a word of it. The chairman's outburst had come as a complete shock, and Wale was trying to gather his wits and consider what his next move should be. He scanned the faces around the table as the managers quickly switched their eyes from him and back to the speaker. Tan returned his gaze with a look that was both stunned and quizzical,

and Wale knew that they were thinking the same thing: "What is the old bugger up to?"

Wale was not about to stand aside. For the rest of the day, he continued to facilitate the meeting, but there was almost no free exchange of ideas from the managers from that point on. Everyone seemed to be concerned about saying something that might lead to another controversy. Meanwhile, the chairman continued to chime in, making it perfectly clear who he thought was in charge of the proceedings.

Wale wondered what his next move should be. He wondered what the chairman's next move would be. The man did have connections, and the merger was six months, at least, from completion. Having a retired bureaucrat who knew nothing about business attempting to run the show certainly was not going to help things along. And what about the other managers? Wale had never considered questioning their loyalty, but this episode put everything in a new light.

STEP 1: Read the case.

STEP 2: Prepare the case for class discussion.

STEP 3: Answer the following questions, individually, in small groups, or with the class as a whole, as directed by your instructor.

DESCRIPTION

1. How would you characterize the Malaysian culture?

DIAGNOSIS

2. What issues does working in Malaysia create?

3. How is working in Malaysia different from working in New Zealand, Hong Kong, or the United States?

4. What challenges does Wale face in dealing with different cultures?

5. How should Wale treat the chairman?

STEP 4: Discussion. In small groups, with the entire class, or in written form, share your answers to the preceding questions. Then answer the following questions:

1. What symptoms suggest that a problem exists?

2. What problems exist in the case?

3. What theories and concepts help explain the problems?

4. How can the problems be corrected?

5. Are these actions likely to be effective?

Trojan Technologies Inc.: Organizational Structuring for Growth and Customer Service

In March 1998, a group of Trojan Technologies Inc. (Trojan) employees grappled with the issue of how to structure the business to effectively interact with their customers and to manage the company's dramatic growth. The London, Ontario, manufacturer of ultraviolet (UV) water disinfection systems believed that strong customer service was key to its recent and projected growth, and had come to the realization that changes would have to be made to continue to achieve both simultaneously. The group hoped to develop a structure to address these issues. Marvin DeVries, executive vice-president, was to lead the development and implementation of the new structure. The transition to the new structure was to begin as of September 1998 to coincide with the new fiscal year.

THE BUSINESS

Technology

Since 1977, the company had specialized in UV light applications for disinfecting water and wastewater. In essence, Trojan's products killed micro-organisms using high-intensity UV lamps. Water was channeled

---

past the lamps at various speeds, based on the clarity of the water and the strength of the lamps, to achieve the required 'kill' rate.

Trojan's UV technology had proven to be an environmentally safe and cost-effective alternative to chlorination, and was gaining wider recognition and acceptance. Even so, a significant market remained to be tapped, as the company estimated ". . . that only 5 percent to 10 percent of municipal wastewater sites in North American use UV-based technology . . . [and] of the approximate 62,000 wastewater treatment facilities operating worldwide, only 2,500 currently utilize UV disinfection systems."[1]

Trojan Technologies Inc.[2]

Trojan was established in 1977 with a staff of three with the goal of developing a viable UV wastewater disinfection technology. Following several years of work, the first UV disinfection system (System UV2000™) was installed in Tillsonburg, Ontario, in 1981. It took another two years, however, before the regulatory approvals were in place to market the technology for municipal wastewater treatment in Canada and the United States. During this time, the company generated revenues through the sale of small residential and industrial cleanwater UV systems.

By 1991, the company had sales in excess of $10 million, and had introduced its second-generation technology in the System UV3000™ wastewater disinfection system. As the company's growth continued, a staff of 50 was in place by 1992. The following year, due to capital requirements created by the company's strong growth, an initial public offering on the Toronto Stock Exchange was completed. Also in 1993, a branch office was established in The

---

[1]From Trojan 1998 annual report.
[2]The information in this section was primarily gathered from Trojan 1997 annual report.

Hague, Netherlands, expanding Trojan's reach across the Atlantic.

The year 1994 saw the launch of the System UV4000™, the construction of a new head office, and sales exceeding $20 million. In 1995, a branch office was opened in California to service the enormous market for wastewater treatment in that state. Two years later, an expansion doubled head office capacity to house 190 staff and to meet the demand for sales of more than $50 million.

Well into 1998, the expectation was that sales would reach $70 million by year-end and continue to grow by more than 30 percent per year over the next five years, reaching $300 million by 2003. The company was in the process of planning additional capacity expansion in the form of building and property purchases adjacent to the head office, and expected to quadruple its headcount by 2003 to more than 1,000 employees.

Products

In 1997, 93 percent of Trojan's sales were of wastewater products (System UV4000™ and System UV3000™). These systems were designed for use at small to very large wastewater treatment plants and more complex wastewater treatment applications with varying degrees of effluent treatment. The remaining 7 percent of sales were cleanwater products (primarily the System UV8000™ and Aqua UV™) for municipal and residential drinking water and industrial process applications. Growth in the coming year would be driven by increased sales of the wastewater disinfection products in both current and now new geographic markets. In the longer term, new products such as the A•I•R• 2000™, which was to use UV light with an advanced photocatalytic technology to destroy volatile organic compounds in the air, were expected to further Trojan's sales growth.

Products were typically assembled from component parts at the Trojan head office. The complexity of the product design, manufacture, and service arose from the integration of skills in electronics, biology, controls programming, and mechanical engineering. The company owned patents on its products and was prepared to defend them to preserve its intellectual capital.

Customers

Trojan sold its wastewater treatment products to contractors working on projects for municipalities or directly to municipalities. Typically, the process involved bidding on a project based on the Trojan products required to meet the municipality's specifications, and, therefore, engineering expertise was required as part of the selling process. Project sales typically fell in a $100,000 to $500,000 range, and given the large value of each sale, the sales and marketing function was critical to the company's success. However, for marketing to be effective, this new technology had to be well-supported. Municipalities purchasing the wastewater disinfection systems required rapid response to any problems and expected superior service given the consequences of breakdowns for the quality of water being discharged from their facility. Municipalities also had the ability to discuss Trojan and their UV products with other municipalities before deciding to make their purchase, further underlining the importance of warranty and after-market service to customers to ensure positive word-of-mouth advertising.

Trojan's smaller product line, the cleanwater segment, focused on a different customer base from wastewater, and it was difficult to generalize about the nature of this segment's customers. These customers ranged from municipalities to industrial companies to individuals.

INTERACTION WITH CUSTOMERS

The Process

The main points of customer interaction in the wastewater product line included:

1. Quote/bid process
2. Configuration of project structure
3. Project shipment and system installation
4. Technical support and warranty claims
5. Parts order processing

Each of these is described briefly below:

The quote/bid process was a major function of the marketing department, with support from the project engineering department. Although the marketing department took the lead role in assembling the appropriate bid and pricing, the customer would on occasion wish to speak directly to the project engineering department on specific technical questions related to the function of the UV unit within the particular wastewater setting.

After winning a bid, the configuration of project structure involved working with the customer on the detailed specifications for the project and applying the appropriate Trojan systems in a configuration that would meet the customer's needs. The project engineering department took the lead role in this work, and either worked through the marketing representative in transmitting technical information to and from the customer or communicated directly with the customer's technical personnel.

Once the project had been configured, it was scheduled for manufacture by the operations department. On completion, and when the customer was ready to integrate the UV system into their wastewater facility, the service department completed the installation and start-up of the unit. The service department would also be involved in demonstrating the proper use of the system to the customer.

After the system was in use by the customer, further interaction came in the form of technical support. The service department would deal with phone calls, site visits, and warranty claims and was the primary contact point for the customer. By its nature, most service work at this stage of the process was completed on an "as-needed" basis by the first available service representative. As a result, it was difficult or impossible to have the same service representative available to respond to a particular customer on every occasion. The service department, therefore, kept a detailed file on each UV installation and all customer contact to ensure the most informed response on each service call.

The final stage of customer interaction was the ordering of replacement parts by the customer after the warranty period was complete. This was handled by a call centre at Trojan head office in London that was separate from the other departments that had dealt with the customer. The call centre was staffed to receive orders for Trojan replacement parts, but not to provide technical support as with the service department, and would generally not access customer service files in taking the order.

In summary, customers would deal with as many as four different departments during their interaction with Trojan. During the early days of Trojan's growth, the "close-knit" nature of Trojan's workforce allowed a seamless transition between "departments." However, as described below, the company's continued growth began to complicate the transition between departments.

Customer Support in the Early Days

In the 1980s and early 1990s, when Trojan had less than 50 employees and worked on a limited number of wastewater bids and projects during the course of the year, customer support was a collective effort across the entire company. In fact, it was not unusual that virtually everyone in Trojan knew the details of all the major projects in process at any given time. There was a common knowledge base of customer names and issues, which resulted, in DeVries' words, in an 'immediate connectivity' to the job at hand. At times, during those early days, there were as few as two employees in a "department." Under these conditions every project received immediate and constant attention from start to finish, ensuring the customer was satisfied and potential issues were addressed in a proactive manner.

Challenges Created by Growth

As the company grew, departments grew. Very quickly the number of projects multiplied and it became impossible for everyone to know all the customers and active projects, or even all the people in the organization. As departments grew from two to five to 10 people, communications became focused internally within the departments. This made it progressively more difficult to ensure timely and effective communication on project status between departments, and the "immediate connectivity" described by DeVries began to break down. The situation was described by many as one where "things began to slip between the cracks" in terms of customer service excellence, because it was no longer possible for employees to shepherd a project through the company from start to finish as had been done in the early days. Once a particular department had finished their component of a project, they immediately had to turn their attention to the other projects they had ongoing, creating the potential for a lag before the next department picked up the customer file.

Project Engineering

Project engineering was one example of a department that had begun to experience problems maintaining service levels to the end-customer as a result of growth. By 1997, there were seven engineers in the department handling the regular support to the marketing department and acting as 'specialists' for the various technical components of the products. When engineers were hired into this group, there was no formal training or apprenticeship program in place. The new hire would simply follow along as best he or she could and attempt to learn the complex product line through observation and assistance from others in the department. This type of training was strained by the demand for project engineering services brought on by Trojan's growth.

A "specialist" role, in addition to their support of the marketing department's project bids, had evolved within the project engineering group. To handle specific technical requests, this informal addition to the project engineer's role had occurred somewhat spontaneously within the department. For example, if one of the project engineers had developed a detailed understanding of the electronics included in the System UV4000™ products, that employee acted as the reference point for most detailed queries on this subject and was considered the "electronics specialist." There was no specific training or support to develop these specialists for their roles in place in 1997, nor was hiring particularly targeted at filling the specialist roles described above, as it was a secondary role for the department. As a result of the dual roles and the company's rapid growth, project engineers could not take responsibility to guide a project from bid through customer queries to production and commissioning of the project. The demand for assistance on many bids, coupled with the need to respond to queries in their "specialist" area on active projects prevented project engineers from acting as a steward on specific projects as they passed through the company. Instead, the department operated more as a pooled resource that was accessed as needed by the marketing department to support bids and by the service group to assist with product support.

Service

The growth of the company and the establishment of new product lines had caused an amplified growth in the service group, because for each new project installed there was a long-term source of potential queries and service needs. The service group covered a broad spectrum of needs, from the initial setup of UV systems to emergency responses to equipment problems or queries (which frequently required site visits). A formal training program had been instituted during early 1998 when the new service manager recognized the need to quickly develop new employees to ensure they could contribute a strong technical background and familiarity with the product. An existing service group member typically instructed new employees for approximately one week, and new employees learned the balance "on the job" through observation and discussion of issues with other service employees. Again, company growth had caused some difficulty in ensuring that new employees received adequate training before they were needed to actively service customer inquiries.

There was a fundamental structuring conflict within the service area on how to best serve the customer. On one hand, customers appreciated the ability to contact one person whenever they had a concern or question. Also, customers frequently needed quick response times to their site for in-person assessments and action by the service employee. This appeared to suggest a need to place service employees physically as close to the end-customer as possible, especially given the company's expanded geographic marketing area. However, the timing of service work was very uncertain. Whereas the project engineering department had some ability to prioritize and schedule their workload, the service department typically had to respond to customer calls immediately, and the geographic distribution of calls was not predictable. Therefore, if Trojan received significant service requests in California, the company could be forced to respond by sending all available service employees there. The uncertainty of the timing and geographic distribution of service calls lent itself more to the centralized pooling of resources that Trojan currently used.

As Trojan had a significant geographic distribution of sales, service work involved substantial travel. In fact, the constant travel presented an additional risk of "burnout" that was unique to the department. To address this, and to ensure a reliable response to calls for assistance from customers, a head office call centre was created in 1998. The call centre was staffed by service technicians who could respond to many customer situations over the phone and by using sophisticated remote monitoring of the UV installments in some cases. The call centre also provided a place where experienced service personnel who were at risk of burnout from constant travel could use their expertise. Also, the call centre provided another opportunity to train new employees before dispatching them directly to customer locations on service calls.

RELATED ISSUES

Career Ladders

In a small company, career progression and satisfaction typically comes with successes achieved that significantly affect the organization. There was generally not the expectation or the possibility of significant promotion or role development, but this was offset by the potential for involvement of everyone in several major components of company activity. This was certainly the case at Trojan in the early days. As the company grew, however, a need to distinguish between and recognize the various levels of experience developed. The current department structure did not provide for much differentiation of job requirements within the departments, and, therefore, did not recognize the significant difference in experience levels between new and veteran employees.

Training Issues

As Trojan's sales continued to grow, the need to increase staffing was accelerating. In the early days,

the addition of a person to the company was informal and supportive. The new employee would be introduced to everyone and would easily be able to approach the appropriate person to ask questions and to learn their role within the company. Given the rapid expansion of the company, this informal introduction to the company and its processes was rapidly becoming insufficient to allow new employees to become effective in their new position. Training, therefore, needed to be addressed in many areas.

DECISIONS

Given the issues developing as Trojan grew, the structuring issue was becoming steadily more important. The structuring team under DeVries envisioned a regional, team-based approach to customer interaction that would replicate the structure used by the company in the early days. One of the difficulties in implementing such a structure, however, would be ensuring that the groups still operated as though they were one company, sharing knowledge and resources as appropriate. Another would be determining what level of centralized support would be appropriate, bearing in mind the need to avoid duplicating activities at head office that should be handled by the regional teams. Employees were now aware that there would be a change in the company structure, and there was a need to come to some conclusions on the new structure quickly to reduce anxiety about the change within the organization.

STEP 1: Read the case.

STEP 2: Prepare the case for class discussion.

STEP 3: Answer the following questions, individually, in small groups, or with the class as a whole, as directed by your instructor.

DESCRIPTION

1. How would you characterize the challenges faced by Trojan Technologies?
2. How have these changed since its founding?

DIAGNOSIS

3. How should the company handle customer service?
4. How does technology affect the business?
5. What issues should management consider in dealing with the company's workforce?
6. What ethical issues is the company likely to face?
7. Should management empower the workers in the new structure?
8. What competencies should managers at Trojan Technologies have?

STEP 4: Discussion. In small groups, with the entire class, or in written form, share your answers to the preceding questions. Then answer the following questions:

1. What symptoms suggest that a problem exists?
2. What problems exist in the case?
3. What theories and concepts help explain the problems?
4. How can the problems be corrected?
5. Are these actions likely to be effective?

Chapter 2

Perception, Attribution, and Learning

Learning Objectives

After completing Chapter 2, you will be able to

1. Diagnose deficiencies in the process of perception.
2. Define four perceptual biases and offer ways of making more accurate perceptions.
3. Offer three ways of managing impressions.
4. Describe the process of attribution and the role played by the individual and the situation.
5. Describe five attributional biases, diagnose their influence on a manager's actions, and show how to increase the accuracy of attributions.
6. Compare and contrast three key approaches to learning.
7. Offer a plan for increasing learning at work.
8. Identify the key issues for ensuring accurate perceptions, correct attributions, and effective learning in the dot-com, global workplace.

A Manager's Preview

Describe . . . Diagnose . . . Prescribe . . . Act

- Select and organize information carefully.
- Create scripts that lead to effective action.
- Manage the impressions you create and understand how others manage theirs.
- Avoid perceptual distortions—stereotyping, the halo effect, projection, and the self-fulfilling prophecy.
- Make correct attributions of employees' and other managers' behaviors.
- Encourage learning with the right cues, rewards, and models.
- Understand how culture affects perceptions and attribution.

New Technology Disasters: Who or What Is Responsible?

*F*ailed information technology implementations have created serious financial problems for a number of corporations. Hershey Foods Corporation, for example, issued a major profits warning because of massive distribution problems following the flawed implementation of an Enterprise Resource Planning (ERP) System. This resulted in many stores lacking Hershey products before Halloween and Christmas. Whirlpool Corporation had similar problems due to a problematic ERP implementation. Problems with an ERP implementation at the pharmaceutical distributor FoxMeyer caused the company to announce a $500 million lawsuit against SAP and Andersen Consulting (now Accenture). British organizations, including the BBC and Newcastle University, also experienced major ERP implementation problems.

Who is responsible for these problems? Some executives blame the vendor and consider technical problems the basis for the failure. Others say the failures result from companies not addressing the human side of change. Still others blame deficiencies in the training of managers to understand the flow of information through the business. Senior management's attitude toward the system, communications dysfunctions, and lack of understanding of the business affected by the system have been cited as causes. Misperceptions about the likelihood of successful ERP implementation also result from management's failure to recognize that the new system provides the infrastructure for a different way of doing business, management's faulty belief that the information system will impose discipline on the system and encourage cross-functional process integration, and management's perception that ERP should result in improved baseline operating measures. Senior managers tend to underestimate their role in ensuring the effectiveness of the ERP implementation.[1]

What really caused the problems in the ERP implementations? Would SAP executives and executives at companies such as Hershey, Whirlpool, and the BBC perceive the situation in the same way and agree about its cause? Questions like these are fundamental to the diagnostic approach, since they deal with the description of events and the reasons given for them. As the preceding case suggests, different observers of an incident may describe and diagnose it very differently. They in turn act based on their different understandings of the situation.

In this chapter, we explore three areas of organizational behavior. *Perception* deals with the way we perceive and so describe events or other people. *Attribution* focuses on the way we understand, analyze, or diagnose the events and people we perceive. *Learning* refers to the way our past experiences and acquisition of knowledge and information influence this description and diagnosis. We conclude the chapter by exploring perception and attribution in the dot-com, global workplace.

▌ THE PERCEPTION PROCESS

Let's start with a close look at implementing an ERP system. We can view the problem from several perspectives. First, think of the project manager of SAP, the system provider. Which features of the implementation would stand out for him? He might focus on top management's role in the situation or his feelings of frustration with the process. Now think of the project manager at one of the companies implementing the ERP system. What features of the situation would she notice? She might feel annoyed that SAP and its partner consulting companies can't provide enough support. Now think of the information technology employees at Hershey, the BBC, or one of the other companies implementing the ERP. How would they experience this situation? They might feel that their company did not provide enough resources for the implementation, or they might believe that the vendor, SAP, didn't provide enough technical knowledge or staff for a successful implementation. These different perceptions affect how these people deal with the implementation problem.

When you put yourself in these different positions, you probably focus on different aspects of the situation. Your experience of this event—your perception—varies when you put yourself in the shoes of different participants. You then act based on your perception.

Perception refers to the active process of sensing reality and organizing it into meaningful views or understandings.[2] Often managers, their co-workers, subordinates, or customers perceive the same situation differently. For example, many consumers view Coca-Cola as the premier soda. Many of the company's employees, in contrast, have a different perception of the company after the 1997 death of its long-time chairman, recent employee lawsuits over diversity issues, worsening relations with its bottlers, and a major product recall in Belgium.[3] Because different people generally perceive a situation differently, presenting a clear, well-documented, agreed-upon description of a situation—the first step in the diagnostic approach—is key. Understanding the perceptual process and the factors that affect it allows us to improve our diagnoses of events and the resulting prescription and subsequent actions. In this chapter, we describe perception as having two parts, as shown in Figure 2-1: attention and organization.

FIGURE 2-1

The perception process includes attention and organization.

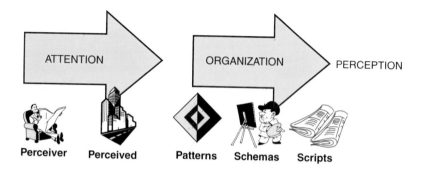

Attention → Organization → Perception

Perceiver   Perceived   Patterns   Schemas   Scripts

Attention

So much bombards our senses that we cannot take it all in. We screen out many sensations and attend to certain features of the situation. Different observers, such as managers and employees dealing with an ERP implementation, often select different information to pay attention to. For example, Hershey's employees might focus on either their company's or SAP's failure to deliver enough support, whereas SAP's employees might focus on an insufficient budget or timeline or lack of cooperation from the customer in looking at the ERP implementation.

We tend to focus on only selected and limited features in any situation. We might focus on the behaviors of a poor performer and ignore those of a top performer. We might focus on the loudest and most persistent customer and ignore the one who quietly and patiently waits for help. This selection process helps us avoid information overload, and focusing on relevant information saves time.

Characteristics of the Perceived.   We tend to pay attention to people, objects, and events that are larger, more intense, in motion, repetitive, either novel or very familiar, or in contrast to their background.[4] We tend to overlook stimuli that are small, less intense, or stationary, or that blend with their background. For example, a quality control manager might return for rework only products with major flaws and overlook minor ones. A salesperson answers a ringing telephone and ignores the person standing next to him (unless the person whines or complains loudly) because he attends to the more intense noise of the telephone.

Characteristics of the Perceiver.   We also attend to sensations according to our motives, personality, personal characteristics, and experiences. For example, we more likely will attend to food commercials before a meal than after one. In business situations, we in the United States used to pay more attention to comments by managers wearing business suits than to the ideas of those wearing patched blue jeans. Now, with the great impact of dot-com companies that typically have more informal dress codes, even very traditional law firms are matching this informal dress code so that their attorneys are perceived as "one of us" by dot-com managers.[5] Food Lion recently installed the option of self-checkout for its customers. Even though cashiers process orders faster, customers perceive self-checkout as speedier.[6]

Let's look at the situation of Joseph Sparks. One year after accepting a new job, Sparks became a parent and decided to use the paternity leave to which he was entitled.

When you think of Sparks, do you focus on the person, his work performance, or his taking a leave? The answer will depend, in part, on cultural expectations, which differ among companies and countries. If you are a manager or co-worker, you might perceive his leave in terms of your own motivation or personality. The more diverse the workforce, the more likely it is that individuals see events differently.

Organization

Once we have selected relevant information, we categorize and organize it so that the new material makes sense to us. For example, Eckert Seamans Cherin & Mellott, a national law firm with 230 attorneys, has announced a long-term branding initiative as a way of differentiating itself from its competitors. The focus of this initiative is to organize perceptions of potential clients to encourage them to think about the law firm in particular ways, such as having particular areas of expertise.[7]

Our brains follow certain laws in seeking physical patterns in the information, as shown in Figure 2-2. These same laws apply to the way we seek behavior patterns in work situations, as follows:

- **Figure-Ground.** Salespeople at exclusive boutiques fade into the background so customers can focus on their products.
- **Similarity.** At work, people with degrees from the same M.B.A. program are considered to resemble each other in preferences, interests, and abilities.

| FIGURE 2-2 |

People use common patterns in organizing their sensations.

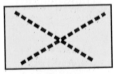

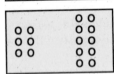

Figure-Ground
We tend to organize sensations into figures and backgrounds.

Similarity
We tend to group similar items. Do you see alternating rows of O's and X's or columns of alternating O's and X's?

Proximity
We tend to group elements that are close together. How many groupings do you see at the left?

Closure
We tend to fill in the gaps in incomplete stimuli. Do you see a rectangle or four lines?

Continuation
We tend to organize stimuli into continuous lines or patterns. Do you see two intersecting lines or four lines?

Simplicity
We tend to reduce stimuli to their simplest shapes or patterns. Do you see an overlapping rectangle and triangle or an unnameable polygon?

- **Proximity.** A manager might evaluate an employee's attitude by looking at her friends or co-workers. If the employee spends free time with union representatives, the manager may assume that the employee shares those attitudes and will support a labor walkout.

- **Closure.** An employee assumes that his computer has the necessary software for various office tasks.

- **Continuation.** A manager assumes, based on past performance, that an employee will continue to come to work late or prepare low-quality reports.

- **Simplicity.** Customer support staff sometimes try to reduce a customer's problems to simpler components and address them one at a time.

Faulty organizing contributes to the perceptual distortions discussed later in this chapter.

Schemas and Scripts. People also use *schemas,* cognitive frameworks that include descriptions of the characteristic features of other people, situations, or objects, obtained through experience.[8] These schemas help managers organize information by grouping objects, individuals, and situations in their thought processes.[9] They may form several types of schemas:

- **Person schemas.** Managers build *prototypes* about the characteristics of good and poor workers. A prototype of successful founders of dot-com businesses might be a person with technical knowledge, propensity for risk, and a previous successful venture. Managers also match new sensations to *exemplars,* which represent concrete examples (rather than general characteristics), such as the dot-com founder whose company most recently went public.[10]

- **Role schemas.** People may form a schema based on a role they or others hold, such as working mother. These roles have various characteristics that influence perceptions about that role. For example, some managers (incorrectly) perceive that an older worker is not technically savvy.

- **Self-schemas.** Individuals can generalize about their own behavior based on present situations and past experiences. For example, individuals may demonstrate self-schemas of competence, showing that they feel they have the skills to accomplish a particular goal or perform a particular task.

- **Events schemas.** *Scripts,* or schemas about a sequence of events, provide a mental representation of the events that guide our behavior.[11] For example, managers develop scripts about the process for increasing sales, going public, or even selling their business.

Managers can use schemas and scripts to help them really understand a situation they face and then determine the most appropriate action. They may need to specify the schemas and scripts they use and then alter them so that they act more effectively.

PERCEPTUAL DISTORTIONS

Managers rarely make truly objective perceptions. Most of their perceptions suffer from inaccuracy and distortion. Think about a product that doesn't meet its sales expectations. Typically, everyone has slightly different and often distorted versions of the events relating to its failure. Distorted perceptions can lead to poor decisions, as well as to unfair hiring, discipline, or evaluation practices. Lack of experience with a different culture, for example, can hinder expatriates working in that culture for the first time. Although many types of distortions can affect perceptions, we discuss stereotyping, the halo effect, projection, and the self-fulfilling prophecy in greater detail here.

Stereotyping

Stereotyping occurs whenever we assume others have certain characteristics or attitudes simply because they belong to a certain group or category. "Blondes have more fun" and "all managers are smart" illustrate stereotyping. We frequently stereotype members of ethnic groups, women, managers, high-technology employees, dot-com executives, and so on. Although stereotypes can be correct, generally they lack accuracy and result in uninformed action.

Why does stereotyping occur? It's a shortcut. Often people don't collect enough information about others to describe their behaviors or attitudes accurately. They may lack the time or patience to do so and instead rely on stereotypes to categorize people and events. For example, African women journalists fight both gender and racial stereotyping. They receive stereotypical "female" assignments, such as "soft" interviews and features, and face sexual harassment from their bosses.[12] Stereotyping more often occurs when individuals experience stress in their work or personal situations.[13]

Some people have personal biases against certain groups of individuals. Historical attitudes toward certain cultural groups may result in stereotypes. Americans may have certain views of Europeans and different views of Asians based on their historical experiences with people from the two regions. Ethnic stereotyping seems to occur in the delivery of health care in the United States: In one study, physicians assumed that Asians would not discuss symptoms or complain and that African Americans and Hispanics would not eat healthy diets or lose weight; minority consumers believed that those with health insurance received a better quality of care.[14] One study of Indian and Israeli businessmen indicated that almost all used very consistent stereotypes about their business partners. They drew these stereotypes from direct experience with their partners and indirect sources of information, such as the media. These stereotypes influenced the conduct of business; for example, Indian managers initiated business with the Israelis because of their perceived work ethic; Israeli managers selected partners, determined the method of payment, and considered information provided by their Indian partners in accordance with their stereotypes of the Indian businesspeople.[15]

Sex role stereotyping often occurs. When you think of female managers, what images and characteristics come to your mind? Are the images and characteristics the same for male managers? Managers may believe that women and men can't hold the same jobs. Or, they may believe that women should be soft-spoken and demure and men outspoken and aggressive. A survey of 461 female executives in Fortune 1000 companies indicated that 52 percent saw male stereotyping of women and preconceptions about women as the biggest barrier to women's advancement.[16] Participants in other recent research believed women experienced and expressed the majority of the 19 emotions studied more often than men.[17] Recent court decisions in the United States require that companies not commit sexual stereotyping and develop strategies to avoid it.[18]

Halo Effect

The halo effect occurs when an individual lets one key feature or trait dominate her evaluation of a person or thing. A manager might judge a person who works long hours as highly cooperative and productive. She might judge a person with a very neat personal appearance as precise and reliable in his work.

Managers frequently use the halo effect when assessing employee performance. In one study, for example, a supervisor evaluated two female workers differently according to their personal appearance. Attractiveness increased the performance evaluations, pay raises, and promotions of women in nonmanagerial positions, but decreased these same outcomes for women in managerial positions.[19]

The halo effect extends beyond appearance. For example, when a product features a health claim on its label, consumers are more likely to attribute appropriate health benefits to it.[20]

Projection

Projection occurs when an individual attributes his attitudes or feelings to another person. People use projection as a defense mechanism—to transfer blame to another person or to provide protection from their own unacceptable feelings. For example, they frequently attribute their own prejudices against minorities, managers, or employees to others. Projection and its dysfunctional consequences can increase as the workforce becomes more diverse. People who lack understanding or mistrust those who differ may project these insecurities onto others.

Projection involves an emotional biasing of perceptions. Fear, hatred, uncertainty, anger, love, deceit, or distrust may influence a person's perceptions. In union–management relations, for example, each side attributes feelings of mistrust (often its own) to the other side. Managers believe that the union members mistrust them when, in fact, the managers distrust the union. They project their own feelings onto the other group, representing them as that group's feelings.

Self-Fulfilling Prophecy

In many situations, the participants expect certain behaviors from other participants and then see these behaviors as occurring whether or not they actually do. Their expectations become self-fulfilling prophecies. Fears of the Y2K computer bug, for example, led to concerns that motorists might top off their gasoline tanks in the last 10 days of 1999 to avoid possible shortages created by reports of potential Y2K glitches; this "topping off party" could have created a self-fulfilling prophecy of gasoline shortages.[21] Advanced Micro Devices has suffered from stockholder perceptions that the company has lax managers who have never developed an interest in increasing stockholder value—and so stockholder value has remained stagnant.[22]

Managers who demonstrate the self-fulfilling prophecy may expect workers to be lazy, bossy, or tardy and then perceive them as actually being lazy, bossy, or tardy. These expectations may either cause the employee to act in the expected way or to aggressively act to counteract the expectations. Employees, in turn, may expect managers to be authoritarian, uncaring, and inflexible and then perceive them as authoritarian, uncaring, and inflexible, causing them to react negatively to the supervision they receive. Other times, employees may perceive that their managers set high standards, and these perceived expectations challenge the employees to work harder and perform better.[23] Sometimes these expectations accompany stereotyping, the halo effect, or projection, or they can occur independently of other biases.

Assume you are the marketing vice president of a high-technology company, and two employees report to you. The first employee has demonstrated initiative and high productivity in his accounts. The second precisely follows your directions, but has shown neither initiative nor enthusiasm for his work. You have just found on your desk a high-quality report about the market potential for a new product that you have not requested from either employee. Which employee do you congratulate for the excellent work? A self-fulfilling prophecy would cause you to approach the first employee. Could you be wrong? Of course. The second employee might have the same capabilities as the first, but never demonstrate initiative because he knows you will attribute the excellent or unexpected performance to his co-worker.

Self-fulfilling prophecies occur often in cross-cultural situations. We frequently have expectations about how people in other cultures will act based on similar experiences in our own culture. Cultural differences, however, can make seemingly identical situations quite different. In the United States, for example, we commonly accept the price on an item as nonnegotiable, whereas in many other countries buyers can negotiate any price. Similarly, in the United States, many workers expect and willingly work overtime, whereas in many European countries time outside the normal workday is protected for family activities.

■ MANAGING IMPRESSIONS

People often try to influence others' perceptions of them through *impression management,* controlling the impressions others form. Managers can use impression management tactics to positively influence their employees' ratings of them.[24] In addition, recent research suggests that employees' ability to use impression management is positively associated with their ability to adapt cross-culturally.[25] We might manage impressions by the way we dress, speak, or otherwise present ourselves. We might manage impressions by the projects we undertake, the causes we support, or the people we associate with. Managers can use their offices to convey impressions of status, power, or informality, for example. The position of their desk, tidiness of their office, and office decor contribute to the impression conveyed to others.[26] Recent research suggests that organizational citizenship behaviors result from impression management motives. Of course, not all impressions are positive.[27] Managers can easily create negative impressions at work and should try to avoid doing so.[28]

Impression management has three components; Figure 2-3 shows the interaction of these components and the influence of both the social context and the individual on them:[29]

- **Impression monitoring** refers to the extent to which people are conscious of the impressions they make. They may pay attention to their impressions because of either their situation or their personality.
- **Impression motivation** refers to the extent to which people actively manage the impressions they make. People might actively try to manage the impression they create for their boss, but not concern themselves with the impression they create for friends.
- **Impression construction** refers to people choosing the image to convey and how to convey it. New job applicants often tailor their resume, even having several versions, to create a particular impression.

■ FIGURE 2-3 ■

Impression management involves monitoring, motivation, and construction.

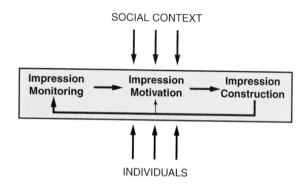

Managers can manage impressions by using tactics aimed at making other people like them, promoting themselves as highly competent, intimidating others, behaving in ways to emphasize self-sacrifice, or making excuses before undesired events happen.[30] Employees in turn might manage their impressions to create perceptions of competence, effort, and quality performance. Impression management can affect performance appraisals, hiring, training, career development, and other human resources activities.[31] For example, one study indicated that subordinates who build coalitions rather than trying to ingratiate themselves with managers tended to create more favorable impressions and receive more positive appraisals.[32]

Organizations, too, try to manage the public's impression of them through their advertising, products, and charitable work. Gifts in Kind International, for example, partners with businesses and charities, including 26 of the Fortune 100 companies, to give products and services to needy communities worldwide. According to a 1999 survey, retailers in the United States contributed an average of $5.8 million to various charities.[33]

Changing an impression can pose major challenges to companies that have created a particular image. Managing impressions involves first assessing the situation, setting impression management goals, and then selecting the best tactics. After producing the impression management behaviors, managers can then assess their effectiveness and modify the goals or tactics used.[34]

■ MANAGING THE PERCEPTUAL PROCESS

How can managers and employees reduce perceptual distortions? Here we offer five steps to increase perceptual accuracy. To see how this works, let's take another look at the ERP implementation.

1. **Gather sufficient information about other people's behavior and attitudes to encourage more realistic perceptions.** Managers, for example, should judge a person's performance on his observed behavior, rather than on the behavior of a group to which the person belongs or the manager's expectations about the employee's performance. The executives of all of the organizations involved need to document both the technical problems and their employees' behavior relative to the implementation.

2. **Check conclusions to ensure their validity.** To the extent possible, the employees of Hershey, the BBC, and Whirlpool should determine the true reasons for the problems in the implementation.

3. **Differentiate between facts and assumptions in determining the basis of perceptions.** The employees need to check whether technical or human considerations created the problems.

4. **Distinguish among various aspects of a person's behavior.** Managers need to separate appearance from performance, productivity from attendance, and personality from creativity. The employees of the companies involved need to carefully identify the behaviors of top management, the information technology department, and others involved in the ERP implementation.

5. **Identify true feelings as a way of eliminating or reducing projections.** Do the employees feel frustrated or distrustful? After recognizing these feelings, the manager or employee can assess whether and how these feelings influence the perceptions of others.

▍THE ATTRIBUTION PROCESS

As part of the diagnosis stage, managers who use the diagnostic approach determine why events occur. *Attribution* refers to their specifying the perceived causes of events. Not surprisingly, different people often attribute different causes to the same event.

When people try to understand the reasons for their own or another's behavior, they focus on personal or situational factors:

- **Personal factors** include people's habits, needs, abilities, or interests.
- **Situational factors** include increases in competition, poor supervision, shortages of resources, the nature of the work, or the organization's characteristics.

For example, a research study indicated that people were more likely to attribute the performance of men to ability than the performance of women. They were less likely to attribute black managers' performance to effort and ability and more likely to the help of others.[35] Another study suggested that top managers on management teams that had replaced many top executives were more likely than top managers on teams with little turnover to attribute performance problems to causes internal to the firm and controllable.[36]

How might managers at Hershey or Newcastle University explain the failure of their ERP implementation? The attribution process occurs in three steps, as shown in Figure 2-4:[37]

1. **The behavior occurs and the employee observes it.** A manager learns about the failure of the ERP implementation.

2. **Having identified the action, the employee determines if the observed behavior—the flawed ERP implementation—was intended or accidental.** If the employee assumes that the failure occurred accidentally, she will attribute its cause to fate, luck, accident, or a similar uncontrollable event. If, however, she assumes that the implementation failure was controllable, she will then move to stage 3.

3. **The employee questions whether situational causes or personal characteristics explain the behavior.** If the employee thinks the vendor failed to provide the appropriate services, she will attribute the lack of computers to situational factors. If, instead, she believes that her company's top executives or employees purposefully hindered the implementation, she will attribute the problem to personal factors.

FIGURE 2-4

Managers and employees make attributions in three major steps.

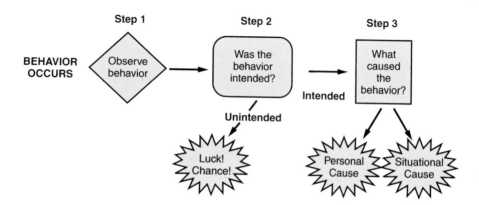

While both situational and personal factors may have influenced the computer situation, those involved often simplify their understanding and attend primarily to only one cause. For example, people who demonstrate continued uncertainty about the causes of behavior more often fail to adjust for situational factors in making an attribution.[38]

ATTRIBUTIONAL BIASES

Without training, people make predictable attributions and attributional errors. Three common factors influence attributions, as shown in Figure 2-5:

- **Consensus**—how many other people behaved in the same way as the individual. We tend to assign personal causes to unique behaviors and situational causes to behaviors performed by many others.
- **Distinctiveness**—how consistent (or unusual) a person's behavior is across situations. We tend to assign personal causes to common behavior and situational causes to unusual behavior.
- **Consistency**—how consistent an individual's behavior is over time and situations. We tend to attribute consistent behavior by an individual to personal causes and situational causes to behaviors that represent isolated instances.[39]

FIGURE 2-5

Consensus, distinctiveness, and consistency influence people's attributions.

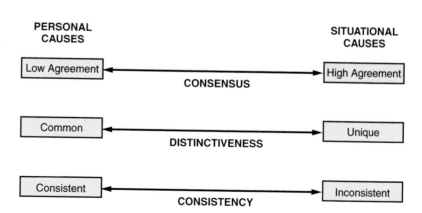

Five additional factors can influence attributions: the individual's point of view, the appropriateness and impact of the behavior, the success or failure of the outcomes, the ease of response, and the person's self-concept. We discuss these factors in detail next.

Point of View

A person can participate in a situation as an actor or an observer. In looking at the ERP implementation, we can view SAP's managers as the actors and the managers from Hershey, the BBC, or Newcastle University as observers, or vice versa. Which group we label as "actor" or "observer" depends on the behavior we are trying to understand.

Actors tend to emphasize the situational causes of a behavior and deemphasize personal factors as a way of protecting their self-image and ego; observers do the reverse.[40] For example, a textbook salesperson who loses a potential adoption more often attributes the loss to the customer (part of the situation) than to her own sales technique.

In addition, actors are less likely to assume moral responsibility for an action because they attribute it to external causes.[41] If a mid-level manager engages in financial fraud, for example, he most likely attributes this behavior to external circumstances, such as top management's directive or changes in relevant laws. These biases may extend to ethical judgments through the moral evaluation of one's own or another's behavior.[42]

Appropriate Behavior

If a person acts in inappropriate ways, an observer will usually attribute that person's behavior to personal characteristics.[43] If a top executive saw an advertising copywriter making false claims about a product (acting in an inappropriate way), the manager would attribute this action to the employee's personal characteristics because the behavior violates agreed-upon standards of behavior. Similarly, an observer who believes that a person has acted to specifically influence the observer will attribute the actor's behavior to his personality traits. If a manager felt that an employee "blew the whistle" on questionable business practices to "get back at management," she likely would attribute the cause of that worker's behavior to his personality.

Successes and Failures

The perceived success or failure of a behavior may also complicate the attribution of its cause, as shown in Figure 2-6. Managers view successes as behaviors that help accomplish the organization's goals, such as increases in performance, efficiency, or adherence to work rules. Failures include increased turnover or absenteeism, declining productivity, decreasing morale, or other unacceptable behaviors. Evidence suggests that actors tend to attribute successes to personal factors and failures to situational factors; observers do the reverse.[44] Training managers in feedback skills may decrease their tendency to attribute subordinates' problem behaviors to personal factors.[45]

Ease of Response

Managers' tendencies to make the easiest response can also affect their attributions.[46] Managers more easily assume that a worker, rather than the situation, is responsible for a problem. To identify a situational cause, a manager typically must

FIGURE 2-6

Managers' attributions consider successes and failures, as well as a person's role as an actor or observer.

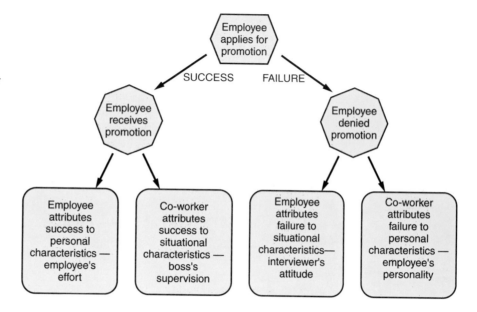

spend time investigating the situation in great detail. Correcting the situation is harder than dealing with the "responsible" individual since the manager may have little or no control over the organizational factors. In this case, the manager attributes the cause to the worker.

Self-Concept

Efforts to maintain a positive self-concept—or people's attitudes about their own abilities, behaviors, and attitudes—also can modify perceptions and attributions. Managers, for example, may view their employees' behavior as a reflection of their own. Maintaining their own self-esteem causes the managers to attribute employees' successes to the manager's contributions (part of the situation) and employees' failures to their own personalities. Successes then reflect the manager's behavior and attitudes; failures reflect factors outside the manager. Because of low self-confidence, women tend to explain away their success, take responsibility for failures, and believe that ability has a greater influence on their subordinate's success than on their own.[47]

▌MANAGING ATTRIBUTIONS

Managers should test their attributions to avoid making costly mistakes, such as blaming the wrong person for low productivity in assembling a product. Managers are more likely to make accurate and complete attributions if they gather enough information and analyze it well enough to determine causes correctly.

Managers and employees who use the diagnostic approach presented in this book will regularly test the nature of their attributions. A manager who has a regularly absent employee can ask the worker about the reasons for his absenteeism, rather than assuming that personal characteristics cause it. In this book, we explore numerous explanations for behavior so that managers can attribute causes as accurately and completely as possible and then act on the basis of correct attributions.

The diagnostic approach encourages us to first describe the situations completely. Then, as part of the diagnosis stage, we attribute the causes of events in the situations we describe. Boots the Chemist PLC, a British pharmacy chain, gives tests to potential sales assistants to assess their customer-focus. The company bases the items on the principles of attribution theory, predicting that employees who tend to blame the customer when faced with a difficult situation are least likely to provide good customer care. In validating the questionnaire, the company learned that the most successful sales performers and those who received the highest ratings for customer care more often attributed the outcomes to personal or internally controllable factors, while those rated as poor performers made external or situational attributions more often.[48]

▌LEARNING IN ORGANIZATIONS

In addition to perception and attribution, *learning*, which refers to the acquisition of skills, knowledge, ability or attitudes, influences both the description and diagnosis of organizational behavior. Dell Learning, the division responsible for all education in Dell Computer Corporation, has four main objectives: align learning with key business initiatives, make learning directly available to anyone who needs it, create clarity around competencies required for continued success, and provide consistency through global curricula. Employees, managers, and sometimes even customers and suppliers participate in programs sponsored by Dell Learning.[49]

In this section, we focus on the way individuals learn. First we examine three learning theories. Then we consider the managerial implications of learning.

The Power of Rewards for Learning

Managers and employees can learn because the repeated pairing of a stimulus and response yields rewards. Recall Pavlov's ground-breaking work with dogs.[50] When a dog received meat (unconditioned stimulus), the dog salivated (unconditioned response). When the dog heard a bell ringing (neutral stimulus), the dog did not salivate. After pairing the ringing bell with the meal several times, Pavlov rang the bell without the meat, and the dog salivated (conditioned response). In *classical conditioning*, as illustrated by Pavlov's experiment, after repeated pairing of neutral and unconditioned stimuli, the neutral stimulus alone led to a conditioned response.

Operant conditioning extends classical conditioning to focus on the consequences of a behavior, what we often call rewards, as shown in Figure 2-7.[51] While a stimulus can still cue a response, the consequence that follows the behavior determines whether the behavior will recur. For example, an employee who receives a bonus (a positive consequence) after creative performance (behavior) on a work assignment (stimulus) will be more likely to repeat the creative behavior than if her manager ignores her performance (a negative consequence). Amoco developed a safe driver training program that incorporates the principles of operant conditioning. First managers and employees identified the behaviors that reduced accidents, such as pulling forward when driving out of a parking space. Second, work groups looked for the root causes of the unsafe behaviors; they identified antecedents and consequences of unsafe driving. Third, they observed and measured the frequency of the targeted safe behaviors. Fourth, safety teams provided the results of their observations as feedback to various teams of drivers. They collected data weekly, discussed it,

FIGURE 2-7

Operant conditioning gives a person a positive consequence or reward after a desired behavior, causing the behavior to recur.

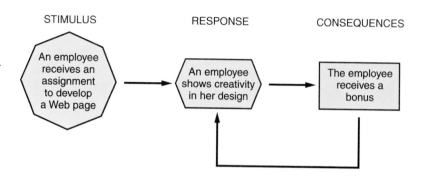

and identified improvements. Fifth and finally, they used positive reinforcement by celebrating the accomplishment of subgoals. At one location, safety team members put recognition notes under the windshield wipers of employees who parked in the correct position. At other locations, team leaders served a burrito breakfast when the team reached a subgoal. The Amoco teams experienced success: Targeted and untargeted behaviors changed, improving driving safety in the company.[52]

Cognitive Approach

Managers' internal mental processes also influence learning, which occurs when various cues in the environment form a mental map for them. In early cognitive experiments, for example, rats learned to run through a maze to reach a goal of food.[53] Repeated trials caused the rats to develop and strengthen cognitive connections that identified the correct path to the goal.

People can also develop cognitive maps that show the path to a specific goal, as illustrated in Figure 2-8. Here the cognitive processes act on the stimulus to result in a given behavior. On-the-job training in new work processes should result in a new cognitive map of job performance for the employees. They should develop and sustain new links between the tasks that comprise their job and optimal ways of linking and performing them.

Miller/Shandwick Technologies, a public relations firm that earned the account of Xerox Engineering Systems, sent their top account executives to the

FIGURE 2-8

Managers and employees can develop cognitive maps that show the path between stimulus and goal.

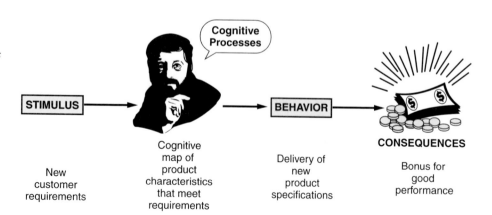

Xerox Document University. There they participated in a three-day course about the reprographics marketplace. Perhaps more important for their learning was the opportunity to play with Xerox and competitors' products. Through this type of training, they developed the mental maps to understand the way the product functioned and the best way to represent their client.[54]

Expert computer systems, frequently used to automate training, provide instructions to employees about how to perform a task or solve a problem. These systems use the cues inherent in the situation to help managers develop cognitive maps around the specific tasks. They then can identify, correct, and explain errors that trainees might make in addressing the problems.

Social Learning

People can also learn by modeling or imitating behaviors, as described in social learning theory.[55] This theory, which integrates the behavioral and cognitive approaches, has several steps:

1. Learners watch others, who act as models.
2. Learners develop a mental picture of the behavior and its consequences.
3. Learners try the behavior themselves.[56]
4. Learners repeat the behavior if positive consequences result; learners don't repeat it if negative consequences occur.

An analysis of the studies of the impact of this approach, often known as OB Mod, indicates an average gain of 17 percent in performance.[57] Different types of reinforcers, such as money, performance feedback, social attention and recognition, or some combination of these, produce different outcomes. For example, performance feedback had a greater impact than monetary reinforcers in manufacturing organizations, whereas the reverse was true in service organizations.[58]

Modeling and imitating behaviors as a way of learning can apply to both on-the-job and off-the-job training. Trainers present models of good performance, and the trainees see the relationship between these desirable behaviors and the consequences, such as praise, promotions, or customer satisfaction. Trainees then rehearse the behaviors and consequences, building cognitive maps that intensify the links and set the stage for future behavior. The learning impact occurs when the subject tries the behavior and experiences a favorable result, as in operant conditioning.

At the same time, the learner develops a cognitive image of the situation, which provides a way of thinking about the steps in acquiring new skills, knowledge, or even attitudes. Some companies use artistic performance techniques to demonstrate and then model the desired behaviors. "U.S. conductor Roger Nierenberg sits managers among orchestra members in rehearsal exercises to make them aware of the professional mastery of individual players, their willingness to play for each other—and, soberingly, their ability to self-organize and play coherently without a conductor at all."[59] Managers then learn leadership behavior by trying to conduct the orchestra.

▌ MANAGING LEARNING IN THE WORKPLACE

How can managers encourage learning in the workplace? Hard Rock Café has designed a training program that specifically aligns with the way its Generation Y employees think and learn. Their staff handbook, for example, emphasizes energetic visual presentations, provides information in an easily accessible manner, and stresses fun, such as by putting employee-drawn collages of famous rock and roll musicians on the covers of each department's manual. An approach such as this encourages learning in several ways:

- **Creating appropriate conditions.** Managers should provide employees with complete and understandable information.

- **Reinforcing desired learned behaviors.** Managers should praise employees' behaviors that result in customer satisfaction.

- **Providing environmental cues that encourage learning.** Managers should structure a physical and emotional context that supports learning, such as off-site workshops that eliminate the distractions of day-to-day work.

- **Using a modeling strategy.** Managers can identify target behaviors, select a presentation method, verify the employee's technical skills, and then structure a favorable learning environment. Then the managers can model, support, and reinforce the target behavior.

Increasingly, companies provide computer-based learning for their employees. IBM rolled out an experimental version of Basic Blue for Managers, which translates a five-day classroom experience into 50 weeks of online learning. The electronic format allowed participants to spend more time on difficult concepts and proceed at their own pace. Participants generally liked the new format, although they believed that traditional classroom presentations were more appropriate for learning certain types of behavioral skills.[60]

Distance learning, in which students participate in online instruction from remote locations, has become increasingly common in industry and higher education. Instructional designers at the World Campus, Pennsylvania State University's distance education division, convert traditional college courses into online courses for use by the university's students and corporate clients.[61] In one distance learning experiment, six professors from six colleges teach an advanced Latin course together. About 30 students in total tune into an online audio broadcast of a lecture. They can ask questions and make comments in a live chat room during the lecture. Students meet weekly with the professor at their college for a tutorial session and also participate in an ongoing online discussion with all class participants and faculty. The creation of a "virtual classics department" coordinates teaching by a similar method for 15 colleges in the Associated Colleges of the South.[62]

PERCEPTION, ATTRIBUTION, AND LEARNING IN A DOT-COM, GLOBAL WORKPLACE

The rapid speed of change experienced in today's workplace can influence the accuracy of perceptions and attributions. Consider the rapid rise of e-business and the great attractiveness of working in a dot-com company in the late 1990s. This rapid rise was quickly followed in 2000 by a decline in stock value and a reassessment of the attractiveness of such companies. The perceptions of the value of various types of businesses changed almost overnight, depending on the business's economic situation at the time. Individual differences in perceptions accompany these large-scale changes in corporate value. So do patterns of attributions of behavior in the dot-coms. Managers need to carefully assess the causes of behavior in these organizations so that corrections can occur to ensure the success of such ventures. Managers in dot-com organizations also need to expedite their employees' learning. Because the environment changes so rapidly and technological advances repeatedly occur, workers' knowledge can quickly become obsolete. Ongoing training and development are essential for employees to meet the challenges posed by the twenty-first century economy.

Cultural differences can also affect the way individuals process information. They affect the stimuli we select to perceive, the way we organize them, and the way we interpret them. They affect the content and structure of schemas used to understand the environment and influence behavior.[63] Our cultural background may cause us to distort our perceptions and attributions in predictable or unpredictable ways. Cultural differences can also affect our approach to and style of learning.

We saw that problems with ERP implementation existed outside of the United States. How might managers and employees in different countries have dealt with these problems? The interaction between the customers and vendors may have differed, depending on cultural influences on perceptions and attributions. Our cultural heritage, for example, may cause us to ignore certain stimuli and focus on others: An American may ignore certain gestures as part of normal conversation, whereas a Japanese businessperson might find them offensive.

Cross-cultural misperceptions occur for four reasons.[64] First, we have subconscious cultural blinders that cause us to interpret events in other countries as if they were occurring in our own. Second, we lack a complete understanding of our own culture and its influence on our behavior. Third, we assume people are more similar to us than they are. Finally, our general lack of knowledge about other cultures contributes to our misperceptions. An awareness of these differences can help us consider and represent the perspectives of several different observers when we describe events or people. If we can incorporate many people's perceptions into an account of a person or event, our description should be more accurate than if we attend only to our own perceptions.

Cultural sensemaking involves the following events. First the individual pays attention to stimuli that give cues about the situation. Next the person analyzes the cues within the appropriate cultural context. Then she should select the correct cultural schema and develop scripts for action. Multinational organizations can then select expatriate employees who can think more complexly and handle ambiguity and different perspectives. For expatriates already placed in jobs, executives can assess the extent of their cultural knowledge and remedy any deficiencies with training or other methods of knowledge exchange.[65]

Making attributions in cross-cultural situations calls for a familiarity with the culture in which the situation occurs. For example, managers of a multicultural workforce should not equate poor grammar or mispronunciation with lack of ability.[66] Managers should also recognize that multicultural employees may differ in the extent to which they accept responsibility for particular events. The high failure rate for expatriate leaders may be a function of culturally based attributional biases that create incongruent perceptions when leaders and followers come from cultures that differ along the individualism-collectivism and low-high context dimensions.[67]

The context in which learning occurs can significantly influence outcomes. Training employees in different countries, which typically have significantly different approaches to learning, may influence the training's effectiveness. British universities, for example, emphasize tutorials, whereas schools in the United States more commonly use larger group learning experiences. Different cultures may stress one type of personal learning style more than another. Japanese reasoning has been characterized as analytical, in which the whole is broken into parts, and Western reasoning as comprehensive, in which the parts are combined into a whole.[68]

Diversity or cross-cultural training often incorporates a social learning approach.[69] Trainees view models of cross-cultural interactions, rehearse the same types of behaviors, and then build cognitive maps of actions that, when reinforced, serve as the basis of future effective action. Diagnosing the nature of learning and constructing experiences that maximize it are essential for functioning in a global environment.

▌ Summary

1. Perception, or the selection and organization of information, influences the way people describe organizational situations.
2. Characteristics of the stimulus and the perceiver influence the way managers perceive a person, object, or event, and the manager organizes stimuli by setting them against a background or grouping them into patterns.
3. People store sensations into schemas, including scripts of behavior.
4. Managers and employees distort perceptions through stereotyping, the halo effect, projection, self-fulfilling prophecy, and other mechanisms, resulting in inaccurate descriptions or diagnoses.
5. Managers may consciously manage the impressions they create in the workplace.
6. Managers and employees attribute reasons for behavior in predictable ways: according to the individual's point of view, the appropriateness and impact of the behavior, the nature of the outcomes, the individual's response tendency, and the individual's self-concept.
7. Managers can increase learning, which refers to the acquisition of skills, knowledge, ability or attitudes, by understanding the links between behaviors and their consequences, rewarding desired behaviors, incorporating mental images into learning, and modeling and imitating desired behaviors.

A Manager's Diagnostic Review

▢ Choose and organize information carefully.
- What factors influence the selection of stimuli?
- How are sensations organized?

▢ Create scripts that lead to effective action.
- What scripts and schemas do managers and employees use?

▢ Manage the impressions you create and understand how others manage theirs.
- What impressions do people try to create?
- To what extent do people monitor, motivate, and construct impressions?

▢ Avoid perceptual distortions.
- What perceptual distortions occur?

◻ Make correct attributions of employees' and other managers' behaviors.

- What factors influence individuals' attributions?
- What biases exist in their attributions?

◻ Encourage learning with the right cues, rewards, and models.

- What behaviors are reinforced as part of the learning process?
- What cues encourage learning?
- What modeling strategies exist, and how are they supported in the organization?

◻ Understand the nature of perception, attribution, and learning in a dot-com, global workplace.

- What special challenges in perception, attribution, and learning do employees in dot-com companies face?
- How accurate are cross-cultural perceptions, attributions, and learning?

Visit the Gordon homepage on the Prentice Hall Web site at

http://www.prenhall.com/gordon

for recommended readings, additional activities, Internet exercises, updated information, and links to related Web sites.

▌ Thinking Critically About Organizational Behavior

1. What mistakes can managers make in their perceptions of people, objects, and events?
2. How do managers use schemas in their perceptions?
3. How would the use of prototypes and exemplars differ in their impact on a manager's behavior?
4. How can managers avoid perceptual distortions?
5. Why do workers and their organizations try to manage impressions?
6. Can impression management result in dysfunctional behavior?
7. What happens when people experience contradictions in their attributions of the causes of organizational events?
8. What factors affect how a manager attributes the cause of poor performance by an employee?
9. What steps should a person take to ensure accurate attributions?
10. How does the environment affect perception, attribution, and learning in dot-com companies?
11. What differences likely exist in perceptions and attributions in the United States, Germany, Singapore, and Australia?
12. How can managers use their knowledge of the processes of perception and attribution to improve description, diagnosis, prescription, or action?

ACTIVITY 2-1: FACTS AND INFERENCES

STEP 1: Carefully read the following report and the observations based on it. Indicate whether you think the observations are true, false, or doubtful on the basis of the information presented in the report. Circle **T** if the observation is definitely true, circle **F** if the observation is definitely false, and circle **?** if the observation may be either true or false. Judge each observation in order. Do not reread the observations after you have indicated your judgment, and do not change any of your answers.

A well-liked college teacher had just completed making up the final examinations and had turned off the lights in the office. Just then a tall, broad figure appeared and demanded the examination. The professor opened the drawer. Everything in the drawer was picked up and the individual ran down the corridor. The dean was notified immediately.

1. The thief was tall and broad.   **T   F   ?**
2. The professor turned off the lights.   **T   F   ?**
3. A tall figure demanded the examination.   **T   F   ?**
4. The examination was picked up by someone.   **T   F   ?**
5. The examination was picked up by the professor.   **T   F   ?**
6. A tall figure appeared after the professor turned off the lights in the office.   **T   F   ?**
7. The man who opened the drawer was the professor.   **T   F   ?**
8. The professor ran down the corridor.   **T   F   ?**
9. The drawer was never actually opened.   **T   F   ?**
10. In this report, three persons are referred to.   **T   F   ?**

STEP 2: In small groups, discuss your answers and then reach consensus about the answers. Write these answers in a separate place.

STEP 3: The instructor will read the correct answers. Score the questions, once for you as an individual and again for your group.

STEP 4: Discussion. Did your score change? Why do people answer these questions incorrectly?

Source: This exercise is taken from Joseph A. Devito, *General Semantics: Guide and Workbook*, rev. ed. Deland, FL: Everett/Edwards, 1974, p. 55, and is reprinted with permission.

ACTIVITY 2-2: PREJUDICE AND STEREOTYPES

STEP 1: Individually or in small groups, as directed by your instructor, make a list of groups of people that tend to be targets of prejudice and stereotypes in our culture.

STEP 2: For each group, identify two to four common (positive and negative) stereotypes associated with it.

STEP 3: With the entire class, identify the issues that underlie the stereotypes. What effect do these stereotypes have in the workplace? How can managers help employees correct inaccurate stereotypes?

STEP 4: You will receive three 5×8-inch cards. On each card write about an experience you had in which you were stereotyped as a member of a group. Be as specific and detailed as possible. Consider the following questions while thinking about these incidents:

1. What group do I identify with?
2. What was the stereotype?
3. What happened, exactly? When did the incident occur? Where did it occur? Who said what to whom?
4. What were my reactions when the incident occurred? How did I feel? What did I think? What did I do?
5. What were the overall consequences? How did the incident affect me in the future? Did it change my expectations of myself? Of others?

STEP 5: In small groups, discuss your experiences. Each student should share one or more personal incidents, describing it and then discussing how it felt to be stereotyped and prejudged.

STEP 6: Each group should select one incident and prepare a role-play of the incident for the class.

STEP 7: With the entire class, discuss the role-play. Identify the prejudice or stereotype portrayed, the thoughts and feelings the scene evoked, and the consequences that might result from such a situation. Then summarize the discussion by answering the following questions:

1. How easy is it to stereotype?
2. Who can be the target of stereotyping?

STEP 8: Students should think about prejudices and stereotypes they personally have. They should answer the following questions in writing:

1. What groups do I feel prejudice toward?
2. What stereotypes do I hold about members of each of these groups?

STEP 9: Students should select one of these prejudices or stereotypes and write about how they think it developed.

STEP 10: With the entire class, students should discuss the nature of personal prejudices and stereotypes and how they likely arise. Then they should answer the following questions:

1. How do prejudices and stereotypes help us? Hurt us?
2. How can we begin to change ourselves? To change others?
3. How do prejudices and stereotypes affect organizational life? Managers? Workers?

Source: Adapted from A. McKee and S. Schor, Confronting prejudice and stereotypes: A teaching model, *Journal of Management Education* 18(4) (November 1994): 447–467.

ACTIVITY 2-3: MANAGING IMPRESSIONS IN THE WORKPLACE

STEP 1: Read each of the minicases below. For each minicase, develop a plan for creating or managing the impression desired by the manager.

Case 1

Sam Cornwall was the new kid on the block. He had just joined McDermott and List, a medium-sized accounting firm, as a senior auditor. Sam had developed an impressive resume in the four years since he had received his CPA. His major problem, however, was that he looked as if he were 15 years old. He wanted to impress his new bosses and his clients. How could he create the desired impression?

Case 2

Susan Everett assumed responsibility for the Fresh-Frozen account in her advertising agency. The previous account manager had created a fairly traditional media campaign for selling FreshFrozen—it featured a housewife using FreshFrozen foods to feed her hungry husband when he came home from work. Susan felt that this image was outdated and even sexist. She wanted to give FreshFrozen a more contemporary image, one that would appeal to the increasingly diverse workforce. How could she manage impressions in the workplace?

Case 3

Emily Fitzgerald was the founder and president of Beta Technologies, a new start-up that sold sophisticated design software for the Web. Fitzgerald knew that her company's product was superior to those already on the market, but although the company was making some inroads into the marketplace, its market share was not increasing at the rate she and her management team had projected. She learned from potential buyers that her company was viewed as an upstart that was trying to bulldoze any competitors that got in its way. Emily herself was viewed as overly aggressive and not someone the distributors wanted to do business with. Emily believed that many of these views resulted because she and many of her top managers were female. Emily wanted to show that her company had the best product and could deliver it to the marketplace.

How might she manage the impressions of her company and herself?

STEP 2: In small groups or with the entire class, share your plans. Identify the common elements in each plan. Then answer the following questions:

1. How easily can an individual manage impressions in an organization?
2. What impact does managing impressions have on an organization?
3. What effect does managing impressions have on an individual's career and performance?

ACTIVITY 2-4: THE PERCEPTUAL DISTORTIONS TRAINING PROGRAM

STEP 1: You are the director of training for the General Computer Corporation. You have read a great deal about programs that use social learning theory to help people function more effectively. You have noticed that the managers in your company have been guilty of numerous perceptual distortions in dealing with their subordinates. You believe that a training session that includes extensive role-playing could help reduce the perceptual distortions in the company. Your task is to design a training module that incorporates both role-playing and the modeling strategy of learning described in the social learning approach.

STEP 2: Share and critique your designs in small groups or with the entire class. Check that each

design incorporates the steps in the social learning approach. If possible, pilot one of the training modules. Consider the following:

1. What behaviors were taught?
2. How did your module incorporate the social learning approach?

STEP 3: Discussion. In small groups or with the entire class, answer the following questions:

1. What behaviors did each module try to teach?
2. How were the modules similar and different?
3. How effective was using the social learning approach?

ACTIVITY 2-5: DEVELOPING GLOBAL MANAGERIAL TRAINING

STEP 1: Read the following scenario:

HR Internet, Inc., began as a partnership of five MBAs who developed and sold computer software for human resources applications for small businesses. Clients could pay a fee and then download the software from the Internet. The company quickly grew as the demand for this type of human resources software boomeranged. The company grew from the original five to more than 150 employees in less than a year. Because most of the managers had risen through the ranks, from programmers to programming consultants to senior consultants and then to project managers, they lacked the training to supervise employees and projects effectively. In particular, they often made mistakes in describing both employees' and customers' behavior and understanding its causes.

STEP 2: HR Internet has hired you to develop a managerial training program for the company that will address these deficiencies for both managers and employees. Individually or in small groups, outline the key perceptual and attributional skills needed by the managers and the employees.

STEP 3: Assume that the company has just opened branches in Nice, France, and Barcelona, Spain. What changes in the training program are necessary to best prepare workers in these locations? Do the basic principles of perception and attribution differ in different countries and cultures? How can managers of global companies ensure consistency in their worldwide management?

ACTIVITY 2-6: LEARNING MODEL INSTRUMENT

STEP 1: For each statement, choose the response that is more nearly true for you. Place an X on the blank that corresponds to that response.

1. When meeting people, I prefer
   _____ **a.** to think and speculate on what they are like.
   _____ **b.** to interact directly and ask them questions.

2. When presented with a problem, I prefer
   _____ **a.** to jump right in and work on a solution.
   _____ **b.** to think through and evaluate possible ways to solve the problem.

3. I enjoy sports more when
   _____ **a.** I am watching a good game.
   _____ **b.** I am actively participating.

4. Before taking a vacation, I prefer
   _____ **a.** to rush at the last minute and give little thought beforehand to what I will do while on vacation.
   _____ **b.** to plan early and daydream about how I will spend my vacation.

5. When enrolled in courses, I prefer
   _____ **a.** to plan how to do my homework before actually attacking the assignment.
   _____ **b.** to immediately become involved in doing the assignment.

6. When I receive information that requires action, I prefer
   _____ **a.** to take action immediately.
   _____ **b.** to organize the information and determine what type of action would be most appropriate.

7. When presented with a number of alternatives for action, I prefer
   _____ **a.** to determine how the alternatives relate to one another and analyze the consequences of each.
   _____ **b.** to select the one that looks best and implement it.

8. When I awake every morning, I prefer
   _____ **a.** to expect to accomplish some worthwhile work without considering what the individual tasks entail.
   _____ **b.** to plan a schedule for the tasks I expect to do today.

9. After a full day's work, I prefer
   _____ **a.** to reflect back on what I accomplished and think of how to make time the next day for unfinished tasks.
   _____ **b.** to relax with some type of recreation and not think about my job.

10. After choosing the above responses, I
    _____ **a.** prefer to continue and complete this instrument.
    _____ **b.** am curious about how my responses will be interpreted and prefer some feedback before continuing with the instrument.

11. When I learn something, I am usually
    _____ **a.** thinking about it.
    _____ **b.** right in the middle of doing it.

12. I learn best when
    _____ **a.** I am dealing with real-world issues.
    _____ **b.** concepts are clear and well organized.

13. In order to retain something I have learned, I must
    _____ **a.** periodically review it in my mind.
    _____ **b.** practice it or try to use the information.

14. In teaching others how to do something, I first
    _____ **a.** demonstrate the task.
    _____ **b.** explain the task.

15. My favorite way to learn to do something is
    _____ **a.** reading a book or instructions or enrolling in a class.
    _____ **b.** trying to do it and learning from my mistakes.

16. When I become emotionally involved with something, I usually
    _____ **a.** let my feelings take the lead and then decide what to do.
    _____ **b.** control my feelings and try to analyze the situation.

17. If I were meeting jointly with several experts on a subject, I would prefer
    _____ **a.** to ask each of them for his or her opinion.
    _____ **b.** to interact with them and share our ideas and feelings.

18. When I am asked to relate information to a group of people, I prefer

_____ **a.** not to have an outline, but to interact with them and become involved in an extemporaneous conversation.

_____ **b.** to prepare notes and know exactly what I am going to say.

19. Experience is

_____ **a.** a guide for building theories.

_____ **b.** the best teacher.

20. People learn easier when they are

_____ **a.** doing work on the job.

_____ **b.** in a class taught by an expert.

Abstract/Concrete		Cognitive/Affective	
Column 1	**Column 2**	**Column 3**	**Column 4**
1. _____	2. _____	11. _____	12. _____
3. _____	4. _____	13. _____	14. _____
5. _____	6. _____	15. _____	16. _____
7. _____	8. _____	17. _____	18. _____
9. _____	10. _____	19. _____	20. _____
Total Circles			
Grand Totals			

STEP 2: For each item, place the letter of your response next to the item number in the chart in the next column.

STEP 3: Now circle every *a* in Column 1 and Column 4. Then circle every *b* in Column 2 and Column 3. Next total the circles in each of the four columns. Then add the totals of Columns 1 and 2; plot this grand total on the vertical axis of the Learning Model for Managers (Figure 2-9) and draw a horizontal line through the point. Now add the totals of Columns 3 and 4; plot that grand total on the horizontal axis of the model and draw a vertical line through the point. The intersection of these two lines indicates the domain of your preferred learning style.

Source: Copyright 1987 by Dr. Kenneth L. Murrell, President of Empowerment Leadership Systems and Full Professor of Management and Organization Development, the University of West Florida. Used with permission.

◼ FIGURE 2-9 ◼

Use this grid to determine your type of learning style.

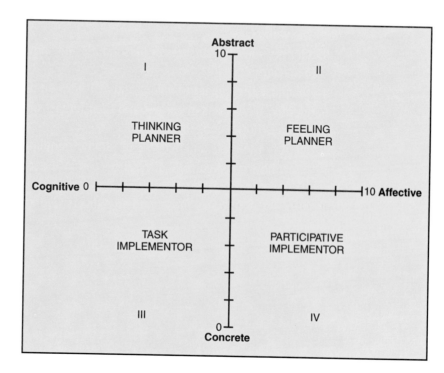

Chapter 3

The Diverse Workforce: Individual Differences, Personality, and Career Development

Learning Objectives

After completing Chapter 3, you will be able to

1. Discuss the advantages of diversity in the workplace.
2. Diagnose the impact of gender, race, age, and physical disabilities in the workplace.
3. Identify some dimensions of personality, and show how they influence behavior in organizations.
4. Diagnose the impact of values and attitudes on organizations.
5. Identify new forms of careers and their impact on individual and organizational performance.
6. Identify the costs and benefits of family friendliness in the workplace.
7. Show how cross-cultural differences can influence behavior and attitudes in the workplace.
8. Offer two strategies for managing a diverse workforce.

A Manager's Preview

Describe . . . Diagnose . . . Prescribe . . . Act

- Acknowledge the value of diversity in the workplace.
- Remove obstacles encountered by women, minorities, older workers, and physically challenged employees.
- Know how personality differences affect a person's work.
- Recognize the role values and attitudes play in job performance.
- Help workers build effective careers.
- Develop programs to help workers create work–life balance.

Companies That Seek Diversity Outperform the S&P 500[1]

Numerous companies have discovered that increasing the diversity of their workforce pays off in improved performance, happier customers, and more satisfied employees. Consider Wal-Mart. "Much of Wal-Mart's substantial growth has come in urban areas, prompting the retailer to diversify its humongous 800,000 workforce to capitalize on local talent pools and do what it does best: sell. Catering to minority customers is far more effective when a company addresses the distinctions that drive purchasing decisions among various ethnic groups. So putting more people of color on the sales floor—and in executive positions—is really a no-brainer in this company."[2]

Now consider the role Glen Toney plays at Applied Materials, a $4 billion manufacturer of semiconductor equipment. A 20-year employee of the company and group vice president of corporate affairs, Toney mentors several of the company's minority employees and keeps top executives informed about promising minority workers. He notes that "people who come aboard here have to move faster than they ever have before, and the organization is complex and can be frustrating." The fatherly role Toney and others play helps explain the company's reputation in the Silicon Valley as a good place for people of color to work.[3]

Toyota tries to locate highly competent minority candidates. A member of the minority advisory board commented, "They'll go outside the automobile industry to get somebody who is energetic and shows promise and wants to become an automobile dealer. Then that person will take an awful lot of schooling and training." This enthusiasm about minority employees attracts many minority customers who recognize a company's reputation as being minority-friendly.[4] Other global companies also benefit from having a diverse workforce that can relate to its customers from many cultures.

Maria Elena Lagomasino, the senior managing director of Chase Manhattan's Global Private Banking Group, oversees the investments of some of the world's wealthiest people. Her effectiveness stems in part from her ability to understand people from diverse cultures. Her Cuban roots have helped. "If you are bicultural, you understand that there are different ways of doing things. . . . When I got into private banking with Latin American customers, I found my ability to understand their reality a great advantage."[5]

These companies recognize the value of a diverse workforce. Each of them has acknowledged the importance of minority customers and employees. Other companies recognize the value of having women, older workers, and physically challenged employees as part of their workforce, and meet the challenge of ensuring that they have a diverse group of employees.

In this chapter, we look at individual differences that affect performance. We first look at the nature of workplace diversity. Then we examine a series of demographic characteristics of the workforce that affect the workplace. We next explore the impact of personality, followed by attitudes and values, on individual behavior. We then examine the ways people build careers and how they handle the work–life challenges they face. We conclude with a return to issues of diversity in the dot-com, global workplace.

▌ THE DIVERSE WORKPLACE

Demographics, competition for talent, marketplace demands, and the changing environment call for a diverse workforce. This workforce includes (and treats equally) men and women, employees with differing ethnic backgrounds, younger and older workers, physically challenged employees, and other workers who differ from the dominant group of white, male employees in the United States. By bringing a greater pool of talent to the workplace, diversity often results in better decision making, an increased understanding of customers' needs, and a greater staffing ability.

Changes in the workplace have made *cultural ethnocentrism,* the belief in the preeminence of one's own culture, dysfunctional in a global economy. Managers in the United States have rejected cultural ethnocentrism for the following reasons:

- respect for individual and cultural differences;
- a legal system that values equal opportunity and nondiscrimination in the workplace;
- a global economy that markets goods and services to diverse cultures;
- belief in the benefits of hiring workers that resemble their customers; and
- an already-changing workforce.

Managers at companies such as Wal-Mart, Applied Materials, Toyota, and Chase Manhattan who understand the uniqueness of each employee can create collaborative relationships among people with different skills, abilities, experiences, aspirations, and expectations. Some managers need encouragement to develop positive attitudes about people different from themselves and to recognize the unique contribution and potential of each employee. Understanding the ways people might differ is a first step in dealing with diversity.

The number of women, racial and ethnic minorities, older workers, and physically challenged workers has increased in the last decade. These groups will remain a significant part of the workforce. They bring different and important perspectives to the workplace that can help companies attain a competitive advantage. In this section, we briefly comment about the issues related to managing these groups of workers.

Women in the Workplace

A dramatic increase in the numbers and percentage of women in the workplace has occurred. This change has resulted from equal employment and affirmative action legislation, the feminist movement, and economic realities. Even today, women still earn less than their male counterparts. For example, full-time working women's earnings were 76 percent of men's earnings in 1998. White workers, middle-aged workers, older workers, and those with only a high school education experienced the greatest gender earnings wage gap. Earnings of women with college degrees increased by close to 22 percent in the past two decades. This improvement contributed in part to an increase in the earnings differences between white women and black and Hispanic women in the same time period.[6]

As their representation has increased, women continue to experience unique concerns and problems. Women's lives differ from men's because they have responsibility for child bearing and generally assume primary responsibility for child rearing. Women more often than men choose to reduce their work commitment to part-time or conduct their careers in a serial fashion, spending time as a full-time wife and mother before reentering the workplace. In one study, part-time work was associated with less interference between work and family responsibilities, better time management ability, and greater life satisfaction for women.[7] In a different, three-year study of 1,000 female managers by Catalyst, a New York research firm that focuses on women's issues, the women who worked part-time said they were happier and more productive than when they worked full-time.[8] Part-time work generally allows women to better balance work and family needs. Yet part-time work can also slow a person's career advancement and result in lower salaries.

The *glass ceiling* may hinder women's advancement.[9] This invisible barrier to movement into top management results from discrimination in the workplace, the inability of women and minorities to penetrate the "old boys' network," and the tendency of executives to promote others like themselves. While the number of top women business leaders has increased, their movement onto boards of directors and top executive positions remains stalled. For example, the chemical industry has few women in top-level positions, and women represent less than 10 percent of board seats in a survey of 48 companies.[10] Sex role stereotyping is more problematic in firms with relatively low proportions of senior women.[11]

Yet some firms have overcome the glass ceiling. Zale Corporation, a large jewelry retailer, has nine women among the 25 in the company's management group and three of five executive officers. Neiman Marcus has its first woman CEO; Avon and J.C. Penney have significant numbers of women in top positions. The increase in the number of women in top positions has resulted from women professionals who entered companies in the 1970s and 1980s and now have the bottom-line experience to assume top-level jobs.[12] Even very traditionally male countries have begun to see cracks in the glass ceiling. Maria Asunción Aramburuzabala, a vice president of Grupo Modelo, the family-run maker of Corona beer, has broken new ground for women in Mexico. She recently led her company in obtaining a 20-percent stake in Grupo Televisa, a Mexican media giant. Compaq Computer's Mexican subsidiary also has a woman leader.[13]

The same problems apply to women in Europe. While the European workforce includes 41 percent women, they hold only 29 percent of management jobs, less than two percent of senior management jobs, and only one percent of board seats. Women earn up to 40 percent less in manufacturing jobs and 35 percent less in service jobs. The slow progress results from lack of child care, as well as women's unwillingness to ask for flexibility.[14]

Women hold only 14 percent of international management assignments, primarily because companies have been unwilling to send them overseas. Myths that women do not want to be international managers and that foreigners may be prejudiced against women expatriate managers have been shown to be untrue. The senior manager of human resources in Asia for Cisco Systems argues that Western women are generally well received in other countries because they're not expected to conform to the same standards as local women and so can function more as they would in the same job in the United States. Women's desire and ability to do high-quality work, as well as support from senior management, further bolster their position abroad.[15]

Companies can increase the likelihood that high-potential women will accept overseas assignments in a number of ways. First, they can help them break through the glass ceiling and assume top-level management positions. Second, they can create career development programs that include international assignments. Third, they can develop a systematic way to identify potential expatriates and convince them to seek international assignments. Fourth, top executives can make sure women receive predeparture cross-cultural training. Fifth, they can provide support that helps women address family needs, such as child care and relocation for their spouses. Finally, they can publicize successful women expatriates.[16]

Race in the Workplace

The percentage of African Americans in the workplace has increased significantly in the past 25 years, due in large part to affirmative action requirements.[17] Now African Americans have assumed more jobs in the executive suite. Lloyd Ward, for example, who began his life in a 400-square-foot house with no running water, rose to become CEO of Maytag Appliances after successful stints at Procter & Gamble and Pepsico. Ward notes, "There are many who are systematically excluded. But the oppressed have to overcome the prejudices of society. Knock on the door, pull on the handle, and, if you have to, dismantle the hinge."[18]

Race combined with gender can create a particularly potent barrier that prevents women of color from advancing into executive positions.[19] Some African American women have made it to the upper echelons of power and influence.[20] They work for companies such as American Express, Kraft Foods, IBM, and Xerox, and hold executive positions such as president, chief executive, executive vice president, and vice president. Reducing stereotypes and promoting workers on the basis of ability and demonstrated competence presents a major challenge for managers. The Corporate Few, an informal network of African American employees initiated in 1971, mentors young African Americans.[21]

In spite of these advances, discrimination continues to exist. Major League Soccer (MLS) fined a New England Revolution player $20,000 for using a racial slur against a teammate during a practice. The MLS then used the fine to pay for diversity training seminars for all league teams' players, coaches, and administrative personnel.[22] NASCAR, the automobile racing organization, suspended two white crew members who mimicked the Ku Klux Klan in a prank on an African American crew member; the drivers who employed the suspended crew members later terminated their employment.[23]

Racial incidents also occur outside the United States. Ford Motor Company's Dagenham, England, plant experienced a series of racial incidents that contributed to a one-day wildcat strike that shut down the assembly line for Ford Fiestas. The most recent racial incident occurred when Ford failed to punish a supervisor accused of pushing an Asian employee; Ford had previously acknowledged that managers had abused this employee for four years, including making him work in an oil-spraying room without protective clothing. Ford CEO Jacques Nasser agreed to establish committees at each of the company's 13 British plants to ensure that managers pay attention to discrimination complaints.[24]

Reducing stereotypes and promoting workers on the basis of ability and demonstrated competence present a major challenge for managers. Texaco, which agreed to pay $175 million to settle a racial discrimination suit, is becoming a model employer in diversity initiatives. Three years after the settlement, four in ten new hires and 20 percent of promotions were minorities. The CEO has helped establish goals and timetables designed to transform the culture to one that supports and encourages minority retention and advancement.[25]

Older Workers

Organizations face a dramatic increase in the number of older workers as the baby boomers age. Predictions call for almost a doubling of the number of senior citizens by 2025.[26] At the same time, current and projected labor shortages make older workers an important source of employees. Wells Fargo & Company, for example, buses retirees from Sun City, Arizona, to the bank's operations center in Tempe, Arizona.[27] Problems in the hiring and advancement of older workers can arise from stereotypes about their skills, energy, and interests. Managers should recognize that the myths about older workers' inability to learn, slow speed of response, and inflexibility are not true. Older workers can demonstrate the same creativity, adaptability, and manageability as younger workers.

Some companies discriminate against older workers. The Equal Employment Opportunity Commission has accused TJX of harassing and firing workers over age 40 because of their age. TJX has also been blamed for subjecting older employees to a hostile work environment due to verbal harassment, unfair discipline, and overt hostility.[28] Age combined with gender or race can have a particularly powerful effect in encouraging wage disparities.[29]

Some companies have begun to institute part-time and modified full-time work arrangements for older workers. This schedule allows them to avoid the boredom often associated with retirement and to earn additional income. REH Marketing pays senior citizens an hourly rate to ask supermarket shoppers to sample different products.[30] Managers will need to work with many of these older Americans who remain in the workforce after the age of 70.[31]

Physically Challenged Employees

The Vocational Rehabilitation Act of 1978 and the Americans with Disabilities Act of 1990 have made the workplace in the United States more accessible to people with physical disabilities. While certain disabilities may prevent a person from performing particular jobs, managers cannot discriminate in hiring, promoting, evaluating, or compensating physically challenged workers. For example, managers can't prevent blind, physically handicapped, or deaf workers from holding jobs for which they are qualified. The increased success of disabled workers has helped overcome myths about their inability to perform jobs, fit into a company's culture, or socialize with other workers. Managers should look for qualified people to perform specific jobs and then make reasonable accommodations for a disability that doesn't create undue hardship for the employer.[32] Microsoft, with the National Business and Disability Council, helped create a coalition of 23 firms that agree to hire disabled professionals.[33]

By law, organizations must remove physical barriers that prevent access to job locations for physically impaired employees; for example, they might install special ramps or elevators for wheelchair-bound workers. Some companies even make special provisions, such as specialized reading equipment for blind employees, to allow physically challenged employees to perform their jobs. Advances in computer software have helped some disabled workers perform more successfully. For example, voice recognition and interpretation and speech recognition software support the work of blind or partially sighted employees; IBM's Home Page Reader lets a blind employee surf the Web and use it for research, shopping, and e-mail.[34] Recent legislation also awards states $150 million over five years to develop programs to support disabled citizens who want to work.[35]

Some argue that the Americans with Disabilities Act has had the unintended consequence of increasing the cost of employing disabled workers so much that firms find employing them unattractive.[36] Increased numbers of lawsuits may have benefited attorneys more than the disabled employees they represent.[37] Yet, particularly in a tight labor market, employees have begun to view disabled employees as an important source of workers. A Sears store manager in Massachusetts, for example, built a stockroom next to an employee's work area when he realized that a physically challenged employee couldn't walk to the stockroom on another floor because of her disability.

▋ PERSONALITY

We can describe workers according to other individual characteristics besides gender, race, and age. An individual's *personality* influences his job performance.

What Is Personality?

Personality refers to a set of distinctive personal characteristics, including motives, emotions, values, interests, attitudes, and competencies. How would you describe Glen Toney's personality? We might describe him as extroverted and competitive. We might describe him as having a Type A personality or being high in self-efficacy. His heredity and his social, cultural, and family environments likely influenced his personality. His personality in turn influences the way he acts. For example, his personality might cause him to naturally set challenging goals and rely on his relationships with others to achieve them. How would you describe the personality of other employees of Applied Materials? Of Toyota, Wal-Mart, or Chase Manhattan?

The personalities of top executives can help explain dysfunctional organizations.[38] For example, an executive who believes that no one can be trusted often creates an organization in which secrecy and guardedness characterize the culture. Or a manager whose personality reflects a need for control will often create an organization that relies too much on formal controls and direct supervision to accomplish the organizational goals. An attempted merger between SmithKline Beecham and Glaxo Wellcome collapsed the first time in part because of a clash between the charismatic CEO of SmithKline and the strong-willed top executive of Glaxo Wellcome over who should run the new company. Now they have given the leadership of the combined company to a third person, characterized as a patient, highly disciplined executive who can provide calming and authoritative leadership.[39]

Measuring Personality

Trained and certified professionals generally assess personality in three ways:

- **Personality inventories** require the person to answer questions that describe the respondent's personality.
- **Projective tests** require the person to describe what she sees in a picture or relatively ambiguous stimulus, such as an inkblot. A detailed scoring protocol places the person along numerous personality dimensions.
- **Simulations, role-playing exercises, and stress interviews** require the person to behave in specific situations. An observation and scoring protocol categorizes the person along dimensions such as adaptability, assertiveness, or dominance.

Managers might use information collected from these instruments as part of the pre-employment screening process or promotion decisions. A 1997 survey by the Society for Human Resources Management indicated that 22 percent of U.S. companies use personality tests to screen candidates. For example, companies use the 50-adjective Predictive Index to help determine the most suitable type of work for potential and current employees. Others use the Sales Success Predictor to measure confidence, aggressiveness, initiative, and creativity for potential salespeople.[40] After administering a test to help understand an employee's personality, the manager can examine how personality affects the worker's behavior. Will the employee likely work well on a team? Does the employee have a drive to succeed, demonstrate compatibility with others, and have positive feelings of self-worth?[41] The manager can then adjust the work situation to better match workers' personalities and hence obtain better outcomes. For example, BellSouth and TManage have agreed to sell Team Telework Connections, which helps set up telecommuting programs. The package includes personality tests that can help determine whether employees are suitable for telecommuting.[42]

Personality Traits and Attributes

Psychological research has identified many traits and attributes, some measured by the previously mentioned instruments, that compose a person's personality. In this section, we examine five personality dimensions, composed of these traits and attributes, that managers could consider in assessing on-the-job behavior. Managers can benefit by knowing how these dimensions might influence employee behavior.

Describing and analyzing a person's personality can suggest some issues managers should consider in managing that employee.

Internalizers–Externalizers. People differ in the extent to which they believe that their behaviors influence what happens to them:[43]

- **Internalizers** feel that they control their own lives and actions.
- **Externalizers** believe others control their lives.

Assume that a manager has two subordinates: Jeff Smith is an internalizer, and Stan Jenkins is an externalizer. How might these two men differ in their views of the best way to advance in an organization? Smith might believe that he can control his advancement, whereas Jenkins might not. Smith might take personal responsibility for implementing advancement strategies, while Jenkins would probably rely on his manager's guidance. Managers need to recognize the nature of employees' personalities as part of coaching and developing them. For example, they can answer the questions shown in Activity 3-3 to help them assess whether their employees are internalizers or externalizers.

Type A–Type B. Type A or Type B characteristics reflect an individual's desire for achievement, perfectionism, competitiveness, and ability to relax.

- **Type A** individuals feel competitive, are prompt for appointments, do things quickly, always feel rushed, and are often angry and hostile.
- **Type B** individuals are relaxed, take one thing at a time, and express their feelings.[44]

If you complete the scale in Figure 3-1, you will have a sense of whether you have a Type A or a Type B personality. In general, Type A employees are more prone to stress and may suffer more often from poor cardiovascular health.[45] A group of Type A Canadian nurses, for example, showed greater job stress and role pressures, but also higher job involvement, effort, and attendance, than a group of Type B nurses.[46]

According to one Silicon Valley consultant, Type A executives can exhibit stress in one of four ways:

- **Hostility/impatience.** They believe that everyone is incompetent and so intimidate others, who then fear them.
- **Compulsiveness/perfectionism.** They want to do everything themselves because they can't live with their own or others' mistakes.
- **Competitiveness.** They want to win at all costs.
- **Chronic tension.** They are multitaskers who make others ill at ease by their hyperactivity.[47]

Finding ways to recognize and correct the causes of stress becomes critical. Yet, some Type A characteristics, such as time urgency and ambition, may decrease as people age.[48] The positive aspects of Type A behavior may contribute to success, whereas the negative aspects can affect a person's health and interpersonal relationships.

Introversion–Extroversion. The Myers-Briggs Type Indicators (MBTI), a test based in Jungian psychology, uses people's preferences to indicate their overall personality type.[49] The information can help managers assess how their employees gather information, make decisions, and evaluate alternatives.

FIGURE 3-1

Completing this questionnaire can help determine whether you have a Type A or Type B personality.

Circle the number on the continuum (the verbal descriptions represent endpoints) that best represents your behavior for each dimension.

Am casual about appointments	1 2 3 4 5 6 7	Am never late
Am not competitive	1 2 3 4 5 6 7	Am very competitive
Never feel rushed, even under pressure	1 2 3 4 5 6 7	Always feel rushed
Take things one at a time	1 2 3 4 5 6 7	Try to do many things at once; think about what I am going to do next
Do things slowly	1 2 3 4 5 6 7	Do things fast (eating, walking, etc.)
Express feelings	1 2 3 4 5 6 7	"Sit on" feelings
Have many interests	1 2 3 4 5 6 7	Have few interests outside work

Now score your responses by totaling the numbers circled. Then multiply the total by 3. The interpretation of your score is as follows:

Number of Points	Type of Personality
Less than 90	B
90 to 99	B+
100 to 105	A−
106 to 119	A
120 or more	A+

Source: Adapted from R.W. Bortner, A short rating scale as a potential measure of pattern A behavior, *Journal of Chronic Diseases* 22 (1966): 87–91 with kind permission from Elsevier Science Ltd, the Boulevard, Langford Lane, Kidlington OX5 16B, United Kingdom.

First, we can classify people according to their basic interactions with others.[50] *Introverted (I)* types tend to be shy; they like quiet for concentration, dislike interruptions, and work contentedly alone. Having the ability to concentrate intensely and develop ideas, this type tends to be reflective and inwardly directed. *Extroverted (E)* types tend to be outgoing and sometimes aggressive. They like variety, enjoy functioning in a social environment, often act quickly without thinking, and may dominate situations or people. This type focuses on people and things.

Second, people acquire information by either sensing or intuition. *Sensing (S)* types like action and getting things done. They focus on facts, data, and details. Although they tend to be pragmatic, precise, and results-oriented, they can reject innovations. They work steadily and reach a conclusion step-by-step. *Intuitive (I)* types dislike doing the same thing repeatedly and enjoy learning new skills. They may leap to conclusions quickly and often follow their inspirations and hunches. They tend to be imaginative, creative, and idealistic, but can be unrealistic or scattered.

Third, people make decisions by thinking or feeling. *Thinking (T)* types excel at putting things in logical order and respond more to people's ideas than to their feelings. Characterized as analytical, rational, logical, and impersonal, they can undervalue feelings or be overly critical. They need to be treated fairly and tend to be firm and tough-minded. *Feeling (F)* types like harmony and respond to individuals' values and feelings, as well as to their thoughts. They tend to be persuasive, sympathetic, sensitive, and loyal. They enjoy pleasing people, but can be overly sensitive or moody.

Fourth, people also differ in the way they evaluate information about the world. *Judging (J)* types like to get things finished and work best with a plan. They are organized, settled, and structured, but dislike interrupting their tasks and can be closed-minded and inflexible. *Perceiving (P)* types adapt well to changing situations and do not mind last-minute changes. They tend to be open-minded, curious, and flexible. They may begin many projects but have difficulty finishing them, or they may postpone unpleasant tasks.

Managers can think of employees along combinations of the four dimensions—for example, introverted-sensing-thinking-judging (ISTJ). Figure 3-2 shows the 16 combinations, or personality types. Such a categorization may help managers understand their employees' actions, match employees to jobs, and explain differences in employees' perceptions of various situations. Diagnosing these types may also help managers understand why different employees demonstrate different styles in performing their work. Managers can then respond to the unique aspects of each worker's personality.

Managers can also think of their own personality types and use this diagnosis to explain their reactions to work situations. Some evidence suggests that managers with different types of personalities differ in conflict resolution, risk taking, and task performance.[51] Consider a manager with a poorly performing employee. A manager with a thinking personality type conducts a logical, systematic inquiry into the situation before acting. A feeling-type manager, in contrast, might first assess the employee's feelings. The effectiveness of the manager's interaction with the employee will depend on both the manager's and the employee's personalities and resulting behaviors.

Machiavellianism.   An individual with a Machiavellian personality demonstrates manipulative and unethical behavior and attitudes.[52] (The term can be traced back to the principles for government analyzed in a treatise titled *The Prince,* written by the Italian political philosopher Niccolò di Bernardo Machiavelli around 1500.) The 20-question Mach IV scale, typically used to measure Machiavellianism, indicates the degree to which the respondent believes others can be manipulated in interpersonal situations.[53] High scorers tend more than low scorers to manipulate, persuade others, win, and regard persons as objects; these are not necessarily negative characteristics

ISTJ	ISFJ	INFJ	INTS
ISTP	ISFP	INFP	INTP
ESTP	ESFP	ENFP	ENTP
ESTJ	ESFJ	ENFJ	ENTJ

FIGURE 3-2   *The Myers-Briggs Scale identifies sixteen types of personalities. (I = introverted, E = extroverted; S = sensing, I = intuitive; T = thinking, F = feeling; J = judging, P = perceiving.)*

for particular types of job holders.[54] Salespeople with high Machiavellian traits, for example, show higher sales volume but receive lower overall ratings from their managers, likely because of some friction between the manager and salesperson.[55]

Self-Efficacy.   Self-efficacy refers to people's perceptions about whether they can successfully perform a task. It influences the difficulty of goals, commitment to goals, and tasks selected by employees.[56] A manager can help increase a person's self-efficacy by giving him a better understanding of a task and its environment. The manager can also provide training for the employee to help him use his abilities more effectively and develop better strategies for doing the task.[57]

Increasing self-efficacy seems to increase an individual's performance in organizations.[58] Self-schemas (see Chapter 2) influence an individual's self-efficacy. An individual's knowledge about himself also influences his self-efficacy. So do his beliefs about the nature of specific aspects of his social situation.[59]

▌INDIVIDUAL VALUES AND ATTITUDES

A person's values and attitudes develop over time, beginning in early childhood. Values and attitudes are linked to personality and can influence behavior. If managers understand how values and attitudes affect workers, they can diagnose the reasons for workplace problems more effectively. Once diagnosed, they can also prescribe ways to solve such problems.

Values

Values refer to the basic principles and tenets that guide a person's beliefs, attitudes, and behaviors. Values tend to be relatively stable characteristics, often developed throughout childhood. They become evident in work and nonwork settings throughout adulthood. People's values can influence their beliefs about money, social interactions, the importance of work, and other aspects of their work and nonwork lives. People who demonstrate a work ethic, for example, believe that they should "do a good day's work for a good day's pay" and live a simple life.

Core values are more susceptible to change, and *peripheral values* are less susceptible. A research study of Israeli workers indicated that organizational influences affect peripheral values, and nonwork influences affect core values.[60] Managers would have difficulty changing a worker's core values through training or other interventions, but a parent, spouse, or friend, or even a powerful religious experience, might alter them. Diagnosing the impact of core values on work situations helps managers place workers in appropriate situations.

Attitudes

An *attitude* refers to a person's tendency to consistently respond to various aspects of people, situations, or objects. We infer attitude from a person's statements about their beliefs and feelings. We infer people's attitudes from what they say, what they do, and how they react. We might, for example, determine a person's job satisfaction by inferring it from her general demeanor on the job or by asking her to describe her satisfaction. We can also use attitude surveys or other attitude scales to assess employees' attitudes toward their job, co-workers, supervisor, or the organization at large.[61]

Diverse workforces include people with varying attitudes. People have an array of beliefs, formed in large part from their socioeconomic and cultural backgrounds and other experiences. These varying beliefs likely result in different attitudes. Research about the relationship between attitudes and behaviors has primarily studied U.S. workers. Would South African, Dutch, or Chinese workers have the same attitudes? Would the same behaviors result from the same attitudes? Because we can only conjecture about the association of attitudes and behaviors outside the United States, we need to describe and diagnose situations as accurately as possible. Once we understand particular attitudes and their impact on specific work situations, we can prescribe ways of changing either the attitudes or the situation to result in more productive outcomes.

Components of Attitudes.   Attitudes have a cognitive, affective, and behavioral component.[62]

- **Cognitive.** Individuals have beliefs about a certain person, object, or situation that they accept as true based on their values and experiences. These learned beliefs, such as "you need to work long hours to get ahead in this job," lead to specific attitudes. Although we have many beliefs, only some lead to attitudes that have an impact on our behavior in the workplace.

- **Affective.** People have feelings that result from their beliefs about a person, object, or situation. A person who believes extra effort deserves praise may feel angry or frustrated when she puts in extra effort but her manager doesn't acknowledge it. The affective component becomes stronger as a person has more frequent and direct experience with a focal object, person, or situation and as the person expresses her feelings about that object, person, or situation more frequently.[63]

- **Behavioral.** Behavior occurs as a result of a person's feeling about a focal person, object, or situation. A person may complain, request a transfer, or be less productive because he feels dissatisfied with work. The minority employees at Wal-Mart, Toyota, Applied Materials, and Chase Manhattan have a series of beliefs and values about their jobs. These may result in feelings of job satisfaction that in turn affect their performance.

Attitudes can also result from a person's experiences.[64] How easily a person can call on an attitude affects its impact.[65] Personal experience with the object and the repeated expression of the attitude increase its accessibility, and the attitude more frequently affects behavior.[66]

Cognitive Dissonance.   People may experience *cognitive dissonance*, which describes their attempts to deal with situations in which they have contradictory knowledge, information, attitudes, or beliefs.[67] An employee tries to reduce the contradictions by redefining the situation. For example, a company might relaunch an existing product so that it fits better with customers' perceptions of what the brand should be. In this way, the company may recapture customers who previously spurned the brand.[68] Theorists argue that dissonance is short-lived. People reduce dissonance by changing their attitudes, forgetting about the inconsistency, reaffirming their core values, trivializing the dissonant elements, or misattributing the cause of the dissonant events.[69]

Job Satisfaction

Satisfaction results when a job fulfills or helps attain an individual's values, expectations, and standards, and dissatisfaction occurs when the worker perceives that the job blocks attaining them.[70] In one study, for example, the empowerment of customer contact employees to make day-to-day decisions in the workplace was positively associated with job satisfaction.[71] In another study, the motivation of classroom teachers was associated with job satisfaction.[72] Flexibility to balance professional and personal responsibilities also contributes to job satisfaction.[73] Researchers and practitioners have paid attention to job satisfaction because they believe it affects workers' commitment and performance, although a more complicated relationship may exist between satisfaction, commitment, turnover, and productivity.[74]

▌ CAREER PLANNING AND DEVELOPMENT

A *career* refers to a lifelong sequence of related jobs and experiences. As companies have downsized and employed more knowledge workers, new types of careers and career development have become more common.

New Forms of Careers

The globalization of business, rapidly changing environment, and downsizing of organizations has called for new types of careers. Dot-com companies have experienced rapid growth, rapid collapse, and frequent movement of employees. Companies more often outsource activities, rely on part-time or contract employees, decentralize decision making, and create free-form organization structures. Online recruiting has made job searches more efficient and effective. No longer do people work for the same company their entire lives. Instead, they move away from traditional career arrangements and take responsibility for managing their own careers.

In these new career forms, known as *protean careers* or *boundaryless careers,* people's needs and search for self-fulfillment guide and shape their career choices.[75] A psychological contract that focuses on an individual responding to his own needs and values rather than to the organization's needs and values has replaced the contract that offers job security in exchange for hard work and loyalty. The new career has peaks and valleys, turns in all directions, and takes a path unique to the employee. As part of the process, employees cultivate networks as a way of learning. The lack of a single-minded direction combined with the need to interact with networks of people requires employees to develop multiple and collaborative skill sets so that they can take advantage of opportunities as they arise. The new career also involves continuous learning, necessitated by increasingly common short-term assignments, job rotation, and lateral moves.

Companies strive to develop high-potential employees. These people show a fast rate of lateral movement through various roles in the company. Managers identify them as future leaders and so move them quickly into new positions, giving them special coaching and mentoring.[76] Executives today appear to work harder but show less commitment to remaining with their companies. Many practice defensive career management, which involves knowing about available job prospects, even if they don't plan to change jobs.[77] Some professional-level employees have switched jobs frequently, taking advantage of offers of promotions and higher salaries. Even in the dot-com world, some have begun to view this job hopping with skepticism, questioning its value for employers and recognizing its toll on employees' personal and professional lives.[78]

Career Stages

Many adults pass through clearly defined stages of biological, social, family, and career growth and development. People at a particular stage often have common needs or similar ways of coping with and responding to situations they encounter. Of course, differences in personality, interests, values, and experiences may cause variations within stages.

This section presents a career progression that is common in the United States. In Israel and other countries with mandatory military service for all men (and women in some cases), the sequence of career stages presented here may be delayed or altered. Countries such as Sweden, with liberal maternity and paternity leave policies, may also have workers with different career patterns from the one described here. Increasingly in the United States, too, individuals pursue serial careers, a set of unrelated, sequential careers over an individual's life span—for example, teacher–banker–bed-and-breakfast owner or homemaker–travel agent.

Figure 3-3 presents one timeline of career development. People in the *entry stage* try to become effective and accepted members of their organizations as quickly as possible while they learn the job's ropes and routines. Newcomers seek information about role demands, feedback about their performance, and technical information from their supervisors. They seek information about organizational norms and social relations from their peers.[79] How well they seek and acquire information influences their mastery of their job, definition of their role, acquisition of knowledge about the organization's culture, and extent of social integration.[80] They must spend time learning to get along with their boss and co-workers, as well as trying to become an effective member quickly.

People in the *early career stage* become more concerned with advancement and establishing a career path. In multinational companies, rapid advancement may require taking overseas assignments.

FIGURE 3-3

People move through numerous stages as they progress through their careers.

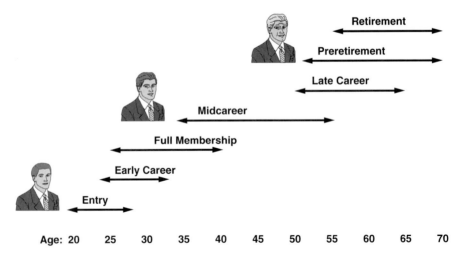

Workers who are typically in their late twenties or early thirties strive for *full membership* in an early career. The primary emphasis of such employees must be on performing effectively, accepting responsibility, managing subordinates, discharging duties, and developing special skills.

Workers at this stage also should assess to what extent they wish to remain as technical experts or advance into a managerial position. If they choose to remain technical, they must ensure that they maintain up-to-date knowledge in their career field. Today, employees at this stage increasingly find teams supporting and even replacing middle managers, requiring them to develop new skills and potentially new ways of advancing in organizations.

Midcareer refers to the period that follows establishment and perceived mastery and precedes career disengagement.[81] These employees, who typically are between the ages of 40 and 55, may face a challenging midlife transition in their careers as well as in their personal lives as they reappraise their accomplishments to date. Some men at midcareer experience a need to disrupt their habitual behavior and initiate career exploration, whereas women become concerned with balancing the various aspects of their lives and ensuring that they have not sacrificed too much time with their families in favor of career activities and advancement.[82] Resolving these dilemmas may result in new choices about career and family or an acceptance of old choices as appropriate.

Once past midcareer, individuals in organizations must find a way in late career to continue to contribute. Depending on the person's skills, interests, and motivation, and the organization's culture and goals, such employees might help shape the direction of the organization by sponsoring the career advancement of younger workers. For executives, this might mean payback—frequent job changes with final grooming or competition for the top executive position—or payoff—attainment of the CEO position.[83] At the end of this stage, most employers enter pre-retirement, which may involve reducing work hours and demands, and eventually retirement.

Another model of career development is possible. Rather than going through a single set of stages during their adult lives, individuals may progress through a series of the same stages several times during their lives. As shown in Figure 3-4, they begin

FIGURE 3-4

People may progress through several sets of the same sequence of career stages during their lives.

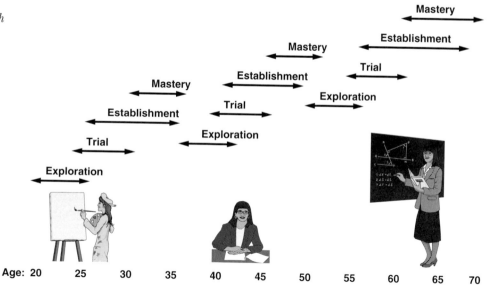

Age: 20   25   30   35   40   45   50   55   60   65   70

with the exploration stage (similar to the entry stage) and continue with the trial stage (which resembles the early career stage). Next they experience the establishment stage, which resembles full membership. They conclude with a mastery stage before proceeding to exploration of a new career. This iterative approach fits well with new forms of careers in which people frequently change organizations and jobs.

Career Planning

Career effectiveness and the individual job effectiveness that accompanies it often arise from the organization's ability to integrate the employee into the organization and to help that employee make career transitions effectively. Both employees and their managers should assume some career planning and development responsibilities. Use of the Web can support information searches, resume development and posting, and networking regarding career planning. Some executives hire coaches for their managers to help them develop better skills.[84]

Employees should know and understand the implications of their particular career stage for their satisfaction and job performance. Managers should provide opportunities to discuss career development issues. They should also give feedback about reasonable expectations for employees, identifying the employees' potential and providing relevant growth opportunities. Linking employees to appropriate resources can also help their career development. A lack of such information, in addition to the dilemmas experienced at various stages of career development, may contribute to confusion and conflict in the performance of work and nonwork roles.

Employees can benefit by finding a *mentor,* usually a more senior executive who helps influence their movement through the organization and affects their career success. Glen Toney, for example, served as a mentor for employees at Applied Materials. A mentor typically provides the career and psychosocial functions shown in Table 3-1.[85] Alternatively, employees can seek developmental support from peers by becoming part of a *relationship constellation,* a group of individuals from various departments in the organization who provide mutual support, friendship, and sponsorship.[86] Mentoring becomes particularly important in a multicultural environment where nonperformance-related factors can block career progress. In one study of cross-race mentoring, a supportive mentor–protégé relationship only occurred when both parties preferred to either deny or openly discuss their racial difference.[87] Employees who have experienced extensive mentoring report receiving more promotions, having higher incomes, and being more satisfied with pay and benefits.[88]

Diversity appears to affect the mentor–protégé relationship. A study of 138 interns on a six-month overseas assignment indicated that those who differed from their mentors in gender and nationality were less likely to receive support related to their tasks, careers, or social interactions. In turn, the lack of mentoring was associated with less learning about international business, poorer socialization during their assignments, and less impact of the internship on job offers.[89] Organizations also benefit from mentoring because mentors help perpetuate or change the organization's culture; improve worker motivation, performance, and retention; or act as a less formal, less costly monitoring and control system.[90]

Professional employees who bring specialized expertise to organizations, such as scientists, engineers, teachers, and accountants, face unique career and organizational issues. These knowledge workers have become particularly valuable in today's economy. Dot-com companies rely on experts in various functional areas of management, scientific areas, and graphic design to ensure that their Web businesses are successful.

TABLE 3-1

Mentors Can Fulfill Numerous Functions for Employees.

Career Functions	**Psychosocial Functions**
Sponsorship	*Role Modeling*
Opening doors. Having connections that will support the junior's career advancement.	Demonstrating valued behavior, attitudes, and/or skills that aid the junior in achieving competence, confidence, and a clear professional identity.
Coaching	*Counseling*
Teaching "the ropes." Giving relevant positive and negative feedback to improve the junior's performance and potential.	Providing a helpful and confidential forum for exploring personal and professional dilemmas. Excellent listening, trust, and rapport that enable both individuals to address central developmental concerns.
Protection	
Providing support in different situations. Taking responsibility for mistakes that were outside the junior's control. Acting as a buffer when necessary.	*Acceptance and Confirmation*
Exposure	Providing ongoing support, respect, and admiration, which strengthens self-confidence and self-image. Regularly reinforcing both as highly valued people and contributors to the organization.
Creating opportunities for the junior to demonstrate competence where it counts. Taking the junior to important meetings that will enhance his or her visibility.	
Challenging Work	*Friendship*
Delegating assignments that stretch the junior's knowledge and skills in order to stimulate growth and preparation to move ahead.	Mutual caring and intimacy that extends beyond the requirements of daily work tasks. Sharing of experience outside the immediate work setting.

Source: Reprinted with permission from K. E. Kram, Mentoring in the workplace. In D. T. Hall and Associates, eds., *Career Development in Organizations* (San Francisco: Jossey-Bass, 1986), p. 162. © 1986 by Jossey-Bass Inc., Publishers.

Managing career development in today's dynamic environment poses significant challenges to managers. Low rates of unemployment, high demand for skilled workers, and rapid turnover in dot-com, other high-technology, and related industries have made hiring a major preoccupation of some executives. Other companies have experienced the losses resulting from mergers and acquisitions. While many workers have left traditional employment for the fast pace and challenges of dot-com companies, increasingly managers and other professionals have subsequently returned to more traditional organizations. The Big Five accounting firms, for example, changed their image so that they could compete with the dot-com companies: They offered signing bonuses, gave stock options to secretaries, flattened their organizations' structures, and reemphasized merit pay. Freddie Mac, the mortgage investor, had 14 former employees return to the company after sojourns in high-tech companies; now executives scan Monster.com for the names of former employees to court.[91] Workers should also ensure that they do not become *plateaued performers,* executives and workers who cannot advance because of limited advancement opportunities and whose job responsibilities never change.[92] Companies that once had single advancement paths offer alternatives. Procter & Gamble, for example, has given some of its marketing executives the chance to move off the traditional management ladder and act as strategic counselors for marketing, with the opportunity to return to the management track if they wish.[93]

■ DEALING WITH WORK–LIFE CHALLENGES

Responding to issues associated with the interaction between work and family has become particularly important in managing a diverse workforce in the United States. Family issues vary significantly, depending on the age, marital, parental, and economic status of employees.

Workplace issues seem to be most critical for adults with child-care responsibilities. The commonality of two-career families, as well as the rise in such nontraditional family styles as single parents, stepfamilies, and divorced parents alternating child-rearing responsibilities, call for greater attention to work–family interaction. For example, both men and women relocate their families because of workplace promotions. Persuading valuable employees to relocate may mean offering incentives for the trailing spouse. Companies often help the trailing spouse land a new job or even start a new career.

As the workforce ages, concerns about elder care for parents and aging relatives have become more prominent. More recently, the set of work–family issues has expanded to include decisions about how to treat gay and lesbian employees, such as whether to offer them benefits comparable to those of married workers.

Family-Friendly Benefits

The Family and Medical Leave Act passed in 1993 provides up to 12 weeks of unpaid leave to all workers employed by companies with 50 or more employees for the birth of a child, adoption of a child, or care of a seriously ill child, spouse, or family member, with a guarantee of the worker's old job or equivalent job upon return. While increasing numbers of workers take advantage of the provisions of this bill, many men, in particular, feel compelled to choose work over family concerns. Leaves of absence in a financial services industry were associated with fewer promotions and small salary increases; the leaves were negatively related to performance ratings during the year of the leave.[94]

The United States lags significantly behind other industrialized countries in dealing with work–family issues. Many European countries, for example, have liberal parental leave policies and provide convenient, affordable day-care options for workers. Japan, in contrast, lags behind the United States; there are no provisions for maternity leaves or company-sponsored day care.[95]

Organizations benefit from helping workers manage the work–family challenges. For example, flexible and innovative managers do the following:

- ■ seek equitable, not uniform treatment for workers;
- ■ recognize that employees perform better free from personal pressures;
- ■ realize that flexibility is a competitive issue and management tool;
- ■ measure performance based on value added, not hours worked;
- ■ meet business objectives by helping employees meet personal needs;
- ■ willingly take risks;
- ■ focus on results, rather than rules and procedures;

- respect individuals but acknowledge and respond to differences;
- gain top-level support and backing from peers; and
- produce change within the organization that outlives themselves.[96]

Organizations have become more family friendly by introducing programs that help employees balance the various aspects of their work and family lives in the following ways:

- **flexible work arrangements,** such as part-time work, job sharing, and flexible hours;
- **parental leaves,** such as maternity or paternity leaves, family-care leaves, and personal days;
- **dependent-care services,** such as day care, vacation care, sick child care, and elder care; and
- **work–family stress management,** such as workshops, private counseling, and employee assistance programs.

Alltel Information Services of Little Rock, Arkansas, introduced a telecommuting program (employees work at home) that has reduced turnover, increased job satisfaction, and resulted in significant cost savings. Employees find that the extra time available to spend with children, even though telecommuters must arrange for primary caregivers for children under the age of 10, has been a major attraction.[97] PNC Bank in Pittsburgh offers 200 employees in corporate finance extra-long shifts with every tenth working day off. Daimler/Chrysler AG includes a work–family account in its benefits that employees can use for child care, elder care, retirement savings, adoption assistance, and education accounts for dependents, among other uses.[98] SAS Institute, a software company, built a 200-child day-care facility at its headquarters, bringing the company's capacity for preschool child care to 700. Employees can take their children from the day-care center and have lunch with them in the company cafeteria. The company also offers a full-time elder-care consultant for employees.[99] Strong Investments gives expectant fathers beepers and three days off with pay after the birth of a child as part of its "father-friendly" benefits. Marriott offers effective fathering classes for employees.[100]

Other employees are not satisfied with options offered by their employers. They have chosen to get off the career ladder as a way of achieving more balance in their lives. These *downshifters* value their personal life over their career accomplishments. While downshifting may be extreme, the trend to simplify their lives has become more common for U.S. employees.[101]

MANAGING DIVERSITY IN A DOT-COM, GLOBAL WORKPLACE

As companies continue to search for ways to improve their bottom line and ensure employee retention and performance, managing issues of diversity, individual differences, and professional and personal development become key. Organizations can take one of three approaches to managing diversity:

- **episodic,** in which diversity initiatives are isolated from core management activities, such as by sending employees to short seminars on diversity;

- **freestanding,** in which managers formalize diversity initiatives but don't fully integrate them into core management activities, such as by creating an intercultural exchange program; and
- **systemic,** in which diversity initiatives are linked with existing systems and core activities, such as by being made a component of all employee, customer, and vendor programs.[102]

Bestfoods, a global consumer foods business that includes Hellmann's Mayonnaise and Entenmann's baked goods, uses the last strategy. It links its diversity initiative closely to the company's business objectives, including both in its core values. The company wants employees who mirror its customers. This diversity strategy includes five key principles: (1) Management is accountable for ensuring diversity in every division; (2) representation of women, as well as various racial, ethnic, and other minority groups, goes beyond quotas to ensuring the ability to spot and hire the best talent; (3) corporate-wide initiatives regarding retention, development, and advancement focus on recommendations regarding career development, diversity, and work–life balance; (4) the company administered and still analyzes an employee survey; and (5) diversity training supports skill development and performance expectations. In 1998, the Women's Global Leadership Forum met with senior executives from Bestfoods for shared learning and making recommendations for change. They offered specific proposals in the areas of career development, diversity, and work–life balance.[103]

Several human resources professionals in the Seattle-Tacoma area started the Professional and Technical Diversity Network as a way of promoting and supporting a diverse workforce throughout the region.[104] Managers can promote diversity in the workplace in a number of ways:[105]

- focus on bringing in the best talent, not on meeting numerical goals;
- set up mentoring programs among employees of the same and different races;
- hold managers accountable for meeting diversity goals;
- develop career plans for employees as part of performance reviews;
- promote minorities to decision-making positions, not just staff jobs;
- ensure that succession planning helps maintain diversity at all levels of the organization;
- make managers accountable for ensuring diversity in their divisions or groups; and
- diversify the company's board of directors.

Top management needs to develop corporate policies that foster diversity. They may need to give managers rewards for hiring, developing, and promoting women, minorities, and older workers. They may need to institute programs to support the diverse workforce. They may need to help managers and other workers learn how to deal with workers different from themselves. To make the most of the diverse workforce, managers can follow the advice shown in Table 3-2. In addition to following this advice, managers should conduct diversity training and create structures that support diversity.

Diversity Training

Many companies conduct diversity training, programs and activities that highlight differences among workers and offer strategies for handling them. The Society for

TABLE 3-2

Building a Diverse Workforce has Positive Consequences for an Organization's Bottom Line.

Advice to managers regarding diversity:

- Understand that a diverse workforce has different perspectives and approaches to work and must truly value variety of opinion and insight.
- Recognize both the learning opportunities and challenges that the expression of different perspectives gives organizations.
- Create an organizational culture that
    - → expects high standards of performance from everyone.
    - → stimulates personal development.
    - → encourages openness.
    - → makes workers feel valued.
- Develop a well-articulated and widely understood mission for the organization.
- Implement a relatively egalitarian, nonbureaucratic structure.

Source: Based on D. A. Thomas and R. J. Ely, Making differences matter: A new paradigm for managing diversity, *Harvard Business Review* (September–October, 1996): 79–90.

Human Resource Management sponsors courses about diversity. Towers Perrin, a major human resources consulting firm, offers "learning rooms" where panels talk with clients' employees about racial and ethnic differences, generational issues, religious questions, and sexual orientation issues.[106]

Diversity training helps managers understand and value individual differences and develop strong diagnostic skills. Dissemination of factual information may change some beliefs, but more emotion-oriented persuasive techniques and longer-term educational efforts may be needed to alter them. For example, Bank of America offers mentoring programs and support/discussion groups based on race, ethnicity, or sexual orientation.[107]

Cross-Cultural Issues

As organizations have become more multinational or even drawn on workers from different cultures in the same country, the importance of integrating home country and foreign workers has increased. The effects of cultural diversity on firm performance depend on a firm's strategies and the way managers and employees handle diversity.[108] For example, Smurfit Flexible Packaging, a midwestern manufacturer, decided to improve its safety. The company faced special challenges because the cultural diversity of the workforce created language barriers that made understanding difficult. Training workers and ensuring the right attitude toward safety became a major priority.[109]

Managers and employees of organizations that operate in more than one country must deal with the diverse cultures of the global marketplace. Implemented in 1985, Japan's Equal Employment Opportunity Act emphasized voluntary compliance and gradual change. Yet, gender inequality persists in the Japanese workplace.[110] Even there, however, women have begun to speak out about sexual harassment in the workplace. A 1999 law makes sexual harassment a criminal offense and requires all companies to have written policies prohibiting sexual harassment, although compliance has been somewhat spotty.[111]

Cultural differences affect the way people perceive each other in the workplace, and these different perceptions affect behavior. Language differences reflect unspoken attitudes, assumptions, and even attributions. They can shape workers' views of the world and actions in the workplace. Some argue that only English should be allowed in U.S. workplaces because employees who speak limited English may have difficulty communicating with other employees and with customers. Rituals and customs can also influence people's perceptions about their jobs and co-workers. Americans, for example, value efficiency and speed, while the Japanese place a higher value on ceremonies and practices that reflect social standing and mutual respect.

Workers from different cultures may also lack knowledge about the ethical appropriateness of various practices, causing them to act in unacceptable or unexpected ways. For example, paying an official to sanction a business act may be standard operating practice in some South American and Middle Eastern countries, but not in the United States. Political and economic differences among nations also create significantly different cultural patterns that may affect the level of education, experience, and expertise of various workers. Managers need to diagnose cultural differences and understand their impact in the workplace. Then they can prescribe ways to ensure effective behavior in cross-cultural situations.

Structures That Support Diversity

Two-career couples benefit from flexible work arrangements and flexible benefits, where the ability to select from an array of benefits prevents, for example, duplication of medical benefits and the possibility of selecting child-care reimbursement.[112] Older workers too can benefit from part-time employment or greater flexibility in their work schedules.

Sharing power and influence throughout the organization also encourages diversity.[113] An organization's culture should reflect the diverse cultural and social groups that compose it and attempt to eliminate discrimination in the organization. Although more than three-fourths of the largest companies in the United States have diversity programs, not all succeed.[114] A growing number of companies have special positions that focus on diversity, such as vice president of diversity, director of multicultural affairs, manager of workforce development, and vice president of diversity management. The inability of top management to consider discrimination a major business issue or to spend sufficient time on training can hinder the success of diversity programs.

▌ Summary

1. A more diverse workforce often results in improved decision making, better understanding of customers' needs, and increased flexibility in staffing.

2. The number of women, minorities, and older workers continues to increase; companies must ensure that they meet the needs of these workers and do not discriminate in their human resources policies and practices.

3. Organizations now employ more physically challenged workers and must ensure that the workplace does not provide obstacles to their performance.

4. A diverse workforce typically includes people with a variety of personality types, such as internalizers and externalizers, Type A and Type B, introverted

and extroverted, sensing and intuitive, thinking and feeling, judging, and perceiving, high and low Machiavellianism, and high and low self-efficacy.

5. An individual's values and attitudes also influence behavior in the workplace; values describe a person's underlying beliefs, whereas attitudes refer to people's tendencies to respond consistently. Attitudes include cognitive, affective, and behavioral components.

6. Individuals have careers that generally progress through a series of stages that each have a different set of concerns and issues, although boundaryless careers have become more common.

7. Companies have introduced family-friendly benefits, such as flexible work schedules, liberal leave policies, dependent care, and work-stress management seminars, to help workers meet the challenges faced by two-career families, single parents, and gay and lesbian workers, among others.

A Manager's Diagnostic Review

■ Accept the value of diversity in the workplace.
- What types of diversity characterize the workforce?
- What cross-cultural issues does the organization face?

■ Remove obstacles encountered by women, minorities, older workers, and physically challenged employees.
- What special challenges do women, minorities, older workers, and physically challenged employees face?
- What programs exist for managing diversity?

■ Know how personality differences affect a person's work.
- How would you characterize the personalities of particular employees and managers?
- Do their personalities fit with the situation?

■ Recognize how values and attitudes affect job performance.
- What beliefs and values do managers and employees hold?
- How do these beliefs and values influence their attitudes?

■ Help workers build effective careers.
- What career stage characterizes each manager and employee?
- What career development problems do employees and managers experience?
- Does the organization have career development programs?

■ Develop programs to help workers handle work–life challenges.
- What family issues do workers face?
- How well does the organization help them in meeting family and other nonwork needs?

■ Manage diversity and individual differences in the dot-com, global workplace.
- Does the organization have diversity programs and offer diversity training?
- Do managers effectively handle a multicultural workforce?

Visit the Gordon homepage on the Prentice Hall Web site at

http://www.prenhall.com/gordon

for recommended readings, additional activities, Internet exercises, updated information, and links to related Web sites.

■ Thinking Critically About Organizational Behavior

1. Why should managers strive for a diverse workforce?
2. How can managers prepare for an increasingly diverse workforce?
3. Will true equality in job opportunities ever exist in the United States?
4. Should managers assess their employees' personalities?
5. Should companies attempt to have a workforce with an array of personality types?
6. Can managers change their employees' values and attitudes?
7. Do divergent attitudes cause problems in organizations?
8. What are the implications for managers and employees of the new forms of careers?
9. Do all adults pass through the same career stages?
10. Should all companies institute family-friendly benefits?
11. Do other countries have the same issues as the United States about employing a diverse workforce?
12. Does diversity training work?

ACTIVITY 3-1: UNDERSTANDING RACE AND GENDER DIFFERENCES

STEP 1: Draw a picture of yourself on a large piece of newsprint with colored markers, making the following assumptions:

Pretend you are to be reincarnated and you can choose how you will come back . . . as long as you choose a different race and gender.

STEP 2: On the left side of the paper, answer the following questions:

1. Why did you choose this persona?
2. What do you like about your choice?

On the right side of the paper, answer the following questions:

1. What do you dislike about your choice?

2. What are you concerned about as you face the future as this new persona?

STEP 3: Discussion. Your instructor will direct the students to present their pictures in small groups or to the class as a whole. Share your answers to the preceding questions. Then answer the following questions:

1. What are the advantages and disadvantages of each choice?
2. What issues concern you in facing the future as your new persona?

Source: Adapted and reprinted with permission of the authors, Bonita L. Betters-Reed and Lynda L. Moore.

ACTIVITY 3-2: TRAVELING TO FOREIGN CULTURES

STEP 1: Your instructor will divide the class into two groups and provide each group with color-coded badges. Print your name in bold letters on the badge and wear it throughout the exercise.

STEP 2: Working with your group members, your first task is to invent your own cultural cues. You are to think about the kinds of behaviors and words that will signify to all members that they belong together in one culture. For each of the following categories, identify and record at least one important attribute for your culture:

Facial expression

Eye contact

Handshake

Body language

Key words or phrases

STEP 3: Now that you have defined desirable cultural aspects for your group, practice them. It is best to stand with your group and to engage one another in conversations involving two or three people at a time. Your aim in talking with one another is to learn as much as possible about each other—hobbies, interests, where you live, what your family is like, courses being taken, and so on, all while practicing the behaviors and words identified in Step 2. It is not necessary for participants to answer questions of a personal nature truthfully. Invention is permissible because the conversation is only a means to the end of cultural observation. Your aim at this point is to become comfortable with the indicators of your particular culture. Practice until the indicators are second nature to you.

STEP 4: You now should assume that you work for a business organization that operates in the culture you defined and practiced. This business has decided that it would like to explore the potential for doing business with companies in a foreign culture. Your awareness of the global marketplace tells you that to plan an effective approach to a foreign country's business leaders you must first understand the culture of that country.

You are to learn as much as possible about another culture. To do so, you will send from one to three representatives, when designated by your instructor, on a "business trip" to the other culture. These representatives must, as much as possible, behave in a manner that is consistent with your culture as defined in Step 2. At the same time, each representative must endeavor to learn as much as possible about the people in the other culture, while keeping eyes and ears open to cultural attributes that will be useful in future negotiations with foreign businesses. (Note: At no time will it be considered ethical behavior for the representative to ask direct questions about the foreign culture's attributes. These cultural attributes must be gleaned from firsthand experience.)

While your representatives are away, you will receive one or more exchange visitors from the other culture who will be interested in learning more about your organizational culture. You must strictly adhere to the cultural aspects you defined in Step 2 and practiced in Step 3 as you respond to the visitor(s).

STEP 5: When told to do so by your instructor, all representatives return to their native cultures. Each group then discusses and records what it has learned about the foreign culture based on the exchange of visitors. The aim is to try to decipher the behaviors expected of members of the other culture. This information will be shared with all group members and will serve as the basis for orienting the next representatives who will make a business trip.

STEP 6: The instructor will select one to three different group members to make another trip to the other culture to check out the assumptions that your group has made about the other culture. This "checking out" process will consist of actually practicing the other culture's cues to see whether they work. Both groups will be standing and conducting their business of getting to know one another as in Steps 3 and 4.

STEP 7: The travelers return and report on findings to the home group, and the group then prepares to report what it learned about the other culture.

STEP 8: Discussion. With the entire class, answer the following questions:

1. What did you learn about the other culture?
2. How easily did you learn about the other culture?
3. What is the effect of having people from two different cultures interact?

Source: By Susan R. Zacur and W. Alan Randolph, Traveling to foreign cultures: An exercise in developing awareness of cultural diversity, *Journal of Management Education* 17(4) (November 1993): 510–513. Reprinted with permission of Sage Publications, Inc.

ACTIVITY 3-3: LOCUS OF CONTROL TEST

STEP 1: Answer the following questions about the way you feel. In the column, mark a Y for yes and an N for no next to each question.

_____ 1. Do you believe that most problems will solve themselves if you just don't fool with them?

_____ 2. Do you believe that you can stop yourself from catching a cold?

_____ 3. Are some people just born lucky?

_____ 4. Most of the time, do you feel that getting good grades means a great deal to you?

_____ 5. Are you often blamed for things that just aren't your fault?

_____ 6. Do you believe that if somebody studies hard, he or she can pass any subject?

_____ 7. Do you feel that most of the time it doesn't pay to try hard because things never turn out right anyway?

_____ 8. Do you feel that if things start out well in the morning, it's going to be a good day no matter what you do?

_____ 9. Do you feel that most of the time parents listen to what their children have to say?

_____ 10. Do you believe that wishing can make good things happen?

_____ 11. When you get punished, does it usually seem it's for no good reason at all?

_____ 12. Most of the time, do you find it hard to change a friend's opinion?

_____ 13. Do you think that cheering more than luck helps a team to win?

_____ 14. Did you feel that it was nearly impossible to change your parents' minds about anything?

_____ 15. Do you believe that parents should allow children to make most of their own decisions?

_____ 16. Do you feel that when you do something wrong there's very little you can do to make it right?

_____ 17. Do you believe that most people are just born good at sports?

_____ 18. Are most of the other people your age stronger than you are?

_____ 19. Do you feel that one of the best ways to handle most problems is just not to think about them?

_____ 20. Do you feel that you have a lot of choice in deciding who your friends are?

_____ 21. If you find a four-leaf clover, do you believe that it might bring you good luck?

_____ 22. Did you often feel that whether or not you did your homework had much to do with what kind of grades you got?

_____ 23. Do you feel that when a person your age is angry at you, there's little you can do to stop him or her?

_____ 24. Have you ever had a good-luck charm?

_____ 25. Do you believe that whether or not people like you depends on how you act?

_____ 26. Did your parents usually help you if you asked them to?

_____ 27. Have you felt that when people were angry with you it was usually for no reason at all?

_____ 28. Most of the time, do you feel that you can change what might happen tomorrow by what you do today?

_____ 29. Do you believe that when bad things are going to happen, they just are going to happen no matter what you try to do to stop them?

_____ 30. Do you think that people can get their own way if they just keep trying?

_____ 31. Most of the time, do you find it useless to try to get your own way at home?

_____ 32. Do you feel that when good things happen, they happen because of hard work?

_____ 33. Do you feel that when somebody your age wants to be your enemy, there's little you can do to change matters?

_____ 34. Do you feel that it's easy to get friends to do what you want them to do?

_____ 35. Do you usually feel that you have little to say about what you get to eat at home?

_____ 36. Do you feel that when someone doesn't like you, there's little you can do about it?

_____ 37. Did you usually feel that it was almost useless to try in school because most other children were just plain smarter that you were?

_____ 38. Are you the kind of person who believes that planning ahead makes things turn out better?

_____ 39. Most of the time, do you feel that you have little to say about what your family decides to do?

_____ 40. Do you think it's better to be smart than to be lucky?

STEP 2: Scoring the scale. Using the following scoring key, compare your answers to the ones on the key. Give yourself one point each time your answer agrees with the keyed answer. Your score is the total number of agreements between your answers and the ones on the key.

Scoring Key

1.	Yes	21.	Yes
2.	No	22.	No
3.	Yes	23.	Yes
4.	No	24.	Yes
5.	Yes	25.	No
6.	No	26.	No
7.	Yes	27.	Yes
8.	Yes	28.	No
9.	No	29.	Yes
10.	Yes	30.	No
11.	Yes	31.	Yes
12.	Yes	32.	No
13.	No	33.	Yes
14.	Yes	34.	No
15.	No	35.	Yes
16.	Yes	36.	Yes
17.	Yes	37.	Yes
18.	Yes	38.	No
19.	Yes	39.	Yes
20.	No	40.	No
		Total Score:	

INTERPRETING YOUR SCORE

Low Scorers (0–8)

Scores from zero to eight represent the range for about one-third of the people taking the test. As a low scorer, you probably see life as a game of skill rather than chance. You most likely believe that you have a lot of control over what happens to you, both good and bad. With that view, internal-locus-of-control people tend to take the initiative in everything from job-related activities to relationships and sex. You are probably described by others as vigilant in getting things done, aware of what's going on around you, and willing to spend energy in working for specific goals. You would probably find it quite frustrating to sit back and let others take care of you, since you stressed on the test that you like to have your life in your own hands.

Although taking control of your life is seen as the "best way to be," psychologists caution that it has its own set of difficulties. Someone who is responsible for his or her own successes is also responsible for failures. So if you scored high in this direction, be prepared for the downs as well as the ups.

Average Scorers (9–16)

Since you've answered some of the questions in each direction, internal and external control beliefs for you may be situation specific. You may look at one situation—work, for example—and believe that your rewards are externally determined, that no matter what you do you can't get ahead. In another situation—love, perhaps—you may see your fate as resting entirely in your own hands. You will find it helpful to review the questions and group them into those you answered in the internal direction and those you answered in the external direction. Are there any similarities in the kinds of situations within one of those groups? If so, some time spent thinking about what it is in those situations that makes you feel as though the control is or is not in your hands can help you better understand yourself.

High Scorers (17–40)

Scores in this range represent the external control end of the scale. Only about 15 percent of the people taking the test score 17 or higher. As a high scorer, you're saying that you see life generally more as a game of chance than as one where your skills make a difference.

STEP 3: Discussion. In small groups or with the class as a whole, answer the following questions.

DESCRIPTION

1. What was your score?
2. What type of personality does this represent?
3. How does this compare to scores of others in the class?

DIAGNOSIS

4. What behaviors and attitudes is each personality type likely to demonstrate?
5. What are the implications for encouraging organizational effectiveness?

Source: By Stephen Nowicki, Jr., and B. Strickland in *The Mind Test* by Rita Aero and Elliot Weiner (New York: William Morrow, 1981), pp. 20–23. Reprinted with permission.

ACTIVITY 3-4: FAMILY FRIENDLINESS AT ABC MANUFACTURING

STEP 1: You have just been appointed the first Work/Family Director at ABC Manufacturing, a Fortune 200 manufacturer of consumer goods such as personal grooming products, stationery products, cleaning products, and food products. The new CEO of ABC has stated that one of his top priorities is to make ABC more "family friendly."

The new CEO believes that making the company more family friendly will reduce its turnover rate, attract better-quality employees from across the country, and increase the productivity of its current workforce. His first step was to create and fill the position you now hold. The company has experimented with flexible working hours and job sharing in a few, selected divisions. When the sponsoring managers changed, these programs generally became defunct. No organization-wide policy or set of programs exist.

ABC currently has 20,000 employees worldwide. It has 20 manufacturing plants, 45 regional sales offices, and a large corporate office that includes marketing, research and development, engineering, human resources, financial, and administrative staffs.

The new CEO has given you a first-year budget of $500,000 and a staff of four. He has promised that both the budget and staff can increase if the new programs show tangible results.

STEP 2: Individually or in small groups, as directed by your instructor, develop a comprehensive plan for making ABC Manufacturing more family friendly. Consider the different types of workers ABC employs and the various locations in which ABC operates. Include in your plan the programs you want to introduce, the priority you assign to each program, the expected costs of the programs, and their likely impact. Develop a timeline for introducing the programs.

STEP 3: With the entire class, share the plans you developed. What elements do they have in common? What costs and benefits will likely accompany these plans? What options will likely have the greatest impact? How do programs differ for the various locations outside the United States? Is family friendliness the same in all cultures?

ACTIVITY 3-5: DESIGNING A DIVERSITY PROGRAM

STEP 1: You have just been hired as the new Director of Diversity for StateBank, one of the top 50 banks in the United States. While StateBank began several diversity initiatives about five years ago, it limited these activities to workshops that help employees become more sensitive to gender, racial, ethnic, and religious differences.

Although surveys suggest that attitudes among StateBank's employees are changing, you believe that the company has not done all it can to address diversity in the workplace. For example, more than 90 percent of top and middle managers are males, while 50 percent of new hires at lower levels are females. African Americans hold 15 percent of entry-level positions but only 3 percent of middle management positions and no top-level positions.

Three bank tellers recently filed a sexual harassment suit against their branch manager.

The bank has renewed its commitment to addressing the diversity issue, particularly because its customer base has become more diverse as the bank has grown. Top management has given you a large budget and a small staff to improve the diversity program in the bank.

STEP 2: Individually or in small groups, as directed by your instructor, develop a comprehensive diversity program for StateBank.

STEP 3: Share your plans with the entire class. Identify the key elements of a comprehensive diversity program. What would the program you proposed cost? What benefits would it likely offer to StateBank?

ACTIVITY 3-6: SELECTING A DIVERSITY CONSULTANT

STEP 1: You are the vice president of human resources for a growing high-technology company. The company's executive team has agreed that employees should participate in a diversity training and awareness program. The consultant has designed a program that company employees will conduct for other company employees. In fact, you have been asked to select a group of five people from your existing employees to form a "train-the-trainer" group. These five people will train a group of 20–30 other employees, who will then actually conduct the training.

STEP 2: Individually or in small groups, prepare a list of criteria for selecting individuals to join the "train-the-trainer" group. Offer a rationale for the list you prepare.

STEP 3: Share your conclusions in writing or orally with the entire class. Consider the following questions:

1. What qualifications make a person a good diversity trainer?
2. How can you validate these qualifications?
3. Does a person need to be a member of a minority group to conduct this training?

Chapter 4

Motivating and Rewarding Employees

Learning Objectives

After completing Chapter 4, you will be able to

1. Describe and evaluate the major needs theories.
2. Diagnose the impact of equity and inequity on motivation.
3. Offer four ways of reinforcing behavior.
4. Comment on the impact of various schedules of reinforcement on behavior.
5. Discuss the impact of the elements of expectancy theory on motivation.
6. Show how to motivate workers by setting goals.
7. Discuss how to motivate a multinational and multicultural workforce.
8. Describe the role of wages, benefits, and incentives in motivating employees.

A Manager's Preview

Describe . . . Diagnose . . . Prescribe . . . Act:

- Identify workers' needs and then meet them.
- Create an equitable workplace.
- Set challenging, focused, and acceptable goals jointly with employees.
- Design and implement a fair wage system.
- Offer an array of benefits tailored to individual employees.
- Pay for performance.
- Motivate employees in the dot-com, global workplace.

Rewarding Salespeople Using ClickRewards

Companies face new challenges in rewarding their salespeople and other employees. As technology has changed, the demands on workers have forced companies to become more creative in finding ways to motivate them. Netcentives, a San Francisco–based marketing company, offers "loyalty awards," such as gift coupons and other incentives to employees. Employees can earn airline frequent flyer miles or various types of merchandise, such as digital cameras.

Netcentives sells ClickRewards@Work, an online, turnkey incentive program. For example, one Netcentives client, which we will call TechProducts, Inc., has 17,000 resellers who access the ClickRewards Internet site to receive various rewards they've earned for acting in prespecified ways. The resellers can take an online new-product quiz that provides them with information about the company's new products. If they answer all of the items correctly, they receive points that they can later redeem for rewards.

Cisco Systems uses ClickRewards@Work to motivate its customer service representatives to encourage clients to submit their orders using the Web. Companies can award points to their employees for increasing sales, improving customer service, or increasing employee performance in various business areas.[1]

Every day, managers must motivate workers. Companies such as Netcentives offer new ways of motivating workers in today's dot-com, global world. Because each person thinks, feels, and acts differently, the factors that motivate each person differ. Motivation theory helps us understand what motivates workers, to what extent, and how to increase motivation. Downsizing, mergers, and takeovers often create special challenges in motivating workers. So do the characteristics of the dot-com, global workplace that many employees experience.

In this chapter, we begin with a brief comment about motivation basics. Then we examine needs, equity, reinforcement, expectancy, and goal-setting theories of motivation. These theories focus managers on the content (needs) and process (equity, reinforcement, expectancy, and goal setting) of motivation. We show how managers can apply those theories to motivate employees to perform more effectively. Finally, we explore ways that managers can create effective reward systems for motivating employees.

▌ MOTIVATION BASICS

Motivation concerns getting the desired outcomes from employees that help attain goals. Employees may be motivated to put in extra effort to meet all the standards and specifications of a job in a short time. They may be motivated to perform better if they receive rewards, such as special bonuses, awards, or extra time off from work, for their performance. Managers may have the following specific concerns when motivating their employees:

- how to keep a high performer challenged and productive;
- how to challenge workers to use their capabilities more fully;
- how to make unproductive workers perform;
- how to encourage employees to act creatively; and
- how to ensure that employees focus on customers' needs.

What motivates people to behave, think, or feel in certain ways? What factors make you willing to work, be creative, achieve, and produce? Some people work to satisfy their *needs,* deficiencies in their basic requirements for living and working productively. For example, some employees use work as a way of making money to meet their basic survival needs. Others use work to satisfy their need for self-esteem. Managers may motivate workers by helping them meet their needs. The diverse workforce includes workers such as senior citizens, single parents, two-career couples, and disabled workers who have special needs that organizations try to meet.

Sometimes workers like to receive *rewards,* outcomes that they find desirable and that accompany specific behaviors. Managers can motivate employees by offering rewards in exchange for certain actions. For example, managers can give the salespeople who open the most new accounts special awards. The award may motivate them to find even more new customers in the future. Workers differ in whether they are motivated by *intrinsic rewards,* aspects of the job's content such as its challenge, opportunities for creativity, responsibility, autonomy, and opportunities for growth, or *extrinsic rewards,* aspects apart from the job's content such as pay, job title, or other perks.

Managers may find it difficult to determine what motivates workers because usually a combination of factors influences employee behavior. Often employees have many unsatisfied needs. Managers might try to satisfy some of these needs as a way of motivating their employees. Also, employees may respond differently to rewards at different times, depending on their personal situation at a particular time. Diagnosing the most potent rewards becomes an issue in motivation. Managers need to continually reassess what motivates workers to encourage their performance and satisfaction.

NEEDS THEORIES

Think about the situation at TechProducts, Inc. How do managers there motivate their salespeople? In part, the managers motivate their workers by meeting their needs. How would the managers know their employees' needs? To do a good job of identifying them, a manager probably would spend a great deal of time talking with her employees and observing their behavior both in and out of the work situation. Some workers might have basic physiological and safety and security needs; others might have needs for esteem or growth.

In this section, we examine the following needs theories: hierarchy of needs theories, McClelland's needs theory, and motivator-hygiene theory. We show not only how they help managers think about motivating workers, but also their limitations.

Hierarchy of Needs Theories

Abraham Maslow and Clay Alderfer both offered simple schemes that managers can use in thinking about needs. Maslow developed his in the 1950s; Alderfer presented a modified version in the 1970s.[2] According to Maslow's hierarchy of needs, people have needs that range from very basic, low-level physiological needs to high-level self-actualization needs, as shown in Figure 4-1.

People work partly to satisfy their needs. Maslow felt that employees first try to satisfy their basic physiological needs, and then progress over time to safety and security, belongingness, esteem, and self-actualization needs.

- **Physiological needs** refer to an individual's most basic needs for food, water, shelter, and sex, or more broadly, from an employer's perspective, the need to care for workers' children and provide medical or dental coverage. Some companies offer family-friendly benefits, such as medical and dental care, child care, elder care, and flexible work hours, to address these needs (see Chapter 3).

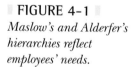

FIGURE 4-1

Maslow's and Alderfer's hierarchies reflect employees' needs.

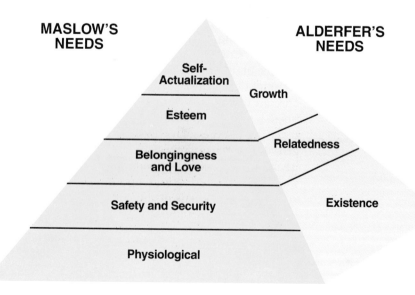

■ **Safety and security** needs describe a person's desire for security or protection. While safety needs once focused on the handling of hazardous materials and problems with remote parking locations, now managers have to deal with problems associated with workers' use of video-display terminals and secondary smoke in the workplace. Some companies attempt to meet safety needs by instituting extensive safety programs that may involve watchdog committees and stringent corporate oversight of the use of hazardous materials. Other organizations have instituted no-smoking policies and special security precautions for workers who must walk to remote parking areas. Security needs can also focus on short-term and long-term job protection, often guaranteed in union contracts.

■ **Belongingness and love** needs focus on the social aspects of work and nonwork situations. Traditionally, organizations have held regular social activities, such as sports leagues and holiday parties, to meet social needs. Some companies in Silicon Valley, for example, even had "fun managers," people responsible for organizing sports tournaments, talent shows, charity volunteering, and even paintball tournaments as a way of building team spirit and meeting the social needs of their young employees.[3] Other managers use teams (see Chapter 6) as a way to meet social needs, and accomplish the organization's goals.

■ **Esteem** needs refer to a person's concern for mastery, competence, and status. Some people who show esteem needs desire recognition for their accomplishments. They may want the material symbols of success—a large office or an executive job title, public recognition, or other special privileges or rewards associated with success, such as a country club membership or a luxury car. Other people with esteem needs wish to master their work, demonstrate competence and accomplishments, or build a reputation as an outstanding performer.

■ **Self-actualization** needs reflect an individual's desire to grow and develop to his or her fullest potential. An individual often wants the opportunity to be creative on the job or desires autonomy, responsibility, and challenge. Although Maslow believed that needs for self-actualization may be difficult to meet, managers can provide employees with the opportunity to learn on the job and grow as individuals through training or increased challenges.

According to Maslow's theory, the lowest unsatisfied need became primary (or *prepotent*). Consider a recent college graduate, who has taken out extensive loans to finance his education and joins Netcentives immediately after receiving his degree. He might be concerned about repaying these loans and at the same time earning enough to meet his basic needs for food and shelter. In this case, his prepotent need is physiological. If, instead, the new hire has no outstanding loans and is receiving a large salary, basic survival needs no longer dominate, but esteem or growth needs may. Simply, according to Maslow, managers motivate workers by satisfying their prepotent needs. A manager meets the needs of the college student with loans by offering him a position with wages that meet his basic needs. A manager meets the needs of the college student without loans by offering more challenges and opportunities for growth and development in the position.

Alderfer collapsed the five needs into three—existence, relatedness, and growth, also shown in Figure 4-1. Existence includes physiological and safety needs. Belongingness corresponds to social needs. Growth needs include esteem needs and the need for self-actualization.

Although Alderfer agreed with Maslow that workers first satisfied lower-order and then higher-order needs, Alderfer felt that satisfying higher-order needs caused them to increase in importance. For example, as a worker began to satisfy her social needs, they became more intense, and she continued to try to satisfy them.[4] In some circumstances, an individual might experience *frustration* in satisfying a higher-level need, which would cause her to return to a lower-level need. For example, if a worker failed to satisfy her social needs, she might try to meet security needs instead.

McClelland's Needs Theory

David McClelland and his associates offer a different way for managers to think about needs.[5] They identify three types of needs: need for achievement, need for affiliation, and need for power.

- **Need for achievement (nach)** reflects an individual's desire to accomplish goals and demonstrate competence or mastery. People high in this need focus their energies on getting a job done quickly and well.
- **Need for affiliation (naff)** resembles Maslow's belongingness need and Alderfer's relatedness need. It describes the need for social interaction, love, and affection.
- **Need for power (npow)** reflects the need for control over a person's own work or the work of others. Ruling monarchs, political leaders, and some executives in large corporations typically have a need for power.

McClelland and his colleagues argue that they can teach people to increase their need for achievement and so improve their performance. Striving to meet the need for achievement is associated with sales performance.[6] A person may demonstrate each need overtly or covertly. For example, a worker at Netcentives may seek a job with more autonomy or may work harder when given it. She may visibly delight in social activities or complain about always working alone. Although each person has all three needs to some extent, generally only one of them tends to motivate an individual at any given time.

A longitudinal study of workers' career advancement in a utility company suggested that, although the overall pattern of motives of successful male and successful female managers did not differ significantly, they used power differently in their work. Men used power to counteract specific behaviors they encountered in the workplace, and women used it to gather resources necessary to perform their jobs better.[7] A study of the motivations of a group of Australian female entrepreneurs indicated three types. Need-achiever entrepreneurs had high need-for-achievement scores; managerial entrepreneurs had high need-for-power scores; and pragmatic entrepreneurs were moderate in their needs for both achievement and power.[8]

Managers can diagnose the level of their workers' needs and then decide how to best motivate them. They can ask the questions shown in Figure 4-2 to identify the dominant need. Take a few moments and answer the questions posed here for someone you manage or for yourself.

Managers can also hire experts to administer the projective *Thematic Apperception Test (TAT)* to measure these three needs. The employee describes what she sees occurring in a series of pictures, such as the picture in Figure 4-3, and in this way *projects* her needs into the description of the picture. Professional test administrators have detailed protocols for scoring the pictures included in the TAT and similar tests.

FIGURE 4-2

Answers to this test can help identify your need for achievement, need for affiliation, or need for power.

- Do you like situations where you personally must find solutions to problems?
- Do you tend to set moderate goals and take moderate, thought-out risks?
- Do you want specific feedback about how well you are doing?
- Do you spend time considering how to advance your career, how to do your job better, or how to accomplish something important?

If you answered *yes*, you probably have a high need for achievement.

- Do you look for jobs or seek situations that provide an opportunity for social relationships?
- Do you often think about the personal relationships you have?
- Do you consider the feelings of others to be very important?
- Do you try to restore disrupted relationships when they occur?

If you answered *yes*, you probably have a high need for affiliation.

- Do you try to influence and control others?
- Do you seek leadership positions in a group?
- Do you enjoy persuading others?
- Are you perceived by others as outspoken, forceful, and demanding?

If you answered *yes*, you probably have a high need for power.

Because of the time and skill required in giving and scoring the test, its cost is high, and only a trained professional can administer and score it.

Motivator-Hygiene Theory

Frederick Herzberg and his associates focused on job satisfaction as a key component of motivation.[9] They divided work into hygiene factors and motivators, as shown in Figure 4-4.

- **Hygiene factors** are features of the job's *context,* including company policies and practices, wages, benefits, and working conditions. Managers who improve hygiene factors reduce a person's dissatisfaction with his work situation and increase the impact of the motivators. Although hygiene factors themselves do not encourage workers to exert more effort, they must be at an acceptable level

FIGURE 4-3

The Thematic Apperception Test includes pictures such as this one.

FIGURE 4-4

According to Herzberg's theory, motivators can increase worker satisfaction, and hygiene factors can reduce worker dissatisfaction.

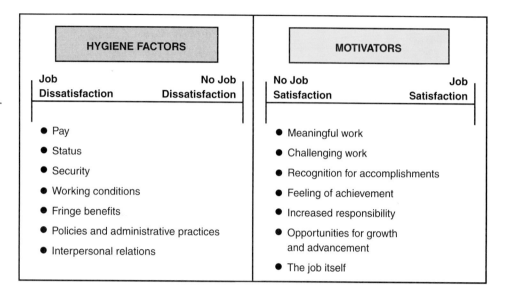

before motivators can have a positive effect. For example, offering autonomy and responsibility to employees with poor working conditions results in worker dissatisfaction and hinders motivation. Managers increase overall satisfaction by reducing dissatisfaction and increasing satisfaction.

■ **Motivators** are features of the job's *content,* including responsibility, self-esteem, autonomy, and growth; they satisfy higher-order needs and result in job satisfaction. Managers can increase motivators by giving workers more autonomy, responsibility, and creativity in their jobs, and thereby encouraging them to exert more effort and perform better. Turner Bros. Trucking Inc., based in Oklahoma City, created self-directed safety teams that gave employees more autonomy and responsibility as a way of increasing their commitment to company safety and productivity.[10]

Evaluating and Applying Needs Theories

Managers find needs theories intuitively appealing and easy to apply. However, research has questioned their validity, focusing specifically on the number and order of needs and whether people have a single dominant need.[11] McClelland and his associates continue to study the three needs and provide consultation about their effects. Yet the measurement of needs using projective instruments is cumbersome, and support for the theory is inconsistent. Although Herzberg and his associates have conducted numerous empirical studies that support the motivator-hygiene theory, its research support too is limited.[12] Problems exist in labeling a work characteristic as either a hygiene factor or a motivator; some factors, such as pay, can be both.

Overall, the concept of needs is difficult to prove or disprove.[13] Managers can have difficulty specifying and measuring needs. They also have problems in showing that satisfying needs depends on various job or organizational characteristics, such as specific benefits or wage plans. For example, when lavish benefit programs become standard, employees take them for granted and the programs lose their power to motivate. Needs theories fail to account for the large variety of behaviors and attitudes of workers and often do not consider that external factors may cause workers to act in certain ways. Finally, categorizing people according to their needs may result in stereotyping behavior and ignoring its subtleties and complexities.

In spite of the limitations of needs theories, a manager can use them to help motivate workers. The manager can ask questions such as the following:

- What needs do employees have?
- What needs have they satisfied, and how have they satisfied them?
- Which needs remain unsatisfied?
- Have some higher-order needs been frustrated?
- How can managers help their employees satisfy unsatisfied needs?
- What motivators and hygiene factors exist in the situation?
- How can managers increase motivators?

▌EQUITY THEORY

Managers also motivate workers by ensuring that fairness exists in the workplace. *Equity theory* has evolved from a social psychological theory called *social comparison theory*. It suggests that people compare their own job situation to another person's, their *comparison other*. The judgments people make about equity between themselves and their comparison other influence their motivation.

Consider, for example, Alexa Rodriguez. Her manager gave her a 4 percent pay increase. Will this motivate her to perform better? Andrew Merchant received a 3 percent increase from the same manager. Will this motivate him? Their manager can use equity theory to answer these questions. Rodriguez and Merchant would make comparisons of the outcomes (e.g., wages, benefits, promotions, job titles, and job content) from their work relative to their inputs (e.g., effort, education, and experience). To determine the equity in the situation and how it would affect their motivation, Rodriguez and Merchant would then assess the ratio of their outcomes to inputs and compare this ratio to their perception of the outcome-to-input ratio of the other person, as shown in Figure 4-5.

According to equity theory, perceptions, not facts, influence motivation. For example, employees who perceive inequitable benefits will be less satisfied with their level of benefits.[14] Culture can also influence perceptions of equity, which may depend on expectations associated with social class, job category, or educational status.

Dealing with Inequities

Equal ratios of outputs to inputs lead to high worker motivation and ultimately high outcomes.[15] Unequal ratios cause the worker to alter either her own inputs or outcomes, or her perception of the comparison person's inputs or outcomes. A worker may exert less effort, work fewer hours, distract herself on the job, or refuse additional training. She may attempt to secure additional pay or a job promotion, change her job title, or request increased or different job responsibilities. Figure 4-6 on page 110 shows some of the responses to perceived inequity.

In theory, workers make the same adjustments when they perceive that they receive too much reward for the input or have too complex a job in comparison to others.[16] For example, they may work harder to change the ratio of outputs to inputs. If you were overpaid, would you work harder to create equity? A study of 342

FIGURE 4-5

According to equity theory, employees are most motivated when the ratio of their inputs to outputs equals that of a comparison other.

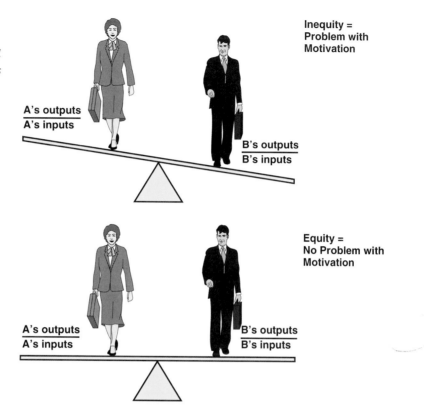

Major League baseball players showed that overpayment resulted in positive changes in performance, while underpayment resulted in negative changes.[17]

Research has reported this *overjustification effect*, but mixed evidence of it exists.[18] Some people respond to inequities by adjusting their perception of the comparison person's inputs or outputs, ignoring the situation, or even choosing a new comparison person. Some people find calculating equity difficult.[19] They may look instead for long-term rather than short-term equity in work situations and see equity as a goal to work for over time.[20]

Managers can determine whether equity exists in the workplace by assessing how fairly individuals are treated, also known as *organizational justice.* For example, an employee may evaluate whether the rules for giving pay raises, the procedures for administering pay, the level of pay, the distribution of jobs, and the pace of work is equitable between him and selected co-workers.[21] Workers can make judgments about fairness about outcomes, such as pay or promotions, known as *distributive justice;* procedures that result in the outcomes, such as the rules for distributing pay, known as *procedural justice;* and the system that generates the procedures and outcomes, such as the organizational reward system, known as *interactional justice.*[22] Procedural justice may further focus on the process itself, the extent to which an individual receives information about the process, and the extent to which an individual agrees with the process.[23] Men seem more concerned about the fairness of the outcomes and women about the fairness of the procedures, tying them to decisions about commitment to their organization and intent to stay employed by the organization.[24] The acceptability of arbitrators to the parties in a dispute-resolution process depends, in part, on their implementation of distributive, procedural, and interactional justice.[25] Managers need to pay careful attention to ensuring organizational justice in the workplace.

What happens when inequities exist?

If person A believes an inequity exists and her ratio is too small, she may
- reduce her inputs
- ask for more outputs
- change her comparison person
- rationalize that equity exists
- leave the situation

If person B believes an inequity exists and his ratio is too large, he may
- increase his inputs
- ask for reduced outputs
- change his comparison person
- rationalize that equity exists
- leave the situation

Evaluation of Equity Theory

Although equity theory makes sense, empirical support has been mixed.[26] *Equity sensitivity* helps explain these findings by suggesting that people have different preferences for equity (e.g., a preference for higher, lower, or equal ratios). Their preferences cause them to react consistently but differently to perceived equity and inequity.[27] Some people may not react immediately to inequity but only perceive it if it persists.[28] Differences in intelligence, social values, personality, and gender may also influence an employee's perception of inequity.[29] Women and minorities today may be particularly attuned to inequity because of the extensive and intense discrimination many of them have experienced. People from different cultures likely have different equity sensitivity.[30]

Equity theory oversimplifies what motivates workers by ignoring individual needs, values, or personalities, as well as cross-cultural differences in preferences for equity and responses to inequity. Still, managers can diagnose and then reduce inequities in the workplace by identifying workers' inputs, outcomes, and comparison others. Managers can then check that perceived comparability exists among workers. They can also encourage employees to make equity judgments on the basis of accurate information. Recognizing that some information about performance and pay must remain confidential, managers should inform employees about reasons for particular wages, promotions, or job changes. Finally, they must ensure that outcomes match inputs. For example, they should pay for performance rather than for non-job-related and potentially discriminatory factors such as age, race, or gender.

▌ REINFORCEMENT THEORY

In addition to trying to meet workers' needs and treat them equitably, managers can motivate their employees by giving them bonuses for attaining certain goals. They apply the basic principles of *reinforcement theory* by encouraging desired behaviors and discouraging undesired behaviors through the use of *reinforcers* such as pay, promotion, challenging assignments, or praise. For example, Wells Fargo Corporation gave its employees Monopoly money, which they could in turn "award" to fellow employees who had helped them achieve their goals. The company then converted the Monopoly money into U.S. currency.[31]

Types of Reinforcement

Reinforcement techniques can either encourage or eliminate the desired behavior by applying or removing reinforcers. Managers can choose among positive reinforcement, negative reinforcement, extinction, or punishment, as shown in Table 4-1.

- ▪ **Positive reinforcement** means giving rewards or feedback when the desired behavior occurs. For example, an employee who delivers home appliances receives a fee for each one delivered. The manager thus encourages the reinforced or rewarded behavior to recur. If the employee does not act as the manager wants, the manager may selectively reinforce behaviors, each time encouraging the employee to act closer to what the manager wants. For example, each time a supermarket cashier processes an order quickly, his boss might praise him. Praise would continue until the cashier handles all orders very quickly. The manager would discontinue praising the cashier when he slowed down.

- ▪ **Negative reinforcement** describes encouraging a person to avoid undesirable consequences and removing the person from an undesirable situation when the desired behavior occurs. A building contractor may try to complete a project as soon as possible to stop penalty payments for late completion. Managers may monitor telephone salespeople until they consistently meet acceptable standards of speed, courtesy, and so on.

▌ TABLE 4-1 ▌

Managers Can Encourage or Discourage Behaviors by Applying or Withholding Various Types of Reinforcements.

	Apply Reinforcement	**Withhold Reinforcement**
Encourage Behavior	**Positive reinforcement** Sales commission	**Negative Reinforcement** Relieving an army private of KP (kitchen patrol duty)
Discourage Behavior	**Punishment** Docking an employee's pay for tardiness	**Extinction** Giving no pay increases

- **Extinction** eliminates an undesired behavior by a manager's withholding positive reinforcement. A person who gives a customer more than they want but receives neither thanks nor praise from his manager for this added effort likely will stop the extra, undesired attention. By withholding reinforcement, a supervisor may also cause desired behaviors, such as productivity, creativity, or attendance, to stop.

- **Punishment** eliminates an undesired behavior by having a negative event follow the behavior. In this way, it differs from negative reinforcement in which the subject acts to stop or avoid an undesirable consequence. A manager might punish a tardy employee by giving him undesirable assignments. Punishment should be used as a last resort because it often creates secondary consequences of tension and stress and may result in unpredictable outcomes. Punishment may not permanently eliminate undesired behavior because it does not offer an alternative to the desired behavior. If a worker repeatedly misuses a piece of equipment and receives punishment each time, her behavior may not change because she hasn't learned the correct way to use the equipment. Punishment may also have consequences for observers: It may deter similar behavior in observers or motivate it to occur.[32]

Schedules of Reinforcement

The timing of reinforcers or rewards can affect their impact. Compare the behavior of an employee who receives a weekly paycheck to that of one who gets paid for each product he sells. How would the behavior of these workers change if they received an unexpected bonus? The timing and frequency of the reinforcement has different consequences, as shown in Table 4-2.

- **Interval schedules** apply reinforcers after a certain amount of time elapses (e.g., weekly or monthly paychecks, yearly bonuses, or biyearly salary increases).

- **Ratio schedules** apply reinforcers after a certain number of behaviors occurs (e.g., a certain wage for a set level of production or sales, known as *piecework* and *commission* systems, respectively).

TABLE 4-2

Managers Can Encourage Behavior in the Short Term and Long Run by Using Different Schedules of Reinforcement.

	Fixed	Variable
Interval	Give reward after the first proper response following a specified time period.	Give reward after a certain amount of time with the amount changing before the next reward
	Regular paycheck	*Unexpected merit bonus*
Ratio	Give reward after a specified number of proper responses	Give reward after a number of responses, with that number changing before the next reward
	Commissions or piecework pay	*Team-based bonus*

- **Fixed reinforcers,** such as the weekly paycheck, occur at a predetermined and expected time.
- **Variable reinforcers** occur at unpredictable and varied times. A manager may praise a worker once a day for a week and then not again for another three weeks.

In general, interval and fixed schedules encourage the behavior in the short term; ratio and variable schedules motivate behavior in the longer run. Assume that a manager of an online bookstore wants her employees to fill orders correctly. To establish the desired behavior, the manager should begin with a fixed-interval schedule of reinforcement. The manager might review the completed orders hourly and praise the employees each day for correct ones. In the medium run, the manager might switch to a variable-interval schedule, offering praise every three days for good performance. Sustaining the behavior in the long term probably calls for a variable-ratio schedule, unexpectedly offering praise or even monetary bonuses after an unspecified amount of error-free orders. Pacific Gas & Electric, for example, uses several types of variable pay, including signing bonuses and stock options, as well as performance-based pay, to keep salary increases stable. Walt Disney Company successfully controlled its workers' compensation costs by linking managers' bonuses to their employees' safety records.[33] High-performing companies give their high-performing employees a larger share of merit pay increases than low-performing companies, according to a recent study of 770 organizations in North America.[34]

Evaluating and Applying Reinforcement Theory

While reinforcement theory is simple and clear, explains behavior relatively well, and has generated extensive research, its focus on the individual and the methodological problems in studying it may limit its usefulness.[35] Managers typically overuse pay as a motivator and underuse praise. They must ensure that they reinforce the behavior they desire; often they "reward A while hoping for B."[36] Often universities, for example, reward research but hope that good teaching will follow. Managers might say that they encourage workers to do quality work, but then give pay raises and promotions to employees based on the greatest quantity of work, the number of clients serviced, or the number of patents obtained, regardless of the work's quality. The "pay for performance" controversy emphasizes that managers should assign reinforcers to the desired behavior, not automatically give pay increases for seniority or effort.

To diagnose the behavior of workers at Netcentives or TechProducts using reinforcement theory, we can ask the following questions:

- What behaviors do managers want from their employees?
- What reinforces these behaviors?
- When are the reinforcements applied?
- What consequences result from these reinforcements?
- How can managers improve the reinforcement pattern?

EXPECTANCY THEORY

Motivating employees involves meeting their needs, ensuring equity in the workplace, reinforcing desired behaviors, and setting specific, challenging, and accepted goals. Expectancy theory provides a view of motivation that integrates these elements into a single theory.

Basic Elements

Expectancy theories include three basic elements—expectancy, instrumentality, and valence:

- **Expectancy** refers to an individual's perception that his effort (E) will result in performance (P), such as higher productivity or increased sales.
- **Instrumentality** refers to a person's perception that performance will result in certain positive or negative outcomes (O), such as promotion, increased wages, greater fatigue, or loneliness.
- **Valence (V)** refers to the value the person attaches to various outcomes that result. She may assign a positive valence to a promotion but a negative valence to fatigue.

Victor Vroom popularized this theory in the 1960s. In his model,

$$\text{Motivation} = \text{Expectancy} \times \text{Instrumentality} \times \text{Valence}[37]$$

Consider the motivation of a TechProducts employee responsible for developing a new product. She has high expectancy if her effort, such as working long hours, results in higher performance, such as a product that has a high market share. Lack of training or proper equipment can reduce her expectancy and motivation. High instrumentality exists for the employee if new product development results in a pay increase; poor reward systems can reduce instrumentality and motivation. A pay raise may have a high valence and fatigue a low valence for the employee. As expectancy, instrumentality, or valence increases, so does motivation; as any of them decreases, so does motivation.

Employers can use this model to help employees act ethically. First, they can determine which rewards have the highest valence for employees and use these when ethical behavior occurs. Second, they can foster a motivational environment by defining and communicating the kinds of ethical behavior expected from employees. Finally, they can link the desired ethical behaviors to the rewards the employees desire or prefer. Bausch & Lomb, a manufacturer and distributor of eye-care products, in an attempt to maintain high-level sales and earnings growth, created pressures on employees to "make the numbers," which resulted in unethical behavior. Managers routinely sold the company's sunglasses through gray market distributors to meet quotas. The company shipped contact lenses to physicians who had not placed an order. Distributors received two years of unwanted inventories to increase managers' sales figures. The motivational structure rewarded questionable behavior by failing to communicate ethical policies to its employees and thereby creating a motivational climate that seemed to foster unethical behavior.[38]

A more recent formulation of expectancy theory reflects the role of unsatisfied needs, equity, reinforcements, and goal setting in motivation:[39]

$$\text{Motivation} = [E{\rightarrow}P] \times \Sigma\,[(P{\rightarrow}O)(V)]$$

Here, $E{\rightarrow}P$ is the same as expectancy and refers to the worker's perception of the likelihood that effort leads to performance. Setting specific, difficult, and accepted goals can increase this expectancy. $P{\rightarrow}O$, akin to instrumentality, refers to the employee's perception that performance results in certain outcomes. V again refers to valence, or the value of the outcome, which is closely tied to a person's needs. To diagnose the work situation using expectancy theory, a manager can ask whether expectancies, instrumentalities, and valences are high. If not, he can then seek ways to increase them.

We can examine the case of a worker, Jennifer Levitz, using this formulation of motivation. If Jennifer perceives that working more hours will result in better performance, then $E{\rightarrow}P$ will be positive. If she perceives that she receives pay and praise if she performs her job well, then $P{\rightarrow}O$ will be positive. If Jennifer likes receiving money and praise, then V will be positive. If, instead, Jennifer receives no praise or pay raise for good performance, then $E{\rightarrow}P$ and V remain positive, but $P{\rightarrow}O$ is negative, reducing her motivation.

Because performance can lead to multiple outcomes, each with different valences or values, each performance-to-outcome expectancy is multiplied by the corresponding valence. For example, consider a Web designer who knows that if she produces a sufficient number of Web pages, she will receive pay, resulting in one positive performance-to-outcome link. But this worker may also know that if she produces too many Web pages, the quality of the designs will not be as high and so this performance-to-outcome link is much less positive. These products are then summed before being multiplied by the effort-to-performance expectancy.

In some countries, however, strengthening the effort-to-performance links or performance-to-outcome links may be viewed as a function of uncontrollable change, rather than as a result of managerial or worker control.[40] Expectancy theory best explains motivation in cultures where workers believe that they can control their environment.[41]

Evaluating and Applying Expectancy Theory

Evidence for the validity of the expectancy model is mixed.[42] The limitations to expectancy theory include the interpretation and operationalization of the key constructs.[43] Although the expectancy equation may oversimplify the motivational process, managers can still use it to diagnose motivational problems or to evaluate effective motivation by asking the following questions:

- Does the employee perceive that effort will lead to performance?
- Does the employee perceive that certain behaviors will lead to specified outcomes?
- What values do people attach to these outcomes?

▌GOAL-SETTING THEORY

Goal-setting theory states that the process of setting goals can focus behavior and motivate employees. As people receive ongoing feedback about their progress toward achieving their goals, their motivation increases and remains high. At Squar, Milner and Reehl, a Newport Beach, California, accounting firm, all managers can participate in a "variable compensation award" program in which they receive from $5,000 to $10,000 in the first year if they meet their goals; compensation for reaching their goals then increases in subsequent years.[44]

Characteristics of Goals

Goals, which any member of an organization can set, describe a desired future state, such as reduced costs, lower absenteeism, higher employee satisfaction, or specified performance levels. For example, an executive of a dot-com company may wish to double the company's sales every six months for the first two years after the company's founding. The sales manager of a cable company might want to increase the number of customers using the company's Internet service by 30 percent each month. Goals such as these help focus an individual's or a group's behavior and help them perform. Goals can vary in at least three ways:

- **Goal specificity** refers to the extent to which the accomplishment is observable and measurable. "Increasing sales by 30 percent" or "reducing absenteeism by 15 percent by December 31" are more specific goals than "improving sales" or "reducing turnover." Specific goals motivate workers more than less specific goals, in part because workers can more easily visualize the target.

- **Goal difficulty** refers to how hard a person or group finds accomplishing the goal. Increasing sales by 5 percent may be easy, by 10 percent may be moderately difficult, and by 25 percent extremely difficult. Motivating employees requires setting increasingly difficult goals up to a reasonable level of challenge, since recent research suggests that performance increases as the difficulty of goals increases until the goals become impossible to accomplish.[45]

- **Goal acceptance** refers to whether those who must accomplish the goal accept it as their own—that is, whether they "buy into it." Involving the person expected to accomplish the goal through joint goal setting increases its acceptance. The authority of the person who sets the goal influences motivation. More senior bosses typically have greater influence, but co-workers can also influence a worker's motivation to accept a goal.[46]

The limitations to expectancy theory include the interpretation and operationalization of the key constructs.[47] Increasingly, companies and other organizations have focused on developing S.M.A.R.T. goals. Such goals are strategic, measurable, attainable, results-oriented, and time-bound.[48]

Evaluating and Applying Goal-Setting Theory

Managers may have trouble applying goal-setting theory if they oversimplify the motivational issues so that they conform to the theory. Effective motivation may require establishing an array of goals at all levels of the organization. Performance depends on the employees' ability, their acceptance of goals, the level of the goals, and the interaction of the goal with their ability.[49] Feedback must accompany goal setting because workers need information about their effectiveness in meeting their goals as part of continuing to work toward them.[50] Acceptance of the goals also has consequences for the goals' difficulty level. Workers are likely to perform a task if the goals are difficult and accepted, but not difficult and rejected.[51] When joined with attempts to raise the expectancy that effort leads to performance, setting difficult goals can boost productivity.[52]

Studies of setting multiple goals suggest that accomplishing one goal may result in sacrificing the second, reflecting the limited cognitive capacity of people.[53] In very complex jobs, however, goal setting may not be feasible because the job may require setting too many goals. Or goal setting may lead to bureaucratic behavior, in which setting the goals becomes an end in itself. The effects of goal setting may also differ across cultures.[54]

Figure 4-7 offers a summary model of the factors that link goal setting to performance. People set goals in response to work-related demands placed on them, which in turn lead to performance. The worker's ability, commitment to the task, receipt of

FIGURE 4-7

Individual and situational factors affect the relationship between goals and performance.

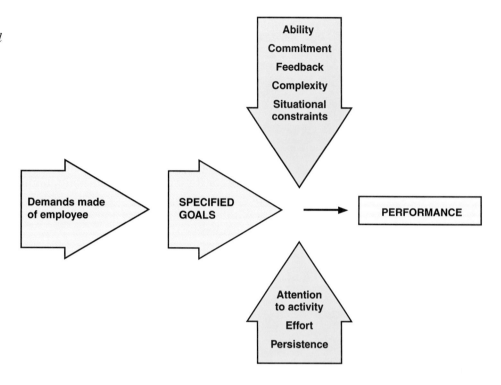

feedback about performance, the complexity of the task, and other situational constraints affect the relationship between goals and performance. Performance increases when workers pay attention to a task, exert effort on it, and persist over time in doing it. In diagnosing worker motivation, we can evaluate each of the factors shown in Figure 4-7 and offer ways of improving them. In particular, we can ask whether the worker has goals, accepts these goals, and has received feedback about the goals.

CREATING EFFECTIVE REWARD SYSTEMS

An organization's reward system incorporates the motivational principles described in this chapter into formal mechanisms, such as wages, benefits, incentives, and employee ownership, for encouraging high performance and meeting organizational goals. It includes both compensation and nonpay components, such as promotions, flexible hours, or even praise.

Wages in Organizations

Pay acts as a powerful reward and can motivate workers to perform better.[55] It can meet diverse needs and reinforce desired behaviors. However, organizations frequently misuse it. They may give all employees the same pay increase, regardless of their performance, or they may fail to use pay to help satisfy workers' needs.

In theory, wages should reflect the performance of an employee. In practice, organizations develop systematic wage systems that are tied to the nature of a person's job and her longevity with the organization. Some workers receive *hourly* wages, so their total pay depends on the number of hours they work. Other workers earn *salaries,* fixed yearly rates earned regardless of the precise number of hours they work. Usually, hourly workers hold lower-level jobs in the organization, and salaried workers hold managerial or professional positions. Because of the status differences often inherent in the allocation of wages, some organizations have eliminated hourly employees and classified all employees as salaried employees. The Saturn division of General Motors created a precedent in the U.S. auto industry by paying salaries to all employees, including union members.[56]

Moderate to large organizations frequently design a *wage system* that formalizes the pay structure in the organization. Each job is placed in a wage grade that determines the range of pay available to a particular job holder. Adjustments in the actual wage may occur for length of employment, higher educational degrees, level of performance, or entering salary. Two managers in a company may both be at wage level 12, but their actual salaries may differ by $10,000 or more because of the length of time each has held the job.

Recently, many organizations have reduced the number of wage levels, typically from 30 or more to 10 or fewer. *Broadbanding* places more jobs within the same wage level and allows more flexibility in moving workers among jobs. Jobs in the same level have approximately the same value to the organization. One band might include all nonsupervisory professionals, whose salary might range from $36,000 to $72,000.[57] Such systems also tie compensation to specific competencies demonstrated by the employees. For example, numerous states, including New Jersey and Florida, are reducing the number of Civil Service job titles through broadbanding. In New Jersey, there were more than 1,200 job titles held by just one employee, such as Assistant Curator for Natural Science Collection and Exhibits, which differs from Assistant Curator for Natural Science Interpretation.[58] Broadbanding helps support the reorganization of work, reduces the traditional emphasis on organizational hierarchy, helps employees manage their careers, and reduces the emphasis on pay comparisons among employees.[59]

Broadbanding has attracted attention worldwide. Companies in Belgium, Austrialia, Switzerland, Canada, India, and Mexico, for example, have used broadbanding as a way of ensuring that their compensation system is strategically tied to their business goals. In Japan, 90 percent of companies use a broadbanding approach. Companies in these countries believe that broadbanding increases organizational flexibility, departs from traditional systems, and supports the flatter organization that is now viewed as more effective. It also supports other organizational changes directed at accomplishing business goals and reduces compensation administration.[60] Nokia, for example, designed a broadbanding system that reduced 40 salary ranges to five broad career bands. Such companies, however, need to carefully consider local differences when designing and implementing such a system.[61]

Managers choose whether to pay according to workers' jobs or their skills and competencies.[62] *Job-based pay* rewards people for performing specific jobs and moving up the hierarchy. Job-based pay reinforces the link between an individual's job and organizational outcomes. It supports a culture that emphasizes bottom-line performance. *Skill-based* or *competency-based pay* rewards people for building more competencies and increasing their skills. Skill-based programs support a culture that reflects a concern for individual development and learning and an environment that requires greater flexibility from a relatively permanent workforce.[63]

Pay inversion, in which new job holders earn more than current job holders, is a major problem in organizations. *Pay compression,* in which the differences in wages between new and long-term employees shrink over time, also creates challenges for fair compensation. For example, an employee is hired at $45,000; a second employee is hired the next year for the same job at $51,000 because the job market demanded that pay level for new hires. The first employee desires a salary adjustment so that his salary is comparable to the second employee's. Frequent adjustments in the wage scale may need to occur in some industries to ensure equity in the workplace. Top executives must also ensure that the wage scale remains competitive with other organizations in the same industry. Particularly in a tight labor market, organizations must offer competitive wages to retain a motivated and productive workforce.

Wage systems must also consider the market position of the pay offered. Why? Some companies prefer to take a leadership position in compensation because they assume that paying well will result in their attracting the best people. Others willingly risk attracting somewhat less qualified workers by offering lower financial rewards. The market position chosen influences the organization's ability to cope with its environment. When a tight labor market exists, organizations with an aggressive, "leader" strategy typically fare best in securing the workers they need. When, on the other hand, labor is very available, these compensation leaders may unnecessarily spend a premium.

Executive pay has received a great deal of attention. People ask, "Are they worth it?" as wages, benefits, and stock options paid to top executives skyrocket. Many companies tie executive pay to performance, but this practice can result in arbitrarily inflated stock prices. Charles Wang, CEO of Computer Associates International, held the honor of being the executive with the highest pay in a 1999 survey of top-paid chief executives. He received $4.6 million in salary and bonus, and $650 million in long-term compensation.[64]

Some companies offer their executives stock options as a way of reducing the current payroll and tying compensation to longer-term performance. When stock prices fluctuate wildly, the value of stock options as compensation can also decrease. Executives at Borders Group Inc., the parent company for Borders bookstores, recently decided to take their pay in the form of salary instead of stock options because of the flagging performance of Borders stock.[65]

Executives also receive "golden parachutes" or even "platinum parachutes" for leaving companies after they restructure. When NationsBank bought Barnett Banks for $15.5 billion, Barnett's CEO, Charles Rice, received $150 million, as well as free lifetime travel on the company's corporate jet, as part of the buyout.[66] The former chairman of US West, Sol Trujillo, was scheduled to receive a total of $36.9 million after the merger with Qwest Communications International.[67] In an unusual case, the golden parachute contracts negotiated for the former CEO and CFO of Harvard Pilgrim Health Care, a financially troubled organization, were rescinded when the state placed the HMO into receivership.[68]

Top management must also determine which organizational members will make pay decisions. Responsibility can be decentralized throughout the organization to supervisors or can be centralized and systematized in a corporate compensation system. Communication of compensation decisions varies from very secretive to very open. The processes chosen frequently complement the organization's structure and reinforce its culture. As companies have moved toward more employee involvement in decision making, compensation decisions have become more open and available for employee action.

Benefits as Motivators

Most organizations offer employees an array of benefits, as shown in Table 4-3. Originally intended to increase worker motivation, benefits more often attract and retain employees than affect their performance. By law, all organizations must offer

TABLE 4-3

Employees May Receive an Array of Benefits.

Health Protectors

Medical insurance

Dental insurance

Income Protectors

Accidental death insurance

Disability insurance

Life insurance

Pensions

Retirements benefits

Supplementary unemployment benefits

Workers' compensation

Time Off with Pay

Holidays

Personal days

Maternity or paternity leave

Sabbaticals

Sick leave

Vacations

Income Supplements

Bonuses

Profit-sharing plans

Stock bonus plans

Stock options

Other Benefits

Professional memberships

Club memberships

Company automobiles

Concierge services

Child care

Education costs

Elder care

Flexible work arrangements

Housekeeping services

Lawn care

Recreational facilities

Subsidized housing

Subsidized meals

their workers time off for certain holidays, as well as workers' compensation insurance in case they are injured on the job. Almost all organizations offer a minimum of one week of vacation a year, which workers might accrue at a specified rate, such as one day for every two months worked. Larger organizations add medical insurance, pension plans, and other income protectors to the array of benefits. Reducing the cost of health care benefits currently provides a major challenge for top executives. Managers must balance the cost of benefits with their value for attracting, motivating, and retaining employees.

Companies now often look for new benefits to meet their employees' needs. Community Hospitals in Indianapolis agreed to hire a lawn service for a cardiovascular nurse they wanted to hire; they also provided a year of free maid service to other nurses they recruited.[69] Employee Solutions in Phoenix provides massages for employees every two weeks.[70] This desire to meet employee needs has prompted the start-up of new businesses such as Circles, a Boston-based online concierge service. The company has met such unusual requests as sending a chainsaw to a hotel room and finding a circular staircase for a dollhouse, as well as the more mundane requests for theater tickets, restaurant reservations, dog walking, and vacation planning. Circles sells its services to companies that in turn offer them to employees who lack the time to handle their personal business.[71]

In selecting benefits, managers must assess cost-effectiveness and how well each benefit responds to workers' needs. Some organizations offer *flexible benefits plans,* in which workers receive a fixed amount of dollars or points to allocate to various medical, pension, vacation, child-care, or other benefits. Such a choice prevents the duplication of benefits and ensures that benefits better respond to worker needs. Some employers create *flexible spending accounts* or *deferred compensation,* which allow workers to pay for benefits with before-tax dollars, thereby creating tax benefits and reducing the "real" cost of the benefits.

Devising Incentive Systems

Incentive programs pay a person or group of people only for what they produce. If a worker packs shipping containers, he receives a certain amount of money for each container filled—the more containers filled, the more pay the worker receives. Or a salesperson receives a fee for each container sold.

Piecework systems, commission plans, merit bonuses, and gainsharing plans are the most common incentive systems. They directly link pay to performance, as follows:

- **Piecework systems** tie compensation to individual performance by paying workers for each item produced. Asian immigrants in the Silicon Valley are paid to assemble electronic parts in their homes for some of the area's high-technology companies and are paid for each component produced. Questions about the legality of this type of piecework, which has allowed high-technology companies to significantly reduce manufacturing costs, have arisen because the pay may not meet minimum wage requirements.[72]

- **Commissions** link pay to sales levels rather than production rates. Employees may receive a certain percentage of total sales or new sales, or they may receive compensation for reaching a sales quota. Most mutual funds, for example, have sales commissions, or load, that traders receive when customers buy the fund.

- **Bonuses** are one-time, lump-sum payments that are tied to exceptional performance. Increasingly, organizations use these instead of merit increases because they do not add to the base wages of the worker. Marjorie Scardino, the first woman CEO at Pearson, the British media and publishing conglomerate, increased employee performance by offering incentives for double-digit earnings growth; in 2001 all employees likely receive at least $3000 for producing margins greater than 28 percent.[73]

- **Gainsharing** programs, such as the Scanlon Plan, Improshare, or Rucker Plan, allow workers to share in productivity improvements by earning bonuses based on group performance.[74] One U.S. furniture company implemented a gainsharing program in which it compared actual to projected labor costs. Employees shared 50/50 with the company in the savings or gain between the cost target and the actual costs. During one month, the employees received a gainsharing bonus of $22,450, which when divided among 152 employees, resulted in $148 for each employee.[75]

Incentives can reinforce organizational goals. They support an emphasis on "bottom-line" performance. Studies show that an award should be at least 10 to 20 percent above a person's base salary to motivate him.[76] Although these awards can increase productivity and lower production costs, they can also adversely affect the quality of the product, cause workers to trade off long-term for short-term gains, and ignore the means by which employees attain results.[77]

Motivating Through Employee Ownership

Perhaps the ultimate reward for workers is to own part of the organization. Among the possible options are employee stock ownership, often incorporated in an employee stock ownership plan (ESOP); the outright sale of stock; the offering of options or appreciation rights (in which the individual gets the increase in the value of the stock without stock ownership); and stock bonus programs.[78] For example, in many organizations with ESOPs, workers sit on the corporate board and top management teams and thus can exert control over the organization's direction and operation. Employees who share in the company's equity through stock ownership begin to think and act like owners, who typically work harder than employees.[79] Capital One Financial Corporation awarded stock options to entry-level associates who began employment there between May 1, 1998, and April 29, 1999. Top executives believe that "a strong sense of ownership is closely linked to Capital One's success."[80]

While employee ownership was initially not well received in the United States, recent opportunities for employee ownership have increased. Home Depot's stock ownership program resulted in more than 1,000 millionaires in 1998.[81] United Airlines gave its employees a 55 percent share of its parent UAL in 1994, and for most, the ESOP lived up to its expectations; the company has experienced job security, positive labor–management relations, worker influence on company management, a large and profitable airline, and significant retirement funds for its employees. In spite of its success, not all employees support the idea of replacing it with a second ESOP when it expires, primarily because of the high cost to employees and the lack of liquidity of their stock shares (employees can only cash them when they retire).[82] Even small, privately held companies can have employee ownership. Sage Electronics increased employee ownership from 16 to 30 percent of the company to signal that the company is not looking for a buyer.[83]

Employee ownership has increased outside the United States as well. German companies have allowed worker representation on boards of directors as a form of worker ownership. Known as *codetermination,* this structure gives workers a direct voice in the operation of their companies. In Russia, companies with more than 200 employees have typically been sold to their employees as part of the restructuring of business there. In China, millions of employees have become corporate owners; there, too, local governments have sold their businesses to employees.[84]

Motivation in the Dot-Com, Global Workplace

Managers in the new workplace face a number of challenges. Traditional pay structures don't work well in dot-com companies for several reasons. For example, dot-com companies frequently reward top executives with stock options rather than direct compensation. Competencies and skills, rather than position, determine an employee's value to these companies. The rapid change experienced by such companies typically makes salary rankings and offerings out-of-date very quickly. Some technical employees often deserve the large rewards typically allocated to high-level managers. Ensuring that the reward system meets the needs of these dot-com workers and motivates their high performance is essential.[85]

Theories of motivation do not apply in the same way in every type of company or every culture. Workers' main needs as well as their order vary in different cultures.[86] For example, workers in countries characterized as high on uncertainty avoidance (e.g., Japan) value security over self-actualization.[87] Different cultures may also place relatively more value on lower rather than higher needs, or vice versa. In France, belongingness heavily influences motivation, whereas in Holland and the United States, fairness and recognition, respectively, are most influential.

Differences in individuals' views of equity in a situation may also vary. In newly formed Web companies, for example, employees may not have great concerns about equity because the potential for gain is so great. We might also predict that equity sensitivity would be greater among employees from the United States and Canada, where power and status differences are less tolerated than among workers from China, Japan, or South America, where power and status differences are more accepted. In fact, recent research suggests that business students in central and eastern Europe were more likely than U.S. students to have an entitled attitude— that is, they prefer that their outcomes exceed their inputs.[88]

Different reinforcers may also be useful in the new workplace. Certainly stock options have increased in value as dot-com companies' stock prices have soared. Yet, fluctuations in the stock market may make such incentives less attractive than traditional pay. In some countries, praise may be valued over pay increases, job flexibility and autonomy over job titles. Managers need to be attuned to variations in attitudes and behaviors in different cultures regarding expectancies and goal setting as well.

The growth of U.S. corporations abroad and foreign-owned corporations in the United States has created challenges in designing effective and equitable multinational reward systems. Variations in the standard of living in different countries, the need to offer incentives to attract workers to certain locations throughout the world, and the desire to maintain a degree of consistency across work sites influence compensation and other, nonmonetary rewards offered. Selecting rewards that motivate employees in these situations and determining appropriate wages and benefits becomes a major challenge for executives of such organizations.

▌ Summary

1. Managers in the dot-com, global workplace can meet unsatisfied workers' needs in a variety of ways that involve altering the job's responsibility, challenge, autonomy, pay, or title, among others.

2. Equity theory suggests that people compare and try to equalize the ratio of their own outcomes, such as pay or promotions, to inputs, such as effort or experience, to those of another person.

3. A manager who applies reinforcement theory encourages desired behaviors and discourages undesired ones by applying appropriate reinforcers.

4. Expectancy theory directs managers to increase an employee's expectancy, instrumentality, and valence.

5. Goal-setting theory says that managers can motivate workers by setting specific, moderately difficult, and accepted goals.

6. A comprehensive reward system motivates employees with wages, benefits, incentives, and employee ownership and ties an array of rewards to performance.

A Manager's Diagnostic Review

☐ Identify workers' needs and then meet them.

- What needs do individuals have?
- How can managers satisfy these needs?

☐ Create an equitable workplace.

- Are rewards given fairly and consistently?
- Do managers help workers provide appropriate inputs for the outputs they desire?
- Create positive expectancies in the workplace.
- Do employees have the skills, tools, and materials to do their jobs well?
- How can managers help them acquire the needed skills, tools, and materials?

☐ Reward employees for high performance, commitment, and creativity.

- Are different rewards used to sustain behavior in the short and long run?
- Do people value the rewards they receive?
- Do managers reward desired behaviors and attitudes?

☐ Set challenging but specific goals jointly with employees.

- Do managers and workers set goals that are specific, challenging, and accepted?
- Do managers give workers feedback about their goal accomplishment?

☐ Design and implement a fair compensation system.

- Are fair wages offered?
- Does the company pay for performance?
- Do the benefits offered meet individuals' needs?
- Does the company offer incentives that encourage high-quality performance?

Visit the Gordon homepage on the Prentice Hall Web site at

http://www.prenhall.com/gordon

for recommended readings, additional activities, Internet exercises, updated information, and links to related Web sites.

▌ Thinking Critically About Organizational Behavior

1. Do employees really progress up a hierarchy of needs?
2. How do managers ensure equity and still meet workers' differing needs?

3. What approaches do workers most commonly use to deal with inequities in the workplace?

4. How does equity theory help explain the impact of discrimination?

5. Does punishment work?

6. Is negative reinforcement the reverse of positive reinforcement?

7. Are the same rewards effective inside and outside the United States?

8. How can managers ensure that workers have high expectancies and instrumentalities?

9. How can a goal-setting program be part of a positive reinforcement program?

10. Do motivation theories offer ways to motivate teams of workers?

11. What are the drawbacks to the new approaches to wages, such as skill-based pay and broadbanding?

12. Do incentive systems work in the long run?

ACTIVITY 4-1: EXPECTANCY QUESTIONNAIRE

STEP 1: Answer Questions 1, 2, and 3 by circling the answer that best describes your feelings.

Question 1: Here are some things that could happen to people if they do their jobs **especially well.** How likely is it that each of these things would happen if you performed your job **especially well?** (You may use your job as student.)

	Not Likely			Somewhat Likely			Extremely Likely
a. You will get a bonus or a pay increase.	(1)	(2)	(3)	(4)	(5)	(6)	(7)
b. You will feel better about yourself as a person.	(1)	(2)	(3)	(4)	(5)	(6)	(7)
c. You will have an opportunity to develop your skills and abilities.	(1)	(2)	(3)	(4)	(5)	(6)	(7)
d. You will have better job security.	(1)	(2)	(3)	(4)	(5)	(6)	(7)
e. You will be given chances to learn new things.	(1)	(2)	(3)	(4)	(5)	(6)	(7)
f. You will be promoted or get a better job.	(1)	(2)	(3)	(4)	(5)	(6)	(7)
g. You will get a feeling that you've accomplished something worthwhile.	(1)	(2)	(3)	(4)	(5)	(6)	(7)
h. You will have more freedom on your job.	(1)	(2)	(3)	(4)	(5)	(6)	(7)
i. You will be respected by the people your work with.	(1)	(2)	(3)	(4)	(5)	(6)	(7)
j. Your supervisor will praise you.	(1)	(2)	(3)	(4)	(5)	(6)	(7)
k. The people you work with will be friendly with you.	(1)	(2)	(3)	(4)	(5)	(6)	(7)

Question 2: Different people want different things from their work. Here is a list of things a person could have on his or her job. How important is each of the following to you? (You may use your job as student.)

How important is . . . ?	Moderately Important or Less			Quite Important		Extremely Important	
a. The amount of pay you get.	(1)	(2)	(3)	(4)	(5)	(6)	(7)
b. The chances you have to do something that makes you feel good about yourself as a person.	(1)	(2)	(3)	(4)	(5)	(6)	(7)
c. The opportunity to develop your skills and abilities.	(1)	(2)	(3)	(4)	(5)	(6)	(7)
d. The amount of job security you have.	(1)	(2)	(3)	(4)	(5)	(6)	(7)
e. The chances you have to learn new things.	(1)	(2)	(3)	(4)	(5)	(6)	(7)
f. Your chances for getting a promotion or getting a better job.	(1)	(2)	(3)	(4)	(5)	(6)	(7)
g. The chances you have to accomplish something worthwhile.	(1)	(2)	(3)	(4)	(5)	(6)	(7)
h. The amount of freedom you have on your job.	(1)	(2)	(3)	(4)	(5)	(6)	(7)
i. The respect you receive from the people you work with.	(1)	(2)	(3)	(4)	(5)	(6)	(7)
j. The praise you get from your supervisor.	(1)	(2)	(3)	(4)	(5)	(6)	(7)
k. The friendliness of the people you work with.	(1)	(2)	(3)	(4)	(5)	(6)	(7)

Question 3: Below you will see a number of pairs of factors that look like this:

Warm weather → sweating (1) (2) (3) (4) (5) (6) (7)

You are to indicate by circling the appropriate number to the right of each pair how often it is true for you personally that the first factor leads to the second on your job (or your job as student). Remember, for each pair, indicate how often it is true by circling the number under the response that seems most accurate.

	Never		Sometimes		Often		Almost Always
a. Working hard → high productivity	(1)	(2)	(3)	(4)	(5)	(6)	(7)
b. Working hard → doing my job well	(1)	(2)	(3)	(4)	(5)	(6)	(7)
c. Working hard → good job performance	(1)	(2)	(3)	(4)	(5)	(6)	(7)

STEP 2: Using the questionnaire results.

The results from this questionnaire can be used to calculate a work-motivation score. A score can be calculated for each individual, and scores can be combined for groups of individuals. The proce-dures for obtaining a work-motivation score are as follows:

a. For each of the possible positive outcomes listed in questions 1 and 2, multiply the score for the outcome on question 1 ($P \rightarrow O$

expectancies) by the corresponding score on question 2 (valences of outcomes). Thus, score 1a would be multiplied by score 2a, score 1b by score 2b, and so forth.

b. All of the 1-times-2 products would be added together to get a total of all expectancies-times-valences.

c. The total should be divided by the number of pairs (in this case, 11) to get an average expectancy-times-valence score.

d. The scores from question 3 ($E \rightarrow P$ expectancies) should be added together and then divided by 3 to get an average effort-to-performance expectancy score.

e. Multiply the score obtained in step c (the average expectancy-times-valence) by the score obtained in step d (the average $E \rightarrow P$ expectancy score) to obtain a total work-motivation score.

STEP 3: Discussion. Answer the following questions in small groups or with the entire class:

DESCRIPTION

1. What score did you receive? Compare it with the scores of other class members.

DIAGNOSIS

2. How motivating is your job?
3. What factors influence your score?
4. How does the content of your job relate to your score?
5. Can you explain the score using expectancy theory?
6. Can you explain the motivation potential of your job using
   a. reinforcement theory?
   b. equity theory?
   c. needs theories?

PRESCRIPTION

7. How would you improve the motivating potential of your job?

Source: Reprinted by permission from D. A. Nadler and E. E. Lawler III, Motivation: A diagnostic approach. In *Perspectives on Behavior in Organizations,* ed. J. R. Hackman, E. E. Lawler III, and L. W. Porter (New York: McGraw-Hill, 1977).

ACTIVITY 4–2: MOTIVATING DIVERSITY IN MIDDLE AND TOP MANAGEMENT

STEP 1: Consider the following situation.

You have recently become the chief operating officer of a large high-technology company that specializes in telecommunications. You are very committed to increasing the diversity of your workforce, but know that you must develop a master plan to help motivate other managers in the company to support this goal. To date, your organization has primarily included white males born in the United States. The previous COO was reluctant to promote women and minorities into top management because he felt that they would have difficulty fitting into the executive ranks. As a result, very few women and minorities currently hold top-management positions, and about 20 percent hold middle-management positions. The lower ranks of the organization have a significant number of women and minorities who have entered the organization in recent years.

STEP 2: Individually or in small groups, incorporating your knowledge of motivation theories, design a motivational plan for reaching this goal.

STEP 3: Discussion. In small groups or with the entire class, share the plans you developed. Then answer the following questions.

1. What motivation theories have you incorporated into your plans?
2. How do your plans reflect elements of an effective reward system?
3. How effective do you expect these plans to be? Why?

ACTIVITY 4-3: REWARDS AT THE ICE CREAM CREAMERY

STEP 1: Read the following description of the Ice Cream Creamery.

Jason Mento owns 10 ice cream shops in a mid-size city and its suburbs. Each shop sells homemade ice cream and frozen yogurt in cones, cups, pints, quarts, and half gallons, and in other forms, such as milkshakes, sundaes, and sodas. The stores employ high school and college students to work behind the counter. Mento makes the ice cream and yogurt for all of the stores in a central location and then ships it to the individual shops. Mento pays his employees by the hour. Recently, however, he has noticed that they do not serve the customers as quickly as he would like. Also, there is great variation in the product they deliver, with some employees offering generous portions and others offering very skimpy ones. Mento believes that he can improve customer service and product consistency by introducing a new compensation and reward system for his employees. He has read a great deal about reinforcement theory and believes that instituting its principles will help him accomplish his goals.

STEP 2: In groups of three to five, design a reward system for the employees using only principles from reinforcement theory.

STEP 3: Discussion. In small groups or with the entire class, share your designs. Then answer the following questions:

1. What do these reward systems have in common?
2. How do they differ?
3. Which principles of reinforcement theory do they illustrate?
4. What are their strengths and weaknesses?
5. What changes would you recommend for each?
6. What other motivation theories might Mento incorporate into the reward system?
7. What changes would these theories suggest for the proposed systems?

ACTIVITY 4-4: COMPENSATION RATINGS

STEP 1: You are the president of a rapidly growing e-commerce business. Your company has grown from a handful of employees to more than 300 in the past three years. Many of your employees have skills that are highly in demand by your competitors. However, as your firm has grown, you have not been able to screen employees as well as you would like. You have been lucky so far because you have been able to offer competitive salaries and have retained most of your workforce. You want to be sure to continue to keep those who work hard and make significant contributions to your firm. You must determine pay increases for the employees listed here. Beside each name, write the percentage increase you would give that person, as well as any other actions you would like to take. Each person currently earns between $45,000 and $90,000; some already have stock options.

Howard Hanscomb   Howard has been with your firm over two years. While his work was quite good during his first year on the job, it has gotten progressively worse, even though he works quite hard at it. His co-workers have complained to you that he doesn't do his share—that he tries to get by on his old accomplishments and by his occasional, brilliant insights. Others say his rich bride takes all his time and attention.

Emily Everest   Emily's rich husband can't understand why she works so hard. She's always the first in the office and the last to leave. During her three years with the firm, she has become a leader among her peers because of her hard work. And you couldn't ask for better work from an employee. She uses her excellent skills to do highly creative work in great quantities.

Sidney Smith   Everyone thinks Sid is a goof-off except you. He certainly leads the irresponsible bachelor's life off the job, or so you've heard. His work is some of the best in his department, which surprises you since he never seems to work hard and you hired him a year ago, not for his skills, but because he is the boss's son.

John Melchior   John always looks as if he is working so hard he'll drop. Even though his co-workers praise his work, when you review it, the quantity does not seem up to par. Maybe he hasn't had a chance to make up for the deficiencies in skills you knew he had when you hired him a year ago. Still, he really needed a job then, and still does because of his mother's huge medical bills.

Carol Cassidy   Carol was one of the first employees you hired. Recently, you have noticed that the quality of her work has declined significantly. She just doesn't seem to be trying. Her co-workers have started to refuse to work with her. They say she isn't up to date and doesn't try to improve her skills. You know she isn't desperate for money since she has no dependents and already earns a nice salary.

Hester Stockton   Hester and her three fatherless children are struggling to make ends meet. She always works extra hours, generally taking piles of work home with her. She joined your firm a year ago; her strong recommendation as a hard worker from her previous employer got your attention even though you felt her academic background was outdated. You were right—the quality of her work has been below average. Even her co-workers have commented about it.

Mark Maccoby   Mark is a hotshot e-commerce expert who has been with your firm for two years. His impressive academic credentials called him to your attention originally—and he hasn't disappointed you yet. His work is of high quality, but he puts in a lot of overtime to make sure it's perfect. Everyone else says he does terrific work too. Mark married when he was in college; his salary barely makes ends meet for his wife and two children.

Jessica Prime   Even though Jessica is easily distracted by her family's financial and health problems, her work is of high quality. Her co-workers don't seem to think too much of her though, perhaps because she doesn't seem to work too hard—she's often late for work and leaves early. You're a bit surprised by the high quality of her work since she was not one of the stronger applicants when you hired her a year ago.

STEP 2: Now, in groups of four to six, reach a consensus about the percentage increase each person should receive. Be prepared to justify the increases.

STEP 3: Discussion. In small groups, or with the entire class, answer the following questions:

1. Explain your reasons for each increase.
2. Use any relevant theory of motivation to justify your compensation plan.
3. Which factors influence pay decisions? Should these factors be influential?

ACTIVITY 4-5: THE EASTWOOD OUTDOORS COMPANY

STEP 1: Read the following description of the Eastwood Outdoors Company.

Eastwood Outdoors Company was founded in 1945 in a small midwestern manufacturing town. It grew from a small job shop of 10 employees to a highly automated factory employing 800 workers. In 1980, the company moved into retail sales of moderately priced outdoor equipment. Beginning with two outlets, the company expanded to 10 outlets throughout the Midwest.

Eastwood employs a diverse group of individuals. The factory organization includes hourly workers, supervisors and plant managers, a small staff in the marketing, finance, and human resources departments, and executives in each functional area. The sales outlets include full-time and part-time salespeople, assistant managers, and store managers.

Eastwood has always been known for its generous compensation. The wages received by the manufacturing and retail workers are among the highest of its competitors. Recently, however, employees have been complaining that their benefits are much too limited. The company offers full individual medical coverage or its equivalent, seven paid holidays, and 10 paid sick days. It also contributes to an employee pension plan after an employee works for the company for five years.

The workforce at Eastwood has also changed in the past 15 years. For example, it now includes more women, more older workers, more MBA graduates, and more members of dual-career families with children of all ages.

STEP 2: Propose a benefits program for Eastwood Outdoors Company. Consider the different types of employees as well as their different needs. List the benefits you want to offer. Specify who is to receive each benefit as well as the conditions that are required to receive it, such as length of employment, job category, or family status. To the extent possible, estimate the costs of various benefit combinations.

STEP 3: Discussion. Individually in writing, in small groups, or with the entire class, share your benefits plans. Then answer the following questions:

1. Which benefits are mandatory?
2. Which benefits are voluntary?
3. Which benefits are more costly? Less costly?
4. To what needs does each benefit respond?
5. Should or must all employees receive the same benefits?

ACTIVITY 4-6: THE NEW TEAM INCENTIVE SYSTEM

Safeway Manufacturing Company, a large producer of circuit boards for computers and other digital applications, recently reorganized its factories. Previously, each employee assembled a small part of the circuit board. Employees' pay was tied to their production, with no penalty for defective parts, since defects were not discovered until the entire circuit board had been assembled. This piecework system encouraged each employee to produce as many boards as they could as fast as possible.

Recently, Safeway reorganized its factory workfloors to allow a team-based approach to production. Instead of individual workers assembling parts of circuit boards with little discussion with co-workers about the product, the company assigned a team of employees to assemble an entire circuit board. The team is responsible for assigning work, making sure that products aren't defective, and assigning pay.

STEP 1: Assume that you are a member of one of these teams. You are meeting with other members of the team to determine an acceptable pay plan. You have 20 minutes to reach an agreement.

STEP 2: Share your plans with the entire class. Then answer the following questions:

1. What types of pay plans are possible?
2. Should a team incentive plan be introduced?
3. What are the advantages and disadvantages of a team incentive plan?
4. How do you ensure pay for performance in a team structure?

Chapter 5

Making Effective Decisions

Learning Objectives

After completing Chapter 5, you will be able to

1. Analyze how well a decision meets four characteristics of a good decision.
2. Characterize six types of decisions.
3. Discuss the major influences on decision making.
4. Identify the steps in a rational decision-making process and apply them to a decision.
5. Compare and contrast the rational process to four alternative decision-making processes, identifying the advantages and disadvantages of each.
6. Offer five techniques for improving decision making.
7. Describe how managers can make effective decisions in different cultures.

A Manager's Preview

Describe . . . Diagnose . . . Prescribe . . . Act

- Know what makes a decision effective.
- Understand what factors influence decision making.
- Reduce cognitive biases.
- Eliminate organizational barriers.
- Use the rational decision-making process where appropriate.
- Know when to use nonrational decision-making processes.
- Apply techniques to improve decision making.
- Make effective decisions in cross-cultural settings.

Federal Employees' Decisions Contribute to Los Alamos Fire

Many of Los Alamos, New Mexico's 11,000 residents were evacuated on May 10, 2000, when a controlled burn in nearby Bandelier National Monument went out of control. The burn resulted in the torching of hundreds of homes, the evacuation of more than 20,000 people, and the destruction of 200 houses. "This prescribed fire was based upon a flawed plan, and required fire management policies were not followed," according to a report prepared by government wildfire specialists who investigated how the controlled burn became New Mexico's worst wildfire in history. Not only did the U.S. Forest Service employees underestimate the risks of their decision, but they failed to get the necessary wind forecasts, to have enough firefighters at the site initially, and to observe federal guidelines for wildfire management. Members of Congress have lambasted the decision to set fires, and plan to call for further study on prescriptive burning. Still others have noted the fire hazard created by the fire suppression policy (as contrasted with the prescribed burning policy) of putting out fires as soon as they are discovered, resulting in an extensive buildup of highly flammable forest vegetation. The Forest Service may need to switch to mechanical means for removing this vegetation.[1]

As part of their responsibilities regarding forest preservation in Bandelier National Monument, federal employees made many decisions, the latest a catastrophic one. How did they make these decisions? Why was the decision about the controlled burn ineffective? What could have prompted a better decision? How can poor decisions be avoided? Making decisions in this informational age has both assets and liabilities. Clearly, managers can easily acquire large quantities of information relatively quickly and inexpensively. Yet, the ability to process so much information often impedes decision making. How can managers use the right information in the most timely way to make effective decisions?

In this chapter, we examine the nature of decisions and the decision-making process. We first look at the four characteristics of a good decision. Next we investigate the types of decisions managers and other organizational members make. We then examine the influences on decision making, including the decision maker, his cognitive biases, and organizational barriers. We next explore the steps in the rational decision-making process and look at alternatives to that process. Finally, we offer five techniques for improving decision-making effectiveness before concluding with comments about decision making within the dot-com, global workplace.

▌CRITERIA OF DECISION EFFECTIVENESS

What does a manager or executive strive for in making a decision? How does a manager know that she has made a good decision? The decision's quality, timeliness, acceptance by those affected, and ethical appropriateness determine its effectiveness, as shown in Figure 5-1.

Quality

Quality refers to the content or substance of the decision being made. A good-quality decision results in desired outcomes while meeting a series of specified criteria or constraints. A staffing decision has high quality if the employees hired complete their work well and on time and if their salaries fall within a specified budget. The decision to launch a new product has high quality if it results in increasing the reputation, profits, or market share of the company.

A high-quality decision helps an organization accomplish its strategic goals. It likely results in increased profits, service, or performance. A high-quality decision also meets the needs of the organization's employees, executives, stockholders, customers, or suppliers. It may, for example, improve the working conditions of employees, increase the stock value for stockholders, or help a manager advance.

High-quality decisions are not necessarily the same as optimal decisions. *Satisficing*, or selecting a satisfactory or acceptable decision, may be adequate, given time, financial, and staffing constraints. A sales decision that limits the number of

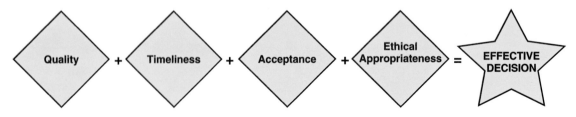

▌ **FIGURE 5-1** ▌   *Four factors influence the effectiveness of a decision.*

customers but tries to increase sales to individual customers may be as good as one that results in doubling the number of customers if the time, personnel, or other resources required justify the tradeoff.

What is the difference between satisficing and simply being lazy or negligent in gathering the information needed to make an effective decision? Managers make mistakes in decision making by paying too much attention to information that they can access easily. Sometimes they rely more heavily on information that causes an emotional reaction. They may overreact to information that is important only for a limited number of unusual situations. Or, managers may overemphasize the most recently received information.[2] Managers need to collect reliable and relevant information and allow enough time to use the information once they collect it. The park officials at Bandelier seemingly did not collect appropriate information and then did not use what little information they had collected.

Timeliness

Managers need to make decisions within an acceptable time frame. What would happen if a quality control inspector decided the products did not meet basic safety standards after the first 4,000 had been shipped to customers? What would happen if employers did not change their payroll withholdings to match changes in federal or state tax laws? What would happen if a retail executive waited five years before deciding which stores to remodel in the second phase of the turnaround program? Alcoa has introduced a decision-making process in its manufacturing plants where any worker with a problem, such as a defective machine, calls a leader with the intention of fixing the problem or implementing the new idea immediately. This approach has had positive results, such as improved inventory turnaround and reduced costs.[3]

Failures to make timely decisions in these situations would result in inefficient use of resources, some unhappy workers, and an inability to compete effectively in the marketplace. Even the best decision loses its value when made too late. Managers need to develop a reasonable timetable for making both major and minor decisions. This means understanding the interrelationships of the various decisions and who has responsibilities for making and implementing them.

Acceptance

Good decisions also result when those affected by the decision understand it, accept it, and can implement it. Consider the decision to redesign the Web site design process in an e-commerce company. Workers resistant to this decision may fail to respond to requests for information for the Web site. In contrast, worker support for the redesign may increase the speed and responsiveness of providing information. Top managers know that they must have the support of workers at all levels when implementing significant decisions. For example, employee participation in the performance appraisal process has been linked to their satisfaction with and acceptance of the system.[4]

Ethical Appropriateness

Managers and other decision makers should also evaluate a decision according to its *ethical justness*. Multiple and potentially conflicting stakeholders, interests, and values, as well as ambiguous laws, often give rise to ethical dilemmas.[5] The ethical violations related to the 2002 Salt Lake City Winter Olympics stemmed from extensive lobbying that resulted in major payoffs by organizing committee members to certain members of the International Olympic Committee (IOC), including thousands of dollars of tuition assistance to children of IOC members.[6]

Although ethical considerations receive the highest priority in many organizations, some managers still disregard them in making decisions. Consider, for example, the number of people in the financial services industry who have used insider information. Some have been punished for violating the laws, but others have escaped unnoticed. One Dreyfus portfolio manager, for example, bought shares in two companies in which he personally owned stock, and Dreyfus vigorously defended him. Although Dreyfus reached a financial settlement with the Securities and Exchange Commission, the firm was not required to admit wrongdoing in this case.[7]

Some organizations have countered this trend by introducing extensive training in ethical decision making. The Canadian Department of National Defense sponsored the Defense Ethics Program, which fosters the shared ethical values common in Canadian society, as a way of reemphasizing ethical decision making and integrity in government for its employees.[8] Companies such as United Technologies and Boeing have established an office of ethics. Nike, among other organizations, has a vice president of corporate and social responsibility whose charge is to make social and moral responsibility a key component of Nike's culture.[9]

Tough standards of ethical behavior are spreading outside the United States, and corporations increasingly believe they have a responsibility to ensure human rights. Reebok, for example, funds the annual Reebok Human Rights Awards and in the early 1990s wrote one of the first human rights codes of ethics. Reebok and musician Peter Gabriel founded a program that gives activists hand-held video cameras to document human rights violations. Activists discovered that subcontracting manufacturers of Reebok products had tampered with leather-stamping machines to speed production by enabling operators to use one rather than two hands to operate them. Reebok replaced the equipment with safer machines, but found tampering within six months, necessitating increased vigilance.[10]

Managers can evaluate the ethical justness of a decision by first recognizing the decision as involving a moral issue. They can ask whether the decision will hurt or help others and make a moral judgment about what is the "right" decision. Then they can prioritize these moral concerns and act accordingly.[11] Men and women, as well as employees of different ages, may differ in how they evaluate others in ethical situations; for example, in one study older participants were more attuned to the legality of the ethical dilemmas presented.[12] Managers who operate in cross-cultural situations must deal with variations in personal and societal definitions of ethical or moral behavior. In these situations, they need to determine their own and their company's ethical standards and use them as guidelines for making a particular decision.

Managers and employees can assess the ethics of their decisions by applying personal moral or societal codes of values or applying philosophical views of ethical behavior. They might also assess the potential harmful consequences of behaviors to certain constituencies. For example, asking "Would my co-workers be upset about my decision?" or "Would I prefer to avoid the consequences of this decision?" might reveal its ethical appropriateness.[13] Companies that help businesses clean up their ethical problems have become more common. Both KPMG Peat Marwick and

Arthur Andersen have ethics units to help companies with their ethics overhauls.[14] Sotheby's opened an $11 million investigation of charges that employees had illegally obtained and sold antiquities from the Middle East and Mediterranean. As a result of this effort, Sotheby's created a new compliance department, expanded its legal department, and introduced training programs to ensure that employees question the provenance of the art sold.[15]

▌TYPES OF MANAGERIAL DECISIONS

What types of decisions do managers make? They might decide whom to hire or fire, where to place a new plant, when to advertise or launch a new product, or how much to budget for R&D. They might decide workers' schedules, new equipment to purchase, or pay increases for subordinates. Or, as the park officials at Bandelier did, they might decide whether to start a controlled burn in a national forest. Classifying decisions allows managers to diagnose the specific challenges or opportunities individual decisions provide. In this section, we classify decisions as programmed versus nonprogrammed, strategic versus operational, and top-down versus worker-empowered.

Programmed Versus Nonprogrammed Decisions

Which employees will receive increased wages? Which managers will be laid off in a downsizing? What resources will be necessary to introduce a new product line? Should a company open a manufacturing branch in Asia? Answering these questions requires either programmed or nonprogrammed decisions.

- **Programmed decisions** describe relatively structured solutions to specific problems. They involve performing tasks by following a well-defined set of rules or standard operating procedures tested through past experience.[16] For example, determining whether a person should receive pay for a sick day is a programmed decision in most companies.
- **Nonprogrammed decisions** refer to relatively unstructured solutions to more complex and ambiguous problems. Standard policies and procedures cannot handle them. Deciding whether to introduce a new product is a nonprogrammed decision.

Once a manager or employee identifies a decision as programmed, he next identifies and then applies the appropriate rules or procedures to result in a quality outcome, such as assigning pay raises as a result of yearly performance reviews. As an alternative, employees can use *rules of thumb* to make programmed decisions whenever they have significant experience with similar decision-making situations.

Nonprogrammed decisions, such as whether to create a learning organization or redesign an organization's reporting relationships, are relatively unstructured and often unique. They require special treatment and typically call for innovative solutions or unusual applications of existing rules of thumb or policies. Nonprogrammed decisions can pose significant challenges for managers, who must go beyond their repertoire of experience to find good solutions. Breaking new ground takes time, expertise, and creativity.

To further complicate matters, decisions that may be programmed in one situation may be nonprogrammed in others. For example, the procedure for handling defective merchandise may be a programmed decision in a large company that has a historical record of dealing with returned merchandise, but not in a small start-up. Nonprogrammed decisions call for a manager to verify first that the problem lacks both structure and a ready solution and then to apply a high-quality decision-making technique.

Strategic Versus Operational Decisions

Strategic decision making focuses on decisions related to the long-term direction of the company. Strategic decisions include plans for accomplishing the long-term goals of market share, profitability, return on investment, service, and performance. As part of strategic decision making, managers determine the organization's distinctive competence. For example, if executives of traditional retail stores such as Nordstroms, Macy's, or Lord & Taylor needed to determine whether they should introduce an e-commerce component to their business, they might ask questions such as the following:

- What kind of business should we be in?
- What should be our markets?
- What products or services should we offer?
- What technological investment should we make?
- What human resources are available and required?
- What financial, time, material, or other resources are available and required?

The Risk & Insurance Management Society chapter in Fairfield, Connecticut/Westchester, New York, held a strategic planning meeting to determine if their chapter, which was experiencing a major downswing, could remain alive. After surveying chapter members, the executives made a strategic decision to reduce the frequency of meetings and limit attendance only to risk managers, not to brokers who used them for merchandising.[17]

Managers can make strategic decisions at three levels:

- **Corporate-level strategic decisions** focus on which lines of business a company should pursue. They include whether to acquire new businesses, divest old ones, establish joint ventures, or create alliances with other companies. Deciding how to use the Web to support or extend their businesses has been a major strategic decision for many companies. Egg, an online savings and loan operator in the United Kingdom, made the strategic decision to start its Internet-based financial services apart from its other businesses, emphasize relationships, and use multiple computer platforms.[18]

- **Business-level strategic decisions** focus on the way each business unit can earn the largest profit or greatest return on investment. This type of strategic decision involves determining what products or services the business should offer, which customers it should serve, and how it will use its resources for advertising, customer service, staffing, and other activities. The Reader's Digest Association made the strategic decision to outsource the building and maintaining of its Web site, Reader's Digest World, rather than to hire the capability internally.[19]

■ **Functional-level strategic decisions** focus on how business functions such as marketing, finance, human resources, and engineering can best support business-level strategies. For example, should the company borrow extensively or rely on current earnings to support projects? Should the company provide in-house training for employees or outsource all training and development activities?

Managers who make strategic decisions usually can take a relatively long time to reach their decisions. Because strategic decisions have long-term consequences, evaluating an array of possibilities and having the information to do this evaluation are important.

Operational decisions, by contrast, focus on the day-to-day activities of the company. Managers need to make decisions about work schedules, employee assignments, and equipment utilization. They may need to handle crises that arise, such as unexpected absenteeism, unexpected delays in receipt of supplies, power outages, or equipment failures. Managers who make operational decisions need the ability to quickly set objectives, determine and evaluate alternatives, and then make the decision. They don't have the luxury of examining many alternatives over a long period of time.

Top-Down Versus Worker-Empowered Decisions

Who should have decided whether to implement a controlled burn at Bandelier National Monument? Who decides the pay increments received by the federal employees at Bandelier? Traditionally, top-level managers have made these decisions and then passed them to lower-level managers or employees for implementation. This top-down, directive approach to decision making may result in timely and high-quality decisions, but employees may not "buy into" the decisions.

Now many companies have organized their workers into teams that bear the responsibility for most aspects of production or service. Accompanying the widespread use of teams has been an empowerment of workers in making decisions. Employees, not managers, make decisions about staffing, ordering supplies, and delivering products or services. For example, in many companies, multifunctional teams either act as advisors to those making decisions about suppliers or themselves decide about suppliers, negotiate contracts, and then require users to buy from the corporate contracts.[20] Wal-Mart's philosophy is to push decision making down to mid-level managers and international executives.[21] Many companies believe that workers can make better decisions because they know best what's necessary to do their jobs well. Workers who make decisions more readily accept the outcomes of the decision and so become more vested in making high-quality decisions.

■ INFLUENCES ON DECISION MAKING

Employees at Bandelier National Monument did not make good decisions about the controlled burn. Of course, not all decisions have such disastrous consequences. Many managers make good decisions. The effectiveness of a decision—its timeliness, quality, acceptance, and ethical appropriateness—depends on factors such as the characteristics of the decision maker, various cognitive biases, and organizational barriers, which are discussed in this section.

Characteristics of the Decision Maker

Managers vary in the amount of information, skills, or experience they can bring to decision making. They use different styles in making decisions. Some focus primarily on the details of a situation and then accumulate them into a sensible decision. Others rely on their intuitive sense about a situation or focus on the "big picture."

Managers who function in a global environment face particularly great challenges in making effective decisions because of the complexity and uncertainty inherent in the situations they face. Diagnosing the factors that likely influence decision makers can help improve effectiveness because managers and workers can better understand the way the decision-making process may unfold.

Three Types of Decision-Making Skills.   The quality of the decision depends in part on the level of the decision maker's skills, as shown in the skill triangle of Figure 5-2.

- **Technical or task skills** refer to the individual's knowledge of the content area of the decision. For example, the task skills of the person giving the final orders to light the controlled burn should have incorporated knowledge of forestry principles and information about weather conditions.
- **Interpersonal or leadership skills** relate to the way individuals lead, communicate with, motivate, and influence others. These skills greatly affect the acceptance of a decision. The key decision maker in the Forest Service must be able to communicate well with his superiors and subordinates to ensure that the correct decision is made and implemented.
- **Decision-making skills** refer to the basic abilities to perform the components of the rational decision-making process, including situational analysis, objective setting, and generation, evaluation, and selection of alternatives, as described later in this chapter. The Forest Service managers must be skilled at using the rational approach or an alternative means of decision making.

Personal Decision-Making Style.   A person's personality can also influence the decision-making process. Managers who can identify a person's style can better match work assignments to this style. One useful way of thinking about personal style characterizes a person in terms of how well he tolerates ambiguity (degree of cognitive complexity) and whether he values task/technical concerns or people/social concerns.[22] Combining these two dimensions results in four

▌FIGURE 5–2 ▌
The decision maker's skill triangle shows key competencies required for effective decision making.

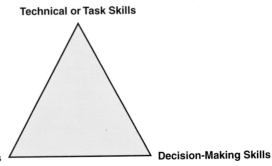

styles—analytic, conceptual, directive, and behavioral, or decision makers who solve problems, see the big picture, expect results, and need affiliation, respectively, as shown in Figure 5-3. These styles suggest the way the manager would approach the decision-making process. People called leaders in this schema tend to have either analytic or conceptual styles, depending on their values orientation. Individuals called managers have directive or behavioral styles. A decision maker with an analytic style, for example, has a high tolerance for ambiguity and focuses on solving particular problems, whereas a decision maker with a conceptual style also has a tolerance for ambiguity, but is concerned with relationships and so "sees the big picture."

Think of a manager you know. What type of style does he have? How does this affect his decision-making process and the decisions he makes? His style may affect his ability to use the rational decision-making process, as well as the type and amount of information he seeks and uses.

Cognitive Biases

The way managers and workers process information also affects decision making.[23] Decision makers who use simplifying strategies, called *heuristics,* to guide their judgments in decision making more often make mistakes.[24] These heuristics cause decision makers to process information inaccurately, resulting in poor decisions.

Values Technical/Task Issues　　　　　　　　**Values People/Social Issues**

High Cognitive Complexity

ANALYTIC
A problem solver who analyzes alternatives and innovates

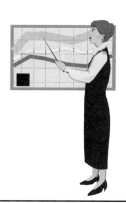

CONCEPTUAL
A socially oriented person who sees the big picture

Low Cognitive Complexity

DIRECTIVE
A rapid decision maker who expects results and relies on rules

BEHAVIORAL
A person who needs affiliation and wants to help others

FIGURE 5-3　　*A manager's decision-making style will influence the way he or she attacks problems.*

The Three Biases.   The availability bias, the representativeness bias, and the anchoring and adjustment bias are the most common heuristics that result in erroneous decisions.[25]

- **Availability bias.** Individuals tend to overestimate the likelihood that an event will occur when they can easily recall past instances. Such availability results in a systematic bias in estimating frequencies. A recruiter may overestimate the likelihood of receiving enough resumes for a job opening if he knows that in the past the company has received large numbers of resumes for advertised jobs. Employees in dot-com companies may place an inflated value on stock grants because of the recent run-up in their value.[26] In addition, individuals also tend to overestimate the likelihood of disasters and underestimate the probability of more common events.[27]

- **Representativeness bias.** Individuals judge an event in terms of their perception of its absolute frequency, ignoring its frequency relative to some base rate of occurrence, sample size, or probability. For example, they give as much or more credence to small samples as to larger, more representative ones. They may view a 10 percent reject rate in the past five months as more accurate than a 2 percent return rate in the past three years. Although special circumstances may make the 10 percent rate more descriptive of the current situation, ignoring the historical or base rate at which certain events occur may cause individuals to act too hastily and make unwarranted changes.

- **Anchoring and Adjustment Bias.** Individuals make assessments by beginning with or *anchoring* onto an initial value and then *adjusting* it before making a final decision. Thus, subsequent estimates of frequency are based on initial estimates and may ignore whether events occur together or separately. For example, the manager budgeting for a new production facility may consider $25 per square foot a reasonable estimate for the building rental, but fail to recognize that square-foot estimates for telecommunications costs need to be added to the cost per square foot. Decision makers further err by demonstrating overconfidence in the infallibility of their judgments.

Framing the Problem.   The way a decision maker *frames* a problem—for example, whether she describes a situation as a winning or losing situation—has a significant impact on its outcome.[28] Managers tend to take fewer risks regarding choices they frame in a positive fashion and more risks about choices they frame negatively.[29] For example, they avoid risks by choosing a sure gain of $250 over a 25 percent chance of winning $1,000 and a 75 percent chance of winning nothing. They take a greater risk by choosing a 75 percent chance of losing $1,000 and a 25 percent chance of losing nothing over a sure loss of $750. Individuals value a series of small gains more than a single gain of the same summed amount. For example, they would respond differently to a situation framed as a gain of $1,000 a week for two months as opposed to a lump-sum profit of $9,000 at the end of two months.

We also assume that people can estimate the likelihood of uncertain events, even though their estimates tend to be inaccurate. This assumption causes a decision maker to err in the evaluation of alternatives by using inaccurate probabilities. Research has shown, for example, that groups increased their commitment to investment decisions in a failing course of action because they inaccurately assessed the probability of a turnaround. They kept trying to recoup their losses, even when a realistic assessment of the situation would have caused them to cut their losses.[30]

Organizational Barriers

In addition to characteristics of the decision maker, characteristics of the organization can influence decision making and its effectiveness. Structural factors can determine who can legitimately make decisions. The extent of the organization's hierarchy and its chain of command may legitimize certain decision makers. For example, managers and employees in state government often look to their supervisors for approving decisions and handling exceptions. In contrast, many dot-com companies give their employees great leeway in making decisions. Flattening the organization by reducing the hierarchy gives more decision-making responsibility to lower-level managers and employees. When Curtis Crawford, who had risen through the executive ranks of IBM and AT&T, took over leadership of Zilog, Inc., a microprocessor manufacturer, he hoped to improve morale by delegating authority to employees. At AT&T, Crawford had taken a similar approach, which helped make its semiconductor operation a leader in growth and profits within the company.[31]

Companies that emphasize specialization of functions often limit decision-making responsibilities to those with extensive expertise. While such expertise can be valuable, insisting on it in all situations can slow down routine decisions.

The company's reward system can also influence decision making. Companies can reward either the quality or quantity of decisions made. Too often, however, they reward one type of behavior while desiring a different type; for example, they might reward employees' face time—that is, spending visible hours at work—but actually desire high-quality effort and performance.

Companies can encourage worker initiative in reaching good decisions by rewarding creativity, effort, and outcomes. They can also provide the tools workers need to get the information required for high-quality decision making. Making appropriate computerized systems available to workers helps improve decision making.

▮ THE RATIONAL DECISION-MAKING PROCESS

Managers who use a systematic or *rational* process for making decisions should make better decisions than managers who don't. Often this type of step-by-step decision-making process, as shown in Figure 5-4, increases the likelihood that a high-quality, accepted, and ethical decision will result.[32] Consider the decision made at Bandelier. The Forest Service officials responsible for ordering the controlled burn should have followed the rational decision-making approach to increase the likelihood of an effective decision. Of course, managers who make very complex decisions may have difficulty following these steps precisely, but considering them should improve the quality of decision making even in these situations. In the next sections, we examine each of these steps.

Analyze the Situation

Decision makers who use a rational process begin by determining the key elements in the situation. They identify the problem to be solved or the decision to be made.[33] They need to answer questions such as the following: Who are the

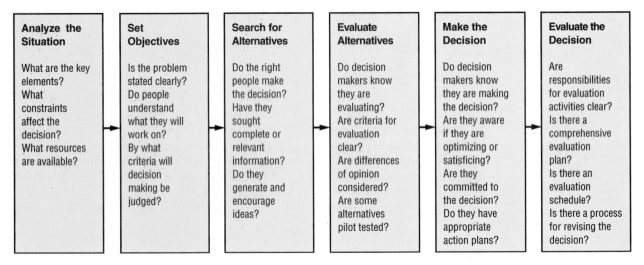

Analyze the Situation	Set Objectives	Search for Alternatives	Evaluate Alternatives	Make the Decision	Evaluate the Decision
What are the key elements? What constraints affect the decision? What resources are available?	Is the problem stated clearly? Do people understand what they will work on? By what criteria will decision making be judged?	Do the right people make the decision? Have they sought complete or relevant information? Do they generate and encourage ideas?	Do decision makers know they are evaluating? Are criteria for evaluation clear? Are differences of opinion considered? Are some alternatives pilot tested?	Do decision makers know they are making the decision? Are they aware if they are optimizing or satisficing? Are they committed to the decision? Do they have appropriate action plans?	Are responsibilities for evaluation activities clear? Is there a comprehensive evaluation plan? Is there an evaluation schedule? Is there a process for revising the decision?

FIGURE 5-4   *Using the rational decision-making process should result in more effective decisions.*

important individuals and groups involved and affected? What organizational characteristics affect the decision? How does the environment influence the outcomes?

Next the decision maker identifies the situation's constraints and their effect on the decision. These constraints might include legal, geographic, demographic, or other factors. Closely related to the constraints are the resources available. Managers should know the financial, time, staff, and material resources that affect particular decisions. Consider, for example, a manager who plans to introduce a new product. What is the timetable for designing, manufacturing, and marketing the product? How should she price the new product? What types of additional resources will be necessary to support sales of the new product? From this situational analysis, the decision maker begins to formulate the major issues to consider in making the decision. Deciding whether to expand a product line to include new variations will depend on the firm's goals, available resources, types of current customers, and competitors' plans.

Set Objectives

The decision maker next identifies the goals and objectives that the decision must accomplish. Setting objectives frees people to look extensively for solutions to problems and so lowers the chance of failure.[34] The way a decision maker frames the problem affects the ultimate solution. Does a manager view a problem as cost-cutting or revenue-maximizing? Does she view it as a performance problem or a working conditions problem?

Errors at this stage ultimately reduce the quality of the decision.[35] Identifying and correcting them may be difficult when goals are too dynamic, general, or unstated. The decision maker needs to carefully identify the goals and objectives that the decision must accomplish and specify the criteria that will be used to assess its quality, timeliness, acceptance, and ethical appropriateness. Table 5-1 lists some questions that can help decision makers with this step. For example, a health care administrator might set a goal of reducing the number of patient beds by 5 percent. The president of a dot-com start-up might set a goal of 5,000 new customers each week for the first

TABLE 5-1

Managers Can Ask a Series of Questions to Assess the Quality of Objectives Set as Part of Decision Making.

1. Do the objectives relate to and support the basic mission of the organization?
2. Do the objectives relate to and support the basic strategies of the organization?
3. Do the objectives acknowledge constraints on the decision?
4. Can managers quantify the objectives?
5. Have managers specified interim points for checking the status of objectives?
6. Are objectives flexible?
7. Have managers allocated enough time to accomplish the objectives?
8. Will the objectives help the organization grow, not just survive?
9. Will the objectives' expected benefits outweigh their costs?

six months. The accomplishment of goals such as these serves as the basic measure of the effectiveness of the decision and the decision-making process.

When possible, the objectives should state observable and measurable results. Some objectives, such as reducing absenteeism or increasing profits by a specified percentage or amount, are clearly observable and measurable. Managers have more difficulty measuring or observing objectives related to employee attitudes, such as satisfaction, commitment, or involvement. In such cases, the decision maker needs to skillfully craft goals. For example, a manager might decide that absenteeism and turnover both reflect employee satisfaction. In setting a goal to increase employee satisfaction by a certain percent, the manager will set an objective to reduce absenteeism and turnover by the same percent.

Managers and other decision makers should not confuse objectives with the action steps needed to accomplish them. Setting goals should precede determining a plan and implementing it. For example, a plan to advertise in national newspapers helps accomplish the goal of increasing market share for a product or service.

Search for Alternatives

The decision maker next identifies a set of realistic and potentially acceptable solutions to the problem or ways of accomplishing the stated objectives. These *alternatives* should achieve the decision objective without producing undesirable consequences. For example, an executive of a consumer company that relies on the Web for sales but has products that are selling below expectations can revamp the site, link it to other sites, offer incentives for visiting the site, or offer discounts on the price of products advertised on the site. Mercuri Urval, a recruitment firm, uses forms-processing software to record information from a detailed questionnaire administered to recruits.[36] Analyzing these data allows executives to generate options for meeting their client's employment needs. Techniques for improving decision making described later in this chapter can help generate more possibilities.

Generating ideas should occur without evaluating them. Often decision makers shift too quickly into evaluation, rather than developing many alternatives. Even poor possibilities may lead to better ones. Some managers and other employees overlook information they have, gather irrelevant information, or look for information too late—after the decision has been made as a way of justifying it.[37]

Evaluate Alternatives

Now the decision maker evaluates each alternative in terms of whether it will result in a good decision. The decision maker first determines the feasibility of each alternative. Assume that you are the manager in charge of increasing the number of hits to your Web site. Additional advertising may be too expensive, but linking the site to other ones may be cost-effective. In addition to the varying cost of these alternatives, the alternatives also differ in their potential benefits, risks, and negative consequences. Decision makers frequently make tradeoffs among the desired and undesired outcomes of various decisions before arriving at the best one.

Managers may use a systematic procedure for evaluating alternatives. They might use quantitative techniques such as linear programming or regression analysis. Quantifying the alternatives, even in less sophisticated ways, can systematize their evaluation, dramatize differences among them, and even improve the quality of decision making. For example, a manager might assign numerical values to each alternative according to its feasibility, cost, potentially adverse consequences, and probability of success. Summing the scores for each alternative would allow a rank ordering of alternatives. The quantitative approach works well when large numbers of alternatives exist or when complex choices create interdependencies among alternatives. More commonly, however, decision makers use a qualitative rather than quantitative evaluation of alternatives. They rely on their judgment and experience, as well as the experiences of others, to select the best alternative.

Make the Decision

Ideally, the decision maker chooses the alternative that best meets his objective within the constraints of the situation. For example, as part of a strategic refocusing, Thomaston Mills, a family-held mill in Georgia, decided to shut its denim and sales yarn businesses and retain its home fashions business, resulting in a loss of 700 jobs.[38] Sometimes, as we noted earlier, the decision maker chooses an acceptable decision because the best decision has high costs. At other times, decision makers become committed to poor alternatives and cannot halt the course of action. Managers may become more committed to a decision when they feel responsible for irrevocable actions and their consequences. They may also become more committed if they believe poor performance reflects their own (not the system's) abilities. Acting in public rather than in private will also increase commitment.[39]

Evaluate the Decision

Too often, selecting an alternative and reaching a decision comprise the final step. Before finalizing the decision, managers or other decision makers should review the decision. This review creates a final chance to reassess the situation, adjust the objectives, and ensure that sufficient alternatives were examined. The decision maker can assess the likely outcomes of the decision and compare them to objectives set earlier. Once the official decided to set a controlled burn in Bandelier, he should have reviewed the steps that led to that decision, verifying his thinking with his supervisors and other experts in the field.

▌ALTERNATIVES TO RATIONAL DECISION MAKING

The rational process may not work well for very complex decisions. Why? Decision makers may not completely analyze the situation. They may have difficulty generating a complete, high-quality set of alternatives. They may not succeed in assessing the quality of each alternative. Given the realities of opposing stakeholders, limited information, time and cost constraints, communication failures, legal precedents, or perceptual limitations, they may not find the best alternative.[40] As a result, researchers have proposed a number of models to help managers make decisions in these "real-world" circumstances.

Bounded Rationality

Herbert Simon, a Nobel prize winner and early critic of the rational model, called his model *bounded rationality*. It reflected the limits placed on the rational decision-making process by such real-world considerations as a decision maker's inability to secure and process complete information relevant to the decision.[41] According to Simon, managers and other decision makers take three steps:

1. **Scan** the environment for conditions that call for a decision. The Forest Service manager operates at the *intelligence* stage when he begins a program to control the growth of underbrush at Bandelier.
2. **Design** possible solutions to the problem by developing and analyzing possible courses of action. The Forest Service manager decided to institute a controlled burn at Bandelier, although leaving the forest in its current state or chopping down trees would have been other possible solutions.
3. **Choose** among the available alternatives. Individuals choose an acceptable, but not necessarily the best, alternative at this stage. They satisfice. The Forest Service manager decided to implement the controlled burn rather than other solutions.

Intuitive Decision Making

Some researchers argue that managers should completely replace the rational approach with *intuitive* decision making, in which a manager relies on his "gut feeling" about the best decision. Good intuition occurs unconsciously and after years of experience in making the same decision.[42] A recent nationwide survey of marketing and advertising professionals indicated that 89 percent of those polled use intuitive decision making frequently.[43]

In normal circumstances, intuitive decision making uses a *compatibility test* to assess alternatives.[44] The decision maker compares each alternative to a set of standards, such as values, morals, beliefs, goals, and plans, called *images*. She then chooses the decision that fits best with the standards, rather than systematically evaluating this or other alternatives. Intuitive decision making can use the same or even less information than the rational approach and result in faster decisions, but it may not result in as high a quality decision.[45]

Decision Making by Objection

Managers seek the least objectionable course of action—that is, one that does not have a high probability of making matters worse, according to the objection model.[46] In choosing between two recruits, a manager would want to hire the recruit who would perform better, although he might select the one who would at least perform satisfactorily.

According to this model, decision makers first produce a rough description of an acceptable resolution of the situation. Next they propose a course of action, accompanied by a description of the positive outcomes of the action. They secure objections to the action from interested managers, co-workers, or other parties. These objections set the boundaries of the problem and define an acceptable resolution. The decision makers repeat this process, creating several courses of action, each one having fewer objections than the previous one. A manager in a dot-com company, for example, might choose to change the way work assignments are allocated, secure objections, and refine the decision until she eliminates all objections.

The Garbage Can Model

Some organizations have unclear goals and no clear ways of achieving whatever goals exist. Often the personnel participating in decision making in such organizations change as the complexity of the goals change over time. In these organizations, problems and solutions often present themselves simultaneously, as shown in Figure 5-5. For example, the people a manager meets or the pressure to address

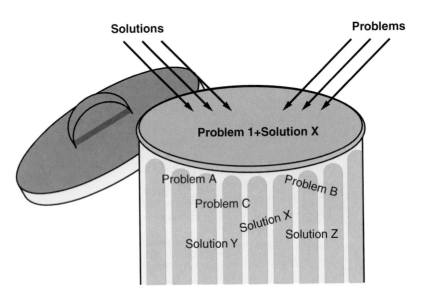

FIGURE 5-5   *Problems randomly attach to solutions in the "garbage can."*

unexpected, critical problems may influence her decisions.[47] Recognizing the complex and unsystematic quality of much decision making, the *garbage can model* uses the image of a garbage can to describe the serendipitous pairing of seemingly unrelated problems and solutions.[48] Compatible problems and solutions that appear at the time a decision is needed result in a decision; otherwise, no decision results.[49]

Good decisions only occur when solutions and problems meet at the same time and the decision maker matches appropriate problems and solutions.[50] For example, the manager who hires a new employee may interview an inappropriate candidate for the open position, but recognize that this candidate can fill another vacant position in the company. Thus, a possible but inappropriate solution to one problem can solve another problem, removing both a problem and a solution from the garbage can. Because unexpected pairings of solutions to problems can occur, decision makers often make decisions about problems that are less significant than the major one they are trying to solve. Similarly, solving a new problem may solve a previously unsolved one as well. Setting and implementing work agendas can help managers take hold of the problems and solutions in the garbage can. The managers' personal characteristics, as well as characteristics and conditions of their work, influence the agendas.[51]

■ TECHNIQUES FOR IMPROVING DECISION MAKING

Managers can use a variety of approaches for improving decision making. In this section, we consider creative problem solving, brainstorming, affinity diagrams, the nominal group technique, and delphi technique.

Creative Problem Solving

Decision makers can treat decision making as an exercise in *creative problem solving*. Creative thinking skills, combined with expertise and motivation, comprise creativity.[52] Managers and employees may generate many alternatives or try to view a problem in new ways rather than clinging to a single preconceived idea. Look at the problem in Figure 5-6 as an example. To solve the problem, you need to literally think "outside of the box" by drawing the first line beyond the three lines of dots

FIGURE 5-6

Connect the nine dots using only four straight lines without lifting your pencil from the paper and without retracing any lines.

before taking the next line through the next dot. Creative problem solving attempts to change traditional patterns of thinking. Rather than thinking of a glass as half empty, it figuratively means thinking of the glass as half full. In the case of the Los Alamos fires, creative thinking might have meant looking for alternatives other than a controlled burn to deal with overgrown vegetation. Individuals may suspend judgment as a way of more carefully exploring possibilities or delay judgment about the relevance of information to the decision. By not drawing conclusions too soon, ideas survive longer and lead to other ideas. Workers may also offer ideas they normally would reject, resulting in developing a new, more useful frame of reference for assessing them.[53] Brainstorming, described later in this chapter, also leads to more creative decision making.

A variety of techniques reduce the perceptual, emotional, cultural, environmental, intellectual, and expressive blocks that hinder effective decision making:[54]

1. using alternative thinking languages, such as expressing a problem in mathematical rather than verbal language or using visual models rather than verbal expressions of a problem;
2. making lists as a way of better processing information;
3. developing a questioning attitude by taking a devil's advocate approach that questions all assumptions and conclusions; and
4. creating analogies, reversing situations, or breaking decisions into their component parts.

Managers and other employees may fail to think of creative alternatives and solutions.[55] They may argue with, misunderstand, disagree with, or challenge new ideas. They may point out only the flaws in a different perspective. They may not listen well, or they may fail to provide feedback about possibilities. They may act critically, disapprovingly, or judgmentally about new ideas. Organizational barriers, such as lack of communication, emphasis on the status quo, and "turf issues," can hinder creativity. Enthusiastic bosses, teams with diverse membership, challenging projects, and other environmental stimulants more often result in high-creativity outcomes.[56]

Brainstorming

Brainstorming refers to a technique by which individuals or groups generate large numbers of ideas or alternatives without evaluating their merits. For example, a research and development team might list as many design options for a new product as they can before pursuing a limited number of them. A home furnishings store might list many ways of informing customers about their products before doing a cost/benefit analysis of selected ones. The owner of CINI Cacak, a heating appliances manufacturer in Serbia, convened his small research and development team a day after NATO bombs destroyed a competitor's factory. As a result of brainstorming sessions, they developed a small, cheap combination heater and cooking stove, designed as a temporary solution to the electricity and gas shortage. The new product, a miniature wood-burning stove called Spasjevo, has had tremendous sales.[57] Listing alternatives without evaluating them encourages people to generate ideas rather than defending or eliminating existing ideas. Table 5-2 offers advice to managers leading a brainstorming session.

TABLE 5-2

Managers Should Follow This Advice for Successful Brainstorming.

- List all ideas.
- Do not evaluate any ideas during the initial stages.
- Encourage creativity.
- Record all ideas.
- Offer ideas related to those already listed.
- Ask each participant to offer a specific number (e.g., five to ten) new ideas.
- Set a time limit for brainstorming.

Brainstorming typically helps decision makers think of unexpected and potentially useful possibilities for attacking a problem. It does not contribute significantly when specialized knowledge is required because it sacrifices the quality of an idea for a quantity of ideas.[58] While brainstorming can result in many shallow and useless ideas, it can also push members to offer new ideas and typically increases the overall creativity of individuals and work groups.

Now managers can use software to encourage brainstorming. For example, software called Knowledge and Innovation Server helps make brainstorming sessions among engineers more productive. The software gives the engineers access to a database of scientific effects and technical applications. It helps them generate and apply an array of potential solutions.[59] Managers can also encourage brainstorming by creating the proper environment for it. The United Kingdom's Post Office management training center includes an innovation lab used for brainstorming sessions that may involve scribbling on walls and throwing things to spur creativity.[60]

Affinity Diagram Technique

Affinity diagrams offer a special way of structuring brainstorming. This technique allows groups of workers to organize ideas, show their interrelationships, and develop action steps. Managers commonly use affinity diagrams as part of continuous improvement efforts, as shown in Figure 5-7. Working on an affinity diagram helps promote teamwork, break down communication barriers, increase understanding in a group, and gain consensus among people with different viewpoints.

Team members generate ideas related to a theme, such as "The number of defects has increased 10 times in the past year." They then group and regroup these ideas until they have about 5 to 10 groupings. They attach a priority to each grouping and then write a summary sentence. (See Activity 5-5 for the detailed steps in drawing an affinity diagram.)

The process allows team members to identify causes of problems and possible solutions. It highlights important interdependencies that need to be considered in addressing the problem. It focuses team members on areas of agreement, so that the process reduces potential conflict over causes of problems and potential solutions. Finally, it gives team members an equal voice in specifying the key issues.

FIGURE 5-7

Managers use an affinity diagram to organize brainstorming in a group of employees.

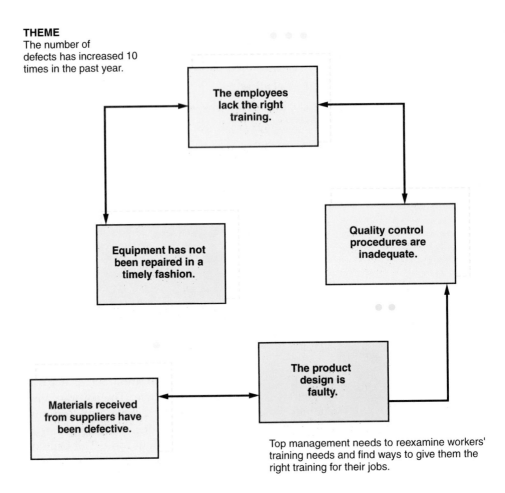

THEME
The number of defects has increased 10 times in the past year.

The employees lack the right training.

Equipment has not been repaired in a timely fashion.

Quality control procedures are inadequate.

Materials received from suppliers have been defective.

The product design is faulty.

Top management needs to reexamine workers' training needs and find ways to give them the right training for their jobs.

Nominal Group Technique

The *nominal group technique (NGT)* describes a structured group meeting in which individuals brainstorm and then rank-order a series of ideas as a way of resolving differences in the group's opinion.[61] The group reviews a problem, and each member individually offers alternative solutions in writing. The group then shares the solutions and lists them on a blackboard or large piece of paper, as in brainstorming. They discuss and clarify the ideas before ranking and voting their preferences. If the group does not agree, they repeat the ranking and voting procedure until the group reaches some agreement. Table 5-3 presents a leader guide for NGT meetings. One study, for example, used the NGT to assess clients' reactions to the Assertive Community Treatment model, which supports people with psychiatric disabilities who live in community settings. The decision-making technique helped uncover the perceived strengths and weaknesses of this approach to clients and staff members.[62]

An *improved nominal group technique* offers a number of advantages over the standard nominal group technique.[63] It requires members to anonymously offer their input to the list of solutions and then vote secretly. Each group meeting has a clearly focused agenda that limits discussion to a single aspect of the decision. This technique delays evaluation of ideas until all inputs are displayed. It also ensures

TABLE 5-3

Leaders of NGT Meetings Should Perform Six Steps in Sequence.

Step 1: Silent Recording

1. Present a written problem statement and a written outline of all process steps.
2. Resist all but process clarifications.
3. Maintain atmosphere by also writing in silence.
4. Discourage members who attempt to talk to others.

Step 2: Round-Robin Recording

1. Indicate the purpose of Step 2 (to create a record of the meeting).
2. Ask members to present their problems briefly and clearly.
3. Accept variations on a theme, but discourage duplicate items.
4. Ask if an idea has been correctly recorded to gain approval before proceeding.
5. Keep the list visible to all members by taping it on the wall.

Step 3: Interactive Discussion

1. Indicate this step's purpose (to explain and consolidate).
2. Skirt arguments, but accept both opinions when a difference arises.
3. Give all items some consideration.
4. Encourage elaborations from everyone without reference to who proposed them.
5. Gain the group's agreement to merge similar ideas, keeping the ideas separate when the group objects.

Step 4: Prioritization

1. Indicate the purpose of Step 4 (to set priorities).
2. Explain the procedure.

Source: Adapted from A. L. Delbecq, A. Van de Ven, and D. H. Gustafson, *Group Techniques for Program Planning* (Middleton, WI; Greenbrief, 1986). Reprinted with permission from P. C. Nutt, *Making Tough Decisions* (San Francisco: Jossey-Bass, 1989), p. 364.

that participants have opportunities to discuss displayed items before voting. Discussion of items focuses solely on the advantages and disadvantages of various alternatives. Individuals can reword alternatives to improve them. Now computerized software exists to support the improved technique.

The nominal group technique becomes more useful as a group increases in size and diversity of expertise. Because of its structure, the NGT gives individuals time to think about the key issues before offering solutions, and provides a mechanism for reaching a decision expediently through the ranking-voting procedure.[64] It fosters creativity by allowing extensive individual input into the process. Strong personality types will less often dominate the group because the NGT provides all group members with an opportunity for systematic input. In sum, it encourages innovation, limits conflict, emphasizes equal participation by all members, helps generate consensus, and incorporates the preferences of individuals in decision-making choices.[65]

Delphi Technique

The *delphi technique* refers to a structured group decision-making technique that uses repeated administration of rating scales to obtain opinions about a decision. It begins with unfocused ideas, and then through exploration of these ideas increasingly focuses them until a decision is reached.[66] Research suggests that the delphi technique outperforms standard interacting groups.[67] One southeastern university used the delphi technique to prioritize the capabilities suggested by the Accounting Education Change Commission for business school graduates. Using this technique allowed them to gather input from participants at multiple locations.[68]

Group members first explore the subject individually. In the conventional delphi technique, a small group of these people designs a questionnaire and then polls a larger group. It tabulates and feeds back the results for discussion. The process repeats until group members reach agreement and develop a common view of the issues.[69]

Consider how the delphi technique might help the president of a rapidly growing e-commerce business decide what benefits to offer his employees. First, he identifies a small group of key players to consider the decision. This group then develops and administers a questionnaire about the possible benefits to employees. They tabulate and share the results, which might uncover agreement about the value of certain benefits, but questions about others. Then they administer a more focused questionnaire, and the process continues. The use of computer software makes this technique easier and faster. The computer program summarizes the results and essentially replaces the small group.[70]

The delphi technique works well when face-to-face conversation is not possible but the input of many people is valuable. It provides a systematic way for considering all ideas that is particularly useful in the case of significant disagreements and protects individual anonymity. The delphi technique also helps managers who cannot apply precise analytical techniques to solving the problem, but prefer to use subjective judgments on a collective basis. It can increase the effectiveness of group meetings when they occur and reduce the likelihood of the group developing a sense of invulnerability and infallibility. Particularly if the individuals involved have historically failed to communicate effectively in the past, the delphi procedures offer a systematic method for ensuring that their opinions are presented.[71]

▌DECISION MAKING IN THE DOT-COM, GLOBAL WORKPLACE

Intense competition and rapidly changing economic, social, political, and technological environments increase the complexity of the decision-making process and limit an organization's ability to control the outcomes of its decisions.[72] To be effective, managers need to develop effective tools for making decisions in the dynamic environment they face both domestically and globally.

Making decisions in dot-com organizations poses special challenges. Not only does the marketplace change quickly and financing of the company's efforts remain unstable, but the rapid growth experienced by many dot-com businesses results in hiring untrained and inexperienced managers. Decision making needs to be particularly timely. Decisions should be carefully considered, yet responsive to unremitting demands for information and progress. Retaining an ethical culture also seems to be difficult for many dot-com companies. Companies have been charged with stealing their competitors' intellectual property and employees, as well as reading employees' e-mail. They also have been guilty of cheating employees out of stock options, giving "directed shares" to family and friends who sell them immediately for an easy profit, having CEOs who sell their stock early and not necessarily to the company's benefit, instituting small boards of directors dominated by insiders, and lobbying stock analysts.[73]

A culture's underlying values affect an individual's approach to decision making, particularly to problem recognition. U.S. managers, for example, see situations as a problem to be solved, but Thai and Indonesian managers perceive that situations should be accepted as is, not changed.[74] Managers in countries characterized as collective likely seek consensus more often than those in countries characterized as individualistic. Values may also affect the type of alternatives selected. European countries may rely more on historical patterns as the source of alternatives. Countries such as Israel with more future-oriented cultures may generate more new, untested alternatives.[75]

The speed of and responsibility for decision making is also culturally based.[76] More rapid decision making characterizes the United States, whereas many Middle Eastern cultures downplay time urgency. Responsibility for decisions may rest on the individual, as in the United States, or on a group, as in Japan. Factors considered irrelevant in the United States, such as face-saving, can be crucial in the decision-making processes of Asian groups. Countries can also differ in the place in the hierarchy where decisions typically occur. For example, Swedish workers are more comfortable with decentralized decision making than are Indian or French employees, and in Africa, middle managers rarely delegate authority.[77]

Cultural diversity poses both advantages and disadvantages for decision makers. Individual decision makers must reconcile their own views with potentially different perspectives offered in another culture. Individuals who are members of diverse groups must find effective ways to cope with differences in experience, customs, language, and other characteristics.

▌ Summary

1. Managers and other organization members can judge the effectiveness of decisions in terms of their quality, timeliness, acceptance, and ethical appropriateness.

2. Programmed decisions describe problems that have a relatively structured solution; nonprogrammed decisions cannot be handled by standard rules and policies.

3. Strategic decisions focus on the long-run goals of the company, whereas operational decisions focus on its day-to-day functioning.

4. Top-down decisions begin with executives and move downward through the organization's chain of command; worker-empowered decisions give workers control over their work setting.

5. Diagnosing influences on decision making, including the characteristics of the decision maker, cognitive biases, and organizational barriers, helps improve decisions.

6. A rational decision-making process, which involves analyzing the situation, setting objectives, searching for alternatives, evaluating the alternatives,

making the decision, and evaluating the decision, generally results in improved decision making.

7. Alternatives to rational decision making include bounded rationality, intuitive decision making, decision making by objection, and the garbage can model.

8. Decision makers can improve the decision-making process by using creative problem solving, brainstorming, affinity diagrams, the nominal group technique, and the delphi technique.

9. The dot-com, global workplace creates special challenges for effective decision making.

A Manager's Diagnostic Review

■ Know what makes a decision effective.

   • Do decision makers make high-quality, timely, accepted decisions?

■ Understand what factors influence decision making.

   • Do managers diagnose their skills and style?

   • Do managers employ strategies to reduce cognitive biases in their decision making?

   • Do decision makers use strategies to overcome organizational barriers?

■ Use the appropriate decision making process.

   • Do decision makers follow the steps in the rational approach when feasible?

   • Do decision makers use alternative processes when appropriate?

■ Apply techniques to improve decision making.

   • Do decision makers use creative decision making, brainstorming, affinity diagrams, NGT, and the delphi technique?

■ Make effective decisions in the dot-com, global workplace.

   • Do decision makers consider the rapidly changing environment in making decisions?

   • Do decision makers consider cultural influences in making decisions?

Visit the Gordon homepage on the Prentice Hall Web site at

   http://www.prenhall.com/gordon

for recommended readings, additional activities, Internet exercises, updated information, and links to related Web sites.

▌ Thinking Critically About Organizational Behavior

1. Can a decision realistically meet all four criteria of effectiveness?

2. Should managers use the same process for various types of decisions?

3. What major factors influence decision making?
4. Is using the rational decision-making process feasible?
5. Do you agree that managers can never identify all possible decision alternatives?
6. How systematically should managers evaluate decisions, and what techniques should they use?
7. Does intuitive decision making lead to effective decisions?
8. Do the elements of a decision act as if they were in a garbage can?
9. Are the alternative approaches to the rational model more valid?
10. What steps should managers take to encourage more creative problem solving?
11. Can managers use computers to help improve decision making?
12. How can managers ensure that cross-cultural differences do not impede the effectiveness of their decisions and decision making?

ACTIVITY 5-1: THE NASA EXERCISE

STEP 1: Read the following instructions.

You are a member of a space crew originally scheduled to rendezvous with a mothership on the lighted surface of the moon. Due to mechanical difficulties, however, your ship was forced to land at a spot some 200 miles from the rendezvous point. During landing, much of the equipment aboard was damaged, and since survival depends on reaching the mothership, the most critical items must be chosen for the 200-mile trip. The 15 items left intact and undamaged after the landing include a box of matches, food concentrate, 50 feet of nylon rope, parachute silk, a portable heating unit, two .45-caliber pistols, one case of dehydrated milk, two 100-pound tanks of oxygen, a stellar map (of the moon's constellations), a life raft, a magnetic compass, 5 gallons of water, signal flares, a first-aid kit containing injection needles, and a solar-powered FM receiver-transmitter.

Your task is to rank-order the available supplies in terms of their importance to your crew in reaching the rendezvous point. Using a scoring sheet like the one in Table 5-4, place the number 1 by the most important item, the number 2 by the second most important, and so on, through number 15, the least important. You have 15 minutes to complete this phase of the exercise.

STEP 2: After the individual ranks are completed, your instructor will direct you to form groups of four to seven members. Each group should then rank-order the 15 items as a group. This group ranking should be a general consensus following a discussion of the issues, not just an averaging of each individual ranking. While it is unlikely that everyone will agree exactly on the group ranking, an effort should be made to at least reach a decision that everyone can live with. It is important to treat differences of opinion as a means of gathering more information, clarifying issues, and encouraging the group to seek better alternatives. The group ranking should be listed in column 2.

STEP 3: The instructor will provide the expert's rankings. Enter them in column 3.

STEP 4: Each participant should compute the absolute differences as follows:

- between the individual ranking and the group ranking (place the numbers in column 4);
- between the individual ranking and the expert's ranking (place the numbers in column 5); and
- between the group ranking and the expert's ranking (place the numbers in column 6). Then total the scores for columns 4, 5, and 6.

STEP 5: Discussion. In small groups or with the entire class, answer the following questions:

TABLE 5-4

Complete This Scoring Sheet For the NASA Exercise						
Items	Individual Ranking	Group Ranking	Survival Expert's Ranking	Influence	Individual Accuracy	Group Accuracy
	Column 1	Column 2	Column 3	Column 4	Column 5	Column 6
Box of matches						
Food concentrate						
50 feet of nylon rope						
Parachute silk						
Portable heating unit						
Two .45-caliber pistols						
One case dehydrated milk						
Two 100-pound tanks of oxygen						
Stellar map (of the moon's constellations)						
Life raft						
Magnetic compass						
Five gallons of water						
Signal flares						
First-aid kit containing injection needles						
Solar-powered FM receiver–transmitter						
				Individual Influence Score	Individual Accuracy Score	Group Accuracy Score

DESCRIPTION

1. Describe your group's operation.
2. Describe the decision-making process used by your group.

DIAGNOSIS

3. Which steps occurred in decision making?
4. Which steps did you skip?

PRESCRIPTION

5. How could your group have made a more effective decision?

ACTIVITY 5-2: THE PROBLEM WITH VANATIN

STEP 1: Read the following background information.

You are a member of the Booth Pharmaceutical Corporation board of directors. You have been called to a special board meeting to discuss what should be done with the product Vanatin.

Vanatin is a "fixed-ratio" antibiotic sold by prescription. That is, it contains a combination of drugs. On the market for more than 13 years, it has been highly successful. It now accounts for about $18 million per year, which is 12 percent of Booth Company's gross income in the United States (and a greater percentage of net profits). Profit from foreign markets, where Vanatin is marketed under a different name, is roughly comparable to that in the United States.

Over the past 20 years, numerous medical scientists (such as the AMA's Council on Drugs) have objected to the sale of most fixed-ratio drugs. The arguments have been that (1) there is no evidence that these fixed-ratio drugs have improved benefits over single drugs and (2) the possibility of detrimental side effects, including death, is at least double. For example, scientists have estimated that Vanatin is causing about 30 to 40 unnecessary deaths per year (that is, deaths that could be prevented if the patients had used a substitute made by one of Booth's competitors). Despite recommendations to remove fixed-ratio drugs from the market, doctors have continued to use them because they offer a shotgun approach for doctors who are unsure of their diagnoses.

Recently, a National Academy of Science–National Research Council panel composed of impartial scientists carried out extensive research studies and recommended unanimously that the Food and Drug Administration (FDA) ban the sale of Vanatin. One of the members of the panel, Dr. Peterson of the University of Texas, was quoted by the press as saying, "There are few instances in medicine when so many experts have agreed unanimously and without reservation [about banning Vanatin]." This view was typical of comments made by other members of the panel. In fact, it was typical of comments that had been made about fixed-ratio drugs over the past 20 years. These impartial experts believe that, while all drugs have some possible side effects, the costs associated with Vanatin far exceed the benefits.

The special board meeting has arisen out of an emergency situation. The FDA has told you that it plans to ban Vanatin in the United States and wants to give Booth time for a final appeal to them. Should the ban become effective, Booth would have to stop all sales of Vanatin and attempt to remove inventories from the market. Booth has no close substitutes for Vanatin, so consumers will be switched to close substitutes currently marketed by rival firms. (Some of these substitutes apparently have no serious side effects.) It is extremely unlikely that bad publicity from this case would have any significant effect on the long-term profits of other products made by Booth.

The board is meeting to review and make decisions on two issues:

1. What should be done with Vanatin in the U.S. market (the immediate problem)?
2. Assuming that Vanatin is banned from the U.S. market, what should Booth do in the foreign markets? (No government action is anticipated.)

Decisions on each of these issues must be reached at today's meeting. The chairman of the board has sent out this background information, and he also wants you to give some thought as to which of the following alternatives you would prefer for the domestic market:

1. Recall Vanatin immediately and destroy it.
2. Stop production of Vanatin immediately, but allow what has been made to be sold.
3. Stop all advertising and promotion of Vanatin, but provide the drug for doctors who request it.
4. Continue efforts to most effectively market Vanatin until its sale is actually banned.
5. Continue efforts to most effectively market Vanatin and take legal, political, and other necessary actions to prevent the authorities from banning Vanatin.

A similar decision must also be made for the foreign market under the assumption that the sale is banned in the United States.

STEP 2: Prepare your role.

STEP 3: The chairperson of the board will conduct the discussion of the Vanatin problem. By the end of 45 minutes, the group should reach a decision on what to do about both domestic and international distribution of Vanatin. At the end of the meeting, each chairperson should record the decisions of the group on the recording form.

STEP 4: Your instructor will tabulate the types of decisions made by all the groups for the U.S. and foreign markets. You may record the decisions on the following table.

1. Record in columns 1 and 2 the actual decisions made by the discussion groups.
2. Privately note to yourself what you think Booth actually did in this case. The instructor will tally the predictions, and you may record these predictions in columns 3 and 4.
3. Record in columns 5 and 6 what Booth actually did.

Decision	Decision Made by Groups*		What do You Think Happened?		What Actually Happened?	
	United States	Foreign	United States	Foreign	United States	Foreign
a. Recall immediately						
b. Stop production						
c. Stop advertising and promotion						
d. Continue to market						
e. Block FDA						
	(1)	(2)	(3)	(4)	(5)	(6)

*Record the letter designation of the group decision in the proper place.

STEP 5: Discussion. In small groups or with the entire class, answer the following questions:

1. What decisions did each group reach?
2. How ethical were the decisions reached?
3. What criteria did you use to evaluate the decisions?
4. How could you ensure the decision making is more ethical?

Source: This is adapted by Roy J. Lewicki, Duke University, from an exercise developed by J. Scott Armstrong, University of Pennsylvania. It is reprinted from Douglas T. Hall, Donald D. Bowen, Roy J. Lewicki, and Francine S. Hall, *Experiences in Management and Organizational Behavior,* 2d ed. (New York: John Wiley & Sons, 1982). For a report on research involving this exercise, see J. Scott Armstrong, Social Irresponsibility in Marketing, *Journal of Business Research* 5 (1977): 185–213.

ACTIVITY 5-3: ETHICAL DILEMMAS

STEP 1: Individually or in small groups, determine how you would act in the following situations:

Situation 1: You are an accountant who prepares the annual tax returns for a small retail store. You know that the owner of the store has adjusted some of the sales figures to reduce his taxes. What do you do?

Situation 2: You are the product manager for a detergent that is being sold for the first time outside the United States. You have talked with the manager of a large grocery chain in the country where you want to sell the soap. He insists that you must give him a "special payment" to stock the detergent in his stores. What do you do?

Situation 3: As head of Quality Control for a medium-size manufacturer of lighting products, you are responsible for ensuring the quality of all products that leave the company.

You know that one of the manufacturing supervisors has made some unauthorized adjustments to the last batch of lamps so that they meet the written standards. You think these adjustments may ultimately result in unexpected fires. You've talked to the manager, who has insisted on shipping the defective lamps because he needs to reach a certain quota to obtain his annual bonus. What do you do?

Situation 4: You must decide which employee to promote to the vice president position. You believe that Janet Smith has worked the hardest of her peers and deserves the promotion. You also know that Janet is pregnant, although she hasn't yet told anyone else in the company. Although Janet has assured you that she will return after her maternity leave, you think perhaps you may bypass her and promote Jerry Davidson. What should you do?

Situation 5: The plant manager who oversees the cereal production line has asked you to reset the scales so that each box actually weighs one ounce less than required. You know that he will make life very unpleasant and perhaps even fire you if you don't follow his directions. What do you do?

STEP 2: In groups of four to six students, reach consensus about how to handle each situation.

STEP 3: Discussion. In small groups, with the entire class, or in written form, as directed by your instructor, answer the following questions.

DESCRIPTION

1. What decisions did each group reach?

DIAGNOSIS

2. How ethical were the decisions reached?
3. What criteria did you use to evaluate the decisions?

PRESCRIPTION

4. How could you improve your decision making to make it more ethical?

ACTIVITY 5-4: HOW BIASED IS YOUR DECISION MAKING?

STEP 1: Answer each of the following problems.

1. A certain town is served by two hospitals. In the larger hospital, about 45 babies are born each day, and in the smaller hospital about 15 babies are born each day. Although the overall proportion of boys is about 50 percent, the actual proportion at either hospital may be greater or less than 50 percent on any day. At the end of a year, which hospital will have the greater number of days on which more than 60 percent of the babies born were boys?
   a. The large hospital
   b. The small hospital
   c. Neither—the number of days will be about the same (within 5 percent of each other)

2. Linda is 31, single, outspoken, and very bright. She majored in philosophy in college. As a student, she was deeply concerned with discrimination and other social issues, and participated in antinuclear demonstrations. Which statement is more likely:
   a. Linda is a bank teller.
   b. Linda is a bank teller and active in the feminist movement.

3. A cab was involved in a hit-and-run accident. Two cab companies serve the city: the Green, which operates 85 percent of the cabs, and the Blue, which operates the remaining 15 percent. A witness identifies the hit-and-run cab as Blue. When the court tests the reliability of the witness under circumstances similar to those on the night of the accident, he correctly identifies the color of a cab 80 percent of the time and misidentifies it the other 20 percent. What is the probability that the cab involved in the accident was Blue, as the witness stated?

4. Imagine that you face the following pair of concurrent decisions. Examine these decisions, and then indicate which choices you prefer.

Decision I

Choose between:
   a. A sure gain of $240
   b. A 25 percent chance of winning $1,000 and a 75 percent chance of winning nothing

Decision II

Choose between:
   c. A sure loss of $750
   d. A 75 percent chance of losing $1,000 and a 25 percent chance of losing nothing

Decision III

Choose between:
   e. A sure loss of $3,000
   f. An 80 percent chance of losing $4,000 and a 20 percent chance of losing nothing

5. You have decided to see a Broadway play and have bought a $40 ticket. As you enter the theater, you realize you have lost your ticket. You cannot remember the seat number, so you cannot prove to the management that you bought a ticket. Would you spend $40 for a new ticket?

   You have reserved a seat for a Broadway play for which the ticket price is $40. As you enter the theater to buy your ticket, you discover you have lost $40 from your pocket. Would you still buy the ticket? (Assume you have enough cash left to do so.)

6. Imagine you have operable lung cancer and must choose between two treatments—surgery and radiation therapy. Of 100 people having surgery, 10 die during the operation, 32 (including those original 10) are dead after one year, and 66 are dead after five years. Of 100 people having radiation therapy, none dies during treatment, 23 are dead after one year, and 78 are dead after five years. Which treatment would you prefer?

STEP 2: Your instructor will give you the answer to each problem.

STEP 3: Discussion. In small groups, with the entire class, or in written form, as directed by your instructor, answer the following questions.

DESCRIPTION

1. How accurate were the decisions you reached?

DIAGNOSIS

2. What biases were evident in the decisions you reached?

PRESCRIPTION

3. How could you improve your decision making to make it more accurate?

Source: From D. Kahnemann and A. Tversky, Rational choice and the forming of decisions, *Journal of Business* 59(4) (1986): 5251–5278; A. Tversky and D. Kahnemann, The framing of decisions and the psychology of choice, *Science* 211 (1981): 453–458; D. Kahnemann and A. Tversky, Extension needs intuitive reasoning, *Psychological Review 90* (1983): 293–315; K. McKean, Decisions, decisions, *Discovery Magazine* (June 1985).

ACTIVITY 5-5: AFFINITY DIAGRAM EXERCISE

An affinity diagram is a problem analysis technique for collecting ideas and analyzing their similarities and relationships. You can use an affinity diagram to brainstorm ideas, promote teamwork, break down communication barriers, facilitate understanding in a group, and gain consensus among people with different viewpoints.

   Team members should follow four general rules in constructing an affinity diagram:

1. Team members have complete freedom to express their ideas.

2. Criticism is not allowed.

3. Team members list as many ideas as possible within the specified time period.

4. Team members can combine and improve on the ideas of other team members.

STEP 1: Select a theme for the affinity diagram. The theme should be capable of being addressed by the people in the time available. The theme is a brief statement that presents the question or problem of concern. Weakness-based themes are frequently easier to work with.

STEP 2: Write the theme or problem on the top corner of a large sheet of newsprint or poster board.

STEP 3: Each team member should write a series of succinct sentences that address or answer the theme or problem statement. Each sentence should include a single idea. Print each sentence on a separate self-stick note using black ink. Often the number of sentences (and notes) will be limited due to time or space constraints. A typical affinity diagram might result in 40 to 60, but as many as 100, items.

STEP 4: Put all notes in random order on the print so that everyone on the team can read them.

STEP 5: Team members should read and review all notes to ensure that the meaning of the ideas expressed is clear. Where clarification is necessary, rewrite the note.

STEP 6: Team members should group the notes into similar ideas. Generally place no more than three notes in a group. This number may be increased to four or five in a grouping if team members generate a large number of sentences in Step 2. All team members should do the grouping simultaneously, without discussion. A team member may move or regroup ideas during this period. The grouping process should continue until all team members are satisfied with the groupings. The team should strive to have between 5 and 10 groupings. Groupings can contain one note. The team should check that no important ideas have been omitted and add them to the groupings as necessary.

STEP 7: The team should write a sentence that describes the essential idea of each grouping in blue ink, stack the notes that compose the group, and place the new sentence on top of that grouping. You do not have to write a new title for a grouping that contains a single note.

STEP 8: Rearrange the groupings, with those having the greatest similarity near each other so that interrelationships can be indicated. Draw arrows to represent causality or contradictions: $\rightarrow$ for causality and $\succ\!\!\prec$ for contradiction.

STEP 9: Indicate the importance of each grouping by voting. Each individual has three votes. To vote, place a red dot next to the grouping with the highest priority, a blue dot next to the grouping with the second highest priority, and a green dot next to the grouping with the third highest priority. Each person should put one red, one blue, and one green dot on the affinity diagram.

STEP 10: Write a one-paragraph summary about the results and place it in the lower corner of the newsprint sheet.

ACTIVITY 5-6: CREATIVE THINKING PROBLEMS

STEP 1: Complete the following problems.

Problem 1: Think of as many uses as you can for an orange.

Problem 2: Determine how to drop an uncooked egg from the top of a six-foot ladder without breaking it and using materials that cost less than one dollar.

Problem 3: Design a portable desk lamp.

Problem 4: How would you divide a rectangle into four equal pieces?

Problem 5: What is the fewest number of coins required to make 91 cents?

Problem 6: Offer several analogies for "the early bird gets the worm."

Problem 7: Design an egg-cracking machine.

Problem 8: List as many words as possible that can be formed from the letters in "Silence is Golden."

Problem 9: Build a bed for a cricket.

Problem 10: Design a combination pen and paper holder that attaches to a computer.

STEP 2: Discussion. Share your solutions with the class. Then think of additional possible solutions.

David Shorter

David Shorter sat back in his chair and thought about what he should say to Bob Chen when they met in a few minutes. Three weeks ago when David had left for holiday, he had regarded Bob as an up-and-coming member of the James-Williams team. David had seen Bob as a solid performer who wanted a career at James-Williams and who could be developed over time into a manager and perhaps eventually into a partner. David had even thought that Bob could help attract to James-Williams some of the new entrepreneurial Hong Kong companies that were coming to Toronto. Now David heard from Bob's managing partner, Jane Klinck, that Bob was threatening to resign.

David's First Day Back

David thought about the steady stream of people who had been in to see him this first morning back in the office. Jane Klinck was worried and upset. She felt that Bob was acting "crazy" and that there might be some sort of personality conflict between Bob and Mike McLeod. She hoped that David would be able to sort out the problem and find a solution that would keep Bob in the company. Mike McLeod had been in to see David, too. Mike was a fairly new part-ner who attracted a lot of business to James-Williams. He felt that he had not only been through the proper channels to have Bob assigned to the Softdisk Computer audit, but that he had been extremely patient with Bob. Mike said the other partners were shaking their heads about his behaviour, wondering why he was being so patient when it was standard procedure for partners to make such an assignment. Joe Silverman had been in as well. Joe was the tax partner Bob would report to starting in September, just five weeks from now. Joe hotly protested Bob's behaviour: "We can't have staff refusing assignments! Bob is way out of line! The customers must come first and this behaviour sheds a poor light on Bob. If he doesn't take the Softdisk job, he should be fired!"

The New Enterprise Group at James-Williams

David Shorter was the Practice Director of the New Enterprise Group at James-Williams. James-Williams was one of the six largest public accounting firms in Canada with 400 partners practising in 30 Canadian cities. James-Williams was the sole Canadian member of James-Williams International which provided audit, tax, consulting and other services to individuals, private businesses and governments in the Americas, Europe, the Middle East, Africa, Asia and the Pacific.

The New Enterprise Group had been set up seven years ago to provide service to smaller growth companies managed by entrepreneurs. David had been the Practice Director for the past four years. James-Williams believed that companies with gross annual revenues of between $5 and $100 M were often neglected as potential customers by Canadian public accounting firms because of their small size. Yet these companies had need of a variety of services that could be provided by James-Williams and these companies would pay high fees for their relative size. When these companies had grown beyond gross revenues of $100 M, their business could be transferred from the New Enterprise Group to the main auditing and consulting services of James-Williams and a solid relationship would exist. This was an important consideration in a mature industry where public accounting firms competed on service, reputation

Neil Abramson prepared this case under the supervision of Professor J. J. DiStefano solely to provide material for class discussion. The authors do not intend to illustrate either effective or ineffective handling of a managerial situation. The authors may have disguised certain names and other identifying information to protect confidentiality.

and price. Often, it was a long-term relationship that kept a client with a public accounting firm. These relationships enabled partners of the public accounting firms to have such an intimate knowledge of their clients' activities that they could anticipate problems and become indispensable to their clients' planning process.

The New Enterprise Group provided a range of consulting services geared to the needs of growing entrepreneurial companies. In addition to accounting and auditing services, the partners acted as principal business advisors. Client companies were particularly interested in the subjects of corporate finance and tax consulting, as well as the problems of acquisition and divestiture. Consulting was also available on strategic planning, development of business plans, marketing, human resource management, and information systems.

The New Enterprise Group was organized as a collegial system of partners who managed their own clients and activities within the performance objectives established by James-Williams, and under the general supervision of the Practice Director, who was also a partner (see Exhibit 1). Staff members below the partner level were organized on the staff system. A staff usually consisted of one or two senior staff accountants and several intermediate or junior staff accountants under a manager. A partner would have one, two or three managers and several staff reporting to him/her.

Most of the staff were either chartered accountants or in the process of becoming chartered accountants. Usually, staff would be hired out of business school as junior staff accountants and would work on staff over a two-year period while they studied for their char-

tered accountant examinations. At the beginning of their second year, they were promoted to intermediate staff accountants at which level they remained until they passed the chartered accountant exams. At the beginning of their third year they wrote their exams, and, if they passed, they were promoted to senior staff accountants. If they did not pass, which was fairly common, they would have another year to prepare for a final chance at the exams.

The normal promotion process at James-Williams was for staff to remain as senior staff accountants for two years while they developed a consulting specialty of their choice. Then they might be promoted to manager and supervise six to nine staff. Most partners were selected from the ranks of the managers after they had been with the firm for ten to eleven years.

Bob Chen's Background with New Enterprise Group

Bob Chen was born in Hong Kong and came to Toronto as a high school student for Grade 13. He graduated with a Bachelor of Commerce from Queen's University in Kingston. At Queen's he achieved an overall grade point average of 75%[1] and was the treasurer of the Chinese Students' Society. He was recruited for James-Williams in the spring of his final year at Queen's, and began as a junior staff accountant at the New Enterprise Group in the following September.

---

[1]In Canada, the grade point system follows the British model. At Queen's, a 75 average is a B+ and is considered evidence of high achievement.

EXHIBIT 1   *James-Williams: The New Enterprise Group Organizational Chart (Reporting relationships prior to Bob Chen's reassignment to tax)*

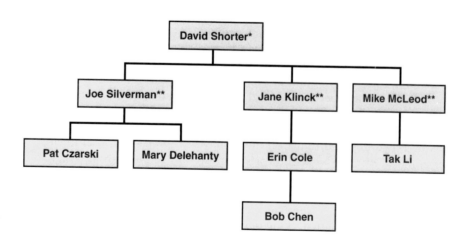

Bob was seen as quiet and soft-spoken. One of his managers described him as "shy and accommodating. He does what he is asked to do and a bit more. Casual requests get immediate results." He was also a very private person whose politeness often meant not saying exactly what he wanted out of a situation or from another person. His civility may have masked from his colleagues his strongly felt desire for success and strongly held views about his possible contribution to the firm.

Bob was well liked by the people around him, most of whom viewed him as Westernized. Some partners and staff thought that Bob "was fairly outgoing for an Oriental" and had much better oral communications skills than previous staff from Hong Kong hired by the firm. His colleagues believed that Bob had good potential with James-Williams and hoped he would stay with the firm.

Previous Contacts Between David and Bob

Two years after joining the firm, Bob wrote his chartered accountant examinations and in the following December learned the good news that he had passed. He was transferred as an audit senior to Jane Klinck, because the partner Bob had previously reported to was leaving the company. Bob was to report to Erin Cole who was the manager working under Jane.

Early in the new year, David Shorter followed his usual custom of having one-on-one meetings with staff who had passed their examinations and been promoted to senior staff accountant positions. The purpose of the meetings was not only to congratulate them on their success, but also to begin to identify their interests in professional specialization so that David could plan appropriate assignments for them within the New Enterprise Group. New assignments were usually announced after the annual performance appraisal in May, and were effective by September.

When he met with Bob in January, David was pleased with Bob's success because he had thought that Bob was a solid, but average performer and might not pass his examination the first time he wrote it. Now David decided that Bob might have higher potential within the New Enterprise Group and suggested that Bob might like to work to build a practice around attracting entrepreneurial, Hong Kong-based companies to use the New Enterprise Group's services. David explained, "One of our goals is to build up our business with Hong Kong companies. Up to now, we haven't had much success because most Hong Kong money has been invested in real estate. Now, however, Hong Kong money is being invested in businesses which are in the New Enterprise Group's target market."

To be able to attract a Hong Kong practice, Bob would have to build up his auditing skills for another year, because audit was the initial function which brought companies to the New Enterprise Group and stimulated their interest in other consulting services. David remembered that he had two goals in suggesting further auditing experience for Bob. First, the New Enterprise Group had a shortage of senior auditors for this year. Second, he felt that Bob was a "keeper" who could have a long and mutually valuable future with the firm. Bob's auditing skills needed strengthening since he had done very little auditing in his first two years. David had seen previous staff with similar limitations fail as both managers and partners, because without auditing experience they could not understand the practical nature of most business problems. David noted, "Without more seasoning, he would not be as valuable to us. He would get weeded out as a technician."

But Bob had other ideas; he indicated to David that now that he had his C.A. designation, he wanted to develop a specialization in tax. He was open to the idea of developing a Hong Kong practice, but in the meantime he wanted an assignment that would teach him tax. David told Bob that he didn't believe Bob was ready for a tax assignment, because tax was a practical discipline that needed the ability to find creative tax solutions to business problems. Without a firm grounding in audit, staff had a tendency to quote tax regulations, rather than use the tax regulations to the advantage of their clients. "I didn't think he was ready and believed that his chargeable activity time would fall. I was under pressure to keep up the chargeable activity time of all staff." David thought that by the end of the interview he had convinced Bob of the soundness of his argument and that Bob had agreed to defer his request for a tax position.

In May, Jane conducted Bob's annual performance appraisal during which time Bob repeated his request for an assignment in tax. Her reply was similar to David's earlier commentary. Jane told Bob that she thought he needed another year of auditing work. "He had one year of decent audit work with me, but his junior year had not been enlightening in the area of audit. I thought he agreed that his junior year had not been productive in the area of audit." Jane asked David to review the performance appraisal because Bob had only been transferred to her in December. When David met with Bob in June, Bob again asked for an assignment in tax. David said no, reiterating his earlier argument that Bob needed more auditing experience. He added that Jane supported this recommendation. It was both David's and Jane's opinion that Bob was only now doing his first and second comprehensive audits. Bob seemed to accept this judgement, though he did not appear to be satisfied by it.

Over the next month, Bob requested and received two more interviews with David to request a tax assignment. David was pleased to talk with Bob because he felt that Bob's concern showed he was highly interested in his career and also highly committed to James-Williams. At the first meeting, David offered the compromise that if Bob would continue as an auditor for a year, then David would send Bob on a comprehensive three-year tax training program that was a much prized opportunity among tax consultants. "I offered to send him on this expensive course fully funded by the firm if he would agree to wait another year for a tax assignment." Bob seemed initially to agree but then asked for another meeting. At the second meeting, David finally agreed to assign Bob to a tax partner, Joe Silverman, to work in tax starting in September. "I told him that even though he could make the move into tax in September, he'd have to do some audits during his first year in tax. The firm needed to take advantage of his auditing skills as a senior. It would also keep his activities time up." Bob agreed to the conditions and David left for holidays shortly after.

Events Occurring During David Shorter's Absence

David Shorter left the New Enterprise Group to attend a Partner Development Program and for holidays at the beginning of July. During this time, Mike McLeod realized his upcoming need for a senior auditor for an important account, the Softdisk Computer Company. Softdisk's year-end required that the audit had to be done in September and October. The audit would fully occupy the time of the senior auditor during those two months. In order to make preparations for the job, the senior auditor had to be

assigned to the audit by the end of July at the latest. It was more desirable for the senior auditor to be in place by July 13 in order to attend the client's physical inventory being conducted on that date. This would also provide an opportunity for the client and senior auditor to meet each other and work together prior to the actual audit.

Mike found that Bob Chen was the only senior auditor in the New Enterprise Group who might be available in September and October. Policy in the New Enterprise Group was to use internal staff as senior auditors whenever possible because the cost for hours of internal staff was less than if an auditor had to be "rented" from another division of James-Williams. Also, it would be easier for Mike to manage someone from inside the New Enterprise Group.

Since the actual audit work was to be conducted in the fall, Bob would be "officially" working for Joe Silverman in tax. Mike approached Joe Silverman and his manager, Pat Czarski, to see whether he could use Bob Chen for the audit. Joe and Pat told him that Bob was to be assigned to Joe's other manager, Mary Delehanty, who was away on holiday. But Joe and Pat thought it was a very good idea to assign Bob to the audit. The arrangements for Bob to be transferred to Joe had only been made in June and there was no tax work available for him. Further, with Mary on holiday, it was unlikely that she could find tax work for Bob to do in September and the Softdisk audit would keep Bob's billable hours at an acceptable level until they could use his services effectively.

With this approval, Mike approached Bob on July 10. He asked Bob to take the Softdisk audit and provided Bob with information on the company. In particular, Mike wanted Bob to know that the Softdisk audit would fit in with Bob's career path in tax. The audit would include international multi-jurisdictional tax issues, tax problems concerning research and development being done in Quebec, and a high-technology emphasis much valued by staff who worked in the New Enterprise Group. The tax issues were so complex and interesting that the audit had been supervised last year by a tax partner who was now in New York. Mike reassured Bob that this partner would be available for consultation if Bob had problems. Further, once Bob had done the audit, he would have first call on any further, special tax work which might be required by Softdisk. Mike suggested that Bob should contact Dominick Sousa, a manager in the New Enterprise Group who had acted as senior auditor for Softdisk last year, to confirm these details.

Mike also noted that because the prior year's work with Softdisk had been a first audit by James-Williams, extra efforts had been taken. Therefore Bob would benefit from a better planning package being in place and a high client commitment for the second year. In addition, two James-Williams staff members from last year's audit would be carried over to Bob's team, further strengthening the continuity. Finally, Mike assured Bob that Mike and Tak Li would also be available to assist as needed. Altogether, he sought to assure Bob that taking on this audit would be consistent with his professed career objectives.

It was Mike's impression that Bob had agreed to do the Softdisk audit once he had confirmed the information Mike had given him with "due diligence." "He didn't refuse. Basically, he did not say yes, but he said, 'Yes, I'll consider it and will talk to the people.' I was led to believe that he would seriously consider it and I got the impression he would do it. I thought we had a reasonable exchange and that we were both being open with each other." Bob agreed to attend the physical inventory conducted on July 13. The key contact at Softdisk was also of Chinese origin, liked Bob, and was pleased to have him for the audit.

Then Mike heard from Pat Czarski and from his own manager, Tak Li, that Bob had told them privately that he did not intend to do the audit. Given that Mike had thought the matter settled, he was shocked by this turn of events. He was especially surprised because Bob's attendance at the physical inventory sent a clear signal to Mike of Bob's acceptance of the assignment. Over the next week when Mike saw Bob in the office corridor or in the washroom, he checked if Bob was planning to do the audit and got the impression that Bob was still agreeable to the arrangements made earlier. But then he would hear more secondhand reports from Pat and Tak that Bob was not planning to do the audit. So Mike decided to be more direct. "I guess that I precipitated a crisis from Bob's perspective. I said, 'Don't BS me. Tell me up front. What are you going to do instead?' We had frequent contact in the hallways. I would ask him if he'd had a chance to talk to Dominick Sousa. But Bob wouldn't say anything about it." At this point, Mike decided that Bob was

not being straight with him. He asked Pat and Tak to act as agents to see how Bob was reacting to the Softdisk project. "They would report one day that he was committed. Then the next day he had thought about it and wasn't committed any more."

This situation frustrated Mike immensely. His parents had lived in Hong Kong while Mike was growing up. His sister still lived there. "I have a better than average knowledge of cultural differences between Canadians and people from Hong Kong. I thought I was being effective." Mike decided an open discussion was necessary and wondered if Bob had not understood what a developmental opportunity the Softdisk audit was for furthering his professed career interest in tax consulting. Mike needed a fast and firm resolution to the problem because an auditor had to be in place by the end of July. If Bob would not do the job, then Mike would have to borrow a senior auditor from another James-Williams office, and the time pressure to brief such a replacement adequately would be extreme.

Mike decided to call a meeting with Bob, Pat and Tak for July 20. "I didn't want a fight but I wasn't going to take any BS. Tak and Pat weren't getting the same story that I was. Bob was telling them 'no' and me 'maybe.' I wanted to get all four of us in a room and finally get some straight answers. I was going to tell Bob, 'You want to be a tax consultant. Well, here is the opportunity.' "

On July 19, Bob met with Jane and asked for her help. Jane had supported Bob at partners' meetings and he felt she was an ally. Bob told Jane that he wanted to refuse the Softdisk job. He said he was concerned that the amount of planning time required for the Softdisk audit would interfere with a complex audit he was currently doing with a film company. He was afraid he might have to take leave from the film company audit. Jane asked if scheduling was his only concern. "Bob told me there was a bigger problem than scheduling. He didn't want to do the audit. He said he couldn't work for Mike but he wouldn't say why." Jane told Bob that he was crazy and not to do anything rash.

On July 20, Mike, Pat, Tak and Bob met for three hours. Most of the discussion centered around Mike's reemphasizing how the Softdisk job fit with Bob's career goals in tax consulting. "I kept dragging Bob back to the career goals he said he had and showing him that if he was serious about tax then this was an opportunity. I answered all of his objections. Pat, Tak and I left the meeting once again thinking that Bob had agreed to do the job."

Meanwhile, Joe Silverman had heard about the situation and started to have doubts about the desirability of Bob joining his tax group in the fall. Since he had never worked with Bob, he approached Jane and asked for more information. Joe said the grapevine was giving him a poor impression of Bob. In Joe's view, not only was it out of line for staff to refuse assignments from partners, but also the clients' interests were the number one concern of the firm. Yet Bob did not seem to be acknowledging either of these values. If Bob would not do the Softdisk audit, then Joe thought Bob should be forced out.

Jane agreed with Joe. She was shocked by Bob's behaviour and felt, as Bob's key backer in partners' meetings, very unhappy to be caught in the middle. She called Bob into her office and told him that both Mike and Joe were furious. She told Bob that his behaviour had put him in a bad position with Joe, who was to be Bob's new managing partner. Joe was very client-oriented and was unlikely to give Bob the benefit of the doubt, because he had never seen Bob's hard work firsthand. "I told him that it didn't seem to be the right time for taking a stand. He said he believed it was a serious enough problem to resist. He was willing to leave the firm rather than work with Mike on the audit. I was shocked. I thought he enjoyed working for the firm and that he saw himself as having a good long-term career here. I don't know if he had a personal problem about working with Mike. I've talked to Mike and he doesn't know either."

On Sunday night, July 22, Bob phoned Pat to say that he would not do the Softdisk audit. Pat informed Mike who washed his hands of the matter and obtained another senior auditor from the Richmond Hill office of James-Williams.

On the morning of July 23, Bob came to see Jane. He said he would have to resign because he could not work for Mike. He also said he realized he had ruined his relationships with the partners and could not expect good performance appraisals even if he did do the audit. Jane told him he was crazy to throw away his career at James-Williams. Jane thought that maybe he was right about getting a poor performance appraisal because Joe "was fit to be tied," but she suggested that Bob wait and talk to David who was returning from holiday the next day. Perhaps David could transfer Bob since David had a high opinion of Bob's worth to the company.

David's Decision

David Shorter returned from vacation on July 23. His first day back he met with Jane Klinck and Mike McLeod who briefed him about the trouble with Bob. He also met with Joe Silverman who came to express his outrage about Bob's behaviour.

On July 24, David sat at his desk thinking. Bob would be here in a few minutes. David had some decisions to make. He knew that Bob was threatening to resign rather than do the Softdisk audit. He knew that both Mike and Joe were furious, but if Bob worked hard in the future, he did not think that Joe would give Bob poor performance appraisals. He knew that Jane had a high opinion of Bob and could not understand what was causing Bob to act this way.

David knew he had to make a decision that balanced the needs of all the people involved. On the one hand, Bob had offended some fairly important partners with whom David had to work and maintain good relationships. David was under no illusion that he could tell these partners what to do or think. They were all partners together, and they decided together. Besides, David agreed with them that it was inappropriate to let an employee with the capacity and the time to do a job refuse it. The Softdisk job also looked like a good opportunity for someone who wanted to specialize in tax. David did not know why Bob had turned it down.

On the other hand, Bob was a valuable employee given his skills and his potential for helping the New Enterprise Group attract business from Hong Kong investors. In addition to his knowledge, as reflected by his passing the uniform C.A. exam on his first attempt, he spoke and wrote Chinese fluently, skills relevant to James-Williams's stated goal of attracting Hong Kong business. That objective was one reason why the James-Williams office had been opened in Hong Kong. Yet the office had not done well and was now closed, so David was uncertain of the importance of Bob to the Canadian strategy.

There was the possibility of a transfer. The "Tower" (James-Williams's main group in Toronto) had been requesting that seniors interested in specializing in tax be transferred to them because they anticipated a future demand for tax specialists. Maybe that was what Bob was hoping for. David suspected that some of Bob's friends had been transferred to the Tower without any audit responsibilities and that Bob had been comparing notes with them.

David was sure of one thing. He did not want to offend the other partners in the New Enterprise Group. Perhaps he could persuade Bob to stay, and do the job, and then start tax work. Bob was an emotional kind of guy. Maybe David could get him to see reason.

STEP 1: Read the David Shorter case.

STEP 2: Prepare the case for class discussion.

STEP 3: Answer the following questions, individually, in small groups, or with the class as a whole, as directed by your instructor.

DESCRIPTION

1. What was Chen's perception of his meeting with Shorter?
2. What was Chen's attribution of his not being assigned to tax?
3. Why did Chen refuse to do the Softdisk audit?
4. What did Shorter think about Chen's career steps?
5. What did Chen think about his own career?

DIAGNOSIS

6. Why are Shorter's and Chen's perceptions different?

7. What perceptual distortions occurred?
8. What were Chen's, Shorter's, and the other managers' attribution of Chen's refusal to perform the Softdisk audit?
9. What attributional biases occurred?
10. Do cross-cultural differences explain the perceptual and attributional differences?

PRESCRIPTION

11. What should Chen do?
12. What should Shorter do?

STEP 4: Discussion. In small groups, with the entire class, or in written form, share your answers to the preceding questions. Then answer the following questions:

1. What symptoms suggest that a problem exists?
2. What problems exist in the cases?
3. What theories and concepts help explain the problems?
4. How can the problems be corrected?
5. Are these actions likely to be effective?

LINK.COM–Mariana Torcelli's Story

After two years of working and developing the Eastern European and Middle Eastern region with very little support and resources, I went back to headquarters to make a case for more resources. They were surprised at what I had accomplished in that region. Revenue per capita in my region was the highest. This was not something that they liked to acknowledge, yet there it was. But when it came time to allocate resources, they didn't seem to take this fully into account.

Jerry, my boss's boss (Senior V.P. of Sales), said to me, "Mariana, you are really very highly regarded. People love you." I heard that over and over, to the point that I hate the word. It's like he was saying, "You are very highly respected, you are very well liked, so be satisfied with that." Yet I wanted resources so that I could grow my region even more, not just kind words.

Professor Joanne Martin and Visiting Professor Debra Meyerson, of the Graduate School of Business, Stanford University, prepared this case as a basis for class discussion rather than to illustrate effective or ineffective handling of an administrative situation. The organizational name, the people involved, and some details of the case have been disguised to protect anonymity and for teaching purposes. The preparers thank the individuals who contributed from their experience to build this case. The case was made possible by the generous support of the BankAmerica Foundation.

Yet, in general, I felt OK about my experiences at Link.Com because I did what I wanted to do. I felt competent. I knew I could do it and that helped my self-esteem, knowing that I had done it in a very tough region. Nobody expected me to succeed to the extent that I had. There's no doubt about it. It was a good experience.

Mariana joined Link.Com in late 1990 as Manager of International Marketing. She had been recruited to Link.Com by Natalie Kramer (then Vice President of Marketing) with whom she had previously worked at another high-growth computer company. In August, 1993, Mariana shifted her focus from marketing to sales, assuming the title of Regional Manager of Eastern European/Middle Eastern Operations. Her move over to sales enabled Mariana to gain more experience and visibility within a regional market and to build on her considerable skill in learning languages and cultures. Mariana became so successful developing this region that she was promoted to Director of Eastern European/Middle Eastern Operations in November of 1995, exactly five years after she had joined the company.

I developed Eastern Europe/Middle East and became the operations manager for this region, establishing channels, presence, everything that had to be done to get this huge thing going.

Mariana Torcelli: Against the Odds

When Mariana decided in 1993 to shift her focus from international marketing to sales within Eastern Europe and the Middle East, most colleagues who understood the company and the prospects for developing this region tried very hard to dissuade her from making this move. Mariana herself wondered why this transition appealed to her, given the region's image as a low-priority, low-potential market. Yet, from Mariana's perspective, the low visibility of this region also had its advantages.

Actually one of the things I enjoyed was that nobody knew anything about this region. So I had a free hand to do what I wanted to do, although investment-wise it was a little bit scary. Because it was not an important region, I really had to fight, to do lots of internal selling of the region myself.

Nobody really cared about this region and it wasn't important to the company. In fact, when I took this region, David Seidel (Senior Vice President, later to become CEO of Link.Com) told me that it's very dangerous and that I should not go there. And others, like Ricardo, the Director of European Sales, who asked me to go work in Europe instead, said, "Mariana, you will be making a stupid mistake. And you will regret it."

So I just said, "I love doing mistakes."

It was like Mariana to view this challenge as a great opportunity for professional development.

The reason I thought this would be great is if I failed, who would care? Nobody cared about it anyway. They would have all said, "I told you so." So if I succeeded, it would be fantastic because everybody thought it was nothing. So that was really to me a win-win situation. I was excited about learning new languages. And nobody will give me suggestions, because nobody knows and nobody cares. I didn't like someone telling me how to do things.

With limited resources beyond her persistence and skills, Mariana was determined to prove her colleagues wrong.

For two years, it was myself and one technical person. It was just in the last year that they let me hire other people to open offices.

The Link.Com Culture: Conformity, Confrontation, Resistance

The dominant culture at Link.Com during the early days was described by several employees and ex-employees as strong and "macho." This culture evoked a variety of behaviors ranging from resigned conformity to confrontation among people who didn't neatly "fit" into the dominant culture. Vivid and vocal expression of anger and aggression had been the norm among senior executives. To get what one wanted and needed within this culture, one had to be "outspoken," which often meant you had to yell and scream. Mariana looked at it this way:

The higher you screamed, the more powerful you were and the more you proved the point.

Those who learned to play by the dominant rules, learned to fight and fend for themselves.

Natalie would say to me, "Mariana, you should go and say that to Henry or to Steven and go to them and do this." I think in this way Natalie was my mentor in terms of telling me how to step out and fight for myself. I didn't like to fight; that was not my nature. I liked to work hard and have them recognize me, but that was not happening here. To get things done and to get what you needed you really had to go for it.

Mariana resisted conforming to these behavioral norms and instead chose to "go for it" in a manner that was more consistent with her own style, sense of self, and values. It was hard for her to determine whether her refusal to conform to these norms ultimately cost her.

In other ways, however, Mariana did conform to norms about emotional expression (and suppression). While some emotions, like anger, were seen as appropriate emotional expressions, others, like sadness and frustration, were viewed as signs of weakness. So Mariana and others learned to contain these feelings.

I wanted to stay up emotionally. Even when my father died, I kept my feelings to myself. I used to go back to my office and cry but I did not allow myself to show them emotion and that upset me. I didn't want anybody to say "woman's emotion."

In other ways, Mariana learned to work within the dominant culture without compromising her own beliefs about appropriate and inappropriate ways to communicate and conduct business. At Link.Com, there were ways to request resources that had proven to be more effective. Mariana learned to confront and work around dominant norms of the culture to secure what she needed and to work in a way that felt appropriate. For example, within Link.Com there existed norms about not giving positive feedback, although people openly and frequently expressed criticisms. This was not acceptable to Mariana. In one instance, after completing what had been an extremely smooth and successful tour of her region with Jim Nelson (then President and CEO of Link.Com) and his wife, Mariana wanted feedback from the CEO.

So when Jim was leaving, I went there and said, "Let's wrap up this trip. Just want to get your feedback, your recommendations, what you think of the trip and anything new you recommend." I wanted some feedback. So he sat and he gave me some recommendations, input about what he thought was good or bad within the region. He talked about others and said nothing about me. And I was really dying to hear how he perceived this whole thing.

And then Susan, his wife, said, "Jim, why don't you tell her something about how she did." Like this was a revolutionary idea. It was so obvious, the questions I was asking, the way I was putting it. I said everything short of "Jim, what do you think of me?" It was not ok within this culture to ask for feedback, particularly positive feedback. She picked it up. I'm sure he did, but he didn't want to say.

And then he actually said to her, "Susan, you know that we don't like to say good things about people." But she kept on. She said, "Go ahead, Jim. You don't want to lose her. Say something." Finally, he said to me "Okay, you did very well." I was right there, in front of him, during this whole conversation. He said, "You did very well." And that was it. It was a good trip, everything went on time, the distributors were just panicking that everything should be perfect. Perfect. And it was. Nothing was late, for a change.

Mariana's stance with respect to the dominant values and norms varied, depending on the circumstance and the extent to which she would have to change or bend her own beliefs and values to "fit" into the dominant culture. Under certain circumstances, she conformed, and under others she resisted, worked with, worked around, and even confronted aspects of the dominant culture.

Helping Others: Role Modeling and Mentoring

According to other women at Link.Com, Mariana represented the image of a determined woman persisting, overcoming obstacles, working steadily and effectively. Mariana had proven that women could be successful in sales, even in seemingly low-potential regions with limited resources, visibility, and support. One of her colleagues (Patricia Sullivan, Director Software) commented on how she and others looked up to Mariana.

Mariana was a tremendous role model in terms of what a woman at Link.Com could do because she made this move from marketing into sales—which is very difficult for anybody to do, male or female—and was extremely successful at it. She learned to speak Polish almost immediately. She had the distributors over there eating out of her hand. I think there was a lot of public perception of her as having been extremely successful. (Patricia Sullivan)

This sort of role modeling was not terribly visible, nor was it deliberate or heroic. It was role modeling alternative patterns of behavior, styles of management, and ways to work that were both successful and authentic, that neither emulated the dominant aggressive patterns nor rejected them outright.

Receiving Help and Support: Locating Mentors, Models, and Colleagues

Mariana developed a network of colleagues, including Natalie, who had hired her, and a few other women and men to whom she went for support, advice, and friendship. This network was limited. It was difficult for senior women to find suitable models of behavior and colleagues who could provide them support during difficult situations. On at least one occasion, Mariana had gone directly to Jim Nelson for advice about building a developmental network of colleagues and models for herself. He seemed surprised at just how difficult it was to locate others to whom Mariana or other senior women could turn.

I said to him "What do I do, Jim?" He said, "Well, I don't know. There are not too many women at the higher levels and you really have to do more networking. You have to get a mentor in the company." I said, "Who, Jim, who do you recommend?" And then he said, "Well, I'm very busy." He thought I was trying to ask him to be my mentor. I said, "I know you are very busy, so who should I get as a mentor? Definitely not Seidel." So, he said, "As you know, it's difficult for a woman to have that type of a relationship in Link.Com."

I was really surprised that he said that. He said, "It's difficult; it's not as easy but, you know, go and find a way." He acknowledged that it was difficult, but he would not push. He wouldn't make the case that we needed to do something about me and the other women in the company, or show that we were appreciated, or give us a chance to compete on an equal level.

Those people who were frequently excluded from important channels of communication had fewer opportunities to develop mentor relationships, which further excluded them from informal channels of advice and information. Mariana recalled a time when she would have benefited professionally from some simple advice and feedback.

Rather than telling me to shut up, or "Mariana, you really don't understand what we're trying to say," or, "No, we don't agree with you," they just let me get away with it. Maybe in my review or something they could have said, "You are not supposed to do something," but they would let me get away with it and do whatever I was doing that wasn't working well. My peers would say to me, "We went out for drinks and he (our boss) told me you shouldn't have done that." But our boss would never confront me that directly, at least when I could do something about it. For example, my boss said to me, "You know when we had that meeting a year ago, you were supposed to do this . . ." I said, "Why didn't you tell me a year ago? All along I thought I was doing the right thing." He just said, "I don't remember why; it was a year ago." I think he didn't tell me because he didn't know how to do it. Like he wasn't comfortable taking me out for drinks to tell me.

On more than one occasion, Mariana was denied some simple instrumental advice that would have helped her do her job more effectively. In addition, each of Mariana's male counterparts benefited from senior colleagues and mentors who helped champion their causes.

If Ricardo did anything wrong, nobody said anything. We had to just accept it and swallow it. Because David Seidel happened to be his mentor, when someone said something about Ricardo, who Seidel was really protecting, that meant you were insulting Seidel directly.

You made him look bad if you didn't protect someone he mentored. Natalie used to back me up. (And they would say) "How could you back her up?" I remember once I had lunch with Seidel, and he said, "Yes, I heard, Natalie said something about you." It was like he didn't believe it. Like I had done something positive and Natalie mentioned it to him. He said, "Yes, I heard about it." And then he discounted it. He would never say, "I'm really happy about it. This is great. You did good work." I never hear those words, only what I could do better.

For this reason, colleagues like Natalie Kramer and some of the other women and men at Link.Com were especially valuable and important to Mariana, and she regularly turned to them for advice about how to work effectively and survive within the Link.Com culture.

Natalie did encourage me to really get into that, and to develop the confidence necessary to really stand up for what I feel and just keep pushing and to do it the right way. And although she criticized herself sometimes, she would tell us how to do it in a way that she wouldn't necessarily do it, because it wasn't her style. But she'd tell us, "This could be done this way if you want to get along." For example, she'd help us be political with the men and get what we need in a situation.

She helped me talk to David Seidel to get what I needed. She encouraged me to push myself to be as open as I could to describe my agenda, and to let him know what I was doing, because nobody else was talking about me to him. She made me realize that I had to promote myself to some extent and to keep people informed about what I was doing and what I needed.

Although isolated in many respects, Mariana felt fortunate to have developed a small network of women colleagues. Even though scheduling around everyone's travel was very difficult, Mariana and these other senior women managed to meet periodically for dinner, support, and some good laughs.

(In)equities in Pay and Promotion

Mariana developed the Eastern European/Middle Eastern Region with very limited resources, particularly in comparison to those with which her peers launched their regions. Most of her counterparts started out with resources that would support the projected growth of their regions; they were staffed up to *create* the projected growth. Mariana had to first create the growth in sales, and then use this growth to justify the resources to support it. This meant that Mariana had to work extraordinarily hard, without sufficient resources, to build her region to earn more resources ultimately to support further growth.

At the time I needed people for my region, I learned to spell out (and create) the return on the investment, rather than just say up front that I needed it. Other regions just had to say what they needed to start. And management would come back and say, "Okay, maybe we will need to put that up front, although we don't have that visibility of the return right away."

Despite the limited resources and support given to her, Mariana was successful beyond anyone's expectation in developing her region. However, compared to her counterparts in other regions, Mariana felt that she had not received the visibility and rewards she had earned. Although she was usually reluctant to attribute discrepancies to gender differences, Mariana was certain that being a woman played a part in how she was treated relative to her male counterparts. However, the nature and extent of this bias was difficult for her to determine.

I'm sure if I were a man I would have definitely been recognized faster, and I would have been considered for other positions.

I don't know how much the men were paid. I didn't know what was the equivalent. I knew we had a scale for the bonus plan, but the base salary and the stock options, I had no idea.

The possibility of inequity within the sales function is notable given the clarity of performance criteria in this area. Patricia Sullivan, one of Mariana's colleagues, pointed to this as blatant and visible evidence of bias.

I think the very frustrating thing about Mariana's situation was that in non-sales jobs there were all sorts of ways to fool around with the metrics including not establishing them, or not being clear about what they are. The image, certainly, that I have always had looking from the outside in is that sales was the one area where metrics were absolutely clear. You met your revenue numbers or you didn't. You met your stretch goal or you didn't. There was no way to fudge on that, no way to be inconsistent about that. It is extremely frustrating when there is a situation like that, where you knew you had your revenue targets and you had your stretch targets and you were performing to those targets and there was still no reward and there was still no recognition. What else was there? What else was standing in the way? I think it was a lot easier in non-sales areas to fall back on the fact that the expectations really weren't clear; the metrics really weren't clear. It's whether you did or didn't fit into the culture. I think you can argue, to some extent, whether that was right or wrong from the standpoint of the company—whether cultural fit, how somebody integrates in the environment, should or shouldn't have been a metric of performance. But in a sales environment, it didn't seem like it should ever have been an issue. (Patricia Sullivan)

Yet when it came time for pay and promotion, the more nebulous criteria, such as "fit" or "lack of fit," seemed to play a part. Mariana sensed that she had been passed over repeatedly for promotions that she rightfully had earned.

When they hired my counterpart for Asia, that person was not experienced with our products and didn't know how we did things within the company. He was a very good person, a very good salesperson, but they hired him at the director level, virtually. He walked into an already developed region. Yet he was made a director. At that time I was a regional manager. Yet I had grown my entire region and had all of the responsibilities he had as a director. I wanted to say, "You hired this person immediately at a director level, and I am proving myself to you every year?"

To Mariana, this was another example of having to go beyond what was expected to prove herself, while her male counterparts were given the benefit of the doubt up-front. When she felt the situation and her own integrity demanded that she call attention to a perceived inequity, she confronted her managers. This had been such a situation:

They said, "No, but this is different. You have to really show us how things are." They never explained why they (hired him as a director and kept me as regional manager). Which to me meant that this happened because I was a woman. That's what I think. I went to Jerry (the Vice President who hired my boss) and said, "Why wasn't I considered for that position? Do you think I am not capable?" And he said, "No. You are capable. Mariana, we really have to consider many people" and so on. And I said, "Was I considered?" He as much as said "No." I said, "Why? You've seen me perform—I've been at Link.Com for over 4 years. Why? Why wouldn't you even have that thought?" And then I said, "Were my (male) counterparts considered?" He said, "Yes."

Mariana took pride in her ability to manage her emotions. However, in this instance, it was difficult to contain her outrage.

Mariana and some of her women colleagues explained the persistence of this pattern of inequities and "oversights" as "the glass half-full vs. half-empty" phenomenon. This bias in interpretations consistently gave men credit and the benefit of any doubt, particularly before they had the chance to earn respect, resources, or status. Under similar circumstances, women were primarily given only the doubt and therefore had to work extra hard to prove themselves worthy of comparable credit and resources.

This bias and the perceived inequities generated mixed feelings about Link.Com. Mariana had become tired of swallowing her frustration. In addition, after being passed over for promotion for so long, when she finally did receive her long-awaited promotion to Director, it had lost much of its significance. However, Mariana had also profited enormously from her experience at Link.Com and felt great loyalty and gratitude for the opportunities she had had at the company.

You know, they really didn't treat me badly. They didn't appreciate me as they would have appreciated other people. I don't think they were mean to me or anything. And my style was really to focus on the job, ignore the different messages I was getting, and not get into the politics of the company. I just got out and did the job. I had wonderful people that I was working with. I worked with the people. We just kept going. So when I was finally given the promotion, it didn't mean anything to me because in my mind I had already received it.

At times, she was even willing to overlook and discount the pay and promotion inequities, given the wealth that had been created for her (and others) through her stock options.

The Future at Link.Com?

Mariana's success in her region eventually translated into a reputation within the industry.

I had earned a lot of visibility in the industry in the market and received lots of phone calls from people wanting me to do the same thing in different companies.

Shortly after receiving her promotion to Director, Mariana received an outside offer that was hard to ignore—the title of Vice President at a competitive firm, ample resources, growth opportunities, the ability to become an important and visible member of an executive team. With mixed feelings, Mariana recalled the attractiveness of the offer.

I never gave a presentation to the Executive Staff or Board at Link.Com. I always made the presentation to my boss, because I needed his approval. At first I ignored (this problem). If I take this job, I want to give presentations to the board. I've never done that.

However, the thought of leaving Link.Com, particularly her region, was painful to her. She had finally received her hard-earned promotion to Director, she had become part of the senior team, and she still had much to do in her region. She felt that leaving the region she had nurtured would be, in a sense, leaving her "baby."

I had this opportunity and I really thought it was good for my career. However, it was really difficult for me because I did develop the Eastern European and Middle Eastern markets and I really felt that this region was my baby. And it was so hard to let go. I was supposed to have received the promotion a year earlier and I had fought for it. My counterpart never (had to fight for it). It was just handed to him with great love. I had to fight for it and I had to prove myself every time. I should not have had to request it. I have had to swallow my anger because I really (loved) the region. And I cared so much

about my people. I had real trouble with leaving something half or almost done.

Mariana's dedication to her region and concern for her staff had overshadowed much of the resentment she had felt toward her managers. In the past, she had swallowed her feelings in an effort to keep going and not disappoint her staff, even during extremely trying times. She didn't want to let them down.

STEP 1: Read the case.

STEP 2: Prepare the case for class discussion.

STEP 3: Answer the following questions, individually, in small groups, or with the class as a whole, as directed by your instructor.

DESCRIPTION

1. How was business conducted at Link.com?
2. What positions did Torcelli hold in the company?
3. How did Torcelli interact with other employees and managers?

DIAGNOSIS

4. What types of personality issues existed?
5. What were Torcelli's values, and how did they fit with the company's culture?
6. Were pay and rewards allocated equitably?
7. What were the norms in the company?
8. What types of mentoring existed (and didn't exist)? Were they effective?

PRESCRIPTION

9. How could the situation have been improved?

ACTION

10. What should Torcelli do now?

STEP 4: Discussion. In small groups, with the entire class, or in written form, share your answers to the preceding questions. Then answer the following questions:

1. What symptoms suggest that a problem exists?
2. What problems exist in the case?
3. What theories and concepts help explain the problems?
4. How can the problems be corrected?
5. Are these actions likely to be effective?

Chapter 6

Creating High-Performing Work Groups and Teams

Learning Objectives

After completing Chapter 6, you will be able to

1. Identify the types of teams and work groups typically found in organizations.
2. Diagnose the basic characteristics of groups and teams at work.
3. Comment about the advantages and uses of group decision making.
4. Discuss the use of electronic and other group decision-making techniques.
5. Discuss ways of empowering members of teams and groups.
6. Offer four strategies for managing teams effectively.
7. Specify the issues that affect team behavior in the dot-com, global workplace.

A Manager's Preview

Describe . . . Diagnose . . . Prescribe . . . Act

- Understand the basics of team functioning.
- Know when to use group and individual decision making.
- Have a repertoire of group decision-making techniques.
- Create high-performing teams.
- Empower team members to lead and make decisions.
- Reward team members for performance.
- Manage teams effectively in cross-cultural settings.

Creating Teams for a Competitive Edge at Brunswick and Marriott

*I*ncreasingly, companies are creating teams that include information technology (IT) staff and members of other functional areas as a way of gaining an advantage over their competitors. For example, Brunswick Corporation, a manufacturer of recreation equipment, combined members of its purchasing and IT departments to design agreements with two telecom suppliers for the company, resulting in a 20 percent cost savings on its annual $7 million expense. The company uses a multifunctional team called TAG, technology acquisition group, for this and other nonroutine purchases. Because the company believes that purchasing is the key to the successful leveraging of technology, integrating the two functions provides opportunities for Brunswick in areas such as e-commerce and vendor selection. IT has learned that a partnership with purchasing improves their supplier management; purchasing has learned that the partnership creates new opportunities for cost savings across the organization, not just in the products the company sells. Working together, IT and purchasing can better accomplish the organization's objectives.[1]

Marriott International, Inc., has attempted to increase its competitive advantage by aligning its IT group with its business strategy, thus creating partnerships with business units instead of limiting them to the purchasing function. For example, Marriott formed teams of business and IT managers that benchmarked existing processes and then developed short-term and long-term action plans for improving them. The chief information officer participated in the company's quarterly meeting with top-volume business customers to address ways of improving relationships with them. Most IT projects have an executive sponsor, a project owner from the business, often a department manager, and a project owner from IT, typically an IT manager. The business and technology project leaders share accountability for the project. Such partnerships allow Marriott to consider the technological aspects of new initiatives at early stages of project development. In addition, IT executives participate in all business strategy review meetings.[2]

Brunswick and Marriott created two types of teams commonly found in the workplace today. Changes in work have encouraged multifunctional teams, the alignment of various functions with corporate strategy, the elimination of layers of management, and increases in workers' responsibilities. We can use traditional concepts about groups and new ways of thinking about teams to improve organizational behavior.

In this chapter, we first look at some types of teams and work groups. Then we consider the basic characteristics of groups and teams at work. We next examine decision making in groups. We then investigate ways of empowering members of teams and groups. Next we offer ways of managing teams for effectiveness. We conclude with issues for groups and teams in the dot-com, global workplace.

▌TYPES OF TEAMS AND WORK GROUPS

In this chapter, we use the labels "work group" and "team" relatively interchangeably, although subtle differences in the terms exist for some people. For example, some consider that a work group includes two or more people who may work independently in a work setting with a common goal, whereas teams generally call for collaboration in accomplishing the goal. Like work groups, teams generally pass through similar stages of development and focus on a common goal. Members develop norms and roles for performing. Unlike work groups, managers generally create teams for a specific purpose, often with a short-term horizon. Teams often differ from work groups in the intensity with which they work on specific tasks or projects. Project teams are generally time limited and produce a new product or service, new internal system, new program, and so on. Teams may contrast with *informal groups,* which arise spontaneously and may form around friendships between co-workers or interests shared by employees in different formal groups. Increasingly, however, the distinction between work group and team has become blurred since most work groups act as teams on some occasions. Both teams and work groups can exist at various levels in the organization, ranging from top-management teams to teams of lower-level employees.

Traditionally Managed Versus Self-Managed Teams

Teams or work groups can either be traditionally managed or self-managed. *Traditionally managed* teams have a designated individual who serves as the official leader or manager. *Self-managed* teams have members who share responsibility for managing the work group without an officially appointed leader. Such a team has full responsibility for completing a well-defined part of the work, generally the finished product or service or a significant component of it, and members have discretion over decisions.[3] Asea Boveri Brown, a Swedish-Swiss company, introduced self-managing teams to make employees more accountable for their performance by giving them control of day-to-day activities, many of which managers had previously controlled.[4]

While managers do not oversee the daily work activities of self-directed team members, they may continue to coach the team, develop an overall strategy for the teams in their area, champion innovation, provide resources for the team, and reinforce the team's accountability. The manager also serves as a liaison to other parts of the organization, suppliers, and customers. U.S. companies such as General Electric, 3M, and Intel also use self-managing teams. 3M, for example, has teams that help create new products and operate well in a risk-taking, creativity-focused environment.[5]

Permanent Versus Temporary Teams

Teams can also be *relatively permanent* or *temporary*. Relatively permanent groups work together for long periods of time, generally at least one year, on a repetitive set of tasks. Temporary teams form for short, prespecified amounts of time to complete a unique set of tasks or projects. Often this type of team draws its members from different functional areas or other work groups in the organization. For example, a bank may form a temporary team to manage its acquisition of another bank. David's Bridal created a temporary team to oversee the temporary technical staff that supports its e-commerce business start-up. The team also trains call-center employees who handle sales from the bridal-clothing retailer's Web site.[6] The introduction and use of problem-solving teams in an aluminum manufacturing plant resulted in increased productivity in both the short term and the long run.[7]

Sometimes companies that introduce an enterprise resource planning system (a comprehensive information system) use a temporary team to cover old jobs while other workers make the transition to the new information system. The New York law firm of Skadden, Arps, Slate, Meagher, and Flom used a temporary team of about a dozen employees to implement an integrated payroll and human resource system. Two of these people served full-time on the team at a time, while the remainder covered the employees' regular jobs.[8]

Single-Discipline Versus Cross-Functional Teams

Teams can contain individuals from *single* or *multiple* disciplines or functions. Cross-functional work groups, such as the TAG team at Brunswick, have become increasingly common in organizations because they bring diverse expertise to complex problems. They also improve coordination and integration among groups, break down organizational boundaries, and reduce cycle time in new product development.[9] The plant manager at Burlington Industries' Klopman Fabric dyeing and finishing complex established 24 cross-functional teams. They posted strategy boards in each department to encourage communication and goal setting relating to a series of problems encountered in the plant. The creation of the teams resulted in improved communication and better employee morale. Plant performance also increased, resulting in fewer seconds, reworks, and late deliveries, as well as lower supply costs.[10] General Electric created cross-functional teams in every business unit to present a hypothetical Web-based business plan for e-commerce. As part of the planning, they assessed competitors' strengths and weaknesses, their own products and services, and the economics of ordering through the Web versus other channels. Known as "Destroy Your Business," this exercise focused on helping business units visualize the future and how e-commerce would affect them.[11]

THE BASIC CHARACTERISTICS OF WORK GROUPS AND TEAMS

Managers and other employees can create and participate in effective work groups and teams by understanding their basic characteristics and how they contribute to effectiveness. The reasons for group formation and the nature of their development—as well as the way groups use member resources, set goals, establish norms, and determine roles—play a major part in ensuring group or team effectiveness.

Why Work Groups Form

Work groups form for a variety of reasons:

- **Common needs.** Members of groups such as cycling or triathalon teams may need variety or challenge. Others, such as members of a food cooperative or a neighborhood watch, may join to satisfy their basic needs for food, shelter, and security.
- **Common interests.** Professors join professional associations to share their interests in specific research or teaching areas, furthering their knowledge and enhancing the image of their profession. Employees from various departments in an e-commerce business may join a task force to work on improving the quality of working life.
- **Common goals.** Employees in the purchasing department at a company may share the common goal of finding the best vendors and securing the best prices for products purchased by their companies.
- **Physical proximity.** Often employees who work in the same department or in the same type of job share social activities. IT staff who work in one functional area typically develop a group identity that affects their work reputation.
- **Cultural similarity.** New immigrants join organizations where their fellow countrypeople work. U.S. workers living abroad join groups with other Americans both on and off the job.

Although work groups may form because of common needs, physical proximity, or even cultural similarity, such groups generally are less effective than those that form because they have common goals and interests. Increasingly, groups or teams form to take advantage of diverse experiences and skills, often resulting in a culturally diverse work group.

Group Cohesion.   Effective groups generally are attractive and cohesive. *Attractiveness*, the extent to which groups appeal to people so they want to belong, increases as people outside the group view it as more cooperative, prestigious, smaller, successful, and interactive.[12] Group membership can lose its attractiveness if the new members of a work group feel that the group makes unreasonable demands on them, if some members dominate the group too often, or if competition exists between members. When a group no longer meets an individual's needs, membership becomes less attractive. As the attractiveness of group membership falls, individuals make less effort to perform well and reach the group's goals.

   Cohesive groups have a tendency to stick together and remain united in pursuit of their objectives or their members' satisfaction.[13] Those groups with a strong interpersonal attraction among group members demonstrate increased performance, satisfaction, quality of interaction, and goal attainment.[14] Coaches of sports teams work hard at building cohesion among their players because it enhances performance.

Cohesiveness develops most easily in small, homogeneous, and stable groups; too many changes in membership in a short time hurt cohesion.[15] So cohesion can change over time.[16] Highly cohesive groups attract workers because the groups show high commitment to the task and provide a strong identity for organizational members. As cohesive groups work together, they become even more cohesive. While increased cohesiveness can have positive results, in some situations it may result in lowered productivity because group members focus on social interactions rather than task performance.

How Work Groups Develop

Work groups and teams change over time as their knowledge and involvement with their task increases, as they develop better (or sometimes worse) ways of working together, or as the time to complete a project gets shorter. Managers can diagnose a group's stages to expedite its progress and performance.

Progressive Model of Development.   The traditional view of group development looks at development as a five-stage process, as shown in Figure 6-1.[17] Each stage involves activities directed both at performing the task (*task activity*) and dealing with the interpersonal interactions within the group (*group process*) needed to accomplish the task. The solid arrows represent the typical development of a group from one stage to the next and within stages. Creating an effective group requires dealing with the challenges and issues of each stage and moving to the next stage. Note that this model may have some limitations in diagnosing team behavior, particularly because teams often have a different, less formalized leadership structure. In addition, its application to virtual teams has not been tested.

1. **Orientation to task (forming).**   The work group looks at its task and determines what information it needs to perform it. Group members try out various roles, such as leader, gatekeeper of information, or agenda setter, testing their functioning. Each person individually and through negotiating with other group members tries to determine the interpersonal behaviors required to perform the group's task. In groups with formally appointed leaders, during the first stage the leader will provide a structure by conducting regular meetings and encouraging widespread participation of the group. Sometimes, chaos and less systematic functioning and processing of information characterize the first stage. The team members need to find an effective way to focus on the team's goal and on their individual contributions. A group may not progress beyond the first stage if it lacks the skills to screen out irrelevant information and behavior or if members can't find effective ways of working together.

2. **Redefinition of appropriate behavior (storming).**   The group redefines its task based on the information acquired during orientation and the abilities and preferences of the group members. The task activities of this stage focus on team members offering emotional responses to the demands of the task. They determine whether they like the task and their degree of commitment to it. Disagreements by members of the group in their reactions to the task demands often lead to the group process of *intragroup conflict*.

FIGURE 6-1

Groups pass through a series of predictable stages as part of their development.

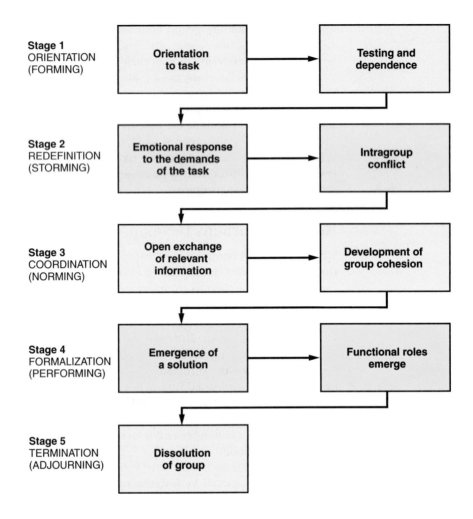

Stage 1 ORIENTATION (FORMING)	Orientation to task → Testing and dependence
Stage 2 REDEFINITION (STORMING)	Emotional response to the demands of the task → Intragroup conflict
Stage 3 COORDINATION (NORMING)	Open exchange of relevant information → Development of group cohesion
Stage 4 FORMALIZATION (PERFORMING)	Emergence of a solution → Functional roles emerge
Stage 5 TERMINATION (ADJOURNING)	Dissolution of group

Members may differ in the amount of time they will devote to a particular task, the priority they assign to the task, or the means they feel will best accomplish it. The sharper these differences, the greater the intragroup conflict that results. A manager who anticipates such differences may be able to reduce the conflict or make it functional for the group. Because group interaction typically increases, conflict over control among the group's members and with the group's leader may occur. Group members attempt to gain influence; they also test, judge, and evaluate each other. The effective leader at this stage encourages team members to express their ideas and concerns. Typically, at this stage of development the group lacks good mechanisms for dealing with conflict.

3. **Coordination of group behaviors (norming).**   An open exchange of relevant information occurs. Group members acknowledge that different emotional responses to the task are legitimate. For example, some workers may become frustrated about lack of progress toward a goal, while others just become more determined to accomplish it. IT and purchasing at Brunswick may disagree about the best vendor for particular hardware or software. IT and the business

unit may disagree about a project timeline at Marriott. This stage often lasts longest due to the time needed to collect and interpret information and to resolve disagreements about the meaning of the data, the nature of the task, and alternative tactics. Ideally, the members resolve their differences after an open exchange of relevant information and opinions, and begin to act as a cohesive group.

Group cohesion typically develops at this stage as the group once again becomes focused on task accomplishment. Members can now voice their disagreements. The leader encourages the team members to openly express their concerns. He assigns challenging problems for the group to solve by consensus and begins to delegate significant amounts of responsibility to team members. Note that some groups do not complete this stage. They disintegrate because they cannot resolve the intragroup conflict of the previous stage and group cohesion does not develop. "Hot groups," which originated in the start-ups of the Silicon Valley and Route 128 in Massachusetts, are goal-focused, tough-minded, task-focused groups of workers who develop social relationships later if they develop them at all.[18]

4. **Formalization of functional group behavior (performing).**   The group performs its task by making final decisions, concluding projects, or creating a solution to a problem. At this stage, the team must effectively resolve issues that arose at previous stages of group development, including their various emotional responses to the task, their differing interpretations of relevant information and opinions, and their specific proposals for action. In the group process component of this stage, *functional roles* emerge as a way of problem solving. These roles match the group's needs for leadership and expertise, the members' abilities and attitudes, and the group's tasks.

5. **Termination of the group (adjourning).**   Some groups recycle through the stages of development, particularly as changes in the group's membership, task, or environment occur. They begin again with Stage 1 and repeatedly proceed through the stages with each new project or decision. Some groups dissolve after Stage 4 either because they have accomplished their goals or are unable to do so.

Punctuated Equilibrium Model of Development.   Managers can think about group development as a noncontinuous model, also known as the *punctuated equilibrium model.*[19] As Figure 6-2 shows, a project team with the job of designing a new information system to expedite purchasing decisions drops its old behavior patterns, adopts new ones, and makes immediate and significant progress toward accomplishing the goal halfway through the time allocated for the project. This pattern fits with our image of people working toward a deadline: At first they don't focus intensely, but as the deadline approaches, they work much harder and ultimately finish the project on time.

Think about a newly created e-commerce business development team at a well-established retailer. During their first few meetings, team members keep discussing ways of proceeding. Not all members agree, and the group appears to reach a stalemate. At the fourth meeting, they agree to an acceptable way of proceeding and begin to work on the project. According to the punctuated equilibrium model, this approach to the project will continue until about halfway to the deadline for completing the project. The group will then move from Phase 1 through the transition period into Phase 2. During Phase 2, they will work together differently, in more productive ways that result in completing the project on time. The break and significant reorientation during the

▌FIGURE 6-2 ▌

Project groups may focus more clearly on their goal and change their ways of working at the midpoint of their existence.

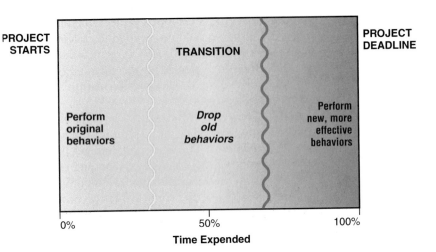

transition period characterize the punctuated equilibrium model, in which a smooth, continuous development of the work group does not occur.

Recent research questions the punctuated equilibrium model. It concludes instead that the pattern of activity and reorientation reflects the pacing of task activities under a deadline rather than group development.[20]

Habitual Routines of Groups.   As part of their development, groups that focus on task performance, such as special project groups, frequently develop *habitual routines* that affect group performance.[21] The routines begin at the start of the project and continue until halfway through it. Some routines may try to get the job done or coordinate activities. Other routines may help maintain the team's energy and spirit. Still others may focus on evaluating and improving team performance. For example, members of TAG may have standard ways of proceeding with decisions about new vendors.

Such routines help groups save time and energy, develop a shared agreement about the situation, and develop a shared plan about proceeding. The routines can also foster coordination among group members, often freeing some to work on new challenges. Because of the comfort created by routines, they also contribute to members' confidence in performing their roles and reduce the likelihood that the group members will perceive their peers as behaving in unacceptable ways. Groups, like individuals, can develop bad habits, causing habitual routines to result in reduced performance, decreased innovation, or other undesirable outcomes. Work teams may import, create, or develop such routines over time. As decision making occurs lower in the organization, workers may develop new routines for agenda setting, task performance, and job sequencing.

Obviously, managers may want to encourage certain routines and discourage others to ensure high performance. For example, in an IT–business unit partnership, such as at Marriott, if IT always leads project development meetings and delays have occurred in implementation, the company may want the business unit managers to lead project development. Changing routines often requires significant attention and effort. The impetus for such a change may occur when groups encounter a novel or changed situation or when they experience failure. Change can also occur when they reach a milestone in group life or cope with a change in the group's structure, task, or authority. Both the timing of the change and the tenacity of the routine affect the ease with which it can be altered.

External Relations and Group Development.   Understanding group development also involves considering the group's external relationships. Teams that interact frequently with groups outside their work group move through five stages.[22] Consider these stages for a group developing a new product:

1. **Creation.**   Group members converse extensively with other members and with people outside the team.
2. **First transition.**   The members move from recognizing the feasibility of a product to committing to a single product idea.
3. **Development.**   The group spends a lot of time coordinating activities with external groups. This stage begins with ensuring that the technical work groups who help develop the product function effectively. Then the group shifts to building and maintaining relationships with other groups.
4. **Second transition.**   The team then moves from "owning" the product to making sure that the rest of the organization values it and works to get it to market.
5. **Ending.**   The group spreads its knowledge to others outside the group. It increases its external activities. The group continues to transfer information about the product to other marketing and manufacturing groups, making sure that they have assumed ownership of the product.

Group Member Resources

A work group's performance depends in part on the resources of its members. These include the skills, experiences, and personalities of group members. For example, group members bring skills both in performing the group's task and in implementing an effective group process. They may either have a lot of experience functioning on teams or have worked solely as individual contributors in their organization. Differences in personality can affect group functioning. Introverted team members may find it challenging to work with extroverted members, and vice versa. Employees with Type A personalities may approach their work with more intensity than those with Type B personalities.

Increasingly, managers deal with a diverse workforce that results in equally diverse teams. Diverse team membership should enhance group decision making by bringing more perspectives, creative ideas, and potential solutions to the problem being discussed. It should also increase the synergy within the group as members interact and develop group ideas. Functional diversity, for example, was correlated with new development efforts, resulting in a faster time-to-market in the computer industry.[23]

Diversity can also reduce group performance because of a detrimental effect on cohesion when members focus on the other group members who are most like themselves, often contributing to confusing expectations and unequal power among members. Recent research suggests that a small amount of diversity may be most desirable; perceptions of effectiveness decline as the diverse subgroup exceeds about one-third of the group.[24]

Managers must develop the skills for managing and reaping the benefits of such diversity. Managers need to diagnose the resources that individuals bring to their teams and help them use them advantageously in accomplishing team and organizational goals. SBC Communications, for example, offers significant training to managers regarding diversity. The company also has significant policies that foster diversity and expects its managers to adhere to them.[25]

Setting Goals

The Brunswick TAG may have had a goal of reducing the cost of telecom services by 15 percent. The Marriott IT–business unit teams may have had a goal of reducing customer complaints by 10 percent. Goals such as these help members of high-performing work groups focus on common expectations and results. *Formal goals,* those specifically stated orally or in writing, typically relate directly to the organization's goals and mission. *Informal goals,* those implied by the team members' actions but not explicitly stated, can either contribute to or impede an organization's goal accomplishment. Agreement about group goals increases the group cohesiveness, or bonding. Agreement also helps focus team activities and the creation of appropriate roles and norms, as described in the next sections.

As noted in Chapter 4, the most effective goals are challenging, specific, measurable, and accepted by group members. For example, "reducing the cost of word processing software by 5 percent" is more specific than "getting better prices from software suppliers." In addition to broad goals, most groups also have subgoals or objectives that identify milestones to attaining the group goal. For example, a new product team may have the objective of obtaining the results of a market research study within one month, having a completed prototype of the product three months later, test-marketing it for six months, and then making revisions to the product plan.

Lack of clear, performance-related goals causes team failures.[26] Unfortunately, groups frequently do not have such goals. Instead, the members' individual goals dominate the group's goal. What would happen if one group member wants to use performance on the project as a springboard to a job in another company? What would happen if one of the team members wants to sabotage the project? These individual goals, often referred to as *hidden agendas* because individuals hide them from the group, can hinder team performance. A well-functioning group develops ways to regularly surface hidden agendas.

Establishing Norms

Norms refer to the unwritten and informal expectations that guide the behavior of group and organizational members. In the Marriott IT project teams, one norm might be that business needs take priority in the design of all information systems, independent of the newest technology available. In other situations, the norms might include primary decision making by IT specialists and little involvement of business unit leadership.

Sometimes norms develop through the interaction of team members as they reinforce certain behaviors and discourage others. For example, if team members encourage participation in agenda setting and decision making from all team members, involvement becomes a norm. If a first and then a second employee consistently comes to work late and the team accepts tardiness from these workers, tardiness may become a norm.

Sometimes the initial pattern of behavior becomes a norm. At other times, supervisors or co-workers may explicitly state certain expectations.[27] Group members can also transfer behavior from other groups; this behavior then becomes the norm in their present group. For example, a group member may bring a "work ethic" from a previous job, which she then practices in her new job, causing other group members to practice it as well. Alternatively, critical events, such as the appointment of a new leader, may establish norms.

Types of Norms and Their Impact on Performance.   We can classify norms according to their importance to organizational functioning, as follows:

- **Pivotal norms** guide behavior essential to the core mission of the organization. Pivotal norms include expectations about attendance, production, involvement in decision making, and acceptance of leadership.
- **Peripheral norms** guide behaviors that are important, but not essential, to achieving the organization's goals or mission. Peripheral norms include expectations about dress or social interactions outside the workplace.

We can also classify norms according to the amount of a behavior expected.

- **Unattainable-ideal norms** describe behavior in which "more is better":[28] for example, the more customer inquiries answered by customer service, the better.
- **Preferred-value norms** refer to behavior that either too much or too little of elicits disapproval from group members. For example, the workers in a self-managing team may disapprove if one worker outshines the others in productivity or if a worker does not produce his or her share.
- **Attainable-ideal norms** describe a particular behavior that group members approve increasing amounts of until they reach their goal, but do not value beyond the goal. An advertising executive will receive approval for each new campaign idea she suggests until the client chooses one, at which point thinking of additional ideas will not be useful.

Generally, a work group's norms help accomplish its goals. Pivotal norms of high productivity, participation, and openness contribute to improved group performance. Group performance norms correlate positively with team ratings of performance, although not with managers' ratings.[29] In contrast, violation of peripheral norms by employees typically has fewer negative consequences for the worker and the organization. If a worker wears a suit on "dress-down day," his co-workers may tease him but will not shun him.

Compliance with Norms.   A group reinforces norms that express its central values, help it survive, and clarify the group's identity. Groups also encourage norms that predict the behavior of group members and prevent embarrassing interpersonal problems from arising.[30] Groups can apply *sanctions*, coercive measures adopted to encourage agreement among the group members and compliance with the norms. Sanctions include verbal reprimands or ridicule, formal punishments such as fines or firings, or informal actions such as isolation from the group. Compliance with norms tends to increase as the group's size decreases or as its homogeneity, visibility, or stability increases.[31] Diagnosing a team's norms and its compliance with them can help a manager understand and improve group performance.

Determining Roles

Roles refer to the set of expected behaviors associated with particular work and nonwork functions or positions. A male executive may hold the roles of manager, vice president of engineering, husband, father, and chairperson of the United Way drive. We can think of roles as generally falling into three categories, as shown in the role checklist in Figure 6-3: task, maintenance, and individual roles.[32]

- **Task roles.** Task roles focus on task or goal accomplishment. Think of the purchasing–IT teams at Brunswick. What tasks do they have to accomplish? They need to find the best vendors for various IT and other functional-area services and supplies. What roles are required to accomplish this task? A team member may act as a coordinator of activities, seeker or giver of information, evaluator of problem-solving strategies, or implementor of these strategies.

- **Maintenance roles.** Roles such as harmonizer, encourager, and gatekeeper help build and maintain group performance. These *maintenance roles* focus less on task and more on group process. For example, these roles may alleviate tension among group members or support the learning of individual workers. They may also encourage individual participation and communication. The person fulfilling the maintenance role of group observer makes a major contribution to the group's effectiveness by monitoring group operations and providing feedback about the quality of team performance.[33]

- **Individual roles.** While both task and maintenance roles tend to be functional and constructive, *individual roles* tend to be dysfunctional or destructive for the group, simply because they place individual needs above those of the group. Think of a team or group to which you have belonged that was ineffective. Did one individual try to dominate the group? Did that person interrupt others and attempt to gain attention? Other individual roles reflect recognition-seeking behavior, resisting group progress, or passively avoiding group activities.

A group member may perform more than one role, or several members may perform the same role. Frequently, a pattern of roles emerges for each group member, which over time should be adjusted to help accomplish the group's goals and

FIGURE 6-3

Managers can use this checklist to diagnose the roles played by each team member.

Task Roles	Maintenance Roles	Individual Roles
✓ Agenda setter	—— Encourager	—— Avoider
—— Analyzer	—— Follower	✓ Blocker
—— Coordinator	—— Gatekeeper	—— Clown
—— Evaluator	✓ Group observer	✓ Dominator
—— Information giver	—— Harmonizer	—— Recognition seeker
✓ Information seeker	✓ Standard setter	—— Other:
—— Initiator	—— Other:	
—— Other:		

meet the individual's needs. Introducing self-managed work teams can change the roles of group members. For example, self-managed teams frequently rotate roles so that everyone has the chance to develop expertise or make contributions in various ways. Early in the team's existence, former managers may begin as team leaders, helping to keep the projects on track and making sure that all team members have comparable information, goals, and vision. As the team develops, the team leaders give specific decision-making responsibilities to team members.[34]

■ DECISION MAKING IN WORK GROUPS AND TEAMS

Managers often choose between using individuals or groups to make decisions. In this section, we look at the advantages and disadvantages of group decision making and some guidelines to use in choosing group decision making. Then we explore ways of overcoming groupthink. We examine a variety of group decision-making techniques, including electronic group decision making.

Advantages of Group Decision Making

The advantages of group decision making include the synergy created, the potential creativity that results, and the increased likelihood of acceptance of the decision.

- **Synergy.** Group decisions tend to combine and improve on the knowledge of the group members. This synergy results when each individual brings additional knowledge and skills to the decision. It leads to decisions that are better than the sum of individual decisions.[35]
- **Creativity.** Increasing the group's diversity in its attitudes, thoughts, and behaviors helps it become innovative in dealing with difficult, discretionary tasks. Such diversity allows members to offer a variety of ways of viewing a problem because their different worldviews influence their perspectives. Diversity has greatest value for groups that work on complex, novel tasks; it decreases for groups that work on simple, repetitive, and routine tasks.[36]
- **Acceptance of the decision.** Because group decision making reflects a consensus, it more readily leads to acceptance of the decision than does individual decision making. When a person makes a decision, group members have no commitment or loyalty to that decision and find it easier to reject or ignore it.

Disadvantages of Group Decision Making

Disadvantages of using groups instead of individuals include the longer time frame required, the likelihood of more extreme decisions, and the ignoring of individual expertise.

- **Longer time frame.** Groups generally need more time to make decisions than individuals, since a group exchanges information among many individuals and then obtains consensus. As a result, groups may try to save time or achieve consensus by satisficing, rather than seeking an optimal solution.
- **More extreme decisions.** Early research suggested that groups tend to make riskier decisions than individuals.[37] Because no single person shoulders the consequences of a decision made by a group, individuals may feel less accountable and will accept more risky or extreme solutions. More recent

research suggests instead that groups actually make decisions much closer to their initial predominant view, which may make them appear risky because they are less likely to take a middle ground or compromise position.[38]

■ **Individual expertise ignored.** Groups may ignore individual expertise, opting instead for group consensus. As a member of a group of peers, an individual may reluctantly choose among individuals on the basis of their expertise. Groups may not critically evaluate their decisions or decision-making process. When group members choose a colleague's solution that they consider good, however, the resulting decision equals the quality of a decision obtained by group decision making and is no riskier than a group decision.[39] But the effectiveness of such a *best-member strategy* depends both on the probability that the group will select the real best member and on the potential for subjectivity in the solution.[40] Even then, many groups can perform better than the most knowledgeable member acting alone.[41]

Circumstances That Favor Using Groups

In deciding whether to use a group or individual decision-making process, decision makers should evaluate the type of problem, the importance of having the decision accepted, the desired solution quality, individual characteristics, the organizational culture, and the time available. Table 6-1 summarizes the circumstances that favor group or individual decision making.

■ **Type of problem or task.** Group decision making leads to better results when a task or problem requires a variety of expertise and when problems have multiple parts that a division of labor can address. Group decision making also results in better decisions when problems require estimates because the diverse expertise and experience available result in improved information for making the estimates. Individual decision making leads to more efficiency in

TABLE 6-1

Managers Should Consider Six Factors in Choosing Group or Individual Decision Making.

Factor	Group	Individual
Type of problem or task	When diverse knowledge and skills are required	When efficiency is desired
Acceptance of decision	When acceptance by group members is valued	When acceptance is not important
Quality of solution	When the input of several group members can improve the solution	When a "best member" can be identified
Characteristics of individuals	When group members have experience working together	When individuals cannot collaborate
Organizational culture	When the culture supports group problem solving	When the culture is competitive
Amount of time available	When relatively more time is available	When relatively little time is available

situations where policy dictates the correct solution. Individual decision making also tends to lead to more effective decisions for problems that require completion of a series of complex stages, as long as the individual receives and coordinates input from many sources.[42]

- **Acceptance of decision.** Creating a group consensus increases the group's acceptance of the decision because individuals involved in making a decision generally become committed to that decision.

- **Quality of solution.** Group decision making generally leads to higher-quality solutions, unless a person with excellent information and knowledge, known as *a best-member strategy*, can be identified in the beginning. Otherwise, using the group provides a way to solicit a range of ideas.

- **Characteristics of individuals.** The personalities and capabilities of the people involved in the decision will help or hinder group decision making. Some people have difficulty collaborating in a group setting, whereas others can deal with diverse viewpoints and attitudes. Also, group members can ignore the expertise of other members, creating tension, distrust, and resentment, which can hinder the identification of effective solutions.

- **Organizational culture.** The organizational culture provides the context in which the decision-making process occurs. Supportive climates encourage group problem solving; competitive climates stimulate individual responses. The culture at Marriott seems to encourage collaboration between IT and business units on project development teams. Outside the United States, countries value and reward group-oriented behavior and hence favor group decision making.[43]

- **Amount of time available.** The amount of time available will determine the feasibility of group problem solving, since group decision making takes relatively more time than individual decision making.

Overcoming Groupthink

Groupthink occurs when members of a decision-making group avoid a critical evaluation of alternatives so that they can preserve a sense of group unity and consensus.[44] The attempt to reach consensus at any cost causes members of such decision-making groups to avoid judging other group members' ideas too critically. For example, Primecap, a stock-picking team, attempts to avoid groupthink by having each portfolio manager decide how to invest one part of the portfolio rather than making the decision by committee.[45]

Table 6-2 lists the symptoms of groupthink. Groups that experience groupthink include members who develop a feeling of invulnerability; they feel safe and protected from the consequences of bad decisions or ineffective actions. Such groups and their members also ignore external criticism by rationalizing their own or others' behavior. Members tend to believe their actions are inherently moral and ethical. They also pressure all individuals in the group to conform to the group decision, by allowing no debate about alternatives. When faced with threats, groups of executives likely procrastinate, "pass the buck," or support other members' rationalizations about the appropriate decision.[46] Recent research suggests that groups that experience groupthink demonstrate a lack of awareness of the potential downside of decisions and a preference for risk largely because they have perceptions of their competence that exceed their actual capabilities.[47]

TABLE 6-2

Groupthink Generally Results in Inferior Decisions.

Symptom	Description
Invulnerability	Members feel they are safe and protected from dangers, ostracism, or ineffective action.
Rationale	Members ignore warnings by rationalizing their own or others' behavior.
Morality	Members believe their actions are inherently moral and ethical.
Stereotypes	Members view opponents as truly evil or stupid and thus unworthy of or incompetent at negotiations around differences in beliefs or positions.
Pressure	Members pressure all individuals in the group to conform to the group's decision; they allow no questioning or arguing of alternatives.
Self-censorship	Members do not express any questions about the group's decision.
Unanimity	Members perceive that everyone in the group has the same view.
Mindguards	Members may keep adverse information from other members that might ruin their perceptions of consensus and the effective decision.

Groupthink occurs most frequently in highly cohesive groups, particularly in stressful situations. Multicultural groups experience it less frequently because individual members have inherently different perspectives. Groupthink alone does not explain decision-making fiascoes because groupthink fails to take into account a group's tendency to exaggerate the value, relevance, and perceived quality of the group's initial decision, which would counterbalance a groupthink mentality.[48] Recent evidence provides less support for the groupthink hypothesis that striving for consensus influenced decision making; instead, the actual options identified by the leaders influenced the decision making.[49]

To limit the likelihood of groupthink, groups and their leaders should do the following:

- ensure an open climate of discussion;
- avoid overcontrolling the group's decisions;
- implement a specific decision-making or problem-solving process;
- actively seek dissenting voices;
- not mistake silence for consent;
- get feedback from informed outsiders; and
- provide group members with enough time to study the problem and solutions.[50]

Groups that rank order alternatives rather than choosing the best one tend to more fully consider all alternatives, exchange information about unpopular ones, and make the best decision.[51]

Group Decision-Making Techniques

Managers can use the nominal group technique and the delphi technique, described in detail in Chapter 5, to support and improve group decision making.

- **Nominal group technique** is a structured group meeting in which group members brainstorm and then rank-order a series of ideas to reach consensus.

- **Delphi technique** is a structured group decision-making technique in which managers or consultants repeatedly administer rating scales to obtain opinions about a decision.

Groups that use a structured, conflict-enhancing, dialectical inquiry approach rather than a consensus approach achieve group consensus about the decision, higher acceptance of it, and greater member satisfaction with it.[52]

Electronic Decision Making

Groupware or *group decision support systems (GDSS),* computer software that helps groups make decisions, has become widely used in organizations. It includes, among other features, electronic mail, electronic messaging, and electronic meeting capabilities. The Winnipeg Public Schools use Doc-IT, which allows users to create private Web sites called topic areas on which people can post notices, hold discussions, distribute forms, and keep spreadsheets and other documents. Doc-IT has become the main form of communication in older school buildings that lack intercom systems.[53]

Groupware lets workers share ideas and hold meetings online, even though they are in different locations. It supports the coordination of groups and the exchange of ideas, making it easier to reach consensus on difficult problems. Electronic notes let authorized group members send a message to a common mailbox or read messages from it. Project teams can modify electronic notes to update specifications for new products. Electronic bulletin boards allow team members to post notes related to agreed-upon topics. Groupware can also coordinate concurrent decision making by individual participants that contribute to a larger decision. It can even poll members electronically to make sure they can offer their opinion anonymously.[54] Lotus is developing advanced groupware software that will support knowledge management within companies. The new software will include an expertise locator for finding people with specific knowledge within the company and a content management system for locating data and documents.[55]

Groupware seems to maintain the benefits of group decision making over individual decision making regarding audits. Groups using GDSS analyze problems more thoroughly and are more likely to accept the group decision.[56] Groups that used groupware also developed more nonredundant, realistic ideas.[57] Multinational companies face the challenge of choosing groupware systems that have enough uniformity to support coordination while still meeting local differences. Allianz, the German insurance company, moved from supporting 11 messaging systems to almost total reliance on a single one. The implementation of Lotus Notes/Domino began with e-mail, added information and document sharing, and now is adding shared applications.[58]

▌EMPOWERING MEMBERS OF GROUPS AND TEAMS

Managers use teams as a way of responding quickly to a changing environment. Teams encourage workers to take initiative, use their expertise, and make suggestions for improving products and processes. Teams also place responsibility for decision making lower in the organization, typically with workers who have the knowledge to make the best decisions.

Eskom Transmission abolished its management hierarchy and restructured its 2,000-person workforce into self-directed functional process teams that focused on meeting customer needs. After its formation, each team developed a business plan that outlined its responsibilities, proposed outputs, and stated the roles and accountability of each team member. Because Eskom operated solely in teams, employees recognized that they had to become functioning team members to remain employed. The company implemented performance management, job opportunity, and team bonus systems that encouraged employees to take responsibility and evaluate members' contributions to the team effort. Empowering these employees required individuals' commitment to change, an organizational structure that supports the change, and training and education to prepare people to perform in their new roles.[59]

Team functioning generally improves when managers empower workers to make decisions or solve problems without managerial intervention. Highly empowered teams are more productive, satisfied, and committed than less empowered teams, and they provide better customer service.[60] Many organizations today have given employees more control over their work and decisions because they believe they have the best knowledge about it. They also believe that workers can respond more quickly to customers' requirements when they can make changes without getting approval from higher-level managers. Yet, empowerment can also result in team members creating dysfunctional control structures that replace rather than improve team functioning.[61]

Empowering work teams occurs along four dimensions:

- **potency**—the team's perception of is own competence;
- **meaningfulness**—the team's experiencing of its tasks as worthwhile;
- **autonomy**—the extent to which team members have freedom, independence, and discretion in their work; and
- **impact**—the extent to which the team produces significant and important work for the organization.[62]

Of course, empowering workers also means giving them the skills to take responsibility for decision making. Teams that move in the direction of increased self-management generally participate in extensive training. Such training often focuses on conflict resolution, problem solving, decision making, and other collaborative skills. Training also helps managers work with self-directed teams; they must develop skills in coaching and counseling.

Successful self-management requires numerous conditions:[63]

- **Commitment from top management.** Top management must provide sufficient time and resources for self-managed teams to develop and function.
- **Mutual trust between employees and managers.** A willingness to take risks and share information will flow from this trust.
- **Commitment to training.** Employees must be trained in technical skills and managerial skills such as budgeting and scheduling. Other types of external support, such as group observers or facilitators, may also be needed.
- **Selection of appropriate operations.** Not all jobs or activities fit well with the use of self-managed teams. Appropriate operations allow autonomy of decision making and benefit from team performance.
- **Union support in unionized organizations.** Labor–management relations change in self-managed teams, generally eliminating the adversarial relationship. These companies often must negotiate new forms of compensation.

Managers at all levels need to create a culture that supports collaboration in order for team performance to endure. They need to feel comfortable with relinquishing authority to nonmanagerial employees. Many managers in a team environment act as coaches to employees, providing them with guidance about ways to do the job better without specifically giving them directives.

Changing the Form of Leadership

Most teams, and self-directed teams in particular, require a new type of leadership. They need leaders who excel in coaching and counseling skills. They need leaders who are comfortable empowering their workers and sharing or relinquishing control over day-to-day decisions. A senior manager at the Norwegian subsidiary of British Petroleum describes how one project leader reacted when two teams asked if they could remove a wall between them; the leader told them to do what they thought was right. When the two groups next asked if they could relocate a piece of equipment, the leader told them that he wasn't sure why they were asking him that question. When the two teams decided they only needed one rather than two lathes, they finally made the decision without consultation and eliminated one of them.[64]

Team leadership generally moves from a single, appointed leader to a responsibility widely shared among group members. The leadership transition accompanies the change from conventional to self-directed teams, as shown in Figure 6-4.[65]

1. **Start-up.**   After initial planning, the executive team convenes the group and provides it with extensive training. Executives retain responsibility for determining most team activities, although they try to give team members more control over their work.

2. **State of confusion.**   Teams may have difficulty adapting to their new roles and may resist the movement to self-directed teams. Managers too may obstruct the change because they perceive (correctly) that their role has been reduced.

3. **Leader-centered teams.**   Persistence during the transition, however, typically results in teams becoming functional, often by relying on an internal leader. These *leader-centered teams* usually experience less conflict with their managers and develop functional norms for conducting meetings and accomplishing assignments.

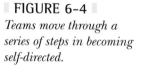

FIGURE 6-4

Teams move through a series of steps in becoming self-directed.

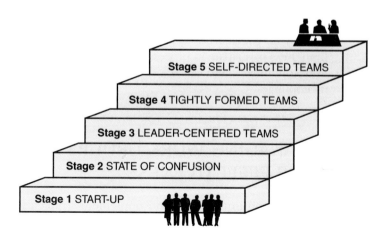

4. **Tightly formed teams.**   Teams that function effectively at this fourth stage may have difficulty assimilating new members and dealing productively with other teams. They generally develop strong internal leadership, either centered in a single person or rotating throughout the team.

5. **Self-directed teams.**   The eventual evolution to self-directed teams involves expanding organizational loyalties beyond the narrow team loyalties and developing a commitment to both team and organizational goals. Team members continue to acquire new skills and perform new technical tasks. They deal effectively with other groups inside the organization, improve their support systems, and improve the way they do their work, such as selecting and ordering the tasks to perform. Team members handle administrative and other leadership responsibilities. Not only do the members exert significant control over individual performance, but they can even exceed the control provided by a more traditional manager, potentially with dysfunctional consequences.

The development of truly self-directed teams at Eaton Corporation's Aeroquip Global Hose Division (see Chapter 1) took five years. Initially, team members thought it was a fad. They were unwilling to talk about their feelings or concerns, refusing to complain to management. Top management had to convince employees that their contributions would make a difference. One year after introducing teams, Eaton removed managers from the team floor, giving managerial roles to the team. Team training helped them perform the required skills. Management showed employees that they would listen to and implement their suggestions. They rewarded teams that accomplished their goals with cookouts and pay increases. Eventually, employees accepted and thrived on the new structure.[66]

Evaluating and Rewarding Team Members

A reward system and a performance management system that support collaboration are critical for effective team performance. Through compensation, praise, or other reinforcers, organizational members must receive a clear message that collaboration is a priority. Companies can attach rewards to team rather than individual performance. They may introduce gainsharing systems (see Chapter 4), in which team members receive bonuses according to the extent their teams attain goals, meet budgetary requirements, or exceed standards. Such rewards should fit with the tasks, and not use individual rewards for group tasks or vice versa.[67] AmeriSteel introduced gainsharing as a way of distributing profits to high-performing teams. Employees participate in process improvement teams, safety committees, and productivity committees, and can see their unit's productivity numbers using computers in their lounges.[68]

MANAGING WORK GROUPS AND TEAMS FOR EFFECTIVENESS

Managers continually seek and implement strategies for improving team performance. In this section, we examine ways of keeping teams performing well, developing trust, keeping lines of communication open, and acting innovatively.

Keeping Teams Performing Well

Assuming that organizations form the right kinds of teams for the right purposes, strategies for improving group performance often include team building and improving group process. Team-building activities typically begin by collecting data about team functioning using instruments such as the one shown in Figure 6-5. Team members or special observers, called *process observers,* may gather information about the team's communication, decision making, and leadership.[69] They may use specially constructed observation schedules or questionnaires to secure the necessary data or may obtain information about group functioning in less formal ways. For example, at Brunswick or Marriott, individual team members can observe and document the nature and quality of group interactions.

The next step involves analyzing the data and presenting the results to team members. Often this feedback improves team performance. Team members receive new insights about how effectively they act. Someone outside the team can also help the team develop an agenda for improving its performance. These objective outsiders may coach the group about ways to perform better. Team members also try to identify factors that facilitate or hinder their performance. Typically, this means clarifying their expectations about their own and the team's functioning and focusing on what each person needs to do differently to accomplish the team's and the organization's goals. This feedback and discussion of results help the team face its problems, evaluate its behaviors, and identify its challenges for future performance by answering questions such as the following:

- What is it like to work here?
- What helps or hinders working together?
- What is our job and its responsibilities?
- What are our expectations of our team and each other?
- What changes could be made to improve performance?
- What does each group member need to do differently?
- What can this unit do to work more cooperatively?
- How do other teams or work units perceive us, and vice versa?
- What commitment is each member willing to make to increase our effectiveness?[70]

Team members can also contribute to better performance by exerting more effort, bringing sufficient knowledge to the task, and using appropriate strategies for performing the task. Changing the organizational reward system will encourage ample effort from employees. Adjusting the group composition will help ensure that the group has sufficient knowledge and skills. Changing the organizational information system should foster appropriate strategies.[71]

Addressing the underpinnings of team performance—goals, norms, and roles—also improves team functioning. First, managers must try to focus all team members on a common goal. Identifying and dealing with hidden agendas is a first step. Working with group members to articulate specific but challenging goals encourages high performance.

Making sure that norms produce effective group performance is also key. Managers can play a particularly pivotal role in identifying and supporting appropriate norms. They can reward behavior that sets high standards, focuses on goal accomplishment, and supports collaboration. In addition, managers can identify leaders within the work groups who can help facilitate desirable norms.

Using the scale below, circle the number that corresponds with your assessment of the extent to which each statement is true about your team:

5 = strongly agree; 4 = agree; 3 = neutral; 2 = disagree; 1 = strongly disagree

1. Everyone on my team knows exactly why the team does what it does. 5 4 3 2 1
2. The team leader consistently lets the team members know how we're doing on meeting our customers' expectations. 5 4 3 2 1
3. Everyone on my team has a significant amount of say or influence on decisions that affect his or her job. 5 4 3 2 1
4. If outsiders were to describe the way we communicate within our team, they would use such words as "open," "honest," "timely," and "two-way." 5 4 3 2 1
5. Team members have the skills they need to accomplish their roles within the team. 5 4 3 2 1
6. Everyone on the team knows and understands the team's priorities. 5 4 3 2 1
7. As a team, we work together to set clear, achievable, and appropriate goals. 5 4 3 2 1
8. I would rather have the team decide how to do something than have the team leader give step-by-step instructions. 5 4 3 2 1
9. As a team, we are able to work together to solve destructive conflicts rather than ignoring conflicts. 5 4 3 2 1
10. The role each member of the team is expected to play makes sense to the whole team. 5 4 3 2 1
11. The team understands how it fits into the organization. 5 4 3 2 1
12. If my team doesn't reach a goal, I'm more interested in finding out why we have failed to meet the goal than I am in reprimanding the team members. 5 4 3 2 1
13. The team has so much ownership of the work that, if necessary, we would offer to stay late to finish a job. 5 4 3 2 1
14. The team leader encourages every person on the team to be open and honest, even if people have to share information that goes against what the team leader would like to hear. 5 4 3 2 1
15. There is a good match between the capabilities and responsibilities of each person on the team. 5 4 3 2 1
16. Everyone on the team is working toward accomplishing the same thing. 5 4 3 2 1
17. The team has the support and resources it needs to meet customer expectations. 5 4 3 2 1
18. The team knows as much about what's going on in the organization as the team leader does, because the team leader always keeps everyone up-to-date. 5 4 3 2 1
19. The team leader believes that everyone on the team has something to contribute— such as knowledge, skills, abilities, and information—that is of value to all. 5 4 3 2 1
20. Team members clearly understand the team's unwritten rules of how to behave within the group. 5 4 3 2 1

Scoring:

Team mission:	Add scores on items 1, 6, 11, and 16 _____
Goal achievement:	Add scores on items 2, 7, 12, and 17 _____
Empowerment:	Add scores on items 3, 8, 13, and 18 _____
Open, honest communication:	Add scores on items 4, 9, 14, and 19 _____
Positive roles and norms:	Add scores on items 5, 10, 15, and 20 _____

FIGURE 6-5   *Managers can use this checklist to assess the effectiveness of a team.*

Source: Reprinted and adapted with permission from V. A. Hoevemeyer, How effective is your team, *Training & Development* (September 1993): 68.

Finally, managers must ensure that team members can perform task and maintenance roles. The particular roles required may vary in different groups. Unlike traditional work groups, for example, self-managed teams may need more members who assume leadership roles. Using a checklist to tally the nature and frequency of role behaviors and individuals' interactions in a group, an observer can identify the roles played by group members, as shown in Figure 6-3. Such a diagnosis should precede prescriptions for improving group functioning and effectiveness. After diagnosis, managers can fit the most appropriate individual to each role. Changing the roles of group members might require giving them special training or feedback about the new roles they perform.

Developing Trust

Building trust allows members to remain focused on the problem. It encourages better communication and coordination and improves the quality of the results of collaboration. Members who trust each other pick up the slack for one another more often and consequently improve overall team performance.[72]

Managers can create trust among their employees in several ways. First, careful selection of team members is critical. Sensitivity to major differences that easily lead to misunderstandings can limit the potential for trust. Second, managers can model trusting behavior. Demonstrating a willingness to delegate key responsibilities to employees lets the workers know that the manager trusts and values them. Third, managers can create a culture that conveys trust. Allowing open access to offices, files, and other work-related materials lets employees know that secrets won't be tolerated.

Keeping Lines of Communication Open

Team members may check perceptions, practice active listening, give feedback, and redesign jobs to increase trust, improve communication, and encourage confrontation of conflict. They may also participate in training programs to learn to become more effective group members.

To be effective, a team must develop ways of interacting with those outside the group and keep the lines of communication open externally as well as internally. The team can use these external strategies:[73]

- **informing**—describing what happens in the group to those outside it;
- **parading**—seeking visibility by showing others how well the team functions; and
- **probing**—interacting with others outside the team to learn about the environment.

Some conflict can improve communication and lead to more effective problem solving. Although managers may want to encourage conflict that helps build a team, they simultaneously need to minimize the amount of conflict that results in undesirable outcomes. To do this, they can attempt to resolve the conflict directly or change the organization's structure to reduce conflict. Managers can also resolve conflict through negotiations. This formal process of trying to resolve differences can highlight the competitive differences between individuals and reach a solution acceptable to both parties.

Acting Innovatively

Managers in today's organizations need to act innovatively in creating and using teams. They need to think about doing work in different ways, often bringing together workers from different functions, levels, or locations. Creating teams to do work traditionally done by individuals also brings new ideas to projects and products.

GROUPS AND TEAMS IN THE DOT-COM, GLOBAL WORKPLACE

Perhaps the biggest change experienced by companies in the past decade has been the widespread introduction and acceptance of teams as the basic way to organize work. Yet, the success of different types of teams can vary in different geographical locations. Mexican companies, for example, may experience special problems in introducing self-managing teams. Although the collectivist culture might suggest that Mexicans would embrace self-managed teams, their low tolerance for ambiguity and preference for formal rules makes the introduction of self-managing teams particularly challenging.[74]

The development of electronic communication has fostered the existence of virtual teams and multicultural teams. Teamware, computer applications aimed at improving team effectiveness, support such teams.[75]

Virtual Teams

Virtual teams describe groups of employees who work at different sites and do not have face-to-face access to each other. They perform team activities primarily using electronic communication. Virtual teams have become more common for a number of reasons: (1) Many organizations have moved to flatter structures; (2) more cooperation and more frequent competition between organizations is needed; (3) employee expectations about how they will use new technology have changed; (4) a continued shift to service and knowledge work from manufacturing has occurred; and (5) the increasing globalization of the workplace has fostered virtual teams.[76]

One of the earliest challenges such teams face is building shared understanding among team members. Developing virtual teams involves developing the hardware and software infrastructure, as well as the teams themselves. Possible resistance includes fear of the new technology, problems in trusting other team members, stress, and resistance to organizational restructuring.[77] Culturally diverse teams face special challenges in the areas of communication, culture, technology, and project management.[78] Such teams may experience "swift trust," which is very fragile and often short-lived.[79] Finding ways to extend the trust becomes a priority. Virtual teams also face the challenge of ensuring that team members receive the correct and appropriate amount of information. General Electric has given its 340,000 employees Web-based collaboration tools to help them improve the sharing of information and break down geographic and cultural barriers.[80]

Companies may put their own employees on virtual teams or use a variety of independent workers instead. The top executives of Dynamic Alternatives and Commdisc, Inc., two Illinois-based companies that provide software consulting, use a group of independent specialists when the companies have a large database-customization project. Each person works on the project from her own home or office.[81]

Virtual teams require members to act more independently of direct supervision. Virtual cross-functional teams, in particular, frequently must deal with nonrecurring problems and the lack of a routine approach to solving problems and making decisions.[82] Managers must find a way to effectively supervise members of such virtual teams. They might use teleconferences to help coordinate team members' activities. At Cisco, for example, managers can read an intranet-based virtual team guidebook to provide suggestions about how to build team spirit, monitor the team's performance, and resolve conflict.[83]

Multicultural Teams

A multicultural team can pose special challenges, since differences in language and culture may exacerbate problems that interfere with high-quality performance. Diversity of group members due to age, sex, race, or ethnic origin can have consequences for team behavior and performance.[84] Specifically, they may have different needs, interests, goals, and perspectives. At the same time, diversity can also enrich the team's performance. A multinational team of researchers, for example, is tracking destruction in the Amazon rainforest. A dozen researchers from the United States and Brazil interviewed about 1,400 wood mill operators on their logging practices and 200 landowners about fire damage.[85] A team of scientists from Great Britain, Germany, and Cameroon have worked together to develop a drug that would eradicate a parasite that causes river blindness in Africa.[86]

Table 6-3 summarizes the advantages and disadvantages of cultural diversity in groups. Multiculturalism results in multiple interpretations, greater openness to new ideas, increased flexibility, increased creativity, and improved problem-solving skills.[87] Cultural diversity also fosters increased creativity, better decisions, and ultimately improved team effectiveness. A diverse work team makes dealing with a particular country or culture easier because the team likely has a member who understands the foreign environment and workers.

At the same time, the diverse perspectives in a multicultural group may increase ambiguity, complexity, or confusion in certain situations because group members may fail to reconcile different perspectives and use them constructively. Miscommunication and difficulty in reaching an agreement may result. Diversity can also lessen

TABLE 6-3

Diverse Teams Offer Both Advantages and Disadvantages in the Workplace.

Advantages	Disadvantages
• Increased number of perspectives	• Increased ambiguity
• Multiple interpretations likely	• Increased complexity
• Greater openness to new ideas	• Increased confusion
• Increased flexibility	• Increased mistrust
• Increased creativity	• Potential miscommunication
• Improved problem solving	• Difficulty in reaching agreements
• Improved understanding of foreign employees or customers	• Difficulty in reconciling diverse perspectives
	• Difficulty in reaching consensus
	• Decreased group cohesion

team cohesion due to miscommunication and mistrust, which results in decreased ability to reach decisions and, consequently, decreased effectiveness.

The society in which an organization operates provides a clue to the prevailing cultures that provide the context for team functioning.[88] Many U.S. companies reflect a cultural orientation of individualism. Japanese companies typically reflect their culture's orientation of collectivism. Teams flourished in Japan long before their widespread use in the United States. Now compare the United States, which emphasizes capitalism, to the Scandinavian cultures, which emphasize socialism. Again, teamwork fits better with Scandinavian than U.S. culture, and may require more supports in the United States until it becomes an accepted way of doing business. Arab cultures, which value personal relationships and trust, provide yet another different context for team functioning.[89]

A culturally diverse work group's potential for effective or ineffective performance depends on the nature of the group's task, the stage of development, and the leader's skill in managing diversity. One study of culturally homogeneous and diverse groups, for example, indicated that homogeneous groups initially scored higher on process and performance effectiveness, but over time both homogeneous and heterogeneous groups improved and eventually demonstrated no significant differences in process or overall performance.[90]

We can diagnose the effectiveness of a culturally diverse work group by asking the following questions:

- Do members work together with a common purpose?
- Has the team developed a common language or procedure?
- Does the team build on what works?
- Does the team attempt to spell out things within the limits of the cultural differences involved?
- Do the members recognize the impact of their own cultural programming on individual and group behavior?
- Does the team have fun?[91]

The protocol for building an effective multicultural team often begins with diversity training. In addition, group members should acknowledge cultural differences while minimizing cultural stereotypes. Managers can use quality feedback to reinforce desirable group behaviors and extinguish undesirable behaviors and attitudes.

Summary

1. Work groups and teams can be traditionally managed or self-managed, permanent or temporary, or composed of members from one or more than one discipline.

2. Work groups and teams form because people have common needs, interests, goals, physical proximity, or cultural similarity.

3. Groups develop in predictable ways—progressively, noncontinuously, using habitual routines or focused externally.

4. Effective work groups begin with a shared goal; teams develop norms that set expectations about acceptable behaviors and attitudes for the team; and team members assume specific task, maintenance, or individual roles.

5. Group decision making offers the advantages of synergy, creativity, and acceptance of the decision and the disadvantages of taking more time, resulting in more extreme decisions, and potentially ignoring individual expertise.

6. Group decision-making techniques and the use of electronic decision making can increase the effectiveness of group decision making and help avoid groupthink.

7. Managers need to empower team members by changing the form of leadership and rewarding team behaviors.

8. Managing teams for effectiveness means keeping them performing well, developing trust among members, and keeping the lines of communication open.

9. Managers need to identify key issues associated with using virtual teams and multicultural teams.

A Manager's Diagnostic Review

Understand the basics of group and team functioning.
- What types of work groups exist?
- How do effective work groups form and develop?
- Do the groups have functional roles?

Know when to use group and individual decision making.
- What factors influence the choice of group versus individual decision making?

Have a repertoire of group decision-making techniques.
- Do teams use brainstorming, delphi, and NGT techniques?

Empower team members to lead and make decisions.
- Do managers share authority?
- Do self-managing work teams exist, and are they functional?

Reward team members for performance.
- What team-based rewards exist?

Manage teams effectively in the dot-com, global workplace.
- How do groups function differently in various types of companies and industries?
- How do groups function differently in various cultural settings?

Visit the Gordon homepage on the Prentice Hall Web site at

http://www.prenhall.com/gordon

for recommended readings, additional activities, Internet exercises, updated information, and links to related Web sites.

▌ Thinking Critically About Organizational Behavior

1. Does the reason groups form influence their performance?
2. How can we reconcile the progressive and noncontinuous views of group development?
3. How can managers ensure that team members bring the necessary resources to the team?
4. Do hidden agendas interfere with team goals?
5. Can individual roles ever be functional?
6. When should managers use groups to make decisions rather than making the decision themselves?
7. Can teams overcome groupthink?
8. How can managers use computers to improve decision making?
9. What is the difference between groups and teams?
10. How can managers act innovatively in using teams?
11. What steps should managers follow to ensure that teams are effective?
12. How do cross-cultural issues affect team performance?

ACTIVITY 6-1: GENERAL WAINWRIGHT

STEP 1: Your instructor will divide the class into groups of six to eight students and assign each student one or two of the following roles: agenda setter, analyzer, evaluator, information giver, information seeker, encourager, gatekeeper, group observer, or harmonizer. During this activity, you are to primarily play the role assigned to you by your instructor. Try not to play roles assigned to other group members.

STEP 2: It is 1941, and General "Hawk" Wainwright, Commander of the U.S. Air Force, needs fighter planes. Your team is to produce aircraft according to his top-secret plans (Figure 6-6). You will be paid for each flight-certified aircraft, but fined for each crash and for each work-in-process plane at the end of the time period.

Production bids are in units of 5 (such as 5, 10, 15, etc.) plans that pass flight certification. A crash is defined as a plane that does not "hit" the wall area designated by the instructor. All crashed planes are unrecoverable.

STEP 3: Your team has five minutes to decide on and submit your aircraft production worksheet for the current production round (Figure 6-7), or the team is ruled unsuitable for government production. The person assigned the observer role may not engage in production.

STEP 4: When the General says, "Up we go into the wild blue yonder," you have 15 minutes to complete production, including flight certification.

FIGURE 6-6
Use General Wainwright's secret plans to produce aircraft.

Airplane Assembly

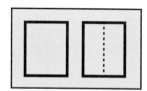

1. Fold a sheet of paper in half. Then open it back up.

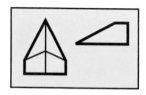

4. Fold in half.

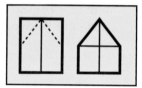

2. Fold corners into middle.

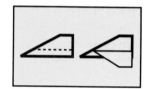

5. Fold both wings down.

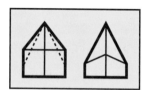

3. Fold corners into middle again.

6. Fold tail fins up for final airplane.

FIGURE 6-7
Use this worksheet for evaluating production.

AIRCRAFT PRODUCTION WORKSHEET

Team #:   **Team Observer:**

Team Leader: **Team Timekeeper:**

Categories/Figures	Round #1	Round #2	Round #3
"Bid" production units			
+ Flight certified @ $100 each			
− Work in process	− $50 each	− $100 each	− $100 each
− Crashes	− $50 each	− $100 each	− $200 each
Profit			

STEP 5: When the General signals the end of the production run, you should calculate your team's profit as directed by your instructor. Your instructor will tell you how many rounds there will be.

STEP 6: Discussion. In small groups or with the entire class, answer the following questions:

    1. How effectively did each person "stay in role"?

    2. Did the group perform effectively?

    3. What changes would have improved the group's performance?

Source: This exercise was adapted and reprinted with permission from Peter Mears and Frank Voehl, *Team Building: A Structured Learning Approach.* (Delray Beach, FL: St. Lucie Press, 1994).

ACTIVITY 6-2: GROUP MEETING AT THE COMMUNITY AGENCY

ADVANCE PREPARATION: Gather role sheets for each character and instructions for observers. Set up a table in front of the room with five chairs around it, arranged in such a way that participants can talk comfortably and have their faces visible to observers.

INTRODUCTION: The Community Agency is a role-play exercise of a meeting between the chairman of the board of a social service agency and four of his subordinates. Each character's role is designed to recreate the reality of a business meeting. Each character comes to the meeting with a unique perspective on a major problem facing the agency as well as some personal impressions of the other people developed over several years of business and social associations.

CAST OF CHARACTERS:

John Cabot, the chairman, was the principal force behind the formation of the Community Agency, a multiservice agency. The agency employs 50 people, and during its 19 years of operations has enjoyed better client relations, a better service record, and a better reputation than other local agencies because of a reputation for high-quality service at moderate cost to funding agencies. Recently, however, competitors have begun to overtake the Community Agency, resulting in declining contracts. John Cabot is expending every possible effort to keep his agency comfortably at the top.

Ron Smith, director of the agency, reports directly to Cabot. He has held this position since he helped Cabot establish the agency 19 years ago.

Joan Sweet, head of client services, reports to Smith. She has been with the agency 12 years, having worked before that for the Department of Education as a contracting officer.

Tom Lynch, head community liaison, reports to Joan Sweet. He came to the Community Agency at Sweet's request, having worked with Sweet previously at the Department of Education.

Jane Cox, head caseworker, also works for Joan Sweet. Cox was promoted to the position 2 years ago. Prior to that time, Jane had gone through a year's training program after receiving an MSW from a large urban university.

TODAY'S MEETING: John Cabot has called the meeting with these four managers to solve some problems that have developed in meeting service schedules and contract requirements. Cabot must catch a plan to Washington in half an hour. He has an appointment to negotiate a key contract that means a great deal to the future of the Community Agency. He has only 20 minutes to meet with his managers and still catch the plane. Cabot feels that getting the Washington contract is absolutely crucial to the future of the agency.

STEP 1: Prepare for the meeting as follows:

1. Five members from the class are selected to role-play one of the five characters.
2. All other members act as observers.
3. All participants read the introduction and cast of characters.
4. The participants study the roles. All should play their roles without referring to the role sheets.
5. The observers read the instructions for observers.

STEP 2: Conduct the meeting.

1. When everyone is ready, John Cabot enters his office and joins the others at the table, and the meeting begins.
2. Allow 20 minutes to complete the meeting. The meeting is carried to the point of completion unless an argument develops and no progress is evident after 10 or 15 minutes of conflict.

STEP 3: Discussion. In small groups or with the class as a whole, answer the following questions:

DESCRIPTION

1. Describe the group's behavior. What did each member say? What did each member do?

DIAGNOSIS

2. Evaluate the effectiveness of the group's performance.

3. What effects did such characteristics as group development, resources, goals, norms, and roles have on its effectiveness?

4. Did any problems exist in leadership, power, motivation, communication, or perception?

PRESCRIPTION

5. How could the group's effectiveness be increased?

ACTIVITY 6-3: THE TINKER TOY EXERCISE

STEP 1: Your instructor will organize the class into groups of five to eight people. Four members of the group will serve as builders and can actually touch the Tinker Toys. The remaining members are divided into consultants and observers. Consultants give advice to the builders and may act as timekeepers. Observers remain silent and report on the group process during the discussion.

STEP 2: Each group will receive one set of Tinker Toys. Each group has 15 minutes to plan the tallest free-standing Tinker Toy tower they can. They must observe the following rules:

1. Only 15 minutes are allowed to plan how to build.
2. No more than two Tinker Toy pieces can be put together during the planning period.
3. All pieces must be put back in the box with the lid on before the competition begins.
4. Observers may not speak.
5. Neither the Tinker Toy box nor classroom desks can be used to increase the height of the tower.
6. Only the four students who are builders may touch the toys during the building phase.
7. The completed tower must stand alone.

STEP 3: Your instructor will signal the end of the planning period. The groups should return all Tinker Toy pieces to the boxes with the lids in place. Your instructor will give the start signal, and each group then has 60 seconds to build the tower. When your instructor calls time, all hands should be removed from the towers.

STEP 4: The instructor will appoint several students to measure the towers. The winner is announced.

STEP 5: In your small groups, answer the following questions:

1. What percent of the plan did each member of your group contribute?
2. Did your group have a leader? Who? How was he or she chosen?
3. Which roles did each person perform during the planning session? During the building session?
4. How effective was your group?

STEP 6: Discussion. With the entire class, answer the following questions:

1. How did the groups' behavior differ?
2. What characterized effective groups?
3. How does your knowledge of group dynamics—specifically resources, norms, roles, and goals—explain your own and other groups' behavior?
4. How could the behavior of the groups be improved?

Source: This exercise is based on B. L. McNeely, Using the Tinker Toy exercise to teach the four functions of management, *Journal of Management Education* 18(4) (November 1994): 468–472.

ACTIVITY 6-4: DIAGNOSING GROUP DYNAMICS

STEP 1: Your instructor will arrange for you to watch a video such as *Twelve Angry Men* or another that depicts a group in action.

STEP 2: During the video, keep a log of (1) examples of roles performed by members of the group; (2) group norms; and (3) hidden agendas of group members.

STEP 3: Share your logs in small groups.

STEP 4: Discussion. In small groups or with the entire class, answer the following questions:

1. What roles did various members of the group play?
2. What norms existed in the group? Which were peripheral norms, and which were pivotal norms?
3. What hidden agendas did individuals demonstrate? How did these fit with the group's goal?

ACTIVITY 6-5: EVALUATING A SPORTS TEAM

STEP 1: Choose a professional or college sports team to study. Make sure that the team has received extensive coverage in local newspapers.

STEP 2: Collect all articles written about the team.

STEP 3: Observe the team during at least two practice sessions and two regular games.

STEP 4: Evaluate the team's effectiveness by answering questions such as the following:

1. What stages did the team experience in its development?
2. Does the team have common goals?
3. How well do team members cooperate, share, and demonstrate unselfish behavior on the field?
4. What roles do team members play? Do individual-oriented roles dominate?
5. What norms exist among the team?
6. What type of leadership exists?
7. Are team members empowered to make improvements?
8. What rewards support team performance?
9. What conflicts exist? How are they resolved?

STEP 5: Discussion. Share your observations and evaluation with the class. Then answer the following questions:

1. What characterizes an effective team?
2. How could the team become more effective?

ACTIVITY 6-6: PROBLEMS IN PROJECT GROUPS

STEP 1: Read the following:

MGT 857, a course required of all new MBAs at Hypothetical University, requires a semester-long group project involving teams of five MBA students. Students will analyze a company's financial situation, strategy, structure, and managerial decision making over the course of the semester. The project will culminate in a 50-page written report. Fifteen-minute oral reports on various phases of the analysis will be made to the class three times during the semester. The project is worth 50 percent of the grade in the course. The instructor has assigned the following five new MBA students to work together as a team to analyze a small new firm in the biotechnology field:

Mike Randolph.   24-year-old single male from the West Coast, undergraduate finance major, two years of experience working in a bank. Tends to be outspoken and impatient with those who do not agree with him. Generally dissatisfied with work done by anyone other than himself. Has a strong desire to excel and is likely to volunteer to take on more than his share of the project "to see that it's done right." Believes in managing "by the numbers," has little respect for "soft" data. Prefers to have group meetings on Sunday afternoons.

Helen St. Thomas.   27-year-old female, married, with a small child, commuting from a town 60 miles from the university. Undergraduate degree in biology, 4 years of experience as a medical lab technician and then lab supervisor. Likes to plan well in advance, uneasy if assignments are not completed at least a week before they are due. Highly intelligent but a bit uncertain about her ability to handle MBA work with no prior background in the area. Willing to meet only on Monday, Tuesday, and Thursday when she is in town for classes.

Peter Christian.   39-year-old male from the Midwest, recently and bitterly divorced. No undergraduate degree. Worked 18 years as an entrepreneur who started and then sold two successful businesses in the publishing field. Has also worked as a consultant to publishing companies. Excellent ability to deal with "soft" data and understand how various organizational systems interact in the real world. Widely read in the management literature. Given to bouts of depression and intolerant of women in general at the moment. Unwilling to meet on weekends because he has custody of his teenage sons on Saturdays and Sundays.

Lee Sing How.   24-year-old Taiwanese male just arrived in the country for schooling. Has honors undergraduate degree in economics and statistics plus 3 years of experience with the World Bank. Strong skills in financial analysis and forecasting. Reads and writes English well but is hesitant to speak it, especially in front of large groups. Tends to be silent unless he is very sure of what he is about to say and what is expected. Unlikely to volunteer to take on tasks in the group, but quite willing to help if asked to do a clearly defined task. Sensitive to real or imagined slights and believes that it is very important to maintain "face." Very serious about his studies, but would much prefer to work alone. Taking five difficult courses this semester, but is willing to meet any time he's not in class.

Richard White.   Divorced 30-year-old male from Dallas, 8 years of experience in used car sales. Planning to specialize in marketing. Rather dissatisfied about required courses in areas he sees as "irrelevant" to his career goals in marketing. Intends to spend most of his effort on marketing courses and just scrape by in his other courses. Needs to be reminded repeatedly to do his part of this group project, but very insightful regarding the marketing and strategy aspects of the case being analyzed. Has an active social life and is reluctant to commit to meetings very far in advance. Works best under pressure with a close deadline.

STEP 2: In small groups, answer the following questions:

1. What are the strengths of this group?
2. What are the potential problems that this group may confront?
3. What can group members do early in their time together to improve their ability to work together during the semester?
4. How should the group organize itself to accomplish the project?

STEP 3: Read the following:

It is now Monday, four weeks into the semester, and the group's first oral report is to be presented tomorrow afternoon. Mike has been acting as the informal leader of the group, although Peter has occasionally challenged his leadership. Over the last four weeks, Helen has made some very good suggestions in group meetings, but Peter seems absolutely unwilling to listen to her. Sing How has attended every meeting and was given a task by Mike two weeks ago. At each meeting, Sing How has assured the group that things are going well, but he has not been willing to say anything more about his progress. Today, the group discovers that Sing How has done almost nothing. He did not understand Mike's terse assignment and was unwilling to ask for clarification for fear of looking incompetent. Richard has missed the last three meetings. The group was getting worried about what they would say about marketing in the presentation. However, Richard just phoned Helen and told her that he is hard at work on the project. He says he

will definitely have his piece done by 10 A.M. tomorrow morning. Mike volunteers to put the whole presentation (except Richard's part) together tonight, including doing Sing How's missing work. The group agrees to meet again tomorrow morning.

STEP 4: In small groups, answer the following questions:

1. What has gone wrong?
2. How do you think each group member feels about the situation and about each other?
3. What can the group members do to ensure that they do not have a repeat of this scenario before the next presentation?

STEP 5: Read the following:

It is now two weeks after the first presentation. Richard completed his work for the first presentation and arrived with it at 1 P.M. (not 10 A.M. as promised). The presentation at 2 P.M. went reasonably well, although Richard's section was not as good as the rest of the group had expected, given his expertise. Mike has backed off since the big push to finish the first presentation. He has been busy with projects in other classes, has missed one group meeting, and came an hour late to another. Sing How faithfully attends meetings, but has said almost nothing since the misunderstanding about the first assignment. When asked for an opinion, he often denies having one. Helen and Peter have suddenly become friends and are now acting as co-leaders of the group. However, their attempts to impose structure and gain agreement from other members are not always successful. Richard has been busy preparing for a midsemester exam in marketing, but has promised to start work on the second presentation early next week. The oral report is due at the end of next week. As the meeting convenes, everyone suddenly seems to realize that it is almost halfway through the semester and the major written report is due in six weeks. Panic sets in.

STEP 6: In small groups, answer the following questions:

1. Have the resources readily available to the group changed by this point in the semester?
2. How should the group proceed?

STEP 7: Discussion. With the entire class, answer the following questions:

1. What characterizes effective groups?

2. How does your knowledge of group dynamics—specifically, resources, norms, roles, and goals—explain the behavior in this group?

3. How could the group's behavior be improved?

Source: Reprinted with permission from C. D. Fisher, J. B. Shaw, and P. Ryder. Problems in project groups: An anticipatory case study, *Journal of Management Education* 18(3) (1994): 351–355.

Chapter 7

Improving Communication

Learning Objectives

After completing Chapter 7, you will be able to

1. Discuss the impact of electronic communication on businesses.
2. Describe the two-way communication process and its components.
3. Cite the five functions of nonverbal communication.
4. Describe typical listening problems, and show how active listening addresses them.
5. Discuss the impact of the structure of communication on its outcomes.
6. Discuss six major barriers to communication and ways to overcome them.
7. Specify the components of effective performance management.
8. Offer four techniques for improving communication.
9. Identify the major issues related to communicating in the dot-com, global workplace.

A Manager's Preview

Describe . . . Diagnose . . . Prescribe . . . Act

- Use electronic communication effectively.
- Diagnose dysfunctions in the communication process.
- Avoid information overload and underload.
- Use formal and informal communication appropriately.
- Diagnose and eliminate barriers to communication.
- Conduct 360-degree performance evaluations.
- Use techniques that improve communication.
- Give employees voice in the workplace.
- Communicate effectively in cross-cultural settings.

E-Mail and The NBA

"Call me Mr. E-Mail."

Know this about Mark Cuban. Despite the dreamy predictions of a sports world in the throes of an Internet revolution, the tech billionaire-cum-owner of the NBA's Dallas Mavericks isn't one to speak his mind.

More often, he types it.

For this article, like other recent ones about him in the national press, Cuban declined to be interviewed in person or by telephone. "Best is to answer question via e-mail. m" he tapped out in the first of a series of electronic exchanges.

The next day he was holding firm: "What is the problem with e-mail?" Four days later, he dashed off a new message restating his opposition to phone and face time: "It's time to try something different."[1]

Communication involves the exchange of information, including facts, assumptions, behaviors, attitudes, and feelings, between two or more parties. In today's dot-com world, the ease and speed of communication have increased dramatically. Electronic communication systems have overtaken other forms of information exchange as the media of choice for many managers and employees. Effective communication forms the building block of effective organizations.

In this chapter, we first look at this change in communication—the impact of electronic communication. Then we examine the communication process in more detail, including the structure of communication. Next we investigate barriers to communication and ways to overcome them. We consider the use of communication in performance management. Then we explore four techniques for improving communication in organizations. We conclude with comments about communication in the dot-com, global workplace.

▌ THE IMPACT OF ELECTRONIC COMMUNICATION

Electronic communication systems have changed the way managers do business. Internal and external messaging systems speed communication and make remote locations accessible. The Internet and intranets make huge quantities of information available to employees and managers.

Messaging Systems

Electronic media for communication include electronic messaging, voice messaging, conferencing systems, and integrated systems.[2] Managers and other employees use these messaging systems to leave and retrieve either voice or written messages in the following ways:

- **Electronic messaging** substitutes for telephone or face-to-face interactions by creating a formal document that conveys the desired information across the telephone lines or computer network.
- **Voice messaging** supplements telephone communication and typically includes the ability to store, retrieve, edit, and forward voice messages, as well as to distribute them to a prespecified list. Managers and other users receive their messages in an electronic in-basket, ready to be answered, filed, or discarded.
- **Conferencing systems** add an interactive component to messaging systems. Audio systems resemble a telephone conference call and so substitute for face-to-face communication. Videoconferencing systems transmit voice and visual images of participants. Computer systems conduct the conference electronically, with participants responding to messages as they are delivered.
- **Integrated systems,** such as groupware, supplement traditional written communication with messaging, word processing, and data processing. They can create, edit, store, retrieve, and forward shared documents, as well as develop electronic calendars and scheduling.

Electronic messaging and conferencing help managers by making it easier to interact, speeding the ease and time of responding, and disseminating information more widely within and from organizations. In the 2000 presidential campaign, electronic messaging speeded the cycle of response and counter-response between the Gore and Bush campaigns. Dozens of e-mail messages reached reporters each week. For example, according to a press secretary, the Democratic National Committee daily wrote quick fact pieces in response to Bush's statements.[3] SouthTrust Bank, like other financial institutions, uses electronic messaging services based on its Web site to communicate with its clients.[4]

Companies are beginning to use the voice capabilities of the Internet to support communication. Students in the Spokane, Washington, school district can listen to a teacher giving a lesson using the Internet. They can also ask questions through their computers. Merrill Lynch is installing Internet phones that allow employees to conduct free conference calls over the Net and simultaneously trade instant text messages. Compaq lets people click on an icon on its Web site and speak live to company representatives.[5] "Personal rich" media, including images, video, and sound, are expected to replace e-mail within the next five years.[6]

Computer conferencing allows for private communication among participants. It offers particular advantages for small businesses, which may lack the travel budget to visit vendors and suppliers around the world.[7] Because it can poll conference participants, computer conferencing can support the use of the nominal group and delphi decision-making techniques. Computer conferencing also provides a transcript of the proceedings, which employees can use to prepare and edit shared documents.

Videoconferencing can increase accessibility among employees at widely dispersed locations. Rather than communicating solely through e-mail or other messages, videoconferencing participants can see each other. This often improves communication because individuals can use both verbal and nonverbal communication. The Cheesecake Factory, a national restaurant chain, is planning trials of videoconferencing and training.[8] The New York State Teacher's Retirement System offers videoconferencing consultations between staff and members about retirement benefits.[9] Of course, the cost of this "face-to-face" medium may affect its use.

The Internet and Intranets

The Internet is an international network of computer networks that offers low-cost global communications. People can use the Internet for electronic mail and access to newsgroups that have common interests. They can also use the Internet to access the World Wide Web. This collection of Web sites provides huge quantities of information about products, companies, technologies, countries, and a host of other topics. A manager can book travel arrangements, research a new technology, order books, subscribe to magazines, and do many other tasks on the Web. Companies can market new products, publish information about the company, and solicit customers using the Web. The Web has changed the way people do business by making information-sharing fast and inexpensive. By providing so much information, however, the Web has increased the potential for information overload. Screening relevant information has become a major challenge for companies and their employees. Sieve, an emerging technology, screens and files e-mail messages before they enter a person's in-box.[10] Table 7-1 offers some advice for individuals who must deal with a glut of e-mail.

An intranet resembles a World Wide Web site, but is used only within a company. Companies use intranets as a place to store information that employees need and to centralize data in easily accessible ways. Managers can easily update or add new information to the intranet. PricewaterhouseCoopers uses its intranet to provide employees with information such as collections of best practices, consulting methodologies, news services, and directories of experts. The intranet site receives 18 million hits each month.[11] Great Lakes Credit Union, an Illinois financial institution, uses its intranet to post job openings. Employees who refer colleagues for jobs receive bonuses based on how long the referred employee works at Great Lakes Credit.[12] Maimonides Medical Center in Brooklyn, New York, uses its intranet to allow employees to read reports in electronic form and print desired sections from their desktops.[13]

TABLE 7-1

***Managers and Employees Can Use a Variety of Techniques to Deal
With E-mail Overload.***

1. Triage e-mail for importance, such as by carefully reading the headers.
2. Avoid reading junk mail.
3. Selectively respond to messages.
4. Identify specific times of the day for e-mail correspondence.
5. Limit e-mail access by controlling who has your address.
6. Prepare brief and readable e-mail to avoid the need for future correspondence.
7. Avoid e-mail when problem solving is necessary.

Source: R. Davidhizar, R. Shearer, and B. Castro, A dilemma of modern technology: Managing e-mail
overload, *Hospital Materiel Management Quarterly* 21(3) (2000): 42–47.

Advantages and Limitations of Electronic Communication

Electronic communication offers the advantage of rapid exchange of information
across potentially great geographical distances. Managers can send messages to
employees working at different sites around the world, and the employees can
receive and respond to them almost immediately. The cost of e-mail when compared to other media is relatively low. It also eases collaboration among team members on many types of projects.

Yet, the speed and ease of such communication also has liabilities. As noted earlier, the ease of sending such messages often creates information overload for workers. Managers often replace necessary face-to-face communication with e-mail,
resulting in miscommunication or even dissatisfied workers. Communication errors
also occur because people don't carefully write their messages. For example, Gad-
zoox, a California-based data storage company, posted a message that said it would
be releasing its earnings on a specific date. Because the traders expected the
announcement at a particular time, missing the date could have major consequences. Unfortunately, the date posted was incorrect. Fortunately, the company
uses NetCurrents as an electronic monitor; NetCurrents found the mistake and
posted the correct message.[14]

Employees and managers may also send messages too quickly without recheck-
ing the content, or they may unintentionally hit the send button. Many people
assume that e-mail messages are only read by the recipient and so send confidential
information electronically. Later they may discover that members of the information technology staff or other organizational members have access to the message,
creating security issues. In addition, employees are increasingly spending time on
nonwork-related Internet surfing, such as shopping, planning vacations, or day-
trading their portfolios. More companies are checking their employees' use and
misuse of the Internet because it has significant economic consequences; cyberloaf-
ing explains 30 to 40 percent of lost worker productivity.[15] Finally, electronic messaging can become dictatorial. Because of its easy accessibility, e-mail can control
employees' time both at work and at home.

FIGURE 7-1
*Managers and employees
should use two-way
communication.*

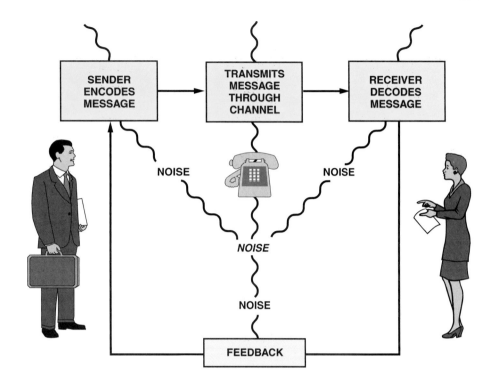

FIGURE 7-1
Managers and employees should use two-way communication.

▮ THE COMMUNICATION PROCESS

Effective communication using electronic or other media calls for a flow of information from one person or group to another and then back to the original person. This two-way flow makes a closed loop, as shown in Figure 7-1. To get a better understanding of this process, we first examine its components. Then we investigate the use of language, nonverbal communication, effective listening, and information overload and underload.

Components of Communication

Looking again at the two-way model of communication, we can see that communication includes the following components: encoding, transmission, decoding, feedback, and noise.

Encoding.   A person with a meaning to convey first determines how to express that meaning. As background for encoding information, the sender uses his personal frame of reference. This includes the individual's view of the organization or situation, resulting from his education, interpersonal relationships, attitudes, knowledge, and experience. The comments that precede the encoding also give meaning to it.[16] The manager of the Beiersdorf, Inc., plant in Cincinnati was given primary credit for helping save the plant from closing because of his exceptional ability to communicate the rescue plan to senior managers.[17]

Encoding the message requires the sender to evaluate the most effective way to convey the information. Think about Mark Cuban's response about communicating only by e-mail: "Best is to answer question via e-mail. m." How else could he indicate his preference: "Could you please send me an e-mail message?" or "I won't answer you unless you send me an e-mail." Obviously the language he uses will affect the message the reporter ultimately hears. Most likely, he will use the reporter's native language. He might also use special jargon that he knows the reporter will understand. The nonverbal messages he encodes will also have an impact. Should he use a pleading tone, an arrogant one, an indifferent one, or some other tone? Should he stomp his feet and wave his hands, stand quietly, or sit in a relaxed position when asking? Because e-mail eliminates the nonverbal aspect of communication, some information in the encoding is lost.

Transmission.   After encoding, the sender transmits the message. Cuban uses e-mail to share information with the reporter, the commissioner, and other basketball executives. What other media alternatives could he use? Cuban could send a memorandum or convene a meeting, although he clearly prefers the speed and ease of e-mail. Table 7-2 shows the characteristics of a variety of media that managers and employees can use in their daily activities.

TABLE 7-2

Specific Media Have Assets and Liabilities for Transmitting Messages.

	Generally Available	Relatively Low Cost	High Speed	Immediate Interaction	High Impact and Attention
Written					
Letters	X	X			
Memos and reports			X		X
Telegrams			X		X
Newspapers and magazines	X				
Handbooks and manuals	X	X			
Bulletins and posters	X	X			
Inserts and enclosures	X	X			X
Oral					
Telephone	X	X	X	X	X
Intercom and paging	X		X		X
Conferences and meetings	X			X	
Speeches	X			X	
Electronic					
Fax			X	X	X
Electronic mail			X	X	
Voice messaging			X		X
Computer conferencing			X		X
Audio conferencing				X	X
Videoconferencing				X	X
Groupware				X	

Source: Adapted with permission from Dale A. Level Jr. and William P. Galle Jr., *Business Communications: Theory and Practice* (Homewood, IL: Business Publications, Inc./Richard D. Irwin, Inc., 1988), pp. 91, 93.

FIGURE 7-2

Media vary considerably in richness.

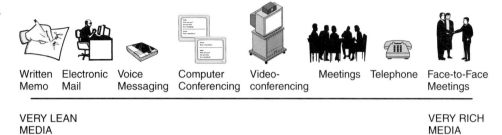

| Written Memo | Electronic Mail | Voice Messaging | Computer Conferencing | Video-conferencing | Meetings | Telephone | Face-to-Face Meetings |

VERY LEAN MEDIA   **VERY RICH MEDIA**

In determining the appropriateness of the medium used, the manager should consider the medium's *richness,* which refers to the amount of information it conveys and how well it encourages understanding. How quickly the medium provides feedback and how many communication channels it uses influence its richness. So do the extent of personal interactions allowed and the vividness of language it allows.[18] Figure 7-2 shows how media vary in richness. As tasks become more ambiguous, managers should increase the richness of the media they use. For example, they should send routine, simple communications through a lean medium, such as a memo, and nonroutine, difficult communications through a rich medium, such as face-to-face communication.[19] They should also use rich media to increase their personal visibility and implement company strategies.[20]

Decoding.   After receiving the message, the receiver must determine its content. He decodes it, trying to give it the same meaning as the sender intended. He must consider the language used to express the message and also pay attention to nonverbal cues, such as body language or tone of voice. Effective listening, which we discuss in greater detail later in this chapter, increases the accuracy of decoding. Often with electronic communication, the recipient infers the emotion associated with a message inaccurately because of the absence of body language to clarify it.

Decoding occurs within the receiver's frame of reference, which again results from her education, interpersonal relationships, attitudes, knowledge, and experience. A receiver who has a similar frame of reference to that of the sender will experience less difficulty in decoding than one whose frame of reference differs considerably. One of the major challenges of communicating globally is developing common frames of reference and bridging cultural differences.

Feedback.   Feedback refers to the receiver's acknowledgment that the message has been received. It provides the sender with information about how the receiver understands the message. Quality feedback should indicate whether errors occurred in encoding and decoding. Feedback can also signal problems during transmission. Feedback limits the errors and inaccuracies that occur in transmission. Feedback may even call for a new transmission of the same or a related message.

Without feedback, one-way communication occurs; the receiver does not inform the sender about how she received the message. Too often, one-way communication occurs between managers and their employees. Faced with differences in power, lack of time, and a desire to save face by not passing on negative information, managers may not ask for feedback, and employees may not provide it.

Why do some managers fail to engage their employees in two-way communication? These managers often experience conflict between their roles as authorities and their desire for employees to like them. Other managers over-rely on written memoranda and electronic mail as a way of communicating with employees. Managers may also use one-way communication because they lack the self-confidence needed to accept possible suggestions, criticisms, or new ideas from their employees.

Employees can also discourage two-way communication. Why? Just as managers may attempt to protect their power positions, their employees may try to manipulate their boss's image of them. Employees may withhold negative information about themselves or their activities. Impression management may play a role in whether individuals seek feedback: Employees assess how their manager will interpret a request for feedback and how the resulting information will affect their public image.[21] Cuban reinforces the impression that he is a high-tech owner by relying on an electronic medium for communication. Some employees fail to tell their manager about needs, interests, and values that don't fit with the organizational culture. For example, attorneys don't tell their bosses that working overtime poses a hardship on their families because the organization values billable hours and expects overtime from its employees. Other employees mistrust their managers and so withhold any information from them.

Noise.   Noise refers to interference in the communication process. Fire engine sirens, building construction, and loud side-conversations can interfere with accurate communication. Noise can include psychological interference that might stem from communicators' education, values, and experiences.

Cultural differences can also create noise. Imagine the interference created when American-born managers in the United States and Chinese-born managers in China attempt to speak in English on the telephone. Can you list the potential sources of noise in that situation? Noise might include static or delays on the line, different experiences of the U.S. and Chinese managers, or cultural variations in tone of voice. Even the presence of a silent third party during a conversation may act as noise that distracts the receiver from hearing what the speaker says.

Differences in roles in the organization, biases in attributions, and various perceptual predispositions can also cause noise. Diagnosing these sources of noise improves communication.

Language and Communication

Often we fail to recognize the impact of subtleties in language, ignoring the fact that shades of meaning can have significant consequences for communication. Yet, the words we use to encode a message influence its quality. In most languages, words have *denotations,* or literal meanings. Many denotations are abstract or vague and leave room for interpretation. As a result, different people may use the same word to mean different things. For example, managers and employees may assign different degrees of probability to the words "very likely," "probably," and "reasonably likely." Such *bypassing,* in which individuals miss each other with their meanings, occurs most often in cross-cultural or stress situations.[22]

The use of *jargon,* or technical terminology, can create distortions unless all parties understand it. Consider the conflict that might arise when a store manager asks the marketing department to put together a "marketing campaign" in a week. The store manager may use the term to denote a single newspaper advertisement. The professionals in the marketing department, however, may use the term to describe an elaborate, coordinated effort that might involve everything from advertisements to publicity and promotional contests.

Words also have *connotations,* or emotional messages that affect their meaning. Advertisers, for example, use "perfume-free" instead of "nonscented" because "free" has powerful, positive connotations. Managers who have to cut their staffs prefer to speak of "right-sizing" instead of "downsizing." Think about the experience of shopping for a PalmPilot or other hand-held organizer. If the salesperson thinks the customer is a "power user," she may use very technical jargon to describe its speed, storage, and display. If, on the other hand, the customer seems to be a "technophobe" or novice, the salesperson may use very simple language.

Nonverbal Communication

Nonverbal communication refers to the use of gestures, movements, material things, time, and space to clarify or confuse the meaning of verbal communication. For example, the kind of facial expressions that accompany a request for a higher salary may indicate its importance. If no one greets a new employee on his arrival at a new job, the employee may form a different impression of the company than if someone meets him in the parking lot. People may also differ in their sensitivity to nonverbal language. Women, in particular, seem more likely than men to respond to body language.[23]

Nonverbal cues serve five functions:[24]

1. **Repeating** the verbal message. An employee who nods after she answers affirmatively confirms the verbal message with the nonverbal gesture.

2. **Contradicting** the message the individual is trying to convey. A manager who pounds the table while stating that he doesn't care about the situation being discussed uses verbal and nonverbal communication that disagree.

3. **Substituting** for a verbal message. A manager with "fire in his eyes" conveys information without using verbal messages.

4. **Complementing** the verbal message. A manager who beams while giving praise increases the impact of the compliment to the employee.

5. **Accenting** the verbal message. Speaking very softly or stamping her feet shows the importance a person attaches to a message.

Senders can intentionally use nonverbal communication to increase the impact of their verbal communication. But nonverbal signals can also deliver unintended messages. English-speaking managers who supervise non-English-speaking workers often experience this problem.[25] A gesture, for example, may have different meanings in different cultures. Consider the A-OK gesture, or the thumb and forefinger circled. In the United States, it means that things are fine; in Brazil, it is an obscene gesture; in Japan, it means money.[26] Two Arabs discussing a business proposal will change the tone and volume of their voices dramatically depending on the subject matter because in Arab culture increased volume or pitch indicates a greater interest in the subject; an American interacting with them should follow the same approach in varying tone.[27] A Japanese manager may have a continuous smile on his face in a meeting. Does this mean he is pleased with the meeting's progress?

Because Japanese tend to communicate with minimal eye contact, facial expressions, or hand gestures, the smile may hide discomfort or embarrassment.[28]

Listening Effectively

Whereas language and nonverbal cues primarily influence the encoding of information by the sender, listening affects decoding. Receivers can listen in five main ways:[29]

1. **Directing.** The listener guides the direction of the conversation.
2. **Judgmental.** The listener injects personal value judgments into the conversation.
3. **Probing.** The listener asks many questions to explore key issues.
4. **Smoothing.** The listener makes light of the speaker's problems and urges resolution of conflicts.
5. **Empathic/Active.** The listener tries to create an encouraging atmosphere for solving problems, often by offering neutral summaries of what she heard.

Deficiencies in listening can result when people don't pay careful attention to the message being transmitted or ignore the nonverbal cues that accompany the verbal message. Listening problems also occur when people don't understand the language used to encode the message or don't spend enough time decoding the message. Managers and their employees can avoid these deficiencies by practicing *active listening*—that is, listening for both the content of and the feelings behind the message.[30] This means that managers and employees should demonstrate both cognitive and affective empathy for the receiver, whether she is another employee, a manager, or a customer.[31] If an employee says, "I think I'll have trouble meeting this deadline," the manager must determine whether the employee means that he can't possibly meet the deadline, feels frustrated with how the work is proceeding, wants recognition, lacks the skills to complete the job, or has some other feeling.

A person who actively listens looks for the total meaning of what the speaker says, not just the superficial or partial meaning. After an active listener has analyzed the feelings that accompany a communication, she must also acknowledge these feelings as part of the feedback. The boss might say to the employee who claims he can't meet a deadline, "I know this is hard work and sometimes you find it frustrating, but let's see if we can figure out a way to make it less frustrating for you."

Managers and other employees can use three major techniques for active listening:

- **Paraphrasing.** The receiver restates the sender's message. For example, if a manager (the sender) states, "I don't like the work you've been doing," his employee (the receiver) might paraphrase it as "you are saying that you are dissatisfied with my performance" or "you are saying that you want to assign me different types of work to do." Note that these ways of paraphrasing the original message suggest very different understandings of the original statement. The manager, upon receiving this feedback from the employee, can then clarify his meaning.

- **Perception checking.** The receiver describes her view of the sender's inner state at the time of communication to check her understanding of the message. For example, if a manager (the sender) states, "I don't like the work you have been doing," the employee (the receiver) might check his perception of the statement by asking, "Are you dissatisfied with me as an employee?" or "Are you dissatisfied with the quantity of my output?" Note that the answers to these two questions will identify different feelings.

- **Behavior or feelings description.** The manager or employee reports specific, observable actions of others without making accusations or generalizations about their motives, personality, or characteristics. Similarly, the person can label others' feelings by name, analogy, or some other verbal representation, as a way of increasing active listening.

Information Overload and Underload

Often people send too much or too little information. Information *overload* or *underload* may result for the person receiving the information. Have you ever received very complicated instructions that you can't follow? In this situation, you might experience information overload. It often occurs when a person doesn't have enough time, has too many job demands, or has a job that requires extensive coordination with other jobholders.[32]

Information overload can become particularly problematic when people use electronic mail and messaging systems that readily increase information sharing. Too much e-mail can quickly overwhelm a customer service department or Web team. E-mail management systems have emerged as a way to solve this problem. They include software that sends incoming e-mails to the correct person, tracks the status of e-mails, and produces reports on the performance of customer service employees. Some systems, such as Brightware's Answer Agent, can even provide automatic answers directly to customers.[33] On the other hand, sometimes managers and other employees do not receive enough information to do their jobs. Such information underload occurs when the sender has a low desire to communicate, a person isolates himself from other organizational members, or great physical distance prevents frequent communication. The advent of electronic communication and decreased costs of telecommunications have decreased the occurrence of information underload.

Figure 7-3 illustrates the personal and organizational factors that influence the amount of information transmitted. Information underload typically occurs with job holders who don't need to coordinate with others, work physically distant from them, have highly routine jobs with few time constraints, make few decisions, and lack the ability and desire to communicate. Underload can result in alienation, lack of motivation, and apathy. Overload tends to occur with job holders who must coordinate with others, don't work physically distant from them, don't have routine jobs, have high time constraints and many decisions to be made, and have both a high ability and desire to communicate. Overload can result in high stress, confusion, and mistakes.[34]

Managers can increase the efficiency of information use in a number of ways.[35]

- **Change the physical setting.** Reducing noise and distractions or changing the physical layout can improve the flow of information.
- **Use filtering or screening devices that improve access to information.** Changing the organization of bulletin boards, color-coding information, or eliminating junk mail can improve access. Message-screening software helps eliminate junk e-mail.

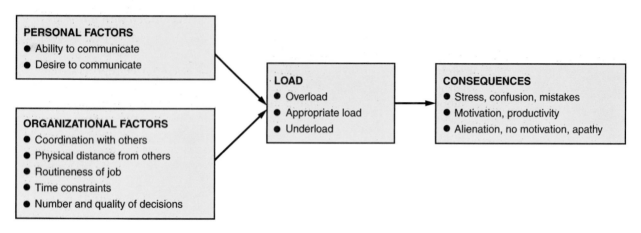

PERSONAL FACTORS
● Ability to communicate
● Desire to communicate

ORGANIZATIONAL FACTORS
● Coordination with others
● Physical distance from others
● Routineness of job
● Time constraints
● Number and quality of decisions

LOAD
● Overload
● Appropriate load
● Underload

CONSEQUENCES
● Stress, confusion, mistakes
● Motivation, productivity
● Alienation, no motivation, apathy

FIGURE 7-3   *Personal and organizational factors affect information load and the resulting consequences.*

■ **Install technical devices such as software, videotapes, audiotapes, or an improved phone system.** These devices can help screen information or present it more conveniently. Some executives subscribe to e-mail services that prescreen newspapers, magazines, or other publications for relevant information. Intelligent agent software automatically screens information using prespecified key words.

■ **Train the users to encode, transmit, and decode information more effectively.** When information is put into a form such as electronic mail, it is more easily and efficiently disseminated.

Companies can also use *information architects,* people who cut through the clutter and help deliver important information concisely. Information architects at Sapient help translate clients' ways of doing business and the needs of the users of their Web sites into functional requirements. They develop blueprints that include defining and documenting a Web site's structure, ways of navigating it, and ways users interact with it.[36] Information architects also interview and observe users to learn about their needs, as well as lead design sessions in which users participate. The information architect for InfoWorld.com's Web site spent more than a month collecting information—using phone and online surveys, user forums, and individual interviews with site visitors—to best understand the site's audience.[37] Many information architects work as members of multidisciplinary project teams that help develop or support customers' e-business strategies.[38]

■ THE STRUCTURE OF COMMUNICATION

Communication becomes patterned over time. Such patterns influence the speed, accuracy, and impact of communication. In this section, we first examine the directions of communication. We next compare and contrast formal and informal communication. We then investigate the use of communication networks in organizations. Finally, we look at official corporate communications.

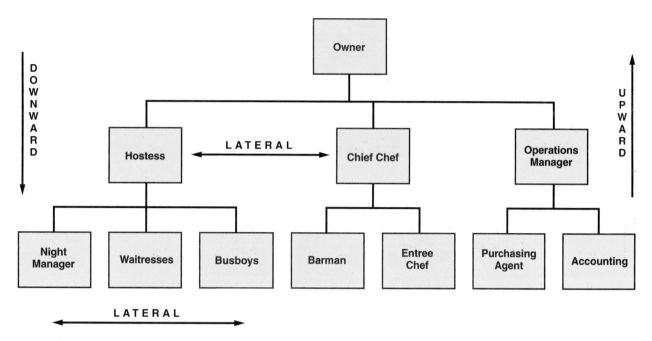

FIGURE 7-4   *Managers and employees can use downward, upward, and lateral communication.*

The Directions of Communication

Managers and employees can communicate downward, upward, and laterally in an organization, as shown in Figure 7-4. For example, the entire staff of Insurance Management Company, a Pennsylvania insurance agency, meets every day at 8:15 A.M. to discuss the previous day and future opportunities.[39]

Downward Communication.   Downward communication refers to sending messages to people lower in the organization's hierarchy. The president of a company communicates to the vice presidents; the middle managers disseminate information to their first-line managers; lower-level managers convey messages to staff members. Managers typically use such downward communication to give information, orders, and directives to employees.

Managers need to seek regular ways to share information, ideas, and both good and bad news with employees. All managers can encourage face-to-face communication with their direct reports by scheduling frequent staff meetings, making periodic contact by telephone, or using traditional or electronic mail to send information that doesn't require an immediate response. They communicate more easily with employees by regularly touring work sites, creating departmental, divisional, or company newsletters, organizing a communication hot line in the organization, or using electronic mail to widely disseminate specific information.

Although most managers intend to communicate accurately to their employees, some may consciously or unconsciously distort downward communication. They may give inaccurate, incomplete, or inconsistent information. They may withhold, screen, or manipulate information.[40] For example, they may delay news about staff cutbacks because they feel such news will affect employee morale. During crisis events, such as downsizing, managers should communicate often and accurately, even overcommunicating, by giving full information and increasing employees' access to them.[41] The South Texas Project, the second largest nuclear plant in the United States, won the Federal Emergency Management Agency's highest award for communicating during a crisis in its handling of a FEMA drill. The company illustrated technical terms with large drawings and used other messages that conveyed South Texas's concern for the community, clearly explained the emergency situation, and offered a plan for preventing a similar crisis.[42]

Sometimes downward communication begins with accurate and complete information, but becomes distorted as the information moves through various levels of management. Such distortion may result from encoding, decoding, or transmission dysfunctions in the basic communication process, particularly if no feedback occurs.

At other times, distortions may occur because managers lower in the hierarchy want to consciously or unconsciously change the message they pass down to the next level. For example, a middle manager may incorrectly feel that her employees will work harder if they don't receive top management's praise for their performance to date. Power differences (see Chapter 9) can result in distortions. Distortions may also result when managers send information to others lower in the organization but outside their own work unit.

What happens when a manager frequently distorts information? Her employees may become distrustful and circumvent the manager to obtain more accurate information. If a new employee in an e-commerce business feels that the president is hiding plans for selling the business, which might mean a reduction in the number of employees, he might seek other ways of verifying the information. Sometimes employees respond to distorted information over the long term by relying more on rumors or the informal network of contacts in the organization than on the formal chain of command.

Although open communication, disclosure, and directness generally benefit both managers and their employees, this approach can backfire if employees are not prepared to receive the information being sent, or if managers are unwilling to deal with employees' reactions.[43] When could this happen? In discussions about their performance, employees may not want to hear about poor results, or managers may not handle an employee's angry reaction well. In discussions about layoffs, employees may try to deny that such actions affect them and their co-workers.

Upward Communication.   Upward communication refers to messages employees send to their managers or others who hold higher positions in the organization. An employee might initiate a weekly meeting with her boss to provide a status report of an ongoing project. Upward communication serves primarily as a feedback vehicle, closing the loop in downward communication to ensure that accurate encoding and decoding of information has occurred.

Upward communication can also occur outside an individual's work unit. The manager of staffing may communicate with the vice president of engineering to determine the specific type of employees to recruit. An employee in the travel department of a large company may send information about reduced airfares to managers of other departments for use in making travel plans. Increasingly, executives empower low-level managers and nonmanagerial employees to make significant decisions. This change calls for high-quality upward communication so that top executives have access to the decision outcomes.

Sometimes employees attempt to save face by delivering only positive information to their bosses. This commonly occurs when bosses don't receive negative news well. Either they blame subordinates for problems outside their control, or they fail to develop joint solutions with employees. While this type of censorship may result in the boss viewing the employee positively in the short run, it may backfire in the longer run and cause the boss to consider the employee untrustworthy. An employee can create misunderstandings by distorting information upwards in the following ways:

- telling the boss only good news;
- paying the boss compliments whenever possible;
- always agreeing with the boss;
- avoiding offering personal opinions different from the boss's;
- insulating the boss from information detrimental to him;
- covering up information potentially damaging to the employee; and
- selecting words that project only favorable impressions.[44]

Managers can create a culture that encourages upward communication by encouraging their employees to share information about their successes and failures, attitudes, work developments, and mistakes. Employees must feel that they can trust their supervisors to receive whatever information they transmit to them, regardless of whether it is positive or negative. For example, an employee who has legitimate reasons for missing a deadline should know that her boss will carefully evaluate the reasons for the delay and help the employee meet her goals by offering constructive comments. Such a culture promotes honest upward communication as a way of counteracting employees' tendencies to hide potentially damaging information. It encourages employee participation in decision making, rewards openness, and limits inflexible policies and arbitrary procedures. By acting constructively on upward communication, a manager reinforces it and prevents his own isolation.

Lateral Communication.   Often individuals send messages to people at the same organizational level, both in their own or other departments or divisions. Communication directly between employees has greater speed and accuracy. Although distortions can still occur in encoding, transmission, or decoding, lateral communication helps managers solve problems and coordinate work. It also encourages workers to develop a common view of organizational goals and concerns.

Although lateral communication can occur through formal channels, more often it occurs informally. Using the formal hierarchy slows down lateral communication. Still, some managers insist that workers rely on the hierarchy for exchanging information. Passing information from employee to manager to top manager to second manager to second employee allows managers to check decisions, stay informed, and reinforce the chain of command. The use of e-mail has greatly expedited all forms of communication.

Many organizations develop special roles to ease lateral communication. *Boundary spanners* exist where two groups or units interact. A product manager, for example, serves as the interface between the marketing and production departments. A technical liaison may ease communication between engineering and marketing. A purchasing agent acts as the interface between a vendor and the manufacturing department. *Gatekeepers,* a special category of boundary spanners, screen information and access to a group or individual; they funnel information into the organization from outside.[45] The chief of staff of the president of the United States acts as a gatekeeper, determining who will have access to the president. The executive secretary of the president of a company serves as a gatekeeper. Electronic communication can remove major obstacles between employees in different or distant departments.

Formal Versus Informal Communication

Managers and other employees can transmit messages formally or informally.

- ■ **Formal communication** refers to transmissions that use formally established or regularly scheduled channels, such as from boss to employee. Formal communication typically follows the organizational hierarchy and formal chains of authority and command.

- ■ **Informal communication** refers to more spontaneous communication that occurs without regard for the formal channels of communication. The organization's grapevine serves as a major vehicle of informal communication.

Formal communication can use oral and written media, such as staff meetings and written memoranda. However, executives often look for new ways to formally promote communication throughout the organization. Companies can develop speak-out programs that include suggestion boxes and rewards for winning or cost-saving suggestions. Company newsletters or information bulletins also regularly disseminate information to large numbers of employees.

The *grapevine* refers to the pattern of communication created outside the formal organization and official channels. The grapevine serves as an excellent source of information about employee attitudes, as well as an emotional outlet for workers.[46] The grapevine often distorts information, just as in the game of telephone, presenting incomplete or inaccurate information. It can replace formal communication, removing management's ability to control the accuracy of information disseminated in the organization.

Increasingly, managers use the grapevine to acquire more information about the problems, attitudes, and information gaps of workers. Managers also use the grapevine to reinforce information they convey to employees through formal channels. For example, a manager might comment about the effectiveness of individuals working on a new project both formally and informally.

Communication Networks

Communication networks represent patterns of formal or informal communication throughout an organization, as illustrated in Figure 7-5.[47] A *total systems network* describes the communication patterns throughout the entire organization, such as communication in a small distributor of soft drinks. A *clique network* describes a group of individuals or departments who communicate exclusively with each other, such as the credit department. A *personal network* represents individuals who communicate with specific individuals.

Networks vary in size, interconnectedness, and the extent to which a person or clique dominates the total network.[48] *Network analysis* shows the pattern of interactions and allows managers to diagnose effective and ineffective patterns. Managers can use network analysis to identify groups or clusters that comprise the network, individuals that link the clusters, and other network members.[49] Network analysis helps diagnose communication patterns and, consequently, communication effectiveness.

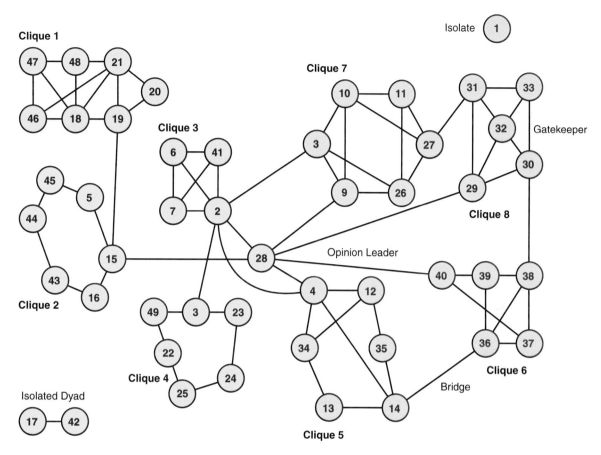

FIGURE 7-5 *A total systems network describes the exchange of information in an organization.*

Communication networks can also exist outside a company. WomenAngels.net, a group of women based in Washington, D.C., have created a total systems network which they use to make investment decisions. They have invested more than $6 million in high-tech start-ups. They generally provide financing after an entrepreneur has obtained seed capital but before the owner receives money from professional venture capital groups. Women who can tolerate the risk associated with such investing have started similar angel networks in Boston, New York, and Seattle.[50]

Official Corporate Communications

Companies communicate official information in a variety of ways. Mission statements, corporate logos, and other company documents provide information and present an identity for the company. A mission statement (see Chapter 11) expresses a company's values and beliefs and generally reflects its way of doing business. Corporate logos offer a pictorial representation of the company's identity. Beginning with the introduction of the new Sable sedan by Mercury, Ford Motor Company featured the Barnes & Noble.com logo in all of its print, mail, and other advertising efforts. Barnes & Noble.com provided a link to Mercury's Web site in exchange.[51]

Although an organization's mission statement and logo offer a snapshot of its philosophy, strategy, and even basic operations, most companies disseminate extensive formal communications about their strategy, goals, operations, financial situation, and employees to many audiences. Managers need to ask, "What do we need to communicate to the workforce?" and "What do employees want to know?" Retail companies often create stores that communicate a particular message. Rue 21, a low-budget fashion retailer, gives its stores an industrial warehouse feel. It has a metal conveyor, wooden crates, and shelving that uses rotary bins; the company displays humorous graphics to support the image. For example, its signature icon is an image of a woman outfitted in a big wooden barrel; the question "What to wear?" accompanies the icon.[52]

Companies frequently send official communications when crises occur. Product failures, hostile takeovers, strikes, or downsizing, for example, call for clear, widely disseminated communications. Managers need to develop a proactive not a reactive strategy that quickly and effectively addresses employee questions and concerns. Such communications should tell audiences how they should behave, help them cope with the emotional aspects of the situation, and help them internalize information and form long-term judgments about the situation.[53]

Organizations must ensure that any published information meets legal criteria. Information disseminated to the public serves as a kind of contract that may fall under legal scrutiny. Particularly when marketing goods and services, conveying investment information, specifying safety information, and writing employee handbooks, employees need to ensure the accuracy and legality of their communication.[54]

▌ BARRIERS TO COMMUNICATION

The basic communication process may appear relatively straightforward, but most organizations have communication problems. Perceptual and attributional biases, interpersonal relationships, top management's role, gender differences, physical distance, and organization structure can create barriers to communication.

Perceptual and Attributional Biases

Perceptual biases, such as stereotyping, the halo effect, projection, and other self-fulfilling prophecies, (see Chapter 2), can distort communication. Stereotyping causes senders to assume that the receivers have certain characteristics based on the group to which they belong without validating that they in fact have these characteristics. Like stereotyping, the halo effect can affect the accuracy of communication by causing managers and others to make inaccurate assumptions about their co-workers or subordinates. Because projection involves an emotional biasing of perceptions due to fear, hatred, anger, uncertainty, love, deceit, or distrust, it colors the message sent and received. This causes errors in subsequent communications.

Errors can also occur in attributing the causes of certain behaviors, events, or situations, as discussed in Chapter 2. Individuals who incorrectly attribute certain behaviors to personal versus situational causes may consequently err in communicating about these behaviors and their causes.

Interpersonal Relationships

The way managers and workers have interacted over time influences their communication:

- Trust tends to encourage more accurate and open communication.
- Power can inhibit communication, causing people to use it to advance their personal agendas.
- Norms can determine the types of acceptable communication media used by individuals.
- Groups with competitive attitudes can hinder effective communication.

Ineffective interpersonal interactions can significantly affect the quality of communication. Lack of trust, power differences, dysfunctional norms, and employee attitudes can create major barriers. As team-based work has become more common in organizations, creating quality interpersonal relationships is essential for effective performance. People should become sensitive to the way they present and listen to ideas. They need to develop interpersonal interactions that help, not hinder, communication.

Top Management's Role

Top management's lack of commitment to effective communication can create a major barrier. Because top managers both set policies and serve as role models, their support for quality communication is critical. Managers who isolate themselves in executive suites or at remote locations may miss the daily contact with employees that encourages good communication. Managers who walk around the plant floor or talk informally with subordinates frequently learn more about their performance than during formal appraisal sessions.

Too often managers just use meetings to convey bad news. For example, the chairpersons of Chase Manhattan and J. P. Morgan and Company met with groups of employees after the $33 billion acquisition of Morgan was announced. The meeting was intended to get employees enthusiastic about the merger, even though about 3,000 people (about 10 percent of the employees in the asset management and investment banking groups) would lose their jobs as a result of the acquisition.[55]

Managers may also take responsibility for communication during a crisis. In the aftermath of the bombing of the federal building in Oklahoma City, the executive management team of Kerr-McGee, a company located two blocks from the bombing site, became the corporate communications team. They combined with members of the company's public relations staff to accomplish their major objective of letting employees know what was going on.[56]

Gender Differences in Communication

Male and female managers often have different ways of communicating.[57] A classic story illustrates a basic difference between male and female communication:

> A man and a woman were driving to a meeting at a location they had never visited before. After 50 minutes of driving around in circles, the woman was visibly upset. When asked why, she responded that she was not upset about being lost, but she was furious that her male companion had repeatedly refused to stop and ask directions.

Women ask for information, and men resist asking for it. Women tend to use rapport-talk, which focuses on building relationships and establishing connections, whereas men tend to use report-talk, which emphasizes demonstration of knowledge and skills and focusing attention on themselves.[58] On the job, women more often use apologetic language, even if they do not mean to apologize; say thanks ritualistically but for no apparent reason; give praise more frequently; and make more indirect comments.[59]

In one study, women sounded more polite but also more uncertain, whereas men used more informal pronunciations and sounded more challenging, direct, and authoritative. The feminine style seemed more accommodating, intimate, collaborative, and facilitative, whereas the male style was more action-oriented, informational, and controlling.[60] Recognizing such patterns should help managers diagnose communication problems caused by gender differences.

Gender may also affect communication in the organizations of the dot-com workplace. For example, in a recent study of communication among virtual teams, the women were more satisfied than the men; the women more than the men also perceived that the group stayed together and helped each other.[61]

Physical Distance

Physical distance obviously affects communication. Employees near each other can more easily communicate face-to-face, check the accuracy of their communication by requesting feedback, and revise their communication. As their physical distance increases, noise also increases, creating greater communication distortions. A global marketplace has become a reality because telecommunications and other electronic media bridge large distances and reduce the problems created by physical distance. Many executives spend large amounts of time touring company sites and speaking with employees as another way of dealing with physical distance.

Companies also design the workplace to reduce physical distances within a single location and encourage communication among employees. Companies have built open offices without windows. They have also constructed common meeting areas to encourage communication among employees in different departments. General Mills' Bassett Creek building was designed with 30,000 square feet of open office floors. The company wanted the ability to bring groups of people together from different departments and the flexibility to create and configure teams in collaborative settings.[62]

Organization Structure

Structural factors can both help and hinder communication. While the organizational hierarchy and chain of command provide direction for downward and upward communication, they may unnecessarily restrict the channels of transmission. Too often, employees feel that they can't violate the hierarchy to communicate with the best or most appropriate person in the organization.

Centralization of authority restricts the sharing of information because different members and groups in organizations have access to different information. The extent to which organizations have specialized work groups also hinders communication, since departments or groups with different goals and expertise often experience difficulty in communicating effectively. Often they must seek ways of overcoming potential conflict to allow quality communication to occur.

New forms of organization that emphasize lateral communication, such as alliances, team-based, and network organizations, call for extensive and effective communication. Although such structures can ease communication, any dysfunctions have major consequences for individual and organizational performance. Chapters 12 and 13 examine the impact of structure on communication in greater detail.

▌ PERFORMANCE MANAGEMENT

Performance management refers to an ongoing process of assessment in which managers and their employees share information about the employees' performance and their future development.

Communication for Evaluation and Development

Performance management typically has two components: evaluation and development.

- **Evaluation** refers to the assessment of past performance and often affects compensation decisions.
- **Development** focuses on future performance and career development and may influence job assignments and promotions.

Performance management involves extensive feedback to employees. Generally, managers and employees meet annually or even more frequently to discuss evaluation and development. The quality of communication during these meetings can support or defeat employees; it can increase commitment and motivation or make an employee defensive. In a performance appraisal meeting, the discussion should rely on direct observations rather than hearsay reports to describe specific employee behaviors. Managers should describe both positive and negative behaviors and use the same basic form and level of detail for each subordinate.

Managers often differ in their comfort and ability to provide such feedback. You can assess your own attitude toward giving feedback by completing the questionnaire in Figure 7-6. The higher your score, the more discomfort you feel in giving feedback. A manager who understands her feelings about feedback can adjust and improve her two-way communication.

As part of performance management, managers should also focus on ways an employee can improve his performance. Such improvement might respond to deficiencies in performance or in planning for advancement. For example, the manager might discuss with the employee what he needs to do to get the credentials or experiences to receive a promotion or a transfer into a different type of job.

Performance management systems in global companies must consider both international and local conditions. Nokia Telecommunications managers discovered that performance management needed to respond to the special characteristics of the situations in which their expatriates worked. A single performance management system for the entire company wouldn't work.[63]

360-Degree Feedback

To increase the effectiveness of communication and the reliability of appraisals, many companies have turned to *360-degree feedback*, which refers to the involvement of multiple raters, including superiors, co-workers, subordinates, and the worker herself, in performance evaluations. BP Amoco initiated a 360-degree system for

Indicate the degree of discomfort you would feel in each of the following situations by circling the appropriate number:

1 = high discomfort; 2 = some discomfort; 3 = undecided; 4 = very little discomfort; 5 = no discomfort.

1 2 3 4 5	**1.** Telling an employee who is also a friend that he or she must stop coming to work late.
1 2 3 4 5	**2.** Talking to an employee about his or her performance on the job.
1 2 3 4 5	**3.** Asking an employee if he or she has any comments about your rating of his or her performance.
1 2 3 4 5	**4.** Telling an employee who has problems dealing with other employees that he or she should do something about it.
1 2 3 4 5	**5.** Responding to an employee who is upset over your rating of his or her performance.
1 2 3 4 5	**6.** Responding to an employee who becomes emotional and defensive when you tell him or her about mistakes in the job.
1 2 3 4 5	**7.** Giving a rating that indicates improvement is needed to an employee who has failed to meet minimum requirements of the job.
1 2 3 4 5	**8.** Letting a subordinate talk during an appraisal interview.
1 2 3 4 5	**9.** Responding to an employee's challenge to justify your evaluation in the middle of an appraisal interview.
1 2 3 4 5	**10.** Recommending that an employee be discharged.
1 2 3 4 5	**11.** Telling an employee that you are uncomfortable in the role of having to judge his or her performance.
1 2 3 4 5	**12.** Telling an employee that his or her performance can be improved.
1 2 3 4 5	**13.** Telling an employee that you will not tolerate his or her taking extended coffee breaks.
1 2 3 4 5	**14.** Telling an employee that you will not tolerate his or her making personal telephone calls on company time.

FIGURE 7-6   *Answering the questions shown here can help you assess your attitude about giving feedback.*

senior managers that focused on specific competencies; such a focus increased the likelihood of their accepting the results of the system. At British Nuclear Fuels, Ltd., employees participate in a one-day workshop for eight to twelve people in which they receive feedback and learn its meaning.[64] Getting managers committed to the feedback process can result from showing its relationship to business activities and goals, getting their input on the process, and identifying the key decision makers and stakeholders.[65]

Using this type of feedback, managers obtain complete descriptions and evaluations of employee behavior from many sources. When organizational members rely on a single source of information, persistent biases occur. For example, raters who felt positive emotions toward ratees were most lenient, and those with negative emotions were least lenient.[66] Raters who thought a worker did well in one area, such as dependability, tended to think the employee did well in several areas.[67] Maintaining a daily or weekly record of employee performance helps managers reduce such biases.

Some question whether managers in other countries can use the same performance appraisal procedures as managers in the United States. For example, performance appraisal in Malaysia doesn't involve employees in the evaluation process. Performance appraisal in Indonesia, unlike that often done in the United States, measures performance on a group basis.[68]

■ TECHNIQUES FOR IMPROVING COMMUNICATION

Managers and other employees can improve their communication by diagnosing problems in encoding, transmitting, decoding, and feedback. They can also try to overcome the communication barriers described earlier. In this section, we examine improving interpersonal interactions, conducting productive meetings, and changing the organization's structure as three approaches to improving communication.

Improve Interpersonal Interactions

Managers can begin to improve communication by increasing the level of trust. They do this by creating a supportive climate, speaking openly to employees, and communicating assertively, not aggressively.

A Supportive Climate.   A supportive communication climate uses communication for effective problem solving, rather than for evaluation that can make employees feel defensive and threatened. A supportive climate also ensures that individuals do not disparage, or otherwise fail to affirm, others' communications.[69] Managers can create a supportive atmosphere in six specific ways:[70]

1. They use descriptive rather than evaluative speech; they give and ask for information rather than praising, blaming, or passing judgment.
2. They take a problem-solving orientation in which they collaborate to explore a mutual problem rather than trying to control the other person.
3. They are spontaneous and honest, and they reveal their goals, rather than trying to manipulate others.
4. They convey empathy for the feelings and problems of their listener, rather than appearing unconcerned or neutral about the listener's welfare.
5. They indicate that they feel equal rather than superior to the listener.
6. They communicate a willingness to experiment with their own behavior and ideas, rather than to be dogmatic about them.

Open Communication.   Managers and other employees can also improve communication by using knowledge of themselves and others that is as complete as possible. The *Johari Window,* shown in Figure 7-7, provides an analytical tool that people can use to identify information that is available for use in communication.[71] Note that this model presents information about a person along two dimensions—(1) information known and unknown by the self and (2) information known and unknown by others—and then combines this into four categories:

- ■ **open self,** information known by you and known by others;
- ■ **blind self,** information unknown by you and known by others, such as others' perceptions of your behavior or attitudes;

	KNOWN BY SELF	UNKNOWN BY SELF
KNOWN BY OTHERS	Open Self	Blind Self
UNKNOWN BY OTHERS	Concealed Self	Unconscious Self

■ **FIGURE 7-7** ■   *Managers can use the Johari Window to help diagnose the openness of their communication.*

Source: Based on a model developed by Drs. Joseph Luft and Harry Ingham and described in *The Personnel Relations Survey* by Jay Hall and Martha S. Williams, Teleometrics International, The Woodlands, Texas.

■ **concealed self,** information known by you and unknown by others (secrets we keep from others about ourselves fall into this category); and

■ **unconscious self,** information that is unknown to you and unknown to others.

In most cases, people should communicate from their open self to another's open self and limit the amount of information concealed or in the blind self. They may resort to guarded communication, however, if one party has violated trust in the past, if the parties have an adversarial relationship, if power and status differentials characterize the culture, if the relationship is transitory, or if the corporate culture does not support openness.[72]

Communicating Assertively.   An assertive style, which is honest, direct, and firm, also improves communication. With this style, a person expresses personal needs, opinions, and feelings in honest and direct ways and stands up for his rights without violating the other person's.[73]

Consider the situation of a boss whose subordinate has missed two important deadlines in the last month. How would the boss respond assertively? The boss might say to the worker: "I know you missed the last two deadlines. Is there an explanation I should know? I need you to meet the next two deadlines. I need to know as soon as possible when you are facing problems, so that I can understand the situation." Note that an assertive response can include the expression of anger, frustration, or disappointment.

We can contrast an assertive style with nonassertive and aggressive styles. A person with a nonassertive style does not stand up for his personal rights and indicates that his feelings are unimportant; the person may be hesitant, apologetic, or fearful. A person with an aggressive style stands up for her rights without respecting the rights of the other person, and attempts to dominate and control others. Men often mislabel assertive communication by women as aggressive because the honesty and directness does not fit with their preconceptions about female communication.

Conduct Productive Meetings

Most managers spend large amounts of time in meetings with their subordinates and bosses, as members of cross-functional work teams, or as participants in special taskforces. Conducting productive meetings poses a major challenge. Managers need to ensure that meetings provide the best vehicle for communicating the necessary information. Too often, managers use meetings inappropriately—to share information they could better disseminate by a short memorandum or a quick telephone call. Other times, they schedule meetings to resolve complicated problems before they gather sufficient information for making decisions.

Managers and other employees who conduct effective meetings implement the following steps:

- **Determine the goal.** What do they want to accomplish by the end of the meeting?
- **Prepare.** They must reserve an appropriate location, set a time limit, identify the right participants, develop an agenda, and distribute advanced materials.
- **Set the agenda.** The agenda specifies the major topics, questions, and information for the meeting. It states how much time each item will receive.
- **Conduct the meeting.** The manager or other employee needs to convene the meeting on time, observe the time limits in the agenda, and encourage widespread participation.
- **Conclude the meeting.** The participants should recap any decisions, specify next steps, and assign responsibility. They should plan to distribute minutes of the meeting within several days.

Change the Organization's Structure

Recent changes in the design of organizations have reduced the hierarchy, flattening the structure and thereby increasing lateral communication. Alliances, network structures, and team-based structures encourage continuous and extensive communication among employees (see Chapter 12). Such changes increase interpersonal interactions, give more responsibility and autonomy to lower-level workers, and empower workers at all levels.

These restructurings, combined with the widespread use of electronic communication, can increase the amount of communication required in the company. Managers need to ensure, however, that quality communication accompanies the restructuring; otherwise, even new structures can create barriers to information sharing.

▌ GIVING EMPLOYEES VOICE

Managers look for ways to allow employees to express their opinions about their work situation and share their work with other employees. Speak-out programs and improvement contests provide two outlets for such expression. Some employees report company malpractice and illegal activities to the public. Whistle-blowing in the workplace can have both positive and negative consequences for individuals and their employers.

Speak-Out Programs

Companies often use suggestion programs as a way for employees to speak out about issues that affect them or concerns they have about the workplace. Such programs provide a simple but effective way of improving operations and encouraging continuous improvement behaviors in an organization. Suggestion programs allow employees to anonymously offer ways to improve company operations. Employees at Haworth Inc., a Michigan manufacturer of office furniture, receive monetary rewards for their ideas. A supervisor may first discuss the suggestion proposed by the employee, but can't dismiss it. Then a committee of eight to ten people reviews the suggestion. The committee either decides to implement it, forwards it to an engineer or specialist, or declines to use it. Even if a suggestion isn't used, the employee receives a thank you, an explanation for the decision, and $1 for that idea. American Axle & Manufacturing, another Michigan manufacturer, saved almost $370,000 and paid $73,000 in rewards to employees for their suggestions in less than a year.[74]

Improvement Contests

Some companies introduce improvement contests in which teams of employees present improvement projects they have conducted. Generally done as part of continuous improvement efforts, companies hold these competitions at least yearly and sometimes more often. Top executives act as judges and select the team that has performed the best improvement project. The winner generally receives some form of company-wide recognition or a monetary prize. These contests serve as a way of communicating about new programs and rewarding improvements throughout the company.

Whistle-blowing in the Workplace

Whistle-blowers voice their views of fraudulent or illegal company activities by reporting them to governmental agencies. They are typically above-average employees who are committed to the organization, not disgruntled.[75] They frequently can play a positive role in organizations by identifying safety hazards, legal violations, sexual harassment, or other unacceptable organizational practices.

While monetary incentives and legal protections can encourage whistle-blowing, employees often receive uneven and sometimes ineffective protection.[76] Many are harassed by their organization and, fearing such retaliation, are reluctant to file complaints. The False Claims Act encourages employees to sue employers committing malpractice in federal programs. The act protects whistle-blowers from dismissal and gives them as much as 30 percent of the damages arising from the case.[77] Most states protect public employees from retaliation, and about one-third protect private sector employees. Human resources managers need to educate managers and supervisors about whistle-blowing and tell them not to retaliate against whistle-blowers. Some organizations, such as Sundstrand Corporation, an Illinois defense contractor, instituted programs to make internal whistle-blowing a valued part of their culture. The program included employee and managerial training, as well as development of a formal code of conduct.[78]

▌ COMMUNICATION IN THE DOT-COM, ▌ GLOBAL WORKPLACE

Today's global marketplace requires more rapid and accurate communication than at any time previously. Consider the way shipping by air courier, such as Federal Express, UPS, or Airborne, has routinely replaced the United States mail. Consider also the widespread use of e-mail and other forms of electronic communication. For example, managers at corporate headquarters in the United States can easily communicate with staff at sales subsidiaries or off-shore manufacturing plants using e-mail, videoconferencing, or computer conferencing.

Business reporters have become so pressured to deliver information quickly that accuracy has suffered. Fake press releases can send financial markets into turmoil. A report that the chief executive of Emulex, a fiber-optic equipment manufacturer, had resigned and that the company would restate its earnings was untrue. Before the error was discovered, investors had sold large amounts of the stock, causing its value to drop from $103 to $45 in 15 minutes before the Nasdaq stopped trading.[79]

Language differences clearly affect global communication. Some U.S. companies have considered instituting English-only work rules to ensure effective communication, although these attempts have often faced legal challenges.[80] Consider the foreign language mistakes companies have made in marketing their products: Kentucky Fried Chicken translated its "Finger Lickin' Good" slogan into "eat your fingers off" in China; Leona Helmsley compared one of her hotels to the Taj Mahal in India, a mausoleum for dead people. Situations such as these have increased the demand for translators in large corporations.[81]

Cross-cultural issues may affect the quality of communication. Effective communication requires deciphering the basic values, motives, aspirations, and assumptions that operate along geographical, occupational, functional, or social class lines. For example, Germans have a high regard for authority and structure, which contrasts markedly with Americans' easygoing, more familiar demeanor.[82] Managers need to see their own culture as different, but not necessarily better.[83]

Consider the following example. An American manager works in a Japanese company in the United States. He notices that the Japanese explain only their conclusion to Americans when they address a problem, rather than discussing the steps to the conclusion. Also, the Japanese employees send reports directly to Japan without showing them to American bosses.[84] In this case, the Japanese are not communicating in a way that the American manager understands, or they are sending messages that have a different meaning in U.S. culture. Different languages pose an obvious barrier to communication, but differences in the meaning of nonverbal communications can also have a strong and unintended impact. For example, Westerners who do business with Koreans need to understand *nunch'i,* a form of tact and subtlety that governs communication that may be reflected in gestures, word choice, or timing of communication.[85] Different cultures have very different norms for the appropriate amount of interpersonal space. Interpersonal distance is high among South Americans, southern and eastern Europeans, and Arabs, and low among Asians, northern Europeans, and North Americans.[86] Also, different styles can hinder accurate communication. The Japanese use an indirect style and hide the speaker's true intent; Arabs use very expressive and elaborate language; North American communication tends to be direct and succinct.[87]

Cultural differences may cause information overload or underload as well. Latin American cultures encourage verbal and nonverbal expression, whereas Asian cultures support lower levels of communication. A person's culture helps set expectations about the level of possible communication. Deviations from the expected level may result in overload or underload.

To ensure quality communication in multicultural situations, communicators should first assume that cultural differences exist and try to view the situation from the perspective of their colleagues.[88] They can then adjust their encoding or decoding, use of language, nonverbal cues, or listening skills in response to likely differences. Knowing the characteristics of diverse cultures eases such an adjustment. A *cultural integrator,* a person who understands cultural differences and the ways the organization can adapt to them, can also reduce the barrier of inadequate cross-cultural sensitivity.[89] For example, U.S. companies can select a cultural integrator from among U.S. citizens familiar with the foreign country or from foreign nationals who are familiar with U.S. customs. Until all individuals have cross-cultural sensitivity, such special arrangements may be necessary for quality, multicultural communication.

Summary

1. Electronic communication, including various messaging systems, conferencing systems, the Internet, and intranets, have made communication worldwide fast and accessible for managers and other employees.

2. Effective communication involves a two-way process in which the sender encodes the message, transmits it through various channels to the receiver who decodes it, and then receives feedback from the receiver.

3. The sender can improve the communication process by carefully selecting the most appropriate language for encoding; both sender and receiver should identify the meaning of nonverbal cues; the receiver should listen actively and effectively to improve the decoding process.

4. Information overload and information underload, when the receiver is given too much or too little information, respectively, can reduce the effectiveness of communication.

5. Downward communication emphasizes the dissemination of information from boss to subordinate; upward provides feedback to supervisors about their employees' thoughts and performance; lateral improves interactions between co-workers, departments, or other work groups within an organization.

6. Communication can occur formally through various media or informally through networks of associates or the grapevine.

7. Barriers to communication include perceptual and attributional biases, interpersonal relationships, top management's role, gender differences, physical distance, and organization structure.

8. Performance management relies on quality communication for employee evaluation and development.

9. Managers and employees can improve interpersonal interactions, conduct productive meetings, and change the organization's structure to improve communication.

10. Managers can also give employees voice through speak-out programs, improvement contests, and whistle-blowing in the workplace.

11. Managers in a dot-com, global environment need to diagnose the impact of different cultures on communication.

A Manager's Diagnostic Review

■ Diagnose dysfunctions in the communication process.

- What encoding and decoding errors occur in communication?
- What media are the most appropriate for transmission?

- What types of noise exist in the organization?
- Does quality feedback occur?

Use verbal and nonverbal communication effectively, and listen well when communicating.

- Do senders use effective language?
- What purpose does nonverbal communication serve?

Use formal and informal communication appropriately.

- Do managers and employees use the right channels of communication?
- How powerful is the grapevine?

Diagnose and eliminate barriers to communication.

- What barriers hinder communication?
- How are these barriers overcome?

Conduct 360-degree performance evaluations.

- Do peers, subordinates, supervisors, and customers participate in performance evaluations?

Use techniques that improve communication.

- Do people use active listening, perception checking, and paraphrasing?

Give employees voice in the workplace.

- Do suggestion programs exist?
- Does the company hold improvement contests?
- Does whistle-blowing occur?

Communicate effectively in the dot-com, global workplace.

- Do managers and employees use electronic communication effectively?
- Do managers and employees change their communication styles in different cultural settings?

Visit the Gordon homepage on the Prentice Hall Web site at

http://www.prenhall.com/gordon

for recommended readings, additional activities, Internet exercises, updated information, and links to related Web sites.

▮ Thinking Critically About Organizational Behavior

1. Should two-way communication always be encouraged in organizations?
2. How can managers overcome language differences in global organizations?
3. Should managers and employees receive training in how to communicate effectively nonverbally?

4. Which is more dysfunctional—communication underload or overload?
5. Should managers try to create efficient communication networks or rely on ones that develop informally?
6. Under what circumstances should managers use electronic communication?
7. Should managers always conduct 360-degree feedback?
8. Do gender differences affect communication?
9. How can managers use interpersonal communication to overcome the barrier of physical distance or organization structure?
10. Does whistle-blowing in the workplace have positive or negative consequences for the organization and its employees?
11. Should managers provide workers with the opportunity to "speak out"?
12. Can a manager truly communicate effectively in a different culture?

ACTIVITY 7–1: DIAGNOSING COMMUNICATION

STEP 1: Think about a work situation in which you have been or are currently involved.

STEP 2: Complete the following questions about that situation.

1. *I think my communication with my subordinates:*

	7	6	5	4	3	2	1	
Increases my credibility								Decreases my credibility
Is precise								Is imprecise
Is clear								Is unclear
Answers more questions than it raises								Raises more questions than it answers
Is effective								Is ineffective
Is competent								Is incompetent
Is productive								Is unproductive
Gets the results I want								Does not get the results I want
Is impressive								Is unimpressive
Creates a positive image of me								Creates a negative image of me
Is good								Is bad
Is skillful								Is unskillful
Is relaxed								Is strained
Is self-rewarding								Is not self-rewarding
Does not embarrass me								Does embarrass me

Total Score _____

2. *I think my communication with my supervisor:*

	7	6	5	4	3	2	1	
Increases my credibility								Decreases my credibility
Is precise								Is imprecise
Is clear								Is unclear
Answers more questions than it raises								Raises more questions than it answers
Is effective								Is ineffective
Is competent								Is incompetent
Is productive								Is unproductive
Gets the results I want								Does not get the results I want
Is impressive								Is unimpressive
Creates a positive image of me								Creates a negative image of me
Is good								Is bad
Is skillful								Is unskillful
Is relaxed								Is strained
Is self-rewarding								Is not self-rewarding
Does not embarrass me								Does embarrass me

Total Score _____

3. *I think my communication with my peers:*

	7	6	5	4	3	2	1	
Increases my credibility								Decreases my credibility
Is precise								Is imprecise
Is clear								Is unclear
Answers more questions than it raises								Raises more questions than it answers
Is effective								Is ineffective
Is competent								Is incompetent
Is productive								Is unproductive
Gets the results I want								Does not get the results I want
Is impressive								Is unimpressive
Creates a positive image of me								Creates a negative image of me
Is good								Is bad
Is skillful								Is unskillful
Is relaxed								Is strained
Is self-rewarding								Is not self-rewarding
Does not embarrass me								Does embarrass me

Total Score _____

STEP 3: Score each question by adding the numbers for the responses you gave. If your total score for a question is 15–36, you have analyzed yourself as a very ineffective communicator; if your score is 37–58, you have analyzed yourself as an ineffective communicator; if your score is 59–80, you have analyzed yourself as an effective communicator. If your score is 81 or above, you have analyzed yourself as a very effective communicator.

STEP 4: Discussion. In small groups, with the entire class, or in written form, as directed by your instructor, answer the following questions.

DESCRIPTION

1. In which type of communication are you most effective? Least effective?

DIAGNOSIS

2. What are your deficiencies as a communicator?

PRESCRIPTION

3. How could you improve your communication?

Source: Reprinted with permission from L. Sussman and P. D. Krivonos, *Communication for Supervisors and Managers.* Sherman Oaks, CA: Alfred Publishing, 1979.

ACTIVITY 7-2: NONVERBAL COMMUNICATION

STEP 1: Your instructor will organize the class into groups of five or six people. Two groups will work together; one will act as a decision-making group and the other as observers.

STEP 2: The decision-making group should rank-order the importance of the following eight leadership characteristics. You have approximately 10 minutes to complete the task. During the ranking procedures, the decision-making group may communicate only verbally. You may not use gestures, facial movements, body movements, or any other nonverbal communication.

LIST OF LEADERSHIP TRAITS

_____ extroverted personality
_____ sensitivity to others
_____ technical expertise
_____ strong ethical values
_____ task orientation or concern for production
_____ charisma
_____ internal locus of control
_____ power

STEP 3: After watching the decision making, observers should answer the following questions:

1. How effective was communication?
2. What barriers to communication existed?
3. What purpose does nonverbal communication serve?

STEP 4: Discussion. With the two groups (decision makers and observers) together or with the entire class, answer the following questions:

1. How effective was communication?
2. What happens when nonverbal communication is absent?
3. What purposes does nonverbal communication serve?

Source: Based on "The Blind Decision-Makers" by Jeffrey Powers, *Exchange: The Organizational Behavior Teaching Journal 1* (January 1975): 32–33.

ACTIVITY 7-3: WHAT DOES THE LOGO SAY?

STEP 1: Individually or in small groups, find five to ten corporate logos.

STEP 2: Analyze each logo for the message it communicates.

STEP 3: In small groups or with the entire class, share your observations.

STEP 4: Individually or with a partner, design a corporate logo for your school or university. Consider the message you want it to convey and how to best convey that message.

STEP 5: Discussion. In small groups or with the entire class, answer the following questions:

1. What communication purpose do corporate logos serve?
2. What types of messages do they convey?
3. How well do they convey the intended message?

ACTIVITY 7-4: GENDER IN COMMUNICATION

STEP 1: Select a small work group to observe for 30 to 60 minutes. Make sure that the group includes both men and women.

STEP 2: For each person in the group, check each time you observe the following types of communication: report-talk (focuses on demonstration of knowledge and skills) and rapport-talk (builds relationships and establishes connections).

Person's Name	Report-Talk	Rapport-Talk
1.		
2.		
3.		
4.		
5.		
6.		

STEP 3: Tally the number of instances of report-talk and rapport-talk for each person in the group. Then compare the average number of instances for the men and women in the group. Did men or women use more report-talk? Did men or women use more rapport-talk?

STEP 4: You may repeat Steps 1 through 3 with groups in different settings and composed of different proportions of men and women.

STEP 5: Discussion. In small groups or with the entire class, answer the following questions:

1. Did communication differ between men and women? If so, in what ways?
2. What are the implications for managers' effectiveness in organizations?

ACTIVITY 7-5: PERFORMANCE FEEDBACK EXERCISE

STEP 1: Read the following scenario.

Dr. Brilliant, a professor, and Pat, Dr. Brilliant's student research assistant, are meeting at Dr. Brilliant's request to discuss Pat's performance during the previous semester. The following are their perceptions of the experience of working together.

DR. BRILLIANT'S COMMENTS ABOUT PAT

Pat is a good research assistant. Projects are eventually completed, but only after repeated requests. For example, I have asked Pat three times to give me an updated draft of the summaries of interviews that have been conducted for the Space Project. The project's documentation is also a mess; it's half in my office and half in Pat's cubicle. Pat's computer skills are excellent, and Pat's writing is exceptional for a student. But Pat's quantitative skills are not as strong as I need, particularly for my upcoming research project.

PAT'S COMMENTS ABOUT DR. BRILLIANT

I learn an incredible amount from Dr. Brilliant, and that is very important to me. What I want most from this working relationship is to learn. It is frustrating because Dr. Brilliant is so busy that I feel as if I only get part of the directions or objectives at any one time. I wish Dr. Brilliant and I could schedule regular time together. I know Dr. Brilliant wants a better project system, but I am not sure about how to create one.

STEP 2: You are Dr. Brilliant. Based on the preceding information, prepare a brief performance feedback for Pat.

STEP 3: With a partner, give each other the performance feedback, alternating playing the roles of Dr. Brilliant and Pat.

STEP 4: Compare the content of each person's feedback as well as what was most and least effective in each person's delivery.

STEP 5: Discussion. In small groups or with the entire class, answer the following questions:

DESCRIPTION

1. Briefly summarize the main events of the meetings.
2. Describe the perceptions and attributions Dr. Brilliant and Pat seem to have about each other. What effects do these have?

DIAGNOSIS

3. Evaluate the communication process during the interview.
4. What types of barriers to effective communication occurred?

PRESCRIPTION

5. Is it possible for most interviewers to avoid the pitfalls in this type of situation? How?
6. How can communication about performance feedback be improved?

Source: This exercise was prepared by Dr. Karen S. Whelan-Berry, Samford University, Birmingham, Alabama, and is used with permission.

ACTIVITY 7-6: COMMUNICATING AT ABLEX ADVERTISING

STEP 1: You are the chief operating officer at Ablex Advertising, a major agency in the Pacific Northwest. Your company has just lost two major clients. Unfortunately, this means reducing the workforce by 15 percent. Top management at Ablex has decided to make the cuts across the board and then reassign people as appropriate. The reduction must occur within the next six months for the company to remain financially viable.

Although this is your agency's first experience with downsizing, you have seen similar situations in other agencies. You have watched these agencies alienate their employees by not telling them anything about their specific plans for reducing the work force. This silence seems to have caused high stress and low productivity from everyone. You think there is a better, more open and honest way to deal with the situation. Although you know that layoffs are painful, they are part of the business and should be handled professionally and openly.

You have the responsibility for communicating on behalf of Ablex about the downsizing. Design a communication plan for Ablex Advertising. Be as specific as possible in describing the types and content of communication that will occur.

STEP 2: In small groups or with the entire class, as directed by your instructor, share your communication plans. Then answer the following questions:

1. What elements do they have in common?
2. How effective is each plan likely to be?
3. What are the key communication issues, and how should they be addressed?

Chapter 8

Leading Effectively

Learning Objectives

After completing Chapter 8, you will be able to

1. Describe how a manager's traits and behaviors influence leadership effectiveness.
2. Compare and contrast five theories that focus on the situation, and show how managers can use them to choose an effective style.
3. Compare and contrast two theories that focus on followers, and show how leaders can use them to act effectively.
4. Describe the basics of charismatic leadership and its relationship to transformational leadership.
5. Offer a prescription for becoming a transformational leader.
6. Describe superleadership, and show how it can increase leadership effectiveness.
7. Offer a protocol for leading in a dot-com, global workplace.

A Manager's Preview

Describe . . . Diagnose . . . Prescribe . . . Act

- Recognize the traits of an effective leader.
- Practice the behaviors of an effective leader.
- Perform the roles appropriate to the job.
- Develop and implement a repertoire of leadership styles.
- Diagnose the situation and use a leadership style that fits it.
- Involve followers effectively.
- Act charismatically.
- Set and implement a vision for your company.
- Develop self-leadership skills in yourself and your employees.
- Lead effectively in the dot-com, global workplace.

Carly Fiorina Leads Hewlett-Packard

*C*arly Fiorina, the first female CEO of Hewlett-Packard (HP) and only the third woman to hold the position of CEO in a Fortune 500 company, was hired to help HP handle the challenges of the Internet. Fiorina learned firsthand at AT&T, her former employer, how to transform a stodgy corporate behemoth into a lean and competitive player in the communications and Internet industries. There she led Lucent's launch, initial public stock offering, and final spin-off from AT&T. Directing one of the most successful initial public stock offerings in history gave Fiorina public exposure and an opportunity to exhibit her industry savvy and leadership skills.

Many say that Fiorina is a decisive leader with strong opinions; yet she always takes the time to listen to her employees and her customers. Since arriving at Hewlett-Packard, she has reduced 83 profit centers into 12, changed the compensation system, reorganized the sales staff, and rewritten job descriptions. Although she has an impatient approach to change, her collegial style and respect for other points of view fit well with the leadership needs of the Internet age. Carly Fiorina likely will serve as a symbol of change, as well as be intensively involved in the transformation process at HP. She plans to execute a new vision for HP by motivating managers and employees to focus on the organization's ideals. Her belief that people make a business and her personal touch inspired great loyalty at Lucent. Many see her accomplishing even greater feats at HP as she attempts to drive new dynamism into the company and alter the culture to include new energy and urgency.[1]

What makes Carly Fiorina an effective leader? How do effective managers lead? This chapter examines an array of leadership theories that managers can use to diagnose a situation and select the most effective style. We first examine the early views of leadership. Next we investigate theories that focus on leaders changing with the situation and theories that focus on followers. Then we consider contemporary ways of analyzing and improving leadership. We conclude with issues faced by leaders in a dot-com, global workplace.

▌EARLY VIEWS OF LEADERSHIP

The early views of leadership focused on the leader's personality, abilities, and behaviors. In this section, we examine trait theory, behavioral theories, and McGregor's Theory X and Theory Y.

Trait Theory

Carly Fiorina has energy, expertise, and initiative; she is ambitious and achievement-oriented; she shows originality, enthusiasm, and persistence. Trait theory suggests that leaders have personality, social, and physical characteristics such as these, known as *traits*.[2] First introduced in the 1940s and 1950s, trait theory originally proposed that individuals were born to be leaders. More than 100 early studies on leader traits showed that leaders differed from nonleaders in their intelligence, initiative, persistence in dealing with problems, alertness to others' needs, understanding of the task, desire to accept responsibility, and preference for a position of control and dominance.[3] Leaders also differed from nonleaders in their drive (achievement, ambition, energy, tenacity, and initiative), desire to lead, honesty and integrity, self-confidence, cognitive ability, and knowledge of business.[4] Ann Livermore, the head of Hewlett-Packard's software and services business when Fiorina became CEO, has a strong drive. Although Livermore appears to be a pragmatist, she has a gutsy temperament that she has softened to fit better with HP's egalitarian culture.[5]

More recent research suggests that leaders like Fiorina and Livermore share a high amount of emotional intelligence, which includes the following:[6]

- **self-awareness,** the ability to recognize and understand your moods, emotions, and drives, as well as their effect on others;
- **self-regulation,** the ability to control or redirect disruptive impulses and moods, the propensity to suspend judgment and to think before acting;
- **motivation,** a passion to work for reasons that go beyond money or status, a propensity to pursue goals with energy and persistence;
- **empathy,** the ability to understand the emotional makeup of other people, skill in treating people according to their emotional reactions; and
- **social skill,** proficiency in managing relationships and building networks, an ability to find common ground and build rapport.[7]

Behavioral Theories

Behavioral theorists argued in the 1950s that leaders' behaviors, not their traits, determine their effectiveness. For example, even today, Tom Siebel, the CEO of Siebel Systems, acts swiftly and decisively without a consideration of social niceties.

"He doesn't hold hands, stroke egos, or spend time building consensus. . . . If employees are offended by this perfunctory management style, then they're probably not right for Siebel Systems."[8]

Siebel demonstrates a strong, task-oriented leadership style, one of two dimensions identified by path-breaking studies in the 1950s:[9]

- ■ **Orientation to task,** sometimes called initiating structure or concern for productivity, refers to the degree to which a leader focuses on the task by structuring his role and employees' roles to help accomplish the group's goal, such as scheduling the work of subordinates or co-workers, assigning employees to tasks, maintaining standards of performance, or delineating the specific tasks individuals will perform.

- ■ **Orientation to people,** sometimes called consideration, refers to the degree to which the leader addresses individuals' needs (e.g., two-way communication, respect for employees' ideas, considering employees' feelings, and showing mutual trust between leader and subordinates).

Figure 8-1 shows that, according to studies at Ohio State University, leaders high on both initiating structure and consideration have employees who show high performance, low turnover, and low grievance rates. Leaders low on both behaviors have subordinates with the opposite outcomes—low performance, high turnover, and high grievance rates. A combination of high initiating structure and low consideration resulted in high employee performance, but also high turnover and high grievance rates. A combination of low initiating structure and high consideration resulted in low employee performance, as well as low turnover and low grievance rates. Carly Fiorina demonstrates both types of behaviors in her task-oriented but consensual style of leadership, theoretically resulting in high performance and satisfaction.

Supervisors of highly productive work groups tended to be both production- and employee-oriented, according to studies at the University of Michigan.[10] They

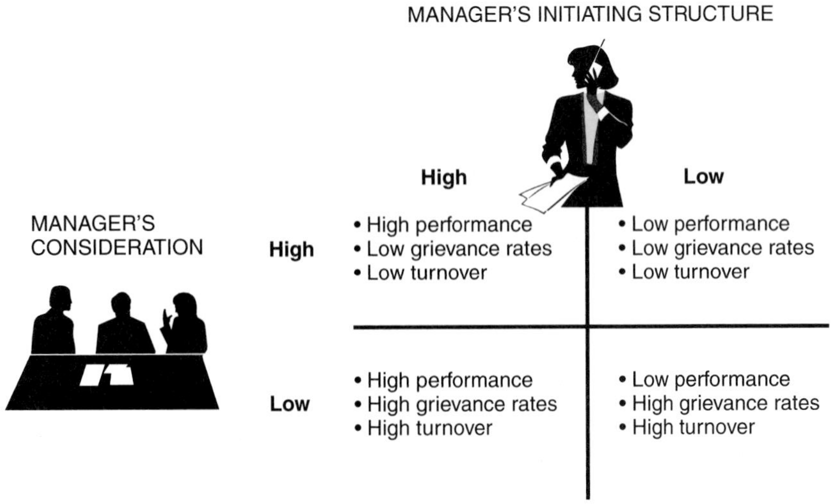

FIGURE 8-1

The Ohio State studies suggested that leaders high on both initiating structure and consideration had the best outcomes.

Source: Based on R. H. Stogdill and A. E. Coons (eds.), *Leader Behavior: Its Description and Measurement.* (Columbus: Ohio State University Bureau of Business Research, 1957.)

MANAGER'S INITIATING STRUCTURE

MANAGER'S CONSIDERATION

	High	**Low**
High	• High performance • Low grievance rates • Low turnover	• Low performance • Low grievance rates • Low turnover
Low	• High performance • High grievance rates • High turnover	• Low performance • High grievance rates • High turnover

spent more time planning departmental work and supervising their employees, less time performing the same tasks as subordinates, and gave their employees greater freedom in accomplishing the task.[11] Louise Kitchen, responsible for developing Enron's business for trading gas contracts online, builds coalitions as a way of demonstrating her orientations toward task and employees. She gathered a group of Enron's top traders as a way of garnering their support for the new business. Her commitment and enthusiasm eventually converted the naysayers to supporters.[12]

Rensis Likert added participative leadership to the behaviors studied.[13] Participative leaders used group meetings to encourage worker involvement in decision making, communication, cooperation, and conflict resolution. Participative leaders supported and guided the group discussions and focused members on making decisions and solving problems. Participative leaders who set high goals, had technical expertise, supported their employees, and acted as an information link had groups with high productivity, high-quality work, low absenteeism, low turnover, and low grievance rates.

Another way to diagnose leader behaviors is to examine the roles a leader performs. In today's global organizations, leaders use a strategic vision to motivate their subordinates, empower employees at all levels, collect and share internal and external information, challenge the status quo, and enable their subordinates to be creative.[14]

Henry Mintzberg said that managers perform ten specific roles, as described in Table 8-1, grouped into three categories:

- **interpersonal contact,** figurehead, leader, liaison;
- **information processing,** monitor, disseminator, spokesperson; and
- **decision making,** entrepreneur, disturbance handler, resource allocator, and negotiator.

Joe Galli, the former president and chief operating officer of Amazon.com and now CEO of VerticalNet, a developer of online business-to-business stores, spent much of his first days as the CEO making interpersonal contacts. Galli met with the company's general counsel on the first day, the company's co-founder and chief operating officer on the second day, and the head of customer service on the third day. He used these meetings to develop a strong management team that supports his vision and goals. Now Galli's planned visits to each of VerticalNet's 18 acquisitions will allow him to perform the roles of liaison and entrepreneur.[15]

Managers and employees can perform additional leadership roles:[16]

- **Sages** expand their knowledge about a wide array of subjects and use it to design strategy.
- **Visionaries** inspire large groups of people to go beyond their previous accomplishments.
- **Magicians** coordinate change by bridging the gap between where the organization is and where it should be.
- **Globalists** consolidate the experiences of people across cultures by demonstrating an interest in the diversity and finding a common ground.
- **Mentors** help employees advance in their careers by helping them learn and work to their potential.
- **Allies** form effective teams and alliances.
- **Sovereigns** take responsibility for the decisions they make even if they involve risk or uncertainty.

TABLE 8-1

Managers Perform Interpersonal, Informational, and Decision-making Roles.

Role	Description	Examples
Figurehead	Acts as a symbol or representative of the organization Performs diverse ceremonial duties	Attends Chamber of Commerce meetings Heads the local United Way drive Represents the president of the firm at an awards banquet
Leader	Interacts with subordinates Motivates and develops employees	Conducts quarterly performance interviews Selects training opportunities for subordinates
Liaison	Establishes a network of contacts to gather information for the organization	Belongs to professional associations Meets over lunch with peers in other organizations
Monitor	Gathers information from the environment inside and outside the organization	Attends meetings with subordinates Scans company publications Participates in company-wide committees
Disseminator	Transmits both factual and value information to subordinates	Conducts staff meetings Sends memos to staff Meets informally with staff on a one-to-one basis to discuss current and future projects
Spokesperson	Gives information to people outside the organization about its performance and policies	Oversees preparation of the annual report Prepares advertising copy Speaks at community and professional meetings
Entrepreneur	Designs and initiates changes in the organization	Redesigns the jobs of subordinates Introduces flexible working hours Brings new technology to the job
Disturbance handler	Deals with problems that arise when organizational operations break down	Finds a new supplier on short notice for an out-of-stock part Replaces unexpectedly absent workers Deals with machine breakdowns
Resoure allocator	Controls the allocation of people, money, materials, and time	Schedules his or her own time Programs subordinates' work effort Prepares the budget
Negotiator	Participates in negotiation activities	Hires a new employee Determines compensation

Source: These roles are drawn from H. Mintzberg, *The Nature of Managerial Work,* 2d ed. (Englewood Cliffs, NJ: Prentice Hall, 1979).

- **Guides** use clearly stated principles based on core values to guide their employees' tasks and attain goals.
- **Artisans** try to improve performance by ensuring the quality of a company's products and production processes.

■ **TABLE 8-2** ■

Certain Jobs Involve Combinations of Roles.		
Managerial Job Type	**Key Roles**	**Examples**
Contact person	Liaison, figurehead	Sales manager Chief executive in service industry
Political manager	Spokesperson, negotiator	Top government, hospital, university manager
Entrepreneur	Entrepreneur, negotiator	Owner of small, young business CEO of rapidly changing, large organization
Insider	Resource allocator	Middle or senior production or operations manager Manager rebuilding after crisis
Real-time manager	Disturbance handler	Plant manager Head of organization in crisis Head of small, one-manager business
Team manager	Leader	Hockey coach Head of R&D group
Expert manager	Monitor, spokesperson	Head of specialist group
New manager	Leader, liaison	Manager in a new job

Source: These roles are drawn from H. Mintzberg, *The Nature of Managerial Work,* 2d ed. (Englewood Cliffs, NJ: Prentice Hall, 1979).

Consider some managers and leaders you have observed. How would you describe the roles played by your former boss? The dean of your school? The CEO of IBM, Dell, or Compaq? Carly Fiorina? Now consider your own performance in managerial and leadership roles. What roles did you perform? How effectively did you perform them? Managers can diagnose their own and others' role performance and then implement strategies for improving them. The choice of roles depends to some extent on the manager's specific job description and the situation in question, as shown in Table 8-2.

Theory X and Theory Y

Douglas McGregor described leadership behaviors based on a manager's assumptions about other individuals.[17]

■ **Theory X** managers assume that people are lazy, extrinsically motivated, incapable of self-discipline or self-control, and want security and no responsibility in their jobs.
■ **Theory Y** managers assume people do not inherently dislike work, are intrinsically motivated, exert self-control, and seek responsibility.

Bill Ford Jr., heir to the Ford Motor Company fortune and now chairman of the company, leads with Theory Y assumptions. He believes that Ford will best serve its shareholders if it takes care of its employees, community, and environment.[18]

Characteristics of the individual, the task, the organization, and the environment combine with these assumptions to determine a leader's style.[19] A manager with Theory X assumptions should first verify that the employee requires extrinsic motivation and, if so, use an autocratic style. If the manager has incorrect assumptions, he should try to change them. Some managers with Theory X assumptions can benefit from training about Theory Y and learn ways to tap into workers' inherent pride in their work or desire for responsibility. A manager with Theory Y assumptions, in contrast, should diagnose the situation and then choose the best style for it. Training for this type of manager will focus on assessing the situation and practicing a variety of leadership styles.

Evaluation of the Early Theories

Although traits can contribute to effective leadership, they are not sufficient by themselves for ensuring effectiveness.[20] Managers must consider the effects of different leadership behaviors or situations.[21] According to the Ohio State and University of Michigan studies, leaders should demonstrate both high initiating structure and high consideration. Is this possible? Perhaps, but more likely, individuals need different styles in different situations. Validating the theory requires more careful data collection to precisely determine whether leadership style caused the outcomes observed.[22]

The early theories had limited applications to multinational and multicultural situations. Traits judged necessary for top, middle, and low-level management also differed among leaders of different countries. For example, U.S. and British managers valued resourcefulness, the Japanese intuition, and the Dutch imagination, but for lower and middle managers only.[23] Behaviors of managers in multicultural situations also differed: In the United Arab Emirates, Arab expatriate and national managers used participative styles while foreign expatriates used consultative styles.[24]

Both the theory of managerial roles and Theory X–Theory Y have intuitive appeal, but they describe only a limited aspect of leadership and management behavior. Because the research included limited empirical support, generalizations are problematic.

▌ FITTING LEADERSHIP STYLE TO THE SITUATION

Rather than relying solely on traits or specific behaviors in all situations, effective leaders select a style that fits the particular situation. They diagnose the situation, identify the most effective style, and then determine if they can implement it. Three factors appear to influence the best style:

- **Subordinate considerations** reflect the leader's awareness of employees' expertise, experience, competence, job knowledge, hierarchical level, and psychological characteristics.
- **Supervisor considerations** reflect the leader's degree of upward influence, as well as the similarity of her attitudes and behaviors to those in higher positions.
- **Task considerations** reflect the degree of time urgency, amount of physical danger, permissible error rate, presence of external stress, degree of autonomy, degree of job scope, importance and meaningfulness of the tasks, and degree of ambiguity of the work being performed.

The precise aspects of each dimension that influence the most effective leadership style vary in different situations. Typically, effective leaders develop a repertoire of leadership styles, which they adapt to different situations.[25] In this section, we will examine five theories and their prescriptions for leadership style.

LPC Contingency Theory

Fred Fiedler and his associates argued that, while a leader matches his style to the situation, his style is relatively fixed.[26] The leader prefers one of two styles:

- **task-oriented,** or controlling, active, and structuring; or
- **relations-oriented,** or permissive, passive, and considerate.

Harold Levy, for example, the interim chancellor of the New York City schools, uses a take-charge approach. He insisted on the ability to send e-mail to the city's school principals and demanded that the school board install new software sooner than the six months they said it would take.[27]

Effective leaders seek a match between their preferred style and the situation; if necessary, they change the situation to fit their preferred style. Fiedler and his associates developed the Least-Preferred Co-worker (LPC) scale to help identify managers' preferred styles. Figure 8-2 presents an excerpt from this scale. Those who score high on the LPC scale have a relations-oriented leadership style. Low-scoring leaders have a task-oriented style. The score of 84 shown in the figure would present a hybrid style, with elements of both task and relations orientations.

A leader analyzes three dimensions of the situation to create a match between style and situation:

- **Leader–member relations** refers to the extent to which the group trusts the leader and willingly follows her directions. If Carly Fiorina has employees who readily follow instructions, set goals, and cooperate with her, she has good leader–member relations; if not, she has poor leader–member relations.
- **Task structure** refers to the degree to which the task is clearly defined. A computer programmer's job has a relatively high task structure; a Web site designer's job has less.
- **Position power** means the extent to which the leader has official power to influence others. Typically, a line manager, such as a night supervisor, has position power, whereas a staff member, such as a quality control analyst, does not.

Table 8-3 shows the type of leadership style called for in situations with combinations of these three characteristics. An effective manager diagnoses the situation along these three dimensions and then determines whether her style fits it. Consider the president of a dot-com company where the 10 employees are hand-picked, the tasks are highly ambiguous, but the president's authority is clear. What type of style would best fit the situation? A task-oriented style would work well. If instead the president bought a small company and has disgruntled employees who perform structured tasks, a relations-oriented style would work better.

FIGURE 8-2

The LPC measures a leader's style along two dimensions: task-orientation and relations-orientation.

Source: Adapted from F. E. Fiedler, *A Theory of Leadership Effectiveness* (New York: McGraw-Hill, 1967). Reprinted with permission.

Think of the person with whom you can work least well. Describe this person as he or she appears to you by checking the appropriate place on each scale.

Pleasant	✓ 8	7	6	5	4	3	2	1	Unpleasant
Friendly	8	7	6	✓ 5	4	3	2	1	Unfriendly
Rejecting	1	2	✓ 3	4	5	6	7	8	Accepting
Tense	1	2	3	4	5	✓ 6	7	8	Relaxed
Distant	1	2	3	✓ 4	5	6	7	8	Close
Cold	1	2	3	4	5	✓ 6	7	8	Warm
Supportive	8	7	6	5	4	3	✓ 2	1	Hostile
Boring	1	✓ 2	3	4	5	6	7	8	Interesting
Quarrelsome	1	2	3	4	✓ 5	6	7	8	Harmonious
Gloomy	1	2	3	4	5	6	7	✓ 8	Cheerful
Open	8	7	✓ 6	5	4	3	2	1	Guarded
Backbiting	1	2	3	4	✓ 5	6	7	8	Loyal
Untrustworthy	1	✓ 2	3	4	5	6	7	8	Trustworthy
Considerate	8	7	6	5	✓ 4	3	2	1	Inconsiderate
Nasty	1	2	3	4	5	✓ 6	7	8	Nice
Agreeable	8	7	6	✓ 5	4	3	2	1	Disagreeable
Insincere	1	✓ 2	3	4	5	6	7	8	Sincere
Kind	8	7	6	✓ 5	4	3	2	1	Unkind

TABLE 8-3

The Appropriate Leadership Style Depends on Leader–Member Relations, the Task, and the Leader's Power Position.

Description of the Situation			Effective Leadership Style
Leader–Member Relations	**Task Structure**	**Position Power**	
Good	Structured	Strong	Task oriented
Good	Structured	Weak	Task oriented
Good	Unstructured	Strong	Task oriented
Good	Unstructured	Weak	Relations oriented
Poor	Structured	Strong	Relations oriented
Poor	Structured	Weak	Relations oriented
Poor	Unstructured	Strong	Either
Poor	Unstructured	Weak	Task oriented

More recently, Fiedler proposed a cognitive resource theory that suggested that leader intelligence and experience influence group performance in the following ways:[28]

1. Leader ability contributes to group performance when the leader is directive.
2. In low-stress conditions, high intelligence results in good decisions, whereas no relationship or a negative one exists between intelligence and decisions in high-stress conditions.
3. Experience and quality of leadership decisions are positively related in conditions of high interpersonal stress, but no relationship exists in low-stress conditions.

Path-Goal Theory

Path-goal theory provides a way of diagnosing the leadership style needed in very complex organizational situations.[29] According to this theory, leaders attempt to influence their employees' perceptions of the payoffs for accomplishing their goals and show them ways to achieve the goals. The nature of the situation—specifically, characteristics of the task, subordinates, and environment—affect the impact of the leader's behavior on follower satisfaction and effort.

Basically, the leader chooses among four styles:

■ **Directive.** The leader tells employees what he expects of them, gives them guidance about what they should do, and shows them how to do it.

■ **Supportive.** The leader shows concern for the well-being and needs of her employees by being friendly and approachable.

■ **Participative.** The leader involves employees in decision making, consults with them about their views of the situation, asks for their suggestions, considers those suggestions in making a decision, and sometimes lets the employees make the decisions.

■ **Achievement-oriented.** The leader helps employees set goals, rewards the accomplishment of these goals, and encourages employees to assume responsibility for achieving the goals.

An effective leader tries to increase the employees' expectancies and valences (see Chapter 4 for discussion of expectancy theory). For example, the leader helps ensure that a worker's effort results in performance by improving the tools, techniques, and skills of workers. The leader secures new equipment, introduces special training programs, or removes other barriers to performing. John McCoy, the former CEO at Bank One, used to let the management of the local banks that he purchased retain their own style of doing business. He called this approach "uncommon partnership," and said that he was buying their banks because of their contributions. Yet, this friendly approach, which worked so well when McCoy initially headed Bank One, ultimately resulted in his losing power after the bank merged with First Chicago because his style didn't fit the new situation. Instead, it resulted in an inability to control the sprawling organization after the merger. McCoy became the target for the operating problems that arose, and the board ultimately ousted him from the top position.[30]

To choose a style that fits the situation, a leader such as McCoy should take the following steps:

1. **Diagnose the task.**   Is the task structured or unstructured? Are the goals clear or unclear? Structured tasks and clear goals require less direction than less structured tasks and less clear goals.

2. **Assess the leader's formal authority.**   Managers tend to have more formal authority than nonmanagerial employees, and top executives have more than middle or lower-level managers. Managers with formal authority typically should not use a directive style because it duplicates their authority, but they may use supportive, achievement-oriented, or participative styles.

3. **Diagnose the work group.**   The leader should assess the group's cohesiveness as well as its experience in working together. The more cohesive the group, the less need for supportive leadership since this is redundant with the group's character. Similarly, the more experience the group has in collaborating, the less it requires directive, supportive, or participative leadership.

4. **Diagnose the organization's culture.**   A culture that supports participation also supports a participative leadership style. A culture that encourages goal accomplishment or a results orientation reinforces an achievement-oriented style.

5. **Diagnose the subordinates' skills and needs.**   Employees skilled in a task require less direction than those less skilled. Employees with high achievement needs require a style that helps meet these needs. Employees with social needs require a style that helps meet those needs.

6. **Match the style to the situation.**   Use the information in Table 8-4. The right-hand columns indicate whether a style fits the feature of the situation listed in the left-hand column when considered independently of other situational characteristics. For example, only directive leadership does not fit a structured task—directive leadership is redundant. In contrast, for employees with high achievement needs, only an achievement style will satisfy their needs.

TABLE 8-4

Path-Goal Theory Suggests that the Leader Chooses One of Four Styles to Fit the Situation.

Leadership Styles

Sample Situational Characteristics	Directive	Supportive	Achievement	Participative
Task				
Structured	No	Yes	Yes	Yes
Unstructured	Yes	No	Yes	No
Clear goals	No	Yes	No	Yes
Ambiguous goals	Yes	No	Yes	No
Subordinates				
Skilled in task	No	Yes	Yes	Yes
Unskilled in task	Yes	No	Yes	No
High achievement needs	No	No	Yes	No
High social needs	No	Yes	No	Yes
Formal Authority				
Extensive	No	Yes	Yes	Yes
Limited	Yes	Yes	Yes	Yes
Work Group				
Strong social network	Yes	No	Yes	Yes
Experienced in collaboration	No	No	No	Yes
Organizational Culture				
Supports participation	No	No	No	Yes
Achievement-oriented	No	No	Yes	No

Normative Decision Theory

Managers' leadership styles also relate to their approach to making decisions in work groups or with individuals. The normative theory calls for managers to select a leadership style according to the amount of participation in decision making appropriate for the situation.[31] Leaders use variations of authoritative (AI and AII), consultative (CI and CII), group-based (GI and GII), and delegative (DI) styles, as shown in Table 8-5, in making decisions. These styles lead to different decision-making processes for solving both individual and group problems.

TABLE 8-5

Leaders Choose from Variations of Four Basic Styles in Solving Problems.

For Individual Problems

For Group Problems

AI You solve the problem or make the decision yourself, using information available to you at that time.

AII You obtain any necessary information from the subordinate, then decide on the solution to the problem yourself.

CI You share the problem with the relevant subordinate, getting his or her ideas and suggestions. Then you make the decision, which may or may not reflect your subordinate's influence.

GI You share the problem with one of your subordinates, and together you analyze the problem and arrive at a mutually satisfactory solution in an atmosphere of free and open exchange of information and ideas.

DI You delegate the problem to one of your subordinates, providing him or her with any relevant information that you possess, but giving him or her responsibility for making the decision and your support for any decision reached.

AI You solve the problem or make the decision yourself, using information available to you at the time.

AII You obtain any necessary information from the subordinates, then decide on the solution to the problem yourself.

CI You share the problem with the relevant subordinates individually, getting their ideas and suggestions without bringing them together. Then you make the decision, which may or may not reflect your subordinates' influence.

CII You share the problem with your subordinates in a group meeting in which you obtain their ideas and suggestions. Then you make the decision, which may or may not reflect their influence.

GII You share the problem with your subordinates as a group. Together you generate and evaluate alternatives and attempt to reach true consensus on a solution. Acting as a coordinator of the discussion, you are willing to accept and implement any solution that the entire group supports.

Source: Adapted with permission from V. H. Vroom and A. G. Jago, Decision-making as a social process: Normative and descriptive models of leader behavior, *Decision Sciences* 5 (1974): 745.

A. Is there a quality requirement such that one solution is likely to be more rational than another?
B. Do I have sufficient information to make a high-quality decision?
C. Is the problem structured?
D. Is acceptance of decision by subordinates critical to effective implementation?
E. If I were to make the decision by myself, is it reasonably certain that it would be accepted by my subordinates?
F. Do subordinates share the organizational goals to be attained in solving this problem?
G. Is conflict among subordinates likely in preferred solutions? (This question is irrelevant to individual problems.)
H. Do subordinates have sufficient information to make a high-quality decision?

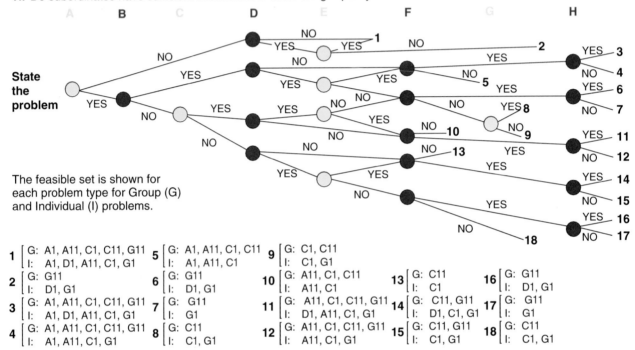

FIGURE 8-3   *Leaders use the decision tree to determine the most effective leadership style in a specific situation.*

Source: Reprinted from V. H. Vroom and A. G. Jago, Decision making as a social process: Normative and descriptive models of leader behavior, *Decision Sciences* 5 (1974): 748.

Leaders should consider numerous factors in analyzing the situation. The eight questions in the decision tree shown in Figure 8-3 reflect these factors. Answers to these questions lead the manager down the appropriate branch of the decision tree, identifying one or more decision-making processes appropriate for the situation.

Applying the Model. To see how this works, let us consider how Carly Fiorina might use the decision tree to decide whether to sell specific computers and printers directly to customers through the HP Web site.

A. *Is there a quality requirement such that one solution is likely to be more rational than another?* Yes. The decision to sell products using the Web cannot be decided by flipping a coin. There are factors that determine whether it is a good decision. [Go to question B.]

B. *Do I have sufficient information to make a high-quality decision?* No. Fiorina probably requires special market and consumer information that other members of her staff have. [Go to question C.]

C. *Is the problem structured?* No. Changing customer preferences and the rapid development of e-commerce influence the decision and prevent its solution by standard procedures. [Go to question D.]

D. *Is acceptance of the decision by subordinates critical to effective implementation?* No. Subordinates would accept a decision made by Fiorina. [Skip to question F.]

E. *If I were to make the decision by myself, is it reasonably certain that it would be accepted by my subordinates?* (This question is skipped.)

F. *Do subordinates share the organizational goals to be attained in solving this problem?* Yes. They seem committed to HP's goals. [Skip to question H.]

G. *Is conflict among subordinates likely in preferred solutions?* (This question is skipped.)

H. *Do subordinates have sufficient information to make a high-quality decision?* No. They need information Fiorina has about the organization's strategy and top management's thinking.

The feasible set is Number 15 for group problems, which calls for extensive employee involvement in making the decision (CII or GII is a feasible approach). Leaders should select the specific approach according to the time available for making the decision and the extent to which they wish to develop the group by involving them in decision making. If less time is available, leaders should use the less consultative styles of the feasible set; if more time is available, they can use the more consultative styles. If the manager wants to help train the group in decision making, he should use more consultative and delegative approaches from the feasible set.

The most recent version of this model uses a computerized question-response format to generate the appropriate decision style. This reformulation uses the same decision processes—AI, AII, CI, CII, GI, GII, DI—as the original model, as well as the criteria of decision quality, decision commitment, time, and employee development.[32] Because it uses a computer to process the data, however, the range of possible responses includes probabilities, rather than "yes" or "no" answers, to each diagnostic question.

Life Cycle Theory

The life cycle theory, also called the situational theory by its authors, states that effective leadership results from the fit between a leader's style and the *readiness* of his followers.[33] A follower's readiness likely increases over the life cycle of her relationship with the leader, calling for a change in the leader's style over time.

This theory focuses on two dimensions of leadership style:

- **Task behavior** refers to behaviors in which the leader specifies an individual's or group's duties, activities, and responsibilities by goal setting, organizing, scheduling, directing, and controlling.

- **Relationship behavior** refers to the communication behaviors of the leaders, such as listening, giving support, facilitating interactions, providing feedback, and supporting individuals and groups.

As shown in Figure 8-4, combining these two dimensions results in four decision styles, labeled S1 through S4, or 1 through 4, in various parts of the figure.[34]

Task Behavior

The extent to which the leader engages in defining roles telling what, how, when, where, and if more than one person, who is to do what in
- Goal-setting
- Organizing
- Establishing time lines
- Directing
- Controlling

Relationship Behavior

The extent to which a leader engages in two-way (multi-way) communication, listening, facilitating behaviors, socioemotional support
- Giving support
- Communicating
- Facilitating interactions
- Active listening
- Providing feedback

LEADER BEHAVIOR

Relationship Behavior (Supportive Behavior)

(HIGH)

3 — Share ideas and facilitate in decision making — Participating

2 — Explain decisions and provide opportunity for clarification — Selling

Hi Rel Lo Task | Hi Task Hi Rel

Lo Rel Lo Task | Hi Task Lo Rel

4 — Turn over responsibility for decisions and implementation — Delegating

1 — Provide specific instructions and closely supervise performance — Telling

(LOW) ◄——— **Task Behavior** ———► (HIGH)
(Guidance)

Decision Styles

1
Leader-made decision

2
Leader-made decision with dialogue and/or explanation

3
Leader/follower-made decision or follower-made decision with encouragement from leader

4
Follower-made decision

Ability: has the necessary knowledge, experience and skill

Willingness: has the necessary confidence, commitment, motivation

FOLLOWER READINESS			
High	Moderate		Low
R4 Able and willing or confident	R3 Able but unwilling or insecure	R2 Unable but willing or confident	R1 Unable and unwilling or insecure
FOLLOWER DIRECTED		LEADER DIRECTED	

When a Leader Behavior is used appropriately with its corresponding level of readiness, it is termed a High Probability Match. The following are descriptors that can be useful when using Situational Leadership for specific applications:

S1	**S2**	**S3**	**S4**
Telling	Selling	Participating	Delegating
Guiding	Explaining	Encouraging	Observing
Directing	Clarifying	Collaborating	Monitoring
Establishing	Persuading	Committing	Fulfilling

FIGURE 8-4   *Leaders select one of four styles depending on the maturity of their employees.*

Source: P. H. Hersey and K. H. Blanchard, *Utilizing Human Resources,* 5th ed. Copyrighted material from Leadership Studies, Inc. All rights reserved. Used by permission.

- **Telling (1 or S1),** high task and low relationship. The leader guides, directs, establishes guidelines, provides specific instructions, and closely supervises performance. A dysfunctional telling-style leader dictates to employees.
- **Selling (2 or S2),** high task and high relationship. The leader explains decisions, clarifies them, and persuades employees to follow them as necessary. Too intense selling, however, can result in badgering employees with too much structure and consideration.

- **Participating (3 or S3),** low task and high relationship. The leader shifts significant responsibility to the followers, encourages employees to participate in decision making, and facilitates collaboration and commitment. In extreme cases, the leader can bend too greatly to the will of his employees, rather than correctly judging the appropriate amount of participation.
- **Delegating (4 or S4),** low task and low relationship. The leader only observes and monitors employees' performance, after giving them responsibility for decisions and implementation. Improper application of this style can result in the leader disengaging too much from the decision-making process.

According to the life cycle theory, selecting the appropriate style requires the leader to determine the readiness of her followers. Follower readiness includes two components:

- **Ability** describes whether employees have the necessary knowledge, skills, and experience to perform the task. New hires, for example, may not have the ability to do the job unless they received specific job-related training prior to securing the job.
- **Willingness** describes whether the employees have the motivation, commitment, and confidence to do the task. Some customer service representatives, for example, have the skills, knowledge, and experience to respond quickly to more customer questions than they did in the previous month, but may lack the motivation and commitment to attain such a goal.

A manager such as Carly Fiorina can use this theory to diagnose the best leadership style. Note in Figure 8-4 that follower readiness (in the middle of the figure) moves from low to high. The curve that represents leadership style over time (in the top of the figure) correspondingly moves (right to left) from telling to selling to participating to delegating. If Fiorina has employees who are unable and unwilling to perform (low readiness), she should use the telling style. If her workers are unable but willing to perform (moderate readiness), she should use the selling style. If the workers are able but unwilling to perform (moderate readiness), she should use the participating style. If her workers are able and willing to perform (high readiness), she should use the delegating style.

The chief technology officer at Embark.com, an education Web site, suggests that the company's new workers tend to demonstrate a maturity and willingness to work. They want guidance and respect, as well as the opportunity to add value to the organization. According to life cycle theory, the leader in this situation probably should use a participative style. The CEO of Eastman Kodak agrees and encourages employee participation by requesting and receiving e-mails from plant workers who update him and make suggestions.[35]

Substitutes for Leadership

Certain characteristics of subordinates, the tasks, or the organization, as shown in Table 8-6, may neutralize or eliminate the need for certain styles of leadership. An established team of skilled subordinates, for example, may not need the task-oriented directions of a new manager.[36] They might even resent the new manager. The organization, too, may have a culture that fosters worker autonomy and responsibility, again mitigating the need for leadership.

TABLE 8-6

Sometimes Characteristics of the Subordinate, Task, and Organization Can Substitute for Individual Leadership.

Subordinate Characteristics	Task Characteristics	Organizational Characteristics
		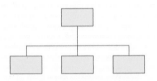
• ability, experience, training, knowledge • need for independence • "professional" orientation • indifference toward organizational rewards	• unambiguous and routine • methodologically invariant • provides its own feedback concerning accomplishment • intrinsically satisfying	• formalization (explicit plans, goals, and areas of responsibility) • inflexibility (rigid, unbending rules and procedures) • highly specified and active advisory and staff functions • closely knit, cohesive work groups • organizational rewards not within the leader's control • spatial distance between superior and subordinates

Source: From S. Kerr and J. M. Jermier, Substitutes for leadership: Their meaning and measurement, *Organizational Behavior and Human Performance* 26 (December 1978): 375–403.

By extension, organizations can manipulate these characteristics to cope with ineffective leadership or eliminate the managers entirely.[37] Many organizations have laid off middle managers who once managed workers now working in self-managed teams. Instead, the teams handle coordination problems by goal setting and using other staff as backup resources.

Evaluation of the Situational Theories

The situational theories have mixed support, and only limited testing of most has occurred. Most theories also suffer from measurement problems. For example, the LPC theory uses the Least-Preferred Co-worker Scale, an instrument of questionable validity, to assess a leader's style.[38] Studies that tried to validate the cognitive resource theory failed to rule out alternative explanations of the results.[39] Most studies to measure the path-goal theory used questionnaires to measure both leadership and its outcomes, which may limit the accuracy of the results.[40] Problems exist in the life cycle theory with the instruments used to measure follower readiness and leader behaviors, particularly the Leadership Effectiveness and Description (LEAD), the instrument most commonly used to measure leadership style.

The theories can also oversimplify the leadership process. For example, the normative theory doesn't capture the complexity of most decision-making and leadership situations. It ignores time constraints, doesn't offer a complete range of style options, and focuses too narrowly on employee involvement in a decision-making situation. The computerized model adds to the time required to use the model and may be more helpful in training than in actual managerial practice.

Generalizing the results has also been problematic. For example, research on the path-goal theory does not conclusively state what outcomes result from particular styles in certain situations, preventing the generalizing of results to different situations. Also, path-goal theory's reliance on expectancy theory means that the validity of this leadership theory depends on the validity of expectancy theory. Only limited testing of the substitutes for leadership theory has occurred. Research still needs to address the ability of specific characteristics to fulfill specific leadership functions. Nevertheless, leadership training needs to more fully consider the importance of situational components.[41]

▌ LEADING BY FOCUSING ON FOLLOWERS

Effective leadership means more than assessing the situation. Diagnosing specific interactions with followers improves leadership behaviors. Exchange theory, attribution theory, and operant conditioning theory can help with this diagnosis.

Exchange Theory

Leaders give followers autonomy or involvement in decision making in exchange for a higher commitment to organizational goals and operations, more effort, or increased performance.[42] For example, Carly Fiorina's giving her employees responsibility for major decisions should result in higher effort and performance. The leader–member relationship is built through interpersonal exchanges where the leader evaluates the follower's trustworthiness in terms of her ability, benevolence, and integrity.[43]

Research suggests that leader–member exchange (often referred to as LMX) is composed of four dimensions: affect, loyalty, contribution, and professional respect.[44] This exchange works somewhat differently for two types of followers.[45] The leader allows a great deal of latitude to the cadre or in-group of followers. This small group of individuals closest to the leader has his greatest trust, often as a result of their competence, dependability, or compatibility with the leader. These workers demonstrate higher performance, lower turnover, and greater satisfaction with supervision than other workers. The remaining employees, known as hired hands or the out-group, receive little latitude from the leader and tend to demonstrate lower performance, lower satisfaction, and higher turnover. An organization's social structure influences which people become members of the in-group and out-group.[46] For example, companies that emphasize research and development are more likely to include members of that department in the in-group. Companies that focus on sales may include salespeople in the in-group and manufacturing people in the out-group.

Managers must recognize that belonging to the in-group versus the out-group has different consequences. They may need to adjust their leadership behaviors to prevent these differences from becoming dysfunctional. Such distinctions may also have ethical implications: Deviating from equal treatment of employees can have significant consequences.

Attribution Theory

Attribution theory suggests that the leader's attribution of the causes of followers' behavior influences his judgment about them.[47] Although biased attributions undermine effective leadership, leaders must recognize their typical attributional biases (see Chapter 2); for example, they link themselves with successes in the group and remove themselves from failures.[48] Thus, they might incorrectly take credit for the group's success by suggesting that it resulted from the interpersonal support or skills of the leader. They might incorrectly attribute the group's failure to external influences, such as time constraints, lack of resources, or absence of member skills. The fairness and accuracy of the attributions also affect the staff's perceptions of the leader and their willingness to follow, cooperate, and perform.[49]

As shown in Figure 8-5, leadership begins with a particular situation—in this case, one of poor-quality production. Leader behavior then involves attributing the cause of the behavior (linkage 1) by determining whether the behavior is unique to a particular task, consistent and frequent, and whether followers demonstrate the same behavior. Once the leader attributes a cause to the situation, she then responds (linkage 2).

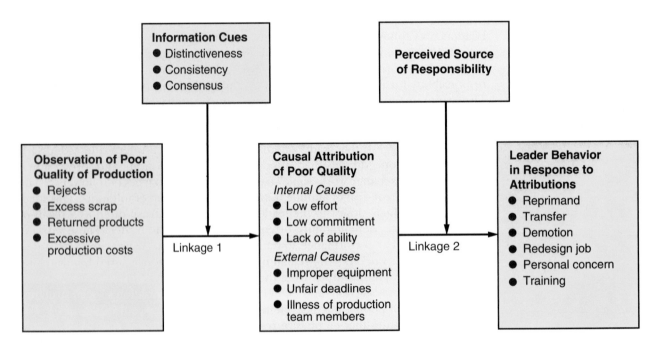

FIGURE 8-5   *Leader and follower attributions influence leadership outcomes.*

Source: Adapted from Terence Mitchell and Robert E. Wood, An empirical test of an attributional model of leader's responses to poor performance. In *Academy of Management Proceedings,* ed. Richard C. Huseman, 1979, p. 94.

Operant Conditioning Theory

We can use reinforcement theory (see Chapter 4) to help diagnose leadership effectiveness and ways employees can work together more effectively. The model has two basic components:[50]

1. **The leader's behavior prompts responses by subordinates.** The employees' responses then reinforce, extinguish, or punish the leader's behavior. For example, a leader may give her employees more autonomy and responsibility. Their increased productivity will reinforce this behavior and cause the leader to continue to empower them in this way.

2. **The subordinates' behavior causes responses in other parts of the organization.** Responses to the employees' behaviors then reinforce, extinguish, or punish the behavior. If, for example, the employees exert autonomy by making too many requests of other departments, the complaints by these departments over time likely will extinguish the employees' autonomous behaviors.

Evaluation of the Theories

Research on leader–member exchange theory has provided mixed validation of the theory. Problems exist with the definition of the concept, measurement of LMX, and level of analysis of the findings.[51] The research relies on very limited data and doesn't explain how individuals become part of the in-group. It doesn't sufficiently study the organizational outcomes associated with the exchange relationship.[52] Researchers have not yet studied the impact of highly similar versus relatively diverse in-groups. They must also examine the process by which the leader–member relations develop; for example, how does an individual become an in-group member?[53]

The attributional model of leadership poses some definitional and measurement problems.[54] No specific instruments have been developed or administered to measure leaders' or followers' behavior in this model. Little empirical data have been collected to validate the model.

The operant conditioning model, too, remains relatively untested. Little empirical research has specifically focused on operant conditioning as an explanation of leadership effectiveness.

▌CONTEMPORARY PERSPECTIVES

Recent thinking about effective leadership has supplemented the situational approach with an emphasis on the leader's charisma, ability to develop and implement a vision of the organization, and ability to teach workers to act as self-leaders.

Charismatic Leadership

A charismatic leader uses self-confidence, dominance, moral conviction, and charisma to inspire his followers and make significant changes in organizational functioning.[55] Michael Capellas, the CEO of Compaq Computer, lighted a bonfire under his employees. "He's got the passion of a Bruce Springsteen—bounding across the stage in a rock star outfit and lip-synching at company events or pumping up the energy daily with electric-guitar tunes blasting from a boom box in his eighth-floor office."[56]

Charismatic leadership occurs in three stages. In the first stage, the leader critically evaluates the current situation. At this stage, charismatic leaders show a sensitivity to environmental constraints and are more sensitive to follower abilities and needs. In the second stage, the leader formulates her vision of the future and relies on impression management skills to convey this impression to others. Finally, in the third stage, the leader deploys innovative and unconventional means, as well as using her personal power to accomplish her vision.[57]

Charismatic leaders emerge more often when an organization experiences stress or transitions.[58] Charismatic leadership may be more appropriate for certain situations, such as dynamic organizational environments, early and late stages of the organizational life cycle, technology with low analyzability, and organic organizations, among others.[59] Followers trust the correctness of a charismatic leader's beliefs, and unquestioningly accept, show affection for, and obey their leader.[60] Charismatic leaders manage others' impressions of their leadership so that others view the leader as competent and successful. Subordinates see their empowered supervisors as innovative, inspirational, and influential up the hierarchy.[61] Ken Chenault, the CEO of American Express, has an understated kind of charisma; Chenault has a quiet warmth that makes people want to be a member of his team and be willing to do anything for him.[62] Such leaders serve as role models to followers, often stating ideological goals for followers and setting high expectations for their behavior. Table 8-7 compares charismatic and noncharismatic leaders. Table 8-8 on page 272 offers some items from a scale of charismatic leadership. You might rate yourself on these items to determine the extent of your own charismatic leadership.

A "dark side" to charismatic leadership may exist if the leader overemphasizes devotion to himself, makes personal needs paramount, or uses highly effective communication skills to mislead or manipulate others.[63] Such leaders tend to be egotistical, focus on their personal power and achievement, and act unethically. They may also have a flawed vision due to seriously miscalculating the resources needed to achieve it or unrealistically assessing the market or changes in the environment.[64]

Transformational Leadership

A transformational leader often has charisma but begins by developing a vision for his organization, department, or work group. This vision guides the manager in attaining quality, performance, and productivity. Transformational leaders motivate workers by focusing on higher ideals. This behavior contrasts with that of transactional leaders, who focus on compliance with existing organizational rules, trade rewards for agreement with the leader's wishes, and even abdicate their leadership responsibility. Is Carly Fiorina a transformational leader? She acted as a transformational leader at Lucent and is expected to be one at HP.

A transformational leader helps employees see a need to revitalize their organization. Real crises may create this need. Employee visits to other organizations can also motivate change. Transformational leaders involve employees in planning for and creating a new vision. The leader helps workers or other managers reframe the way they think about the organization. For example, managers at a graphic design firm might reframe the company's major objective as providing top-quality Web sites for a small, but select group of clients, rather than trying to increase the number of clients they serve. Institutionalizing the change calls for replacing the organization's old culture with a new one.

Rob Glaser, the CEO of RealNetworks, "beats you over the head with concepts—big concepts—and then peppers you with obscure references and tangential observations till your brain stops working, all within a few moments of conver-

TABLE 8-7

Charismatic and Noncharismatic Leaders Differ Significantly.

	Noncharismatic Leader	**Charismatic Leader**
Relation to status quo	Essentially agrees with status quo and strives to maintain it	Essentially opposed to status quo and strives to change it
Future goal	Goal not too discrepant from status quo	Idealized vision that is highly discrepant from status quo
Likableness	Shared perspective makes him/her likable	Shared perspective and idealized vision make him/her a likable and honorable hero worthy of identification and imitation
Trustworthiness	Disinterested advocacy in persuasion attempts	Disinterested advocacy by incurring great personal risk and cost
Expertise	Expert in using available means to achieve goals within the framework of the existing order	Expert in using unconventional means to transcend the existing order
Behavior	Conventional, conforming to existing norms	Unconventional or counternormative
Environmental sensitivity	Low need for environmental sensitivity to maintain status quo	High need for environmental sensitivity for changing the status quo
Articulation	Weak articulation of goals and motivation to lead	Strong articulation of future vision and motivation to lead
Power base	Position power and personal power (based on reward, expertise, and liking for a friend who is a similar other)	Personal power (based on expertise, respect, and admiration for a unique hero)
Leader-follower relationship	Egalitarian, consensus seeking, or directive / Nudges or orders people to share his/her views	Elitist, entrepreneur, and exemplary / Transforms people to share the radical changes advocated

Source: Reprinted with permission from A. Conger and R. N. Kanungo, Toward a behavioral theory of charismatic leadership in organizational settings, *Academy of Management Review* 12 (1987): 641.

sation."[65] Glaser's vision involves bringing a set of disciplines together and then seeing how they can interact in a new way. He has made RealNetworks "the gold standard of the industry," trying to become part of every digital-media niche.[66]

A manager who acts as a transformational leader motivates employees to do better than they expected in three ways:[67]

1. The leader raises their consciousness about the importance of certain outcomes, such as high productivity or efficiency.

2. The leader shows the value of workers concentrating on what benefits their work team rather than on their personal interest.

3. The leader raises the workers' need levels so that they value challenges, responsibility, and growth.

TABLE 8-8

Rate Yourself on These Items to Evaluate Your Charismatic Leadership.

1. Provides inspiring strategic and organizational goals.
2. Consistently generates new ideas for the future of the organization.
3. Recognizes the abilities and skills of other members of the organization.
4. Recognizes the limitations of other members of the organization.
5. Influences others by developing mutual liking and respect.
6. Takes high personal risks for the sake of the organization.
7. Uses nontraditional means to achieve organizational goals.
8. Often exhibits very unique behavior that surprises other members of the organization.

Source: Excerpted from the Refined Conger-Kanungo Scale of Charismatic Leadership, J. A. Conger and R. N. Kanungo, *Charismatic Leadership in Organizations* (Thousand Oaks, CA: Sage, 1998).

Chief executive officers of divisions of corporations who succeeded in developing new businesses differed from those who attempted new business development and failed.[68] These CEOs inspired commitment throughout the division by insisting that the entire division pursue new business development and assigning the best people to it. They demonstrated intense, undistracted, and long-term personal commitment to new business development. They built confidence among their employees by helping them increase their competence and giving them the freedom to take initiative. They applied appropriate discipline to the process by carefully selecting the new venture, using the appropriate strategy, and managing failures.

Top-performing managers also rated higher on transformational leadership than a group of ordinary managers.[69] Because some research suggests that transformational leadership cascades from the leader to his followers,[70] training higher managers in transformational skills should have a more widespread impact than training only lower-level managers. Training managers in two branch banks to act as transformational leaders changed employees' organizational commitment and the branches' financial performance.[71]

Transformational leaders may be so driven to achieve a vision that they ignore the costly implications of their goals. Failed visions result when

- the vision reflects the internal needs of the leaders rather than those of the market or constituents;
- the leader has miscalculated the resources needed to achieve the vision;
- the leader has an unrealistic assessment or distorted perception of market and constituent needs; or
- a failure to recognize environmental changes prevents redirection of the vision.[72]

Superleadership

The superleader goes one step beyond the transformational leader by helping followers discover, use, and maximize their abilities.[73] Similar to the transformational leader, the superleader empowers followers to contribute fully to organizations. She changes employees into self-leaders who take primary responsibility for motivating and directing their personal behaviors.[74]

A leader becomes a superleader by performing the following steps:

1. **Become a self-leader.** As a self-leader, a person may use an array of behavioral and cognitive strategies that include personal goal setting, practice, providing rewards or punishments to oneself, and making sure activities result in a sense of competence, purpose, and self-control.

2. **Model self-leadership.** The superleader displays self-leadership behaviors and encourages others to rehearse and then produce them.

3. **Encourage employees to create self-set goals.** The leader trains and supports others in setting accepted, challenging, and attainable goals.

4. **Create positive thought patterns.** The superleader continuously observes, evaluates, and changes her assumptions, beliefs, mental images, and thinking in general.

5. **Reward self-leadership behaviors and constructively reprimand other behaviors.** The leader uses natural rewards that stem from the task, such as a sense of competence and increased responsibility, and self-administered rewards, such as self-recognition, self-praise, and self-congratulations.

6. **Use teamwork to promote self-leadership.** The leader relies on teams to reinforce principles of self-leadership and provide a context for responsibility and goal setting.

7. **Create a culture of self-leadership.** The superleader extends self-leadership throughout the organization.[75]

Employees in a bankrupt company who received self-leadership training showed increased mental performance, enthusiasm, job satisfaction, feelings of self-efficacy, and optimism about the organization, and decreased nervousness.[76] Employee self-leadership combined with self-leadership systems in the organization, such as a supportive culture, use of teams, and design of work, result in increased employee commitment, motivation, capability, performance, and innovation.

Evaluation of the Contemporary Theories

The theories just discussed have intuitive appeal, and the transformational theory in particular has been widely embraced by practitioners. However, little research has systematically studied their impact. Researchers have relied on interview, questionnaire, historical, and case-study methodology to study the outcomes.[77] Yet, the context of transformational leadership has received little attention.[78] Similarly, a more complete examination of these approaches to leadership in different cultures is also essential. Although one study showed that transformational leadership has some universality across countries, another indicated that charismatic leadership had a greater impact on North American than on Mexican workers.[79]

▍ LEADERSHIP IN A DOT-COM, GLOBAL WORKPLACE

How does leadership need to change in the dynamic environment most organizations are facing? Increasingly, leaders have responsibility for coaching employees. They act as advisors and resources when their employees encounter problems. They highlight key areas for employee development. The leaders themselves may also have personal coaches, who help them function more effectively. GE Equity, a division of General Electric, offers coaching to its senior executives. Coaches serve as a sounding board and help improve the executives' performance.[80]

Team-oriented structures also call for new types of leadership. Individual employees may be called to act as leaders temporarily, frequently shifting roles between leader and follower. Team leaders need to focus the team on its goals, clarifying and gaining agreement about the desired direction. They also need to structure the team for results and find ways to facilitate decision making. Team leaders may train members in the task skills and then maintain standards of excellence. Team leaders also coach team members in interpersonal skills, manage conflict, and build commitment and a feeling of esprit de corps. They look for ways to satisfy the needs of individual team members. Team leaders also should try to model ethical practices, ensuring that they are fair and consistent in dealing with team members. Team leaders may focus their attention externally by networking, representing the team to others, negotiating to obtain necessary resources, and buffering team members from a problematic environment.[81]

Dealing with small, upstart companies whose future is tied more to stock market fluctuations and venture capital than to profitability poses new leadership challenges. First, many employees in these companies are young and enthusiastic, but inexperienced. So are the managers. While they generally bring strong technical skills, they may lack the seasoning of more experienced managers and have difficulty dealing with problem employees, organizational crises, or demanding customers.

Second, leaders in dot-com companies need to make decisions quickly while remaining sufficiently flexible to adapt to rapidly changing market conditions. William Harris moved to the online bank X.com from Microsoft, but lasted only two months. He held endless meetings and instituted a more hierarchical structure, both of which greatly stifled timely decision making.[82]

Third, leaders in dot-com companies need to fit their management style to the special circumstances faced by this new breed of organizations. Managers who move into the dot-com world from old Fortune 500 companies quickly learn that the rules-of-the-game differ. Their mastery of formal managerial techniques often explains their hiring by the dot-com companies. Yet, they quickly face the rapid pace and spontaneity that characterizes and sustains these start-ups. Richard Frank left the top management at Disney to become CEO of Food.com, a multifaceted Web site. When the numbers from a measurement service he hired didn't make sense, his first reaction was to send a press release to the measurement service announcing that he was dropping the service. While using the press in this way may have worked at Disney, this approach would have failed at Food.com. Executives such as Frank and Harris find that they must rethink their assumptions about strategy, management style, and technology when they switch to the dot-com environment.[83]

Leading in a global environment also poses special challenges. Most research and thinking about leadership has used U.S. managers and cultural assumptions. What happens once a manager moves into the global economy and must lead a multinational, multicultural workforce? Can the same theories be used to diagnose these global management challenges? The answer is, "It depends."

A global manager is a sensitive, innovative, and participative leader who builds on cultural differences through international collaboration and leads change in the organization to improve intercultural performance.[84] Such a manager continuously acquires current information about the culture in which he lives and adapts his leadership style to it. How do the key components of a situation change for a leader managing multiculturally and multinationally? Leaders must adjust their style to the cultural norms of a particular work group. We know, for example, that a collectivist orientation characterizes the Japanese culture, whereas an individualistic orientation describes the U.S. culture.[85] The circumstances in which an achievement-oriented style would work likely differ in these two types of cultures. Similarly, cultures with a masculine orientation, such as in Latin America, may have a different attitude toward authoritarian leadership than those with a more feminine orientation.

Summary

1. Trait theory identifies personal characteristics that distinguish leaders from nonleaders.
2. Behavioral theories view a leader's concern for task and concern for people as key to effectiveness. Managers perform interpersonal, informational, and decisional roles.
3. Theory X and Theory Y leaders hold different assumptions about workers and fit their style to these assumptions.
4. Fiedler and his associates said the effectiveness of a leader's style depends on leader–member relations, the task's structure, and the position power of the leader.
5. Path-goal theory states that leadership effectiveness depends on the fit between the style and such situational characteristics as the task, employees, formal authority, work group, and organizational culture.
6. The normative decision model offers a procedure for deciding the appropriate amount of employee participation in decision making.
7. The life cycle model says that leadership effectiveness depends on the fit between the leader's style and the maturity of his or her followers.
8. Substitutes for leadership, such as characteristics of leaders, followers, and the situation, may prescribe effective leadership.
9. Exchange theory emphasizes the leader's interaction with subordinates and superiors.
10. Attribution theory says that individuals' perceptions of the causes of their followers' behavior influence their leadership effectiveness.
11. Operant conditioning theory cites the role of positive reinforcement in encouraging specific leadership behaviors.
12. A charismatic leader uses self-confidence, dominance, moral conviction, and charisma to inspire her followers.
13. An effective transformational leader recognizes the need to revitalize the organization, creates a vision of the new organization, and then implements and institutionalizes this vision.
14. A superleader encourages his followers to act as self-leaders.
15. Leaders in a dot-com, global workplace face special challenges of dealing with a rapidly changing environment and multicultural workforce.

A Manager's Diagnostic Review

■ Know the traits of an effective leader.

- Do the managers have the traits necessary for effective leadership?

■ Display the behaviors and roles of an effective leader.

- Do the managers display the behaviors required for effective leadership?
- Do the managers have Theory Y assumptions?
- Do the managers perform the roles required for effective leadership?

■ Diagnose the situation, and use the leadership style that best fits it.

- Do managers have a variety of styles available for use?
- Does the leadership style fit the nature of the task, leader–member relations, and the position power of the leader?
- Does the leadership style fit the maturity of the followers?
- Do leaders involve subordinates appropriately in decision making?
- Do substitutes for leadership exist?

■ Consider followers when leading.

- Do in-groups and out-groups exist?
- Do correct attributions of leader and follower behavior occur?
- What leadership behaviors are reinforced?

■ Set and implement a vision for your company.

- Do charismatic leaders exist, and are they effective?
- Do transformational leaders exist, and are they effective?
- Do superleaders exist, and are they effective?

■ Lead in a dot-com, global workplace.

- Do leaders understand and face the challenges of their dynamic environment?
- Do leaders change their style to fit the culture of the situation?

Visit the Gordon homepage on the Prentice Hall Web site at

http://www.prenhall.com/gordon

for recommended readings, additional activities, Internet exercises, updated information, and links to related Web sites.

▌ Thinking Critically About Organizational Behavior

1. Can managers lead effectively if they don't have the traits of an effective leader?
2. Do effective leaders demonstrate common behaviors?
3. Should a manager ideally have Theory Y assumptions?

4. What elements of the situation are key to choosing a leadership style?
5. If different features of the situation call for different leadership styles, what style should a leader choose?
6. Do substitutes for leadership effectively replace a leader?
7. Must employees be part of the in-group?
8. Can leaders create specific follower behavior by using reinforcement?
9. How do transformational, charismatic, and superleaders differ?
10. How should a leader in a multicultural setting act?
11. Does gender, race, or ethnic origin influence effective leadership?
12. What advice would you offer the new president of a dot-com start-up?

ACTIVITY 8-1: LEADERSHIP QUESTIONNAIRE

STEP 1: This questionnaire contains questions about different styles of leadership. Indicate how often each statement is true of your own behavior according to the following scale:

1 = Never; 2 = Hardly ever; 3 = Seldom; 4 = Occasionally; 5 = Often; 6 = Usually; 7 = Always

_____ 1. I let subordinates know what is expected of them.
_____ 2. I maintain a friendly working relationship with subordinates.
_____ 3. I consult with subordinates when facing a problem.
_____ 4. I listen receptively to subordinates' ideas and suggestions.
_____ 5. I inform subordinates about what needs to be done and how it needs to be done.
_____ 6. I let subordinates know that I expect them to perform at their highest level.
_____ 7. I act without consulting my subordinates.
_____ 8. I do little things to make it pleasant to be a member of the group.
_____ 9. I ask subordinates to follow standard rules and regulations.
_____ 10. I set goals for subordinates' performance that are quite challenging.
_____ 11. I say things that hurt subordinates' personal feelings.
_____ 12. I ask for suggestions from subordinates concerning how to carry out assignments.
_____ 13. I encourage continual improvement in subordinates' performance.
_____ 14. I explain the level of performance that is expected of subordinates.
_____ 15. I help subordinates overcome problems that stop them from carrying out their tasks.
_____ 16. I show that I have doubts about their ability to meet most objectives.
_____ 17. I ask subordinates for suggestions on what assignments should be made.
_____ 18. I give vague explanations of what is expected of subordinates on the job.
_____ 19. I consistently set challenging goals for subordinates to attain.
_____ 20. I behave in a manner that is thoughtful of subordinates' personal needs.

STEP 2: Scoring.

1. Reverse the scores for items 7, 11, 16, and 18 (score a 1 as 7, 2 as 6, 3 as 5, and so on).
2. Directive style: Sum the scores on items 1, 5, 9, 14, and 18.
3. Supportive style: Sum the scores on items 2, 8, 11, 15, and 20.
4. Participative style: Sum the scores on items 3, 4, 7, 12, and 17.
5. Achievement-oriented style: Sum the scores on items 6, 10, 13, 16, and 19.

SCORING INTERPRETATION

- *Directive style,* a common score is 23; scores above 28 are considered high, and scores below 18 are considered low.

- *Supportive style,* a common score is 28; scores above 33 are considered high, and scores below 23 are considered low.

- *Participative style,* a common score is 21; scores above 26 are considered high, and scores below 16 are considered low.

- *Achievement-oriented style,* a common score is 19; scores above 24 are considered high, and scores below 14 are considered low.

The scores you received on the questionnaire provide information about which style of leadership you use most often and which you use less frequently. In addition, these scores can assess your use of each style relative to your use of the other styles.

STEP 3: Discussion. Answer the following questions in small groups or with the entire class.

DESCRIPTION

1. What score did you receive? Compare it with the scores of other class members.

DIAGNOSIS

2. What style of leadership do you use most frequently? Least frequently?

3. In what situations do you use each of the four styles of leadership?

4. How well do you fit the style to the situation?

PRESCRIPTION

5. How could you improve the particular leadership style you use?

Source: Adapted from J. Indvik, A path-goal theory investigation of superior subordinate relationship, Unpublished doctoral dissertation, University of Wisconsin–Madison, 1986; J. Indvik, A more complete testing of path-goal theory, Paper presented at Academy of Management, Anaheim, CA, 1988. Used with permission.

ACTIVITY 8-2: THE CHIEF EXECUTIVE AS MANAGER

STEP 1: Collect at least 10 newspaper or magazine articles about the two most recent presidents of the United States.

STEP 2: Compile a list of the activities that each president performed according to these articles.

STEP 3: For each activity indicate the work role performed by the presidents.

STEP 4: Discussion. Answer the following questions in small groups or with the entire class.

DESCRIPTION

1. Which activities did the two presidents perform?

DIAGNOSIS

2. Which roles were most commonly performed?

3. Which roles were least commonly performed?

4. How did the two presidents differ in their role performance?

5. What are the implications of these differences for their leadership of the United States?

ACTIVITY 8-3: THE PAT HOWARD ROLE-PLAY

STEP 1: Your instructor will divide the class into groups of eight. Four students in each group will adopt the role of Pat Howard (the supervisor). The remaining four students will adopt the role of one of the four subordinates (Jan Perez, Chris McBride, Jamie Johnson, or Fran Fulton). Your instructor will distribute the appropriate role description to each person. Each person reads background informa-

tion only for his or her own role. The meeting schedule (Table 8-9) lists the names of the three subordinates with whom each supervisor will meet and the order in which they will meet.

STEP 2: Each supervisor should write some notes about what he or she plans to do when meeting with each subordinate.

TABLE 8-9

Use This Meeting Schedule for the Pat Howard Role-Play.

Group Member Number	Assignment
	Supervisor (Pat)
1	Jan, Fran, Jamie
2	Fran, Jamie, Chris
3	Jamie, Chris, Jan
4	Chris, Jan, Fran
	Subordinate
5	Chris
6	Jan
7	Fran
8	Jamie

STEP 3: Each supervisor meets with the first subordinate on his or her schedule. For example, the schedule indicates that person number 1 will play the role of Pat Howard and meet first with Jan, then Fran, and finally Jamie. Person number 2 will also play the role of Pat Howard, meeting first with Fran, then Jamie, and finally Chris. Person number 5 will play the role of Chris, and person 6 will play the role of Jan, and so on. The supervisor–subordinate pair meets one-on-one for 5 minutes. Your instructor will stop you after 5 minutes and ask you to fill out either Table 8-10 or Table 8-11. After 1 minute, your instructor will direct you to proceed to your second meeting. Repeat this process until all supervisors have met with the three subordinates designated on their schedules.

TABLE 8-10

Complete This Leader Self-Evaluation Form if You Played the Role of Pat Howard.

In the role-play with _____ (insert name of subordinate), what leader behaviors did you use?

	Low						High
Supportive	1	2	3	4	5	6	7
Directive	1	2	3	4	5	6	7
Participative	1	2	3	4	5	6	7
Achievement-oriented	1	2	3	4	5	6	7

How successful were you in meeting this subordinate's needs and addressing his/her concerns?

	Low						High
Success	1	2	3	4	5	6	7

To what extent did you influence or motivate the subordinate toward high or better performance?

	Low						High
Influence	1	2	3	4	5	6	7

TABLE 8–11

Complete This Subordinate's Role-Play Evaluation Form if You Played the Role of Chris, Jan, Fran, or Jamie.

In the first role-play, to what extent did Pat Howard use each of the following leader behaviors?

	Low						High
Supportive	1	2	3	4	5	6	7
Directive	1	2	3	4	5	6	7
Participative	1	2	3	4	5	6	7
Achievement-oriented	1	2	3	4	5	6	7

To what extent did Pat seem concerned about your job performance and your job satisfaction?

	Low						High
Job performance	1	2	3	4	5	6	7
Satisfaction	1	2	3	4	5	6	7

How successful was Pat in meeting your needs and addressing your concerns?

Successful	1	2	3	4	5	6	7

To what extent did Pat influence or motivate the subordinate toward high or better performance?

	Low						High
Influence	1	2	3	4	5	6	7

Describe leader behaviors that were effective and behaviors that were less effective:

STEP 4: Each designated subordinate–supervisor pair meets again (in the same order as in Step 3) for 3 minutes to allow the subordinate to provide feedback to the supervisor concerning the effectiveness of the supervisor's behavior. You should avoid vague or very general comments. Instead, describe Pat's specific behaviors, focusing especially on those behaviors that your character found to be effective or ineffective. Contrast the behavior of this "Pat" with the other "Pats" with whom you met. How do you think your character would have felt during your meeting with Pat? Did Pat focus primarily on your job performance or your job satisfaction? What concerns of yours were not addressed during your meeting with Pat? Provide Pat with at least two developmental suggestions. After providing oral feedback, give your copy of the role-play evaluation form to the supervisor. The supervisor should then compare his or her self-ratings to the ratings provided by subordinates.

STEP 5: Discussion. With the entire class, answer the following questions:

1. What differences did you observe in the behavior of the different supervisors? What was effective? Ineffective?

2. Did the supervisors vary their behavior with different subordinates? Did some behaviors appear to be more effective with one person than with another?

3. What leadership style(s) should be most effective for each of the subordinates? Why?

Source: Reprinted with permission from J. Seltzer and J. W. Smither, A role-play exercise to introduce students to path-goal leadership theory, *Journal of Management Education* 19(3) (1995): 380–391.

ACTIVITY 8-4: DECISION-MAKING CASES

STEP 1: Read each of the following cases.

STEP 2: For each case, apply the normative model and indicate the most appropriate decision-making process. Be sure to list your answers to each diagnostic question and the resulting problem style.

Case I

You are president of a small but growing midwestern bank, with its head office in the state's capital and branches in several nearby market towns. The location and type of businesses in the area are factors that contribute to the emphasis on traditional and conservative banking practices at all levels.

When you bought the bank five years ago, it was in poor financial shape. Under your leadership, much progress has been made. This progress has been achieved while the economy has moved into a mild recession, and as a result, your prestige among your bank managers is very high. You feel that your success, which you are inclined to attribute principally to good luck and to a few timely decisions on your part, has one unfortunate by-product. It has caused your subordinates to look to you for leadership and guidance in decision making beyond what you consider necessary. You have no doubts about the fundamental capabilities of these men but wish that they were not quite so willing to accede to your judgment.

You have recently acquired funds to permit opening a new branch. Your problem is to decide on a suitable location. You believe that there is no "magic formula" by which it is possible to select an optimal site. The choice will be made by a combination of some simple commonsense criteria and "what feels right." You have asked your managers to keep their eyes open for commercial real estate sites that might be suitable. Their knowledge about the communities in which they operate should be extremely useful in making a wise choice.

Their support is important because the success of the new branch will be highly dependent on your managers' willingness to supply staff and technical assistance during its early days. Your bank is small enough for everyone to feel like part of a team, and you feel that this has and will be critical to the bank's prosperity.

The success of this project will benefit everybody. Directly, they will benefit from the increased base of operations, and indirectly, they will reap the personal and business advantages of being part of a successful and expanding business.

Case II

You are regional manager of an international management consulting company. You have a staff of six consultants reporting to you, each of whom enjoys a considerable amount of autonomy with clients in the field.

Yesterday you received a complaint from one of your major clients that the consultant whom you assigned to work on the contract with them was not doing his job effectively. They were not very explicit as to the nature of the problem, but it was clear that they were dissatisfied and that something would have to be done if you were to restore the client's faith in your company.

The consultant assigned to work on that contract has been with the company for six years. He is a systems analyst and one of the best in that profession. For the first four or five years, his performance was superb, and he was a model for the other more junior consultants. However, recently he has seemed to have a "chip on his shoulder," and his previous identification with the company and its objectives has been replaced with indifference. His negative attitude has been noticed by other consultants, as well as by clients. This is not the first such complaint that you have had from a client this year about his performance. A previous client even reported to you that the consultant reported to work several times obviously suffering from a hangover.

It is important to get to the root of this problem quickly if the client is to be retained. The consultant obviously has the skill necessary to work with the clients effectively—if only he were willing to use it!

Case III

You have recently been appointed manager of a new plant that is presently under construction. Your team of five department heads has been selected, and they are now working with you in selecting their own staffs, purchasing equipment, and generally anticipating the problems that are likely to arise when you move into the plant in three months.

Yesterday, you received from the architect a final set of plans for the building, and for the first time, you examined the parking facilities that are available. There is a large lot across the road from the plant intended primarily for hourly workers and lower-level supervisory personnel. In addition, seven spaces immediately adjacent to the administrative offices are intended for visitor and reserved parking. Company policy requires that a minimum of three spaces be made available for visitor parking, leaving you only four spaces to allocate among yourself and your five department heads. There is no way to increase the total number of spaces without changing the structure of the building.

Up to now, there have been no obvious status differences among your team, who have worked together very well in the planning phase of the operation. To be sure, there are salary differences, with your administrative, manufacturing, and engineering managers receiving slightly more than the quality control and industrial relations managers. Each has recently been promoted to a new position, and expects reserved parking privileges as a consequence of his new status. From past experience, you know that people feel strongly about things that are indicative of their status. So you and your subordinates have been working together as team, and you are reluctant to do anything that might jeopardize the team relationship.

Case IV

You are executive vice president for a small pharmaceutical manufacturer. You have the opportunity to bid on a contract for the U.S. Department of Defense pertaining to biological warfare. The contract is outside the mainstream of your business. However, it could make economic sense since you do have unused capacity in one of your plants, and the manufacturing processes are not dissimilar.

You have written the document to accompany the bid and now have the problem of determining the dollar value of the quotation that you think will win the job for your company. If the bid is too high, you will undoubtedly lose to one of your competitors. If it is too low, you will stand to lose money on the program. There are many factors to be considered in making this decision, including the cost of the new raw materials and the additional administrative burden of relationships with a new client, not to speak of factors that are likely to influence the bids of your competitors, such as how much they need this particular contract. You have been busy assembling the necessary data to make this decision, but several "unknowns" remain, one of which involves the manager of the plant in which the new products will be manufactured. Of all your subordinates, only he is in the position to estimate the costs of adapting the present equipment to their new purpose, and his cooperation and support will be necessary to ensure that the specifications of the contract are met. However, in an initial discussion with him when you first learned of the possibility of the contract, he seemed adamantly opposed to the idea. His previous experience has not particularly equipped him with the ability to evaluate projects like this one, so you were not overly influenced by his opinions. From the nature of his arguments, you inferred that his opposition was ideological rather than economic. You recall that he was actively involved in a local "peace organization" and within the company, was one of the most vocal opponents to the war in Vietnam.

STEP 3: Compare your responses to those given by your instructor.

STEP 4: Discussion. In small groups or with the entire class, answer the following questions:

1. In what situations would using the normative model improve your decision making?

2. In what situations would the model be of little value?

Source: Reprinted with permission from V. H. Vroom and A. G. Jago, Decision making as a social process: Normative & descriptive models of leader behavior, *Decision Sciences* 5 (1974): 750–753.

ACTIVITY 8-5: ACTING AS A TRANSFORMATIONAL LEADER

STEP 1: Individually or in small groups, identify four businesspeople who you think act as leaders. Learn as much as you can about them from articles, information on the World Wide Web, and film or news clips. (Alternatively, your instructor will show you film clips that depict people acting as leaders. If so directed, use those people as the basis for your analysis.)

STEP 2: For each person, determine whether they are charismatic, transformational, or superleaders. List the characteristics of each type of leader and then give examples to support your conclusions.

STEP 3: Now think of a manager that you know. Describe that manager's behavior in as much detail as possible for the rest of your group. What type of leader is the manager?

STEP 4: Offer a prescription for increasing the person's charismatic leadership, transformational leadership, or superleadership behaviors.

STEP 5: In larger groups or with the entire class, share your responses. What makes each person a leader? What characteristics make them a charismatic leader? A transformational leader? A superleader?

ACTIVITY 8-6: LEADING A CULTURAL CHANGE

STEP 1: Read the following scenario.

You have just been promoted to plant manager at Cybersonics Inc., which manufactures high-technology audio and videoconferencing equipment. The plant, which employs about 200 people, has always been managed fairly traditionally, with a strong and extensive hierarchy. You have read a great deal about self-managing teams and want to change the plant to that structure. You expect some resistance from the three shift supervisors because they have had a great deal of authority in the past.

STEP 2: You will be meeting shortly with these three supervisors. You want to lead the plant into the new structure and know you need their cooperation and enthusiasm in order for the change to succeed. Individually or in small groups, prepare your agenda and approach for the upcoming meeting. Consider which leadership style would work best in this situation and how best to implement it.

STEP 3: Your instructor will organize you into groups of four. Take turns playing the role of the new plant manager.

STEP 4: Compare the way each person led the meeting. Note what style they used and whether it seemed to be effective.

STEP 5: Discussion. In small groups or with the entire class, answer the following questions:

DESCRIPTION

1. Briefly summarize the main events of the meetings.

DIAGNOSIS

2. Analyze the leadership styles used by each plant manager.
3. Which styles seemed most and least effective?

PRESCRIPTION

4. Which leadership style should the new manager use? Why?

Chapter 9

Diagnosing Power and Managing Conflict and Stress

Learning Objectives

After completing Chapter 9, you will be able to

1. Define power in terms of influence, dependence, and exchange.
2. Discuss whether empowerment is a form of power.
3. Describe and illustrate four sources of power.
4. Discuss the impact of organizational politics.
5. Show how sexual harassment is an abuse of power.
6. Describe the levels, stages, and outcomes of conflict.
7. Identify the nature and impact of hidden conflict in organizations.
8. Offer two approaches to managing conflict.
9. Describe the consequences and impact of stress in organizations.
10. Offer three approaches to managing stress.
11. Identify issues of managing power, conflict, and stress in the dot-com, global workplace.

A Manager's Preview ✳

Describe . . . Diagnose . . . Prescribe . . . Act

■ **Know** how to reduce your dependence by using power.

■ **Identify** people who have a need for power.

■ **Empower** workers.

■ **Build** your sources of power.

■ **Use** organizational politics effectively.

■ **Identify** sexual harassment in the workplace.

■ **Diagnose** and manage conflict.

■ **Diagnose** and manage stress.

■ **Deal** with power, conflict, and stress in the dot-com, global workplace.

Power Struggle in the Failed Deutsche-Dresdner Bank Merger

Rolf E. Breuer, the head of Deutsche Bank, was in the center of an unsuccessful, attempted $30 billion merger with Dresdner Bank that left the German banking industry in total confusion. He reneged on his promise to absorb Dresdner's investment bank, in part, because he failed to recognize that it overlapped extensively with Deutsche's investment bank. He failed to consult sufficiently with Deutsch's investment bankers, angering its head, Josef Ackermann. Breuer miscalculated the extent to which power had shifted within his own organization. It had moved from the traditional German commercial bankers in Frankfurt to a team of investment bankers in London. Ackermann had created a financial success that moved Deutsche into close competition with Goldman Sachs and Morgan Stanley; the investment banking unit accounted for 60 percent of Deutsche Bank's profits in 1999.

Breuer also failed to consider Edson Mitchell's clout at the investment banking company. Responsible for the bank's global markets business, Mitchell, an American, succeeded in paying the investment bankers large bonuses, even when the unit was losing money in the mid 1990s. Mitchell insisted that Deutsche sell Dresdner's investment bank, stating that integrating it would be difficult and expensive. One ex-Deutsche executive said about Mitchell, "If you're a shareholder, you have to thank God that he's there because if you strip him out, the stock would halve in value." Mitchell brought 60 bankers with him when he left Merrill Lynch in 1995 to join Deutsche.[1]

Who has power at Deutsche Bank? How did power plays result in conflict? How could the conflict have been resolved? What types of stress did the merger attempt create? How could Breuer have managed the planned merger more effectively? In this chapter, we examine power, conflict, and stress in more detail and show how they influenced the failure of the Deutsche-Dresdner merger.

■ WHAT IS POWER?

Power refers to the potential or actual ability to influence others in a desired direction. Who has power at Deutsche Bank? Breuer, as CEO of the bank, had some power. So did Ackermann and Mitchell because of their roles in creating the successful investment banking enterprise.

Power and Influence

We begin our diagnosis of power by identifying those who exert influence. Heidi Miller left her job as CFO at Citibank to become the CFO and EVP in charge of business development at Priceline.com because she didn't feel she could influence her Citibank boss. At Priceline.com, she believes that she has more power because she has more influence and can more readily implement change.[2] Individual employees, including top and middle-level managers, technical analysts and specialists, support staff, and other workers, can influence the actions an organization takes to reach its goals. Formal groups of employees, such as departments, work teams, management councils, task forces, or employee unions, as well as informal groups, such as workers with offices near each other or those who see each other socially, can exercise power. Nonemployees may also try to influence the behavior of an organization and its members. Owners, suppliers, clients, competitors, employee associations (e.g., unions and professional associations), the general public, and directors of the organization may exert power that affects the organization.[3]

Individuals can exert influence in a variety of ways.[4] They may exert regular, ongoing influence, such as when managers demonstrate authority over subordinates. Or they may exert influence periodically when unique circumstances occur, such as the expiration of a labor contract or a change in the economic or technological environment. Influence can focus on specific individuals, groups, or even events. Or it can occur more generally, with the entire work situation as a target.

Influence can occur in downward, upward, and lateral directions:

- **Downward influence.** Most influence attempts are directed to those lower in the chain of command. Managers, for example, can give direct orders to employees, establish guidelines for their decision making, approve or reject subordinates' decisions, or allocate resources to them. Breuer tried to exert downward influence on the Deutsche Bank units to accept the merger.

- **Upward influence.** Managers and employees can try to influence their bosses. They may control the type of information passed to superiors as a way of promoting or protecting their self-interests or managing other impressions (see Chapter 2). They must understand and respond to their bosses' needs in order to effectively influence them. Ackermann and Mitchell, for example, exerted upward influence.

TABLE 9-1

Individuals and Groups Can Use a Variety of Tactics to Exert Influence.

Scale	Definition
Pressure tactics	The person uses demands, threats, or intimidation to convince you to comply with a request or to support a proposal.
Upward appeals	The person seeks to persuade you that the request is approved by higher management, or appeals to higher management for assistance in gaining your compliance with the request.
Exchange tactics	The person makes an explicit or implicit promise that you will receive rewards or tangible benefits if you comply with a request or support a proposal, or reminds you of a prior favor to be reciprocated.
Coalition tactics	The person seeks the aid of others to persuade you to do something or uses the support of others as an argument for you to agree also.
Ingratiating tactics	The person seeks to get you in a good mood or to think favorably of him or her before asking you to do something.
Rational persuasion	The person uses logical arguments and factual evidence to persuade you that a proposal or request is viable and likely to result in the attainment of task objectives.
Inspirational appeals	The person makes an emotional request or proposal that arouses enthusiasm by appealing to your values and ideas, or by increasing y our confidence that you can do it.
Consultation tactics	The person seeks your participation in making a decision or planning how to implement a proposed policy, strategy, or change.

Source: Gary Yukl and Cecilia M. Falbe, Influence tactics and objectives in upward, downward, and lateral influence attempts, *Journal of Applied Psychology* 75 (1990): 133. Used with permission.

- **Lateral influence.** Sometimes managers exert positive influence on peers, or vice versa, such as when co-workers offer advice or provide service. At other times, lateral influence attempts can result in competition as the parties try to strengthen their power vis-à-vis each other.[5] As their interdependence increases, they may rely more on negotiation and cooperation to resolve their differences.

Managers and other employees can use a variety of tactics to influence others, as shown in Table 9-1. Various factors, including culture, influence the use of these tactics. For example, U.S. and Chinese managers assess influence tactics differently. For example, U.S. managers rated rational persuasion and exchange as more effective than did Chinese managers. Chinese managers rated coalition tactics, upward appeals, and gifts as more effective than did their U.S. counterparts.[6]

We can assess the appropriateness of power efforts by asking questions such as the following:

- Do power efforts result in accomplishing individual, group, and organizational goals?
- Do power efforts lead to desired outcomes?
- Is power being used in ethical ways?

To control abuses and ensure the rights of all organizational members, managers may need to establish informal norms or more formal guidelines for using power.

Power and Dependence

We can also diagnose power by measuring the extent of the dependence inherent in a relationship that includes power behavior.[7] The degree that B depends on A affects the power that person A has over person B. Dependence arises because a person, group, or organization relies on another person, group, or organization to accomplish tasks. For example, subordinates may exert power, such as withholding information or failing to sign a contract, to counteract job-related dependencies on their managers. The power that the Deutsche bank investment unit has over Breuer results in part from Breuer's dependence on it: He depends on it for 60 percent of the company's profits. Candidates for national office in the United States are often dependent on big financial donors who in turn can have power over them. To counteract such dependence, jobholders attempt to garner power from other sources, such as their charisma, expertise, or control of rewards. A recently passed law in Italy attempted to give suppliers who were dependent on their clients or clients dependent on their suppliers more power by protecting them when economic dependence exists. For example, a supplier who sells all of its product to a single client can be considered economically dependent on that client, and the new law regulates termination of the client's contract with the supplier.[8]

A jobholder's dependence relates to characteristics of the organization and its environment. As the organization's goals become more ambitious, managers depend more on others to accomplish these goals. Dependence also increases as the organization becomes larger, causing managers and employees to rely more on the specialized staff that results from the increased division of labor. Because technology increases specialization, it also increases managers' dependence on specialists who can help them perform their jobs. As the uncertainty of the environment increases, managers also depend more on people who can reduce the ambiguity in organizational situations for them. Finally, dependence is a function of the organization's formal structure, measurement systems, and reward systems. Diffusing authority throughout the organization to individuals other than managers, for example, creates greater dependencies. Reward systems that encourage collaboration and team performance also increase dependencies.

Dealing with Dependence   Managers and employees engage in power-oriented behavior to reduce their dependence on others. They also try to increase the dependence of others on them, thus increasing their own relative power. An assistant who must rely on his boss for pay raises may reduce her dependence by becoming indispensable to the boss. By acquiring unique expertise or knowledge, the assistant develops power. The director of human resources may try to reduce her dependence on a supplier of training materials by finding alternative sources of goods or services. To cope with dependence, managers draw from bases of power and establish trade relations and alliances, as described later in this chapter.

Diagnosing Dependence and Power   We can use a power/dependence analysis in diagnosis. To begin this analysis, managers and employees answer the following questions:

- On whom do you really depend?
- How important and appropriate is each dependency?
- What is the basis of each dependency?

FIGURE 9-1

Managers and employees can perform a dependence diagram to help determine where they should develop and exert power.

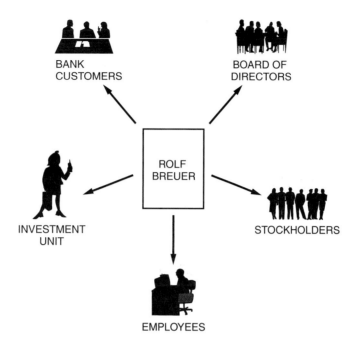

- Does a pattern of dysfunctional dependence exist?
- What created the pattern, and what consequences resulted?
- How much effective, power-oriented behavior do you engage in?
- Do you use enough power-oriented behavior to cope with your job-related dependencies?[9]

To help with our diagnosis, we can diagram the relationships within an organization, as shown in Figure 9-1 for Rolf Breuer at the Deutsche Bank. According to this diagram, Breuer relies on a large number of people. He needs to use many sources of power to reduce his dependencies. The investment unit's refusal to support the merger suggests that he didn't use enough power in negotiations to counteract this dependence.

Power and Exchange

Power goes beyond merely counteracting dependence. Managers can exert power when they exchange services others need for compliance with their requests.[10] For example, a manager such as Edson Mitchell may exchange bonuses for loyalty from his employees.

Sometimes individuals or groups develop a social exchange network to help them negotiate the allocation of valued resources.[11] This network extends the exchange to groups of individuals who control resources. Managers who use these networks may spend more time than usual making deals, interacting across departments, and exchanging resources across organizational boundaries.[12] Some of China's newly rich citizens, for example, have become wealthy as a result of their connections, or *guanxi*. The degree of closeness or affection between people, the trust and credibility between them, and the individuals' public image help determine *guanxi.*[13] High-ranking members of the People's Liberation Army and members of the Communist Party have the best connections. One such person used his connections to start a printing factory in an industry normally only open to state businesses.[14]

Power and Personality

Some people have a need for power.[15] They try to influence and control others and enjoy persuading them to agree with their views. They often seek leadership positions in groups and may act as controllers, dominated by false pride, a reflection of their strong ego.[16] Others perceive them as outspoken, forceful, and demanding. Can you think of people who have high needs for power? Often politicians, top managers, or informal leaders do.

An individual's personality can affect her exertion of power and influence. Personality explains the type of influence tactics used. In one study, people high on Machiavellianism more often used nonrational and indirect tactics (e.g., deceit or thought manipulation). People low in Machiavellianism more often used rational and direct tactics (e.g., reason, persistence, or assertion). Those high on need for approval used rational and indirect tactics (e.g., hinting, compromise, bargaining). Those low on need for approval used nonrational and direct tactics (e.g., threat, evasion, reward).[17]

■ EMPOWERMENT AS A FORM OF POWER

Rather than viewing power as a limited resource that can inspire power struggles and competition, empowerment suggests that managers can increase their power by sharing it with others.[18] In a common scenario, managers give workers the training and authority they need to act with more autonomy. As a result, the empowered workers feel more involved, experience greater job satisfaction, support the manager's goals, and perform better. The manager's influence increases both within the group and within the organization as his employees' productivity rises. Aeroquip-Inoac Company's plant in Livingston, Tennessee, empowered workers by training them in techniques focused on continuous improvement and involving more than 90 percent of them in at least two improvement activities. One year, employees each generated an average of 8.5 improvement suggestions. In addition, the management team rewards innovation. Such empowerment resulted in major gains in process and quality improvements; work teams created over $740,000 in cost savings in a single year.[19]

Empowering workers counteracts powerlessness they may feel from several sources:[20]

- ■ **Organizational culture.** Significant organizational changes, such as reorganizations or downsizings, an excessive emphasis on competition, an impersonal bureaucratic climate, or poor communication, can make employees feel they have little control over their work lives.
- ■ **Management style.** An authoritarian supervisor who emphasizes employee failures but fails to offer reasons for management decisions promotes feelings of powerlessness.

- **Job design.** Employees often feel powerless when their jobs involve little variety, unrealistic goals, too many rules, low opportunities for advancement, and a limited supply of the resources needed to perform the job.
- **Reward systems.** Powerlessness also occurs when the organization does not reward competence or innovation or offers unattractive rewards.

As the workforce becomes more diverse, managers must ensure that they don't contribute to the powerlessness of a jobholder. A manager may empower workers by providing a positive emotional atmosphere and rewarding staff achievements in visible and personal ways. He may express confidence in subordinates' abilities, foster initiative and responsibility, and build on success.[21]

Empowering workers has improved employees' attitudes and resulted in significant financial benefits for them and the organization.[22] It increases task satisfaction and task performance. Monarch Marking Systems, an Ohio manufacturer of electronic bar-code printers, price-marking guns, and product line labels, determined that the hourly workforce had the greatest knowledge of production problems. The team identified lengthy setups as a major cause of low productivity. After considering and testing a number of possible remedies, the team implemented five solutions that reduced changeover time from 60 minutes to 4 minutes. Monarch's Practical Process Improvement program encouraged teams such as this one to drive continuous improvement throughout the organization.[23]

Empowering workers results in more cooperation among group members and ultimately in the group's survival. It leads to greater personal growth and learning for group members. Worker empowerment also helps prevent power abuses. PAC International, a small British company that manufactures electronic access-control systems, currently has six empowered manufacturing teams. Each has a maintenance person, who is responsible for preventative maintenance, and a materials person, who makes sure needed supplies are ordered. PAC managers have attempted to foster a culture of cooperation and respect, where power differences are minimized.[24]

Yet, at the same time, empowerment can have a downside. Empowerment programs have failed for a number of reasons. Some managers give their employees too much control over decision making too quickly. VCS, Inc., a manufacturer of ladders, firehouse poles, and dumbwaiters, transferred decisions from team leaders and shift supervisors to line employees operating as a team. The lack of an orderly transfer of responsibility caused the empowerment to fail.[25] In addition, some companies fail to differentiate among their employees, giving them all the same degree of responsibility. Some middle-level managers may have difficulty passing decision-making responsibility to their subordinates.[26] Managers may need to seek a balance between worker empowerment and managerial control to ensure effective organizational functioning.[27] Empowerment programs may fail for other reasons. The CEO may decree that the employees can make decisions and take actions, and try to make the change too quickly. Companies may try to convince employees that they have more power rather than actually giving real power to them. The company may not selectively empower employees in ways that make sense for them, their jobs, and the organization. Top executives may overlook middle managers' needs for control, achievement, security, recognition, and understanding of events. The organization may take a piecemeal approach to empowerment and not change all the systems required for empowerment to succeed. Finally, the organization may distort the accountability of employees, protecting them from assuming risks associated with their new power.[28]

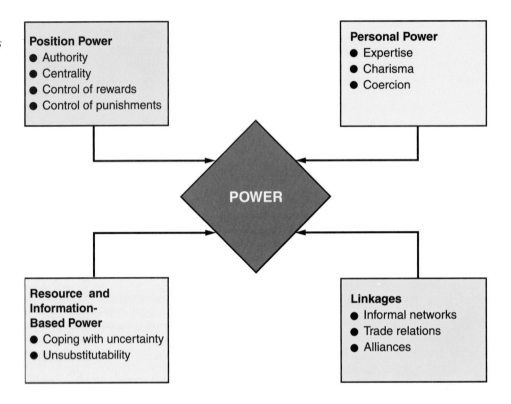

▌ SOURCES OF POWER

How can you and others increase your power? Managers and employees can draw on four major sources of power, as shown in Figure 9-2: (1) their position; (2) their personal characteristics; (3) the resources or information they can access and control; and (4) the linkages they form.

Position Power

People often obtain power from the position or job they hold in an organization. For example, a comparison of 10 public and 35 private sector organizations indicated that private sector supervisors had more position power than public sector supervisors.[29] Men generally have higher levels of legitimate power than women, whereas women have more expert and referent power than men.[30] Authority, centrality, and control of rewards and punishments provide position power to individuals or groups.

▪ **Authority.** Managers can exert influence over others simply because of the authority associated with their jobs. This legitimate power results in employees obeying a manager's rules or orders because they consider them valid due to the manager's position. An organization's culture can affect the way authority is translated into power, such as whether the authority is respected or not based on credible expertise.[31]

- **Centrality.** Other positions accrue power because they link and are important to those of other people or subunits.[32] The director of marketing at an e-commerce company has greater centrality than a Web designer because more jobholders' activities link to the marketing director than to the Web designer. The power that results from centrality increases when managers also use the tactics of upward appeal, coalition formation, and exchange.[33]
- **Control of rewards and punishments.** Managers who can deliver rewards and punishments have more power. Edson Mitchell, for example, has power because he obtained bonuses for his subordinates even when their unit didn't make a profit. Such managers may use rewards, such as pay raises, status, desirable work assignments, praise, recognition, or group sanctions, to encourage others' compliance with desired behaviors or goals. They might also punish workers by demoting or dismissing them, increasing the supervision they receive, or withholding compensation or promotions.

Personal Power

Personal power stems from knowledge or personality traits that allow a person to influence the behavior of others. The success of financial planners, for example, may depend on their ability to influence clients and prospects using such aspects of personal power as their expertise, knowledge of specific information, and likeability.[34] When Debby Hopkins assumed the position of CFO at Lucent, she quickly showed her subordinates that she would support them. She has a "can-do intensity" that impresses executive recruiters and her co-workers.[35] Personal power results from three factors:

- **Expertise.** A person who has unique or special knowledge, skills, and experience may use this expertise as a source of influence and a way of building personal power. As organizations have become more technology-oriented, technical support staffs and employees with e-commerce experience and expertise have acquired increased power in organizations.
- **Charisma.** Some people influence others because they have a personal magnetism that causes others to identify with them and their aspirations. Employees may work long hours to meet difficult deadlines simply because their manager has the charisma needed to convince them the project is worth the extra effort. Charismatic managers look for opportunities, craft a vision related to it, communicate their goals, and may break the traditional rules of their industry to get a competitive edge.[36]
- **Coercion.** A manager who exerts power by evoking fear has coercive power. For example, the president of a company where workers are on strike could threaten to replace any striking workers or take the company into bankruptcy. The risk of retaliation may further prevent the use of coercive power.[37] The use of coercive power often has secondary, dysfunctional consequences, such as stress and anxiety, increased absenteeism and turnover, and even sabotage.

Resource-Based and Information-Based Power

Access to resources, such as money, material, staff, or information, also gives managers and other employees power. People who formulate rules to regulate the control of resources, such as the budget, as well as those who actually possess, allocate, and use the resources, will acquire power.[38] For example, workers who control the scheduling of prized machinery or the allocation of computer equipment can also acquire resource-based power.

We can describe and diagnose the use of resources along three dimensions:[39]

- **Internal-external.** People may rely on resources internal to the organization, such as exchanging favors or forming networks with other employees. When these sources fail or become inadequate, individuals may turn outside the organization for resources by joining professional organizations or forming alliances outside the organization.
- **Vertical-lateral.** People may exert influence by relating to superiors or subordinates as opposed to peers. Mentor–protegé activities occur vertically in the organization; coalition formation occurs laterally.
- **Legitimate-illegitimate.** Power behavior ranges from normal to extreme. A manager exerts legitimate power behavior when he uses his position to influence workers to get their jobs done well. He uses illegitimate power when he influences them to act unethically.

Information-based power can accompany the control of resources, but it can also occur independently in organizations. The first people in a company who can use newly acquired computer software have information-based power. Such power has less permanence than expert power. Information-based power helps explain the importance of office gossip or the grapevine. People who get information first tend to have more power because they can better deal with uncertainty and are less replaceable. Information-based power increases when organizational subunits, including specific departments, individual managers, or ad hoc groupings of workers, can use information to cope with uncertainty and increase their unsubstitutability.

Coping with Uncertainty   Managers and employees can gain power by using information to help others reduce workplace uncertainty caused by unclear task demands, a rapidly changing environment, introduction of new technology, or an ambiguous organizational structure. In a unionized plant, managers who know the provisions of the current contract may secure information-based power because they can help other managers cope with uncertainty in managing the union workers. A customer service department can gain power by informing marketing, engineering, and R&D about the needs of customers.

Boundary-spanner roles, roles associated with positions that interact with individuals or groups in other organizations, have significant power potential. People in roles such as public relations director or purchasing agent deal with the outside environment for the benefit of the organization's members. Coping with uncertainty for others and channeling information to the organization's members gives them power.

Unsubstitutability   In general, the fewer substitutes that exist for the activities of an individual or group, the more power that person or group has. Consider an organization in which you have worked. Who performed activities that no one else could readily perform? The president was probably less substitutable than a secretary. The chief financial officer may have been more substitutable than the chief information officer. A unit that can bring resources into the organization from the outside may also have low substitutability. Who in the situation at Deutsche Bank has power because of lack of substitutability? At the time of the proposed merger, the investment unit did!

Linkages

Individuals and groups can acquire power by increasing their contacts with others. They share information and provide support for them as a way of increasing their power. They can build informal networks, foster alliances, and create trade relations.

Informal Networks Informal networks may result in the transfer of legitimate authority from a supervisor to an influential employee. Supervisors can use three types of informal networks:

- **Advice networks** include the people to whom others turn to get work done.
- **Trust networks** include the people who share confidential or delicate information.
- **Communication networks** include the people who talk to each other about work-related matters.[40]

Developing an informal network of contacts requires spending scheduled and unscheduled time meeting with co-workers and other organizational members. Women and minorities have faced particular challenges in developing networks both in the United States and abroad because they must penetrate the "old boys' network" that controls resources and information in organizations. Gail McGovern, the head of Fidelity Investments' core retail division, says that women feel powerful when they are part of the inner circle.[41] The South Korean Women's Trade Union, for example, is the first union for women in a country where men have typically held all of the power.[42] New Zealand has created a "new girls' network" that begins with top political jobs, including the governor-general, prime minister, attorney general, National Party leader, and mayor of Auckland, and extends into industry, with a woman acting as chief executive at the country's biggest corporation.[43] The Club of 22, an exclusive group of 30 top women executives and politicians in Poland, demonstrates women's success in that developing country. Women hold more seats in the national legislature than in a number of western European countries. Twenty-two percent of Polish women—more than four times the number of German women—hold decision-making jobs.[44] Women in Boston are also forming an "old girls' network" to financially support women candidates and ultimately gain more political power.[45]

Trade Relations *Trade relationships,* reciprocal relations or lateral exchanges between parties, contribute to the acquisition and exercise of power. Managers participate in trade relationships with other managers by exchanging personnel or other resources to get their jobs done.[46] For example, a trainer in the human resources department might exchange a reduction in training budget for help from the marketing department in promoting training programs. Trade relations can create a "quid pro quo" mentality in which a manager has power because a colleague "owes" her for previously given services, resources, or other favors.

Alliances By forming *alliances,* special partnerships that attempt to exert concerted influence within or between organizations, managers and employees can influence others without having or using formal authority.[47] Alliances between two or more people, groups, or organizations form when they have resources or favors to exchange. They might exchange equipment, supplies, assistance, cooperation, recognition, visibility, personal support, and gratitude, among other things. Such reciprocity can occur between peers, between supervisor and subordinate, or between members of different organizations.

An alliance can be organized as a *coalition* in which a group lobbies for a mutual interest. Coalition members bring a larger pool of resources to situations, including greater expertise and commitment. They often act politically to support or oppose an organizational program, policy, or change. They may also use negotiations to achieve their goals. Shifts in the balance of bargaining power among the parties may affect the stability of the alliances. For example, when partners in an international joint venture gain enough knowledge to remove their dependency on their partner, the original bargain becomes invalid and the alliance unstable.[48]

ORGANIZATIONAL POLITICS

Individuals may secure and exercise power from any of the four sources for the sole purpose of advancing their personal goals, causes, ideas, or positions.[49] The resulting actions, which stem primarily from their self-motivations rather than the organization's good, often are viewed as *organizational politics,* or self-serving, power-oriented behavior.[50] Political behavior increases as resources become less available, uncertainty increases, and goals become more complex and difficult to attain. One study indicated that perceptions of organizational politics reduced the job satisfaction of 1,251 public sector employees. The effects of organizational politics were less when employees participated in decision making with their supervisors.[51]

As individuals attempt to exert power for their own purposes, they may conflict with others' attempts, resulting in competing drives for control and power struggles. Stress may also result.[52]

In one study, for example, organizational members saw politics as contributing to declining morale, inferior organizational performance outcomes, and increased organizational control.[53] Another study concluded that organizational politics particularly can damage lower-status employees, who react by demonstrating increasingly negative attitudes toward the organization.[54] In particular, the absenteeism of shorter-term employees increased.[55] In general, political behavior related to negative work outcomes.[56] Playing the political game may become so salient for employees that they lose sight of the real goals of the organization. Ethical concerns often arise about political behavior in organizations. Occasionally, however, organizational politics may result in the airing and interplay of diverse opinions and agendas, resulting in more effective decision making.

SEXUAL HARASSMENT: THE ABUSE OF POWER

Companies have a legal responsibility to keep the workplace free of sexual harassment and intimidation. Title VII of the Civil Rights Act of 1964 and subsequent legislation protect workers from discrimination that includes sexual harassment. Sexual harassment refers to situations in which a person submits to unwelcome sexual advances, requests for sexual favors, or other verbal or physical conduct of a sexual nature. These coerced behaviors become a condition of a person's employment, are used as the basis for an employment decision about that person, or interfere with a person's work performance by creating a hostile, intimidating, or offensive work environment. Such conduct must be "unwelcome" for sexual harassment to occur. Sexual harassment is viewed as a way of exerting power over a less powerful person. Both men and women can be victims of sexual harassment, although women more frequently experience it.

Men who commit sexual harassment may see it as a way of "winning" or being the center of attention; often they feel that women are inferior and don't belong in the workplace, or they insult women in the workplace to impress other men.[57] The Army's highest-ranking woman, Lieutenant General Claudia Kennedy, accused a general of sexual harassment. Many women, however, do not make official complaints as Kennedy did. Instead, they leave the company because they fear that reporting harassment will either damage their careers or go unpunished.[58]

Companies must ensure that the work environment is free from sexual harassment. This means not only ensuring that direct harassment does not occur, but that a hostile environment, as is created by sexually oriented posters or language, does not exist. Managers must take complaints about harassment seriously and have stated policies and procedures for dealing with them. They must also offer training to all workers so that they understand what constitutes sexual harassment, how to recognize it, and how to deal with it. At the same time, companies must make sure that they are not overprotecting women by sending an unintended message about their fragility, implying that they need male-dominated management to protect them from their male co-workers. For example, telling sexist jokes is inappropriate whether or not anyone objects to them, but it must be "objectively offensive" to serve as the basis of a sexual harassment suit.[59] Not all sexual harassment complaints are legitimate. Many attorneys believe that the number of unfounded complaints has increased since the Civil Rights Act of 1991 allowed for compensatory damages.[60]

Companies may have poorly written sexual harassment policies, use vague definitions of sexual harassment, or require cumbersome reporting procedures.[61] Managers may deny the claims, blame the victim, minimize the seriousness of the offense, protect valued employees, ignore habitual harassers, or retaliate against the victim.[62] The U.S. Department of Labor recommends a six-step approach to dealing with harassment in the workplace:[63]

1. Establish a task force to study the problem and recommend solutions.
2. Communicate the plan to top managers.
3. Notify relevant unions of the plan.
4. Distribute a sexual harassment policy statement to all employees and have each person sign off on it.
5. Design and implement a training program.
6. Establish and enforce specific penalties for violations.

Sexual harassment can also be a problem outside the United States. In Mexico, where sexual harassment is a criminal offense, the penal code offers protection for anyone whose job is put in jeopardy because they deny a request for sexual favors. Cross-cultural training for executives in multinational corporations can help them understand legal liability in the workplace. Mitsubishi Motors Manufacturing of America uses cross-cultural training regarding diversity, equal employment, and prevention of sexual harassment for Japanese employees who will work in the United States. Mitsubishi introduced this program after the Equal Employment Opportunity Commission brought one of the largest cases of sexual harassment in terms of potential damages against the company.[64]

▌THE NATURE OF CONFLICT

Conflict refers to a disagreement, opposition, or struggle between two or more people or groups.[65] It results from their incompatible influence and often accompanies differences in power among parties. Breuer, Ackermann, and Mitchell experienced conflict over the decision to acquire Dresdner's investment unit. The likelihood of conflict increases when parties interact, view their differences as incompatible, and see conflict as a constructive way of resolving disagreements.[66]

We can describe conflict along three dimensions:

- **public versus private,** overt, visible, and authorized conflict versus covert, hidden, and unauthorized conflict;
- **formal versus informal,** conflict related to the chain of command versus conflict between ad hoc individuals or groups; and
- **rational versus nonrational,** premeditated or logical conflict versus spontaneous, impulsive, and emotional conflict.[67]

Conflict most commonly arises when[68]

- individuals or groups perceive they have mutually exclusive goals or values;
- people use behavior designed to defeat, reduce, or suppress an opponent;
- groups face each other with mutually opposing actions; and
- a group tries to create a favored position compared to another person or group.

The major causes of conflict include individual characteristics, such as personality, values, and goals, interpersonal factors, such as communication distortions, power imbalances, and previous interactions, and issues that are complex or vague.[69] Conflict can easily occur in multinational or multicultural situations. Basic differences in language, norms, personal styles, and other cultural characteristics hinder effective communication and set the stage for conflict. Cross-cultural sensitivity and understanding are key ingredients for minimizing dysfunctional conflict.

Perceptions play a major role in conflicts. People may perceive conflict along three dimensions:

- **Relationship/Task.** Parties focus either on their ongoing relationships, such as questioning their competence or struggling for leadership, or substance of the task.[70]
- **Emotional/Intellectual.** Parties pay attention either to the emotional or the cognitive components of the conflict.
- **Cooperate/Win.** Each party can try to either cooperate with the other party or win at the other party's expense.[71]

How individuals or groups handle the conflict often depends on the way they frame it along each of these dimensions. For example, by focusing on relationships, the parties more likely maintain respect for others. By focusing on task, the parties may avoid the onus of reacting emotionally.

Levels of Conflict

To manage conflict effectively, managers must diagnose precisely where it exists so they can choose appropriate management strategies. Conflict can occur at the individual, group, and organizational levels.

Role Pressures on Individuals   A person may experience *cognitive conflict,* an intellectual discomfort created by trying to achieve incompatible goals. An accountant, for example, may be forced to sacrifice additional checking of a company's books in order to meet an imposed deadline. *Affective conflict* occurs when competing emotions accompany the incompatible goals and result in increased stress, decreased productivity, or decreased satisfaction for the individual. The accountant may experience both frustration and excitement in trying to reconcile the incompatible goals of speed and accuracy. We can usually trace such individual-level conflicts to role ambiguity, role conflict, or other role pressures.

Each person has a prescribed set of activities, or potential behavior, that constitute a *role* he performs.[72] Roles can be both formal (vice president) and informal (office gossip) and found in both work and nonwork settings. Typically, a person who holds a particular role relates to or interacts with others in comparable or related roles, known as the *role set.* A male may hold the roles of manager, husband, father, and community activist. As a manager, he may even hold the roles of boss and employee simultaneously.

Both role holders and others have expectations of how a role holder will think and behave. These expectations may lack clarity or create conflict. Role ambiguity, overload, and conflict may lead to such dysfunctional work-related behaviors as tension, stress, job dissatisfaction, propensity to leave the organization, and lowered organizational commitment.[73]

- **Role ambiguity.** Although a person usually operates according to expectations associated with her role, occasionally she performs activities typically not associated with it. People's differing expectations about the activities appropriate to a role lead to lack of clarity about the expectations, or *role ambiguity.*

- **Role overload.** When a role holder receives compatible expectations from others about how to perform a role, but these duties require too much time or knowledge, *role overload* occurs. A person who holds a full-time job and has too many tasks to complete in the available time likely experiences role overload. So does a person who is asked to perform tasks that exceed her knowledge, skills, or abilities.

- **Role conflict.** Differing and often incompatible expectations that pressure a role holder to perform in one way rather than another can result in *role conflict.* Complying with one set of role-related pressures hinders or prevents compliance with a different set of role-related pressures. For example, managers who are also spouses and parents might experience role conflict when they must deal with a sick child on the same day a mandatory meeting for all managers is scheduled. A "good parent" will tend to the sick child; a "good employee" will make the business meeting a top priority.

We can identify four types of role conflict, as illustrated in Figure 9-3:

- **Intrasender.** One person sends a role holder conflicting or inconsistent expectations. Customer service representatives whose boss tells them on the one hand to handle as many clients as possible and on the other hand to provide complete, detailed, accurate, and timely information may experience intrasender conflict.

- **Intersender.** Different people with whom the role holder interacts have different expectations of him or her. A laboratory technician may receive one set of instructions about the types of tests he should provide from his supervisor and a different set from other physicians in the practice.

FIGURE 9-3
Role conflict results from differing and incompatible expectations.

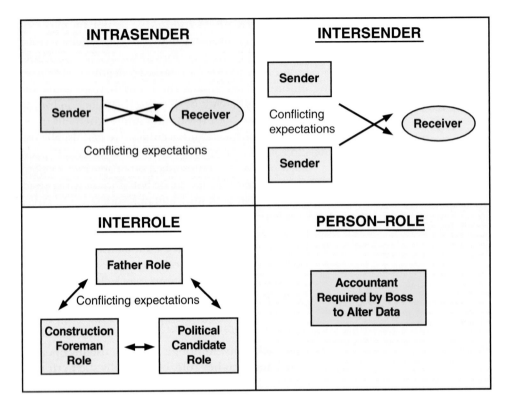

- **Interrole.** The expectations associated with a person's different roles come into conflict. The working mother who has a sick child feels she is expected to be at work and perform her job as well as to be at home and care for her sick child.
- **Person-role** The activities expected of a role holder violate the individual's values and morals. The devout employee who is expected to work on a religious holiday experiences person-role conflict. So does the employee who is pressured to perform unethical acts, such as distorting data to represent the company in a favorable light.

Interpersonal Conflict   Interpersonal conflict describes a situation in which two individuals disagree about issues, actions, or goals, and where joint outcomes become important. Breuer and Ackermann disagree about how to handle the acquisition of the Dredsner investment unit. Internal squabbling at the Sammy Sosa Charitable Foundation, created to send hurricane relief funds to the Dominican Republic, contributed to its demise less than two years after its founding.[74]

Interpersonal conflict often arises from differences in people's status, perceptions, and orientations. A group of physician-managers who attempted to control the performance of physicians and other professional staff in line with insurance company and government guidelines often experienced conflict with their physician colleagues. Some attempted to serve the needs of the physicians, whereas others focused on meeting the needs of the health maintenance organization. The latter group, in particular, experienced conflict with their colleagues over patient care and allocation of resources.[75] Such conflict may motivate individuals to reveal additional relevant issues, or it may prevent any further communication. To further complicate matters, some individuals are more likely to engage in conflict than others. For example, individuals with a Type A behavior pattern (see Chapter 3) had a higher frequency of conflict than those with a Type B pattern. Women reported a lower frequency of conflict than men.[76]

Group-Level Conflict.   Groups may also experience either cognitive or affective *intragroup conflict.* For example, members of a new product development team may draw different conclusions about the best direction for the company regarding new markets and products and hence experience cognitive or substantive conflict. The group members may even feel excited about unfeasible options and so experience affective conflict, which results from their different emotional responses to the same situation.

Intergroup conflict exists between or among groups, such as an engineering and a research and development department. In a nursing home, it can exist between staff and patients.[77] We can often trace such conflicts to competing goals, competition for limited resources, or cultural differences. Power differences and attempts to preserve the groups' separate identities can also contribute to intergroup conflict.[78] It can exist between groups responsible for different aspects of the same process. Marketing and manufacturing, for example, sometimes clash over the best way to create and bring a new product to market.

Organizational-Level Conflict   *Intraorganizational conflict* refers to conflict that characterizes overall organizational functioning. Organizational conflict occurs when widespread conflict exists within organizational units, such as within or between departments or between individual employees.

- **Vertical conflict** occurs between supervisor and subordinates. Managers and employees, for example, may disagree about the best ways to accomplish their tasks or their department's goals. Union representatives and plant managers may argue about work rules throughout the organization.

- **Horizontal conflict** exists between employees or departments at the same level. Marketing and manufacturing may disagree about product specifications or quality standards.

- **Diagonal conflict** often occurs over the allocation of resources throughout the organization—to product development or product sales, for example—or over the involvement of staff in line decisions.

Some intraorganizational conflict can energize workers and inspire innovation because it reveals new ideas and perspectives. But uncontrolled and unmanaged, it can demoralize workers and cause performance to deteriorate because the conflict saps their energy and distracts them from their jobs.

Interorganizational conflict, conflict between organizations, can also exist. Amarillo National Bank experienced conflict with the larger Bank of America in retaining its customers, but Amarillo National succeeds because of its customer focus, early introduction of Internet banking, and continuous upgrading of services.[79] The amount of conflict may depend on the extent to which the organizations create uncertain conditions for competitors, suppliers, or customers and try to access or control the same resources. It may also depend on how much organizations encourage communication, attempt to balance power in the marketplace, and develop procedures for resolving existing conflict.[80] Recent attempts to manage such conflict and ensure that it has a positive impact on organizational performance have emphasized the formation of strategic alliances and partnerships.

Identifying the level of conflict is a prerequisite to selecting appropriate strategies for managing it. Accurate diagnosis also involves specifying the stage of conflict, as described in the next section, since not all conflict involves overt warfare.

Stages of Conflict

The nature of conflict changes over time. When a group can't accomplish a goal or complete a task, its members experience frustration. They may perceive that conflict exists and formulate ideas about the conflict issue. They gather information and consider multiple points of view to gain a better understanding of the conflict issue. Those affected respond, resolving the conflict or igniting more conflict.

Diagnosing the nature of conflict is aided by considering it as a sequence of conflict episodes. Regardless of the level of conflict, a historical but still useful view suggests that each conflict episode proceeds through one or more of five possible stages, as shown in Figure 9-4.[81] By specifying the stage of conflict, a manager can determine its intensity and select the best strategies for managing it.

- **Latent conflict.** Conflict may begin with conditions for conflict, such as power differences, competition for scarce resources, different goals, or diverse role pressures, which provide the foundation for disagreement and, ultimately, for conflict. Departments such as human resources and finance frequently experience *latent conflict* because of inherent differences in perceptions and attitudes.

- **Perceived conflict.** The conflict moves to the stage of *perceived conflict* when differences of opinion are voiced, incompatible goals or values become apparent, or people demean others or try to enact opposing actions.

- **Felt conflict.** When one or more parties feels tense or anxious as a result of such disagreements or misunderstandings, conflict has moved beyond perceived to *felt conflict*. Typically, there is a time lag between intellectually perceiving that conflict exists and its becoming personalized so that you feel it "in the pit of your stomach."

- **Manifest conflict.** Observable behavior designed to frustrate another's attempts to pursue his goals is the most overt form of conflict. Both open aggression and withdrawal of support illustrate *manifest conflict*. At this stage,

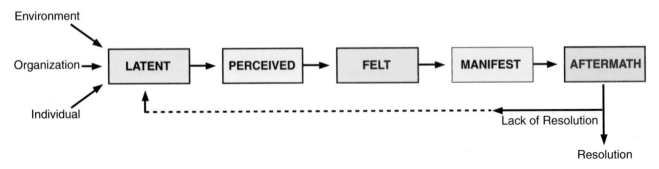

FIGURE 9-4   *Conflict proceeds from latent conflict to conflict aftermath.*

conflict must be used constructively or resolved in order for effective organizational performance to occur.

■ **Conflict aftermath.** The conflict episode ends after the conflict has been managed and the resulting energy heightened, resolved, or suppressed. If the conflict is resolved, the parties may experience a new reality as they adjust their perceptions.[82] Unresolved conflict, which exists everywhere, simply sows the seeds for manifest conflict later. Thus, conflict can be functional or dysfunctional as described in the next section.

Hidden Conflict in Organizations

Not all conflict is overt and public; rather, it can be covert and hidden.[83] For example, individual employees may hold private grievances regarding their managers. Hidden conflict frequently is nonrational—that is, spontaneous, impulsive, and emotional. Those who experience this conflict may vent their feelings, express their displeasure with people or situations, or feel hurt. Hidden conflict typically involves informal disputes, which ignore rank and position in their resolution. For example, managers and employees may disagree over vacation policies, but never formally express their disagreements.

People may air hidden conflict as private grievances or may commit sabotage and other signs of disloyalty instead of overt conflict. Such private conflict occurs out of the public view, even during time-outs or sidebar discussions in negotiations. Sometimes people don't recognize such disputes as conflict, resulting in passive resistance to events. On the other hand, conflicts may be handled in the course of normal, daily activities, keeping them at a relatively low intensity.

Managers need to be sensitive to hidden conflict because it can have significant consequences for organizations. It can also lead to more public and formal conflict, as well as affect organizational performance. Managing hidden conflict may require different strategies than managing more public, overt conflict. For example, managers might need to develop a more collegial way of interacting with employees.

▌ CONFLICT: FUNCTIONAL OR DYSFUNCTIONAL?

Some conflict can encourage organizational innovation, creativity, and adaptation. Conflict also can result in higher worker enthusiasm or better decisions. Can you think of a personal conflict in which a positive outcome occurred? If so, you may realize that you acquired a different perspective on an issue or learned that your own perceptions or information had been inaccurate. By exchanging and clarifying thoughts, you may have gained insight.

Sometimes conflict leads to a search for new approaches that will resolve disagreements or long-standing problems. Conflicting groups may form an alliance as a way of handling competition for limited resources. Conflict, in the form of planned competition, can also energize participants and lead to greater productivity because it results in an intensity about task performance.

Conflict can also result in dysfunctional outcomes, such as reduced productivity, lower morale, overwhelming dissatisfaction, and increased tension and stress. Some people, often the losers in a competitive situation, feel defeated and demeaned. A climate of mistrust and suspicion may arise. Individuals or groups may focus more narrowly on their own interests, preventing the development of teamwork. Production and satisfaction may decline; turnover and absenteeism may increase.

Whether the conflict is functional or dysfunctional depends on several factors:

- **Sociocultural context.** Differences in sociocultural background between parties may exaggerate barriers and reduce the likelihood of functional conflict resolution.[84]
- **Issues involved.** Highly significant, complex issues of long standing more likely cause dysfunctional outcomes than trivial, simple, and recently created issues.
- **Cognitive frame.** Those with cooperative attitudes more likely seek a functional outcome than those with competitive attitudes.
- **Characteristics of the conflicting parties.** The knowledge, experiences, and personal styles of the parties may influence the outcomes of conflict.
- **Misjudgments and misperceptions.** Errors in perceptions and attributions may cause the parties to act on the basis of inaccurate information, often exaggerating existing conflict or creating new disagreements.

Conflict in work groups can be functional or dysfunctional, depending on the type of conflict, the nature of the task, the task interdependence, and the group norms. For example, in groups that performed very routine tasks, disagreements hindered group functioning. In groups that performed nonroutine tasks, disagreements were not detrimental and were sometimes beneficial. Norms that encouraged open discussion of conflict did not always result in positive outcomes, particularly when they increased the number and intensity of conflicts related to interpersonal relationships.[85] Conflict affects individuals and interpersonal relationships. Individuals can become angry, hostile, frustrated, stressed, or exhilarated. Distrust, misunderstandings, absenteeism, or even creativity can result.[86]

Effective managers learn how to create functional conflict and manage dysfunctional conflict. They can develop and practice techniques for diagnosing the causes and nature of conflict and transforming it into a productive force in the organization.

▌ MANAGING CONFLICT

The ease of managing conflict can vary.[87] For example, managers have more difficulty resolving conflict that involves a matter of principle, large stakes, and a single transaction than conflict that involves minor issues, small stakes, and a long-term relationship. They also experience difficulty in resolving conflict in which one party is viewed as gaining at the expense of the other, has weak leadership, and feels harmed. Conflict is harder to resolve when no neutral third party can act as an intermediary because it relies on the two parties understanding and then resolving their differences.

Interpersonal Techniques

Managers and employees can begin by taking the other's perspective as a way of better understanding and then managing conflict.[88] Perspective taking helps individuals disclose more information, express messages in ways that others better understand, and consider and respond to the perspectives of others. By understanding that others have different views, team members can anticipate disagreements. Then they more often respond to the conflict by trying to understand the other person.

FIGURE 9-5

A person can use one of five styles to deal with conflict.

Source: Adapted from K. W. Thomas, Conflict and conflict management. In M. D. Dunnette (ed.), *Handbook of Industrial and Organizational Psychology* (New York: RandMcNally, 1976). Used by permission of Houghton Mifflin Company.

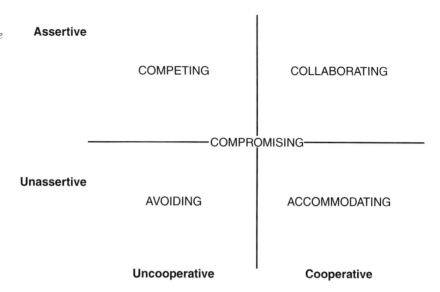

People also can use the five behaviors shown in Figure 9-5, for handling conflict. Competing, collaborating, compromising, avoiding, and accommodating, differ in the extent to which they satisfy a party's own concerns and those of the other party.[89]

■ **Competing.** Individuals who use the competing mode try to satisfy their own concerns. They are unwilling to satisfy others' concerns to even a minimal degree. This strategy works well in emergencies, on issues calling for unpopular actions, in cases where one party is correct in its position, or where one party has much greater power.

■ **Collaborating.** Collaborating emphasizes problem solving with a goal of maximizing satisfaction for both parties. Successful collaboration involves seeing conflict as natural, showing trust and honesty toward others, and encouraging the airing of every person's attitudes and feelings. Each party exerts both assertive and cooperative behavior. Parties can use collaboration when their objective is to learn, use information from diverse sources, and find an integrative solution.

■ **Compromising.** Compromise represents an intermediate behavior on both the assertiveness and cooperative dimensions. It can include sharing positions, but not moving to the extremes of assertiveness or cooperation. It generally doesn't result in maximum satisfaction for both parties. This style works well when the groups have equal power, value the goals enough to act assertively, or experience time pressures.

■ **Avoiding.** Individuals or groups may withdraw from the conflict situation and thus satisfy neither their own nor the other party's concerns. This mode works best when individuals or groups face trivial or tangential issues or have little chance of satisfying their personal concerns. Avoidance also works when conflict resolution will likely result in significant disruption or when others can resolve conflict more effectively.

■ **Accommodating.** Individuals or groups who accommodate demonstrate a willingness to cooperate in satisfying others' concerns, while at the same time acting unassertively in addressing their own needs. Smoothing over conflict in this way can build social credits for later issues, result in harmony and stability, and satisfy others.

Employees in a medical department at a U.S. university who used a collaborating style experienced less task conflict and so less relationship conflict and less stress. Those who used either a dominating or avoiding style experienced more task conflict and so more relationship conflict and more stress.[90]

Organizational Approaches

Managers can use formal processes, such as grievance procedures, mediation and arbitration, and negotiation, to resolve conflicts.[91]

Grievance Procedures.   Grievance procedures provide a formal process by which workers can complain to management if they feel they have not been treated properly or if their rights have been violated. A formal grievance procedure helps managers respond to workers' complaints. It can clarify a worker's contractual work requirements and provide a structure for hearing and resolving the complaint. Workers typically file grievances to protest unfair treatment or contractual violations, draw attention to health or safety hazards, or exercise their power as a test of worker prerogatives. Royal Dutch/Shell tracks the number of employees who use the company's grievance procedures as a way of understanding the workplace culture and atmosphere.[92]

In a unionized situation, the aggrieved employee presents the complaint orally to the first-line supervisor and union steward. Unresolved grievances then can proceed through a series of appeals, as shown in Figure 9-6, until they are satisfactorily resolved. Nonunionized organizations often have less formal grievance procedures. They may appoint an ombudsperson who facilitates the grievance resolution process or represents the worker in dealing with management. They may suggest that the worker meet with a specific manager or a human resources representative. Companies must also develop a grievance procedure for handling sexual harassment complaints. The procedure should encourage victims to make a complaint and make sure that no retaliation will occur. The policy should also state the process for investigating the complaint. The grievance procedure should include the opportunity to file the complaint with individuals other than the complainant's

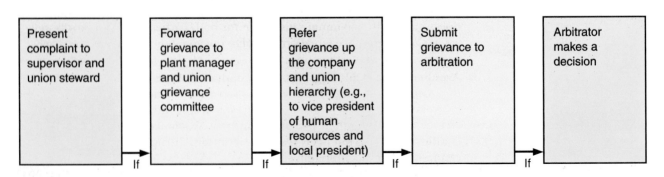

| Present complaint to supervisor and union steward | Forward grievance to plant manager and union grievance committee | Refer grievance up the company and union hierarchy (e.g., to vice president of human resources and local president) | Submit grievance to arbitration | Arbitrator makes a decision |

FIGURE 9-6   *Workers in unionized companies can follow a series of steps when filing a grievance.*

supervisor. Effective policy also means communicating that the firm does not condone sexual harassment and will punish violators.[93]

Mediation and Arbitration   Third-party interventions use trained individuals to help resolve conflict. In *mediation,* a neutral party tries to help disputing parties reach a settlement of the issues that divide them. The mediator focuses on bringing the parties to agreement by making procedural suggestions and keeping the channels of communication open. She may help parties establish priorities or offer creative solutions. A good mediator tries to determine the true intentions of each party and communicate them to the other. Engineers at Purdue University are developing a computer program that acts as a mediator by preparing its own solution or suggesting additional mediators as a way of helping facility designers resolve conflicts over plant layout, product routing, or robotics equipment programming.[94]

   An arbitrator, in contrast to a mediator, acts as a judge in a dispute. *Arbitration* is a quasi-legal proceeding that resembles a formal judicial procedure but does not take place in a court of law. In arbitration, each party presents its position on disputed matters to the arbitrator, who then judges the situation and decides on the disposition of each issue. For example, if a worker files a grievance against his employer that he was unfairly discharged, an arbitrator will listen to evidence about the matter from both sides and reach a judgment about the fairness and appropriateness of the discharge. Algeria, for example, uses arbitration to enforce health and safety laws.[95]

Negotiation   Negotiation, as described in detail in Chapter 10, can help resolve conflict between two groups. The construction industry uses *partnering,* a combination of mediation, negotiation, and facilitation, to resolve disputes that formerly called for legal remedies.[96]

▌ STRESS IN ORGANIZATIONS

Conflict and power struggles in organizations frequently result in stress for individuals. Executives can better manage stressful organizational environments if they have good political skills that allow them to work with scarce resources, satisfy multiple stakeholders, and handle competing interests.[97] Think about a situation in which you felt stress. What contributed to the stress? What alleviated it? How did you perform when you experienced stress? You may have felt stress when you didn't have enough time to finish your assigned tasks, failed to advance in an organization, or received a promotion and didn't think you could do the new job well.

   Stress refers to a psychological and physiological state that results when certain features of an individual's environment, called *stressors,* create discomfort, anxiety, or feelings of being overwhelmed. Stressors include physical challenges, such as heat or disease, as well as role conflict, role overload, task ambiguity, uncertainty, competition, and other aspects of a work or nonwork situation. Some employees, such as firefighters or police officers, are subjected to chronic stressors as part of their jobs.[98] If the stressor persists, individuals try to respond by dealing with it directly or using it to energize them. If the stressors persist and create physiological or psychological damage, exhaustion and other dysfunctional consequences can result. Figure 9-7 illustrates this progression, starting with an alarm that causes stress, followed by resistance or heightened stress, and concluding with exhaustion.

| FIGURE 9-7 |

People experience stress by moving through a series of stages.

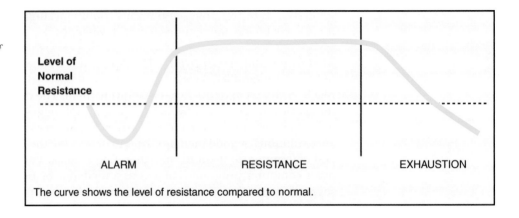

The curve shows the level of resistance compared to normal.

Causes of Stress

Personality traits can contribute to stress.[99] For example, employees in public accounting with a Type A personality or who worked with someone with a different personality type experienced stress.[100]

Individual career characteristics, such as occupational level, career stage, and stage of adult development, may also cause stress (see Chapter 3). People at the beginning of their careers who are trying to establish themselves often experience stress. The midcareer is associated with stress for many people as they recognize that they may not be accomplishing what they planned. Facing the changes of retirement creates significant stress for some individuals. Job stressors that threaten an employee's reputation with his supervisor likely generate anxiety symptoms at work and at home.[101]

Increased job complexity and economic pressures also contribute to stress.[102] Death of a spouse, divorce, marital separation, detention in jail, and death of a close family member head the list of the top 25 life-stress events for people in the United States.[103]

Consequences of Stress

Eustress, a positive form of stress, can energize and stimulate a person to greater creativity and productivity. *Distress,* a negative form of stress, can result in declining performance, satisfaction, and commitment. Other people who are under stress experience gastrointestinal, glandular, and cardiovascular disorders or overeat, drink excessively, or take drugs. Still others become impatient, detached, or filled with despair. Women and men demonstrate different symptoms of stress; for example, women more often have headaches, poor overall physical health, and depression.[104]

Job Burnout   Some workers experience *burnout,* the emotional exhaustion that results from being overworked, overwhelmed, or stressed over a period of time. Burnout results in a variety of physical, emotional, interpersonal, attitudinal, and behavioral consequences.[105] Members of the clergy are prone to burnout because of the exhausting expectations others hold for them. They may experience disillusionment, an ambivalence about their parishioners, or feelings of detachment, helplessness, and hopelessness.[106] Real estate agents have also experienced burnout in the heated market of the past few years.[107] Burned-out workers develop negative or impersonal responses to others. They may lose their self-esteem and have low feelings of accomplishment.[108] One study found that, as a result of burnout, some workers experienced decreased professional commitment and planned to leave their employers.[109]

■ MANAGING STRESS

Using or reducing stress begins with diagnosing its causes and impact. Managers can use a stress audit, as shown in Figure 9-8. They can also ask questions such as the following:[110]

- Do you try to do everything yourself?
- Do you blow up easily?
- Do you seek unrealistic goals?
- Do you act rude?
- Do you get too little rest?

Managers and employees can then find ways to manage stress. Managers and their organizations can try to prevent stress by supporting the training of employees so they can handle the new demands of the workplace, showing more concern about employees during the implementation of change, working on ways to help employees resolve work–home conflicts, and establishing methods to handle employee concerns and distress.[111]

Personal Techniques

Managers can encourage productive stress by helping employees build challenge into their work and assume more responsibility and autonomy over time. At the same time, they try to ensure that workers don't exhibit too much overload, in which the time or content demands of the job create anxiety and stress.

Managers can help workers cope with dysfunctional stress by sponsoring stress management programs. These typically include regular exercise, relaxation techniques

FIGURE 9-8

You can perform a stress audit to help determine the causes of the stress you experience.

⇒ Does anyone have physiological symptoms?
⇒ Is their job satisfaction high?
⇒ Is their job tension high?
⇒ Is their absenteeism high?
⇒ Are they accident prone?
⇒ Does the organization's design contribute to the symptoms?
⇒ Do interpersonal relations contribute to the symptoms?
⇒ Do career-development variables contribute to the symptoms?
⇒ What effect does personality have on stress?
⇒ What effect does sociocultural background have on stress?
⇒ What effect does the nonwork environment have on stress?

such as yoga and meditation, and practice using diagnostic tools for determining the causes of stress.

Managers can also try to eliminate stressors that cause the dysfunctional stress.[112] They can help people label their personalities and understand their typical behaviors. They can support effective career progression by conducting career planning and development activities. They can also help design high-quality job experiences.

Wellness Programs

Wellness programs prevent and combat stress.[113] They focus on reducing or eliminating unhealthy behaviors, such as smoking, alcohol abuse, and overeating, as a way of reducing future health-related costs. Approximately 80 to 90 percent of all employers offer at least one wellness program, and 35 to 40 percent offer a comprehensive program.[114] Siemans Business Communications Systems introduced a Wellness Incentive Program. Employees receive credits toward their share of medical, dental, and life insurance costs for participating in modules related to nutrition, fitness, and stress management.[115]

Health care professionals offer the following advice:

■ **Get regular exercise.** Many corporations provide on-site health clubs where their employees can exercise, relieving some of the physical tension associated with work-related stress.

■ **Eat well.** Most company cafeterias offer a wide variety of salads, fresh fruit, and other healthy foods, along with nutritional information for most offerings.

■ **Monitor personal health.** Many companies sponsor programs that promote healthy lifestyles, as well as programs that help employees stop smoking or using other ineffective techniques for coping with stress.

■ **Learn to identify and reduce sources of stress.** Some companies sponsor retreats or seminars on conflict resolution and other personal skills that help employees identify and eliminate needless sources of stress.

Companies may offer specific programs to attack health concerns, or they may create wellness accounts that employees can use for joining a fitness club or taking a health-related course. Such companies must ensure that programs target the right people, as well as ensure employee privacy.[116] California WorksWell, a collaboration between the state government of California, eight health maintenance organizations, and Merck & Company, offered health-risk assessment screenings to state employees. After the screening, employees had individual meetings with a professional health counselor from one of the health maintenance organizations. California WorksWell also started a major educational effort that included seminars about exercise, cardiovascular disease, cholesterol, and stress management. It began a walking program that included walking clubs and clinics and planned walks. Now its task is to expand the program to include all California state government employees.[117]

Employees at Reynolds-DeWalt Printing in Connecticut take time during the middle of the day to take two- to three-mile walks around the company's property with co-workers. The company's "walking captain" coordinates workers who want to walk together and hands out information about walking. The company will also pay 50 percent of an employee's dues at a nearby health club, as well as give an employee who quits smoking a $500 bonus.[118] Caterpillar, CIGNA Corporation, Daimler-Chrysler/UAW, and Fannie Mae won the ninth annual C. Everett Koop National Health Award. This award recognizes organizations that promote healthy behavior and reduce health costs through programs such as health screenings, immunizations, and health-risk assessments.[119]

Organizational Approaches to Coping

Organizations can also redesign jobs or restructure organizations to reduce dysfunctional stress. This redesign may involve reducing hierarchies and giving more autonomy and control to jobholders. It may mean increasing the lines of lateral communication to speed problem solving and decision making. While many new forms of organizations encourage such decentralization (see Chapter 12), the redesigns also can create new stresses. Managers need to carefully diagnose the impact of such redesigns on themselves and their employees.

Managers can change organizational policies and practices. For example, they can reward managers for delegating more responsibilities to their employees. They can introduce practices, such as mediation and arbitration, as described earlier, to help resolve conflict. They can also introduce more flexibility into workers' jobs, such as through telecommuting, job sharing, flexible hours, and compressed work weeks. Baxter Exports introduced such programs, and employees better managed their stress as a result.[120]

POWER, CONFLICT, AND STRESS IN THE DOT-COM, GLOBAL WORKPLACE

The rapidly changing environment faced by companies in the dot-com, global workplace creates major opportunities for exerting power and experiencing conflict and stress. The early employees in a company frequently have significant power because of their expertise and centrality. Employees in such companies can frequently experience stress and burnout as a result of the pressure for growth. For example, employees of the portable batteries catalog 1-800-Batteries dealt with this as a result of their 2,300-percent growth in five years. The company even elected a "Fun Queen" who plans outings such as bowling, pottery painting, and snow tubing.[121]

Power relations can significantly affect multicultural and multinational organizations in societies that foster power differentials. *Power distance,* the extent to which a society accepts the unequal distribution of power in organizations, affects manager–employee interactions.[122] In high power-distance countries, such as India, Mexico, and France, employees accept the unequal distribution of power and frown on people who bypass their bosses. In low power-distance countries, such as Austria, Denmark, and Sweden, managers and employees expect employees to bypass bosses and go to the best person to get the information or help they need. Power imbalances among culture groups may also have significant consequences.[123] Imbalances may result in intergroup conflict and reduced motivation among the powerless.

Resolving conflict may also have a cultural component. Conflict resolution styles have different effects in different cultural settings. Arab Middle Eastern executives use more integrating and avoiding styles, whereas U.S. executives use more dominating and compromising styles.[124] When conflicts arise between American and Japanese businesspeople, each tends to use resolution methods successful in their country, which may only antagonize the other party.[125] Westerners operating in Asian cultures need to pay attention to the importance of maintaining face in conflict situations. They need to be sensitive to the value of quiet observation, listen attentively and respect the other party's presence, and discard their own model of effective conflict resolution.[126] Asians, in turn, need to pay attention to differences in problem-solving assumptions. They should focus on resolving the substantive issues of the conflict, engage in an assertive style, and recognize individual responsibility for conflict resolution.[127]

Managing stress may also have cultural considerations. Sometimes the causes and consequences of stress resemble those in the United States. For example, Chinese employees from five cities experienced the highest anxiety and depression when their jobs had high demands and they could exert little control over them.[128] Twenty-five percent of CEOs in the top 100 European companies believed that they could suffer from job burnout. These feelings particularly characterized the CEOs younger than age 50 from Great Britain, compared to those from other European Union countries.[129] Japanese executives have been prone to *Karoshi,* death from overwork. Many workers don't take their allotted vacation time. Others reduce stress by smoking and drinking after work.[130] At other times, different cultural factors may stimulate or prevent stress. Attitudes about power distance, the social acceptability of conflict, and preferred styles of conflict resolution may vary and influence the stress felt by workers.

▌ Summary

1. Power refers to the potential or actual ability to influence others in a desired direction. People exert power to influence others, overcome job-related dependencies, or participate in social exchanges. Empowerment results in people increasing their power by sharing it with others.

2. Sources of power include position power, personal power, resource-based and information-based power, and linkages.

3. Organizational politics, generally considered the use of self-serving, power-oriented behavior obtained from any of the power sources, can result in power struggles and other dysfunctional organizational behavior.

4. Sexual harassment illustrates an abuse of power in the workplace.

5. Conflict can exist within and between individuals, groups, and organizations, and typically progresses from latent to perceived, felt, and manifest stages, and finally to a conflict aftermath.

6. Conflict's consequences can be functional, such as increased creativity and exchange of ideas, or dysfunctional, such as increased stress, absenteeism, and turnover, or decreased satisfaction and performance. Managers and other employees can use interpersonal techniques and organizational approaches to manage conflict.

7. Stress experienced by individuals results from a variety of personal, career, and job-related characteristics and can have significant costs to organizations.

People can manage stress using personal techniques, wellness programs, and organizational methods of coping.

8. Managers need to understand the implications of power distance and power imbalances because conflict resolution styles may have different effects in various cultures.

A Manager's Diagnostic Review

Know how to use power to reduce your dependence.
- What dependencies exist in the organization?
- How do people use power to reduce dependencies?

Empower workers.
- How is powerlessness overcome in the organization?

Build your sources of power.
- What sources of power are available?

Recognize organizational politics.
- Do organizational politics help or hinder the accomplishment of organizational goals?

Diagnose and manage conflict.
- Is there conflict in the organization?
- Are the outcomes of conflict functional or dysfunctional?
- What level of conflict exists?
- What stage of conflict exists?

Diagnose and manage stress.
- Do individuals experience stress?
- What causes stress?
- What strategies can help deal with stress?

Deal with power, conflict, and stress in the dot-com, global workplace.
- How is power handled in dot-com companies?
- How do cultural differences affect power in the organization?

Visit the Gordon homepage on the Prentice Hall Web site at

http://www.prenhall.com/gordon

for recommended readings, additional activities, Internet exercises, updated information, and links to related Web sites.

▮ Thinking Critically About Organizational Behavior

1. Which is the best explanation of power—influence, dependence, exchange, or personality?
2. To what extent should managers empower their workers?
3. How can managers expand their sources of power?
4. Which source of power is most valuable for managers?
5. Can managers eliminate organizational politics?
6. Why is sexual harassment an abuse of power?
7. What are the basic elements of conflict across levels?
8. Does all conflict proceed through all stages?
9. How does hidden conflict differ from other types?
10. What are the most and least effective ways of managing conflict?
11. Can stress be avoided?
12. What are the most and least effective ways of managing stress?

ACTIVITY 9-1: TINKERTOY POWER

STEP 1: Your instructor will form you into groups and give you a set of basic Tinkertoys.

STEP 2: You have 10 minutes for planning.

1. You may negotiate/bargain across groups for resources during the planning/building stage.
2. You are competing for the most points.
3. There are no rules other than those explicitly stated.
4. You may not put pieces together until after this initial 10-minute planning period is over.

STEP 3: You are to use your Tinkertoys to build the structure shown to you by your instructor. You have 20 minutes to complete the structure.

STEP 4: Your instructor will award you points for completing the structure, as well as for having excess resources after the structure is completed. Groups that do not complete the structure will not receive any points.

Completed Structure	500 points
Excess Resources	
Blue and yellow sticks	10 points each
White connectors	5 points each
Red and green sticks	1 point each

STEP 5: Discussion. With the entire class, answer the following questions:

DESCRIPTION

1. How were resources allocated?
2. What strategies did the groups use to obtain resources?

DIAGNOSIS

3. What power existed in the groups?

4. What sources of power did the groups or individuals use?
5. Did the power relations change over time?
6. Did all players act ethically?

Source: Based with permission on C. P. Lindsay and C. A. Enz, Resource control and visionary leadership: Two exercises, *Journal of Management Education* 15 (February 1991): 127–135

ACTIVITY 9-2 EMPOWERING THE WORKFORCE

STEP 1: Read the following scenario:

Excelsior Bicycles has a long history of manufacturing top-of-the-line racing bicycles. It has two major plants, each of which runs three shifts. The owner, Fred Jenkins, has always exerted a great deal of control over the design and manufacture of the bicycles. As the founder and person who grew the company from sales of $50 thousand in the first year to $50 million in the most recent financial statements, he has used traditional approaches to lead and manage his employees. As Fred nears retirement, his daughter Sarah has assumed greater responsibility for managing the company. Like Fred, she understands how to design and manufacture a high-quality product. Unlike Fred, however, she believes that the employees of the company should have more power than they currently do. She has read a great deal about worker empowerment and believes that her firm's success in the next century will depend on instituting a new approach to management.

STEP 2: You have been asked to help Sarah develop a plan for empowering the workforce. Include all types of employees in your plan: the design, engineering, manufacturing, sales and marketing, and human resources departments. Individually or in small groups, develop your plan for empowering the workforce at Excelsior Bicycles.

STEP 3: Share and critique your plans in small groups or with the entire class. Identify the ways each plan empowers workers.

STEP 4: Discussion. In small groups or with the entire class, answer the following questions:

DESCRIPTION

1. What approaches to empowerment did each plan incorporate?

DIAGNOSIS

2. Which plan likely will be most effective?
3. What other approaches to empowering the workforce could be included?
4. How effective will these approaches likely be?

PRESCRIPTION

5. What would be the major components of a "master plan" that incorporates the best approaches to empowerment?

ACTIVITY 9-3 KING ELECTRONICS

STEP 1: Divide the class into groups of four people. Read the following general description of the situation. The instructor will distribute four roles to each group. Each person in the group should then prepare one role. In preparing for the role-play, try to put yourself in the position of the person whose role you are playing.

GENERAL BACKGROUND

King Electronics Company, located in the San Fernando Valley outside Los Angeles, manufactures special government orders on precision instruments. The company has no major product but applies its specialized skills to very complex projects and has done this successfully. Its flexibility in moving from project to project has built a reputation for high quality, the ability to manufacture precise instruments, and quick production and delivery.

Many jobs require that proposals with technical and cost information be hand-carried to Washington, D.C., by a specific deadline. While management realizes that the nature of its business necessitates rigid time constraints and short time frames, it has been successful because of this opportunistic reaction time. As a result, King Electronics has been rewarded appropriately for its efforts in meeting its customers' demands. See the accompanying organizational chart of the Cost Proposal Section (Figure 9-9).

STEP 2: Each group of four participants should convene the group meeting in part of the room. Your instructor will tell you how much time you have to reach a solution.

STEP 3: Report your group's solution to your instructor.

STEP 4: Discussion. In small groups or with the entire class, answer the following questions:

DESCRIPTION

1. Characterize each participant's behavior. What style did each use?

DIAGNOSIS

2. What problems did you encounter in reaching an agreement? Why?
3. Evaluate the effectiveness of conflict resolution in this situation.

Source: Reprinted with permission from "Conflict Management" by Randolph Flynn and David Elloy, National Institute for Dispute Resolution (Washington, D.C.), Working Paper, 1987.

FIGURE 9-9

This chart shows the organization of the Cost Proposal Section.

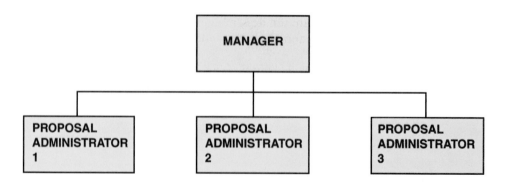

ACTIVITY 9-4 SECURING POWER

STEP 1: You are the newly appointed vice president of human resources for a large online retailer that was founded five years ago. During its short history, the company has grown from a handful of employees to over 1,000 worldwide. Your predecessor served primarily a paper-pushing function, making sure that everyone received the pay and benefits they had earned. You want to expand the human resources function, but you know that this will require both gaining more power and influence for yourself and empowering your staff. Your task is to develop an action plan that will accomplish both of these objectives within a three- to six-month time frame. You know that if you don't succeed in making your department more powerful, your effectiveness in your new position will be very low and you likely will be looking for a new job.

STEP 2: Individually or in small groups, as directed by your instructor, develop two plans: (1) the first plan should focus on how to make you more powerful in your new position; (2) the second plan should focus on how to empower your staff. Be sure to make both plans as specific as possible and show your knowledge of the theory and concepts related to power in your plan.

STEP 3: In small groups or with the entire class, share your plans.

STEP 4: Discussion. In small groups or with the entire class, answer the following questions:

DESCRIPTION

1. What were the key elements of the plans?

DIAGNOSIS

2. What theories and concepts related to power played a role in the plans?

PRESCRIPTION

3. How can you increase your power and empower your employees?

ACTIVITY 9-5 BEHAVIOR DESCRIPTION QUESTIONNAIRE

STEP 1: Complete the following questionnaire.

Consider situations in which you find that your wishes differ from the wishes of another person. How do you usually respond to such situations?

Following are several pairs of statements describing possible behavior responses. For each pair, please circle the A or B statement, depending on which is most characteristic of your own behavior. That is, indicate which of these two responses is more typical of your behavior in situations where you find that your wishes differ from someone else's wishes. In many cases, neither the A nor the B statement may be very typical of your behavior, but select the response you would be more likely to use.

1. **A.** There are times when I let others take responsibility for solving the problem.
   B. Rather than negotiating the things on which we disagree, I try to stress those things on which we agree.
2. **A.** I try to find a compromise solution.
   B. I attempt to deal with all of his and my concerns.

3. **A.** I am usually firm in pursuing my goals.

   B. I might try to soothe the other's feelings and preserve our relationship.

4. **A.** I try to find a compromise solution.

   B. I sometimes sacrifice my own wishes for the wishes of the other person.

5. **A.** I consistently seek the other's help in working out a solution.

   B. I try to do what is necessary to avoid useless tensions.

6. **A.** I try to avoid creating unpleasantness for myself.

   B. I try to win my position.

7. **A.** I try to postpone the issue until I have had some time to think it over.

   B. I give up some points in exchange for others.

8. **A.** I am usually firm in pursuing my goals.

   B. I attempt to get all concerns and issues immediately out in the open.

9. **A.** I feel that differences are not always worth worrying about.

   B. I make some effort to get my way.

10. **A.** I am firm in pursuing my goals.

    B. I try to find a compromise solution.

11. **A.** I attempt to get all concerns and issues immediately out in the open.

    B. I might try to soothe the other's feelings and preserve our relationship.

12. **A.** I sometimes avoid taking positions that would create controversy.

    B. I will let him have some of his positions if he lets me have some of mine.

13. **A.** I propose a middle ground.

    B. I press to get my points made.

14. **A.** I tell him my ideas and ask him for his.

    B. I try to show him the logic and benefits of my position.

15. **A.** I might try to soothe the other's feelings and preserve our relationship.

    B. I try to do what is necessary to avoid tension.

16. **A.** I try not to hurt the other's feelings.

    B. I try to convince the other person of the merits of my position.

17. **A.** I am usually firm in pursuing my goals.

    B. I try to do what is necessary to avoid useless tensions.

18. **A.** If it makes the other person happy, I might let him maintain his views.

    B. I will let him have some of his positions if he lets me have some of mine.

19. **A.** I attempt to get all concerns and issues immediately out in the open.

    B. I try to postpone the issue until I have had time to think it over.

20. **A.** I attempt to immediately work through our differences.

    B. I try to find a fair combination of gains and losses for both of us.

21. **A.** In approaching negotiations, I try to be considerate of the other person's wishes.

    B. I always lean toward a direct discussion of the problem.

22. **A.** I try to find a position that is intermediate between his and mine.

    B. I assert my wishes.

23. **A.** I am very often concerned with satisfying all our wishes.

    B. There are times when I let others take responsibility for solving the problem.

24. **A.** If the other's position seems very important to him, I try to meet his wishes.

    B. I am concerned to work out the best agreed-upon course of action.

25. **A.** I try to show him the logic and benefits of my position.

    B. In approaching negotiations, I try to be considerate of the other person's wishes.

26. **A.** I propose a middle ground.
    B. I am nearly always concerned with satisfying all our wishes.
27. **A.** I sometimes avoid taking positions that would create controversy.
    B. If it makes the other person happy, I might let him maintain his views.
28. **A.** I am usually firm in pursuing my goals.
    B. I feel that differences are not always worth worrying about.
29. **A.** I propose a middle ground.

B. I feel that differences are not always worth worrying about.
30. **A.** I try not to hurt the other's feelings.
    B. I always share the problem with the other person so that we can work it out.

SCORING THE BEHAVIOR DESCRIPTION QUESTIONNAIRE

Below and on the next page, circle the letters you chose on each item of the questionnaire.

Item Number	Competition (Forcing)	Collaboration (Problem solving)	Sharing (Compromise)	Avoidance (Withdrawal)	Accommodation (Smoothing)
1.				A	B
2.		B	A		
3.	A				B
4.			A		B
5.		A		B	
6.	B			B	
7.			A	A	
8.	A	B			
9.	B			A	
10.	A		B		
11.		A			B
12.			B	A	
13.	B		A		
14.	B	A			
15.				B	A
16.	B				A
17.	A			B	
18.			B		A
19.	A		B		
20.		A	B		

(continued)

Item Number	Competition (Forcing)	Collaboration (Problem solving)	Sharing (Compromise)	Avoidance (Withdrawal)	Accommodation (Smoothing)
21.		B			A
22.	B		A		
23.		A		B	
24.			B		
25.	A				B
26.		B	A		
27.				A	B
28.	A	B			
29.			A	B	
30.		B			A
Total number of items circled in each column:	_____ Competition	_____ Collaboration	_____ Compromise	_____ Avoidance	_____ Accommodation

STEP 2: Discussion. In small groups or with the class as a whole, answer the following questions:

DESCRIPTION

1. What did your score pattern look like?
2. Do any patterns emerge among groups in the class?

DIAGNOSIS

3. Which modes have you found to be most commonly used? Least commonly used?

4. Which modes have you found to be most effective? Least effective?
5. In what situations has each mode been most effective?

Source: Reprinted with permission from "Conflict Management" by Randolf Flynn and David Elloy, National Institute for Dispute Resolution (Washington, D.C.), Working Paper, 1987.

ACTIVITY 9-6 THE SUMMER INTERNS

STEP 1: The instructor will divide the class into subgroups of three or four (the latter if an observer is to be used). One person should play the role of Samantha (Sam) Pinder, who will mediate the dispute. The other two parties will play the roles of Brenda Bennett (director of personnel) and Harold Stokes (vice president of engineering), who are having a dispute over the hiring of summer interns.

STEP 2: Each party should read his or her role information and prepare the role. Remember to:

1. Empathize with the role. Try to see the world as your assigned character sees it and behave accordingly.
2. Do not add facts that are not in the case.

3. Stay in role. Do not jump out of the role to comment on the process.

4. Try to make it realistic.

STEP 3: Sam Pinder will "lead" each small group in an effort to resolve the summer interns problem. When you have achieved a resolution, write it down so you can report it to the class later.

STEP 4: Discuss how the mediation session went in each of the small groups. If you had an observer assigned, the observer can comment on the strengths and weaknesses of the mediator's efforts.

STEP 5: Report to the class on the outcome of the mediation session. Describe particular problems that may have occurred with the mediation session in your small group.

1. What were some of the different settlements arrived at by different groups?

2. How did your group's specific settlement emerge? How much influence did Pinder have in shaping the final settlement? How much influence did Stokes and Bennett have?

3. Was the mediation process fair? Was the outcome that was achieved fair? What made it fair or unfair?

4. What tactics did the mediator use that were most effective? Least effective?

5. When would it be most useful to use mediation in an organization? When would it be least useful to use mediation?

6. What are some of the major problems and obstacles for a manager in using mediation?

Source: Reprinted with permission of the National Institute for Dispute Resolution, 1726 M Street, N.W. Suite 500, Washington, D.C. 20036. Call (202) 466-4764 for further information.

Chapter

10

Managing Intergroup Behavior and Negotiating Effectively

Learning Objectives

After completing Chapter 10, you will be able to

1. Describe four types of interdependent groups and their typical behavior and outcomes.
2. Diagnose how perceptual differences, power differences, task relations, and cross-cultural differences affect intergroup relations.
3. Propose three interpersonal techniques for improving intergroup relations.
4. Propose three structural mechanisms for improving intergroup relations.
5. Compare and contrast distributive and integrative bargaining.
6. Identify the steps in effective negotiations.
7. Compare and contrast the use of negotiating strategies and tactics.
8. Offer a protocol for negotiating with and managing relations between culturally diverse groups.

A Manager's Preview

Describe . . . Diagnose . . . Prescribe . . . Act

- Diagnose the type of group interaction and its consequences.
- Know how perceptual differences, power differences, task, relations, and cross-cultural differences affect group interactions.
- Use interpersonal techniques and structural changes to improve intergroup relations.
- Use negotiation strategies and tactics appropriately.
- Negotiate effectively in the dot-com, global workplace.

US Airways and Its Flight Attendants Reach an Agreement

*U*S Airways went to the brink of a debilitating strike with its flight attendants in March 2000. Prompted by an inability to reach an agreement after months of negotiating, the National Mediation Board first attempted to help resolve the dispute. In February 2000, the board released the parties from a failed mediation and gave the Association of Flight Attendants the legal ability to strike. Airline workers, other airlines, airport management, and consumers prepared for a strike unless President Clinton intervened. Stephen M. Wolf, the chairman of US Airways, vowed to shut down the airline rather than allow the flight attendants to resort to a work stoppage that would paralyze the airline.

The major area of disagreement was the airline's desire to match flight attendants' wages, benefits, and work rules with those of flight attendants at the four largest U.S. airlines, and add an additional one percent (known as parity plus one). US Airways management expected the flight attendants to accept this provision since its other unions had accepted that formula. Although the airline had agreed to discuss alternative formulas, no real softening in either side's position occurred.

Negotiators spent seven days prior to the strike deadline holed up in a Washington, D.C., hotel, trying to reach an agreement. The National Mediation Board asked the airlines and the flight attendants to negotiate past a 12:01 A.M. deadline. The two sides reached an agreement three hours after the strike deadline. Two months after the labor agreement was reached, executives at United Airlines and US Airways agreed that United would pay $4.3 billion to buy US Airways.[1]

The situation at US Airways describes an increasingly common one in the airline and other industries: the inability of management and unions to work collaboratively and to easily reach a contract agreement. In this chapter, we investigate the issues associated with managing intergroup relations. We first discuss the nature of group interactions, the factors that affect them, and techniques for improving them. In the second part of the chapter, we examine the process of negotiation, strategies and tactics used in negotiations, and negotiating in a dot-com, global workplace.

▌ THE NATURE OF GROUP INTERACTIONS

Groups interact with other groups all the time. One group may depend on another for resources, such as raw materials, information, or assistance in performing a task. Airline employees, for example, depend on management for their jobs, wages, assignment of responsibilities, and supervision in performing their jobs. Customers depend on pilots to provide safe and on-time flights. Interdependence increases as the amount, frequency, or variety of resources exchanged increases. Interdependence also increases as exchanges become more reciprocal.

Group interdependence can have consequences for both individuals and groups. At the individual level, the interplay of group interactions can affect the way a person constructs his reality. For example, a person's position in the organizational structure (upper, middle, or lower level management or staff groups) will determine that person's perception of events.[2] The top executives at US Airways likely view the flight attendants' demands differently than the flight attendants and other union members do. These differing perceptions will affect the performance of individuals in the various groups.

At the group level, interdependence can increase the likelihood of conflict. Diagnosing such interdependence can alert managers to the potential for conflict between specific groups. US Airways executives who depend on flight attendants to provide service to passengers may experience conflict when the attendants refuse to agree to their proposed contract provisions. The pilots and baggage handlers may experience conflict with the flight attendants when the attendants refuse to accept the same contract other union members have accepted. Top managers at US Airways can anticipate and deal with such conflict in the early stages if they understand the nature of the interdependence.

Types of Group Interdependence

Interdependence occurs in one of four ways, as shown in Figure 10-1:[3]

- *Pooled.* The groups have no direct interactions.
- *Sequential.* Interactions between groups form a definite order.
- *Reciprocal.* Pairs of groups interact in both directions in no prescribed order.
- *Team.* All groups interact in both directions with every other group.

Most groups demonstrate each type of interaction at various times, but often the relationships between groups form a more enduring pattern that can best be described by one of the four types. We examine these patterns in more detail in this section.

Pooled Interdependence.   Groups that rely on each other only because they belong to the same parent organization show pooled interdependence. Two stores in a chain such as Lowes or Best Buy show pooled interdependence because their

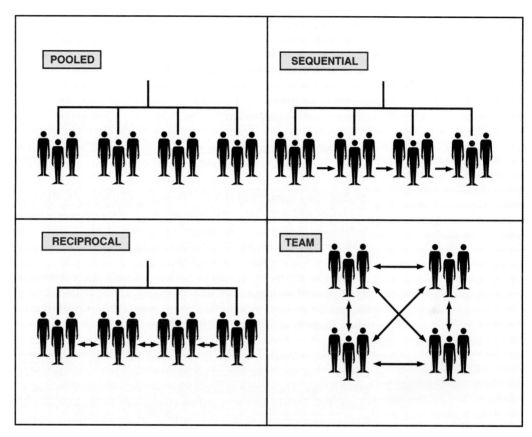

▌ FIGURE 10-1 ▌   *Four types of interdependence differ in the extent of reciprocal interactions between groups and create different potentials for conflict.*

reputations depend on their identification with the parent organization. Two subsidiaries within a conglomerate may show pooled interdependence because they share a common advertising agency or benefit from mass buying power. The maintenance workers and the cafeteria workers in a single organization are two departments that, for the most part, demonstrate pooled interdependence.

Groups with pooled interdependence may obtain their reputation, staff resources, financing, or other services from corporate headquarters. Such groups may sometimes compete for resources, but generally they operate relatively independently. Because these groups have limited interactions, pooled interdependence has few potentially dysfunctional consequences for groups until their representatives need to work together.

Sequential Interdependence.   Sequential interdependence occurs when one group's operations precede and act as prerequisites for the second group's. In a manufacturing plant, the assembly group and the packing group exhibit sequential interdependence. In the post office, the postal workers at the central post office demonstrate sequential interdependence with the letter carriers in the local post offices. In a hospital, the nurses have sequential interdependence with the purchasing department because the nurses use the supplies bought by purchasing.

Problems may arise in this type of interaction when the first group doesn't perform its job effectively. If, for example, purchasing doesn't order required supplies, the nurses may have difficulty meeting the medical needs of their patients. In cases such as this, members of the second group may resent the first group and try to limit their interactions with it, often by using alternative ways to meet their requirements. The nurses, for example, may horde supplies until needed. In extreme cases, sabotage may occur.

Reciprocal Interdependence.   Two groups whose operations each precede and act as prerequisites to the other's have reciprocal interdependence. At airlines, the pilots, flight attendants, and executives have reciprocal interdependence. These groups must repeatedly interact to perform their jobs effectively.

Sales and support staffs typically have reciprocal interdependence. A salesperson selling computer software relies on technical support staff to handle problems that users face. The technical support staff requires the sales staff's input in identifying ongoing customer problems.

As the extent of group interdependence increases—that is, as groups move from pooled to sequential to reciprocal interdependence—the potential for conflict and dysfunctional behavior increases correspondingly. Conflict is common when there is reciprocal interdependence.

Team Interdependence.   Where multiple groups interact, reciprocal interdependencies may multiply. When we look at their functioning over time, we see that each group's operations precede and act as prerequisites for every other group's operations. For example, the various departments supervised by a vice president of human resources—training, staffing, compensation, and organization development—may exhibit this type of interdependence. Or we might characterize the overall interdependence of the various employee groups at US Airways in this way. Groups with team interdependence have the greatest potential for conflict and the highest requirements for effective communication.

▎FACTORS THAT AFFECT GROUP INTERACTIONS

What factors affect the relationship between various groups at US Airways and other organizations? In this section, we examine perceptual differences, power differences, task relations, and cross-cultural differences as influencing intergroup behavior.

Perceptual Differences

Perceptual differences, as shown in Figure 10-2, influence group and intergroup interactions. The perceptions of group members combine to influence their attitude toward their own and other groups. Clearly, the perceptions of flight attendants changed over time toward the value of reaching an agreement with the airline's management. Now the executives' perceptions about operating an independent airline have changed, given their agreeing to a buyout by United.

Orientations.   Differences in focus or orientations influence the way one group views another's actions. Groups' goal, time, and social orientations may differ.

FIGURE 10-2

Differences in orientations, attitudinal sets, and status influence perceptions, which in turn influence intergroup relations.

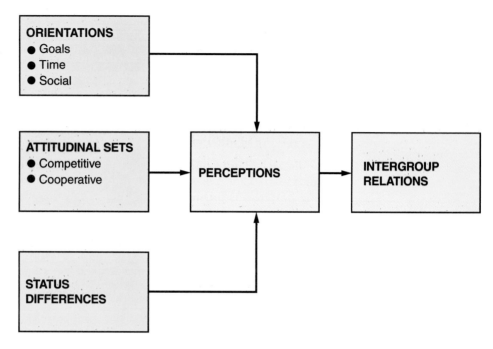

Groups with different goals have a different focus for their activities. Marketing departments highlight the attractiveness of a product to consumers. Research and development groups emphasize the product's innovative characteristics and its value to the advancement of scientific knowledge. Production departments stress a product's ease of production. How do the goals of an airline's top management and its pilots or flight attendants differ? Airline management might focus on reducing costs as a way of ensuring profitability for the airline; the pilots and flight attendants might focus instead on obtaining satisfactory pay, which might inflate rather than reduce costs. How would these differences in goals create perceptual differences? These groups may differ in their perceptions of the desirability of specific provisions in their contracts.

Groups also differ in their time orientation—the extent to which they focus on events now and in the future. A research and development department, for example, has a long-term orientation since new product development takes a long time. A production department, in contrast, has a short-term orientation since it focuses on meeting immediate inventory needs. The marketing department may reflect a short-term orientation in its concern for selling the product now, whereas the technical services staff may have a different time orientation in its concern for keeping the product functional over the medium or long term.

The social or extra-work orientations of groups might also differ. Consider the pilots, flight attendants, and executives at US Airways. The professional allegiances and social interactions of these groups probably differ. The unionized workers might be more involved with union activities and may choose their friends from other union members. The managers would be oriented toward their professional group—other managers.

Attitudinal Sets. The attitudes different groups hold also contribute to their perceptual differences. Diagnosing these differences can help managers and other group members anticipate and even head off possible conflicts. For example, group attitudes may reflect competitive or cooperative feelings about other groups.[4]

- **Competitive attitude.** A group encourages its members to have negative attitudes toward the task, distrust other group members, dislike other group members, and act without considering others.
- **Cooperative attitude.** A group encourages trust, mutual influence, coordination of effort, and acceptance of differences between its members and those of other groups.

The McFarland Clinic, based in Ames, Iowa, tried to acquire the McCrary-Rost Clinic in Lake City. A competitive attitude existed among the various groups related to the hospital: its physicians, the administrator of the local hospital, its board of directors, and many Lake City residents. The residents feared that if McFarland acquired the McCrary-Rost practice, all of its physicians would send their patients to the hospital with which McFarland was affiliated, requiring the closing of the local hospital, a major employer in Lake City. The hospital administrator threatened to lock out of the hospital any physicians who joined McFarland.[5]

Groups can also have different attitudes because of their cosmopolitan versus local orientation.[6]

- **Cosmopolitans.** These employees have highly specialized role skills and thus more orientation to their professional group and relatively little loyalty to their employing organization.
- **Locals.** These employees have relatively unspecialized role skills and thus little or no orientation to a professional group and high loyalty to their employing organization.

Clerical staff might have a local orientation and health care professionals a cosmopolitan one. Production workers might have a local orientation and engineers a cosmopolitan one. If such attitudinal differences exist for these groups, their perceptions will also differ, creating a major challenge for anyone who wants to meld the groups into a strong team.

Status Differences.   Employees' views of their rank and standing relative to others in an organization can also influence their perceptions of people and events. Often these perceptions lack accuracy. If factory workers assembling circuit boards in an electronics plant perceive they have relatively low status compared to their managers, the workers may make few demands on the managers, resulting in feelings of resentment toward the managers.

Differences in education, experience, or background may influence employees' assessment of their status. Traditionally, workers and managers are perceived to have a different status in manufacturing organizations. Engineers and customer service representatives are perceived to have a different status in their organizations. The rewards given in the organization can reinforce these differences.

Differences in identity due to race, gender, ethnicity, and religion can also affect perceptions of status. In managing a multicultural workforce, managers must recognize these differences and make sure they don't play a dysfunctional role in intergroup interactions. The managers can use the conflict resolution approaches described in Chapter 9 and the strategies for managing intergroup relations described later in this chapter for this purpose.

Power Differences

Interacting groups often experience performance difficulties when they differ in the power, or the amount of influence and control, they have over others. We have discussed power in Chapter 9, but this section highlights three ways power differences affect intergroup relations.

Perceptions of Substitutability. Groups able to perform the work of another group can substitute for that group, thereby reducing the power of the replaceable group. Line managers able to recruit and hire employees can substitute for human resources recruiters and reduce the recruiters' power. Quality control officers able to stop an assembly line can substitute for the production supervisors and reduce the supervisors' power. A company that can easily replace one of its suppliers will interact differently with a vendor than if it can't.

Ability to Cope with Uncertainty. How well a group can deal with and compensate for a rapidly changing environment also influences its power.[7] Typically, a group of executives can cope with uncertainty better than various employee groups because of the executives' greater experience and better access to resources. In some organizations, the marketing department can cope with uncertainty better than production because marketing employees can more easily make adjustments for the client; in other organizations, production copes better than marketing. Any difference in the ability to cope with uncertainty would contribute to power differences between the two groups and potentially to dysfunctional intergroup relations.

Control of and Access to Resources. The amount of money, people, and time a group controls also influences its power. The greater the amount of resources it controls, the more power the group has. Managers who control budgets often have more power than those who don't. Groups that have to divide resources often disagree about how to allocate the resources, resulting in conflict between the groups. In hospitals, physicians typically have greater access to resources and more influence over their allocation than do nurses; this may contribute to differences in power between the two groups.

Task Relations

The activities or processes that interdependent groups perform and the way these activities interrelate, known as their *task relations*, play a significant role in the interactions between groups. Both the flow and clarity of task activities affect intergroup relations.

Task Interaction. Group members can perform independent, dependent, or interdependent tasks, as shown in Figure 10-3.

- **Independent.** Independent task relations occur when one group's task can be done without any relationship to another group's. A bank teller and the person refilling the ATM machine can each perform their tasks without any assistance from the other.
- **Dependent.** Dependent task relations occur when one group's task follows and has another's as a prerequisite. Shipping clerks depend on manufacturing for the products they ship.

■ **FIGURE 10-3** ■
The relations between tasks performed by groups can determine whether conflict occurs.

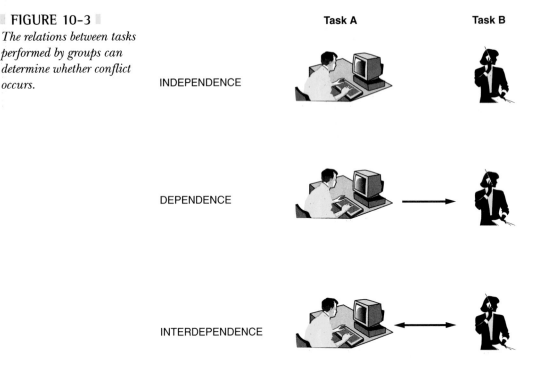

Task A   Task B

INDEPENDENCE

DEPENDENCE

INTERDEPENDENCE

■ **Interdependent.** Interdependent task relations occur when each group's task follows and is prerequisite to the other's. Members of the production department in a publishing firm work on a manuscript provided by their authors who then check the changes made by production.

The nature of task relations generally resembles the nature of interdependence among groups described earlier. Groups showing pooled interdependence most often have independent task relations. Groups showing sequential interdependence most often have dependent task relations. Groups showing reciprocal or team interdependence most frequently have interdependent task relations.

Because the independent task groups interact less, they generally have fewer problems with other groups than do groups with dependent or interdependent task relations. Interdependent tasks most frequently contribute to problems between interacting groups. Yet, increasing the groups' control over decisions may result in high performance when they have interdependent tasks.[8]

Task Ambiguity.   The clarity or ambiguity of the task describes whether the interacting groups have clear, predetermined guidelines to follow. Task ambiguity often contributes to difficulty in groups interacting because a particular group may not understand its responsibilities and the requirements of its task. For example, designers of a new e-business strategy for a consumer goods company may not understand the boundaries of their job, thus infringing on the existing marketing and sales departments.

Cross-Cultural Differences

Groups from different cultures often interact in companies. Heritage College, a small, multiethnic, four-year school in Washington state, experienced problems with intergroup relations between Native Americans, Mexican Americans, and rural Anglo-Americans. Negative stereotypes, misunderstandings, and a strong aversion to the other groups characterized their interaction. To address the intergroup conflict, Heritage developed a mission statement that emphasized obtaining quality information to overcome stereotypes. It also portrayed all groups in a positive light in public arenas. People at the school shared stories as a major means of communicating and developed problem-solving techniques based on positive and caring contacts.[9]

Cross-cultural differences frequently arise in multinational organizations or as part of interorganizational alliances. Differences in time and social orientations, language, and customs may become exaggerated as two or more groups try to work together. Understanding such differences often facilitates intergroup interaction.

Xerox, Sun Microsystems, and iPlanet E-Commerce Solutions created an alliance to develop a computer application that allows financial service and health care organizations to send bills and statements electronically. iPlanet and Sun offer the computer hardware and software development and support; Xerox provides the marketing, selling, installation, and service of the product, Internet Presentment Solution.[10]

▌IMPROVING INTERGROUP RELATIONS

Managers and employees can use interpersonal techniques and structural mechanisms to improve the relations between groups.

Interpersonal Techniques

Managers can focus on improving the interactions between the members of groups that experience conflict. Generally, they or a third party bring the groups together in a structured way that encourages them to air and resolve differences.

Confrontation Meeting. A one-day *confrontation meeting* requires the two interacting groups to share the problems they face and offer solutions for resolving them.[11] First, a top manager introduces the issues and goals for the day. She may have identified these issues on the basis of prior discussions with group members or her own view of the situation. In small subgroups of the various interacting groups, the participants gather more detailed information about the problems they face. Next, representatives from each subgroup report their findings to the entire group. Regrouped into natural work groups, participants set priorities for the problems and determine early action steps for resolving their problems. Finally, they implement their plan. A top management team continues to plan and monitor follow-up action. Four to six weeks later, the group reconvenes to report its progress.

The confrontation meeting effectively deals with intergroup problems under several conditions:

- when the total management group needs to examine its own workings;
- when very limited time is available for the activity;
- when top management wishes to improve the conditions quickly;
- when sufficient cohesion in the top team will ensure follow-up; and
- when top management is committed to resolving the issues in the organization or has recently experienced some major change.

Organizational Mirror.   In the *organizational mirror* technique, a host group receives structured feedback about the way various other groups in the organization perceive it.[12] A consultant first interviews members of all groups. Then he reports data from these interviews to the invited and host groups. The groups next discuss the data presented. Small, heterogeneous groups with representatives from the diverse groups meet, discuss the data further (if appropriate), and develop action plans for the problems identified. Then they implement the action plans. Success requires commitment and follow-up from top management.

Third-Party Interventions.   A third party can act as a mediator, arbitrator, or fact-finder, as well as provide confrontational or procedural consultation.[13] Generally, a third party tries to open communication between the two parties, focus on the key issues and information, and then reach an agreement acceptable to both groups.

In carrying out the intervention, the third party can think about the role she plays in several ways. The third party can actively identify areas of agreement and disagreement among parties where personal chemistry hinders effective face-to-face discussion. Contact between parties occurs primarily through the facilitator, who acts as a go-between, message carrier, or spokesperson for one or both groups. The facilitator deals with the leaders or key members of disputing parties who meet to exchange positions and formulate proposals or counterproposals.[14]

In a different approach, the third party can lead key members of opposing groups through a series of meetings and activities that identify and resolve differences. He sets expectations, establishes group rules, and determines the sequence of speaking. He also ensures candor, curbs expressions of hostility, and avoids evaluations. He introduces procedures to reduce disagreements, ensures understanding of positions or statements, and checks the implementation of agreed-upon changes.[15]

Third parties can also assume peacemaking roles. In these roles, third parties provide support, help reframe people's understandings of a situation, and explain their perceptions of each other. They might even help the parties reveal private conflicts as a way of identifying issues behind their disagreement.

In a potentially risky strategy, a third party may escalate the conflict as a way of increasing creativity or revealing issues in a way that will ultimately defuse the conflict.[16] The third party may stimulate the conflict by teaching the parties to fight fair or showing them effective ways to prove their point. The third party may change the conditions that affect the conflict, such as leadership style or organizational structure. He may extend the conflict issues by stressing differences or introducing new facets of existing issues. Bringing in other parties, which may result in coalition formation, can also increase the conflict. Finally, the third party can identify consequences that encourage escalation, such as convincing a party that it will lose face if it does not fight for its beliefs. Because of potential side effects and lack of qualified change agents, few individuals and groups request an intervention that escalates the conflict.

Structural Mechanisms

Managers can use structural mechanisms, such as redesigning formal reporting relationships, adding special managerial roles, or using standard operating procedures more extensively and effectively, to improve intergroup relations.

Redesigning Reporting Relationships.   Interactions between groups generally improve when a common boss coordinates the work of the interacting groups. The manager of the groups sets priorities for the groups, shares relevant information, and then resolves any disputes as they occur.

Certain organizational structures (see Chapter 12) can encourage lateral interactions in organizations. In a hospital, for example, a medical team made up of nurses, physicians, social workers, and other support personnel may serve a small group of patients with similar illnesses in the same ward. The emphasis on creating cross-functional teams in organizations also reduces potential conflicts between different departments. Roche Pharmaceuticals organized a group of employees from the finance, employee health services, benefits, legal, and public relations departments to develop "Choosing Health," a program to help employees choose healthy lifestyles. This program attempted to reduce the number of claims that resulted from preventable conditions by creating a personalized health profile for each employee and then offering health improvement suggestions.[17]

Cross-functional teams, task forces, and corporate alliances can improve intergroup interactions across companies. A cross-functional team at Detroit Diesel, composed of company employees and representatives from their suppliers, created a fully functioning diesel engine in 7½ months.[18] Cleveland State University's administration created an emergency task force to work with PeopleSoft to fix its software, which caused major problems for the school. The task force identified problems with the software, which they then prodded PeopleSoft to fix.[19]

Introducing Special Roles or Groups. Employees may temporarily assume positions that let them connect interacting groups. Rather than relying on their boss to resolve any differences, groups can use a peer to encourage communication and reduce potential conflict. Although the linking employee can still distort communication and even contribute to conflict by inaccurately passing information, the potential for improving rather than hindering communication is greater.

Some organizations instead appoint a permanent coordinating individual or group of people to act as an interface between interacting groups. A project or product manager, for example, coordinates the decisions of such interdependent groups as sales representatives, research and development engineers, and the production line. A unit manager in a hospital, who may be either a medical or nonmedical person, may fulfill the role of coordinating all activities on a particular medical service, such as outpatient, emergency, or obstetrics.

Boundary spanners shepherd the interaction between groups inside and outside the organization. Industrial salespeople, for example, combine personal selling and customer service and provide the link between an industrial company and its customers. Human resources professionals may serve as boundary spanners between management, staff, and external contacts.[20] Boundary spanners can assume one of two roles in dealing with the environment:[21]

- **Buffers** keep the environment from interfering with internal operations by resisting or controlling change.
- **Bridgers** help the organization adapt to changes in the external environment.

Boundary spanners have unique positions because of their access to and control of the distribution of information. School principals can serve in this role because they manage the interface between the school staff and the community, including parents, community partners, and professional service organizations.[22] Companies may emphasize one or both of these activities as a way of coping with a dynamic, competitive environment.

Sometimes managers convene special groups of representatives from all parties to work on problems faced by the interacting groups. Mayor Daley of Chicago convened a task force that included representatives of the school board, park district, and various city departments to contribute to the redevelopment of the Cabrini-Green area, a public housing complex about a mile north of downtown.[23]

Changing Organizational Procedures, Plans, and Goals.   Introducing new rules and regulations to govern the activities of two groups might also improve their interaction. For example, disagreements between firefighters and police officers in handling traffic at a fire could be resolved by changing and clarifying the procedures for dealing with the public, the media, and the victims. Clearly specified procedures eliminate the ambiguity about responsibility for particular tasks and the best way to perform them. Employees can concentrate on the tasks rather than on interpersonal issues.

Organizations can also use clearly specified plans to direct the activities of interacting groups while minimizing their interaction. By using plans, even the integration of groups geographically distant can be effective. The use of common, or superordinate goals can have an influence similar to plans because they create a common focus for the groups' activities. A clearly stated mission can have a similar effect. For example, successfully creating networks of independent physician practices as part of managed care involves developing common goals and objectives for the participants.[24]

▌ THE PROCESS OF NEGOTIATION

Negotiation refers to the process by which two or more interdependent parties use bargaining to reconcile their differences. Most people have had the experience of negotiating an increase in salary or the price of a car. Many workers negotiate their job assignments or salary. Employees and management at US Airways and other airlines negotiate their labor contracts.

Negotiations typically have four key elements:[25]

- ▪ **A degree of interdependence between the parties.** US Airways relies on its flight attendants, pilots, baggage handlers, and other employees to service its customers.
- ▪ **A perceived conflict between the parties.** Management and flight attendants disagreed about the appropriate wages for the attendants.
- ▪ **An opportunistic interaction between the parties.** In their various negotiations, labor and management look for opportunities to influence the other. Each cares about and pursues its own interests and tries to influence decisions to its advantage.
- ▪ **The possibility of agreement.** Both labor and management expect to agree on contracts that specify wages, benefits, and conditions of employment.

In this section, we examine these elements in more detail by looking first at the distributive and integrative paradigms. Then we trace the four steps of the negotiation process.

Distributive Versus Integrative Bargaining

The negotiating process shows a fundamental tension between the claiming and creating of value.[26] Value claimers view negotiations purely as an adversarial process. Each side tries to claim as much of a limited pie as possible, such as limited financial or other resources, by giving the other side as little as possible. Each party claims value through manipulation, arguments, limited concessions, and hard bargaining.

Value creators, in contrast, participate in a process that results in joint gains to each party. They try to create additional benefits for each side in the negotiations. They emphasize shared interests, developing a collaborative relationship, and negotiating in a pleasant, cooperative manner.

A negotiator incorporates these strategies singly or in combination in one of two basic paradigms. Distributive bargaining takes an adversarial, or win-lose, approach. Integrative bargaining takes a problem-solving, or win-win, approach.

Distributive Bargaining.   The classical view considers bargaining as a win-lose situation, in which one party's gain is the other party's loss. This approach is also known as a zero-sum type of negotiation because one party's gain equals the other party's loss, for a net gain of zero. Examples include the purchase of used cars, property, and other material goods in organizations. This approach has also been applied to salary negotiations and labor–management negotiations.

Distributive bargaining emphasizes the claiming of value. At US Airways, for example, management seemed to view the financial resources of the airline as a fixed pie: Whatever the flight attendants gain, the airline loses. Negotiators carefully make their opening offers, as well as later offers and counteroffers, so they can successfully claim value and "win" the negotiation. Power plays a key role in successful distributive bargaining because it increases a party's leverage and ability to shape perceptions.

Integrative Bargaining.   Recent research encourages negotiators to transform the bargaining into a win-win situation.[27] Here both parties gain as a result of the negotiations. Known as a positive-sum type of negotiation, because the gains of each party yield a positive sum, this approach has recently been applied in international negotiations, labor–management negotiations, and specific job-related bargaining. Ideally, US Airways sees the wages it pays to flight attendants, pilots, and other labor groups as contributing to high-quality service and customer loyalty, ultimately resulting in profits for the airline.

Flash Electronics and Applicast negotiated for two months over a 25-page outsourcing contract that would guide Applicast's support of the SAP application that the CEO of Flash Electronics had purchased. The two parties worked to ensure that they agreed about issues such as performance measurements, service level, and plans for an exit strategy. The CEO agreed, for example, to pay for upgrades as part of the monthly service fee Flash would pay Applicast.[28] Building such a relationship involved jointly developing shared values, taking time for retraining, and developing trust and care. The use of a problem-solving process led to perceptions of greater success in the negotiating process.[29]

Although the negotiation process described in the next section can result in both distributive and integrative bargaining, it helps managers take a win-win approach that will result in mutual gains for both parties. Computer software, such as Negotiator Pro, can also support managers in improving their negotiations.[30]

The Steps in Negotiation

People can follow four basic steps for an effective negotiation.

Step 1: Prepare. Preparation for negotiations should begin long before the formal negotiation begins. Each party gathers information about the other side—its history, likely behavior, previous interactions, and previous agreements reached. Sometimes, particularly in labor–management negotiations, the parties poll their members about their wishes, expectations, and preferences for the new agreement. The parties might even gather information about their competitors to help determine whether they have realistic expectations. An entrepreneur who wanted to open the Rainforest Café in the Mall of America prepared by getting to know everyone connected with the other party in the negotiation, including family, friends, and business associates.[31]

Step 2: Evaluate Alternatives. The two sides attempt to identify the bargaining range—that is, the range in which both parties would find an agreement acceptable. Consider the issue of wages at a unionized company. Assume that the employees represented by a union want an $8.00 per hour wage increase but will settle for $6.00. Figure 10-4A illustrates their target price ($8.00) and resistance price ($6.00). Now assume management wants to pay $2.00 more per hour, but is willing to pay $4.00 more. Figure 10-4B illustrates the target price ($2.00) and resistance price ($4.00). The bargaining range includes the wages that would satisfy both sides; it is the overlap between the parties' resistance points. Figure 10-4C shows that, given the initial resistance points, no bargaining range exists for the employees and management. If, however, the employees' union convinces management's representatives that employee services are more valuable than management originally thought, management may raise its resistance point to $7.00, as shown in Figure 10-4D; then a bargaining range exists between $6.00 and $7.00.

In determining this range, each party asks questions such as the following, known as the min-max strategy:[32]

- What is the minimum I can accept to resolve the conflict?
- What is the maximum I can ask for without appearing outrageous?
- What is the maximum I can give away?
- What is the least I can offer without appearing outrageous?
- What is the minimum the other party can accept to resolve the conflict?
- What is the maximum the other party can ask for without appearing outrageous?
- What is the maximum the other party can give away?
- What is the least the other party can offer without appearing outrageous?

The bargainers determine the alternatives acceptable to them. The more alternatives they have, typically the more leverage they have in the negotiation. For example, the HUB group is building a network of insurance agencies in key regions of the United States. Because HUB's president doesn't have a specific geographic focus, he has many alternatives and so more leverage in negotiating with potential acquisitions.[33]

Negotiators also identify their best alternative to a negotiated settlement, known as their BATNA. In one study, individuals who had a BATNA when negotiating had higher individual outcomes than those who didn't.[34] For some employees,

FIGURE 10-4

The bargaining range depends on the resistance point and target point of each party.

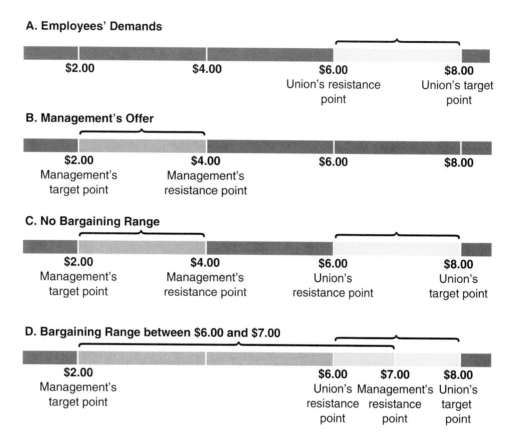

A. Employees' Demands

$2.00 $4.00 $6.00 — Union's resistance point $8.00 — Union's target point

B. Management's Offer

$2.00 — Management's target point $4.00 — Management's resistance point $6.00 $8.00

C. No Bargaining Range

$2.00 — Management's target point $4.00 — Management's resistance point $6.00 — Union's resistance point $8.00 — Union's target point

D. Bargaining Range between $6.00 and $7.00

$2.00 — Management's target point $6.00 — Union's resistance point $7.00 — Management's resistance point $8.00 — Union's target point

for example, striking might be the best alternative. For others, securing a position outside the company might be the best alternative. Identifying a set of alternatives, including the best one, helps individuals determine whether to continue the negotiation or seek another course of action. Negotiators for Colbún SA, a large producer of electric power in Chile, must establish alternatives for any negotiation. When Colbún lacked options for purchasing transmission capacity, it had to create an alternative—developing its own transmission line.[35]

The cognitive biases that affect decision making (see Chapter 5) also influence negotiations. The way a negotiator frames a situation (e.g., describing it as a gain or a loss) and the starting value he uses will affect his view of the alternatives. Similarly, the negotiator's assessment of the frequency of the situation and his analysis of his own abilities to make judgments will also affect the assessment of alternatives and ultimately the progress of the negotiation.[36] Recent research suggests, for example, that bargainers who frame a situation as a possible loss for themselves generally have a better outcome than negotiators who frame the situation as a possible gain. Viewing the outcome as a possible gain, however, results in more integrative settlements.[37]

Step 3: Identify Each Party's Interests.   Negotiators act to satisfy their substantive, relationship, personal, or organizational interests. Managers' interests, for example, can include their reputation, their relationship with other parties, the organization's goals, or the bottom line. Workers' interests might include raising their standard of living, creating a positive working relationship with management, or improving their status when compared to workers in other companies.

In focusing on its own interests, a party often ignores or simplifies the interests of the other party, particularly when uncertain future events play a role in each party's interests.[38] The person or group must assess the other party's interests and then decide how to respond to those interests in their offers.

Even though negotiators try to reach agreements on a specific position or a specific issue, the underlying interests are generally broader, and numerous alternatives may satisfy them. For example, either increasing wages or offering more flexible hours may improve the quality of life for employees. Managers who negotiate effectively satisfy interests by identifying and exploring a range of possible positions on specific issues.

In assessing what interests are at stake, managers can use the following advice:[39]

- Consider both tangible interests and subtler interests, such as reputation, fairness, and precedent.
- Separate interests from issues and positions. For example, meeting security needs differs from insisting on the company paying for the employee's and his family's health insurance.
- Recognize that interests may have either intrinsic or instrumental value. For example, increased autonomy may have value by itself or may help accomplish other personal goals.
- Understand that interests depend on perceptions, which are subjective.
- Note that interests and issues can change intentionally or accidentally.

The Composites Division of Owens Corning negotiated with Excel Logistics to manage a warehouse facility in Tennessee. At the first meeting between representatives of the two companies, Excel presented its capabilities and the scope of the project. At the second meeting, Excel offered a formal proposal for managing the facility and addressed every aspect of the Composites Division's warehouse operations. The manager from Excel described this as "an open-book meeting where we discussed our margins, our return on investment, and our anticipated payroll costs." Excel identified how they would meet Composites' interests in a smooth transition from the current provider within an acceptable time frame.[40] Each party consciously identified and attempted to meet its own and the other party's interests.

Step 4:   Make Trade-offs and Create Joint Gains.   Negotiators use trade-offs to satisfy their own and others' interests. In labor negotiations, the union side may trade wage increases for job security provisions or vice versa. Either position (increased wages or better job security) would meet the interests of maintaining a certain standard of living. US Airways may trade wage increases for more control over working conditions. Either position (higher wages or different working conditions) could meet the interests of serving the airline's shareholders and customers.

People can assess trade-offs by first identifying the best and worst possible outcomes. Then they can specify what impact trade-offs will have on these outcomes. Finally, they can consider whether the changed outcomes will better meet the parties' interests.

In addition to making trade-offs as a way of reaching a satisfactory negotiating outcome, integrative bargaining attempts to create gains for both parties. A party may offer something relatively less valuable to it but more valuable to the other party. Or the parties may build on shared interests. They may also use economies of scale to create joint gains. Negotiators need to overcome the idea that a fixed amount of outcomes exists. They also should try not to escalate conflict unnecessarily.

Effective negotiators pay attention to the other party's beliefs and values and avoid devaluing the others' concessions while overvaluing their own.[41] For example, unions that cooperate with management typically reach agreements that benefit both sides by gradually loosening union work rules and increasing union participation in quality improvement teams. Management also gives the union more flexibility regarding compensation and makes available cost and profit data so that unions can make reasonable compensation requests.[42]

Negotiators can create joint gains in a variety of circumstances:

- They can consider interests separately, rather than bundling them into a single, comprehensive and complex interest.
- They can develop contingent agreements in which outcomes depend on the particular circumstances as they arise.
- They can create agreements in which both parties share the risk.
- They can alter the pattern of payment or actions over time, rather than requiring a consistent set of behaviors from either party.
- They can use a variety of criteria, such as precedence, substance, and fairness, to create joint gains.
- They can use economies of scale to create increased value.[43]

Franciscan Health System in Ohio thought it had entered negotiations to sell its Franciscan Medical Center in Dayton, Ohio, to Vanguard Health Systems. However, the continued losses by the medical center likely caused Vanguard to withdraw its offer. The inability of the two sides to create joint gains contributed to Franciscan's closing rather than selling the medical center.[44]

Negotiators can reach either explicit or implicit agreements, and both can be satisfactory. An explicit, written agreement covers all contingencies and binds the parties by an external enforcement mechanism. The parties have limited, verbal, and formal communication, and use specific terms to exchange promises. The contract has a clear beginning and end, as well as explicit statement of any future interactions. An implicit, oral agreement offers flexibility for responding to unforeseen circumstances and binds the parties by the nature of their personal relationship. The parties use extensive verbal and nonverbal, formal and informal communication, and may make vague, ill-defined promises. The contract involves no clear beginning or end and no specification of future interactions.[45]

▮ NEGOTIATION STRATEGIES AND TACTICS

In effective bargaining situations, the negotiators attack the problem, not the people, and treat negotiation as joint problem solving. They remain open to persuasion and explore interests rather than taking a position. They also create multiple options and try to improve their alternatives in case they do not reach an agreement.[46] In addition, successful negotiators draw upon a variety of negotiation strategies, tactics, and styles, keeping in mind cross-cultural issues.

Strategies

Three common negotiation strategies exist:[47]

- **Competitive.** This strategy frequently accompanies distributive bargaining. It focuses on achieving one party's goals at the expense of the other party's goals. The group (or individual) may use secrecy, threats, or bluffs as a way of hiding its own goals and uncovering the other party's. The group (or individual) creates a bad image of the other party, ignores their logic, and increases hostility. The key attitude is "I win, you lose."

- **Collaborative.** This strategy, typically used with integrative bargaining, emphasizes pursuing common goals held by the two parties. It calls on each party to accurately communicate its needs to the other. It takes a problem-solving approach and looks for solutions that satisfy both parties. The two parties share information and are honest; they treat each other with understanding and integrity. The key attitude focuses on identifying what is best for both parties.

- **Subordinative.** In this strategy, one party puts its goals after the other party's goals in order to minimize or avoid conflict and soothe hostility. The first party becomes overly concerned with the other's goals rather than its own or both parties'. A party may totally expose its own vulnerabilities and weaknesses and relinquish its position to satisfy the other party. The key attitude is "You win, I lose."

Choosing a strategy may depend on the desired relationship between the negotiating parties and the importance of substantive (content) outcomes to the manager.[48] Figure 10-5 illustrates the way these two dimensions can influence the strategy chosen by one party. In Situation 1, for example, the manager should use trusting collaboration because he values both the relationship and substantive outcomes. In Situation 2, a manager should use open subordination, since establishing

Is the **substantive outcome** very important to the manager?

		YES	NO
Is the **relationship outcome** very important to the manager?	**YES**	**Trustingly collaborate** when both types of outcomes are very important Situation 1	**Openly subordinate** when the priority is on relationship outcomes Situation 2
	NO	**Firmly compete** when the priority is on substantive outcomes Situation 3	**Actively avoid negotiating** when neither type of outcome is very important Situation 4

FIGURE 10–5

Managers need to determine the importance of substantive and relationship outcomes when negotiating.

Source: Reprinted with permission from G. T. Savage, J. D. Blair, and R. L. Sorenson. Consider both relationships and substance when negotiating strategically, *Academy of Management Executive* 3(1) (1989): 40.

a relationship overshadows the substantive outcome. Situation 3 demands firm competition to attain the desired substantive results at the expense of the relationship. Situation 4 calls for active avoidance of negotiation, since the negotiator values neither outcome. Negotiators can also act strategically by offering incentives, stepping up the pressure, establishing their authority, enlisting support, and exerting control over the process.[49]

Tactics

Negotiators use a variety of short-term, focused maneuvers, known as *tactics,* to accomplish their objectives.[50] Negotiators can engage the other party in collaboration by appreciating the other person's situation, feelings, ideas, and face.[51] Alternatively, the negotiator can use more competitive tactics. The negotiator can choose to wait out the other party. He can take a unilateral action and treat the negotiation outcome as a fait accompli. Or, the negotiator can suddenly shift his approach and do the reverse of what is expected, thereby catching the other party unprepared. He can withdraw from the negotiation or impose time, dollar, or deadline limits. Finally, the negotiator can grant or withhold favors or show anger, intimidating the other party.

Conflict spirals occur when one negotiator starts a contentious communication, the other negotiator responds similarly, and then the first negotiator responds in the same way. Stopping such spirals is important for increasing the effectiveness of negotiations. Negotiators can stop them by responding with noncontentious communications or a combination of contentious and noncontentious communications, or by labeling the negotiation as unproductive.[52] When tactics involve lying and deception—such as misrepresenting a position to an opponent, bluffing, falsifying information, deception, and selective disclosure of information—questions can arise about ethical appropriateness.[53]

When North Korea delayed their summit with South Korea by one day, in June, 2000 some believe they were using a delaying negotiating tactic to extract more concessions from South Korea.[54] In another case, Catholic Healthcare West and Sutter Health threatened to use a withdrawal tactic and terminate contracts with Blue Cross of California if they didn't receive more favorable terms.[55]

Negotiating Styles

Negotiators can use a variety of styles that they fine-tune to the particular situation. Table 10-1 describes seven types of negotiators, each of whom deliberately chooses a style that supports negotiation tactics. They may take a domineering, aggressive approach or act more collaboratively.

Sometimes a negotiator's style can interfere with effective negotiations because he doesn't relate effectively to the other party. The other party may also view the negotiator's style as inappropriate to particular circumstances. Grupo Financiero Serfin, a large Mexican bank, decided that the bank should change the concession-oriented culture created by their loan officers' negotiating styles. They introduced improved negotiation training. They also encouraged the negotiating team to work closely with analysts who defined the bank's interests in various cases. The bank identified appropriate negotiating strategies for each type of debtor. The bank also established a system by which negotiators could share successful negotiating practices. The establishment of this infrastructure freed the loan officers to become more creative in solving loan-related problems.[56]

▌ TABLE 10-1 ▐

Managers Should Beware of the Types of Negotiators Who Deliberately Choose a Style that Exaggerates Particular Tactics.

Type	Method
Aggressive-opener negotiator	Discomfort the other side by making cutting remarks about their previous performance, their numbers, their unreasonableness, or anything that can be used to insinuate that the opposition is hardly worth speaking to.
Long-pause negotiator	Listen to the other side but do not answer immediately their propositions; rather, appear to give them considerable thought with the result that long silences ensue for the purpose of getting the other side to reveal as much of their case as possible without revealing your own.
Mocking negotiator	Mock and sneer at your opposition's proposals to get them so "uptight" that they say something they will regret later.
Interrogator	Meet all proposals with searching, prodding questions couched in such a way that the opposition feels they have not thoroughly done their homework. Challenge any answers in a confronting manner and ask the opposition to explain further what they mean.
Cloak-of-reasonableness negotiator	Appear agreeable and helpful, while making impossible demands, for the purpose of winning the friendship and confidence of the opposition.
Divide-and-conquer negotiator	Produce dissension among the opposition so that they have to pay more attention to their own internal disagreements than to the disagreements with the other party. Ally with one member of the team and try to play him or her off against the other members of the team.
Simpleton negotiator	Pretend to be particularly dense, and by so doing exasperate the opposition in hopes that at least one member of the opposing team will reveal information as he tries to find increasingly simple ways to describe proposals.

Source: Based on R. Gourlay, Negotiations and bargaining, *Management Decision* 25(3)(1987): 19–20.

▌ NEGOTIATING IN A DOT-COM, GLOBAL WORKPLACE

Managers face new challenges in negotiating in the twenty-first century. The rapid rise and fall of new businesses has made negotiations occur at a dizzying rate. Managers of dot-com companies must be adept negotiators because they interact with a variety of constituencies. They negotiate employment contracts with workers in high demand. They bargain with venture capital firms to determine the amount of financial support the firms will make available. They negotiate with potential customers about realistic deadlines and prices. These negotiations must occur quickly and competently before available opportunities for product development, launch, and growth evaporate.

Buyers and sellers can also negotiate online. General Motors recently introduced BuyPower, which allows customers to start a negotiation process with dealers using e-mail. Users can access more than 6,000 dealerships using this online capability.[57]

Negotiating in the global marketplace requires managers to recognize that the assumptions that underlie effective negotiations differ significantly in various parts of the world. Consider this situation:

> Your company has just received confirmation that a high-level delegation from the People's Republic of China will visit your office. Since the Chinese have already received a sample of your products, the purpose of their visit is probably to
>
> (a) sign an agreement to act as your local distributor in China.
> (b) establish a firm relationship with the company management.
> (c) learn more about your company's technological advancements.
> (d) visit your country as a reward for their hard work at home.[58]

If you chose (b), you answered correctly. Most Chinese begin by establishing rapport and acquiring commitment. Lower-level managers then handle the technical details.

The general approach to negotiations varies in different cultures, although exceptions exist in every culture. In one study of U.S. and Japanese negotiations, joint gains were lower in intercultural than in intracultural negotiations.[59] People in different cultures may have different perceptions of the appropriateness of specific negotiating tactics.[60] In Asia, negotiators focus on saving face for all parties.[61] Being too frank, critical, insincere, impatient, or unadaptable results in ineffective negotiations. Asians ask questions indirectly: "I've developed a shortcut for manufacturing these garments at a lower cost but ensuring higher quality, and would appreciate any suggestions you have for improving it," not "Can you make this garment cheaper but improve its quality?"

Negotiating with Russians, in contrast, has historically posed different challenges.[62] The Russians emphasize building arguments on asserted ideals and deemphasize building relationships. They make few concessions. An opponent's concessions are viewed as weaknesses and almost never reciprocated. Russians have been described as making no effort to build continuing relationships, often offering an extreme initial position, and ignoring any deadlines.

Arabs, on the other hand, use primarily an emotional rather than an ideological or factual negotiating style.[63] They request and make concessions throughout the negotiating process, and almost always reciprocate an opponent's concessions. They start with extreme initial positions, but rarely enforce deadlines. They focus on building a long-term relationship; thus, the business climate and personal relationship are critical.[64]

North Americans, in contrast, appeal to logic and counter their opponents' arguments with objective facts rather than with subjective feelings or asserted ideals.[65] They may make small concessions early and then usually reciprocate an opponent's concessions. But they take a moderate initial position, build only a short-term relationship, and value deadlines greatly.

While these generalities may not always apply, they suggest that all managers who work in cross-cultural situations should think carefully about the context of any negotiations. They should be aware of differences in negotiators' styles and the way negotiators view the process itself.

▌ Summary

1. Groups can demonstrate pooled, sequential, reciprocal, or team interdependence. Groups showing reciprocal or team interdependence experience dysfunctional conflict and other problems more often than those showing pooled or sequential interdependence.

2. Perceptual differences, including goal, social, and time orientations, attitudinal sets, and status differences, create differences between groups.

3. Power differences, including the extent of a group's substitutability, its ability to cope with uncertainty, and its access to resources, influence the effectiveness of its interactions with other individuals or groups.

4. Task relations reflect the nature of group interdependence and can reinforce problematic interactions.

5. Cross-cultural differences can also exaggerate problems of interacting groups. Managers can improve intergroup relations by using interpersonal interventions and structural mechanisms.

6. Negotiation describes a process in which two or more parties attempt to reach an agreement; in distributive bargaining, one party's gain is the other's loss, and in integrative bargaining, mutual gains for both parties occur.

7. Effective negotiation includes preparing, evaluating alternatives, identifying interests, and making trade-offs and creating joint gains.

8. Negotiators may pursue competitive, collaborative, or subordinative strategies, and use an array of tactics to supplement these strategies.

9. Managers who negotiate in different cultures should carefully diagnose the effect of the culture on the process and people involved in the negotiations so that they can bargain effectively.

A Manager's Diagnostic Review

■ Diagnose the type of group interaction, and understand its consequences.
- Do the groups have pooled, sequential, reciprocal, or team interdependence?

■ Know how perceptual differences, power differences, task relations, and cross-cultural differences affect group interactions.
- What factors contribute to the relationships between groups?
- How effective are group interactions?

■ Improve intergroup relations.
- What interpersonal techniques do managers use?
- Do managers redesign the job or the organization to improve intergroup relations?

■ Diagnose the impact of bargaining.
- What type of bargaining occurs?
- Do managers have strategies for dealing with all types of bargaining?

■ Know and use the steps in effective negotiation.
- What types of preparations occur?
- Are interests identified?

- Is the best alternative to a negotiated agreement specified?
- Are trade-offs made?

Use negotiation strategies and tactics appropriately.

- What tactics and strategies are used?
- How effective are intercultural negotiations?

Negotiate effectively in the dot-com, global workplace.

- How does the new dot-com environment affect negotiation?
- How does the culture affect negotiation?

Visit the Gordon homepage on the Prentice Hall Web site at

http://www.prenhall.com/gordon

for recommended readings, additional activities, Internet exercises, updated information, and links to related Web sites.

▌ Thinking Critically About Organizational Behavior

1. Under what circumstances do groups become more interdependent?
2. What are the differences between pooled, sequential, reciprocal, and team interdependence?
3. Can you think of an example of pooled interdependence resulting in conflict between groups?
4. Are differences in time, goal, or social orientation more likely to result in conflict between groups?
5. Should organizations attempt to eliminate all power differences between groups?
6. How can managers improve intergroup relations using interpersonal techniques and structural changes?
7. Under what circumstances should managers use distributive bargaining? Integrative bargaining?
8. What steps should managers follow for a successful negotiation?
9. How can managers create joint gains in negotiations?
10. What are the differences between competitive, collaborative, and subordinative negotiation strategies, and when is each most effective?
11. What types of negotiation tactics should managers use?
12. What cultural characteristics should managers consider when conducting negotiations outside their home country?

ACTIVITY 10-1: THE PRISONERS' DILEMMA

STEP 1: Read the following situation:

Two people are arrested for a crime and put in separate cells so that they cannot communicate. Lawyers are assigned to advise the prisoners. There is not enough evidence to convict either criminal. The prisoners have the choice of either denouncing their accomplice or colluding with their accomplice by remaining silent.

STEP 2: The instructor will make up teams of two people. Each team begins with five tokens and has two cards to play—Denounce or Collude. There is a pot of tokens between the two teams. If both teams play "Collude," each gets two tokens from the pot. If one team plays "Collude" and the other plays "Denounce," the one that plays "Collude" gives one token to the pot, and the team that plays "Denounce" takes four tokens from the pot. If both teams play "Denounce," neither gets anything. The play lasts for 10 rounds.

Round 1: Each team plays a card simultaneously.

Round 2: The teams take turns playing a card, beginning with team 1.

Round 3: Each team plays a card simultaneously.

Round 4: The teams take turns playing a card, beginning with team 2.

Round 5: Each team plays a card simultaneously.

Round 6: The teams take turns playing a card, beginning with team 1.

Round 7: Each team plays a card simultaneously.

Round 8: The teams take turns playing a card, beginning with team 2.

Round 9: Each team plays a card simultaneously.

Round 10: Each team plays a card simultaneously.

STEP 3: Discussion. In small groups or with the entire class, answer the following questions:

1. What is the best strategy?
2. What are the lessons for negotiation?

ACTIVITY 10-2: FAIRFIELD FLYER WAGONS

STEP 1: Students will manufacture wagon parts (wheels, long sides, short sides, bottoms, and handles). These parts will be used during Step 2.

1. Your instructor will pass out the necessary materials:

   Rulers

   Quarters

   Scissors

   Paper

   Pencils

   "Pooled Interdependence Template"
   IN/OUT labels (3 OUT for manufacturing departments; 1 IN, 1 OUT PASSED, and 1 OUT REJECTED for Quality Control). (Pieces of paper with these legends are sufficient.)

2. Your instructor will arrange the room. Use extra chairs or desks for IN/OUT stations, and attach IN/OUT labels with tape.

3. Your instructor will divide the class into four departments. Each will be provided with the following materials:

   a. Wheel Department: "Wheel Department Template," quarters, scissors, paper, pencils.

   b. Sides Department: "Sides Department Template," rulers, scissors, paper, pencils.

   c. Bottom and Handle Department: "Bottom and Handle Department Template," rulers, scissors, paper, pencils.

   d. Quality Control: All department templates, rulers.

4. Appoint or have each department select a manager.

5. Review the following manufacturing procedures.

WHEEL DEPARTMENT

Your job is to produce as many wheels as possible. Make sure that they are the right size (the diameter of a quarter), and do not waste materials. The department manager will distribute raw materials, collect the finished wheels, and deliver them to the OUTPUT table where they will be collected by the instructor for delivery to Quality Control.

SIDES DEPARTMENT

Your job is to produce as many long and short sides as possible. Make sure that they are the right size (see your template), and do not waste materials. You should produce the same number of long and short sides. The department manager will collect the finished sides, separate them into long and short batches, and deliver them to the OUTPUT table, where they will be collected by the instructor for delivery to Quality Control.

BOTTOM AND HANDLE DEPARTMENT

Your job is to produce as many bottoms and handles as possible. Make sure that they are the right size (see your template), and do not waste materials. You should produce the same number of handles and bottoms. The department manager will collect the finished wheels and deliver them to the OUTPUT table where they will be collected by the instructor for delivery to Quality Control.

QUALITY CONTROL

Check each part against the template. Put those that pass inspection on the OUT PASSED table and those that fail inspection on the OUT REJECTED table.

Communication *between* any of the departments is prohibited. Managers may communicate only with the people within their departments.

6. Have a 15-minute production run.
7. Participate in a brief discussion.
   a. Was there a need for communication between the manufacturing departments? If so, what kind? If not, why not?
   b. Was there a need for communication between the manufacturing departments and the Quality Control department? Why or why not?

   c. Did your physical/spatial relationship to any other department influence your ability to do your job? Why or why not?

STEP 2: Students will assemble wagons from the parts manufactured during Step 1. The groups will be sequentially interdependent.

1. Your instructor will pass out the necessary materials:
   Assembly instructions
   Rulers
   Tape
   Pencils
   Wagon parts manufactured during Step 1
   Sample finished wagon
   IN/OUT labels (as indicated on Suggested Room Layout)
2. Your instructor will rearrange the room according to the Suggested Room Layout.
3. Your instructor will divide the class into six departments (a–f) and provide each with the following materials:
   a. Attach handle to bottom: Step 1 assembly instructions, rulers, tape, pencils, handles, and bottoms from Step 1.
   b. Attach long sides to bottom: Step 2 assembly instructions, rulers, tape, pencils, long sides from Step 1.
   c. Attach short sides: Step 3 assembly instructions, rulers, tape, pencils, short sides from Step 1.
   d. Fold and tape sides together: Step 4 assembly instructions, tape.
   e. Attach wheels: Step 5 assembly instructions, rulers, tape, pencils, wheels from Step 1.
   f. Quality Control: All assembly instructions, sample finished wagon, rulers, "Quality Control Guidelines."
4. Appoint or have each department select a manager.
5. Go over the production procedure. Each department should follow the assembly instructions provided.
6. Have a 15-minute production run.
7. Participate in a brief discussion.
   a. What difficulties did you have?

b. Would your task have been easier or would you have been more productive if you could have communicated with the other departments? If so, which departments? What type of communication would have been the most effective? Would memos have helped?

c. Did the spatial relationship between the departments help or hinder your ability to get your work done? How? How would it have affected your ability to get your work done if the departments with which you interacted had been in different rooms? In a different order?

STEP 3: Students will manufacture wagons under two conditions of reciprocal interdependence.

1. Your instructor will provide the necessary materials:

    Assembly instructions

    Rulers

    Tape

    Pencils

    Sample finished wagon

    Paperclips

    Paper cut into 11″ × 3⅝″ rectangles

    "Reciprocal Drawing Template"

    Scissors

    Copies of "Interdepartmental Memos"

    Quality Control Guidelines (attached)

    IN/OUT labels (4 IN, 4 OUT)

2. Your instructor will rearrange the room according to the Suggested Room Layout.

3. Your instructor will divide the class into four departments and provide each with the following materials:

    a. Drawing Department: Paper cut into 11″ × 3⅝″ rectangles, pencils, rulers, quarters, "Reciprocal Drawing Template," copies of Interdepartmental Memo #1, paperclips

    b. Cutting Department: Scissors, pencils, copies of Interdepartmental Memo #2, paperclips.

    c. Assembly Department: Tape, pencils, rulers, Step 1 through 5 assembly instructions, copies of Interdepartmental Memo #3, paperclips.

    d. Quality Control Department: Rulers, sample completed wagon, pencils, "Quality Control Guidelines," copies of Interdepartmental Memos #4, #5, and #6, paperclips.

    Start Assembly Department off with one handle and bottom per person and Cutting Department with one set of long sides drawn per person.

4. Appoint, or have each department appoint, a manager.

5. Review the following manufacturing procedure.

Condition 1

You must follow all directions exactly. You are only permitted to communicate with other departments using the memos provided. Managers may only communicate with the workers within their own department. There is to be no discussion between departments. Your instructor will deliver any necessary memos, which should be placed on your OUT table for pickup.

DRAWING DEPARTMENT

Parts must be drawn according to the drawing template.

Step 1: Draw long sides on paper.

Step 2: Send to Cutting Department (put on OUT table).

Step 3: When paper returns from Cutting Department (on IN table), draw handle and send back to Cutting Department.

Step 4: Repeat above for short sides, wheels, and bottom (in that order), sending the paper to the Cutting Department after each part is drawn (that is, after both short sides are drawn, after four wheels are drawn, after bottom is drawn).

You may work on several sheets of paper simultaneously, but you must follow the steps in order. For example, from one sheet of raw material: draw two long sides, send to Cutting Department; draw one handle, send to Cutting Department; draw two short sides, send to Cutting Department; draw four wheels, send to Cutting Department; draw one bottom, send to Cutting Department.

If you receive requests from the Quality Control Department,

a. Get more raw material (paper).

b. Redraw the part specified on the "Redraw" memo.

c. Send redrawn part to Cutting Department with a "Recut" memo completed and attached (attach memos with paperclips).

d. Put remaining raw material aside for other rejected parts.

CUTTING DEPARTMENT

Step 1: When you receive drawing from Drawing Department, cut out long sides.

Step 2: Send long sides to Assembly Department and paper back to Drawing Department.

Step 3: Repeat above for handle, short sides, wheels, and bottom, each time sending cut parts to Assembly and paper to Drawing.

You may work on different sheets simultaneously, but you must follow the steps in order for each.

If you receive a "Recut" memo from the Drawing Department,

a. Recut part.

b. Send recut part to Assembly Department with "Reassembly" memo completed and attached (attach memos with paperclips).

ASSEMBLY DEPARTMENT

Follow assembly instructions in the following order:

Step 1: Attach handle to bottom.

Step 2: Attach long sides to bottom.

Step 3: Attach short sides to bottom.

Step 4: Fold sides up and tape.

Step 5: Attach wheels to long sides.

Step 6: Send to Quality Control.

If you receive a rejected wagon from Quality Control,

a. Follow the directions on the attached memo. You will either have to reassemble the wagon or hold it until you receive a new part from the Cutting Department.

b. Send the reassembled wagon back to Quality Control with a "Reassembly" memo completed and attached (attach memos with paperclips).

QUALITY CONTROL

Step 1: Check each wagon against the "Quality Control Guidelines" (attached).

Step 2: If the wagon meets specifications, send to shipping.

Step 3: If the wagon is assembled wrong, return to Assembly Department with a "Reassemble" memo completed and attached (attach memos with paperclips).

Step 4: If wagon contains a part that is the wrong size,

a. Remove faulty part from wagon.

b. Send faulty part to Drawing Department with a "Redraw" memo completed and paperclipped to the faulty part.

c. Send remainder of wagon to Assembly Department with a "Hold" memo completed and paperclipped to wagon.

6. Have a 15-minute production run.

7. Participate in a brief discussion.

a. What difficulties did you have?

b. Would your task have been easier or would you have been more productive if you could have communicated with the other departments? If so, which departments? What type of communication would have been most effective?

c. Did the spatial relationship between departments help or hinder your ability to get your work done? What changes would you suggest?

Condition 2

Appoint a single "Plant Manager." (Other managers become members of their departments.)

8. Take the next 20 minutes to decide what type of wagon you would like to make. Use the previous discussion to guide your decisions. You may make changes within the following constraints:

a. You must remain in the same functions—that is, you cannot change jobs.

b. You must follow the same manufacturing procedure in the same order.

9. Have a 15-minute production run.

STEP 4: Discussion. In small groups or with the entire class, answer the following questions:

1. Did the changes you made during Condition 2 improve your ability to do your job? How?

2. How did the need for interdepartmental coordination and communication change as the departments became more interdependent?

3. Did the spatial/physical relationship between departments become more important as technology became more interdependent?

Source: This exercise was developed by Cheryl L. Tromley. It was presented at the Eastern Academy of Management, Buffalo, NY 1990, and appeared in Lisa A. Mainiero and Cheryl L. Tromley, *Developing Managerial Skills in Organizational Behavior,* 2d ed. (Englewood Cliffs, NJ: Prentice Hall, 1994). It is adapted and reprinted with permission.

ACTIVITY 10-3: NEGOTIATION SKILLS: A SELF-ASSESSMENT EXERCISE

STEP 1: Complete the following questionnaire.

Please respond to this list of questions in terms of what you believe you do when interacting with others. Base your answers on your typical day-to-day activities. Be as frank as you can. For each statement, please enter on the Score Sheet the number corresponding to your choice from the following five possible responses:

1. If you have *never (or very rarely)* observed yourself doing what is described in the statement.

2. If you have observed yourself doing what is described in the statement *occasionally, but infrequently:* that is, less often than most other people who are involved in similar situations.

3. If you have observed yourself doing what is described in the statement about *an average amount:* that is, about as often as most other people who are involved in similar situations.

4. If you have observed yourself doing what is described in the statement *fairly frequently:* that is, somewhat more often than most other people who are involved in similar situations.

5. If you have observed yourself doing what is described in the statement *very frequently:* that is, considerably more than most other people who are involved in similar situations.

Please answer each question.

1. I focus on the entire situation or problem.
2. I evaluate the facts according to a set of personal values.
3. I am relatively unemotional.
4. I think that the facts speak for themselves in most situations.
5. I enjoy working on new problems.
6. I focus on what is going on between people when interacting.
7. I tend to analyze things very carefully.
8. I am neutral when arguing.
9. I work in bursts of energy with slack periods in between.
10. I am sensitive to other people's needs and feelings.
11. I hurt people's feelings without knowing it.
12. I am good at keeping track of what has been said in a discussion.
13. I put two and two together quickly.
14. I look for common ground and compromise.
15. I use logic to solve problems.
16. I know most of the details when discussing an issue.
17. I follow my inspirations of the moment.
18. I take strong stands on matters of principle.
19. I am good at using a step-by-step approach.
20. I clarify information for others.
21. I get my facts a bit wrong.
22. I try to please people.
23. I am very systematic when making a point.
24. I relate facts to experience.

25. I am good at pinpointing essentials.
26. I enjoy harmony.
27. I weigh the pros and cons.
28. I am patient.
29. I project myself into the future.
30. I let my decisions be influenced by my personal likes and wishes.
31. I look for cause and effect.
32. I focus on what needs attention now.
33. When others become uncertain or discouraged, my enthusiasm carries them along.
34. I am sensitive to praise.
35. I make logical statements.
36. I rely on well-tested ways to solve problems.
37. I keep switching from one idea to another.
38. I offer bargains.
39. I have my ideas very well thought out.
40. I am precise in my arguments.
41. I bring others to see the exciting possibilities in a situation.
42. I appeal to emotions and feelings to reach a "fair" deal.
43. I present well-articulated arguments for the proposals I favor.
44. I do not trust inspiration.
45. I speak in a way that conveys a sense of excitement to others.
46. I communicate what I am willing to give in return for what I get.
47. I put forward proposals or suggestions that make sense even if they are unpopular.
48. I am pragmatic.
49. I am imaginative and creative in analyzing a situation.
50. I put together very well-reasoned arguments.
51. I actively solicit others' opinions and suggestions.
52. I document my statements.

53. My enthusiasm is contagious.
54. I build upon others' ideas.
55. My proposals command the attention of others.
56. I like to use the inductive method (from facts to theories).
57. I can be emotional at times.
58. I use veiled or open threats to get others to comply.
59. When I disagree with someone, I skillfully point out the flaws in the other's arguments.
60. I am low-key in my reactions.
61. In trying to persuade others, I appeal to their need for sensations and novelty.
62. I make other people feel that they have something of value to contribute.
63. I put forth ideas that are incisive.
64. I face difficulties with realism.
65. I point out the positive potential in discouraging or difficult situations.
66. I show tolerance and understanding of others' feelings.
67. I use arguments relevant to the problem at hand.
68. I am perceived as a down-to-earth person.
69. I go beyond the facts.
70. I give people credit for their ideas and contributions.
71. I like to organize and plan.
72. I am skillful at bringing up pertinent facts.
73. I have a charismatic tone.
74. When disputes arise, I search for the areas of agreement.
75. I am consistent in my reactions.
76. I quickly notice what needs attention.
77. I withdraw when the excitement is over.
78. I appeal for harmony and cooperation.
79. I am cool when negotiating.
80. I work all the way through to reach a conclusion.

STEP 2: Score the completed questionnaire.

Enter the score you assign each question (1, 2, 3, 4, or 5) in the space provided. Please note: The item numbers progress across the page from left to right. When you have all your scores, add them up vertically to attain four totals. Insert a "3" in any number space left blank.

1. _____	2. _____	3. _____	4. _____
5. _____	6. _____	7. _____	8. _____
9. _____	10. _____	11. _____	12. _____
13. _____	14. _____	15. _____	16. _____
17. _____	18. _____	19. _____	20. _____
21. _____	22. _____	23. _____	24. _____
25. _____	26. _____	27. _____	28. _____
29. _____	30. _____	31. _____	32. _____
33. _____	34. _____	35. _____	36. _____
37. _____	38. _____	39. _____	40. _____
41. _____	42. _____	43. _____	44. _____
45. _____	46. _____	47. _____	48. _____
49. _____	50. _____	51. _____	52. _____
53. _____	54. _____	55. _____	56. _____
57. _____	58. _____	59. _____	60. _____
61. _____	62. _____	63. _____	64. _____
65. _____	66. _____	67. _____	68. _____
69. _____	70. _____	71. _____	72. _____
73. _____	74. _____	75. _____	76. _____
77. _____	78. _____	79. _____	80. _____
IN: _____	NR: _____	AN: _____	FA: _____

NEGOTIATION STYLE PROFILE

Now enter your four scores on the following chart. Construct your profile by connecting the four data points.

	Underused	Properly Used	Over-used
Intuitive Style			
Normative Style			
Analytical Style			
Factual Style			

20 25 30 35 40 45 50 55 60 65 70 75 80 85 90 95 100

DESCRIPTION OF STYLES

Intuitive

Basic Assumption: "Imagination can solve any problem."

Behavior: Making warm and enthusiastic statements, focusing on the entire situation or problem, pinpointing essentials, making projections into the future, being imaginative and creative in analyzing the situation, switching from one subject to another, going beyond the facts, coming up with new ideas all the time, pushing and withdrawing from time to time, putting two and two together quickly, getting their facts a bit wrong sometimes, being deductive.

Key Words: Principles, essential, tomorrow, creative, idea.

Normative

Assumption: "Negotiating is bargaining."

Behavior: Judging, assessing, and evaluating the facts according to a set of personal values, approving and disapproving, agreeing and disagreeing, using loaded words, offering bargains, proposing rewards and incentives, appealing to feelings and emotions to reach a "fair" deal, demanding, requiring, threatening, involving power, using status and authority, correlating, looking for compromise, making effective statements, focusing on people and their reactions, judging, paying attention to communication and group processes.

Key Words: Wrong, right, good, bad, like.

Analytical

Basic Assumption: "Logic leads to the right conclusions."

Behavior: Forming reasons, drawing conclusions and applying them to the case in negotiation, arguing in favor or against one's own or others' position, directing, breaking down, dividing, analyzing each situation for cause and effect, identifying relationships of the parts, putting things into logical order, organizing, weighing the pros and cons thoroughly, making identical statements, using linear reckoning.

Key Words: Because, then, consequently, therefore, in order to.

Factual

Basic Assumption: "The facts speak for themselves."

Behavior: Pointing out facts in a neutral way, keeping track of what has been said, reminding people of their statements, knowing most of the details of the discussed issue and sharing them with others, clarifying, relating facts to experience, being low-key in their reactions, looking for proof, documenting their statements.

Key Words: Meaning, define, explain, clarify, facts.

GUIDELINES FOR NEGOTIATING WITH PEOPLE HAVING DIFFERENT STYLES

1. Negotiating with someone having an *intuitive* style:

   ■ Focus on the situation as a whole.
   ■ Project yourself into the future (look for opportunities).
   ■ Tap the imagination and creativity of your partner.
   ■ Be quick in reacting (jump from one idea to another).
   ■ Build upon the reaction of the other person.

2. Negotiating with someone having a *normative* style:

   ■ Establish a sound relationship right at the outset of the negotiation.
   ■ Show your interest in what the other person is saying.
   ■ Identify his or her values and adjust to them accordingly.
   ■ Be ready to compromise.
   ■ Appeal to your partner's feelings.

3. Negotiating with someone having an *analytical* style:

   ■ Use logic when arguing.
   ■ Look for causes and effects.
   ■ Analyze the relationships between the various elements of the situation or problem at stake.
   ■ Be patient.
   ■ Analyze various options with their respective pros and cons.

4. Negotiating with someone having a *factual* style:

    ■ Be precise in presenting your facts.

    ■ Refer to the past (what has already been tried out, what has worked, what has been shown from past experiences . . .).

    ■ Be indicative (go from the facts to the principles).

    ■ Know your dossier (including the details).

    ■ Document what you say.

STEP 3: Discussion. In small groups or with the class as a whole, answer the following questions:

1. What did your score pattern look like?

2. What are the implications of your score for negotiating cross-culturally?

Source: Pierre Casse, *Training for the Cross-Cultural Mind,* 2d ed. Washington, D.C.: Society for Intercultural Education, Training and Research, 1981. Out of print.

ACTIVITY 10-4: REALTIME

STEP 1: Your instructor will assign you to teams. Your instructor will also assign one individual from each team to be the leader and people to serve as team observers. The instructor will introduce the objectives of the exercise.

STEP 2: All participants are given a copy of the Agenda. Each leader receives a copy of the Leader Instruction Sheet, Instructions for All Teams, REALTIME Exercise Scoring Sheet, and the puzzle packet. Leaders should read through their instructions. Each observer should receive a copy of the Observer's Instruction Sheet, Observer's Recording Sheet, Instructions for All Teams, and the REALTIME Exercise Scoring Sheet. Leaders and observers should address any questions to the instructor.

STEP 3: (10 minutes) The teams will meet to prepare to solve the puzzle.

STEP 4: The teams will alternate Assembly Periods and Communication Rounds as shown on the Agenda and described in their directions. Teams will score their activities as shown in the directions.

STEP 5: The teams will submit their scoring sheets to the instructor, who will record the total scores on the blackboard.

STEP 6: Discussion. Your instructor will ask the observers to describe the events that occurred during the exercise. Next your instructor will ask the team members to comment on the descriptions given by the observers. Then the class as a whole will answer the following questions:

1. What types of intergroup behavior did you observe?

2. What types of task relations existed?

3. Did power differences exist?

4. What perceptual differences existed?

5. How can you explain the intergroup behavior you observed?

6. How might you have redesigned your group to make it more effective?

Source: Based on J. E. Garcia and K. J. Lovelace, Realtime: An intergroup problem-solving exercise, *Journal of Management Education* 20 (February 1996): 104–124.

ACTIVITY 10-5: UGLI ORANGE ROLE-PLAY

STEP 1: The instructor will divide the class into groups of three. In each group, one person will play Dr. Roland, one will play Dr. Jones, and one will be an observer. The instructor will then dis-

tribute the roles to each group. After assigning one role for each group member, read the role descriptions. Then spend 5 minutes "getting into your role."

STEP 2: The group leader will read the following:

I am Mr(s). Cardoza, the owner of the remaining Ugli oranges. My fruit-exporting firm is based in South America. My country does not have diplomatic relations with your country, although we do have strong trade relations.

After you have read about your roles, you may negotiate with the other firm's representative. Spend about 10 minutes meeting with the other firm's representative, and decide on a course of action. Be prepared to answer the following questions:

1. What do you plan to do?
2. If you want to buy the oranges, what price will you offer?
3. To whom and how will the oranges be delivered?

STEP 3: The observers will report the solutions reached. Then they will describe the process used in their negotiating team.

STEP 4: Discussion. Answer the following questions with the entire class.

DESCRIPTION

1. What solution did each group reach?

DIAGNOSIS

2. What are some key features of a bargaining situation?
3. What influences the effectiveness of negotiations?

PRESCRIPTION

4. How can the effectiveness of negotiations be improved?

Source: Reprinted by permission of the author, Robert J. House, University of Toronto.

ACTIVITY 10-6: SALARY NEGOTIATIONS

INTRODUCTION

In this simulation, you will play the role of either a manager or subordinate in a negotiation over salary. Both in securing employment and in getting promotions, we frequently are in a position to negotiate with our superiors over salary. And once we achieve managerial rank, we do the same with subordinates. This is one of the most common and, at the same time, most personal forms of negotiation. For many people, it is also the most difficult. Since salary can be a means of satisfying many needs—economic, recognition, status, or competitive success measure—it leads to complex negotiations.

STEP 1: (5 minutes) The class will be divided into groups of three; two will play the roles of manager and subordinate, the other will act as an observer.

Role-players will be assigned either an "A" or a "B" role in one of the salary simulations. Assemble with your trio in the place specified by the instructor.

STEP 2: (5 minutes) Read your assigned role and prepare a strategy. If you are an observer, review the Observer Reporting Sheet (provided here) and make sure you understand what to look for.

STEP 3: (10 minutes) Carry out your discussion with your counterpart. If you finish before the allotted time is up, review the sequence of events with the other party and tell the other what he or she did that was productive or unproductive to the negotiations.

If you are an observer, make brief notes during the role-play on your Observer Reporting Sheet. When the role-play is over, review the sheet and add further details where necessary.

Observer Reporting Sheet

Round _____

How did A open the meeting? _____

_____

_____

How did B respond to the way A opened the meeting? _____

_____

_____

Was an agreement reached? Yes _____ No _____

What was the salary agreed to, if there was an agreement? _____

Were there any other added features in the settlement achieved? _____

_____

Will future relations between A and B be better (+), worse (−), or the same (0) as a result of this meeting? List the opinions of A, B, and the observer.

A _____ B _____ Observer _____

STEP 4: (10 minutes) In your trio, discuss the outcome of the negotiation. The observer should report what he or she saw each party doing. Review what steps or positions seemed most and least useful.

At the end of the time for Step 4, the observer should hand the Observer Reporting Sheet to the instructor.

STEP 5: (5 minutes) In your trio, change role assignments so that the person filling the A role now fills the B role, the person filling the B role now becomes the observer, and the previous observer now fills the A role.

STEP 6: (5 minutes) Repeat Step 2.

STEP 7: (10 minutes) Repeat Step 3.

STEP 8: (10 minutes) Repeat Step 4.

STEPS 9, 10, 11, 12: (30 minutes) Repeat steps 5, 6, 7, and 8.

STEP 13: (30 minutes) The instructor will post the results from the three sets of role-plays. Examine the different outcomes, and explore the reasons they occurred and their consequences.

STEP 14: Discussion. Answer the following questions with the entire class.

1. Were there any differences in the way the negotiations were handled when:
   a. both parties in a role-play were satisfied?
   b. one was satisfied?
   c. both were dissatisfied?

2. Were some people playing the same role dissatisfied with an outcome that others in the same role found satisfying? Why? How do you account for this?

3. Poll quickly those who were satisfied with the outcome. Ask why they were satisfied.

4. Poll quickly those who were dissatisfied with the outcome. Ask why they were dissatisfied.

5. What was the effect of observing another's negotiation on how you negotiated? Did what you saw as an observer affect how satisfied you felt with your own outcome?

Source: Developed by Roy J. Lewicki and published in Lewicki and Litterer, *Negotiations: Readings, Exercises, and Cases*, Richard D. Irwin, Homewood, IL, 1985. Used with permission.

PART III CASES

Lee Coker

INTRODUCTION

Lee Coker is Manufacturing Manager in one of the major plants of a Fortune 100 company. He is known by all, and described by his subordinates as a very bright, innovative, and energetic manager. Talking to another participant on a management development programme in late September, he reflected on his job:

In manufacturing you need people with drive, people who can fix problems. I have five Area Managers reporting to me. They are all fine, but they are not equally willing to stretch themselves. This means that I have to get more involved with some than others.

For the last year or so, I've been very busy planning for a new product line which is considered important for the future of the plant. Because of the attention this product line is receiving from above, I worked closely with the Area Manager responsible for the line. I realized this meant neglecting some of the other Area Managers to a certain extent, but it was a calculated risk. You've got to hope that they'll let you know if they need you. But some of them don't.

Last week, for instance, I had a big problem with a guy called Ed. Out of the blue, the quality department almost stopped one of Ed's lines because quality was too uneven. I hadn't seen it coming, but you can bet your life that from now on I'll give a lot more attention to Ed's lines.

BACKGROUND

The plant is the largest on a site comprising more than ten production facilities. It is part of a relatively successful profit centre, generally meeting the targets set by headquarters. The plant manufactures three major types of products, which are sold in two

Source: This case was written by Jean-Louis Barsoux, Research Fellow, under the supervision of Jean-François Mazoni, Assistant Professor of Accounting and Control, both at INSEAD. It is intended to be used as a basis for class discussion rather than to illustrate either effective or ineffective handling of an administrative situation. Although the case is based on real situations within a single company, the names have been changed and the company's activities disguised to preserve anonymity. Copyright © 1996 INSEAD, Fontainebleau, France.

major markets. The products are precision control devices that regulate electrical current (e.g., circuit breakers), pressure (e.g., pressure valves) or temperature (e.g., thermostats). The devices operate within fairly tight tolerances.

The products vary along several dimensions. One of the product lines involves a very large number of variations; it can only be produced on order, sometimes in batches of a single unit. The production process involves a large amount of skilled labour and the equipment used is fairly old. At the other extreme, another line involves a small number of models manufactured in large volumes on relatively modern equipment; the manufacturing process is very mechanised and is buffered by a small amount of finished goods inventory. The plant's strategy is to target growth in the latter (more recent) product line which, as a result, receives more engineering support than the older lines.

The plant is organised by production lines, each operated by a dedicated team. Manufacturing Supervisors oversee up to three production lines. They report to Area Managers who are responsible for meeting production, quality, and cost objectives for a product group. Lee Coker has five Area Managers reporting to him. Lee himself reports to T. C., the Plant Manager. Both of them have worked their way up through the plant and have, at one time or another managed most of the lines. The organisational chart for this plant is shown in Exhibit 1.

Ed is the newest of the five Area Managers. Lee Coker was very happy when he managed to secure Ed's transfer from another plant on the site in January of this year. Ed's training and solid experience as an engineering manager looked set to strengthen the team. He was put in charge of a group of lines that had proved relatively stable and profitable over the years—they were often used as a first assignment for new Supervisors. Lately, however, some of these lines had been experiencing minor difficulties and Ed was expected to manage their restructuring and revitalisation over time. Two Supervisors reported to him, including a recently hired college graduate.

■ EXHIBIT 1 ■
*Simplified Organization
Chart of the Plant*

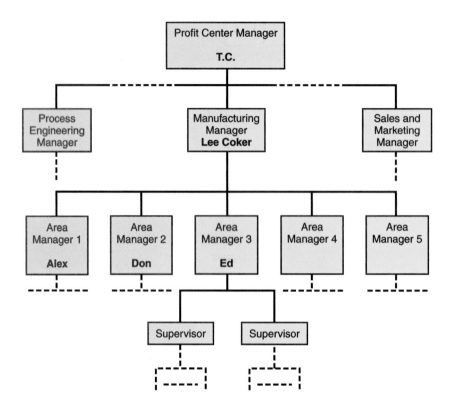

ED'S FIRST NINE MONTHS ON THE JOB

Ed recalls things going pretty well at the start. He immediately hit it off with two of the other Area Managers, Alex and Don. They were especially helpful in telling him what to expect from Lee and how to handle him. They agreed that Lee was the most creative manager they had ever worked for. They also agreed on a few basic dimensions of Lee's management style. First, they said, Lee tends to be more interested in discussing projects and programmes than just "numbers"; the plant had been first on the site to implement Just-in-Time in the late eighties. Lee was now asking Area Managers to focus on the development of self-managed work teams.

Aside from one or two key indicators such as cycle time, Alex and Don pointed out, Lee tends to follow quantitative measures of performance on an exception basis; he is more likely to focus on large, unfavourable variances. This was quite clear in the weekly staff meeting during which each Supervisor and Area Manager reviewed progress against a variety of monthly objectives; units that were on target spoke briefly, while units that might not reach their targets were invited to discuss the causes of their problems and the corrective mechanisms they had set in place.

Alex and Don also emphasised Lee's dislike for "bad surprises." "It's best not to surprise him, " Alex laughed. "The key is recognising the problem as soon as possible, communicating to him what the problem is and what you're doing about it, and giving him a conservative assessment of the problem's consequences, rather than being optimistic and further missing the target."

Alex and Don also reported noticing over the years that Lee tends to devote more attention to problems or variances reported by managers early in their job tenure and thus relatively inexperienced. In this case, Alex and Don added, Ed might escape Lee's normal focus on "rookies" because, over the coming months, Lee would probably be very busy with the new, high-volume line. This new line was receiving a lot of visibility from the top, so Lee would be keen on ensuring a smooth production ramp-up.

Ed quickly found that, as he had been told, Lee did not tend to get involved unless there was a problem or he was asked for help. When he did approach

Lee for advice, Ed often came away dissatisfied. As he explained to Don: "Sometimes you describe a problem to him and he fires off 50 answers, leaving you to choose the best 10 out of 50! He can also be somewhat out-of-date in terms of how the line runs and how the process works."

In addition, Ed himself thought it best not to ask too many questions. His experience in other plants had taught him that, "If you have a question about the way something is working, that means that you have some potential problem coming up on your lines, that you don't have the necessary experience or you haven't done a very good job at researching. Asking questions shows that you don't know everything, and then the boss might think 'if he doesn't know this, maybe he doesn't know something else too!'"

No major problem occurred over Ed's first nine months on the job. Interactions between Ed and Lee were fairly limited and the two developed a courteous, if not warm, relationship.

THE NEXT THREE MONTHS

Following Lee's return from his management development programme, exchanges between Ed and Lee had become more strained. Puzzled, Ed confided to Don:

Of late, he's started asking a lot more questions, being a lot more pressing. When he comes to my area, he often checks up on routine matters and he rarely bothers to comment on improvements. What irritates me the most is that he sometimes asks me questions I'm sure he already knows the answers to—I feel like he's testing me, not just keeping informed.

Ed explained how Lee had started asking him to explain even minor variances and seemed increasingly reluctant to give him the benefit of the doubt. For that reason, Ed did not like to meet with Lee without first holding a meeting with his own subordinates who could brief him on reasons for unfavourable results. Ed realized that he had grown uncomfortable discussing with Lee anything that required more than a quick answer. Partly, it was because he didn't want to expose himself to more negative feedback than was necessary. But he also sensed that Lee was either too busy or not very keen to have an open discussion with him.

After one particularly difficult team meeting, Alex and Don came round to Ed's office to say that they thought Lee had been unfair to Ed in the meeting and to offer him some advice. Ed complained:

I just don't seem to have any freedom anymore. Whenever there's a hiccup, he wants to know what caused it and then he doesn't give me a chance to solve the problem on my own. He'll "suggest" a particular course of action—often it's what I would have done anyhow—and then come back later in the day to see how things are going . . . or maybe it's to check on us!

Don sympathised with Ed:

He does the same thing to me! The communication is pretty much one way, from him to me almost like "this is the way you do it because I'm the boss and you're my subordinate." You say: "Yes, but Lee, wouldn't it be better to do it this way?" But he always seems too busy to have any sort of open discussion about it. Even if he's listening, you don't get the impression that he is—like he'll start doing something else while you're talking to him.

Ed nodded as Don continued:

And he regularly sends me questions or comments written over performance reports. Then I have to go to his office and explain why things happened and what we are doing about them. Then, when he finds my answers unsatisfactory, which is not unusual, I have to do more research on the issue. Once I've presented all the facts and finished answering all his questions, he is capable of understanding that the variance wasn't our fault, but it can take a while to gather all these facts!

Ed was relieved that he wasn't the only one who sometimes found Lee difficult. Don's openness made it easier for Ed to reveal his own frustrations and the two of them compared anecdotes about Lee. They confessed that this constant struggle was taking its toll on them. As Don put it:

You end up simply going through the motions. And you stop bringing up new ideas because you know he'll try to change them to something which is closer to his own view. Sure, you can fight him for three months, but in the end it won't even resemble your idea anymore, so what's the point?

"Yes," agreed Ed, "plus it would be nice, once in a while, to get some praise from him to help us keep up our level of effort!"

Alex joined in the conversation:

It's funny, I listen to you guys talk about Lee, and you'd think we have completely different bosses! He's just not like that with me. I mean, I hardly ever get a query from him on a variance or a problem. Most of our exchanges are routine ones, mandated by the reporting systems; the rest of the time he leaves me alone.

And I certainly don't have any qualms about going to see him when I disagree. Of course, he won't always agree with me but he does listen, and he allows me to vent, which I do often! I would even say that he's often quite helpful when we discuss a problem I face.

Don laughed and pointed out that Alex had not always sung that tune. Alex thought for a minute and smiled:

That's true! We did go through a rough period a couple of years back. For some time he followed up quite closely on us whenever we had a problem. He would set up a daily eight o'clock meeting to review the prior day's results, and my supervisors and I would have to defend the actions we'd taken and those we wanted to take.

I guess that, over the last two years, we have managed to convince him that we are a good bunch of people and that when there is a problem, it's generally not our fault. The success we have had implementing Just-in-Time has probably helped; we followed a different route than the one he believed in, but our approach has worked out well for our area and our type of products. So you see, Ed, you've got to hang in there!

Encouraged by Alex's pep talk, Ed continued doing his job to the best of his abilities, trying to manage his area with a minimum of help from Lee. As Ed saw it, "If there's no trouble, why wave the flag?"

LEE'S PRIORITIES

In June (i.e., about six months after Ed joined the group), Lee had met with his boss, T. C., to discuss the forthcoming mid-year performance evaluations. "I guess there is only one Area Manager that I would put in the excellent category," explained Lee, "and that's Alex. At the other end of the scale, there's Don whose performance is, let's say, adequate. He's not great, but he's not awful either. He does an okay job. The others are somewhere in between, average performers."

"What about the new guy, Ed?" asked T. C.

"It's too early to tell for sure, but he looks fine. He's not a superstar, but he's solid," answered Lee.

"Tell me," continued T. C., "what's the basis for distinguishing between, say, Alex and Don?"

With a bit of prompting, Lee was able to articulate his views on the differences between outstanding performers and adequate performers:

In manufacturing, outstanding performers know how to get things done. What they don't know, they go and find out. They're self-starters, they drive to excellence. Adequate performers tend to accept that "things happen" rather than challenging them. There's also a difference in terms of accountability; I find that lower performers often spend more time trying to escape accountability—trying to explain variances away or resisting stretch targets—than they actually spend trying to achieve the targets! And the last thing is that lower performers generally don't ask for help before it's too late. They allow themselves to get buried. A high performer will ask you for help if they need it.

"And how does that affect the way you manage them?" asked T. C.

Lee thought for a while, then explained:

Well, for instance, I would communicate with Alex on a daily basis: When I see him, I tend to ask him a general question like, "How are things going?" I'm just inviting him to communicate with me. But with Don, say, I tend to ask more specific, detailed questions, like, "How are things going with this?" or "What's happening with a, with b, with c, with d? Are you satisfied that enough is being done about a, b, c, or d? Do you need any help with a, b, c, or d, any more help, and what is that help?" to try and encourage Don to think on his own.

I also monitor Don's decisions and actions—I don't know if you'd say on an ongoing basis, but frequently—because he is not a self-driver, and so he doesn't set stretch targets. And depending on how serious the situation is or how great a variance it is, I may look later on the same day to make sure that he's on track with the corrective action we identified.

"In contrast," Lee added, "I would give Alex, say, a greater opportunity to succeed on his own, without as much monitoring. I wouldn't jump in as quickly. Overall, I would invite Alex to come and get me involved if he needs help instead of imposing myself. I think that if you have a good performer, you need to give that person a chance to succeed on their own."

With a smile, Lee continued:

Also, in terms of praise, there's a little trick I actually picked up from you which I tend to use with the higher performers. Sometimes, I'll ask Alex, in particular, a question about something that I know has already been solved and where he played a critical role. So I'll let him tell me all about it and then I'll give him a positive response, recognition, and say "Gee, you handled that well."

T. C. was impressed by Lee's lucidity regarding his own management style. He also remembered that during last year's performance appraisal meeting, Lee had agreed to try to improve his coaching skills. T. C. decided to take advantage of this discussion to ask Lee to assess his own progress.

Lee confessed that his progress along that dimension had probably been slower than anticipated, largely because of the pressures on his time with the new line. Lee realised that he still had a tendency to be fairly directive, particularly with the Area Managers he did not view as excellent, and that he was not quite as patient when trying to coach these individuals. He acknowledged that he always started the conversation with good intentions, but sometimes resorted to "spoon-feeding the person just a little bit because they were not coming up with the idea." He explained:

The question is, if I had spent another five or another fifteen minutes asking questions, rather than telling the person what I wanted, would the person have got it? I hope so, but I don't know for sure. I have other problems to attend to. It's the time factor; that's no excuse, but it's a fact of life. I am trying to get around to more of a coaching mode and cut down on comments that may stifle their creativity, but I'm involved in so many things—and I guess that, to some extent, I choose to be involved in so many things—that I don't always have the time. But I'm still working on it.

AS ED BEGINS HIS SECOND YEAR ON THE JOB . . . .

Lee's increased contact with Ed proved frustrating. He was devoting more and more time to Ed's lines but Ed did not seem to be responding. On the contrary, Ed seemed increasingly defensive and he certainly wasn't any more forthcoming about problems on the line—if anything, less so. While troubled by Ed's failure to improve, Lee tried to stay upbeat in their conversations. He tried to present things in a "positive light," realising that expressing a lack of confidence in Ed might seriously undermine Ed's motivation.

Ed was also trying to remain upbeat. He kept reminding himself of Alex's encouragement, but he could also see himself become increasingly defensive and stressed. He had more and more difficulty cheering himself up for work in the morning. Fortunately, Don was there to listen when Ed needed to talk.

In early March, Lee and T. C. were reviewing the plant's first-quarter production and sales forecasts when the Quality Manager walked into Lee's office and said: "We're going to have to close down two of Ed's lines; the quality is just too uneven and we can't afford to take any chances with customers. I think you guys should do something!"

T. C. turned to Lee. These two lines represented 15% of the plant's income stream.

EPILOGUE

Lee had worked hard to establish his reputation as an effective and achievement-oriented manager. The performance problem with Ed, together with the effect it was having on team spirit, was seriously jeopardising all that effort. A number of questions preyed on Lee's mind. How could it have come to this? Was Ed a lost cause from the start, or was Lee partly to blame? What signals did he miss? Should he just give up on Ed or could something still be done to retrieve the situation? Most importantly perhaps, how could he avoid a recurrence of this kind of situation in the future?

STEP 1: Read the case.

STEP 2: Prepare the case for class discussion.

STEP 3: Answer the following questions, individually, in small groups, or with the class as a whole, as directed by your instructor.

DESCRIPTION

1. How does Lee define his job and his management style?
2. Describe the relationship between Lee and Ed.
3. How well does Lee work with the Area Managers?

DIAGNOSIS

4. How effective was communication between Lee and Ed?
5. Was Lee an effective leader?
6. What types and levels of conflict existed in this situation?

PRESCRIPTION

7. How could the situation have been improved?

ACTION

8. What should Lee do now?
9. What should the Area Managers do now?

STEP 4: Discussion. In small groups, with the entire class, or in written form, share your answers to the preceding questions. Then answer the following questions:

1. What symptoms suggest that a problem exists?
2. What problems exist in the case?
3. What theories and concepts help explain the problems?
4. How can the problems be corrected?
5. Are these actions likely to be effective?

Pak Somad

Somad sighed and rubbed his eyes as he put down the phone. He had a headache and was tired this morning as he sat in his office in Jakarta. He pondered the conversation he had just had with Paul MacDonald, general manager of P.T.[1] Bara Mulya (PTBM). Somad had requested a meeting with MacDonald in Jakarta at the end of the week, but had said little about the purpose of the visit. Somad had purposely been elusive, because he needed time to formulate what he wanted to say. Somad often thought carefully before acting or speaking, because he was never quite sure how the expatriates would interpret his actions or comments. Despite the fact that he had worked with many foreigners during his twenty years in the mining industry, he was concerned that he might be misunderstood. Nevertheless, he was often at ease with them and was admired within his organization for dealing effectively with foreigners. Indeed, he always enjoyed the interaction he had with non-Indonesians and usually looked forward with anticipation to the bimonthly contractor meetings.

He was not enthusiastic, however, about the next bimonthly meeting. He had been informed that delayed contractor reports were a significant, chronic problem that had never been addressed. He knew that he had to discuss and resolve this unpleasant topic with the contractors. This issue was the only nettle in an otherwise smooth and amicable relationship between Somad's agency, Divisi Kontrak Kerjasama Batubara (KKB), and the eleven coal contractors regulated by KKB's parent organization, PTBA.

THE INDONESIAN COAL INDUSTRY

Indonesia, the largest archipelago in the world, consisting of over 13,500 islands, was a rapidly developing country in a rapidly developing part of the world. Plentiful in natural resources, the Indonesian government had relied heavily on earnings from oil and, more recently, from natural-gas production. With the onslaught of the oil crisis in the 1970s, and the continued depletion of oil reserves, development of alternative energy sources became a priority for Indonesia.

The government targeted coal as an alternative energy source to help fuel industrial development. The high economic growth rates and the subsequent 15 percent per annum growth in demand for electrical-power generation required the development of the coal industry.[2] The Indonesian government at that moment operated two large coal mining companies in West Sumatra (Ombilin) and South Sumatra (Bukit Asam).

In 1978, as part of their efforts to expand the coal industry, the Indonesian government issued limited international tenders for the exploration and development of coal mines in Kalimantan and Sumatra (Exhibit 1). In 1981, a presidential decree established the first three contractual arrangements between foreign companies and P.T. Perum Tambang Batubara (prior to its merger with Bukit Asam, this government agency had controlled coal mining in Indonesia).

In October 1990, in order to enhance the efficiency and productivity of these mines, the two state-owned coal companies were merged into one venture, P.T. Tambang Bukit Asam (PTBA). PTBA was owned by the Indonesian government and received policy guidance from the Ministry of Mines and Energy.

COAL AGREEMENTS

Under the Coal Agreements between each contractor and PTBA, the contractors were required to contribute coal payments to PTBA. The contractors were also liable for corporate taxes of 35 percent for the first five years and 45 percent for any subsequent years. In addition, the contractors were subject to mining-safety and environmental regulations. Finally, the agreements specified that contractors were required to submit to PTBA monthly and quarterly reports and an Annual Work Programme and Budget (Exhibit 2). Besides these specific requirements, the contracts stated: "PTBA shall have and be responsible for the management of coal operations."

---

[1]P.T. stands for Perusahaan Trbatas, the Indonesian equivalent of Company Limited.

Source: This case was prepared by Per Froyen, Edward Gibson, Balbina Hwang, and Patricia Severynse, MBA '93, under the supervision of Reid Whitlock, Associate Professor. Copyright © 1993 by the University of Virginia Darden School Foundation, Charlottesville, VA. All rights reserved.

[2]For a further discussion of the Indonesian government's plans for the development of the domestic coal mining industry, refer to "The Indonesian Coal Mining Industry," copyright © 1993 by the University of Virginia Darden School Foundation. All rights reserved.

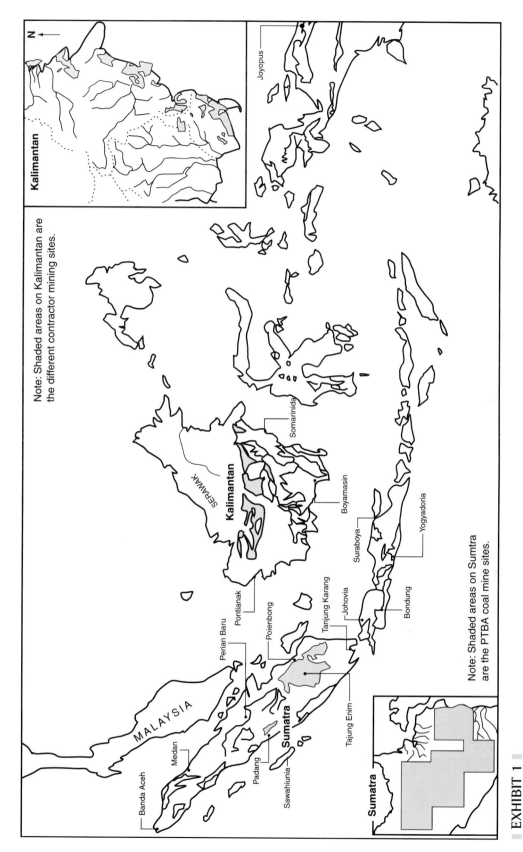

■ **EXHIBIT 1** ■
Coal Resource Map of Indonesia

GROUP (1)	TYPE AND DESCRIPTION OF MACHINERIES, EQUIPMENT (2)	CUMULATIVE 199.				ADDITIONAL QTY (7)	REQUIRED IN 199.					
		QUANTITY		PURCHASE PRICE			QUANTITY		PURCHASE PRICE			
									DOMESTIC		IMPORT	
		C & SC (3)	USE (4)	PLANT (5)	SPARES (6)		DOMESTIC (8)	IMPORT (9)	PLANT (10)	SPARES (11)	PLANT (12)	SPARES (13)
A	HEAVY EQUIPMENT											
B	LAND TRANSPORT											
C	WATER TRANSPORT											
E	COMMUNICATION											
F	LAND SURVEY & RECONNAISSANCE											
G	DRILLING EQUIPMENT											
H	SAMPLING, LABORATORY, UPGRADING											
I	REPAIR AND MAINTENANCE											
J	BUILDING MATERIAL											
K	UTILITIES, FURNITURE, AND APPLIANCES											
L	CONSUMABLE FUEL, OIL, AND GAS											
M	FOODSTUFF											
N	MISCELLANEOUS											
O	MEDICAL, HEALTH, HYGIENE											
P	RECREATION FACILITIES											
Q	POWER STATION AND HYDROPOWER PLANT											
R	PROCESSING PLANT											
T	MARINE EQUIPMENT AND NAVIGATION AIDS											

	DOMESTIC	IMPORT	TOTAL
PLANT			
SPARE			

EXHIBIT 2

Sample Form from Annual Work Programme and Budget

	AI	UI	KPC	KJA	BERAU	ADARO	AIC	CUMO	MHU	TH	IM
SUMMARY											
I. INTRODUCTION											
1. STAGE OF ACTIVITIES											
2. PROBLEMS AND PROGRESS OF THE PREVIOUS YEAR											
3. PROJECTION OF COMMENCING YEAR											
4. OBJECTIVES											
II. SUMMARY OF WORK PROGRESS PREVIOUS YEAR											
III. GENERAL SURVEY AND EXPLORATION											
1. STATUS (AREA TIME)											
2. ACTIVITIES											
a. MAPPING											
b. GEOPHYSICAL SURVEY											
c. DRILLING AND TEST PITTING PROGRAMME											
d. LAND ACQUISITION											
3. TESTING											
a. COAL ANALYSIS											
b. GEOTECHNICAL AND HYDROGEOLOGICAL TEST											
IV. FEASIBILITY STUDY AND ENVIRONMENTAL IMPACT ANALYSIS											
1. REGION											
2. STATUS											
V. CONSTRUCTION											
1. PRE CONSTRUCTION											
2. INFRASTRUCTURE											
3. OTHERS											
VI. MINING OPERATION											
1. OVERBURDEN REMOVAL (PLANNING, LOCATION, VOLUME)											
2. COAL MINING (LOCATION, PRODUCTION, STRIP RATIO)											
3. COAL PREPARATION (PRODUCTION, CAPACITY)											
a. SIZING											
b. WASHING											
c. MEDIA AND REAGENTS											
4. CONSTRUCTION (INFRASTRUCTURE, OTHERS)											
VII. STOCKPILE AND SHIPMENT											
1. STOCKPILE (LOCATION AND CAPACITY)											
2. SHIPMENT (LOCATION, TYPE, CAPACITY, PROGRAMME)											
VIII. MANPOWER AND TRAINING											
1. NUMBER AND STATUS OF MANPOWER											
2. TRAINING PROGRAMME											
IX. ENVIRONMENT											
1. PROGRAMME											
a. RECLAMATION											
b. MONITORING											
2. COMMUNITY DEVELOPMENT											
X. SAFETY											
1. SUMMARY OF THE PREVIOUS YEAR ACCIDENTS, ETC.											
2. PROGRAMME											

EXHIBIT 2 *(continued)*

Evaluation of Work Programme and Budget

	AI	UI	KPC	KJA	BERAU	ADARO	AIC	CUMO	MHU	TH	IM
XI. EQUIPMENT AND SPARE PARTS											
1. EQUIPMENT LIST AND UTILIZATION											
2. SPARE PARTS MANAGEMENT											
XII. MARKETING											
1. CONSUMEN											
2. TONNAGE											
3. PRICE											
XIII. FINANCIAL											
1. EXPENDITURE											
2. SALES											
3. PROJECTED PROFIT											
4. BALANCE SHEET											
5. INCOME STATEMENT											
6. ESTIMATE TAXES											
XII. MISCELLANEOUS											
1. AGREEMENT AREAS											
2. OTHERS											
APPENDICES											
1. COMPANY ACTIVITIES											
2. OFFER OF SALES TO INDONESIAN PARTICIPANTS											
3. EQUIPMENT MASTER LIST (TYPE, CAP, NUMBER)											
4. MAPS											
a. AGREEMENT AREA											
b. MINING ACTIVITIES (EXPLORATION, CONSTRUCTION, MINING OPERATION TRANSPORTATION)											
c. RECLAMATION AREAS											

EXHIBIT 2 *(continued)*
Evaluation of Work Programme and Budget

PTBA'S ORGANIZATION

In addition to operating a state-owned coal mine, PTBA was in charge of administering Indonesia's coal industry. The KKB division within PTBA supervised contractors. As head of KKB, Somad consulted with, and reported directly to, Dr. Ambyo Manjungwidjaya, the president director of PTBA (Exhibit 3). They had a solid relationship, dating back to Somad's days as a student in Dr. Ambyo's classes at the Bandung Institute of Technology.

Dr. Ambyo's[3] background was highly academic, as he had received his Ph.D. in mining engineering in the United States. Although he was a quiet and reserved man, he commanded a great deal of respect within the Ministry of Mines and Energy and was well known throughout the Indonesian mining industry. His approach to the management of PTBA was scientific and analytical.

By contrast, Somad represented a new breed of Indonesian managers: his personality and leadership style were both dynamic and engaging. Like Dr. Ambyo, Somad commanded respect within the coal mining industry, as much for his efficiency in "getting things done" as for his reliability and cooperativeness.

KKB probably had the most direct interaction with the contractors of any PTBA agency. Thus, Somad's visibility was high within the contractor community; indeed, he served as the primary PTBA contact for contractors.

[3]The use of "Dr." denotes Ambyo's level of education as well as the respect that was shown to him in Indonesian society. It is customary in Indonesia to attach titles to first names.

EXHIBIT 3

P. T. Tambang Baturbara
Bukit Asam (PTBA)

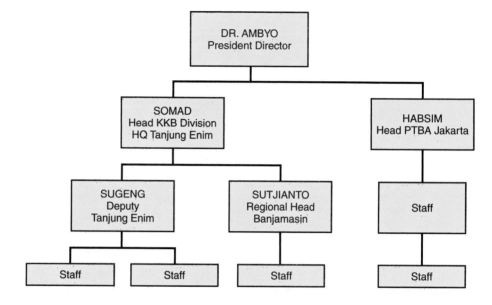

One major hindrance in the development of smooth contractor/PTBA relationships was the geographical locations of the various entities. Ten of the contractor mine sites were located in remote areas of the eastern and southern part of the island of Kalimantan, and one mine was on the island of Sumatra (Exhibit 4). Although all operations were overseen at the mine sites, most contractors had a representative or head office in Jakarta, the capital city and business center of Indonesia. Travel from Jakarta to the mine sites was arduous and time consuming. Communication was difficult; many contractors had established their own systems of telecommunication, such as radio- and satellite-relayed faxes or other special transmission lines, in order to facilitate communication.

Although KKB continued to maintain a licensing office in Jakarta, P. T. Perum Tambang Batubara's headquarters were moved to the site of the Bukit Asam mines in Tanjung Enim after the merger with PTBA. Tanjung Enim was a well-established and developed mining compound similar to a military base. It was remotely located on the island of Sumatra. The compound itself was quite comfortable, but its inaccessible location was a significant drawback. In order to travel from Tanjung Enim to Jakarta, or any of the other major islands, one had to first travel for over four hours to the nearest airport at Palembang by motor vehicle over rugged roads. Then, if the domestic flights were not delayed, one traveled by air for up to two hours to either Jakarta or Kalimantan (where the contractor mines were located).

Although Dr. Ambyo and Somad's official headquarters were in Tanjung Enim, they spent a great deal of time in Jakarta. Somad also traveled frequently to Kalimantan to visit the regional KKB office in Banjarmasin and to the mine sites to meet the contractors. Somad spent his remaining time visiting his family in Bandung, several hours away from Jakarta by train. Many of the KKB staff regularly commuted between Tanjung Enim and Jakarta as well. Because of the varied and distant locations, coordination and communication among the PTBA agencies, contractors, mine sites, and regional offices were hectic and problematic.

BIMONTHLY CONTRACTOR MEETINGS

In an effort to alleviate some of the communication problems, Somad had started the bimonthly contractor meetings, which brought together the general managers or managing directors of each of the eleven contractors. The meetings rotated among the mine sites and usually took place over the weekend. The atmosphere at these meetings was congenial, relaxed, and clubby. The contractors all knew one another and, despite competition in the marketing end of their businesses, generally had cooperative relationships. All were inclined to share experiences and "war stories" with their counterparts, partly because most

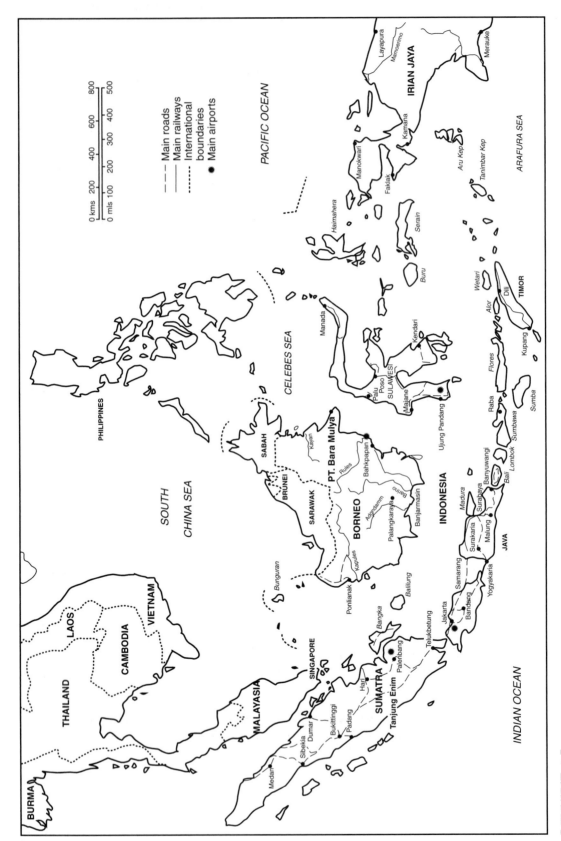

EXHIBIT 4

368

of the group were expatriates. Many had been present from the very birth of the coal industry in Indonesia. They all appreciated the chance to get together, socialize, and visit each other's operations.

Somad himself was quite pleased with the outcome of these meetings because, in addition to the exchange of information and camaraderie, the meetings enhanced his ability to communicate with each individual contractor. He knew that he had a captive audience to whom he could impart any new developments at PTBA.

CURRENT SITUATION

Somad pondered his problem of late reporting. He was exhausted because he had traveled late at night from Tanjung Enim to Jakarta the previous evening. He had arrived in the office early that morning to discover a note from Dr. Ambyo requesting a meeting for later that afternoon. Somad knew that Dr. Ambyo wanted to be debriefed regarding the late reporting problem that Somad was supposed to have resolved just a few days ago at the last contractor meeting. Somad was unsure, however, if he had anything to report.

At the last meeting, Somad had brought attention to the problem by showing an overhead listing the contractors and their report-submission dates. He knew that, in this subtle way, those contractors who were late would "lose face" in front of their peers. He had tried to soften the embarrassment by making a joke; the expatriates, in particular, seemed to be put at ease by his sense of humor and overall congeniality.

Paul MacDonald of PTBM was one of those he had singled out. There had been much laughter and joking among the contractors about the procrastinators "being in trouble now," but Somad was uncertain if he had made his point. Perhaps they had all dismissed it as unimportant: Somad had certainly received that impression from the casual bantering that occurred after his presentation. Indeed, MacDonald had seemed genuinely surprised and even irritated that Somad had brought attention to the late reports. Somad had arranged a meeting with MacDonald later in the week in Jakarta to discuss this issue.

Somad was uncertain if he was reading too much into MacDonald's reaction, but he knew from experience that expatriates, especially Western ones, were straightforward about expressing their emotions by Indonesian standards. Somad sighed. That was one of the main differences between the management styles of Indonesians and foreigners, he had discovered: an even tone of voice and modest action were extremely important in Indonesia, even if one was displeased. Somad sometimes felt inhibited by this indirect style, but, being Indonesian, he never allowed his frustrations to show. That was what made him an effective manager and a respected leader among both Indonesians and expatriates.

Now Somad wondered whether his decision to "embarrass" late reporters had been the best way to point out the problem. Somad was at a complete loss as to why the contractors did not seem to think that the timeliness of reports was extremely important. The report requirement was clearly outlined in the contracts (certainly little else was! Somad muttered to himself) and was an obligation that the contractors had been aware of from the very beginning of their agreements. Somad had to admit that formatting was an issue for the contractors. Currently, there was no universal format for the contractors to follow, so that compiling the reports was difficult for the contractors, and analyzing the data was a challenge for Somad's staff. He and his staff had been working for over a year to put together a new and more efficient format for the reports, but the process was an arduous one in the highly bureaucratic environment of PTBA.

The contractors had to recognize that, as difficult and tedious as the reports were to prepare, they were of the utmost importance to PTBA. Dr. Ambyo had made clear to Somad the urgency of these reports. Apparently, Dr. Ambyo was receiving pressure from the Minister of Mines and Energy (to whom Dr. Ambyo reported) about the reports. Dr. Ambyo had to submit regular reports to the Ministry regarding the progress of the coal industry in Indonesia, and the contractors' figures were critical to the planning and development of the national energy policy.

I wonder if there is another reason why the reports are late, Somad mused. Not naturally a suspicious person, he nevertheless wondered if the contractors were delaying the reports on purpose. Perhaps the contractors were worried about the sensitive nature of some of the required information? He knew that marketing issues were especially sensitive in the coal industry and pricing was guarded with utmost secrecy. PTBA required some pricing information, but surely the contractors trusted PTBA not to leak that information or use it in a dishonorable way. Perhaps he should consider allowing a sealed envelope for the sensitive information, if those were the concerns of the contractors.

At this moment, Somad's thoughts were interrupted by a knock. Pat Sugeng,[4] Somad's deputy from KKB's headquarters in Tanjung Enim, was standing at Somad's open door. Pak Sugeng had made the tiring trip from Sumatra with Somad the night before.

"Come in, Pak Sugeng," Somad gestured to a chair. "I see you have rested after our trip last night. I wanted to speak with you regarding this reporting problem with the contractors. You have been in charge of compiling the data that comes in from the contractors for some years now. Tell me, how do you suppose we can resolve this problem of tardiness?"

"Well, Pak Somad, I'm not certain quite what you mean. It is my impression that several of the contractors have indeed been submitting tardy reports on occasion. As you know, however, it takes us such a long time to analyze the data that even if all the reports were in on time, we probably would not be able to compile it all before the deadline. We have been trying our best but you know better than anyone that our division is understaffed. In any case, we are always able to send the information along to Jakarta within a week or so of the deadline and there has never been much of a fuss."

"Pak Sugeng, this is all very surprising to me. Of course I know that we are understaffed, but I always thought that surely you understood the importance of these reports to PTBA. Are you saying that the delays have been internal?"

"No, no. Of course we try our best to get the reports in on time. We have never before heard from anyone in Jakarta, however, that late reports were a problem. They always seemed to have given us a few days' grace period, so we have never, in turn, pressured the contractors."

"So what actions have you taken with the contractors, then?" Somad was surprised at this news. It appeared that even his own staff did not recognize the importance of the timeliness of these reports.

"Actions? No specific actions. We try to call those who are late, and if it's difficult to get through, then we ask the regional KKB office in Banjarmasin to intervene. That seems to have always worked in the past. No further action seemed necessary."

Somad was stunned. Why hadn't his staff taken any prior action? He supposed he himself was partly

to blame because he had been unaware of his staff's responses to late reports. Now he was really at a loss as to what he should do to correct this problem; its roots seemed to be deeper than he had thought. "I need to discuss this with Pak Habsim," Somad thought to himself. "Perhaps he can shed some light on this situation."

"Thank you for your time, Pak Sugeng. I will meet with you again later to go over the budget. In the meantime, could you ask Pak Habsim if he could see me for a moment?"

"Certainly, Pak Somad," said Pak Sugeng as he exited Somad's office.

A few moments later, Pak Habsim appeared at Somad's door. Habsim was one of the PTBA officers stationed permanently in the Jakarta office. This office handled mostly licensing affairs and thus was rather close to the Ministry of Mines and Energy and other central government agencies. After some minor pleasantries, Somad arranged to meet Habsim for lunch to discuss reporting matters further.

LUNCH WITH PAK HABSIM

Several hours later, Habsim and Somad walked out of the PTBA office building and across the office plaza to the "Tex-Mex" restaurant. After settling down and ordering, they exchanged pleasantries until the main course arrived. Only then did Somad broach the subject of contractor relationships.

"Pak Habsim, I have a problem I would like to share with you, and perhaps you may even be able to help me resolve it. As you know from our last meeting with Dr. Ambyo, we have a problem of late reports from the contractors. I'm not certain how it should be solved, because I'm not sure if either the contractors or my own KKB staff recognize the importance of these reports."

"Really, Pak Somad, there is only one way to deal with it. The contractors must be made to understand that we at PTBA are technically the managers of their operations. We should exert our control over them. I think many of them have become too complacent and do not understand the nature of our relationship. They think that simply by giving us 13.5 percent of their coal production, we will be happy with that. But I believe that it is imperative to make them understand that we are very interested in what they do and how they do it. As these contractors start to increase their annual productions, our interests

---

[4]*Pak*, short for *Bapak*, is the Indonesian equivalent of "Mr." Pak is traditionally used with Indonesian first names.

will be in far more than just the 13.5 percent share. We are talking about the future of our coal industry for Indonesia! The contractors' actions will have a critical impact on what we do at the Ministry."

Habsim's voice softened a bit as he added, "I think your difficult challenge is to somehow make these contractors comply with the deadlines, as difficult as that may be. If they cannot follow simple regulations such as these, is it not the beginning of a much greater problem?"

Now Somad was even more confused. He knew that Habsim's last remark was meant to be sympathetic. It was simply not the Indonesian way, however, to demand that the reports be in on time, even though compliance was explicitly stated in the contracts. Somad was fearful of damaging the congenial personal relationships he had developed with the contractors. He knew that he had their respect, and he allowed himself a bit of immodesty by acknowledging that the mining community, especially the expatriates, held him in high regard.

Nevertheless, was he being negligent in his duties as division head if he failed to get the results that were expected of him? Frankly, he was tired of hearing about the reporting problem from Dr. Ambyo. But what was the best way to go about it?

Somad was unsettled by Habsim's comments, which seemed to imply that PTBA should vigorously control the contractors. Strict government control would have vast implications for the future of Indonesia's coal industry, especially since seventeen new contractors were expected to enter into agreements with PTBA in the next four months. Any problems Somad had with overworked staff would only be exacerbated. And the traveling back and forth would reach intolerable proportions, he was certain.

Somad did not fully agree that PTBA should rigorously control the current eleven contractors. He knew it would damage the good working relationships he and his staff had cultivated with the contractors.

As he ordered dessert, Somad wondered what to do next. What approach should he take during the meeting with Paul MacDonald? What was the most

effective way for him to resolve this reporting issue once and for all? What would he say to Dr. Ambyo at their upcoming meeting?

STEP 1: Read the case.

STEP 2: Prepare the case for class discussion.

STEP 3: Answer the following questions, individually, in small groups, or with the class as a whole, as directed by your instructor.

DESCRIPTION

1. How did Somad communicate with the contractors?

2. Why had Somad's staff done nothing about the late reports?

3. Why did Somad decide to embarrass the late contractors?

DIAGNOSIS

4. Did two-way communication occur?

5. What barriers to effective communication existed?

6. How effective were perception and attribution in the case?

7. What impact did cultural differences have on perception, attribution, and communication?

PRESCRIPTION

8. How can Somad communicate more effectively?

STEP 4: Discussion. In small groups, with the entire class, or in written form, share your answers to the preceding questions. Then answer the following questions:

1. What symptoms suggest that a problem exists?

2. What problems exist in the case?

3. What theories and concepts help explain the problems?

4. How can the problems be corrected?

5. Are these actions likely to be effective?

Chapter 11

Building an Organizational Culture

Learning Objectives

After completing Chapter 11, you will be able to

1. Define organizational culture.
2. Identify types of culture.
3. Describe the dimensions of a culture.
4. Outline the functions of a culture.
5. Specify ways of determining culture.
6. Offer an approach to creating a culture.
7. Comment about ways to sustain a culture using organizational socialization strategies.
8. Discuss ways to change a culture.
9. Highlight the issues related to developing and sustaining a culture in the dot-com, global workplace.

A Manager's Preview

Describe . . . Diagnose . . . Prescribe . . . Act

- Define a culture that would create a competitive advantage for your organization.
- Choose the best type of culture for your organization's goals.
- Create an organizational culture in a new company, division, department, or team.
- Sustain an organization's culture to accomplish corporate goals.
- Change the culture in your organization.

The Corporate Culture in an E-Business Start-Up

*I*carian, a three-year-old start-up in the Silicon Valley, typifies the new breed of e-commerce businesses that have changed the face of industrial America. The company provides online software that helps companies hire and manage their employees. Located in Sunnyvale, California, Icarian has created an extremely informal environment that reflects a friendly culture. The office is filled with roller-hockey gear and balloons; a foosball game happens in the lunchroom; many employees bring their dogs to work. Although the company operates in extremely rapid Internet time, its executives don't believe that a pressure-cooker environment helps the company operate effectively. Rather, the casual culture allows employees to focus on the challenging tasks they face in the pre-initial public offering stage of business.

"Icarian's philosophy is simple: grow, share, and celebrate. People are encouraged to rise in the ranks. . . . In gratitude for hard work, the company hands each employee 50 'Icarian bucks' each month to be spent on gestures such as a massage for a colleague. When the spirit so moves, employees move with it. Somebody pops in a music CD and everybody gets up to dance."[1]

Many companies create a culture that gives them a competitive advantage. They may focus on customer service, emphasize employee involvement, or incorporate technological innovation in their product development or service delivery. They may encourage people to be playful, as at Icarian, or more formal and bureaucratic. In this chapter, we first explore the nature, types, and functions of organizational culture. Then we examine ways of determining culture. Next we investigate how to create, sustain, or change a culture. We conclude with some observations about organizational culture in the dot-com, global workplace.

▌WHAT IS ORGANIZATIONAL CULTURE?

An organization's *culture* describes the part of its internal environment that incorporates a set of assumptions, beliefs, and values that organizational members share and use to guide their functioning.[2] Culture refers to the shared meanings or interpretations that are largely tacit and unique to group or organizational members, and that focus their actions.[3] United Services Automobile Associations (USAA), a large San Antonio–based insurer and financial services provider, has a corporate culture that serves its employees so they can better serve the company's customers. USAA's campus has jogging paths, softball fields, and on-site medical clinics. USAA also provides significant training for its employees; for example, its information technology staff receives eight days of classroom training each year and can attend Twilight University, which offers featured speakers, Tech Days during which the company's vendors offer product demonstrations, and T&T Transitions to New Technology seminar series.[4]

Culture also acts as a tool for achieving organizational goals and helping companies adapt to challenging external forces.[5] For example, Kerry Foods decided to build its delivery van drivers into a sales team as a way of meeting changing environmental conditions. After assessing the culture using a staff survey, the company instituted improvement programs for the entire direct sales division of 500 employees. The salespeople participated in one-on-one meetings and training programs, and the company also modified the incentive program to focus on supporting the new team culture.[6]

Companies such as these believe that their culture gives them a competitive advantage. It also symbolizes meanings and values that guide employees' behavior and helps them integrate diverse internal components. Icarian's culture, for example, creates an environment that supports high-energy and high-level performance by employees. However, because firms in the same industry often have similar cultures, the competitive advantage of corporate culture runs the risk of being overstated.[7]

The culture can affect the way individuals make sense of events, even influencing their schemas for organizing and retaining information (see Chapter 2).[8] At Icarian, for example, the culture focuses on respecting individuals' personalities and outside interests. The company gives one of its employees, a shot-putter who is aiming for the U.S. Olympic Team, time off for training.[9]

Strong, strategically appropriate, and adaptive organizational cultures have a positive effect on an organization's long-term economic performance.[10] In an adaptive culture, people can comfortably handle uncertainty, ambiguity, and change. To create such a culture, organizations must encourage, communicate, and leverage individual learning through the sharing of successes and failures.[11] Procter & Gamble, for example, is instituting a major cultural revolution that replaces an attitude of secrecy and strict discipline with a new open attitude, with the hope of improving the bottom line. The company has eliminated the practice of rewriting memos 20 times and sending new initiatives to review committees that tended to kill them. Employees now wear casual dress to work. The company's president, [Durk] Jager, sponsors a Web site called "Ask Durk" where employees can get a direct answer from Jager; or they can complain anonymously using P&G's intranet. The company has also given away patents to an engineering school and has begun to license technology to competitors.[12]

▮ TYPES OF CULTURES

We can describe an organization's culture in numerous ways. Strong cultures demonstrate internal consistency and so have a major impact on an organization's members. Weak cultures show inconsistency and so have less impact. Efficient cultures fulfill their goals, innovate well, and demonstrate a strategic capacity. Inefficient cultures lack these characteristics.[13] Wal-mart, for example, has a strong culture established by its founder, Sam Walton. Leaders in the company act as servants to the store employees who take care of customers. Management decision making focuses on supporting the front-line employees, even reversing a bad managerial decision when necessary. The company embraces change, including experimentation with products and services and a commitment to technology.[14]

One categorization of cultures looks at whether an organization emphasizes reliability, customers, flexibility, or technology in responding to changes in the environment and describes culture as functional, process-driven, time-based, or network:[15]

- **Functional cultures** focus around specialization of individuals and decision making using the corporate hierarchy, and so emphasize reliability and consistency. Organizations with functional cultures limit downside risks, use proven methods, serve existing markets, and maintain clear lines of accountability. Most agencies of the U.S. government have a functional culture.
- **Process-driven cultures** emphasize quality and customer satisfaction and focus on the processes for improving quality and meeting obligations to customers. Organizations with process-driven cultures deliver on their commitments to customers and so gain their confidence. Cabot Corporation, a manufacturer of carbon black, introduced cross-functional teams as a way of better responding to customer needs.
- **Time-based cultures** attempt to reduce costs and quickly bring new products and services to market. Organizations with time-based cultures decrease cycle times, develop new products and services, maintain a high sense of urgency, and adapt quickly. Many dot-com companies attempt to create this type of culture in their organizations.
- **Network cultures,** which occur with the emergence of virtual corporations, design work around alliances that contain the competencies needed for the organization to compete. Organizations with network cultures develop new products and services, seize windows of opportunity, and effectively use outside resources. A general contractor who uses many subcontractors creates this type of organization.

Managers can think about cultures in terms of their attitudes toward hiring and promotions, and group their company's culture into one of four types:[16]

- **Academy.** These companies help young employees master their jobs and steadily climb the organization's hierarchy. They hire many new college graduates and send them through a number of specialized jobs. An academy, such as IBM, might identify fast-trackers early in their careers and send them to regular and extensive training.
- **Club.** These companies focus on helping managers fit into the organization. Moving ahead depends on seniority with the company, as well as demonstrating a strong commitment to it. These companies groom managers

as generalists, beginning with their first job. Creating a family feeling in the company helps reduce turnover.

■ **Baseball team.** These companies don't attempt to move people through the ranks, but try to secure employees who can perform well immediately without additional training. They seek talented employees of differing ages and experience who already have the required skills or can quickly develop them on the job. They reward employees for what they produce, rather than for seniority or specialized knowledge. Consulting, law, and accounting firms typify this entrepreneurial-type culture.

■ **Fortress.** These companies focus on their survival. They may be companies trying to reverse their failures in the marketplace or companies that regularly experience boom-and-bust cycles. Fortresses make no promises of job security, but can excite managers who like working in a turnaround situation.

The cultures of some companies combine more than one of these four types. Other organizations experience changes in their culture as they grow or diversify. Not only can managers use these four types to assess how well they fit into their own company's culture, but they can consider them as options for creating a more effective culture.

An organization's culture doesn't always offer consistency. It may be a "mosaic of inconsistencies"[17] and have shared meanings only within departments, divisions, or work teams, rather than across the entire organization. These organizational sub-cultures may exist harmoniously or conflict with each other. For example, personnel at the British Broadcasting Corporation have multiple loyalties and multiple identities that have been managed to effectively create a corporate culture.[18]

Sometimes no shared meanings or understandings exist. Consensus depends on the particular issue and constantly changes.[19] Culture in these situations may describe the amalgamation of what workers experience or may be so diffuse that managers and employees can't label it. Even when shared assumptions exist, some employees deviate from the culture; these employees may not fit well with the company and perhaps should seek other employment. On the other hand, such deviations may signal areas in which the company might change its culture to function more effectively.

Dimensions of Culture

We can also examine the dimensions that comprise culture. Managers can use the Organizational Culture Profile to identify specific dimensions.[20] This instrument asks employees to sort 54 value statements, such as fair, supportive, achievement-oriented, and experimenting, that assess a company's attitudes toward flexibility, risk taking, quality, and collaboration.

Employees in 15 U.S. firms, in the areas of public accounting, general consulting, government service, and transportation, identified seven dimensions in their organizations' cultures:[21]

■ **innovation,** risk-taking, experimental, and opportunistic;

■ **stability,** predictable, rule-oriented, clear performance expectations, secure;

■ **people orientation,** fair, respectful of individuals' rights, supportive, nondemanding;

■ **outcome orientation,** action, achievement, and results oriented;

■ **easygoingness,** tolerant, calm, reflective, low conflict;

- **detail orientation,** analytical and precise; and
- **team orientation,** collaborative.

Companies high on team orientation and people orientation likely differ significantly from those high on stability and detail orientation. For example, accounting firms scored relatively high on outcome orientation, detail orientation, and team orientation, but considerably lower on easygoingness, innovation, and stability.[22]

A second set of dimensions includes the following:[23]

- **communications,** the number and types of communication systems and what information is communicated and in what ways;
- **training and development,** management's willingness to provide training and development opportunities and the nature of these opportunities;
- **rewards,** the behaviors that receive rewards and the types of rewards offered;
- **decision making,** the way decisions are made and conflicts are resolved;
- **risk taking,** the extent to which the organization values creativity and innovation, encourages risk taking, and welcomes new ideas;
- **planning,** the relative emphasis on short- and long-term, reactive and proactive planning and the extent of employee participation in planning;
- **teamwork,** the amount, type, and effectiveness of teamwork; and
- **management practices,** the fairness and consistency of the administration of management policies, accessibility of management, the provision of a safe working environment, and the encouragement of diversity.

Although additional dimensions might exist in other companies or organizations, these provide a sense of an organization's culture. Managers who choose to sustain or change their cultures can address the specific behaviors identified in these dimensions. For example, increasing the amount of teamwork changes the culture. So does increasing the percentage of work time employees spend on training and development. Managers can use these dimensions to shape the type of culture they want.

▌ FUNCTIONS OF CULTURE

An organization's culture provides consistency by integrating diverse elements into a coherent set of beliefs, values, assumptions, and consequent behaviors. In fact, the consistency, adaptability, and employee involvement in an organization's culture, and the clarity of its mission, can predict organizational effectiveness.[24] So can involving employees in decision making and fostering a positive response to organizational change.[25] Management at the bakery division of Sweetheart Cup Company embarked on a new process goal called "Business Excellence," which involved all employees in focusing on delivering quality goods. The company formed teams and empowered workers to build their commitment to improving processes. Team meetings, while threatening at first, became fun for the employees, who had significant input into scheduling process improvements. Trust and personal accountability replaced the hierarchical management that had previously guided employees.[26]

Managers use culture for a number of functions:[27]

- **Supporting the organization's business strategy.** As Icarian grows, its managers will grapple with what changes they need to make in the culture to support the growth.

■ **Prescribing acceptable ways for managers to interact with external constituencies,** such as shareholders, the government, or customers. Medtronic, a major manufacturer of medical technology products, invites six patients and their physicians each December to tell Medtronic employees their personal stories about how a Medtronic product changed or saved their life. This holiday program fits with their mission of restoring people to full life and health and the patient-oriented culture they have developed to implement it.[28]

■ **Making staffing decisions.** Workers who don't work hard or don't fit into the informal culture at Icarian likely will experience performance problems.

■ **Setting performance criteria.** Managers and other employees can be evaluated on the basis of their ability to meet standards consistent with the culture. As companies increasingly institute team-based management, performance criteria focus on accomplishing team rather than individual goals.

■ **Guiding the nature of acceptable interpersonal relationships in the company.** Icarian's corporate culture encourages managers and workers to respect each other's skills and contributions.

■ **Selecting appropriate management styles.** Icarian's employees work long hours, but are given time to deal with nonwork concerns.

Culture also provides a mechanism for controlling behaviors. It helps create values that commit employees and customers to the organization's goals. At the same time, the wrong culture can sabotage goals, strategies, and values.[29]

■ WAYS OF DETERMINING CULTURE

Organizational culture exists at three levels, as shown in Figure 11-1: artifacts, values, and assumptions.[30] The artifacts at level 1 refer to the audible and visible patterns of behavior, technology, and art. You can look around any office space and get an idea of a company's culture. Does the company have lots of small conference rooms for informal meetings? Do family pictures adorn employees' desks? How close are managers' and employees' offices? Bradford & Bingley, the second-largest building society in the United Kingdom, redesigned its logos, replacing staid-looking bowler hats with hats in a brightly colored, surrealistic motif.[31]

The values at level 2 refer to the way people evaluate the behaviors of level 1. Values describe the way managers and employees believe they should act, although they may behave differently in some situations. For example, a company's mission statement tends to reflect its values. The mission of the Juvenile Diabetes Foundation is "to find a cure for diabetes and its complications through the funding of research."[32] Colorado's Arrowhead Elementary School's mission statement is "to inspire every student to think, to learn, to achieve, to care."[33] Figure 11-2 shows the corporate mission statement of Dell Computers. Note its emphasis on customer service and customization, two hallmarks of this company.

The most basic ways of determining culture, the assumptions of level 3, refer to people's ideas and assumptions that affect their behavior. Cultures form around assumptions in areas such as the following:[34]

■ **Reality and truth.** What is real? How is truth determined?

■ **Time.** How is time measured? What is its role and importance in the culture?

FIGURE 11-1

We can analyze an organization's culture by looking at its artifacts, values, and assumptions.

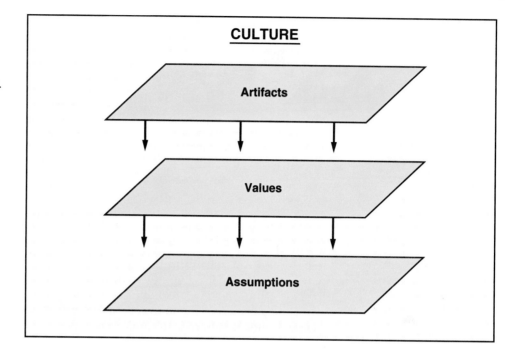

- **Space.** How is physical space allocated and owned?
- **Human nature.** What does it mean to be human? Is human nature good, evil, or neutral?
- **Human activity.** What is the right thing for people to be doing?
- **Human relationships.** How should people relate to each other?

Shared assumptions help managers and employees forge a strong culture that all accept and support. To reveal the culture, you look at the artifacts at level 1. At Icarian, you first look at messages conveyed by the physical working space. What do the roller-blades, dogs, and foosball games tell you about the company? Then

FIGURE 11-2

Dell's mission statement reflects the company's values, beliefs, and way of doing business.

Source: http://www.dell.com/us/ en/gen/corporate/vision_ mission.htm, October 9, 2000.

Dell's mission is to be the most successful computer company in the world at delivering the best customer experience in markets we serve. In doing so, Dell will meet customer expectations of:

- Highest Quality
- Leading Technology
- Competitive Pricing
- Individual and Company Accountability
- Best-in-Class Service and Support
- Flexible Customization Capability
- Superior Corporate Citizenship
- Financial Stability

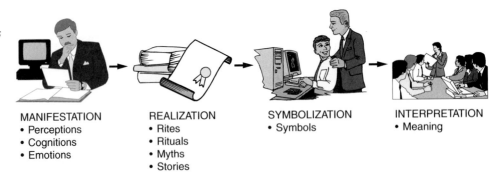

MANIFESTATION	REALIZATION	SYMBOLIZATION	INTERPRETATION
• Perceptions	• Rites	• Symbols	• Meaning
• Cognitions	• Rituals		
• Emotions	• Myths		
	• Stories		

search deeper. Look for underlying values and assumptions. The top executives' work ethic, for example, provides more subtle, less apparent reflections of the culture. Then look at the assumptions that result from these values. Employees interpret the executives' behavior combined with the physical work space as supporting a work ethic that focuses on innovation and creativity.

Organizational culture is dynamic. Assumptions, values, artifacts, and symbols interact in four cultural processes, as shown in Figure 11-3:[35]

- **Manifestation.** The perceptions, cognitions, and emotions of workers reveal cultural assumptions. At Icarian, assumptions about how to attain riches translate into behaviors of working hard.
- **Realization.** Perceptions, cognitions, and emotions are transformed into tangible artifacts. Artifacts can include rites, rituals, myths, and stories. Stories about Icarian's executives create perceptions about their attitude toward work.
- **Symbolization.** Particular artifacts take on a specific symbolic significance. Icarian gives employees "Icarian bucks" to be spent on perks, such as a massage for a colleague.
- **Interpretation.** People inside and outside the organization determine the meaning of various symbols. Employees may value the services they receive from others by spending their "Icarian bucks."

Many companies use surveys to assess the culture experienced by their employees. Table 11-1 lists some statements used to evaluate an organization's culture after a merger. Managers are asked to indicate on a five-point scale the perceived importance of these items to the following questions:

- What values do you feel should be emphasized at a company, whether or not they appear at your present company?
- How were things at your firm before the merger?
- How do things appear now at the buying firm?[36]

Mission Statements

A company's culture reflects the basic organizational philosophy of its leaders. The company's mission expresses this philosophy, as well as the most basic values, beliefs, and assumptions underlying the organization's culture. It provides a sense

TABLE 11-1

Companies Can Survey Their Employees' Views of the Corporate Culture Using Statements Such as These.

1. Encourages creativity and innovation.
2. Cares about health and welfare of employees.
3. Is receptive to new ways of doing things.
4. Stresses teamwork among departments.
5. Bases promotions primarily on performance.
6. Explains reasons for decisiosn to subordinates.
7. Tries to improve communication between departments.
8. Gives recognition when deserved.
9. Challenges persons to give their best effort.
10. Values effectiveness more than adherence to rules and procedures.

Source: J. Veiga, M. Lubatkin, R. Calori, and P. Very, Measuring organizational culture clashes: A two-nation post-hoc analysis of a cultural compatibility index, *Human Relations* 53(4) (2000): 539–557.

of purposefulness and direction for members of the organization. It can also unify employees by providing them with a sense of identity. Johnson Wax, for example, states in the introduction to its corporate brochure "This We Believe" that the company has translated its statement of corporate philosophy and communicated it around the world to both internal and external groups. It informs employees about the basic principles that guide the company and gives people outside the company an understanding of the basic corporate beliefs.[37]

A formal mission statement, as illustrated by Dell's statement in Figure 11-2 and the UCLA police force's statement in Figure 11-4, succinctly states the culture's basic beliefs. The requirements of the industry in which the organization functions, as well as its national culture, may exert an influence on the beliefs expressed in the mission statement.[38] Companies in the health care, education, high-technology, and financial services sectors likely have different emphases in their mission statements.

The University of California Police Department at Los Angeles is a leader in providing progressive law enforcement services to a culturally diverse urban campus and its surrounding community. We actively foster a safe environment by maintaining a high state of readiness, cultivating community partnerships, and creating innovative community programs.

FIGURE 11-4   *This mission statement helps clarify the organization's purpose and direction.*

Source: http:www.ucpd.ucla.edu/ucpd/organization.htm#Mission, October 9, 2000.

Heroes and Heroines

Heroes and heroines are individuals who transmit culture by personifying its corporate values. For example, Michael Dell, Bill Gates, and Lou Gerstener could be viewed as heroes of Dell Computers, Microsoft, and IBM, respectively. A leader whom workers view as a hero or heroine reinforces the basic values of an organization's culture. James Goodnight, the founder of SAS Institute, a company that develops software, leaves the office at 5 P.M. sharp, believing that dinner should be spent with your family. The company offers on-site day care and a six-week paid maternity leave. In this way, SAS's culture supports family values and encourages employee loyalty.[39]

By acting as role models, symbolizing and hence representing the organization to the outside world, these heroic figures preserve the organization's special qualities. They set standards of performance, motivate employees, and make success attainable and human.[40] Managers who create heroes or heroines foster a set of corporate values that may stabilize the current organization or expedite change. Heroes aren't always larger-than-life figures. Goodnight, for example, appears to be a "regular guy" to his employees.

Myths and Stories

Myths refer to stories about corporate heroes and heroines that help managers transmit and embed culture. What does the repeated telling of a story about the spectacular rise of a copy editor to the presidency of a major advertising firm suggest about a company's values? Does a story about the heir to the family fortune being the designated company president give the same impression? Clearly, the themes of such stories provide clues to an organization's culture.

Rituals and Ceremonies

Rituals, such as posting team accomplishments or year-end results, and ceremonies, such as retirement dinners or employee-of-the-month awards, contribute to corporate culture by dramatizing the organization's basic values. Boldt Metronics International hosts lunches every six weeks for its 350 employees; the president considers the sharing of a meal one of the company's core principles.[41] The awarding of a pin for 25 years of service indicates a company that values loyalty. Often linked with a corresponding organizational story about the value of long-term company service, such events can provide an explanation of new behavior patterns or reinforce existing ones.[42] Metromedia Restaurant Group's (MRG) managers receive a sack of rocks when they complete the in-house leadership and training program. One of MRG's nine core values is stamped on each rock. While eight of the rocks are ovals and are stamped with values such as "ownership," "simplicity," and "winning," the ninth rock is triangular and labeled "integrity," which is the foundation of the company's vision and culture.[43]

Rituals or ceremonies can also act as rites of passage, marking entry into an organization's inner circle or expediting transitions in leadership. For example, a breakfast or dinner for a new work team demarcates the change from the former to the current team composition. In addition to celebrating passage into new social roles, rites can also support or distract from a person's social identities and social structures. Rites can reduce conflict and encourage common feelings among group members.[44] The Great Michigan Millers Comeback kicked off a major cultural change at Michigan Millers Mutual Insurance Company of Lansing, Michigan. When employees arrived at work, they saw a blimp flying over the building, heard the Michigan State fight song in the building, and received pom-poms. This symbolized a new way of doing business—a focus on providing service to customers by "walking the extra mile."[45]

Physical Arrangements

The selection and arrangement of offices and furnishings often reveal significant insights into corporate culture and its underlying values. Compare the culture of an insurance agency that provides only a desk and telephone for its agents to a competitor's culture that offers free and open space for its employees. How might the cultures of these two firms differ?

Often the physical arrangements can be used to support the cultural values. Dell's physical space, for example, supports its non-hierarchical approach to management. The company doesn't have fancy corporate offices; in fact, all except four people have a cubicle. The hallways are plain, without art. "There is strictly a start-up, keep-the-costs-down-and-the-options-will-take-care-of-themselves feel to the place."[46] Other companies arrange desks in a bullpen area or provide many conference rooms as a way of encouraging teamwork. The advertising agency Chiat/Day moved its Los Angeles headquarters to a warehouse that has no cubicles, offices, or desks. Called "Advertising City," the physical space includes bright yellow cliff dwellings on the mezzanine level of the 27-foot-high space; here, pairs of employees work together in view of all other employees.[47] E-mail and videoconferencing also encourage communication and teamwork between workers at remote locations, but may reflect a different culture

▌ HOW TO CREATE A CULTURE

Most organizations already have a culture that influences the way its managers and employees act, as well as the way customers, suppliers, and other people view the company. New companies, in contrast, need to determine the kind of culture they want and then find ways to create it. The two owners of Icarian, for example, wanted a high-achieving culture and created it through their use of physical space and acceptable behaviors. Creating a culture involves developing shared assumptions about how to deal with the external environment and internal relationships. Saudi Chevron Petroleum wanted to create a culture that valued safety. To do this, they needed a caring culture that included a commitment to treating all employees with respect and a commitment to having a healthy and safe place to work. Their goal included creating an environment where employees could stop work they believed was unsafe, report near misses, and take responsibility for safety.[48] Figure 11-5 shows the interaction of the external and internal environments in creating a culture. For example, organizations create a culture by encouraging consistency among power, status, and rewards, and the organization's tasks, goals, and mission.

Look again at Figure 11-1. To create culture, you can begin at the deepest level by formulating the assumptions of level 3, which then become the values of level 2, and ultimately are reflected in the artifacts, such as mission statements, of level 1. Although managers most often lead such an effort, lower-level employees can also significantly influence the development of a new culture.

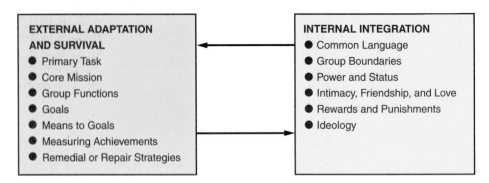

EXTERNAL ADAPTATION AND SURVIVAL	INTERNAL INTEGRATION
● Primary Task	● Common Language
● Core Mission	● Group Boundaries
● Group Functions	● Power and Status
● Goals	● Intimacy, Friendship, and Love
● Means to Goals	● Rewards and Punishments
● Measuring Achievements	● Ideology
● Remedial or Repair Strategies	

▌ **FIGURE 11-5** ▌   *Creating a culture involves dealing with issues of external adaptation and survival and internal integration.*

Source: E. H. Schein, The role of the founder in creating organizational culture, *Organizational Dynamics* (Summer 1983).

Top-Management Directed

Owners and chief executives of companies can most easily create a culture. They set the rules, regulations, and rewards in their organization. Their early behaviors reflect their assumptions and values. These reflect and encourage the desired behaviors that ultimately become the corporate culture. Michael Eisner, CEO of Disney, heads an insular and even arrogant corporate culture characterized by centralization of decision making, a strong hierarchical structure, and corporate synergy. Many believe that Eisner retains control over too many decisions himself, slowing the process.[49] Such a top-down culture can have both positive and negative consequences for employees, customers, and the bottom line. Whereas Disney's culture once allowed the company to execute ideas flawlessly, now its large size and rapidly changing environment make this culture less effective.

Employee Initiated

Culture can also start at the bottom of organizations. Individual teams, departments, or other subgroups often have their own culture, which may differ from each other's and from the corporate culture. As similarities emerge among these subcultures, pockets of cultural influence can develop. Eventually, a subculture can become so pervasive and influential that it becomes the corporate culture.

Consider the role a successful project team can play in developing a company's culture. Think of a team that has a different culture from the rest of the organization. Perhaps the team relied on consensual decision making and rotating leadership. The company, in contrast, had reams of policies and procedures, and most decision making rested with the company's managers. The success of the project team demonstrates that a different way of operating works. Additional teams will try this approach. Their successes will extend the culture into more areas of the company and eventually affect the entire organization. Ames Department Stores fosters its culture of going the extra mile by taking employees' ideas for improvement seriously, helping them develop so they can assume higher-level positions, and offering incentives that encourage employee excellence.[50] The sharing of a culture among many subunits of the organization can also help sustain it, as described in the next section.

▌ HOW TO SUSTAIN A CULTURE

Managers may try hard to perpetuate cultures. One way to sustain a culture is by continuing rituals that reinforce the culture. For example, managers can hold employee recognition days, conduct regular improvement contests, or give employee-of-the-month awards. Employees need to internalize the culture. This means that employees must accurately perceive the behavior expected from them, use the organizational culture to help evaluate information and place behaviors in the "good" and "bad" categories, and finally, receive rewards that reinforce particular types of behavior. Such internalization of the culture has been shown to positively relate to job satisfaction, job commitment, and individual performance.[51]

Managers can also ensure that the reward system encourages behaviors that "fit in" with the desired culture. For example, the investment firm of Donaldson, Lufkin & Jenrette has an entrepreneurial culture. Employees own about 20 percent of the company. The president notes that employees take pride in applauding other employees' successes and retaining a smaller-firm attitude. Employees can participate in the company's venture capital and merchant banking funds as an additional way of having a personal stake in the firm's investing expertise. The company encourages teamwork through its compensation scheme, which includes team members evaluating the performance of others on the team.[52]

Figure 11-6 illustrates another way of thinking about sustaining cultures. Managers can focus on effective staffing as a way of reinforcing the corporate culture:[53]

1. A behavior occurs, such as hiring a new employee.
2. Managers and employees justify the existing culture.
3. Managers and employees communicate the culture's characteristics to people inside and outside the organization.
4. Managers hire and socialize members who fit in with the culture.
5. Managers remove workers who do not.

Organizational Socialization

Managers can use a variety of approaches to help new employees "learn the ropes," understand the organization's goals and the preferred way to attain them, and know their responsibilities and appropriate behavior. Although orientation programs frequently provide the initial socialization of employees, top managers may regularly meet with recent recruits to share and reinforce their vision of the organization. Subsequent on-the-job training and informal interactions with co-workers can reinforce the values, norms, and behavior patterns introduced earlier. Veterans Affairs Eastern Kansas Health Care System, an organization that resulted from the merger of two different medical centers, used training to provide a common language and approach for the new organization. The University of Kansas Division of Continuing Education designed a series of professional development seminars and consultations that helped staff members become effective members of the new organization. For example, each of four seminars focused on several core competencies and encouraged participants to experiment and take risks in identifying the behaviors that will make them successful individuals and an effective organization.[54]

Managers can use the corporate training program to socialize workers in ways that support the corporate culture. The content and delivery of the training can

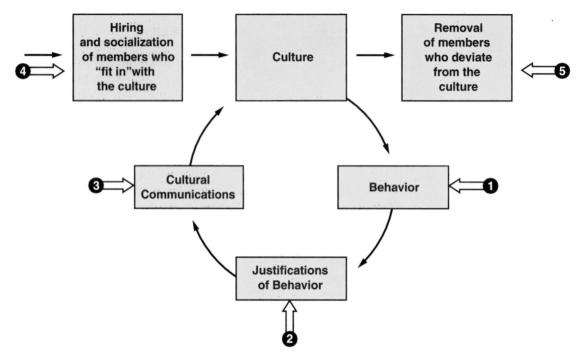

FIGURE 11-6   *An organization's culture sustains itself by socializing people to fit in with the culture and removing people who deviate from it.*

Source: Reprinted from V. Sathe, How to decipher and change culture. In R. H. Kilmann, M. J. Saxton, R. Serpa, and Associates (eds.), *Gaining Control of Corporate Culture* (San Francisco: Jossey-Bass, 1985), p. 245.

reinforce the culture. Managers can consciously choose among a series of socialization strategies, as shown in Table 11-2. For example, from these possibilities, choosing the following strategies will more often result in employees conforming to an existing culture:[55]

- putting new employees through a common set of experiences as part of a group rather than training them singly and in isolation from other new hires;
- segregating newcomers from regular organizational members;
- requiring the new hires to move through a series of discrete and identifiable steps to achieve a defined role, such as specialized medical training;
- treating all new hires as similar, regardless of their education or experience;
- giving recruits a complete knowledge of the time required to become a functioning employee rather than offering an ambiguous timetable;
- providing experienced employees as role models for newcomers to follow; and
- stripping away any personal characteristics of the recruits rather than treating them as individuals.

To support its change to a team-based environment in which two or three agents meet with prospects, develop sales, and then close them, Baltimore Life hired a former leadership training consultant to coach the new teams in group dynamics and communication skills. The training emphasizes relationships as well as tasks, and includes a survival role-play activity.[56]

TABLE 11-2

Managers Can Choose From Seven Types of Socialization Strategies.

Strategy	Definition	Example
Collective	Puts newcomers through a common set of experiences as part of a group	Freshman orientation
Individual	Processes recruits singly and in isolation from each other	On-the-job training
Formal	Segregates newcomers from regular organizational members	Basic military training
Informal	Treats newcomers the same as other members	Transferred employees
Sequential steps	Requires entrant to move through a series of discrete and identifiable steps to achieve a defined role	Specialized medical training
Nonsequential steps	Achieves a defined role in one transitional stage	Promotion
Tournament	Separates clusters of recruits into different programs on the basis of presumed differences	Academic tracked programs
Contest	Avoids sharp distinctions between clusters of recruits	Law school
Fixed	Gives the recruit complete knowledge of time required to complete passage	Six-week training program
Variable	Offers a timetable that does not fix the length of socializaiton	Doctoral program
Serial	Provides experienced members as role models for newcomers	Apprentice program
Disjunctive	Has no role models available for newcomers	First holder of a newly defined job
Investiture	Ratifies and documents the usefulness of personal characteristics of new recruits	New faculty orientation
Divestiture	Seeks to deny and strip away recruits' personal characteristics	Training for the priesthood

Source: Based in part on J. Van Maanen, People processing: Strategies of organizational socialization, *Organizational Dynamics* 7 (1978): 19–36.

■ HOW TO CHANGE A CULTURE

Managers can diagnose an organization's culture to determine whether it supports the company's strategy and goals. If it doesn't, they can change it. Xerox has built a strong knowledge-sharing culture that supports its mission as the "document company." Each senior manager supports the knowledge management effort in his or her business unit, believing that the knowledge of its employees provides a major competitive advantage to Xerox.[57]

Culture change frequently accompanies mergers and acquisitions. Daimler-Chrysler faced the challenge of merging both corporate and national cultures. At the time of the merger, the American employees' pay was as much as four times as great as that of their German counterparts. At the same time, the Germans always had high travel expenses, including routine first-class travel to meetings and stays at top-ranked hotels over weekends. Because neither company conformed entirely to their national stereotypes, compromise was possible. As one board member said, "We have a clear understanding: one company, one vision, one chairman, two cultures."[58] Such a collision of cultures can result in employees of one company making incorrect assumptions about the attributes of the other company's employees. Bringing these assumptions to the surface is critical to successfully changing the culture.

Employees can respond to change in an organization's culture in the following ways:[59]

- **Active acceptance.** Employees unquestioningly adopt, agree to, and participate in the change effort.
- **Selective reinvention.** Employees selectively disguise elements of the old culture in the new culture, such as by relabeling them.
- **Reinvention.** Employees superficially and more radically align elements of the old culture with the new culture, but camouflage them under the guise of the new cultural attributes.
- **General acceptance.** Employees somewhat but not completely adopt the new culture because of existing values and beliefs.
- **Dissonance.** Employees experience confusion about the new culture and so frequently act inconsistently.
- **General rejection.** Employees disagree with the new culture, although some elements of it may occur because of the weakness of the old culture.
- **Reinterpretation.** Employees reinterpret the new culture in a way that results in developing values and behavior consistent with both the old and new cultures.
- **Selective reinterpretation.** Employees reject some elements of the new culture while reinterpreting other elements of it.
- **Active rejection.** Employees cognitively and physically reject the rationale and means of the new culture.

To carry out cultural change, executives have to win over other managers and employees who may be very comfortable with the existing culture. After the NE Restaurant Company purchased Bertucci's, they focused on creating a new culture that incorporates the best of both companies' cultures. As a way of getting the employees on board, the newly appointed vice president of human resources mailed 9,200 surveys to the company's front-line employees; the company also conducted 32 focus groups with employees. Now the company is in the process of sharing the findings with employees as a way of helping create the new organization.[60]

Although many approaches to change exist, managers at all levels need to participate in the change. Top managers should support the change. They need to develop a clear vision of the organization's future direction and the culture required to attain it. Top managers can model the features of the new culture for subordinates. They should behave in ways that reflect the desired values, expectations, and behaviors. "Walking the talk" is a key component of improvement efforts instituted in companies such as Hewlett-Packard, Xerox, and Motorola (see Chapter 14). CEOs can also help create an organizational culture that supports the use of new technologies by modeling such behaviors themselves and paying for training to support employees' acquisition of technology skills.

Mid-level and top-level managers should change their organization's structure, human resource systems, and management styles and practices to support the shift in culture. If an organization assumes an egalitarian, people-oriented culture, managers must encourage, measure, and reward worker participation in decision making. If an organization assumes a more authoritarian, production-oriented culture, managers must encourage, measure, and reward worker obedience to authority and bottom-line performance. Lockheed Martin has focused on identifying the best practices in its various businesses and transferring them to other Lockheed Martin units. Known as LM21, the new initiative expects to achieve savings of between $800 million and $1 billion in its first year.[61]

Changing the reward system also motivates and reinforces a new culture. Travelers Insurance changed the culture of its commercial insurance group by changing the way it rewarded agents. Agents now receive cash bonuses and stock options for selling particular types of insurance. Customers have noted that agents are "hungrier" and want to make deals.[62]

Managers can select and socialize newcomers to fit in with the new culture. They can retrain or terminate existing employees who do not fit in. The merger of two organizations or a radical cultural change in a single organization may result in some employee casualties. The merger of Citibank and Travelers attempted to combine two very different cultures, which never coalesced. As John Reed, the former CEO of Citibank, noted shortly before announcing his retirement: "As you put two cultures together, you get all sorts of strange, aberrant behavior, and it is not clear whether each side getting to know the other side helps, or whether having common objectives helps, or whether it is just the passage of time. . . . The problems of step-parents, the descriptions of some children rejecting one parent, and other children rejecting other parents . . . . is all meaningful. The Travelers people are ticked off that they did the merger, because clearly these Citi people are a bunch of idiots . . . . The Citi people are equally annoyed."[63]

Look again at Figure 11-6. Changing the culture can occur by intervening at any of the numbered points. For example, at (2) if managers can't justify existing behavior, others may change it and culture change may result. Top executives may fail to communicate the nature of the current culture at (3), and instead discuss a preferred culture, which can lead to change. Finally, as part of the hiring and firing processes, managers at (4) and (5) can hire or retain employees who don't fit in with the culture. Such differences may result in culture change.

Different processes may be required to change different cultures. In some situations, consistent but different messages from the top executives can lead to a culture change. Others require a crisis to precipitate the need for a culture change and help employees accept the new culture. The organization's history, stage of development, and general orientation may influence the most effective process.[64] For example, younger organizations with less ingrained cultures may be more prone to change than older, more bureaucratic ones. Because of the complexity of changing an organization's culture, managers may need to experience some trial-and-error before they find the best approach. Changing the culture can also take time, as long as three to five years in many cases. One survey of Fortune 500 companies indicated that 70 percent believed that they lacked the skill and knowledge to address cultural issues.[65]

▌ CULTURE IN THE DOT-COM, GLOBAL WORKPLACE

Executives in the fast-paced dot-com environment must give significant consideration to the type of culture that will work best for them. Icarian's executives created a very informal culture to encourage the intense activity required for the company to be successful. Generally, the dot-com companies have instituted egalitarian cultures that encourage employees to contribute their knowledge and skills to helping the company grow. Ray Sozzi, the CEO of Student Advantage, which provides services for college students, holds town meetings as a way of ensuring employees' voice. Employees at the company's Boston office meet in a conference room and conduct a company-wide conference call with employees at eight other sites. These town meetings are "no-holds-barred, free-for-all forums that tap into employees' attitudes and thoughts."[66]

Often such companies encourage a playful environment because they believe it motivates creativity. Ensuring that the culture supports the company's strategy is key to its ultimate success. Such companies also need to create appropriate incentives to encourage creativity and productivity. Greenfield Online, for example, has a formal recognition program that rewards employees for their commitment, creativity, perseverance, performance, research, and service. They also give unofficial awards, such as "a plastic doll bed for a guy who logged grueling hours at the office [and] a can of spray starch for the staff neatnik."[67]

Multinational companies face special issues in building, sustaining, and changing their cultures. They face the challenge of meshing national cultures with corporate cultures. Grand Circle Corp., a Boston-based tour operator, needed to transfer its corporate culture to a regional office the company opened in Bangkok. Grand Circle's co-owners created a 12-person team called Winning Operations Worldwide (WOW). Team WOW used cross-cultural training to build a bridge between Boston and the company's regional offices. Team WOW first set up the physical office space in Thailand and next trained employees in each department in the Bangkok office. Customer service representatives traveled to Thailand to train their Thai counterparts. After the formal training, the WOW team and Thai staff participated in more informal games and getting-to-know-you activities. The training was quite successful, with the "Jewels of Thailand" trip becoming Grand Circle's fastest-selling tour.[68]

Corporations may more easily flourish if their culture fits with their country's culture. General Electric has taken its corporate culture and employed local talent to allow the culture to suit local conditions. For example, a meeting of the CEOs of GE's businesses in China included a discussion of issues such as "critical to quality" and "Six Sigma," key aspects of GE's culture. Only two of the more than 20 CEOs weren't Asian, and all except one of the Asians were Chinese, either from the mainland, Hong Kong, or Taiwan.[69]

If, however, the corporate culture conflicts with the national culture, performance problems likely will result. Yahoo France faces the challenge of having a free-spirited Silicon Valley culture in a country whose rules-oriented and bureaucratic culture have supported companies with a clear hierarchy, rigid decision-making structure, and layers of management, such as the publishing company Hachette Filipacchi.[70] Performance-enhancing cultures in Russia include company spirit, employee empowerment, training, a team orientation, coordination, implicit behavioral norms, a strong customer focus, and clear strategy. Companies that lack such a culture perform more poorly than those that have it.[71]

▍ Summary

1. An organization's culture describes the part of its internal environment that incorporates a set of assumptions, beliefs, and values which are shared by organizational members and help guide their functioning.

2. An organization's culture helps it attain a competitive advantage and achieve its goals.

3. Organizations can have consistent and inconsistent, efficient and inefficient cultures, differ along an array of dimensions, and serve a variety of functions.

4. A culture has three levels: assumptions, values, and artifacts.

5. We can uncover a culture by examining an organization's mission, heroes and heroines, myths and stories, rituals and ceremonies, and physical arrangements.

6. Founders of companies and other top executives of small companies can create an organizational culture, although a culture can consolidate as a result of the actions of people lower in the hierarchy.

7. Managers can sustain cultures by hiring the right people and then socializing them to desired behaviors.

8. Managers who change the culture must have a clear vision of the organization's future, support the change, and model the new culture for subordinates, as well as change the organization's structure, human resource systems, and management styles and practices to support the new culture.

9. Companies in the dot-com, global workplace may face special issues in building, sustaining, and changing their cultures.

A Manager's Diagnostic Review

☐ Define a culture that would create a competitive advantage for your organization.
- What components should the culture have?
- How do these compare to the components of the current culture?

☐ Choose the best type of culture for your organization's goals.
- What type of culture does your organization have?
- What type of culture should it have?
- What dimensions need to change to attain the desired culture?

☐ Create an organizational culture in a new company, division, department, or team.
- What steps should top management take to create the desired culture?
- Do employees have the power and skills to create a new culture?
- What steps should employees take?

☐ Sustain an organization's culture to accomplish corporate goals.
- What elements of the culture should be sustained?
- What types of socialization programs will help sustain the culture?

☐ Change the culture in your organization.
- What steps should you take to make the necessary changes?

Visit the Gordon homepage on the Prentice Hall Web site at

http://www.prenhall.com/gordon

for recommended readings, additional activities, Internet exercises, updated information, and links to related Web sites.

▌ Thinking Critically About Organizational Behavior

1. What type of culture does your college or university have in terms of its attitudes toward hiring and promotions?
2. Can you think of additional dimensions of an organization's culture beyond those listed in this chapter?
3. Should customers know and understand the culture of their suppliers?
4. Why should employees understand the culture of their organization?
5. Are mission statements really necessary?
6. Can a hero or heroine represent a dysfunctional culture that should be changed?
7. How can myths or stories be used to guide performance?
8. Are top-management-directed and employee-initiated cultures likely to differ in any basic ways across organizations?
9. How long can a culture be sustained?
10. Should an organization consciously socialize its employees in a particular fashion?
11. How would you change your college or university's culture?
12. What are the major challenges of creating, sustaining, and changing cultures in the dot-com, global workplace?

ACTIVITY 11-1: ORGANIZATION CULTURE QUESTIONNAIRE

STEP 1: Select an organization with which you are very familiar. You can choose your college or university or an organization in which you have been employed.

STEP 2: Complete the Organizational Culture Questionnaire in Figure 11-7.

STEP 3: Individually or in small groups, compare your organizations by answering the following questions about each one:

1. What are the dominant values of the organization?
2. What assumptions underlie these values?
3. What artifacts represent these values?
4. What are some of the behavioral norms of the organization that an outsider or a newcomer would quickly notice?
5. How do the leaders of the organization reinforce these values and norms?

6. How are newcomers socialized in this organization?

STEP 4: Discussion. In small groups or with the entire class, answer the following questions:

1. What are the key components of the organizations' cultures?
2. Compare where the organizational culture actually is to where it ideally should be for each organization.
3. How extensive is this discrepancy for the organizations analyzed?
4. What individual and organizational outcomes does organizational culture affect?

Source: From Kolb, Osland, Rubin, *Organizational Behavior: An Experiential Approach* 6/E, © 1995 pp. 34, 346–347, 363. Reprinted by permission of Prentice Hall, Englewood Cliffs, NJ.

For each of the seven organizational culture dimensions described, place an (a) below the number that indicates your assessment of the organization's *actual* position on that dimension and an (i) below the number that indicates your choice of where the organization should *ideally* be on this dimension.

1. **Conformity.** The feeling that there are many externally imposed constraints in the organization: the degree to which members feel that there are many rules, procedures, policies, and practices to which they have to conform rather than being able to do their work as they see fit.

   Conformity is not characteristic of this organization. | 1 | 2 | 3 | 4 | 5 | 6 | 7 | 8 | 9 | 10 | Conformity is very characteristic of this organization.

2. **Responsibility.** Members of the organization are given personal responsibility to achieve their part of the organization's goals: the degree to which members feel that they can make decisions and solve problems without checking with superiors each step of the way.

   No responsibility is given in the organization. | 1 | 2 | 3 | 4 | 5 | 6 | 7 | 8 | 9 | 10 | There is a great emphasis on personal responsibility in the organization.

3. **Standards.** The emphasis the organization places on quality performance and outstanding production, including the degree to which members feel the organization is setting challenging goals for itself and communicating these goal commitments to members.

   Standards are very low or nonexistent in the organization. | 1 | 2 | 3 | 4 | 5 | 6 | 7 | 8 | 9 | 10 | High, challenging standards are set in the organization.

4. **Rewards.** The degree to which members feel that they are being recognized and rewarded for good work rather than being ignored, criticized, or punished when something goes wrong.

   Members are ignored, punished, or criticized. | 1 | 2 | 3 | 4 | 5 | 6 | 7 | 8 | 9 | 10 | Members are recognized and rewarded positively.

5. **Organizational clarity.** The feeling among members that things are well organized and that goals are clearly defined rather than being disorderly, confused, or chaotic.

   The organization is disorderly, confused, and chaotic. | 1 | 2 | 3 | 4 | 5 | 6 | 7 | 8 | 9 | 10 | The organization is well organized, with clearly defined goals.

6. **Warmth and support.** The feeling that friendliness is a valued norm in the organization, that members trust one another and offer support to one another. The feeling that good relationships prevail in the work environment.

   There is no warmth and support in the organization. | 1 | 2 | 3 | 4 | 5 | 6 | 7 | 8 | 9 | 10 | Warmth and support are very characteristic of the organization.

7. **Leadership.** The willingness of organization members to accept leadership and direction from qualified others. As needs for leadership arise, members feel free to take leadership roles and are rewarded for successful leadership. Leadership is based on expertise. The organization is not dominated by, or dependent on, one or two individuals.

   Leadership is not rewarded. Members are dominated or dependent and resist leadership attempts. | 1 | 2 | 3 | 4 | 5 | 6 | 7 | 8 | 9 | 10 | Members accept and reward leadership based on expertise.

FIGURE 11-7 *Organizational Culture Questionnaire.*

ACTIVITY 11-2: CORPORATE CULTURE AFTER MERGERS

STEP 1: Using the newspaper, magazines, the Web, and other relevant sources, trace the merger of two companies.

STEP 2: Analyze the cultures of the two companies that merged. Then analyze the culture of the merged company.

STEP 3: Individually or in small groups, answer the following questions:

1. How did the new company incorporate the cultures of the former companies?
2. What decisions did top management make that affected the new culture?
3. What artifacts reflected the old and new cultures?
4. How did employees, customers, and the general public react to the culture of the merged company?

ACTIVITY 11-3: THE PHYSICAL SIDE OF CULTURE

STEP 1: Select two organizations to visit, or choose two locations on your campus.

STEP 2: Individually or with a small group of students, tour the physical facilities of each organization.

1. Describe the types of office space, manufacturing space (if applicable), conference rooms, and other work spaces in the organizations.
2. Describe the artwork, personal artifacts, or other decorations in the work spaces.
3. Note the settings in which employees interact. What types of interactions occur—meetings, personal conversations, telephone conversations, and so on?

STEP 3: Based on your observations, identify and describe the type of culture that exists in each organization you visited.

STEP 4: Interview at least one person from each organization. Ask them to describe their organization's culture.

STEP 5: Compare their descriptions to your hypotheses about the culture. Did you assess the culture correctly or incorrectly? How does the physical space reflect the organization's culture?

STEP 6: Discussion. In small groups or with the entire class, share your results. Then answer the following questions:

1. How effectively do the organizations reflect their culture in their physical work spaces?
2. What changes can the organizations make to better fit their physical work spaces with their culture?
3. How does a fit between the physical spaces and the culture affect individual and organizational performance?

ACTIVITY 11-4: SOCIALIZATION EXERCISE

STEP 1: Think of two experiences: (1) when you socialized another person and (2) when you were socialized. Describe each of these experiences in a paragraph.

STEP 2: With a partner, identify the socialization strategies used in each.

STEP 3: In small groups or with the entire class, compare the strategies used in these two types of experiences.

1. What strategies did you use most commonly to socialize another person?
2. What strategies were used most commonly to socialize you?
3. List your reactions to each strategy used.
4. List the outcomes of each strategy used.
5. Which strategies were most effective? Why?

ACTIVITY 11-5: CULTURAL STORIES

STEP 1: Think of an organization in which you spent some time as an employee, student, or volunteer, or in some other capacity.

STEP 2: Answer the following question orally or in writing, as directed by your instructor.

During the time you were in the organization, you probably were told stories or anecdotes about it. Perhaps you told some yourself. If you were telling someone a story or anecdote that captures the essence of what it's like to be in that organization, what would you say?

STEP 3: In small groups or with the entire class, share your stories. For each story, reach consensus about the nature of the organization's culture.

1. How would you characterize the culture?
2. What shared meanings do members of all the organizations have?
3. How do your stories reflect these shared meanings?

Source: The idea for this exercise was drawn from W. B. Stevenson and J. M. Bartunek, Power interaction, position, and the generation of cultural agreement in organizations, *Human Relations* 49(1)(1996): 75–104.

ACTIVITY 11-6: CHANGING AN ORGANIZATION'S CULTURE

STEP 1: Pick an organization to which you belong. It can be a club, team, work group, department, or even a living group.

STEP 2: Identify the key elements of the culture. Use the list of dimensions given earlier in this chapter to help you with this step.

STEP 3: Select one dimension. Develop a plan for changing that dimension. Be as specific as possible. Develop a list of action steps and a timetable for altering that dimension.

STEP 4: Implement the change.

STEP 5: Discussion. Individually, in small groups, or with the entire class, answer the following questions:

1. What were the key elements of the culture?
2. Which dimensions did you and your classmates address?
3. How did you plan to change the dimension you selected?
4. What problems did you encounter in implementing the change?
5. Was the change effective?

Chapter 12

Structuring High-Performance Organizations

Learning Objectives

After completing Chapter 12, you will be able to

1. Describe four options for the division of labor.
2. Characterize the basic coordinating mechanisms used in structure.
3. Comment about the values of centralization versus decentralization.
4. Compare and contrast mechanistic and organic structures.
5. Discuss the role of the informal organization.
6. Compare and contrast the basic types of structures.
7. Describe the options for creating a more adaptive structure.
8. Identify the key issues in designing structures in the dot-com, global workplace.

A Manager's Preview

Describe . . . Diagnose . . . Prescribe . . . Act

- Design an organization incorporating division of labor, coordinating mechanisms, and the organizational hierarchy.
- Know when mechanistic and organic structures work best.
- Recognize and delineate the informal organization in your company.
- Choose among functional, market-oriented, and integrated structures for your organization's design.
- Design a more adaptive structure for your organization.
- Structure dot-com and global companies effectively.

Restructuring Didn't Work at Xerox

Rick Thoman lasted little more than a year in his role as CEO of Xerox as he failed to successfully turn around a company that had been experiencing flat revenues, plummeting earnings, and a sinking stock price. The company lost more than $20 billion in stock market value during that time. Thoman's contributions seemed to be a series of unsuccessful reorganizations as he attempted to position Xerox to compete more effectively in the digital era.

The focus of reorganization was the sales force, which under the new structure, would be reorganized along industry lines rather than product lines. A single sales representative would sell all of Xerox's products. This approach required a different set of skills: Salespeople needed to diagnose each customer's situation and determine the best way to manage its information, rather than merely taking orders for photocopiers or other specialized equipment. Although the new structure might have ultimately worked, Thoman implemented it before Xerox's employees had received training about how to operate in this new way. Changes killed the organization's morale; Thoman didn't get enough people to buy into the new way of working.[1]

How would we characterize the change in Xerox's structure? How does a company's structure help it act competitively? In this chapter, we explore the options available for structuring companies and their implications for competing in a global economy. We first investigate the basics of structure. Then we examine three basic types of structure. Next we look at several more adaptive structures. Finally we analyze organizational structures in global organizations.

■ THE BASICS OF ORGANIZATIONAL STRUCTURE

Structure refers to the delineation of jobs and reporting relationships in an organization. It coordinates the work behavior of employees in accomplishing the organization's goals. An *organization chart,* as shown in Figure 12-1, shows how workers group into departments, to whom they report, and how they coordinate their activities. In this section, we discuss the basic building blocks of organization structure: division of labor, coordinating mechanisms, the hierarchy, centralized versus decentralized decision making, and mechanistic versus organic structures.

■ **FIGURE 12-1** ■

This organization chart shows how the Vermont State Treasurer's Office groups its employees.

Source: www.state.vt.us/treasurer/ orgchart.htm, December 17, 1997.

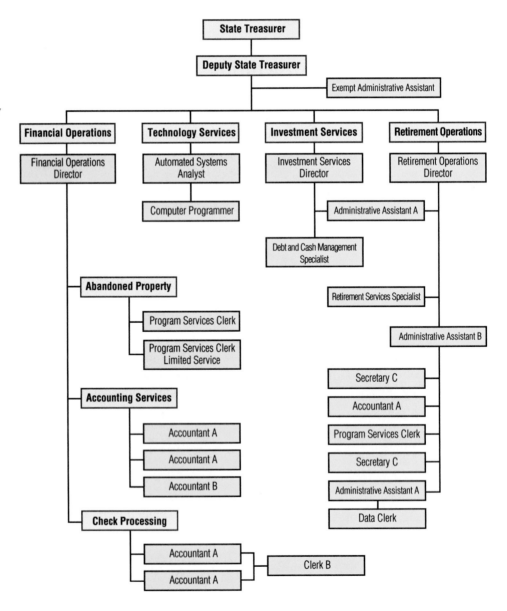

Division of Labor

Organizations allocate responsibilities in a variety of ways. Some workers focus on just a small aspect of the overall task, while others perform many related tasks. For example, an assembly-line worker in a computer assembly plant used to attach a small component of each computer; now a worker assembles an entire computer.

Specialization, or how much a job focuses on a specific and limited set of activities, varies for different positions and at different levels in the hierarchy. A copywriter might perform fewer activities than an advertising account supervisor. Entry-level salespeople perform fewer activities than sales managers. Companies can specialize by using horizontal, vertical, personal, and spatial differentiation.[2]

Horizontal Differentiation.

Horizontal differentiation describes the grouping of jobs at the same level in the hierarchy according to their function, customer, product, process, or geographical area. Look at Figure 12-2, which illustrates two types of horizontal differentiation. The left-hand chart shows an organization with relatively extensive horizontal differentiation. It has many divisions at the level shown. The right-hand chart, in contrast, shows relatively low horizontal division of labor. It has only two divisions at the level shown.

The amount of horizontal differentiation can vary considerably. It depends on such factors as the manager's preference and the employees' abilities, as well as the organization's size, age, goals, and product or service. As horizontal differentiation increases, potential barriers to communication grow. Electronic communication has reduced these barriers since it makes communication across units almost as easy as communication within a unit.

Vertical Differentiation.

Vertical differentiation describes the number of hierarchical levels in a company. Tall organizations, as shown in the left column of Figure 12-2, have many levels in the hierarchy for their size. Flat organizations, as shown in the right column, have relatively few. Compare a medium-sized insurance company, which may have seven or eight levels in its hierarchy, to a comparably sized consulting firm, which often has only three levels. The insurance company has high vertical differentiation, whereas the consulting firm has low vertical differentiation.

Vertical differentiation increases the checks and balances in a company and so can limit the number of mistakes made by employees. In a very hierarchical company, higher-level employees more often check the decisions made by lower-level employees. Tall structures provide more avenues for advancement within the organization since many levels of positions exist. This breadth of opportunity supports a closer fitting of employees' personal needs and abilities to jobs.

But tall structures can slow decision making if people at many levels in the hierarchy participate. Workers low in the hierarchy may have less motivation when only higher-level managers make important decisions. Although flatter structures have the potential for faster communication and greater adaptability, even tall structures can allow the decentralization of decision making.

Personal Differentiation.

Division of labor according to the worker's expertise or training is known as *personal differentiation*. Professional organizations often emphasize personal division of labor. For example, a hospital organizes around the specialties of its physicians, with groups for gerontology, pediatrics, and cardiology. In large hospitals, the groupings occur around subspecialties, such as pediatric cardiology, neonatology,

Structures vary in the extent of their horizontal, vertical, personal, and spatial differentiation.

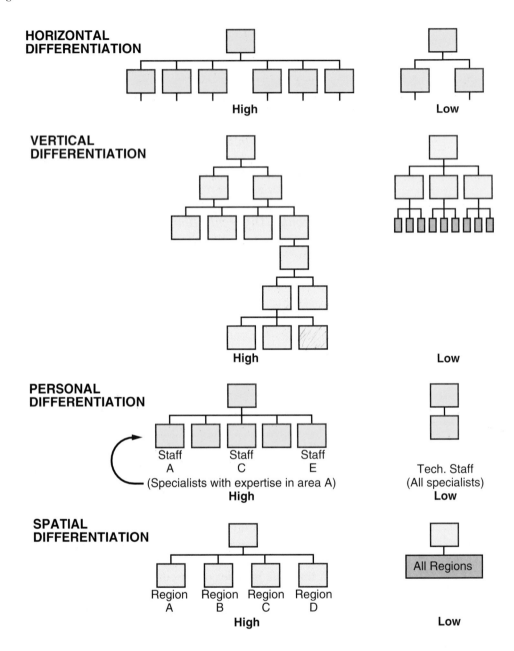

high-risk obstetrics, and so on. Departments within an organization can also vary in their degree of personal differentiation. A large university, for example, may organize groups within its management department around professors' expertise, such as strategy, organizational behavior, human resource management, and social issues in management. This type of organization becomes valuable in business situations that call for special expertise, such as high-technology manufacturing or specialty marketing.

Spatial Differentiation.   Organizations may group jobs or workers according to their geographical location. Known as *spatial differentiation*, this type of division of labor responds best to differences in customers, suppliers, or even regulations in different locations. Certainly, most transnational corporations, such as Gillette, Nestle, Compaq, and Ford Motor Company, consider geographical differences when organizing. So do large national corporations that service diverse regions of a single country.

Coordinating Mechanisms

Once an organization has created positions and departments or other groupings of workers, it must find ways to coordinate the various groups. *Coordination* refers to the extent and means by which an organization integrates or holds together its various parts and helps them work together to accomplish a common goal or activity. It can occur in five ways: mutual adjustment, direct supervision, standardization of work processes, standardization of outputs, and standardization of skills.[3]

Mutual Adjustment. Informal but direct communication between individuals, also known as *mutual adjustment,* is the most common way of coordinating. Two programmers working on a software product who speak often to coordinate their activities use mutual adjustment. Managers at Xerox who regularly attend meetings to discuss strategy or specific operations use mutual adjustment for coordination. Increasingly, mutual adjustment occurs through the use of electronic media. Employees can have immediate access to co-workers around the world through electronic mail, telephone communication, or videoconferencing.

Very simple organizations generally rely heavily on mutual adjustment to coordinate the work. Dot-com start-ups commonly use this type of coordination. Very complex organizations use it to reduce ambiguity in communication and task performance. Large, bureaucratic organizations may rely on mutual adjustment in small departments or among the top management team.

Direct Supervision. More formalized control occurs when a manager directly supervises or has responsibility for the work of one or more other employees. The vice president of human resources may coordinate the work of her employees by using direct supervision. She provides guidance, timetables, and feedback to her employees about their performance. *Direct supervision* uses the chain of command to ensure that workers do their jobs correctly. It can accompany other coordinating mechanisms, such as mutual adjustment or standardization of work processes.

The increased emphasis in organizations on empowering and using teams of workers has changed the roles of managers and reduced the amount of direct supervision used for coordination. Many organizations have substituted mutual adjustment for direct supervision of employees. Horizontal, lattice, modular, and virtual organizations, described later in this chapter, emphasize mutual adjustment rather than direct supervision for coordinating work-related activities.

Standardization of Work Processes. Managers often specify the actual steps employees should follow in performing the work, a practice known as *standardization of work processes.* Production that uses assembly-line technology, such as manufacturing ice cream or preparing hamburgers at a fast-food restaurant, typically involves standardization of work processes. This standardization uses equipment, computer programs, or written directions to define each step in the process. Specifying the procedures in this way reduces the need for other forms of coordination.

In the past, standardization of work processes effectively coordinated both highly specialized and relatively unskilled jobs; it specified repetitive tasks or simplified parts of very complex jobs. Today, however, empowered work teams that have the autonomy to adjust work processes to meet customer needs perform many of these activities.

Standardization of Outputs. Instead of specifying the process, coordination can also occur by specifying the nature of the outputs, known as *standardization of outputs*. For example, managers who are judged on the basis of their groups' productivity or profitability have their work coordinated by standardization of outputs. Insurance agents who must meet a certain quota, regardless of how they accomplish that goal, also have their work coordinated in this way. This focus on outcomes motivated agents from Prudential Insurance, Metropolitan Life Insurance, John Hancock Mutual Life Insurance, and other companies to "churn" policies by persuading policyholders to switch policies in a way that did little to change the insurance coverage but generated commissions for the agent.[4]

Historically, standardization of outputs has coordinated the work of top managers. It allows them discretion to devise the best processes to get the job done. Worker empowerment has resulted in more organizations using standardization of outputs at lower levels, allowing more workers to respond creatively to changing conditions or customer demands.

Standardization of Skills. Teachers, nurses, pharmacists, and other professionals rely on their training and expertise to coordinate their work through the *standardization of skills*. Licenses, certification programs, and training offer ways of standardizing skills. For example, certified public accountants and board-certified surgeons participate in programs directed at creating and maintaining skill standards. Nurses know how to interact with physicians and other medical personnel as a result of the training they receive in school and on the job. Lawyers know their courtroom responsibilities vis-a-vis other courtroom personnel as a result of their legal training. Often, professionals such as these use mutual adjustment to complement the standardization of skills.

The Nature of the Hierarchy

Every organization has a variety of reporting relationships. Sales representatives at Xerox may report to regional sales directors, who may in turn report to the corporate sales director, who may report to the vice president of marketing. This *chain of command* describes the supervisory relationships in an organization. An organization chart presents all the chains of command in a given organization and hence portrays the reporting pattern in that organization.

In most organizations, each individual reports to one and only one supervisor. This results in clear lines of authority. Each person knows to whom to communicate problems or questions. Occasionally, in the matrix organization (described later in this chapter), an individual may have more than one supervisor. While this structure may facilitate communication in an organization, it may also create confusion.

Although each individual typically reports to a single person, many organizational members have more than one subordinate. A manager's *span of control*, the number of people who report to him, can range from one to hundreds, although more typically from one to ten. The appropriate span of control generally depends on characteristics of the supervisor, subordinates, task, and organization. For example, professional employees often need less supervision than less skilled workers. Companies that have moved to team-based structures can also reduce their managers' span of control because the teams assume some managerial responsibilities.

Centralization Versus Decentralization

Organizations differ in the location and nature of decision making. *Centralization* means that the responsibility for making decisions is limited to those at the top of the organization's hierarchy. For example, only the owner of a neighborhood restaurant may make decisions about the items to offer or the hours of service. He centralizes decision making by allowing no other employees to make major decisions. The new COO of store operations at JCPenney decided to decrease inefficiency by centralizing all buying functions. Specialized computer software uses historical data to support inventory replacement. The new system should improve coordination, reduce inventories, and create a consistency among stores.[5]

Decentralization refers to extending the responsibility for decision making to people at all levels in the organization. At Xerox, realigning sales managers and employees lower in the hierarchy according to the industry they serviced gave them more responsibility and autonomy. However, their lack of training in performing these new roles contributed to the reorganization's failure. Decentralization assumes that the people closest to the problem have the most knowledge about it and so can best make decisions about how to handle it. It speeds decision making because decisions don't hit the bottleneck that exists when a small number of top executives must handle all problems. Although decentralization enables an organization to deal with new or sophisticated information more quickly, directly, and effectively, it can also fail to coordinate the activities of its various parts and in an extreme case even send conflicting messages into the marketplace.

Burlington Northern and Santa Fe Railroad combines centralization and decentralization. The company centralized planning and coordination but decentralized responsibilities for execution of crew scheduling, maintenance, and other operations.[6]

Mechanistic Versus Organic Structures

We can combine the building blocks described so far into two general patterns of organization structure: mechanistic and organic.

Mechanistic Structures.   Mechanistic structures have relative stability and inflexibility in the way they organize activities and workers. They most often have centralized decision making accompanied by a unitary chain of command. They rely on extensive horizontal and vertical division of labor to encourage specialization of activities throughout the organization. Although this specialization can work well in relatively predictable situations, it tends to slow decision making and impede effective communication.

Mechanistic structures rely on standardization of work processes and direct supervision, two approaches that limit the discretion of most workers in the organization to make and implement decisions. Such structures typically have a low capacity for processing information because they use the hierarchy for communication and problem solving. Some declining companies have become more mechanistic in an attempt to implement a turnaround. A study showed that 29 declining U.S. firms further centralized decision making, increased the company's reliance on formal procedures, and decreased the information that flowed to top managers. In this way, they restricted their ability to change their strategic orientations in order to halt the decline and help turn around the firm.

Organic Structures.   Organic structures emphasize flexibility and the ability to adjust rapidly to change. They deemphasize job descriptions and specialization, and encourage individuals throughout the organization to assume responsibility for making important decisions. Xerox's organization of its sales representatives around industry groups is a relatively organic structure since they are expected to expand their job description and extend their responsibilities.

Characterized by decentralization of decision making, an organic structure typically relies on a unitary chain of command, but may occasionally shift to multiple lines of authority. Companies with organic structures tend to have less horizontal and vertical differentiation and more personal and spatial differentiation. The organic structure relies on mutual adjustment and standardization of outputs, giving individuals great discretion in how they attain organizational goals. Organic structures have a high capacity for information processing, so they can readily respond to unexpected events. Such structures influence a company's ability to introduce effective change. For example, companies with organic structures have been more able to successfully introduce total quality management programs (see Chapter 14) than companies with mechanistic structures.[7]

The Informal Organization

Most organizations have an informal organization that accompanies the formal organization but reflects the way the work actually is done. For example, a trainer may formally report to the vice president of human resources but actually work more closely with the manager of the plant where he conducts most of the training. Alterations in formal relationships occur when they become too cumbersome or dysfunctional for accomplishing personal or organizational goals.

Differences between the formal and informal structure occur for three reasons:

1. **Employees may lack knowledge about the official channels of communication so use others.** Some lower-level employees, for example, may rely on former supervisors for information, rather than going to their current superiors with questions and problems. Technical employees with a problem may go directly to the person they think has expertise rather than referring it to their boss.

2. **Interpersonal obstacles may prevent workers from using the formal reporting channels.** Some workers may experience personality clashes with their bosses and seek assistance from other managers. For example, the advertising manager may work more effectively with the executive vice president than with the vice president of marketing. Other workers may have difficulty communicating with managers because of different personal styles, experiences, or perceptions of job requirements.

3. **Workers may obtain a faster response if they bypass certain channels.** If a worker can't obtain supplies by using standard procedures, he may call the purchasing agent and make a special request for supplies rather than relying on his boss to obtain them. Often workers use the corporate grapevine rather than formal channels to secure information.

In some organizations, nonofficial relationships become legitimized and substitute for the formal ones. Top managers may eventually redesign the official reporting relationships to reflect the informal ones. They may, for example, eliminate paperwork and substitute direct e-mail or voice-mail contact for securing supplies or other resources.

Diagnosing the differences between the formal and informal structure can help managers redesign organizations. They can use network analysis (see Chapter 7) to identify the nature of the links between individuals or positions, the roles individuals play, and the characteristics of positions in the network, as well as other properties of the network, such as its connectedness, accessibility, and openness to the outside.[8]

▐ BASIC TYPES OF STRUCTURES

Companies can combine the basic characteristics described in the previous section into a prototypical organizational structure. Historically, companies had functional structures. Then they introduced market-based and integrated structures, which better responded to a rapidly changing environment and professionalized workforce.

Functional Structure

A *functional structure* groups employees according to major categories of work activity. At the corporate level, companies may group employees into marketing, information systems, and human resources functions, among others, and then into further groupings within each major function. Marketing, for example, might include separate groups for market research, advertising, sales, and sales support. Springs, a home products manufacturer, recently reorganized its marketing function into three functional groups—sales, merchandising, and marketing—as a way of focusing on key accounts and products.[9] Human resources might include separate groups for staffing, compensation, organizational development, and equal opportunity compliance.

Figure 12-3 shows an excerpt from an organization chart for a functional structure. Note the relatively high horizontal and vertical differentiation that characterizes such a structure. The functional structure works best when

- the roles or jobs in the organization group well into functional areas;
- employees need relatively little communication outside the groupings;
- the organization has a well-developed product or service;
- few exceptions occur;
- the company has a relatively benign environment, such as a stable and predictable market; and
- the organization is small- to medium-sized, making face-to-face communication feasible.

Types of Functional Structures.   Functional structures fall into one of three types:

- **Simple structure.** Small and young organizations that primarily use mutual dependence and direct supervision as coordinating mechanisms have a simple structure.[10] A women's clothing store, an ice cream parlor, and a small accounting firm probably have this structure. The top manager has significant control. As the organization grows, the simple structure either departmentalizes by function or develops a more complex form that relies on other means of coordination.

- **Machine bureaucracy.** As organizations increase in size, horizontal and vertical differentiation tend to increase, leading to the standardized and formalized behavior characteristic of a machine bureaucracy.[11] Direct supervision and

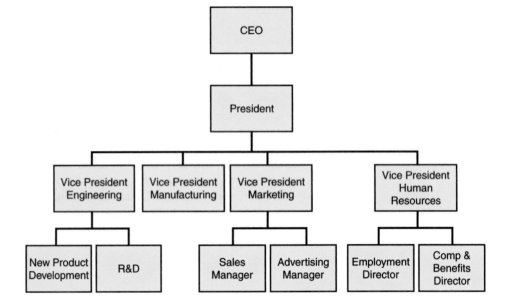

standardization of work processes are the key coordinating mechanisms. Many large-scale companies, such as automobile, steel, equipment, and consumer goods manufacturers, organize in this way.

- **Professional bureaucracy.** This structure has the formalized characteristics of the machine bureaucracy, but emphasizes standardization of skills rather than standardization of work processes for coordination.[12] A professional bureaucracy, such as a university or hospital, typically has little vertical or horizontal differentiation, but extensive personal differentiation. It uses training to ensure that workers have the required skills for effective organizational functioning.

Advantages and Disadvantages.   The functional structure encourages people with jobs in the same area of specialization to work together. This type of interaction builds a strong loyalty to the functional group and offers extensive expertise in specified areas. The relatively high vertical division of labor that often accompanies this structure provides employees with many opportunities for advancement within a functional discipline. This structure avoids duplication of effort in different parts of the organization since typically only a single human resources department, operations division, or accounting group services the entire company.

The high horizontal and vertical differentiation can also cause problems. Limited communication between functional areas can result in dysfunctional performance and even competition. Dealing with problems and exceptions may call for communication up the hierarchy, often slowing response time and hindering the ability to respond to customer demands.

Market-Oriented Structures

Unlike the functional structure, which groups employees according to functional area, the *market-oriented structure* groups workers according to the market they serve, such as product, project, client, or geographical area. Xerox used this structure for

■ FIGURE 12-4 ■

Market-oriented structures can group workers by product, as shown here, or by project.

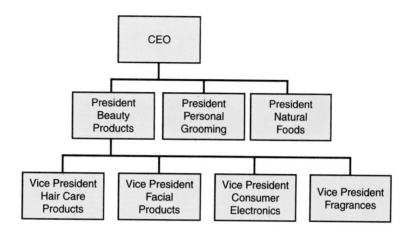

its sales representatives: The old structure at Xerox grouped employees according to the products they sold; the new structure groups them by industry. A consulting firm might organize its workers into projects for particular industry sectors, such as health care, government, and high technology. A computer distributor might separate its salesforce into corporate and personal groups. [Durk] Jager reorganized Procter & Gamble from an international network of 144 regions to seven global business units organized around product lines.[13]

Figures 12-4, 12-5, and 12-6 illustrate some market-oriented structures. In market-oriented structures, a product, project, client, or geographical grouping exists at one level, but other forms may exist elsewhere. For example, in a product structure, a product manager often supervises various functional groups. The top level of a geographical structure emphasizes location, while a more typical functional structure may exist within each geographical division.

Larger companies that implement a market-oriented structure may have market-based divisions or create a conglomerate of separate subsidiaries. Companies such as Unilever that deal with diversified products create major units, or divisions, for each market or product. Unilever has approximately 500 operating companies, each of which has a unique product identity, such as Lipton Tea. United Technologies has

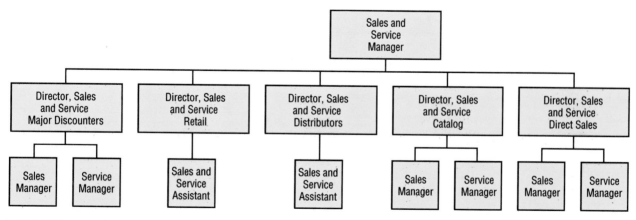

■ FIGURE 12-5 ■ *Market-oriented structures can also group employees according to their clients.*

FIGURE 12-6

Geographical structures group workers according to the areas they serve.

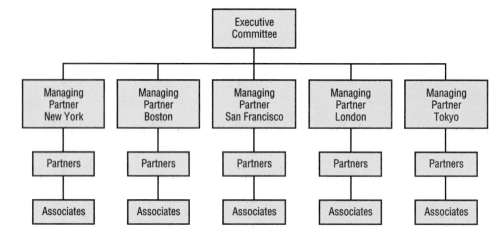

numerous divisions, including Pratt & Whitney Engines, Otis Elevator, and Carrier Air Conditioning. Divisionalized companies emphasize standardization by outputs so that each manager has bottom-line responsibility. This structure allows organizations to respond to a heterogeneous environment, particularly diverse cultures, by setting up mini-organizations that meet the unique needs of various countries and cultures. This structure takes advantage of a diverse product mix by emphasizing rather than ignoring it.

The market-oriented structure responds effectively when

- the company faces a relatively dynamic and unpredictable market situation;
- success requires rapid communication;
- the company must respond to rapidly changing conditions; or
- the organization has abundant resources for meeting customer needs.

Advantages and Disadvantages.   The market-oriented structure focuses on the unique needs of particular products, projects, customers, or geographical areas. Teams develop the common goal of meeting market demands, an advantage when changing market needs require a fast response. When accompanied by decentralized decision making, this structure speeds problem solving and adaptation by the organization. The market-oriented structure also brings the diverse expertise of various functional specialists to bear on problems associated with the particular product, project, or client.

On the downside, this structure can duplicate knowledge throughout the organization and so increase costs. Two groups of advertising professionals with similar experience and skills may service two separate product groups, eliminating any cost savings due to economies of scale. The focus on market requirements may also prevent workers from developing a wider, functional expertise that would let them move from market group to market group as needed.

Integrated Structure

The *integrated structure* is a hybrid structure that can incorporate both functional and market-oriented structures. Sometimes called an *adhocacy*,[14] it responds to the needs of a changing and complex environment.

This structure uses a variety of *ad hoc* or temporary liaison devices (task forces, integrating roles, project teams, and matrix structures) to encourage mutual adjustment among organizational members. An adhocracy has a flexible structure that can respond to a complex, changing environment. It generally incorporates sophisticated information technologies that can support teamwork and information sharing.

The integrated structure has four major characteristics:

■ **Flexible groupings of individuals that change as organizational needs change.** These groupings allow the organization to take a functional, product, project, geographical, or client orientation. For example, teams may form or disband as the organization introduces new products or withdraws obsolete ones.

■ **Groupings of individuals that emphasize a market focus.** A bank may organize temporary or permanent work teams to service small business, institutional, or other special interest group accounts.

■ **Decentralized decision making.** Increasing the autonomy, responsibility, and accountability of all employees lets the company respond faster to changing or unpredictable conditions.

■ **Groupings of employees that combine functional specialties.** Cross-functional teams that include marketing, engineering, and manufacturing representatives share high-quality information during product development and delivery.

Some companies have an integrated structure called a *matrix,* which combines the best aspects of the functional and product structures, as shown in Figure 12-7. Arthur Andersen created a regional matrix to administer its programs across state boundaries.[15] Workers report to two (or more) supervisors, one from their original functional area, the second from the product or project on which they worked, and sometimes a third from a geographical region. The assignment of workers to functional groupings remains relatively permanent, while the assignment to product, project, client, or geographical area changes as necessary.

FIGURE 12-7

A matrix structure combines the advantages of functional and market-oriented structures.

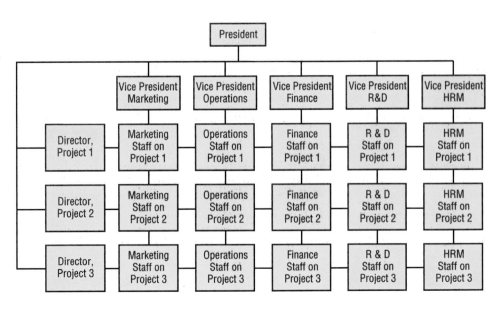

Advantages and Disadvantages.   Because integrated structures group workers along different dimensions and for varying amounts of time, they respond well to a changing environment. Companies can add or delete product or project groups as necessary. They tend to adopt this structure when they have high information-processing requirements.[16] Because project groups share functional resources, some cost economies can occur. Workers retain a strong functional identity that helps them bring special expertise to the unique needs of various products or projects.

The matrix form of an integrated structure has special costs. Overhead costs increase because this structure has relatively more managers than other forms. Reporting to more than one boss may also have personal costs for workers. They may experience conflict and stress from working for people with different standards, expectations, and work priorities. Competition between managers can lead to power struggles as well as difficulty in controlling the work. The matrix structure can also slow time-to-market in new product development.[17]

Although clarifying responsibilities and devising procedures for quickly identifying problems can improve some of these situations, companies have looked for other ways to combine functional and market-oriented structures. The more adaptive forms of organizations described next offer several possibilities.

▌ MORE ADAPTIVE STRUCTURES

The structures described so far vary in their ability to respond quickly, flexibly, and adaptively to the changing demands of the global marketplace. As a result, forward-thinking executives have devised new structures to respond to the continuing challenges of a rapidly changing environment and unpredictable customer demands. In this section, we consider five structures that are more adaptive: (1) horizontal organizations, (2) lattice organizations, (3) alliances, (4) modular organizations, and (5) virtual organizations.

Horizontal Organizations

The *horizontal organization* emphasizes the empowerment of workers by reducing the management hierarchy and focusing on core processes.[18] It encourages employees to focus on customer requirements and satisfaction. Horizontal structures typically include cross-functional teams that manage and run the processes, as shown in Figure 12-8. General Electric's Salisbury, North Carolina, plant links four multiskilled teams into a build-to-order process. A group of associate advisors, former GE managers, offer advice to the teams and provide necessary coaching.[19]

A horizontal structure has the following elements:[20]

1. It organizes work around key processes, not tasks.
2. Process owners take responsibility for an entire core process.
3. It flattens the hierarchy as a result of empowering workers and eliminating non-value-added work.
4. It uses teams to manage everything.
5. It uses information technology to help reach performance objectives and deliver value to customers.
6. It lets customers' satisfaction drive performance.
7. It rewards workers for their team-related performance.
8. It maximizes contact with suppliers and customers.

FIGURE 12-8

Horizontal structures group workers into core processes with cross-functional teams of employees.

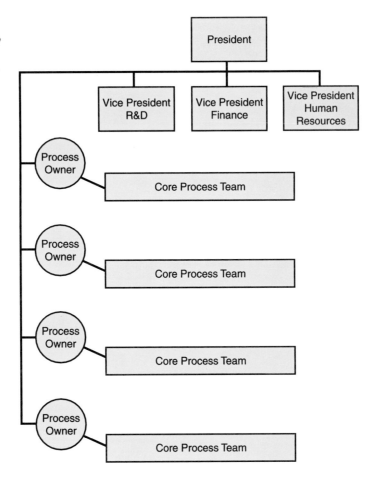

9. Top management continuously informs and trains all employees to help develop multiple competencies.
10. It measures end-of-process performance objectives.
11. It builds a culture of cooperation, collaboration, and openness.

In 1995, Ford Motor Company's Customer Service Division restructured and created a horizontal organization that focused on four core processes: business development, parts supply and logistics, vehicle service and programs, and technical support. Ford established numerous teams to handle these processes around the world. Each process has an "owner" with the responsibility for overseeing the teams' work and making sure they accomplish their goals. Twelve thousand employees use this structure to serve more than 15,000 dealerships worldwide.[21]

Lattice Organizations

The emphasis on teamwork and employee empowerment has resulted in structures that reduce or eliminate the organizational hierarchy. The *lattice organization,* one form of this type of structure, has virtually eliminated assigned or assumed authority.[22] Sponsors (rather than bosses) work with associates (rather than employees). The structure emphasizes strong interpersonal communication. The people who must accomplish various objectives are the ones who set them. In addition, commitments by associates and sponsors help organize tasks and functions.

W. L. Gore & Associates, a manufacturer of medical products, fabrics, electronic products, and industrial products that use the famous goretex material, employs more than 6,200 associates organized with this highly decentralized structure. The company uses a team-based approach to hiring, in which team members interview all candidates. Once they hire a candidate, the team assumes responsibility for the new hire's success. The resulting workforce tends to be entrepreneurial and self-starting.

Alliances

Rather than acquiring and developing their own resources, some organizations find it faster and cheaper to form a mutually beneficial *alliance* with another organization. IBM, for example, has formed alliances with several software vendors, including SAP, Seibel Systems, and SAS Institute. The SAS alliance gives IBM access to software for use in decision support and data warehousing.[23] Firms such as these unite to pursue a set of agreed-upon goals. They share control over the performance of assigned tasks and make continuing contributions to the alliance.[24] Pacific Century CyberWorks Ltd. and Telstra Corporation, both Australian companies, formed a joint venture to build the first pan-Asian mobile-phone network that would have uniform service and branding across the countries it serves.[25]

Prior alliances and strategic interdependencies influence the types of alliances that form.[26] Some companies try to form alliances along the value chain, from suppliers to customers. Iomega Corporation, a manufacturer of personal computer storage devices, first tried to improve relationships with internal suppliers, next with external suppliers, and then with customers.[27] Managers who lead such alliances must blend different cultures and management styles and reconcile variations in job design. They must also develop compatible strategies for staffing, training, performance evaluation, career development, and compensation. They must make sure that the industrial relations systems in the alliance can function compatibly.[28] This can be particularly challenging in international alliances where countries have different industrial relations systems.

The linkages between organizations in alliances strengthen companies by bringing additional resources to solving organizational problems and competing in the marketplace.[29] Fujitsu-ICL Systems, Inc., which supplies Fujitsu products for banks in North America, and Tidel Technologies, Inc., which manufactures automated teller machines, have signed an agreement under which Fujitsu-ICL will supply bill dispensers for a series of Tidel's ATMs and allow Tidel to meet continued demand for its ATMs.[30] In addition, strategic alliances can create opportunities for learning from a partner.[31]

Alliances that work

- view partnership as an opportunity;
- attach importance to the results of the collaborative efforts;
- demonstrate a reasonable level of trust;
- demonstrate a willingness to learn from each other;
- create shared goals and realistic expectations;
- use conflict productively;
- redesign and create integrated systems;
- believe in honest communication;

- have committed leadership;
- plan and budget jointly;
- have congruent measurement and reward systems; and
- provide necessary resources.[32]

Mellon Financial Corporation and Chase Manhattan originally formed a joint venture called ChaseMellon Shareholder Services that maintains shareholder accounts for small, middle-sized, and Fortune 500 companies. Mellon subsequently purchased Chase's share, renamed the company Mellon Investor Services, and added it to its various investment services businesses.[33]

Small businesses can use a variety of strategic alliances to develop and sustain technological leadership. They might create joint ventures with distributors or companies with strong research. Small companies can use contract manufacturers, companies that produce goods that other companies sell, as a way of transforming a small amount of capital into large amounts of sales.[34] They might allow others to invest in their companies or license their technology to another company. They can also make marketing–distribution agreements, manufacturing agreements, or agreements with universities or research institutes.[35] Jabil Circuit, Inc., for example, in St. Petersburg, Florida, designs and constructs personal computers for various PC makers. Celestica, Inc., in Chelmsford, Massachusetts, provides contract design or manufacturing for such PC companies as Dell, Hewlett-Packard, IBM, and Sun Microsystems.[36]

Alliances face two kinds of risk. First, they may encounter relational risk, which refers to the risk associated with unsatisfactory cooperation among alliance members. Second, they may experience performance risks, which include all other factors that negatively affect the performance of the alliance.[37] Firms manage these risks by the following means:

- using patents, contracts, and trademarks to protect their primary physical and financial resources;
- using contracts, equity, and management to exercise control;
- using short-term renewing contracts, as well as limiting commitment and making effective provisions for exiting the alliance, to retain flexibility;
- limiting another company's exposure to their company's knowledge as a way of ensuring security; and
- emphasizing superior alliance performance by encouraging high knowledge productivity and eliminating any internal learning barriers, to ensure increased productivity.[38]

Multinational partnerships offer another way to deal with global competition. Lion Bioscience AG and Bayer AG expanded their 15-month-old research partnership to computerize some chemistry experiments performed by Bayer's pharmaceutical research scientists. The United States–based firm Tripos, Inc., which developed the software for this project, has also joined the partnership. Together, these companies are attempting to use genetic data to discover and develop blockbuster drugs.[39]

Modular Organizations

A *modular organization,* also known as a dynamic network, combines a variety of subcontractors into a working organization, as shown in Figure 12-9.[40] In its simplest form, a modular organization has a small staff that develops strategy, subcontracts

Modular structures combine a number of subcontractors in order to develop and deliver a product.

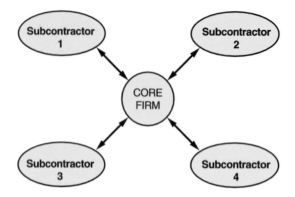

the work to others, and then monitors the interface with the various subcontractors.[41] In particular, it outsources noncore functions. This allows managers to decrease overall costs and speed the development of new products. In this way, the company can hire superior talent to perform certain functions, avoid idle capacity, reduce inventory costs, and avoid becoming committed to a technology that becomes obsolete. Such a company can grow rapidly because it uses its small amount of capital to feed rapid growth.[42]

The core firm may "sell" personal computers, but parcel out design, manufacturing, sales, and distribution to subcontractors. The company can add or subtract subcontractors as needed, giving it tremendous flexibility.[43] Because the subcontractors pursue different strategies, yet complement each other as part of the network, the modular structure meets the need for innovation and efficiency.

The dynamic network takes a variety of forms.[44] For example, individual firms may join in a partnership to work on international projects. In construction, the general contractor and subcontractors may form a stable and continuous network over time. Strategic partnering in high-technology firms also illustrates such network organizations. Nike and Reebok have used this type of structure to drive profits. Nike has very few plants, and Reebok has none. They subcontract their shoe manufacturing to companies in Asian countries with low labor costs.[45]

A modular structure has four characteristics:[46]

1. **Vertical disaggregation,** in which independent organizations within the network perform the business functions, occurs for product design, marketing, manufacturing, and other functions.
2. **Brokers** assemble the business groups by subcontracting for required services, creating linkages among partners, or locating such functions as design, supply, production, and distribution.
3. **Market mechanisms**—such as contracts or payment for results, rather than plans, controls, or supervision—hold the functions together.
4. **Full-disclosure information systems** link the various network components.

A modular structure can also exist inside an organization. The company creates entrepreneurial and market components, such as distribution, information technology, or research and development, that operate as separate divisions or profit centers with bottom-line responsibility.[47]

Virtual Organizations

The *virtual organization* is a network of independent suppliers, customers, and even competitors, generally tied together by computer technology.[48] Information technology allows them to share skills, costs, and access to markets.[49] The World Wide Web and other information technology more readily supports the development of this structure.[50] Once the network achieves its objectives, it may dissolve.[51]

Each organization participating in the network contributes only its core competencies. The frequent regrouping of companies into new virtual corporations creates the flexibility required to seize new opportunities. Virtual organizations tend to have flat structures in which information and decision making move horizontally. The widespread availability of electronic communication systems supports the multidisciplinary work arrangements that link people across formal organizational boundaries.[52] Virtual organizations may be temporary, and firms may participate in multiple alliances simultaneously.

Virtual corporations have five major characteristics:[53]

- **Technology.** Computer networks link far-flung companies and entrepreneurs, and partnerships are based on electronic contracts.
- **Excellence.** Each partner brings its core competencies to the corporation, allowing the creation of a "best-of-everything" organization.
- **Opportunism.** Companies band together to meet a specific market opportunity and then disband after meeting the need. Partnerships are less permanent, less formal, and more opportunistic.
- **Trust.** Members of a virtual corporation must trust each other because they rely on each other to achieve their goals.
- **No borders.** The virtual corporation redefines the traditional boundaries of a company. Increased cooperation among competitors, suppliers, and customers makes it difficult to determine company's borders.

Virtual companies often begin by placing individual employees in remote locations and then relying on electronic communication to coordinate their work. Next they place sales and service groups in the field, close to their customers. Finally, the organization relies on computer systems to work collaboratively with customers and suppliers.[54] The people who most readily adapt to working in a virtual organization are those who have always worked independently, such as consulting teams, and those who have worked closely before but now must work at different locations.[55] AgileWeb offers manufacturing services by gathering expertise from a pool of manufacturing companies to meet a specific client's needs.[56]

Virtual organizations can also exist within a single company. Allmerica created four Centers of Excellence for its information technology staff: software engineering, business services, project management, and systems management. These virtual organizations consist of a pool of employees from whose expertise various business units can draw. This allows all parts of the organization access to a broader pool of talent and enables information technology staff to work on a broader array of projects and problems.[57] The U.S. Department of Defense is formulating plans for a virtual organization of high-technology reservists who would remain in their home units while meeting the broader needs of the military worldwide.[58]

STRUCTURES IN DOT-COM, GLOBAL ORGANIZATIONS

Most dot-com companies introduce highly organic, flexible structures that allow them to grow rapidly and responsively. They may begin as simple organizations, with the CEO working closely with a small group of associates. Then, as the companies grow, they typically introduce more formalized structures. However, many dot-coms continue to function as networked organizations, coordinating their employees' work by using electronic communication. Although dot-coms may adopt a more formal structure and hierarchy as they grow, in order to respond to the rapidly changing environment, they tend to retain organic structures that allow them to be flexible and adaptable.

Although global organizations have the same basic structures as domestic ones, they may face particular challenges in creating a cohesive structure across countries. They must respond to differences in culture, language, and laws while creating an integrated enterprise. Hewlett-Packard reorganized its global structure so that multinational clients can purchase from a single sales and marketing group in their local area.[59] Other companies have moved key operations to specific business locations; for example, Philips's digital set-top box is in California, and its audio business is in Hong Kong, both the hottest regions for those new trends.[60]

Increasingly, organizations form alliances with foreign companies. Eesti Uhispank of Estonia, Vilniaus Bankas of Lithuania, and Unibaka of Latvia formed an alliance in which all three banks develop investment-banking deals, give loans, and issue credit cards.[61] Need2Buy, a California-based online marketplace, recently formed a joint venture with Mitsubishi Electric to develop Need2Buy-Asia, an e-commerce Web site for distributing electronic components in the Far East.[62] Companies that tend to have longer-lasting international joint ventures are those with experience in forming domestic joint ventures and those that are international, wholly owned subsidiaries.[63]

Foreign companies may need to deal with complex legal entities that make competition from outside the country difficult. Japan, for example, has the *keiretsu,* and Korea has the *chaebol;* both terms refer to a family of companies joined under various financial agreements, with interlocking directorates. Ranging in size from ten to hundreds of companies, the keiretsu can be either supplier oriented or bank centered. In a supplier-oriented alliance, companies such as Sony or Honda integrate vertically. In a bank-centered keiretsu, companies such as Mitsubishi integrate vertically and horizontally with 20 to 40 percent of their stock owned by other members of the alliance.[64] Sanwa created a specialist financial keiretsu that joined partners, such as the fund-management company Toyo Trust and the stockbroker Universal Securities, in a loose federation.[65]

Penetrating such alliances has been virtually impossible for non-Japanese companies. Recently, however, U.S. companies have found ways to penetrate them. TRW Systems, for example, has become a second-tier member of the Toyota and Nissan keiretsus, giving it long-term ties as a supplier to these companies.[66]

The Asian financial crisis of the 1990s left some of their keiretsus in shambles. Mitsubishi, one of the most powerful alliances, posted huge losses and sold a 34 percent stake in Mitsubishi Motors to DaimlerChrysler. Unwilling to undergo the restructuring needed to succeed, Mitsubishi failed dramatically.[67] The Daewoo Group, a long-existing Korean chaebol, also illustrates the failures of such closely held alliances, since the government declared it insolvent in 1999. Initial plans to spin off or sell its components have languished because Daewoo executives have been reluctant to accept foreign expertise and investment.[68] In addition, many engineers and managers left the chaebol to start their own companies.[69] Chaebol chairmen have lost millions of dollars due to unilateral investment decisions. Dividends tend to be low compared to profits, and the Fair Trade Commission has examined the likelihood that the top chaebols have used earnings of stronger members to subsidize weaker ones without consulting minority shareholders.[70]

▌ Summary

1. An organization's structure refers to the content of jobs, their grouping, and the reporting relationships in the organization.
2. Structures vary in their division of labor and the mechanisms for coordinating various parts of the organization.
3. Centralized decision making places control of decisions in the hands of a few, whereas decentralized decision making disperses the responsibility for decisions throughout the organization.
4. Each worker usually reports to a single supervisor reflecting unity of command, and these reporting relationships define the chain of command.
5. Mechanistic structures emphasize specialization, have extensive centralization of decision making, and operate best in predictable, relatively simple situations; organic structures deemphasize specialization, support decentralized decision making, and operate well in dynamic, complex, unpredictable situations.
6. The informal structure, which describes the way people actually conduct business in an organization, often operates instead of the formal structure.
7. A functional structure groups employees according to major functions, or categories of work activities; market-oriented structures group employees according to the particular product, project, client, or geographical area on which they focus; integrated structures combine two or more forms of grouping to create more flexible, market-driven organizations.
8. Adaptive structures—such as horizontal structures, lattice structures, alliances, modular organizations, and virtual organizations—respond to a dynamic environment and the demands of globalization.
9. Competing in a dot-com, global environment poses special challenges and opportunities for designing organizational structures.

A Manager's Diagnostic Review

■ Design an organization using variations on division of labor, coordinating mechanisms, and the organizational hierarchy.

- What type of division of labor exists?
- What integrating mechanisms does the organization use?
- Does unity of command exist?

- How large is the span of control of each manager?
- Is decision making centralized or decentralized?

☐ Know when mechanistic and organic structures work best.

- Is the structure mechanistic or organic?
- What are the advantages and disadvantages of the structure used?

☐ Recognize and delineate the informal organization in your company.

- What does the informal structure look like?
- Does the informal organization reinforce or contradict the formal organization structure?

☐ Choose among functional, market-oriented, and integrated structures for your organization's design.

- What structural configuration describes the organization?
- What are the advantages and disadvantages of each structure?
- When should each structure be used?

☐ Design a more adaptive structure for your organization.

- What alternative structures are possible?
- Which structure would work well in your organization?

☐ Structure dot-com and global companies effectively.

- Which structure best meets the challenges dot-com companies face?
- Which structure best meets the challenges multinational and multicultural organizations face?

Visit the Gordon homepage on the Prentice Hall Web site at

http://www.prenhall.com/gordon

for recommended readings, additional activities, Internet exercises, updated information, and links to related Web sites.

▌ Thinking Critically About Organizational Behavior

1. Do certain coordinating mechanisms work best with specific types of division of labor?
2. What problems does unity of command cause?
3. What problems does duality of command cause?
4. Should all organizations decentralize decision making?
5. Should all organizations strive for organic structures?
6. Are matrix structures still feasible?
7. Do more adaptive structures work better for dot-com or traditional companies?

8. Under what circumstances are horizontal organizations and modular organizations most and least effective?
9. Can multinational companies successfully be created as virtual organizations?
10. Under what circumstances are alliances most and least effective?
11. What advice about structure would you offer a manager starting a dot-com company?
12. What unique challenges do multinational organizations face in choosing their structures?

ACTIVITY 12-1: THE DOT-COM START-UP

STEP 1: You have been asked to join the board of directors of a dot-com start-up that your former college roommate has founded. Your roommate believes that renting apartments to college students on the Web has great business potential. So far, your roommate seems to be correct. The company grew from 5 employees after three months of existence to 30 employees after six months. The company's business plan targets a company with 200 employees within 12 more months and 500 employees within 12 months after that. Your roommate knows that you are an expert in designing organizations and wants your input in that particular area. You are allowed to confer with a group of your friends and colleagues.

STEP 2: Individually or in small groups, as directed by your instructor, draw the organization chart for the company at each of the four time periods. You have considerable freedom in creating a structure that you believe would support the growth described. You will need to determine the types of functions and jobs required in the company.

STEP 3: Describe the department's structure at each of the four times. Answer the following questions:

1. How would you characterize the division of labor?
2. How would you characterize the coordinating mechanisms?
3. How would you describe the chain of command and span of control?
4. How would you describe the basic structural configuration?

ACTIVITY 12-2: ORION COLLEGE

STEP 1: Read the following information about Orion College.

Orion College has had a functional organizational structure, as shown in Figure 12-10. Students who are accepted to Orion need to deal with several departments to register. For example, the Admissions Department answers any questions about the admissions process, makes admissions decisions, and communicates with the students until they arrive on campus. Although the Admissions Department sends incoming students information about financial aid, it does not answer questions about it or process aid applications. The Financial Aid Department receives applications for financial aid, makes decisions about financial aid, and then administers it during the

students' four years in the college. The registrar handles all course registration.

Over the past few years, the number of complaints from incoming students has increased markedly. They feel that the college isn't customer-oriented—that they have to deal with too many departments to get answers to simple questions.

STEP 2: The president of Orion has appointed a task force to evaluate the structure of the college. You and a group of classmates have been appointed to that task force. In small groups, review the structure of Orion College. Answer the following questions:

1. Describe the division of labor.
2. Describe the coordinating mechanisms used.

■ FIGURE 12-10 ■
Partial organization chart for Orion College.

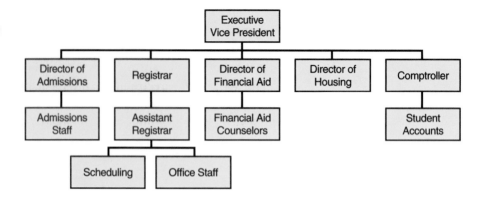

3. What are the advantages and disadvantages of the functional structure?
4. What kinds of problems does this type of organization solve? Create?
5. Is this the most effective kind of organization?

STEP 3: Propose a series of structural changes.

STEP 4: Share your proposals with the entire class. Then answer the following questions:

1. How does the new organization differ from the old one?
2. Will it be more customer-focused?
3. What are its advantages and disadvantages?

ACTIVITY 12-3 MAGNACOMP, INC.

STEP 1: Read the following description of Magnacomp, Inc.

In this exercise you are operating as members of a work team producing Magnaunits. These are assembled from subassemblies, and the subassemblies have to be built from smaller units.

The job of your team is to work together to assemble the final product "Z" at the lowest cost and with acceptable quality. Product cost is measured by the total employee minutes required to produce the product. The labor cost schedule shown in Table 12-1 is the basis for computing the total cost for a team completing the exercise with an acceptable quality

■ TABLE 12-1 ■

Labor Costs for Magnacomp, Inc.

Number of Members	Cost in $/Employee/Minute
3	100
4	125
5	150
6	175
7	200
8	225
9	265
10	305

FIGURE 12-11

Magnacomp, Inc., Project 1, flowchart for manufacturing.

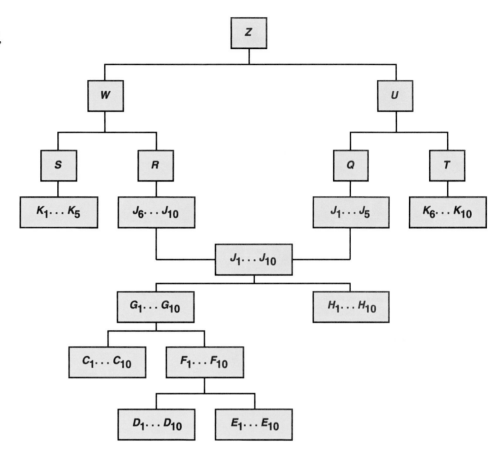

answer. Thus, a team completing the task successfully in 15 minutes with five members would have a total cost of $150 \times 5 \times 15 = \$11,250$.

Quality is determined by the accuracy of the answer. Deviations greater than ± 10 percent will not be acceptable, and a new answer must be computed.

The assembly process is straightforward, and there are no tricks in the method: A deck of cards corresponding to individual parts will be distributed to each company by the instructor. They are identical for each company. These cards, representing raw materials coming into the plant, are in random order. Operation cards also accompany the individual parts cards. Each part is coded by a letter-number combination. Before the parts can be assembled, various indicated computations must be performed. The parts can then be assembled into subassemblies by performing the appropriate operations.

Work flow is indicated by flowcharts (Figures 12-11 and 12-12), which show how assemblies are formed. They do not show the combining of operations. The operations necessary to combine sub-

assemblies are indicated on the operations cards included with the parts and in the description of operations in Tables 12-2 and 12-3 for Project 1 and Project 2.

The team determining the value of "Z" within ± 10 percent at the lowest cost will be declared the winner. If ties in cost occur, the team with the most accurate answer will win.

Two trials will be run: Project 1 and Project 2.

STEP 2: Team leaders will be selected. There will be three to five teams depending on class size. Each leader in turn will select two assistants from the class. Each team will then have 10 minutes for a private preliminary planning session. During this time, decisions should be made as to an initial organizational structure, and an operations plan should be formulated. At this time, each team should estimate its manpower needs for the simulation. Each team will be allowed to select additional persons for the simulation at the end of this planning period. Care should be taken in selecting

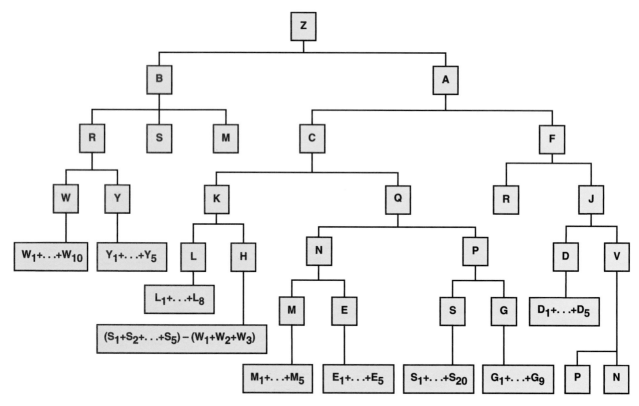

■ FIGURE 12-12 ■   *Magnacomp, Inc., Project 2, flowchart for manufacturing.*

■ TABLE 12-2 ■

Magnacomp, Inc., Project 1.

Operations

1. $Z = W + U$
2. $U = Q \div T$
3. $W = S \div R$
4. $S = K_1 + \ldots + K_5$
5. $R = J_6 + \ldots + J_{10}$
6. $Q = J_1 + \ldots + J_5$
7. $T = K_6 + \ldots + K_{10}$
8. $J_1 \ldots J_{10} = G_1 - H_1, G_2 - H_2, \ldots G_{10} - H_{10}$
9. $G_1 \ldots G_{10} = F_1 \times C_1, F_2 \times C_2, \ldots F_{10} \times C_{10}$
10. $F_1 \ldots F_{10} = D_1 - E_1, D_2 - E_2, \ldots D_{10} - E_{10}$
11. Where $C_1 \ldots C_{10}; E_1 \ldots E_{10}, D_1 \ldots D_{10}, H_1 \ldots H_{10}$ and $K_1 \ldots K_{10}$ are numerical values.

TABLE 12-3

Magnacomp, Inc., Project 2.

Operations

1. $Z = A + B$
2. $B = R - S + M$
3. $R = W + Y$
4. $W = W_1 + \ldots + W_{10}$
5. $Y = Y_1 + \ldots + Y_5$
6. $A = C \div F$
7. $C = Q \times K$
8. $K = L \div H$
9. $L = L_1 + \ldots L_8$
10. $H = (S_1 + \ldots + S_5) - (W_1 + W_2 + W_3)$
11. $Q = P \div N$
12. $N = M - E$
13. $P = S + G$
14. $M = M_1 + \ldots + M_5$
15. $E = E_1 + \ldots + E_5$
16. $S = S_1 + \ldots + S_{20}$
17. $G = G_1 + \ldots + G_9$
18. $F = R \div J$
19. $J = D - V$
20. $D = D_1 + \ldots + D_5$
21. $V = P - N$
22. Where $G_1 \ldots G_9$; $S_1 \ldots S_{20}$; $M_1 \ldots M_5$; $E_1 \ldots E_5$; $L_1 \ldots L_8$; $W_1 \ldots W_{10}$; $Y_1 \ldots Y_5$; and $D_1 \ldots D_5$ are numerical values.

additional personnel since the group's performance evaluation will be affected by the size of the team. If the team is understaffed, it may not be competitive with the other teams in the exercise, and if it is overstaffed the cost of additional personnel will reduce the team's efficiency measure.

STEP 3: The selection of additional team personnel will occur. Those class members not selected will act as observers and report to the class during the discussion period.

STEP 4: A second planning session will now be conducted with the complete team. You will have 10 minutes.

STEP 5: Begin the exercise. Complete the Project 1 phase of the Magnacomp, Inc., simulation. You will have 20 minutes.

STEP 6: At the conclusion of Project 1, a 10-minute period will be provided to allow each team to analyze its mode of operations and make changes if necessary.

STEP 7: Complete the Project 2 phase of the exercise. You will have 20 minutes.

STEP 8: Discussion. After the exercise, each team should analyze its mode of operations, its effectiveness, the organizational structure developed, the communication channels, and the advantages and disadvantages of the system employed.

DESCRIPTION

1. Prepare an organization chart of your company.
2. Is this the initial form of organization you used? If you modified your initial structure, when, how, and why?
3. How did each member feel about his or her role in the simulation? Why?
4. Do differences exist between the various teams in the exercise with respect to these questions?
5. How was the team's performance? How does it compare with that of the other teams?

DIAGNOSIS

6. Can differences be explained in terms of organizational structure?
7. How were the division of labor, coordination, and communication handled in the organization?

PRESCRIPTION

8. What changes would have improved the organization's functioning?

Source: Reprinted by permission from *Managing for Organizational Effectiveness: An Experiential Appraoch,* by F. E. Finch, H. R. Jones, and J. A. Letterer (New York: McGraw Hill, 1976), pp. 82–84.

ACTIVITY 12-4: HOSPITAL DEPARTMENTAL CONSOLIDATION

STEP 1: Read the following description.

Janet Johns is the administrator of Suburban Memorial Hospital, a 275-bed hospital in an upper-class suburb in a western state.

Ms. Johns recently asked the new assistant administrator, Sam Donalds, to investigate whether a consolidation of the ECG, Pulmonary Function, and Cardiopulmonary Rehabilitation Departments would result in a significant savings to the hospital.

BACKGROUND

The three departments do basically the same types of patient tests. As medicine has progressed, there has been a movement away from static (at rest) testing to dynamic (in motion) testing. Dynamic testing is used in the ECG Department for tests on the heart, in the Pulmonary Function Department for lung tests, and in the Cardiopulmonary Rehabilitation Department for both heart and lung tests.

At present there is a duplication of services and equipment among the three departments at Suburban Memorial. In addition, three separate technicians are employed, as well as three part-time physicians who work on a percentage basis, according to the volume of work.

The ECG and Pulmonary Function Departments make a significant contribution to Suburban's revenue. The contribution margin of Pulmonary Function has been 80 percent (for every $100 earned, the hospital spends only $20 to earn it) and that of ECG has been 60 percent.

Revenues for each department have been as follows:

Department	Annual Revenue	Contribution Margin
ECG	$360,000	60%
Pulmonary Function	$520,000	80%
Cardiopulmonary (new department, less than one year)	$80,000	Unknown

The total annual revenue of Suburban Memorial is $16.1 million, and the net income is $1.3 million. Mr. Donalds had calculated that a departmental consolidation could initially save the hospital $100,000 by selling duplicated equipment. In addition, the annual savings would amount to the following:

$44,000	Personnel costs (fewer technicians needed, etc.)
$15,000	Ordering and supplies reduction (no duplication, less ordering)
$125,000	Reduced physician fees (only one physician needed)
$16,000	Plant and facilities (could lease out space not needed after consolidation)
$200,000	Total

Therefore, the total annual savings—in essence, additional revenue—would be $200,000 in addition to the initial $100,000 for selling the equipment.

PHYSICIANS

Dr. Bartl, head of Pulmonary Function, is responsible for 80 percent of the pulmonary admissions to the hospital and about 4.7 percent of the total admissions. He is an extremely popular physician, attracting respiratory cases from well outside the normal service area of Suburban Memorial.

Dr. Neuman, head of ECG, controls 20 percent of the hospital's cardiac/internal medicine cases. She admits about 30 percent of the hospital's patients.

Finally, the head of the new Cardiopulmonary Rehabilitation Department, Dr. Hermann, controls 100 percent of those cases that at this point represent a negligible percentage of the hospital's patient revenue.

All three physicians have more or less equal support from the medical staff.

Ms. Johns is wondering what to do about the physicians if she decides to go through with the consolidation. One of the three physicians would have to be chosen (with a new reimbursement contract) to head the new department, or perhaps a new, salaried physician could be brought in. The combined workload would still be less than full-time.

However, Ms. Johns sees several problems with either of these alternatives. Primarily, the physicians who would be "excluded" from this new department might become resentful and start admitting their out-of-service-area patients to other hospitals. Ms. Johns and Mr. Donalds have estimated a 25 percent probability that the three physicians would do so, which would mean a possible loss to the hospital of 15 percent of these physicians' admissions.

Ms. Johns has asked Mr. Donalds to prepare a report of the situation, including his recommendations, which will be discussed at the next management council meeting.

STEP 2: Assume you are Mr. Donalds, what would you recommend? Prepare the type of report Ms.

Johns has asked for as if it were going to be presented to the management council.

STEP 3: Assuming the council votes for consolidation, prepare another report outlining your recommended strategy, one that would result in the least amount of alienation and maximum cooperation.

STEP 4: Discussion. Share the reports. What are the advantages and disadvantages of each option? What key elements should be included in a redesign of the departments?

Source: From D. Marcic, *Organizational Behavior: Experiences and Cases*, 3rd ed. (St. Paul: West, 1992).

ACTIVITY 12-5: THE JOB-GETTER ENTERPRISE

STEP 1: Read the following:

The Job-Getter Enterprise is a start-up publishing firm. The publication produced by the firm, the Job Getter, is a weekly magazine that publishes listings of available jobs in the area. The magazine is sold in local convenience stores, campus bookstores, and through vending machine newsracks, and it is distributed throughout northern California.

The business has been operating for three years and shows great promise. But the firm has yet to generate a regular profit. The founder, Martin Manicot, is convinced that his firm has grown to the point where he needs some help in redesigning it. He has asked you to serve as a team of consultants to help him redesign his organization.

THE ISSUES

Four key issues plague this entrepreneurial start-up:

1. Obtaining a variety of timely job listings is difficult. Job listings are advertised jobs that appear in the publication. If job listings are not timely, repeat sales for the magazine decline. Customers are unwilling to purchase the publication unless the job listings meet their needs, are timely, and are local.

2. Circulation and distribution remain a problem. Local distributors are not willing to carry an untested publication on their newsracks. Circulation has been low because the number of locations in which the new publication was

sold were few. This is a problem because circulation is traditionally a key factor in attracting advertising for the publication.

3. The success of the publication depends on the number of advertisements sold. Full- and half-page advertisements account for the bulk of revenue. Advertisers include companies such as the local retail stores, employment placement agencies, food-service firms, manufacturing firms, and others who have continuous needs for employment. However, advertisers are reluctant to purchase advertising space unless circulation is sufficiently widespread.

4. Turnover of sales personnel plagues the business. Manicot has continually hired salespeople to sell advertising space. Once they realize the task is difficult, they leave for other jobs posted in the magazine. He has hired a number of college students part-time as salespeople; the continual drain of personnel out the door has taken considerable time away from Manicot's other duties as he spends most of his time on training new salespeople and less of his time on increasing circulation.

It is the task of the new publication to identify and publish timely job listings, while simultaneously increasing circulation and distribution to attract competitive advertising space.

THE DEPARTMENTS AND FUNCTIONS

The key functions of the new enterprise are summarized as follows:

1. **sales,** selling job listings and advertising space;
2. **circulation and distribution,** making the publication available in as many locations as possible, picking up and delivering the publication on a weekly basis; and
3. **production,** putting together the weekly listings, advertising space, formatting, proofreading, and printing the magazines.

Sales encompasses two categories: (1) job listings, listed for free in the publication, and (2) advertising space, for companies who wish to advertise particular positions or continual employment needs. Jobs are gathered by telemarketing (calling local companies to determine if they want to list a job opening). Advertising space is sold through telemarketing and visits. Typically, a company is contacted to determine if it would like to list available jobs for free. After the company receives a response from the publication (for example, 20 applicants say they saw the job listed in the magazine), that company is approached to see if it might like to purchase advertising space.

Circulation and distribution involve making the publication as widely available as possible. Currently, approximately 700 outlets carry the magazine. There is potential for as many as 1,500 outlets or more. Owners of local convenience stores, college bookstores, grocery stores, and other likely locations must be visited regularly to obtain permission to distribute the magazine. As an incentive, store owners receive a small percentage (10 percent) of every issue sold. In addition, the publication is distributed through newsracks in urban areas. The magazine must be picked up and delivered to all these locations on a weekly basis so that timely information is distributed.

Production involves printing the magazine—typing the job listings, designing advertisements, and proofreading each issue. The issue is compiled by using a graphics computer and then sent to a local print shop for presswork and binding.

THE JOBS AND THE PEOPLE

Currently, seven people are employed in sales jobs. Salespeople have been hired on a part-time basis, with only the sales manager, Jennifer, and one other salesperson hired full-time. Full-time salespeople concentrate on on-site visitations for advertising sales; they are paid part salary ($100 per week) and part commission (25 percent of the advertising space sold). Part-time salespeople concentrate primarily on telemarketing sales; they are paid minimum wage on an hourly basis ($4.25 an hour) and receive a 10 percent commission. One employee, Greg, serves as the circulation manager. He is responsible for increasing circulation by improving the number of outlets that carry the publication. The circulation manager is a salaried position, paid $325 per week with no commission. Another employee, Alfred, has been hired on a full-time basis to supervise the drivers who distribute and pick up the publication. This individual is paid a single sum for the distribution and collection of each issue during the month. The drivers who distribute the publication are hired part-time; currently, there are five drivers, paid on an hourly basis. Two part-time secretaries are responsible for the production of the magazine. Their duties involve inputting the job listings, designing advertising space, and proofreading each issue. The production secretaries are paid on an hourly basis and are offered flextime hours to complete their job tasks.

THE PROBLEMS

Manicot has found that his current organization design is not working. The salespeople concentrate on telemarketing (which can be done easily from home) more than on-site visitations to sell advertising space. Advertising sales are much lower than projected. For those salespeople who have attempted on-site visits to sell advertising space, much of their activity has centered around locations close to their homes, rather than larger targeted sales areas. The geographic span includes a territory of over 200 miles, with the Monterey Bay area as one location, Sacramento and points east as another area, and San Francisco and the Silicon Valley–San Jose basin as a third (Figure 12-13). Manicot would like to expand into the Napa Valley area north of San

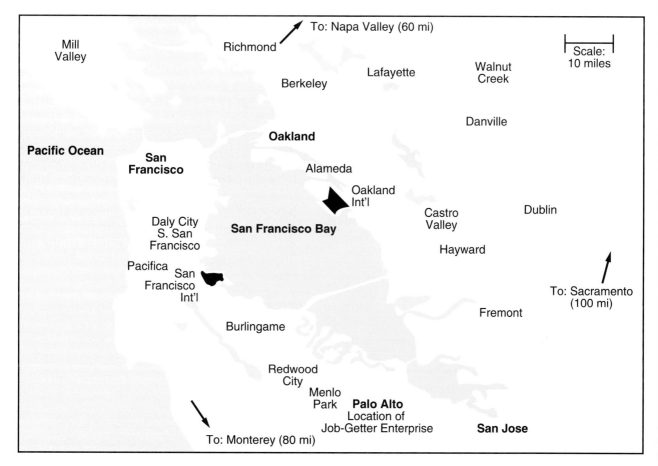

FIGURE 12-13   *San Francisco Bay area.*

Francisco as well, but he can't seem to get his salespeople to concentrate on that area.

The sales manager, Jennifer, complains that she cannot concentrate on sales, telemarketing, training new salespeople, and promotion all at the same time. She recognizes that in a small business it is often necessary to perform more than one task, but the combination of all four tasks is simply too much. As a result, her job performance suffers. Because her pay is directly tied to her sales, she spends most of her time selling rather than training or working on promotional activities.

The circulation manager, Greg, complains that his territory is too large for one individual. This is complicated by his other responsibilities, such as supervising Alfred, who oversees the truck drivers who distribute the publication. He says there is

enough stress in his job battling major distributors who sell publications en masse to local stores. The geographic area for circulation is as dispersed as the sales territory. Additionally, he maintains he cannot sell the publication to new vendors until it is proven via circulation. Circulation will not be boosted until customers get to know the product and are willing to purchase it on a repeat basis.

The distribution manager, Alfred, reports in only once every two weeks. He seems to want to do more than simple distribution and coordination of the drivers, but Manicot is unclear what that could be. Alfred is motivated, interested in earning more money, and a good co-worker. He has mentioned an interest in developing circulation or helping with sales from time to time, but as a part-time worker, it is unclear how much he really could contribute.

The production staff works primarily at home, and Manicot is displeased with the quality of their proofreading. Some of the listings were actually omitted from the last issue by mistake, causing delays in the timeliness of the information. Occasionally, new advertisers have been omitted from the publication, causing delays in revenue.

Turnover has plagued the sales ranks. Four part-timers and one full-timer have left the company during the past three months. Over the past three years, Manicot has lost a circulation manager and two other members of his production staff. Although turnover is to be expected in a small business, each time someone leaves, a new person must be trained properly. New employees cannot work to full capacity until they have been on the job at least two full months. As a result, Manicot always seems to be running behind on his sales and circulation objectives.

Furthermore, Manicot is doing virtually everything himself—training new salespeople, performing on-site visits, proofreading the magazine, manning the phones, and obtaining new vendors for distribution. He feels he needs to create clear-cut jobs that specify the functions and responsibilities so that he can do what he really needs to do for the business—strategic planning and obtaining financing to capitalize the business. If he could get additional financing, he could afford to pay his personnel more competitively, hire more salespeople full-time, and reduce turnover.

STEP 2: Examine the current organization chart for the Job-Getter Enterprise (Figure 12-14). Then, in groups of three to six people, design an organization chart that you feel is most appropriate for solving the problems of the Job-Getter Enterprise. Draw the chart, complete with reporting relationships and functions that describe how you feel the Job-Getter Enterprise should be organized. Be certain that your chart includes spaces for individual position responsibilities, similar to the one drawn for the current Job-Getter Enterprise organization.

STEP 3: Discussion. In small groups or with the entire class, answer the following questions:

1. Which organizational design did you choose?
2. What are the advantages and disadvantages of this design?

Source: Excerpted and reprinted with permission from L. A. Mainiero and C. I. Tromley, *Developing Managerial Skills in Organizational Behavior,* 2d ed. (Englewood Cliffs, NJ: Prentice Hall, 1994).

ACTIVITY 12-6: CREATING AN ALLIANCE

STEP 1: Read the following scenario.

You are the dean of the Fleming Business School. Your board of advisors has recently suggested that the school would benefit from forming an alliance with a medical school in your town. The medical school is part of a medium-sized university that lacks a business school. Market research has suggested that future physicians could benefit from understanding how businesses operate—and that they increasingly want to understand this. Obtaining an MBA in addition to their medical degree would be useful. The medical community could provide a new source of students for both your MBA and executive programs.

STEP 2: Individually or in small groups, offer a plan for creating such an alliance. Consider the following questions in your plan:

1. What form of leadership will the alliance have?
2. What will be an appropriate division of labor?
3. What types of coordinating mechanisms make sense?
4. What will the organization chart look like?

STEP 3: Share your plans with the entire class. Then answer the following questions:

1. How do you create a workable alliance?
2. What are the major issues to consider?

FIGURE 12-14

Current organization chart and financial information: The Job-Getter Enterprise.

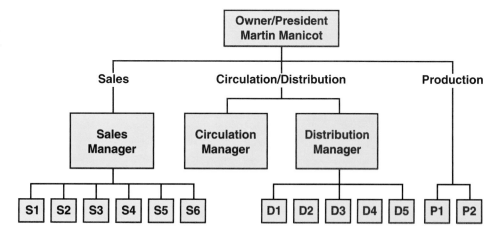

Financial Information: The Job-Getter Enterprise

Revenue per month:

Approximately 4,000 issues sold at $1 per issue: @ $.70 return*	$2,800
Approximately 10 full pages of advertising space sold per month @ $350 per page (after commissions paid)	$3,500
Total Revenue	**$6,300**

Expenses per month:

Office expenses (including office rental, five telephone lines, supplies)	$2,000
Production costs per issue for printing (20,000 issues printed)	$1,400

Compensation costs:

Sales: $100 per week plus 20% commission	$ 400
Telemarketing: Minimum wage ($4.25 per hour) plus 10% commission. Total $2,600 per month	$2,600
Circulation: $325 per week, no commission/ $1,400 per month	$1,400
Production: Minimum wage ($4.25 per hour)/ $200 per month	$ 200
Delivery: Minimum wage ($4.25 per hour)/ $1,100 per month	$1,100
Total Month Expenses	**$9,800**

Net Loss	**($3,500)**

Number of current locations: 800

*$.30 goes to vendors

Chapter 13

Influences on Organizational Structure

Learning Objectives

After completing Chapter 13, you will be able to

1. Identify the components and dimensions of the changing environment and identify the environment's impact on the design of companies.
2. Discuss the impact of changing technology on organizational design.
3. Comment about the changing workforce, particularly the influence of knowledge workers on organizational design.
4. Show how an organization's goals and strategy should affect its design.
5. Trace an organization through its life cycle.
6. Comment about the impact of downsizing and rightsizing on the design of organizations.
7. Indicate how mergers and acquisitions affect organizational design.
8. Specify the unique issues involved in designing organizations in the dot-com, global workplace.

A Manager's Preview

Describe . . . Diagnose . . . Prescribe . . . Act

▢ Design a structure that effectively responds to the organization's environment.

▢ Fit an organization's structure to its technology.

▢ Design an organization to meet the needs and abilities of the workforce.

▢ Design a structure that fits the organization's goals and strategy.

▢ Design a structure that suits the organization's stage of development.

▢ Deal with the impact of downsizing, mergers, and acquisitions.

▢ Effectively structure organizations in cross-cultural environments.

Redesigning Ford Motor Company

As the new CEO of Ford Motor Company, one of Jacques Nasser's highest priorities was to shake up the stodgy, overly analytic culture and equally bureaucratic structure of the giant auto maker. Nasser dramatically moved Ford's units away from the centralized authority that had characterized the company to semi-autonomous businesses focused on the company's brands and regions. Ford of Europe and Ford of South America illustrate the results of such restructuring.

Nasser believed that to compete in the extremely challenging automobile industry, Ford needs to be nimble both in design and manufacturing. He hired new heads of luxury, design, and marketing units as part of a major shakeup. He purchased Volvo; he expects new leadership there to achieve ambitious sales targets by broadening its image and expanding its customer base. He overhauled the way Ford designs cars so that it responds more creatively, quickly, and accurately to consumer demands. He reduced the company's reliance on focus groups and updating of old models to match those of competitors. One of his managers even went club-hopping with a group of 20-somethings! Nasser developed an entrepreneurial style in his previous assignments at Ford and plans to help his managers adopt a similar approach to managing. Nasser intends to reinvent Ford as a "nimble, growth-oriented consumer powerhouse for the 21st century."[1]

What factors determine the most effective structure for Ford? In Chapter 12, we examined the many options available for designing a structure. In this chapter, we focus on how to choose the best option. In particular, we investigate the impact of the following factors on an organization's structure: (1) environment, (2) technology, particularly the electronic revolution, (3) workforce, (4) goals and strategy, and (5) life cycle. We also explore issues of downsizing, mergers and acquisitions, and cross-cultural influences on design.

▌THE ENVIRONMENT

Most organizations face a demanding, intrusive, and somewhat uncontrollable *environment,* those factors outside the organization that influence its functioning. Increasingly, companies function in a global environment, with special challenges described later in this chapter. Managers in high-performance companies structure their organizations in ways that increase the effectiveness of their interactions with the environment. Ford, for example, had a centralized structure that no longer met the challenges of its competitive environment. Nasser instituted a more decentralized structure that would allow managers to respond more quickly and effectively to customer requirements.

Components of the Environment

Economic and market circumstances and technological innovations comprise an organization's environment. So do federal, state, and local legislation and political, social, and cultural conditions external to the organization. Together, these components of the environment influence an organization's functioning and should determine its structure. For example, the changing regulation and structure of the financial industry has removed barriers to geographic expansion, causing a wave of interstate bank mergers, such as Nationsbank and Bank of America.[2]

Economic Environment.   Managers increasingly work in an unpredictable economic environment. Although inflation has remained relatively low during the past decade, swings in the financial markets can significantly affect corporate functioning. Decisions about the prime rate, which influences the cost of funds to an organization, also influence corporate behavior. The impact of financial conditions in a particular country extends well beyond its borders. As more businesses operate globally, the stability of monetary currencies around the world has consequences for organizational performance.

Managers must respond efficiently and adaptively to the changing economic situation. They must reduce costs as necessary or use the ability to borrow money at a low interest rate as an opportunity for innovation or expansion. They must respond quickly to actions by their competitors, suppliers, and customers. Ford plans to remain competitive by increasing profits through cost reduction, introduction of a more effective design process, and more careful response to customer needs.

Technological Environment.   Companies like Ford also face a constantly changing technological environment. Here we refer to the general technological context in which organizations function, rather than the specific technical systems they use, which we examine later in this chapter. Frequent advances in technology require a continued emphasis on research and development. The electronic revolution has had a dramatic effect on companies such as Ford. Innovations in computer design and manufacturing can speed products to market and improve the entire product line.

A company's organization structure should make the acquisition, development, and introduction of new technology easy. First Union, for example, partnered with w-Technologies Inc., which sells software for customizable, wireless applications, to offer its customers wireless access to their accounts. Customers had previously been able to receive alerts about their account balances through their pagers; now they will be able to pay bills, execute trades, and implement other transactions using a variety of wireless devices.[3] The availability of such technology will likely affect the structure of First Union, since new groups or divisions will need to manage these services.

Political/Legal Environment.   Increased government regulations have constrained management's actions in its production and employment practices. In the United States, occupational safety and health guidelines, equal employment opportunity regulations, and foreign trade tariffs and policies influence the way organizations do business.

Outside the United States, laws unique to various countries in Europe, Asia, Africa, and South America create similar constraints on organizational functioning. German law, for example, creates worker councils as a formal component of the structure of unionized organizations. The current political climate in both the host and home countries, which may support or hinder business initiatives, can influence an organization's ability to compete.

Sociocultural Environment.   The sociocultural environment includes a complex web of cultural considerations, such as attitudes toward family life. It also includes an array of social attributes, such as demographics, the makeup of the general population, and the educational experiences of workers. For example, such demographic changes as the aging of the workforce and high educational levels and expectations of workers have caused organizations to decentralize decision making and give workers more control over their jobs.

In the United States, many workers have moved from the industrial northeast and midwest to the south and west, reducing the pool of skilled workers available to companies in some locations. Large numbers of immigrants in the United States and other industrialized countries have altered the available labor pool. As the general population has aged and mandatory retirement has been eliminated, companies have used early retirement incentives to reduce the number of older workers. Companies that extend into international markets deal with additional sociocultural considerations.

Managers who work in different countries often prefer different structures. For example, U.S. managers have traditionally viewed an organization's structure as a means for accomplishing organizational goals, while French managers have seen the structure as a way to create interpersonal interactions.[4] An effective structure considers such cultural differences.

Dimensions of the Environment

An effective organizational structure reflects three specific dimensions of the environment: its complexity, dynamism, and hostility/munificence.[5]

Complexity.   The number and variety of environmental elements that affect an organization vary considerably. A state university must deal with all the environmental components described in the previous section, while a small clothing boutique must respond primarily to the economic environment and secondarily to the sociocultural environment. Hence, the university has a more complex environment than does the local clothing store. An organization that serves retail and wholesale markets faces a more complex environment than a comparable organization that only markets its product through retail outlets. Moving up the scale of complexity, a multinational firm, which must deal with the unique characteristics of numerous cultures and countries, experiences even greater environmental complexity.

As the complexity of the environment increases, organizations generally experience greater success if they decentralize decision making. Decentralizing decision making places expertise and authority in direct contact with the essential information in the environment. Ford has decentralized decision making, giving managers and employees greater control over their work and letting them respond faster to changes in the marketplace.

As the environment becomes increasingly complex, organizations may divisionalize as one way of dealing with a large number of environmental elements. The divisionalized structure works best in larger, relatively older companies that have complex economic, technological, political/legal, and sociocultural environments.

Dynamism.   Although the environment of all organizations changes over time, some companies face a more dynamic environment than others. Regional economic growth rates affect corporate performance and the selection of organizational structures. Ongoing technological advancements also demand reactions from organizations. New or changed immigration or import laws can affect an organization and its choice of structure. Regulatory changes can also affect organizational structures. For example, changes in health care delivery have turned a predictable, highly regulated business into a competitive, dynamic one. High Point Regional Health System in North Carolina responded to mergers of its competitors and development of large physician groups by creating a new vision statement. While still offering a broad array of services, High Point decided not to merge with other systems and not to make insurance products a key component of its organizational offerings.[6] These decisions in turn had implications for the strategy and structure of this organization.

The more frequently and unpredictably the environment changes, the more flexible and adaptable the organization's structure should be. Market-oriented and integrated structures (see Chapter 12) offer flexibility by emphasizing lateral relationships, decentralizing decision making, and deemphasizing status and rank differences. Organizations can create additional lateral linkages to improve the flow of information in the organization or between the organization and its environment. Divisionalized firms facing instability can reduce uncertainty by divesting themselves of "noncore" businesses so that they can better understand the remaining markets.[7] Increased uncertainty in the environment is related to increased use of alliances, particularly when managers have entrepreneurial and collectivist orientations.[8] A study of 230 private colleges indicated that an organization that has strong ties to other organizations can reduce the degree of uncertainty in its environment. Strong ties also encourage adaptation by creating high-capacity information links that facilitate communication and sharing of information between organizations.[9]

Hostility/Munificence.   The degree to which the environment creates conflict, threat, or unexpected or overwhelming competition for an organization reflects either *hostility* or *munificence*. Pinkerton, for example, assists its multinational clients in dealing with a hostile environment, countries where there is high potential for civil unrest, kidnapping, extortion, and terrorism. It recently evacuated more than 400 expatriates from Indonesia during riots in that country.[10]

Hostile environments occur when the following conditions exist:

■ extensive competition, including price undercutting;
■ threatened obsolescence;

- a government investigation;
- new or unexpected government regulations;
- a threatened takeover;
- potential bankruptcy; or
- lack of social responsibility.

Organizations with highly hostile environments require high centralization of decision making. Centralization allows the most controlled means of responding to competition or other threatening events by placing decision making in the hands of a few top executives. Organizations typically use this design strategy in the short run, and it takes priority over other strategies for only a brief period of time. Organizations that must cope with a hostile environment over a prolonged period experience real threats to their survival because operating in a crisis mode tends to sap energy and resources.

Organizations that typically operate in a munificent environment may experience unexpected environmental pressures. They respond by increasing their specialization and deploying more professionals to specialized areas so they can immediately apply their special knowledge to the problem.[11] The Ontario Teachers' Pension Plan Board discovered that for decades the plan had incorrectly paid as many as two-thirds of its participants and that it would cost hundreds of millions of dollars to correct the situation. The board decided to make full restitution. It created a project team headed by a Teachers' senior vice president. The team oversaw the cleanup, which involved computer systems employees, a first-level management working committee to integrate the restitution with ongoing business, and a project advisory council. This relatively centralized structure ensured clear lines of authority and accountability.[12]

Dealing with Design Dilemmas.   Design dilemmas can arise when an organization's environment has competing forces, ones that call for different and even opposing strategies. How, for example, does management reconcile the decentralized structure required for a complex environment with the centralization required to deal effectively with a hostile environment?

A proposed structure may not fit the internal characteristics of the organization. For example, differing goals or different types of workers in different parts of the organization may result in the introduction of inconsistent structures.[13] Resolving these dilemmas generally occurs in one of three ways:

- **Creating diverse structures within the same organization.** The marketing and research and development departments may have one structure while manufacturing has a different one.
- **Redesigning the structure within each work unit.** As task and environmental demands change, units need to continually redefine their structures to respond effectively to the new environmental conditions.[14]
- **Creating temporary structures in times of crisis.** Top executives might convene a management council only in response to hostile environmental events.

▌TECHNOLOGY

Technology refers to the process that converts raw materials into a product or service. Technology can mean the machinery used to alter raw materials into a finished product or the intellectual or analytical processes used to transform information into a product or service. The technical system an organization uses to produce and deliver its product should influence organizational design. In this section, we explore the fit between technical system and structure, rather than the general technological context in which the organization operates, as was described earlier.

The Impact of the Electronic Revolution

Web-based technologies and other aspects of the electronic revolution have had a dramatic impact on the options for structuring organizations. Like many organizations, United States Pharmacopeia (USP) has greatly expanded its information systems and information systems staff to support its new, online dissemination of publications and other information about pharmaceutical standards, one of the company's major activities.[15] The restructuring of the information technology (IT) group has received much attention as a result of the new marketplace demands of the electronic revolution. Many IT leaders have eliminated old IT department structures and sent IT employees to work directly with business units.[16]

Most companies have replaced mechanistic structures with more organic ones that support flexibility and adaptability in product development, manufacturing, and customer service. Overall, more companies have resorted to outsourcing or introducing network forms that allow a clear focus on core competencies while not sacrificing high performance of other organizational functions. For example, many companies outsource major components of their information technology and human resources functions to firms and individuals with special capabilities in these areas. Others rely on off-shore manufacturing to reduce costs and speed product delivery.

Some companies have introduced a chief Web officer, a person responsible for overseeing the harnessing of technology for the organization. The chief information officer of Cisco Systems led the company's efforts in e-commerce that resulted in reducing costs by $1.5 billion as a result of using Net technologies in all phases of its operations. The CIO at Charles Schwab led the company's successful move to online trading, which now constitutes 81 percent of its volume.[17]

The Changing Nature of Technology

Two early ways of looking at technology considered production processes and related task performance, as shown in Table 13-1.[18] A later focus on knowledge technology classified jobs along two dimensions:[19]

- **Task variability,** the number of exceptions that a jobholder encounters. An assembly-line worker has relatively low task variability, whereas a physician in family medicine has high task variability.

- **Problem analyzability,** the extent to which the technology is understood by those who use it. A salesperson's job has ill-defined problems, whereas a quality control engineer's job has better defined problems.

TABLE 13-1

Technology Includes the Traditional Assembly Line, Craft, and Process Forms.

Type of Technology	Technological Process	Task Performance
Craft	*Unit Technology* Craft processes that produce custom-made products, such as housewares, clothing, or artwork, or even services, such as legal and medical needs	*Intensive Technology* Application of diverse techniques and knowledge to various raw materials, with the techniques varying according to the problem or situation, such as treatment of hospital patients
Assembly Line	*Mass Production* Assembly-line operations that produce standardized consumer goods, such as automobile or heavy equipment manufacturing	*Long-linked Technology* The repetitive application of one technology to a standardized raw material, such as mass-production assembly lines.
Process	*Technical Batch (or Unit) Processing* A small scale of operations that requires complex knowledge, such as aircraft production or check processing *Continuous Flow Technology* An unsegmented, ongoing production process, such as chemical or oil refining	*Mediating Technology* Repeated application of a standardized method to unique raw materials, such as a social service agency imparting standardized counseling techniques to diverse clients

Source: J. Woodward, *Industrial Organizations: Theory and Practice* (London: Oxford University Press, 1965); J. Thompson, *Organizations in Action* (New York: McGraw-Hill, 1967).

Combining these two dimensions results in routine, craft, engineering, and nonroutine technology, as shown in Figure 13-1. How would you classify the manufacture of discrete and integrated circuit boards? Is the technology for product manufacture the same as for product design and development? Manufacturing typically uses a mass-production, routine technology. Design and development, in contrast, rely more on an engineering technology.

Today, most companies have incorporated some form of information systems technology into their operations. *Automation,* the use of computers to perform tasks previously done by people, increases the efficiency and reduces the cost of performing various tasks in the workplace. Besides replacing humans with machines, it changes the way jobs are done and the way organizations are structured.

Office automation systems use computer hardware and software to perform the functions of information storage, data analysis, document preparation, time management, and communication. The virtual office allows workers to perform office functions at remote sites, such as a client's company or home. Work-flow automation

FIGURE 13-1

Technology varies according to the variability of the task and the analyzability of the problem.

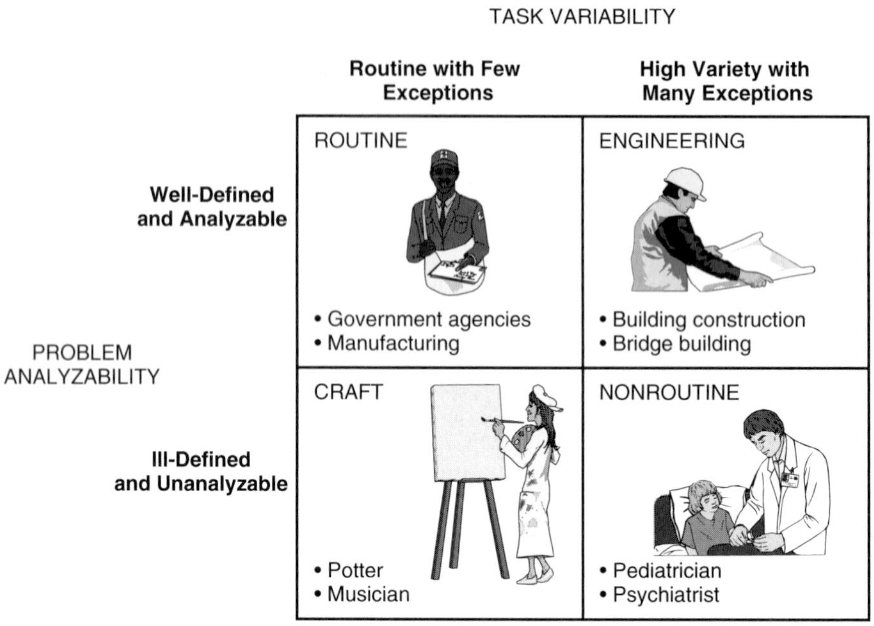

TASK VARIABILITY

	Routine with Few Exceptions	High Variety with Many Exceptions
Well-Defined and Analyzable	ROUTINE • Government agencies • Manufacturing	ENGINEERING • Building construction • Bridge building
Ill-Defined and Unanalyzable	CRAFT • Potter • Musician	NONROUTINE • Pediatrician • Psychiatrist

PROBLEM ANALYZABILITY

refers to the computerized control and coordination of administrative, production, and other business processes. Document management helps users keep track of stored electronic documents.

Sales force automation provides computerized systems for tracking sales leads, sales, service requests, and other sales-related information. Sales support includes a prospect database combined with other applications that provide instantaneous summary reports. Automated customer service systems include automated call directors and computerized databases to track service calls, problems, and repairs.

Computer-aided design (CAD) allows engineers, architects, graphic designers, and others to compose their product and process designs on a computer rather than on paper. Computer-aided manufacturing (CAM) automates machine monitoring and control by using flexible manufacturing, robotics, and automated guided vehicles. Computer-integrated manufacturing (CIM) coordinates CAM and CAD systems into an integrated information system that automates the sharing of data among departments. Virtual reality technology has moved from video arcades to the work area of product designers. For example, General Motors, Ford, and Boeing have significantly reduced cycle time using virtual reality tools to eliminate the development of physical prototypes. In addition, rapid prototyping systems, which speed the steps involved in prototyping, have accompanied the reduction in cycle time. Because of the high cost of such rapid prototyping systems, many companies have relied on outside contractors for these services, which has implications for organizational design.[20]

Technology and Design

A technology's regulation and sophistication, based on the dimensions and characteristics described in the previous section, help determine the most effective structure.

■ **Regulation** refers to the extent to which machinery and equipment control the employee's work. *Regulating technologies* include mass production, continuous flow, long-linked, and engineering technologies, among others. They call for a relatively mechanistic structure since the technology helps predetermine a set of predictable responses to it. A *nonregulating technology*, such as unit, craft, and nonroutine technologies, calls for an organic structure.[21] The less routine the technology, the greater the need for flexibility.

■ **Sophistication** describes the complexity or intricacy of the technology. As the technical system increases in sophistication, the organization requires an increasingly elaborate administrative structure and more support staff who have decision-making responsibilities. Increased sophistication also calls for more integrating and linking devices.

The extensive use of computer-based technologies in companies has significantly increased the need for support staff who can develop, apply, and help others use the new technologies. Computerization also requires a more organic structure because it frees employees to perform more innovative, knowledge-based work.

Effective organizational structures buffer or protect the technology from environmental influences or disturbances.[22] The more specific the technology, such as that of a mechanized bottle capper, the less tolerance the process has for disturbances and the more the organization must elaborate its structure and administration to protect the operation from environmental disturbances. As organizations become more automated, they require increasing rules and regulations, centralized control, and support staff as a way of buffering the technology. New technologies also change how the job is done, and ultimately they affect the division of labor, control and coordination, and organization–environment fit.[23] Organizational design must respond to the complexities created by new technologies.

▌THE WORKFORCE

Managers must realize that some structures support various workers and jobs better than others. A highly creative designer, for example, would chafe at the restraints of a bureaucratic structure. Today's Web-savvy employees also prefer very fluid and flexible structures. The hierarchical structure does not effectively support e-businesses; instead, interconnectedness, such as that provided by a virtual organization, better responds to those needs.[24] An organization's structure might consider employees' professionalism, expertise, and group memberships, such as union affiliation. In addition, the structure might consider workers' education, work experience, and demographic characteristics, such as age, work values, and life and career stages. An effective structure might also fit their personalities and attitudes.

Knowledge Workers

Increasingly, companies rely on *knowledge workers,* employees with specialized skills, such as scientists and technologists, to provide requisite knowledge in the various management areas. These workers develop and retrieve highly specialized information to do their jobs. They rely on information technology tools, such as databases, data mining, or data warehouses, to access and share technology.[25]

Knowledge management involves collecting and organizing a massive amount of information or collective expertise and then making it available to the appropriate people in a timely fashion.[26] PricewaterhouseCoopers manages knowledge by using a team of 300 knowledge workers across industries who conduct research for consultants and work to get the consultants' knowledge into internal repositories at the firm. Consultants then access knowledge resources through their computers. PricewaterhouseCoopers also has a global knowledge help desk called Knowledge Point, which employees can call for specific searches or to access knowledge-based resources.[27]

The increased number of knowledge workers has caused companies to create more organic structures, particularly networks and virtual organizations, that let the company draw on advanced knowledge in other organizations. Cisco Systems, for example, partnered with a few manufacturers to jointly develop equipment because internal manufacturing and hiring alone could not sustain the company's growth rate.[28] A contingent workforce can also help companies accumulate valuable knowledge.[29]

International Workers

Organizations that function in numerous countries likely have employees with different cultural backgrounds, and so different experiences, values, and education. A company's employees within a given country may come from both the home country and the host country. Reconciling differences in employees' perspectives, as well as taking advantage of their different views, becomes a major challenge in designing organizations.

Establishing structures that allow for the fluid exchange of employees at various sites across the world also may be important for some companies. In addition, many companies, including General Electric, Verizon, Citigroup, and Microsoft, have shifted work outside of the United States to locations with lower-cost labor, but large English-speaking populations, such as Ireland.[30] The transfer of skills and the translation of knowledge among locations occur more easily in product or project structures, in which people are used to working with diverse groups. Functional structures, in contrast, tend to perpetuate a more holistic viewpoint. Network structures provide the greatest opportunity for taking advantage of synergy from diverse countries and using it to make the parent organization more competitive.

▌ ORGANIZATIONAL GOALS, MISSION, AND STRATEGY

An organization's goals, mission, and strategy also influence the choice of an effective structure.

Organizational Goals

Goals refer to the desired outcomes of individual or organizational activities and behaviors. They focus on particular activities and provide a rationale for organizing them. Goals offer a standard for assessing performance. They legitimize individual and organizational behavior and provide an identity for employees.[31] Goals communicate higher management's philosophy and intentions, and motivate people to achieve.

Developing Goals.   Goal formation can occur as a result of bargaining among members of a coalition, which can be a formal organizational unit such as a department or work team or an informal group of people with related interests.[32] The coalition members bargain about goals, while competing groups offer inducements to support their own, often different goals. The coalition leaders then attempt to strengthen and clarify their goals by satisfying in some way the goals of all coalition members. Finally, the group leaders and members adjust the goals to reflect experience. For example, the new president of SSM St. Joseph Hospital of Kirkwood, Missouri, a hospital in crisis, first set a customer service goal and then created a structure that combined centralized oversight with a new, more decentralized nursing structure to meet this goal. The hospital created a Nursing Leadership Team composed of all the clinical directors of nursing departments, whose responsibility was to guide everyone through the transition and develop nursing practices and programs around the new mission. The hospital also organized the care of patients around four groups: surgical, cardiovascular, women, and children. Each of these groups was responsible for identifying its patients' needs and providing the appropriate care. As a result of these and related changes, inpatient admissions, surgeries, outpatient admissions, and patient days increased; operating revenues and operating expenses decreased; and the satisfaction of patients, employees, and physicians increased.[33]

Goal formation isn't straightforward. Organizations continually have difficulty specifying clear, responsive, and responsible goals. Organizations such as Ford Motor Company or a large discount store, accounting firm, or university have different and varying goals that might relate to market share, profitability, product innovation, or quality of working life. Table 13-2 reflects some diverse goals that organizations might have. Managers must first identify the goals of all parts of the organization and then choose the structure most likely to facilitate their accomplishment. Goals generally form within a set of constraints.[34] For example, a manager might specify the available financial resources or research expertise for developing a new product and then determine what the organization can do given these conditions.

Goal Incompatibility. Because organizations frequently have multiple goals, goal conflict may result. For example, goals in the area of public responsibility may incur costs that detract from profitability. A goal of providing the highest-quality service may conflict with a goal of minimizing costs. These conflicts frequently arise from a misfit between different goal types, such as innovation and productivity goals or societal and output goals. Or, a conflict between the goals of influential individuals, groups, or departments may prevent top management from agreeing on the organization's overall goals.

Defining an organization's goals requires significant and complex action to reconcile conflicting and incompatible goals. Otherwise, dysfunctional *goal displacement*—in which individuals or groups divert their energies from the organization's original goals to different ones—may occur. Organizational structures can also help companies focus on and accomplish their goals, rather than displacing their energy to other ones. For example, the new structure of Ford Motor Company should help the company introduce products faster and more cost-effectively.

Organizational Strategy

An organization's *strategy*, which includes its basic mission, purpose, and goals, as well as the means for accomplishing them, also influences its structure. We can categorize organizations into four strategic types:[35]

- **Defenders** have a major share of the market and attempt to retain that share. Companies like Federated Stores emphasize planning and cost control rather

TABLE 13-2

Companies Can Have a Wide Array of Goals.

Goal	Definition	Example
Societal	Creation and maintenance of cultural values through production of goods or services	To increase the number of managers on boards of charitable organizations
Output	Kinds and quantities of outputs produced	To increase production by 15%
System	The functioning of an organization's system independent of its production of goods or services	To introduce a project structure
Product	Specific characteristics of goods and services	To develop a line of women's perfume
Derived	The organization's use of power in areas apart from production of goods and services	To introduce a mentoring program
Market standing	The organization's position in the marketplace, including quality and share of market	To become the sales leader in laptop computers
Innovation	The value of new product development	To develop two new products
Productivity	The level of output organization-wide	To increase shoe production by 35%
Physical and financial resources	The nature and extent of resources used in product development and production	To reduce the cost of raw materials by 10%
Profitability	Profit and return on investment	To increase profit by 5%
Manager performance and development	Managerial output, growth, activities, and style	To provide all managers with 70 hours of training each year
Worker performance and attitudes	Individual output, turnover, absenteeism, satisfaction, and morale	To reduce turnover to less than 10% a year
Public responsibility	The organization's use of natural resources and contribution to the public good	To seek alternative sources of raw materials

Source: Adapted from C. Perrow, *Organizational Analysis: A Sociological View* (Belmont, CA: Wadsworth, 1970); P. Drucker, *The Practice of Management* (New York: Harper, 1954).

than a search for new products. They have a relatively bureaucratic structure, with high horizontal differentiation, centralized control, an elaborate hierarchy, and extensive formalization.

■ **Prospectors** find and develop new products and markets. They emphasize innovation and rapid introduction of new products. Companies with this strategy, such as Microsoft, have a more organic structure, with less division of labor, greater flexibility, and more decentralized decision making and control.

■ **Analyzers** enter new markets or introduce new products or services after the prospectors, while maintaining their market share like the defenders. The strategy of analyzers, such as banks, calls for a hybrid structure that has moderately centralized control and encourages both flexibility and stability.

■ **Reactors** design their strategies based on what others in the market have done. These companies may pursue one of the other three strategies incidentally, and so may have a variety of structures. Dell Computers, for example, doesn't focus on research and development but uses a more efficient manufacturing approach to undercut the more innovative pioneers.

How would you characterize Ford's strategy using this scheme? The company has three major focuses: innovation, globalization, and total quality management.[36] The emphasis on innovation makes it a prospector. Its introduction of a highly flexible structure with decentralized decision making fits this strategy. Executives in companies like Ford must identify the organization's strategy and then select the design that best responds to it.

▌ORGANIZATIONAL LIFE CYCLE

Most organizations evolve through a *life cycle*, a series of developmental stages similar to those described for individuals in Chapter 3. These stages reflect the organization's size, age, managerial approach, and product or service delivery, among other factors.

Life Cycle Stages

An organization's movement through its life cycle occurs in a predictable sequence of stages that is not easily reversed.[37] For example, we can trace corporate growth through four stages, as summarized in Figure 13-2: entrepreneurial, collectivity, formalization, and elaboration.[38]

Entrepreneurial Stage.   Managers who create a new organization first develop ideas about the organization. Next they make commitments to a particular direction and begin initial planning. Then the managers make the new organization operational.[39] As part of implementation, managers focus on developing a customer base, reliably delivering the product, building sufficient cash flow to support the company's activities, and generating a profit. At this stage, Apple Computer's Steve Jobs and Microsoft's Bill Gates started their companies by understanding the needs of the market, having a vision of how their company could respond to those needs, and having the entrepreneurial drive for early success and growth.[40]

Collectivity Stage.   Companies typically experience rapid growth in the second stage, also known as the *success stage*. While innovation and expansion continue, some attempts to stabilize and routinize the organization begin.[41] The owner decides whether to stabilize the company at its present size or strive for more growth.[42] She can consolidate the company and professionalize its functional management either by removing herself from an active management role or by retaining

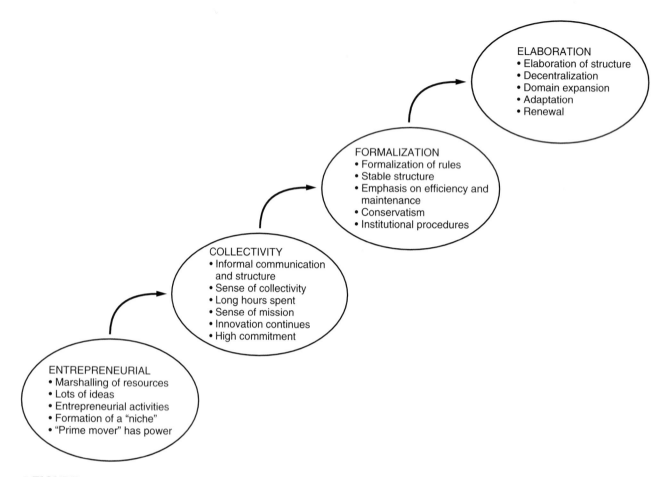

Source: Adapted from R. E. Quinn and K. Cameron, Organizational life cycles and shifting criteria of effectiveness: Some preliminary evidence, *Management Science* 29 (January 1983).

control and reinvesting the profits in growth. Although the founding and early members of the organization remain committed to it, over time their involvement depends on the nonfinancial incentives offered: They must work on challenging and varied tasks, have growth opportunities in the organization, and receive frequent, quality communication from top management.[43]

Formalization Stage.   The maturation of the company signals its complete movement from entrepreneurial to professional.[44] In this *take-off stage,* the owner must address such issues as delegating responsibility and acquiring sufficient cash to finance growth.[45] As the company matures, ownership and management diverge, although the owner maintains stock control. In small businesses, the transition from an owner-manager to a hired manager frequently signals the beginning of this stage. Larger organizations create functional specialties at this stage. They also develop systematic reward and evaluation systems. This stage emphasizes formal planning and goal setting. Increased formalization may cause more entrepreneur-ial, innovative workers to leave the organization to seek new outlets for their cre-ativity. Employees whose goals and orientations fit better with the stabilization and formalization processes replace them.

Elaboration Stage. The mature organization strives to adapt to changing condi-tions, renew itself, and seek continued growth opportunities. The company must consolidate its growth. It expands its management staff and capabilities. It increases the number of special management and staff positions. At this stage, it also must ensure a return on investment.[46]

Some organizations diversify their product markets as a way of ensuring their continued growth. Others search for new products or growth opportunities through acquisitions. Companies that thrive

- **accept change** by continually reviewing and revising goals and procedures;
- **listen to customers** and involve them in new product development;
- **decentralize authority** to encourage rapid decision making;
- **hire skilled workers** who are versatile and responsive;
- **teach and train employees** continuously; and
- **control costs.**[47]

When the mature organization fails to adapt, decline may result.[48] Rubber-maid, once a thriving, highly admired company, was taken over after a major attempt to cut costs failed. Problems at Laura Ashley occurred after the death of the founder; since then, its products have lagged behind the rest of the market.[49] Such companies often must deal with internal or external pressures that threaten their long-term survival.[50] For some organizations, downsizing provides an early signal of organizational decline.

Companies that decline generally pass through a series of stages during which the organization can be salvaged.[51] At first, most managers don't see early warning signs. If they were to use the available information, they could halt the decline at this time. A little later, some managers recognize the need to change but take no action. Prompt action at this stage would stem the decline. In the third stage, top management takes action, but acts inappropriately. Correct action at this time could still reverse the decline. In the fourth stage, the organization reaches the point of crisis and faces its last chance for reversing the decline. Sometimes an effective reorganization (often after declaring legal bankruptcy) can reverse the sit-uation. If the organization reaches the fifth and final stage, it is forced to dissolve. The speed of its dissolution depends on the company's environment.

Diagnosing an organization's position in its life cycle provides managers with data to use in designing an effective structure. Young organizations require a flexi-ble structure that can accommodate innovation and respond to uncertainty. As the organization moves into the collective or success stage, managers can introduce some formal procedures and policies, but overall the organization likely retains rel-atively informal communication and structure. As the organization matures and formalizes, top management typically introduces systematic planning, evaluation, and reward systems. Functional structures with centralized decision making often fit with the control, specialization of tasks, authority, and stability required at this stage. An organization's ultimate survival, however, increasingly depends on having an adaptable and flexible structure.

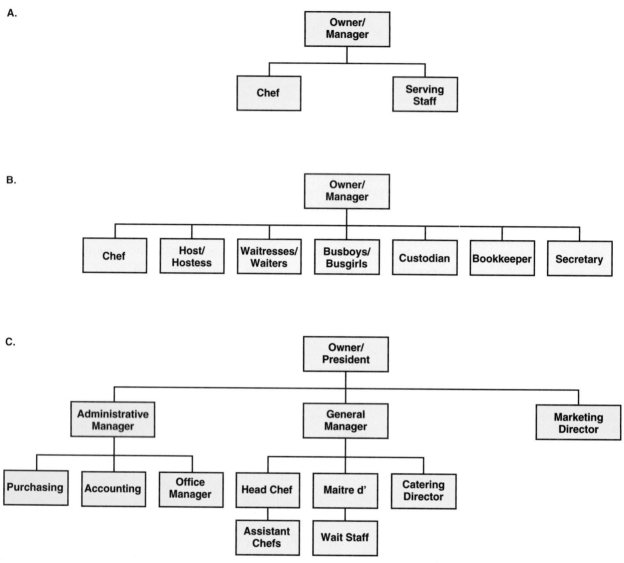

FIGURE 13-3   *A company develops a more complex structure as its size increases.*

Organizational Size and Age

The growth and aging of an organization influence its structure.

Size.   As organizations increase in size, they generally expand their orientation, developing an array of products and services. This change calls for a more differentiated structure. For example, a company may move from a simpler, functional structure to a more complex, product structure. Figure 13-3 illustrates a typical progression.

Managers should consider an organization's size when diagnosing a structure's effectiveness. Size dictates certain structural dimensions—specifically, the structuring of activities, specialization, standardization, formalization, span of control, and centralization.[52] Size also affects the way technology influences structure. Larger organizations generally have a more bureaucratic structure regardless of their technology.[53]

Age. An organization's age, not surprisingly, often correlates with its size. As an organization ages, its behavior tends to become more standardized and formalized. Young companies often use mutual adjustment for coordination. As they get older, the companies tend to standardize more procedures and change to a more mechanized and bureaucratic structure. Companies need to consciously remain flexible and adaptable as they age. This may call for regularly reviewing structures to ensure that bureaucracy doesn't become too firmly entrenched.

▌ DOWNSIZING AND RIGHTSIZING

Some organizations find that they must reduce or downsize their workforce or their product line as a way of responding to environmental or technological changes. The Canadian National Railway and Canadian Pacific Railway sold financially marginal lines and relinquished lines that lost money, resulting in increased profitability.[54] Seagate Technology downsized to reduce the economic impact of the Asian market crisis of the late 1990s. A restructuring accompanied a workforce reduction of more than 10,000 employees.[55]

Often labeled *rightsizing* because of its focus on reducing the workforce to the right size to accomplish the organization's objectives, this change may call for restructuring. The early steps in rightsizing involve carefully diagnosing customers' needs, translating them into organizational requirements, and then revising (if necessary) the organization's mission, strategy, structure, and job descriptions.[56] Declining economic conditions or shifts in demand for a product or service may mandate downsizing. So may ineffective strategy, poor performance, or financial restructuring.[57] A&P restructured and closed 127 stores to improve its profitability by becoming more efficient and reducing overhead.[58] The movement to teams, just-in-time manufacturing, and increased outsourcing also has contributed to corporate downsizing and restructuring.[59] Downsizing can accompany increasing automation when the introduction of new technology reduces the total number of employees needed to do the same job.

Companies use downsizing or rightsizing as a way to renew the organization. Managers can strip away excess jobs and staff and so reclaim some of the vigor associated with younger, smaller organizations. Executives can restructure to increase efficiencies or economies of scale. Sysco Food Services of Houston downsized its credit department and then remodeled it using a number of activities: retooling the way responsibilities were allocated, redefining the process for submitting orders, reducing the processing time, rejecting inconsistent or incomplete information, reviewing all departmental policies, and making sure the company routed all delivered goods properly.[60]

Downsizing has both positive and negative consequences. It can reduce costs, redirect strategy, and increase efficiency. It can also destroy employee morale, injure sales, reduce quality, and result in little improvement in profits.[61] In particular, companies need to avoid significantly understaffing work areas. Although moderate understaffing may improve the commitment and work performance of employees because they perceive increased task scope and use of their skills, too much understaffing lowered group performance among 160 blue-collar and 55 white-collar groups studied.[62]

Downsizing that occurs as a short-term, panic-stricken response to a hostile environment most often results in failure. Many companies that downsized under such conditions did not achieve their desired results, with less than one-half earning increased profits. More than 40 percent of executives surveyed were dissatisfied with the results of their corporations' downsizing.[63] Downsizing as part of a long-term strategy for performance and competitiveness likely has better outcomes.

Managers can answer the following questions as part of strategic restructuring:[64]

- What work should be the object of our most intense improvement efforts?
- What work activities need to be improved together, and which can be improved separately?
- What work should be eliminated?
- What work should be outsourced?
- When are efficiency (doing things right) and effectiveness (doing the right things) the most useful drivers of improvement efforts?

After answering these questions, the company can delineate which work helps accomplish the company's strategy, which supports the business's continuation, and which has lost its usefulness but continues to be done out of tradition. Companies can then eliminate this last, nonessential work.[65] Procter & Gamble's "Organization 2005" initiative eliminated 15,000 workers out of 110,000 worldwide and reorganized the company into seven global business units based on product categories from its geographic structure. The downsizing and restructuring were intended to help the company make decisions faster, cut costs, become more Internet-savvy, and double its revenues.[66]

▌ MERGERS AND ACQUISITIONS

Some companies merge with or acquire other companies as a way of becoming more competitive. Unlike the 1980s when financial buyers drove the market, today mergers and acquisitions are driven by the search for synergy and its translation into reduced costs, increased customer base, and improved and expanded product lines.[67] Unilever's bid for Bestfoods, the manufacturer of Skippy peanut butter and Mazola corn oil, was seen as the first of a series of desired acquisitions of food companies such as Ben & Jerry's or Slim-Fast Foods, that would expand the brands offered.[68]

A changing environment can lead to both mergers and acquisitions. For example, an increasing number of European companies have responded to the coming of the global market place and the accompanying need to cut costs by acquisitions or mergers. The Dutch conglomerate Royal Ahold recently added to its U.S. holdings by purchasing PYA/Monarch, a major U.S. food service distributor that provides food and nonfood items to about 40,000 customers. Royal Ahold also acquired Stop & Shop, an East Coast food retailer, and has a majority interest in the Internet grocer Peapod.[69] Preussag-Thomson became the world's largest travel company after the German company Preussag took over the U.K.'s Thomson Travel group.[70]

Other companies merge as a way to expand their product lines or strengthen the value chain of supplier, manufacturer, customer. Advancing technology can also motivate mergers and acquisitions. Oil and gas companies have made acquisitions that provide access to new technologies and oil reserves. Citicorp and Travelers merged for a different reason: to create a large financial services supermarket that offered every imaginable financial product. The challenge for such companies is finding a structure that works for the combined entity. Initially, Travelers and Citicorp even appointed co-chief executives, although the former CEO of Travelers, Sandy Weill, eventually became the sole CEO.[71] Some companies handle the problem of integrating two companies by keeping them independent. Wells Fargo chose not to combine Van Kasper & Company, a small investment bank it acquired, into the larger bank's existing operations because of significant differences in operations, goals, and cultures.[72]

Mergers and acquisitions can also result in cost savings. Renee Hornbaker, the vice president and CFO of Flowserve, a major provider of industrial flow-management services and equipment, has overseen 16 mergers and acquisitions. One merger allowed Flowserve to reduce its tax rate and save more than $34 million because of its consolidation of a variety of legal entities from the two companies.

ORGANIZATIONAL DESIGN IN THE DOT-COM, GLOBAL WORKPLACE

Organizations that have attempted to start and develop as part of the new wave of dot-com companies have faced numerous challenges in structuring themselves to be nimble and responsive. Many of these challenges have been noted earlier in this chapter—the rapidly changing environment, the constant development and availability of new technology, and the increased number of knowledge workers in the labor force. Companies in this environment have tended to implement organic structures, such as horizontal organizations, network structures, and even virtual corporations. Frequent reinvention and restructuring has also occurred as these companies have responded to new product launches, increased competition, and a general environment that moves so fast they can barely respond. As these companies become more established, more mechanistic structures in parts of their organizations may combine with their overall organic structures to create new hybrid forms.

Organizations that function in the global environment face special environmental pressures.[73] They must respond to local laws and customers, as well as to those of their home country. Multinational companies typically choose the extent to which they create special local structures that respond specifically to conditions in their host countries.

The elimination of economic borders between countries and the increasing similarity of consumer demands also have implications for organizational structure. Whereas organizations once needed to differentiate horizontally into regional divisions or product subsidiaries, global structures now emerge. The impact of improved communication technologies makes coordination across long distances easier. Still, variations in laws and regulations may require special support staffs in various countries to ensure compliance.

Managers of multinational organizations often create structures that respond to their unique strategies. They typically choose one of the following strategies and then design compatible structures:[74]

- **Global management,** typical of many oil companies, has similar products in all regional markets. These organizations compete worldwide by creating few or no distinctions between markets and developing global economies of scale in manufacturing, distribution, and sales.
- **Multinational management,** used by consumer product companies in the food or electronics industries, emphasizes differences in the products and services for each country. These companies design marketing, sales, and even the product itself to meet specific country or regional requirements.

- **International management,** used by pharmaceutical companies, is a style that falls between global and multinational management. These organizations sell similar products in all countries but tailor them somewhat to meet local regulations.
- **Transnational management,** used by companies such as Unilever, combines elements of each of these approaches. Beginning with either global, multinational, or international management, transnational management adds elements from the others to meet special market needs, a changing environment, or cost-reduction pressures.

Flextronics, a multinational contract manufacturer, represents the new breed of multinational companies. Officially based in Singapore, Flextronics has major operations in North America, including California and Mexico. The company has grown from a $93 million organization that assembles printed circuit boards into an $8 billion company with 55,000 workers worldwide. Its Guadalajara, Mexico, site has 4,000 workers who manufacture cell phones, Palm Pilots, circuit boards, and routers for major U.S. companies. Outsourcers such as these offer companies flexibility by focusing on their core competencies, rather than on all aspects of manufacturing and distribution.[75]

Companies that form international alliances need to add a cultural dimension to their normal financial, legal, and strategic planning. Figure 13-4 shows eight stages involved in developing a culturally responsive alliance. To increase the likeli-

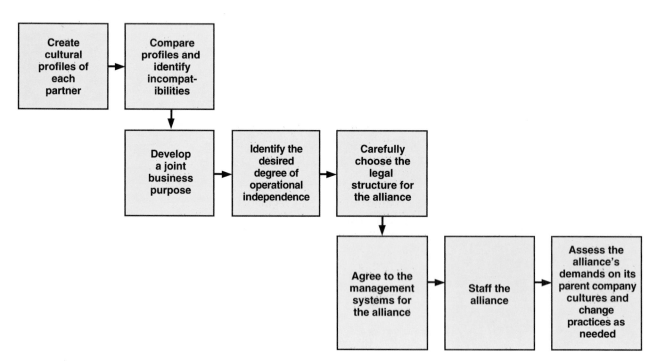

FIGURE 13-4   *Culturally responsive international alliances proceed through eight stages.*

Source: Adapted from K. J. Fedor and W. B. Werther Jr., The fourth dimension: Creating culturally responsive international alliances, *Organizational Dynamics* (Autumn 1996): 39–53.

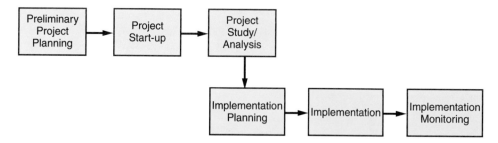

FIGURE 13-5 *Managers lead their companies through six steps when redesigning the organizational structure.*

Source: Adapted from M. W. Stebbins and A. B. Shani, Organization design; Beyond the "Mafia" model, *Organizational Dynamics* 17(3).

hood that the international alliance will succeed, companies may explicitly identify and address cultural incompatibilities. Increasing the involvement of all managers and employees in the alliance can help create a shared vision and smooth its development and operation.[76]

Some companies have moved from high-cost U.S. and European sites to locations in developing countries.[77] Caltex Petroleum, for example, a joint venture between Texaco and Chevron that runs gasoline stations in Asia and Africa, relocated from Dallas to Singapore. It moved its Web site development from the United States to Manila and also moved its accounting division to Manila.

Multinational companies, as well as those not operating globally, should follow the steps in Figure 13-5 when they redesign. Managers must periodically and repeatedly fit the pieces of the organization chart together in a new way. They need to assess what factors have changed and whether or not the structure still works because of these changes. Restructuring must explicitly consider managers' and other employees' abilities to function effectively in the new structure and deal with the resistance they will likely create.

Summary

1. Organizational redesign includes a regular, systematic diagnosis of a company's current organizational structure, the factors that affect it, and the fit between the structure and these factors.

2. Many organizations face changing economic, technological, political/legal, and sociocultural environments. The environment's complexity, dynamism, and degree of hostility or munificence influence the selection of a design.

3. The electronic revolution has affected organizational structures and the design of jobs. A regulating technology calls for a bureaucratic structure; a nonregulating technology calls for a more flexible structure. A sophisticated technology calls for increasing an organization's administrative structure.

4. A diverse workforce calls for varying structural features to respond to the differences among employees.

5. Managers must fit the structure to the organization's goals and strategy.
6. Organizational structure also responds to the unique needs and characteristics of organizations of various ages and sizes and at particular stages.
7. Companies may downsize, merge, or acquire other companies to become more competitive, and these changes should affect their organizational design.
8. Organizations that function in the dot-com, global workplace face numerous challenges as they attempt to structure their operations to respond to a rapidly changing environment, cultural differences, and unique strategies.

A Manager's Diagnostic Review

■ Design a structure that effectively responds to the organization's environment.
  • What is the nature of the organization's environment and subenvironments?
  • Is the environment complex or simple, dynamic or stable, munificent or hostile?
  • What type of structure responds best to the environment?

■ Fit an organization's structure to its technology.
  • How has the electronic revolution affected the organization's structure?
  • What structure does the technology call for?

■ Design an organization to meet the needs and abilities of the workforce.
  • What type of workforce does the organization have?
  • In what structure do the workers function most effectively?

■ Design a structure that fits the organization's goals and strategy.
  • What are the organization's goals?
  • What is the organization's strategy?
  • What structure fits best with its goals and strategy?

■ Design a structure that suits the organization's stage of development.
  • How old and how large is the organization?
  • At what stage is the organization?
  • What structure fits best with the organization's age, size, and stage of development?

■ Deal with the impact of downsizing, mergers, and acquisitions.
  • How has the organization been affected by downsizing, a merger, or an acquisition?
  • What type of structure would be most effective for the new organization?

■ Effectively structure organizations in the dot-com, global workplace.
  • How well does the organization handle new ventures?
  • What cross-cultural factors influence the structure?
  • What design best responds to the dot-com, global workplace?

Visit the Gordon homepage on the Prentice Hall Web site at

http://www.prenhall.com/gordon

for recommended readings, additional activities, Internet exercises, updated information, and links to related Web sites.

▌ Thinking Critically About Organizational Behavior

1. Has the electronic revolution had as big an impact as the industrial revolution on organizational design?
2. Besides the electronic revolution, what other aspects of the environment might influence an organization's design?
3. Can you develop a new and improved typology for characterizing an organization's technology?
4. How will changes in technology in the next decade likely affect the structure of organizations?
5. What additional changes can we expect in the workforce in the next two decades, and how will they affect organizational structure?
6. Should all organizations strive to employ a large number of knowledge workers?
7. Do all organizations pass through the same stages of development?
8. Should all large and old organizations have a mechanistic structure?
9. Is downsizing necessary?
10. Should merged organizations continue to function as separate entities or as a single combined organization?
11. What are the key organizational issues for dot-com companies?
12. Should global organizations have similar structures?

ACTIVITY 13-1: WORDS IN SENTENCES COMPANY

STEP 1: Form companies and assign workplaces. Each group should include between seven and twelve people and should consider itself a company. In this exercise, you will form a "mini-organization" with several other people. You will be competing with other companies in your industry. The success of your company will depend on (a) your objectives, (b) planning, (c) organizational structure, and (d) quality control. It is important, therefore, that you spend some time thinking about the best design for your organization.

STEP 2: Read the following directions and ask your instructor about any points that need clarification.

DIRECTIONS

You are a small company that manufactures words and then packages them in meaningful English-language sentences. Market research has established that sentences of at least three words but not more than six words are in demand. Therefore, packaging, distribution, and sales should be set up for three- to six-word sentences.

The words-in-sentences (WIS) industry is highly competitive. Several new firms have recently entered what appears to be an expanding market. Since raw materials, technology, and pricing are all standard for the industry, your ability to compete depends on two factors: (1) volume and (2) quality.

GROUP TASK

Your group must design and participate in running a WIS company. You should design your organization to be as efficient as possible during each 10-minute production run. After the first production run, you will have an opportunity to reorganize your company if you want.

RAW MATERIALS

For each production run, you will be given a "raw material word or phrase." The letters in the word or phrase serve as the raw materials to produce new words in sentences. For example, if the raw material word is "organization," you could produce the words and sentence: "Nat ran to a zoo."

PRODUCTION STANDARDS

Several rules have to be followed in producing "words in sentences." If these rules are not followed, your output will not meet production specifications and will not pass quality-control inspection.

1. The same letter may appear in a manufactured word only as often as it appears in the raw material word or phrase; for example, "organization" has two o's. Thus "zoo" is legitimate, but not "zoonosis," which has too many o's and s's.
2. Raw material letters can be used again in different manufactured words.
3. A manufactured word may be used only once in a sentence and in only one sentence during a production run; if a word—for example, "a"—is used once in a sentence, it is out of stock.
4. A new word may not be made by adding "s" to form the plural of an already-used manufactured word.

5. A word is defined by its spelling, not its meaning.
6. Nonsense words or nonsense sentences are unacceptable.
7. All words must be in the English language.
8. Names and places are acceptable.
9. Slang is not acceptable.

MEASURING PERFORMANCE

The output of your WIS company is measured by the total number of acceptable words that are packaged in sentences. The sentences must be legible, listed on no more than two sheets of paper, and handed to the Quality Control Review Board at the completion of each production run.

DELIVERY

Delivery must be made to the Quality Control Review Board 30 seconds after the end of each production run.

QUALITY CONTROL

If any word in a sentence does not meet the standards set forth here, all the words in the sentence will be rejected.

The Quality Control Review Board (composed of one member from each company) is the final arbiter of acceptability. In the event of a tie vote by the review board, a coin toss will determine the outcome.

STEP 3: Design your organization using as many group members as you see fit to produce your words in sentences.

STEP 4: Production Run 1. The group leader will hand each WIS company a sheet with a raw material word or phrase. When the instructor announces "Begin production," you are to manufacture as many words as possible and package them in sentences for delivery to the Quality Control Review Board. You will have 10 minutes. When the instructor announces "Stop production," you will have 30 seconds to deliver your output to the Quality Control Review Board. Output received after 30 seconds does not meet the delivery schedule and will not be counted.

STEP 5: While the output is being evaluated, you may reorganize for the second production run.

STEP 6: Production Run 2.

STEP 7: The results are presented.

STEP 8: Discussion. In small groups, and then with the entire class, answer the following questions.

DESCRIPTION

1. Draw the organizational chart for your WIS company.

DIAGNOSIS

2. Analyze your company's structure: Describe (a) division of labor, (b) mechanisms of coordination, and (c) structural configurations.

3. Using your knowledge of organizational design and the contingencies that influence it, evaluate your WIS company's structure.

PRESCRIPTION

4. How could you have designed a more effective organizational structure?

Source: The origin of this exercise is unknown.

ACTIVITY 13-2: ORGANIZATIONAL LIFE CYCLE EXERCISE

STEP 1: Choose two organizations.

STEP 2: Collect written documents that trace the history of each organization. Interview members who are familiar with the development of each organization. Gather any additional data available about the organization's growth and development.

STEP 3: In groups of two or three people, share the data you have collected. Trace the stages in each organization's development. What issues did the organization face at each stage? What

problems did the organization encounter in its development? Compare and contrast the development of the two organizations. How were they similar?

STEP 4: Discussion. In small groups or with the entire class, identify the stages in development you have identified. Which stages do these organizations have in common? How did the development of these organizations differ? How do effective organizations differ from ineffective organizations in their development?

ACTIVITY 13-3: REDESIGN THE SCHOOL OF MANAGEMENT

STEP 1: Interview three staff members in your school of management. (Your instructor may direct you to choose a different organization.) Select people who know the reporting relationships among people in the school.

STEP 2: Individually or in small groups, draw a detailed organization chart for the school.

STEP 3: Analyze the following factors that affect the school: (a) environment, (b) technology, (c) work force, (d) goals, (e) strategy, (f) stage of development, (g) size, and (h) age. What type of structure would best respond to these factors?

STEP 4: Redesign your school of management. Then prepare a brief executive summary describing and justifying the changes.

STEP 5: In small groups or with the entire class, share your designs.

1. What changes did each group propose?
2. Why did they propose these changes?
3. Which designs likely will be most effective?

ACTIVITY 13-4: THE DEVELOPMENT OF AN INTERNATIONAL ALLIANCE

STEP 1: Choose an international alliance to study (e.g., Ford-Mazda, Xerox-Fuji).

STEP 2: Collect written documents (e.g., newspaper articles, magazine accounts, descriptions on the World Wide Web) that trace the formation of the alliance.

STEP 3: In groups of two or three people, share the data you have collected. Trace the stages in the development of the international alliance. What issues did the organizations face at each stage? What problems did they encounter in forming the alliance?

STEP 4: Discussion. In small groups or with the entire class, identify the stages of development you have identified. Which stages do these organizations have in common? Which stages were most critical for the effective development of the alliance? At which stages did they experience problems? How did they resolve them?

ACTIVITY 13-5: THE NEW TRAVEL AGENCY

STEP 1: Read the following scenario.

You are the owner and president of a medium-sized travel agency with four branches in suburban areas of a major midwestern U.S. city. You have steady and loyal clients who have used your services because of the expertise and personal attention they receive from the 30 agents you employ. In fact, many of your customers have commented about the high quality of recommendations for hotels and inns offered by your staff. They have been particularly grateful for assistance in planning trips outside the United States.

You have become concerned, however, that the increasing number of Web sites that enable travelers to make hotel and airplane reservations will cut into your business. You believe that you need to find ways to take advantage of the Web, rather than ignore it. You think that you need to change your organizational structure to respond to this dynamic environment. Until now, you have had a branch manager for each branch, who supervises the travel agents in that branch.

STEP 2: Individually or in small groups, consider how the organizational design should respond to the changing environment. Offer a list of changes you would make in the organizational structure to respond to the environmental changes.

STEP 3: Share your list of proposed changes with the entire class. Then offer an organization design of the agency that would respond best to the environment it faces.

ACTIVITY 13-6: THE DOWNSIZING DEBATE

STEP 1: Your instructor will assign you to teams that will debate either the pro or con side of the following issue.

Resolved: Companies should use downsizing to become more efficient in a highly competitive environment.

STEP 2: Prepare your position.

STEP 3: Conduct the debate with the opposing team.

STEP 4: In small groups or with the entire class, discuss and answer the following questions:

1. Which side was more convincing?
2. What issues should organizations consider before deciding to downsize?

Chapter 14

Managing Change in Organizations

Learning Objectives

After completing Chapter 14, you will be able to

1. Describe the nature of change, including the approaches to and scope of change.
2. Identify forces for and against change.
3. Compare and contrast internal and external change agents, and discuss the value of using consultants.
4. Discuss the issues associated with initiating change from the top and the bottom.
5. Highlight the key aspects of three work redesign strategies.
6. Discuss the advantages and disadvantages of virtual employment and alternative work schedules.
7. Describe ways of implementing business process redesign to improve quality.
8. Delineate the key components of learning organizations.
9. Describe the major issues involved in implementing, evaluating, and institutionalizing change.
10. Highlight the key issues for managing change in the dot-com, global workplace.

A Manager's Preview

Describe . . . Diagnose . . . Prescribe . . . Act

- Increase the forces for change and reduce the forces against change.
- Select the most appropriate change agent.
- Implement the most effective intervention strategies.
- Redesign jobs in your organization.
- Design a program of virtual employment and work schedules.
- Offer a plan for implementing business process redesign and quality improvement.
- Offer a protocol for making a company a learning organization.
- Increase innovation in your workplace.
- Evaluate organizational changes.
- Institutionalize organizational changes.
- Modify change strategies to work in a dot-com, global workplace.

Change at Herman Miller Furniture

Executives recently reinvented the Herman Miller furniture company by turning the country's second-largest manufacturer of office furniture into a Web wizard. Built to experiment with new technology, the Holland, Michigan, plant has dramatically improved its performance. SQA, or "simple, quick, affordable," is the new division Miller started to make furniture for smaller companies (those with five to 150 employees). SQA initially ran the Holland plant and then moved to corporate headquarters to extend its approach company-wide. The company linked all sales and purchasing operations to the Internet. Miller has established Web sites for large corporate customers and for hooking its suppliers into the company's order and accounting systems. This use of the Web, which has resulted in brisk online sales, has allowed Miller to improve customer service, speed deliveries, and significantly reduce costs. In addition, the company uses technology to enable its salespeople to prepare rough furniture plans during sales calls. Herman Miller also has improved its information systems so it can ship products that specifically meet customer requests. Buyers can customize a product's color, size, and style. Herman Miller invested nearly $500 million in technology over a five-year period. Corporate revenues increased by 90 percent between 1995 and 2000, up 8 percent alone in 1999.[1]

How did its executives approach the transformation of Herman Miller? What steps did they take to ensure that the company attains its goals? In this chapter, we focus on organizational change, the *action* step of the diagnostic approach. We begin by looking at some general approaches to change. Then we examine each step in organizational change, focusing on identifying the forces for and against change and selecting a change agent. Next we consider an array of intervention strategies, including work redesign, virtual employment, business process redesign, and learning organizations. We also look at other issues related to interventions, such as innovation and ways of differentiating among strategies. Finally, we examine the evaluation and institutionalization of change before concluding with comments about change in the dot-com, global workplace.

▌ THE NATURE OF CHANGE

Companies like Herman Miller increasingly try to reinvent themselves. *Planned change* describes the systematic process of introducing new behaviors, structures, and technologies for addressing the problems and challenges organizations face. Unplanned or unintentional change can also occur, although in this chapter we focus mainly on planned or intentional change. Companies may take three approaches to planned change:

- **Behavioral approach.** Often known as *organization development (OD)*, the behavioral approach improves communication, group behavior, intergroup behavior, leadership skills, and power relations by changing employees' knowledge, skills, interactions, and attitudes as well as the organizational culture.[2]
- **Structural approach.** This approach focuses on redesigning organizations and jobs or work situations. Companies increasingly move to more organic structures, such as horizontal or modular organizations. New online ventures may require a total restructuring, even introducing virtual organizational components.
- **Technological approach.** This approach changes the equipment, methods, materials, or techniques used to perform jobs, such as by redesigning or reengineering tasks and automating work processes. Herman Miller decided to rely on the Web more extensively for integrating its functions.

Planned change usually involves a *change agent*, a person responsible for overseeing the change effort. This person can work for the organization or for an outside firm. Regardless of her position, the change agent generally works extensively with managers and employees to diagnose problems and implement the changes (prescriptions) required to address them. Sapient Corporation in Cambridge, Massachusetts, an Internet consulting firm, provides Web-savvy change agents to companies, including United Airlines, Kmart, and Compaq, that want to establish an online presence. It drills its new recruits on the company's basic mission—helping other companies quickly get wired to the Web—and how their personal motivations relate to this philosophy. Sapient has succeeded by hiring highly qualified and highly motivated employees who can combine Web-related technical, marketing, and creative advice with the ability to introduce advanced wireless technology.[3]

FIGURE 14-1

Organizational change varies along at least two dimensions: expected-unexpected and incremental-radical.

	Expected	Unexpected
Incremental	TUNING (e.g., new policies, technologies)	ADAPTATION (e.g., new products or new features)
Radical	REORIENTATION (e.g., organizational redesign or reengineering)	RE-CREATION (e.g., new culture or total strategic change)

The Scope of Change

We can manage organizational change by classifying it in one of four ways, as shown in Figure 14-1:[4]

- **Tuning** is incremental change that occurs in anticipation of changes in the environment or attempts to improve efficiency and effectiveness. Tuning can improve policies and procedures, introduce new technologies, and develop employees, among other functions.
- **Adaptation** is incremental change in response to unexpected changes in the environment. For example, organizations may introduce new or improved products to respond to products offered by their competitors.
- **Reorientation** is radical or discontinuous change that anticipates a change in the industry, often involving a fundamental redefinition of the organization, such as a significant change in identity, vision, strategy, or values. This type of change generally requires a visionary leader who can anticipate changes in the environment. It can include organizational redesign and reengineering.
- **Re-creation** is radical or discontinuous change in response to crises or other unexpected changes in the environment. These changes tend to be abrupt and severe and often challenge the organization's core values.

What type of change did Herman Miller experience? Changing its basic way of doing business through the use of new technologies suggests a discontinuous change. Managing such a change poses significant challenges for the people involved.

Reorientation and re-creation both reflect *transformational change* and describe many companies that have attempted to reinvent themselves.[5] The manufacturing facility of C. R. Bard in Glens Falls, New York, underwent a major transformation when it changed to a team-based environment. The change took several years and involved decision, design, and implementation processes. Throughout the change process, Bard used cross-functional, multilevel project teams that often "learned by doing." Bard provided extensive training to all employees and kept the process visible throughout the organization. The transformation resulted in a new, results-oriented culture.[6]

We can think of the transformation process in these types of changes in two ways. First, the transformation can include a *reframing* of the situation by people involved.[7] Often motivated by a crisis, managers challenge the original understanding of the situation. Then they prepare for reframing—that is, they collect and share an array of information about the problems, which should lead to a new understanding of the situation. Then participants develop new and different ways of thinking about and understanding the situation. The transformation concludes with members adopting and accepting the new view or understanding.

Second, we can think of transformation using a *punctuated equilibrium paradigm.* This view suggests that organizational change occurs as an alternation of long periods of stability and short periods of revolutionary change.[8] During the stable or *equilibrium* periods, deep structures—for example, standard operating procedures, performance and reward systems, norms, and roles—anchor its operations. These basic activity patterns of an organization, department, work group, or other subsystem, make incremental adjustments that adapt to external changes. At times, however, *revolutionary changes* dismantle the deep structure. The organizations or its subsystems may outgrow their deep structures, lack sufficient resources for dealing with the environment, or face a traumatic external environment. During the revolutionary period, emotions of participants intensify, and outsiders may play more critical roles. Ultimately, new deep structures develop. Some companies do the reverse and alternate major change with periods of smaller change, called *tinkering* or *kludging,* to create more stability as the change occurs.[9] Managers can create ambidextrous organizations, where they encourage continuous improvement and simultaneously allow experimentation and flexibility so their firm can respond to dramatic environmental shifts.[10]

▌ THE CHANGE PROCESS

What process should people use to successfully manage change? Kurt Lewin offered one of the earliest ways of thinking about change. He described the change process as having three stages:

1. **unfreezing,** creating an awareness of a need for change and removing any resistances to change;
2. **change,** altering the organizational situation; and
3. **refreezing,** stabilizing the organization after the change has occurred.

In the 1960s and 1970s, as employee involvement in change became more valued, some managers adopted an *action research* approach to change, as shown in Figure 14-2. Many organizations still use this approach, in which the change agent collaborates extensively with the client in gathering and feeding back data. Together, they collect and discuss the data, and then use the data for planning future changes.[11]

The approach to managing change described in this chapter incorporates some of the elements of these models, but offers a more flexible, analytical approach to change. It begins with diagnosing the forces that affect change, followed by selecting a change agent, building an action plan, implementing the change, evaluating it, and institutionalizing it, as shown in Figure 14-3.

Forces for Change

Change begins when the person responsible for making the changes or for ensuring that they occur obtains preliminary information about the situation and the people involved. Often that person must negotiate an agreement (either formal or informal) with top executives about the nature of the planned change and who will participate in its implementation.

The change agent then attempts to understand the forces that affect the change. One way to do this is by using an analytical technique called *force field analy-*

FIGURE 14-2

Action research involves both managers and employees in the change process.

Source: W. French, Organization Development: Objectives, Assumptions and Strategies. © 1969 by the Regents of University of California. Reprinted from *California Management Review* 12(2): 26, by permission of the Regents.

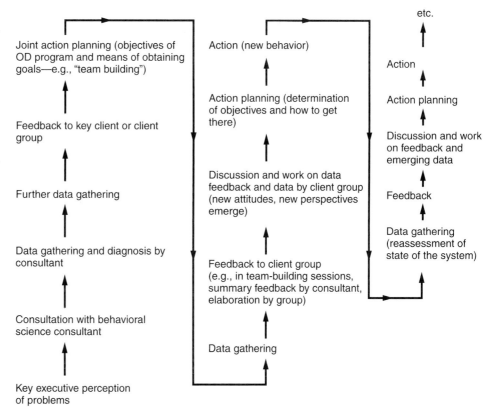

sis, which views a problem as a product of forces working in different, often opposite directions, as shown in Figure 14-4.[12] An organization, group, person, or other entity maintains the status quo when the sum of forces for and against change is zero. When forces in one direction exceed forces in the opposite one, the organization, group, or person moves in the direction of the greater forces. If, for example, a major crisis causes the forces for change to exceed the forces against change, then change is likely. If a strong preference for the status quo causes the forces against change to exceed those for change, change is unlikely.

FIGURE 14-3

Managing organizational change involves a series of steps.

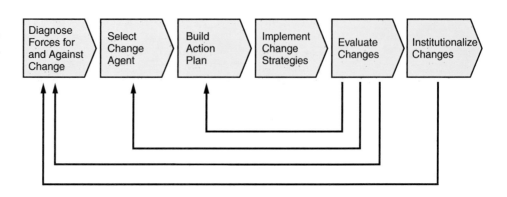

The intensity of the forces for and against change likely will determine the likelihood of change.

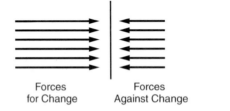

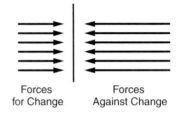

Forces
for Change

Forces
Against Change

Forces for Change GREATER THAN
Forces Against Change

Forces
for Change

Forces
Against Change

Forces for Change LESS THAN
Forces Against Change

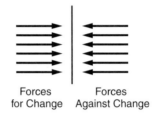

Forces
for Change

Forces
Against Change

Forces for Change EQUAL TO
Forces Against Change

Managers who wish to change a company must either increase the forces for change in that direction, decrease the forces against change, or do both. Generally, reducing resistance to change creates less tension in the system and fewer unanticipated consequences than increasing forces for change. At Herman Miller, the SQA division needed to reduce resistance to the change from board members, dealers, and salespeople. Managing change effectively at this stage calls for managers to diagnose and then plan ways to change the forces for and against change.

Changes in an organization's environment, such as new laws or regulations, rapidly increasing competition, or an unpredictable rate of inflation, may require the organization to implement new structures or reward systems. Other factors that may affect the organization are new product development or product selection due to improved technology, changes in competition in the industry, or the unusual requirements of a new client. For example, strikes at major airlines and other companies often force top management to reexamine the way they deal with employees.

Changes in the workforce, such as more educated workers, more women, or more technically trained management, may call for new forms of decision making or communication. Reduced productivity, product quality, satisfaction, and commitment, or increased turnover or absenteeism may call for changes in relations inside or between departments. Crises in organizations, such as a hostile takeover, potential bankruptcy, industrial accidents, product defects or tampering, major computer breakdowns, or a myriad of other causes, can motivate change. The crisis management process can result in either success or failure. For example, an organization that can maintain business as usual during and after the crisis or can improve its organizational image by its approach to crisis management will experience success. An organization that lacks the essential resources to address the crisis or that makes the same mistakes when similar incidents occur will experience failure.[13]

Forces Against Change

Identifying the forces against change involves two steps. First, the manager or other change agent must identify resistance behaviors. These behaviors can range from lowered productivity, increased absenteeism, and poor morale to slowdowns, strikes, or unionization. Second, the manager or change agent needs to determine the causes of the resistance, such as the following:

- **Employees may feel that managers ignore their needs, attitudes, and beliefs.** Increasing automation in the workplace may threaten workers with high security needs who perceive that layoffs will result.

- **Employees may hold ingrained schemas that prevent them from being able to function in new ways.**[14] Or, they may lack the skills and knowledge required for change.

- **Employees may lack specific information about the change.** Workers may not know when, how, or why the change is occurring.

- **Employees may fail to perceive a need for change.** Employees may feel that their organization operates effectively and profitably. In these cases, they may not voluntarily make or request changes.

- **Employees may demonstrate a "we–they" attitude and so view the change agent as their enemy.** Employees may feel inconsequential to the change, particularly when representatives of a distant corporate headquarters or an outside consulting firm lead the change effort.

- **Employees may view change as a threat to the prestige and security of their supervisor.** They may perceive a change in procedures or policies as an indication that their supervisor's performance is inadequate.

- **Employees may perceive the change as a threat to managers' and employees' expertise, status, or security.** Revising the organization's structure may challenge employees' relative status in the organization. Introducing a new reward system may threaten their feelings of job security. Employees may fear change, desire to maintain power, or act complacent toward the change. Integra Financial, a bank holding company, changed its reward system to support its new focus on teamwork. The company then took market share from long-time regional rivals.[15]

- **Employees may work in rigid organizational structures and so develop rigid thinking.** Conflicts between individual and organizational goals and organizational inertia against changing the status quo can also contribute to resistance to change. Lack of resources to support the change can also cause resistance.

The president and CEO of Telefon AB L. M. Ericsson was forced to resigned after 15 months in part because he encountered resistance to the changes he proposed from inside the organization. He couldn't push needed reforms through an organization that has traditionally relied on a slow, consensus-oriented management style.[16] At North Snohomish County Health System in Arlington, Washington, even the leaders almost succumbed to their own resistance to change as they tried to move from a departmental to a process-based organization. The leaders initially tried to deal with problems by using quick fixes, but soon recognized that they needed to overcome their own resistance to massive change and deal with the problems by continuing to push the change agenda. Eventually, the hospital simplified the work flow, reduced costs, and created greater efficiencies from the new structure.[17] Leaders may need to change the mind-set of their organization's employees by modeling the desired behaviors.[18]

How does a company deal with these forces? After identifying the forces both for and against change, top executives or other managers next select the best person to oversee the change.

▌ SELECTING A CHANGE AGENT

Who should make the changes in companies like Herman Miller? We can think about change agents in three ways:[19]

- ▪ **Change generators** demonstrate the need for change to the organization. These people create a felt need about other managers and employees, demonstrate support for the proposed change, financially or psychologically support the change process, or defend the change at the lower levels of the organization.
- ▪ **Change implementors** carry out the change activities specified by top management. These include the people who are invited from outside or inside the organization to implement the change, as well as the managers who implement and model the change for other units.
- ▪ **Change adopters** practice the changes as part of their daily work. These include the managers who first adopt and practice the change, adopt the change because they see it helps their work, or become more committed to the change as they continue functioning in the new situation.

Effective change agents are empathetic, sensitive, open, tolerant, flexible, patient, friendly, cooperative, and imaginative. They develop and use information to understand situations and identify behavior patterns. They act in a self-reliant fashion, are bold, risk-taking, and initiating. In contrast, the least effective change agents are suspicious, tense, directive, and impersonal. They stay within the bounds of known facts, focus on the practical, secure minimal information, and are more concerned with the "how" than the "why" of situations. They also are shy and aversive to risk.[20]

How can organizations select the most appropriate change agent for a particular initiative? The following steps direct their efforts:

1. Determine the objective of the change.
2. Consider the extent of help and involvement desired.
3. Consider the extent of help and involvement available in the organization.
4. Identify individuals with expertise congruent with the objectives.
5. Identify and specify constraints that affect the choice of change agent: time, cost, effort, involvement, and other resources.
6. Communicate expectations, including needs, constraints, and personal biases, to the change agent.
7. Establish criteria for evaluating the change and change agents (e.g., cost, time, or technical feasibility).
8. Determine the trade-offs in selecting various change agents (e.g., cost versus experience).
9. Assess which change agents fit the organization's needs.

TABLE 14-1

Managers Can Choose Internal or External Change Agents.

	Internal Change Agents	External Change Agents
Advantages	Possess better knowledge of the organization	Have more objective views of the organization
	Are more quickly available	Have more experience in dealing with diverse problems
	Require lower out-of-pocket costs	Can call on more individuals with diverse expertise
	Are a known quantity	Have more technical knowledge, competence, and skills available
	Have more control and authority	Have less knowledge of the organization
Disadvantages	May be too close to the problem	Require higher out-of-pocket costs
	May hold biased views	Are an unknown quantity
	May create additional resistance if viewed as part of the problem	Have longer start-up time
	Must be reassigned; not available for other work	Reflect unfavorably on the image of management

Internal and External Change Agents

Should a company rely on its own employees and managers for implementing change? Should it use outside consultants? Managers can consider the advantages and disadvantages of each option, as shown in Table 14-1. They can then choose the type of change agent that best fits the requirements of the situation.

Internal Change Agents.   Managers and employees have first-hand knowledge of their organization. They probably can work on the change immediately and at no additional out-of-pocket cost. Because of their investment in the organization, however, insiders may not objectively analyze the problems their company faces. In some situations, they may be part of the problem. The time they lose to other projects may also have significant costs to the company.

Increasingly, internal audit departments are acting as change agents. They conduct special consulting projects and develop ways to link control processes to organizational learning.[21] Members of the human resources department also often act as internal change agents. When Sharon Smith became the vice president of human resources for Cox Communications in California, she learned that the department's role was very limited. She reassessed and repositioned the department and helped its staff act as major change agents for the company. Her department helped Cox's managers think differently about recruitment and compensation as a way to attract better employees. Smith regularly provides top management with feedback about the executives' business decisions. She helped the company make a major cultural change, and the human resources staff regularly receives praise from managers they have helped.[22]

External Change Agents and Consultants.   People who work for organizations other than the one experiencing the change can also participate in or lead the change effort. Consultants, accountants, or members of other professional organizations can be hired to fill this role. Consultants often play the following roles:[23]

- assessment, using tools and techniques to help organizations identify change management barriers, opportunities, and networks;
- training in change management principles and methodology or to meet special needs (e.g., helping managers adopt new styles, teaching teamwork skills, and developing change leadership);
- planning for change management, by using tailored workshops and planning processes;
- values and vision development assistance;
- infrastructure design and role development;
- assistance in redesigning organizational factors to support change, such as compensation and performance measurement systems, information systems, and financial systems;
- organizational communication planning and development; and
- project management assistance.

External consultants tend to have more technical knowledge, diverse competencies, and objectivity in instituting change. On the down side, they may lack information about the particular situation, take longer to start implementing the change, and add large out-of-pocket costs. Employees at Battelle & Batelle, a Dayton, Ohio, accounting firm, act as external consultants and offer clients help with strategic planning. The firm also offers other business services, such as assistance with refinancing, performance management, inventory controls, and process management.[24]

Managers who hire consultants need to consider the following to ensure their effectiveness. First, a manager needs to assess the reason he is hiring the consultant and then set objectives for the consulting engagement. For example, he might want the consultant to design a training program, redesign the organization's structure, or provide coaching to top executives. Next, the manager should investigate various choices of consulting firms. As with any type of organization, consulting firms differ in size, expertise, and manner of operation. Choosing one that will best accomplish the hiring organization's objectives is paramount.

Once the consultant has been hired, either the consultant or the client can take the lead in establishing the specific aspects of the consulting engagement. This includes specifying a series of deliverables and a timetable for their delivery. The hiring company should also assign a manager or appropriate staff member to serve as a liaison for the consultant. The liaison can keep other company members informed about the consultant's activities and progress. She can also help arrange any contacts the consultant needs with specific organizational members. Finally, both the hiring manager and the consultant should ensure that quality communication exists throughout the relationship. Failure to keep each party informed about relevant issues can weaken the results of the consultation.

Initiating Change from the Top

Traditionally, top managers have assumed significant responsibility for motivating and supporting change. As noted earlier, their support is particularly important in the case of radical change, where special vision and leadership skills are required.

Because top managers have access to the resources required to implement change, they can often mobilize the change effort more quickly than lower-level managers. The new president of Mazda, Mark Fields, plans to institute cost-cutting measures from the top down. In his previous position at Mazda, he helped close 100 sales outlets and reduced the workforce through attrition.[25] Honeywell instituted a new e-business strategy from the top down. It includes Web sites that offer Honeywell products and services to key customers and information about pensions and benefits to employees. Honeywell also plans to integrate its customer and employee sites with the company's finance, manufacturing, and engineering systems. The corporate e-business president and his staff of six have responsibility for implementing this strategy.[26]

The manager of the group involved in a change often becomes the person responsible for implementation. This selection occurs informally, primarily because the manager is closest to the situation, has greatest knowledge of it, and has control over it. Using a manager can reduce the time required to begin the change. In addition, other organizational members already know the manager and have clear expectations about actions she might take.

Initiating Change from the Bottom

Other organizational members can also lead change. In particular, they can help reduce resistance to change from co-workers. Some focus well on organizational processes and can develop creative ways of improving them. The use of self-improvement teams encourages this type of change. Selected or specially trained employees can coach managers about how to develop others and support problem-solving activities.[27] Increasingly, companies have introduced train-the-trainer approaches to skill development, which can be extended to change efforts.

▌ SELECTING INTERVENTION STRATEGIES

The next step in managing change involves identifying ways to increase the forces for change and reduce the forces against change. Together, these strategies comprise an action plan.

Consider the situation at Herman Miller again. What should the company have done to ensure the success of the changes in operations? First, top managers must overcome employee resistance to the change in the following ways:

- **Extensive communication with employees.** Scheduling regular informational meetings for all employees affected by the change helps involve them in the process and allows them to flag any problems with the proposed change.
- **Educational and training programs.** Educational activities prepare workers for their new job and organizational requirements after the change.
- **Employee involvement in decision making.** Participation in decision making increases employee commitment to the change and can surface valuable ideas.
- **New organizational structures.** Steering committees, task forces, or other temporary structures can help establish a climate of innovation. Experimentation can reduce the organization's tendency to maintain the status quo.
- **Staff changes.** Hiring or transferring staff can help ensure that employees have both the skills and attitudes required for the altered organization.

- **New policies and procedures.** Companies must revise their reward systems to ensure support for the behaviors required by the change.
- **Evolutionary rather than revolutionary changes.** Employees can more easily accept smaller, more deliberate changes than drastic transformations in their work situation. However, sometimes only dramatic changes can accomplish the objectives, and additional preparation for the change must occur.

In the next part of this section, we describe four major types of implementation that can result in large-scale organizational change.

Work Redesign Strategies

The design of work or jobs (terms used interchangeably in this book) involves determining the appropriate task content, sequences, interrelationships, and context. Redesigning work involves changing these aspects of jobs to increase worker performance and satisfaction. Job redesign can reinforce the benefits of new organizational designs (see Chapters 12 and 13) by improving their fit with the new structure, introducing new ways of coordinating work, or modifying the chain of command to allow a more rapid response to environmental changes. Managers have traditionally used work simplification, job enlargement, job enrichment, and the sociotechnical approach to redesign jobs.

Work Simplification.   Work simplification refers to reducing a job to its component parts and then reassembling these parts into the most efficient process. Simplifying the manufacture of computer printers, for example, might divide the process into a series of separate tasks, each performed by a different person. One worker might always insert the circuit board; another might assemble the case; a third might attach the power supply, and so on. Work simplification includes:

- mechanical pacing, or the use of an automated assembly line;
- repetitive work;
- concentration on a fraction of the product;
- detailed specification of the tools and techniques used in production;
- limited social interaction among workers to ensure that they pay close attention to the task; and
- sufficient training to ensure that workers have appropriate skills.[28]

Industrial engineers, staff members who evaluate and improve work processes, study the exact series of motions in a job. They make detailed observations and draw extensive diagrams of the work process to allow them to completely understand it. Next, they monitor the time required for each part of the job. Then they identify and attempt to eliminate all false, slow, and useless movements. Finally, they redesign the job by collecting into one series the quickest and best movements. To accomplish the last step, work simplification typically involves the extensive use and careful design of machines or office equipment, careful spacing of rest periods, high specialization of work activities, and matching of workers to jobs best suited to their abilities, experience, and aptitudes.[29] The process should then operate smoothly and cost-effectively.

Managers who use work simplification to redesign clumsy or overly complex processes may find ways to reposition items between operations. They might also review the grouping of tasks and reassemble them into a more efficient total process.

For example, they might restructure the pace or order of tasks performed to reduce down time in less time-consuming tasks. Pep Boys, a major U.S. auto parts chain, used a flexible plan for its new distribution center. Stock pickers need access to many different units of stock, but in small numbers. The company organized the center into two types of items; they placed faster-moving, more frequently picked items in easily accessible racks. They also placed the more commonly picked items closer to the main pick aisle and the least commonly picked ones farthest from the aisle.[30]

Work simplification can also create significant dysfunctions. Workers may become bored. They may have limited opportunities for individual growth if top management automates and mechanizes production for its own sake rather than for improving worker performance. This form of redesign may also ignore interdependencies between various parts of the job, reducing it to a series of poorly coordinated activities.

Job Enlargement.   Job enlargement expands the scope of the job by increasing the number of different but related processes a person does. Job enlargement offers the opposite solution to work simplification. Rather than encouraging an individual to concentrate on a fraction of the product or service, job enlargement requires a worker to perform numerous, often unrelated, job tasks.

The earliest job enlargement programs involved *job extension*,[31] in which workers did more of the same types of activities. *Job rotation* is a more common form of job enlargement. The worker performs two or more tasks, but alternates among them in a predefined way over a period of time. A worker, for example, might attach the wheel assembly one week, inspect it the next, and organize the parts for assembly during the third.

Job rotation provides a hedge against absenteeism since workers learn how to perform more than a single function. It also supports career advancement by training workers in numerous jobs or tasks. Job rotation has been used to reduce worker injuries, commonly known as cumulative trauma disorders or repetitive stress injuries, which result from tasks involving repetitive manipulations, awkward posture, or forceful exertion.[32] One of the biggest challenges of job rotation is to ensure that it occurs at the right speed; when rotation occurs too quickly, the organization becomes less stable because ripple effects of filling jobs occur throughout the organization. Managing the process effectively is critical to its success.[33] Two units at St. Elizabeth Hospital in New Jersey cross-trained their nurses so they could broaden their competencies. In this way, the hospital could more readily fill vacant positions in the intensive care units (ICU). Nurses were routinely reassigned to the ICU. An experienced intensive care nurse mentored them, and nurse managers and the attending ICU physician staff monitored them. These changes resulted in increased morale and decreased overall patient-care burden for the ICU.[34]

Job Enrichment.   Job enrichment involves changing a job both horizontally by adding tasks and vertically by adding responsibility. The widespread use of self-managed teams in organizations has resulted in significant job enrichment. Employees in these teams perform many types of tasks and receive training on many jobs so that they can exchange jobs with other workers as necessary. Signals of the need for job enrichment include declining work motivation, dissatisfaction with growth opportunities and the job in general, and lack of work effectiveness. Enriched jobs often meet the needs of the increasingly educated workforce many companies employ.

FIGURE 14-5

Managers enrich a job by modifying its characteristics.

Source: J. R. Hackman and G. R. Oldham, *Work Redesign*, Copyright © 1980, Addison-Wesley Publishing Co., Inc. Reprinted with permission of the publisher.

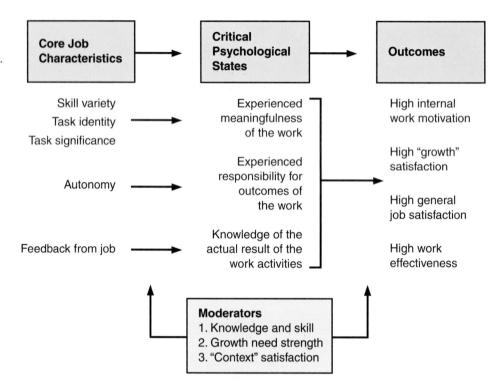

Frederick Herzberg's two-factor model (see Chapter 4) provided the roots for job enrichment programs. He enriched jobs by increasing motivators, such as challenge, autonomy, and responsibility.[35] Managers who jointly set goals with their employees and then make the employees accountable for accomplishing them enrich workers' jobs. Self-managed work teams naturally enrich jobs because they give employees control over managerial activities that others previously held.

The *job characteristics model* of enrichment, shown in Figure 14-5, offers a more complete way of evaluating and enriching a job. This model specifies five core characteristics of the job that significantly influence workers' behaviors and attitudes.[36]

- **Skill variety** means how much a job requires the worker to perform activities that challenge his skills and use diverse abilities. An executive chef's job has more skill variety than a prep cook's job.

- **Task identity** refers to how much a job requires a worker to complete a "whole" and identifiable piece of work—that is, to do a job from beginning to end with a visible outcome. Assembly-line workers in a furniture factory who assemble an entire chair or bookcase have jobs with high task identity.

- **Task significance** means how much a job is perceived to have a substantial impact on the lives of other people. Classroom teaching appears to have greater task significance than lunchroom monitoring.

- **Autonomy** indicates how much a job gives an employee control over her work schedule and how she does her work. Members of self-managed work teams have high autonomy.

- **Feedback** refers to how much a worker receives information about the effectiveness of his work performance. A typesetter who receives a list of typographical errors each day from a proofreader receives feedback.

Three critical psychological states—*experienced meaningfulness, experienced responsibility,* and *knowledge of results*—affect personal and work outcomes.[37] These outcomes include internal work motivation, "growth" satisfaction, general job satisfaction, and work effectiveness. Of the five job characteristics just listed, skill variety, task identity, and task significance influence the extent to which an employee experiences the job as meaningful. As workers use their diverse abilities, complete entire tasks, and view their work as having an impact on others' lives, they are more likely to experience their jobs as meaningful. Autonomy in the job influences the extent to which a person believes he is responsible for outcomes. A person with limited supervision may feel more responsible for his job outcomes than a person who has such tight supervision that the manager corrects all mistakes. Feedback in the job increases the person's knowledge of the actual results of the work. Increasing the amount of information available to a jobholder increases her ability to determine her effectiveness.

A person's knowledge and skill, growth needs (needs for learning, personal accomplishment, and development), and satisfaction with the work context affect the relationship among the five core job characteristics, the three critical psychological states, and the outcomes.[38] For example, employees who have the skills and knowledge to perform enriched jobs will be more satisfied than less competent workers. People with high growth needs typically prefer and work better in enriched jobs than those with low growth needs, who find enriched jobs stressful. Employees satisfied with the work context may be more able to take advantage of the opportunities provided by enriched jobs than those dissatisfied with the work context, who are too preoccupied with the parts of the job that dissatisfy them.

The job characteristics approach calls for enriching a job by increasing one or more of the core dimensions.[39]

- **Combining tasks** increases skill variety and task identity.
- **Forming natural work units,** such as with self-managed teams, increases task identity and task significance.
- **Establishing client relationships** increases skill variety, autonomy, and feedback.
- **Loading a job vertically** to combine implementation and control increases autonomy.
- **Opening feedback channels** increases knowledge of results.

In a study of three U.S. manufacturing plants, continuous improvement efforts, known in Japan as *kaizen* and described later in this chapter, also had a positive impact on skill variety, task identity, task significance, autonomy, and feedback. Both internal motivation and growth need strength also increased.[40]

Sociotechnical Approach.   Building on job enrichment, the sociotechnical approach uses teams to motivate employees and appropriate technologies to improve task performance.[41] Researchers at the Tavistock Institute in England in the 1950s and 1960s first noted the importance of work groups in handling new technology.[42] Later, Scandinavian automobile manufacturers used the concept of autonomous work groups as a way of meeting workers' social needs while introducing technological innovation.[43] In these self-regulating groups, employees worked on interdependent tasks in a single unit, controlled their own task assignments, and performed many roles traditionally assigned to management. According to this sociotechnical paradigm, autonomous work groups integrated and optimized social and technical systems.[44] Volvo, for example, eliminated the assembly line completely at its Udevalla plant, where small groups of workers assembled an entire car. Declining demand resulted in the closing of this and other Volvo plants in the mid-1990s.[45]

The introduction of autonomous or self-regulating work groups reduced the isolation and boredom traditionally felt by manufacturing workers, particularly as automation increased. In an Australian manufacturing setting, introducing semi-autonomous work groups accompanied by weekly meetings of employees and supervisors resulted in positive improvements in worker satisfaction, productivity, and attendance.[46] In other settings, the use of autonomous work groups resulted over time in increased personal stress, lower job satisfaction, decreased organizational commitment, and less trust in management than in comparable, traditionally functioning groups.[47]

Participative design, which focuses on ways to democratize decision making, provides an alternative to sociotechnical systems redesign.[48] It addresses two basic questions:

- What decisions about control and coordination of work are necessary for effective group performance?
- To what extent can these decisions be located within the group doing the work?

Participative design tries to reduce the length and complexity of the redesign process, sustain the redesign over time, and create commitment and energy for change. The introduction of self-managed teams illustrates the principles of this approach.

Virtual Employment and Alternative Work Schedules

Virtual employment, flexible hours, and part-time employment help workers balance the demands of work and family and help employers reduce the costs of maintaining large amounts of office space for workers who spend most of their jobs outside the office.

Telecommuting.   More workers now use information technology to perform their jobs at sites away from the organization's physical plant. These *virtual employees,* connected to their offices through computer networks, have increased in number in the past decade. Most often, these employees already use computers for large parts of their jobs. Salespeople, who spend large amounts of time out of the office, may also base their operations at home. *Hoteling* describes workers who lack a permanent work space. They make reservations for an office cubicle when they want to work in the office. Often this space is in suburban office parks that have lower rents and are more accessible to workers.[49]

Companies can save the overhead costs of providing offices by having these types of employees work away from the corporate location. Workers may telecommute from home or from *telecenters,* satellite offices that more than one employee share.[50] For example, an AT&T sales manager in Virginia manages eight commission-based salespeople from her home two or three days each week. By working at home, she can eliminate almost three hours of commuting time to her primary office in Washington, D.C. A salesperson for Summit Software only visits its main office in Syracuse, New York, several times a year; instead, he works from a small satellite office in Texas about 50 percent of the time, from home about 5 percent of the time, and at his clients' sites the remainder of the time. A Web and multimedia developer for Tmanage telecommutes from home; her employer has an established telecommuting policy for many of its employees.[51]

Some workers prefer telecommuting because it reduces their commuting time and allows them more flexibility in meeting family responsibilities. However, segregating work from family time can provide a challenge in these circumstances. Some employees feel that the lack of social interaction with co-workers creates feelings of isolation.[52] Spending some time, at least one or two workdays each week, at the work site reduces these feelings. Telecommuting can put workers' aspirations for promotion at risk because they don't seem part of the regular work activities.[53] Employees should negotiate the impact of virtual employment on their career advancement before telecommuting. The benefits generally outweigh the costs, according to executives at publishers such as Ziff-Davis, tele.com, *Travel & Leisure,* and *Conde Nast.*[54]

Flexible Hours.   Programs that offer workers flexible hours give employees some discretion in creating their work schedules. Such programs take three basic forms: discretionary systems, part-time employment, and contingent workers.

In *discretionary systems,* workers choose the precise days or hours worked.

- **Flextime,** probably the most common discretionary system, offers workers the choice of starting and ending times as long as they work certain specific hours daily and meet the requirements of a normal workweek (usually 35 to 40 hours). For example, one office clerk might work from 7 A.M. to 3 P.M., whereas another clerk might work from 10 A.M. to 6 P.M. At Cendant Mortgage Corporation in New Jersey, employees work with their supervisors to design alternative work schedules that fit with their personal responsibilities.[55]

- **Staggered week schedules** require employees to alternate between working a four-day, 32-hour week and a six-day, 48-hour week.

- **Compressed workweek** allows employees to work the number of hours in a traditional five-day week (usually between 35 and 40) in four or even three days. Although a four-day workweek may result in greater employee satisfaction, it may also reduce employee efficiency due to the fatigue of the long working hours. Scheduling work in two-week rather than one-week blocks enhances the attractiveness of this option. For example, firefighters often work four days, have a four-day break, and then work four more days, followed by a normal two-day weekend break. AVT Document Exchange Software Group in Arizona, which sells e-document software, allows its general staff to work four 10-hour days and choose their day off; its information technology workers on the swing and midnight shifts work four 9-hour days. Nahan Printing in Minnesota found that a compressed schedule let them better meet their customers' and employees' needs because they had staffing seven days a week without required overtime.[56]

In one analysis, flextime positively affected productivity, performance, job satisfaction, absenteeism, and work schedule satisfaction, while compressed workweeks positively affected all but absenteeism.[57] Marcel Dekker, Inc., an international publisher, uses a combination of flextime and compressed workweek for its employees. The company has found this arrangement to be an excellent benefit that has helped it recruit and retain employees. Most staff work Monday through Thursday for 10 hours a day and begin their days between 7:30 and 9:30 A.M.[58]

Part-time employees work less than whole weeks, with predictable or unpredictable hours. Employers typically don't pay benefits to part-time workers, significantly reducing compensation costs. Employees can also work reduced hours by sharing or splitting jobs. These arrangements offer greater flexibility to workers and give organizations access to employees who otherwise would not be able to work.

- **Job sharing** is when two employees divide a whole job into two parts according to time and day of the week. Although they typically divide the tasks according to time, such as mornings versus afternoons, job sharers may also specialize their tasks somewhat. Baxter Exports includes job sharing as one of an array of alternative work arrangements designed to allow employees to better manage work–life issues.[59]

- **Job splitting** divides a job according to tasks or skills, rather than schedule. In splitting a secretarial job, for example, one person might take all the dictation, while the second might do all the manuscript typing.

Companies hire *contingent workers* to complete specific projects or tasks. More than 93 percent of U.S. firms employ some type of contingent worker.[60] They may be freelance employees who wish to retain their personal flexibility and autonomy by developing their own work schedules. They may be contract workers, employed by outsourcing firms that have contracted to provide certain services to a company, such as managing the mail room or other facilities or working on special medium-term projects. Professional and technical companies, such as those involved in software development or distribution, often hire this type of employee in order to have maximum staffing flexibility.[61]

Contingent employees may become frustrated about pay or benefits differentials, reducing their productivity and value to the company. Increasingly, companies with contingent workers can face litigation regarding their status as employer or contractor, leading to costly lawsuits related to equal employment opportunities.[62] Contingent employees sued Microsoft, arguing that they were common-law employees and so were entitled to corporate benefits. Temporary employees at Allstate Insurance filed a class-action suit claiming that 10,000 temporary employees since 1983 were common-law workers and so entitled to benefits.[63]

Effectiveness of Alternative Work Arrangements.   Managers who implement alternative work options need to screen candidates carefully, set appropriate goals, and develop a good work plan. They need to identify the job designs and personal characteristics that fit best with alternative work arrangements. For example, managers may discover that jobs with little dependence on other jobs make better candidates for flexible hours than highly interdependent ones. Companies should also carefully evaluate the job task before determining whether telework is appropriate.[64] An organization may find that only experienced, highly mature, highly experienced employees make good candidates for telecommuting. Managers must find ways to validate the number of hours worked by employees. In addition, they must maintain open communication, provide ongoing support, and remain flexible in dealing with employees who take advantage of alternative work options.[65]

Studies indicate that alternative work schedules have reduced payroll costs, increased corporate flexibility, and responded well to employee needs.[66] Increased productivity, decreased turnover, reduced absenteeism, decreased overtime, and increased employee satisfaction and morale have also resulted.[67] Flextime doesn't work as well when a company has multiple continuous shifts, machine-paced assembly work, few employees, or highly interdependent operations.[68] Alternative work schedules also have less success when managers perceive that all workers must do all work at the same time.

Business Process Redesign and Quality

Business process redesign takes a comprehensive approach to redesigning work. It combines the tenets of reengineering and total quality management that dominated large-scale change in the 1990s. Because many processes change in business process redesign, managers and employees need to regularly question the old ways of managing and working. Managers must overcome their fears of letting go, losing control, misplacing trust, losing popularity, and failing.

Focus on Core Processes.   Business process redesign identifies the core processes and reorganizes them to eliminate unnecessary processes and steps. It relies on information technology to help reduce the time and number of employees required for particular work processes. It also gives control over tasks to workers on the "front line," particularly those who interact with customers. AFC Enterprises, owners of Church's Chick and Popeye's Chick & Biscuits, uses the Internet-based program AFC-Online to handle communication with its 2,700 restaurants.[69] The city of Chicago also introduced a new enterprise resource planning system to streamline its core purchasing processes.[70] Such redesign efforts attempt to dramatically improve corporate performance, as reflected in cost, quality, service, and speed, in the following ways:

- **Managers combine several jobs** into a single job, similar to job enlargement and job enrichment.
- **Workers make decisions;** they are empowered to solve problems and take action.
- **The steps in each business process are performed in a logical order.** Some steps can be performed simultaneously, in part because information systems often hold much of the information relevant to the tasks. For the same reasons, subsequent steps can begin while the present steps are underway.
- **Processes have multiple versions** so they can fit the situation.
- **Employees perform work where it makes the most sense.** For example, employees in charge of orders might call up and complete all forms required to do their job, rather than passing some to other workers.
- **Checks and controls are reduced.** Checking the accuracy of processes often occurs at the end of a sequence of steps, rather than at each step. Individuals are judged on results rather than on how well they followed the process.
- **Contact with external groups is limited to that essential to the process.** For example, the distribution department might have minimal contact with groups outside that department.
- **A single manager provides a single point of contact.** Information systems give that person all necessary information.
- **Companies have both centralized and decentralized structures,** placing decision making at the most appropriate level and position in the organization. The company uses technology to facilitate the sharing of information.[71]

The Role of Information Technology.   Information technology is essential to business process redesign. Technology removes limits to the way employees perform their work, allowing companies to redefine the way work is done and ultimately achieve a competitive advantage.[72] For example, shared databases allow multiple workers simultaneous access to the same information. Expert systems give generalists access to specialized expertise. Telecommunications technology supports both the centralization and decentralization of decision making. Decision support tools allow managers and employees to make better-informed, more analytical decisions. Effective business process redesign projects include information technologists from the outset, build an electronic model of the business, design prototypes of streamlined processes for the redesign team to review, and use high-level programming tools to speed the creation of applications.[73]

Because of the extensive use of information technology, organizations can often reduce the number of managers, thereby flattening the structure and giving workers more control over their jobs. Such restructuring, however, may require workers to develop a broader range of skills or seek out additional training to perform the new work processes. Ensuring top management's support for reengineering projects is critical, and lack of support often explains why such projects fail.[74] Managers can't just add information technology and expect significant improvements in work processes. They need to carefully think about ways to use information technology to improve the delivery of services and the manufacturing of products.

Customer Satisfaction.   Business process redesign focuses on meeting customer needs, "delighting the customer," and thereby increasing customer satisfaction. Efforts to improve quality begin by working with customers to identify their needs, preferences, and expectations. Teams of employees collect this information, asking questions such as those shown in Figure 14-6, and then translate the information into better products and services. Wachovia Bank, for example, introduced the concept of relationship banking to both its retail and commercial customers. Wachovia promised to consider the customers' best interests and offer the "right products at the right place at the right time" to meet their needs.[75] Universal Underwriters, a member of Zurich Financial Services Group, chose a computerized policy management system capable of helping Universal manage its customer relationships. The software also provides support for direct sales at the agent's office or the customer's site. Account executives can use their laptops to remotely access policyholder information.[76]

Concern for the customer extends to new policies toward suppliers. These include making purchasing decisions in terms of cost and quality, reducing the number of suppliers, establishing long-term contracts with suppliers, and developing cooperative relationships.[77] Each of these changes encourages suppliers to meet specifications faster, more reliably, and at the lowest possible cost.

Continuous Improvement.   Redesign programs foster continuous improvement in both an organization's product and the processes for creating it. Employees use a variety of tools, including control charts, bar charts and cause-and-effect diagrams, to diagnose, control, and improve processes. Continuous improvement attempts to reduce the cost of quality by instituting measures to prevent poor quality. These measures guard against internal failures, such as the need for rework or down time, and external failures, such as customer complaints or returns.[78] Companies often try to create a zero-defect product, one that has no exceptions or defects. A manufacturer attempts to eliminate the need for reworking parts by performing jobs right the first time. A railroad measures on-time delivery of cargo. Quality-focused change also puts demands on suppliers and subcontractors to provide high-quality, defect-free components.

Companies may also benchmark selected processes at the sites of competitors or other industry leaders to identify truly excellent methods. *Benchmarking* involves gathering data about how well a company does in comparison to a "best-in-class"

1. What images come to your mind about using this product?
2. How do you use this product?
3. Have you seen other people using this product? In what way?
4. What are the product's most important features?
5. What additional features do you wish the product had?
6. Which features could be eliminated?
7. Have you ever used this product for a purpose other than the one for which it was intended?
8. Do you consider this product too expensive or well priced?
9. What would you be willing to pay for these features (give a list)?

company in specific areas. The results help create strategies for improvement. Usually, small teams conduct research and field trips to learn about excellent processes in another organization. The Kennedy Space Center created a benchmarking team, the Kennedy Benchmarking Clearinghouse, which included representatives from its major contractors. This consortium created a common process to use in benchmarking best practices in other organizations; members must first check other members of the consortium for best practices, and then, if necessary, the group seeks external partners.[79]

Worker Empowerment. A focus on quality encourages managers to empower workers to make decisions and take responsibility for their outcomes. Some believe that Disney's current problems stem in large part from its hierarchical, centralized, slow approach to decision making.[80] Some public accounting firms have empowered their staff by creating employee advisory boards to tell the firm's executives how to make their workplaces into ones where employees want to stay rather than leave.[81] Inland Steel in Chicago has given its employees representation on the board of directors as a way of improving decision making.[82]

Business process redesign programs create self-managed work teams, cross-functional teams, and task teams as a way of empowering workers.[83] Human resource systems, including selection, training, performance evaluation, and compensation, support worker empowerment. In their empowered role, employees are expected to call attention to specific quality problems in their normal work, look for ways to perform their jobs better, and identify ways to create continuous improvement in organizational processes.[84]

You can assess a work group's readiness for empowerment by asking questions about the individual or group under consideration, such as the following:[85]

- Does the person or group have job or project knowledge?
- Does the person or group have a high desire to achieve?
- Does the person or group communicate effectively at work?
- Is the person or group always trustworthy?
- Does the person or group know the organization as a whole system?
- Does the person or group envision a future and take responsibility for it?

Leadership.   Quality depends on top management having a vision of excellence that it translates into organizational practices. As a leader of a quality-focused effort, you should

- communicate the importance of each employee's contribution to quality;
- stress the quality-related synergies available through cooperation and teamwork;
- empower employees to make a difference; and
- reinforce individual and team commitment to quality with a wide range of rewards and reinforcements.[86]

A successful focus on quality depends on managers "walking the talk." Starting at the highest levels in the organization, executives must support a strong customer focus, continuous improvement, and worker empowerment.

Implementing quality-focused programs requires organization-wide changes. Beginning with their own commitment, top managers must then involve all employees in the change process. Extensive training characterizes quality-oriented companies. Employees learn about techniques for continuous improvement, effective team performance, and customer satisfaction. The reward system must also fit with the new quality goals. Measuring and rewarding quality is a core activity. Reward systems in quality-oriented companies often include both individual and team-based incentives. All human resources systems focus on implementing and then sustaining the changes included in the quality program.

The U.S. government has introduced an award, the Malcolm Baldrige National Quality Award, to recognize and reward manufacturing and service companies that meet certain standards of excellence. An organization is judged on a variety of categories, shown in Table 14-2, which also gives some sample questions in each area from the Self-Assessment Questionnaire. Past winners include Xerox, Ritz-Carlton Hotel Company, General Motors Cadillac Division, Corning Telecommunications Product Division, Dana Commercial Credit, and Granite Rock Company.

Creating Learning Organizations

Managers have created *learning organizations,* ones that have the ability to fundamentally and regularly revitalize themselves,[87] as a way of instituting business process redesign and quality management. Learning organizations, such as Motorola, Xerox, and MCI, can anticipate and more readily transform themselves to respond to change.[88] We can describe a learning organization as follows:[89]

- Continuous learning by individuals, teams, and the organization provides a competitive advantage. Managers complete skill inventories and audits of the learning capacity of individuals and groups. They create systems for sharing learning and using it in business each day.
- Employees have a shared vision, which reflects the organization's underlying assumptions and values. Managers and other organizational leaders help create and nurture the vision, as well as inspire commitment from workers who contribute their ideas and are empowered to implement them.
- The entire organizational system is involved, including its strategy, structure and information flow, work processes, performance goals, training, individual and team development, and rewards and recognition.

TABLE 14-2

These Questions Help Assess How Well an Organization Meets the Baldrige Criteria.

Category	Assessment Criteria
Leadership	• How do the senior leaders' personal leadership and involvement create and sustain values, company directions, performance expectations, customer focus, and a leadership system that promotes performance excellence? • How well are the values and expectations integrated into the company's leadership system, including how well does the company learn and improve continuously and address its societal responsibilities and community involvement?
Strategic planning	• How does the company set strategic direction and determine key action plans? • How are the plans translated into an effective performance management system?
Customer and market focus	• How does the company determine the requirements and expectations of customers and markets? • How effectively does the company enhance its relationships with customers and determine their satisfaction?
Information and analysis	• How well does the company manage and effectively use data and information to support key company processes and the company's performance management system?
Human resource development and management	• How is the workforce enabled to develop and utilize its full potential, aligned with the company's objectives? • How successful are the company's efforts to build and maintain an environment conducive to performance excellence, full participation, and personal and organizational growth?
Process management	• Are the key processes—such as customer-focused design, product and service delivery processes, support processes, and supplier and partnering processes involving all work units—designed, effectively managed, and improved to achieve better performance?
Business results	• How well has the company performed and improved in key business areas—customer satisfaction, financial and marketplace performance, human resource, supplier and partner performance, and operational performance? • How well does the company perform compared to its competitors?

Source: Adapted from the Baldrige Application package.

■ Executives value learning as a continuous process. They believe that intentional activities can increase the quantity and quality of learning, and that shared learning is easiest to maintain. Managers model calculated risk taking and experimentation. They create a culture that rewards employee initiative and encourages feedback by employees to higher-level managers.

■ Managers support decentralized decision making and employee empowerment. They encourage the use of cross-functional work teams.

Is your organization a learning organization? Learning can occur at individual, group, or organizational levels. Rockwell Collins developed a learning strategy that focuses on expanding its training offerings by 40 percent over three years. A learning and development team created a plan that calls for delivering 70 percent of Rockwell's curricula using computer-based methods within a year. Rockwell also plans to create learning councils in all business units to oversee needs assessment and evaluate the use of training as a way of solving particular performance problems.[90]

Creating a learning community, where individuals practice and perform together in the workplace similar to the way musical ensembles or sports teams practice and perform, addresses group-level learning.[91] Communities of practice are informal organizational forms that complement existing structures and facilitate the sharing of knowledge. People join together because of shared knowledge or a common passion for a joint enterprise.[92] Xerox created a strategic learning community through a project called Transition Alliance. This community provided a vehicle for information technology professionals to manage their infrastructure more effectively and provide better solutions to organizational problems. It also offered a means for sharing knowledge throughout the business units. Members investigated solutions to problems, learned from each other, and applied what they learned to the business units. Finally, the Transition Alliance motivated individuals to learn and develop, and ultimately to improve Xerox's performance. Xerox encouraged rather than required membership in the alliance and involved about 50 active members out of 250 information technology professionals in infrastructure management. The alliance included facilitators, who encouraged discussion, and knowledge leaders, who shared their knowledge on specific issues, with the roles changing with regard to particular issues. The Transition Alliance encouraged both the acquisition of information by its members for use in performing their jobs and the dissemination of information throughout the company.[93]

Organizational learning involves the individual-level processes of *intuiting*, which involves recognizing the pattern or possibilities in a series of personal experiences, and *interpreting*, or explaining the insight to oneself or others. It also involves the group-level process of *integrating*, or developing a shared understanding about organizational members and then taking coordinated action. Finally, it involves the organization-level process of *institutionalizing*, or ensuring that routinized actions occur.[94]

Organizational learning must move beyond single-loop to double-loop learning.[95] A *single-loop*, or *adaptive*, organization uses routine learning to accomplish its objectives, without significant changes in its basic assumptions. In contrast, a *double-loop*, or *generative*, organization uses experience to reevaluate its objectives and basic values and to modify its culture. Innovation requires this type of learning.[96]

A learning organization, which can be characterized as a double-loop organization, goes through a continuous cycle of experience, examination of experience, formulation of hypotheses about the experience, experimentation to test the hypotheses, and experience once again (Figure 14-7).[97] Productive organizational learning requires continuous learning, valid information, a willingness to hold one's actions open to inspection in order to receive quality feedback, the judging of opinions based on their merits rather than on the person who holds them, and accountability for one's actions.[98]

Employees who work in a learning organization regularly collect data to help them examine their experiences. They analyze the data to develop hypotheses about their experiences and ways of improving them. They conduct open dialogue, which includes both constructive dissent and acknowledgment of failures, as part of experimenting with the new learning and applying it to organizational situations.[99] Members of learning organizations learn from past experiences and the best practices of others. They transfer the knowledge they acquire rapidly and efficiently

FIGURE 14-7

Learning organizations use double-loop learning.

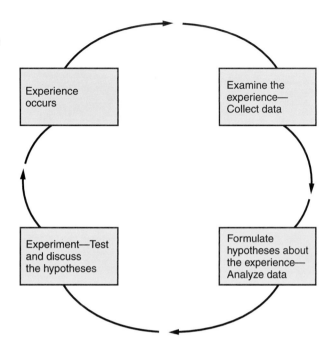

through the organization.[100] Learning organizations also create specific mechanisms for renewal, such as periodic reviews, strategic planning efforts, or system-wide training programs.[101]

Change and Innovation

Approaches to large-scale change represent innovations that organizations have undertaken to become more competitive. In addition to the way work is performed, other innovations in the United States have focused on updating technology and developing and offering new products and services.

How does innovation occur? It begins with the recognition that a demand exists for the new product, service, or process. Next, the basic idea is formulated, integrating the technical and market issues into a design concept. The problem-solving stage follows. Here the design is elaborated; resource and technical problems are addressed. False starts may consume time at this stage.[102] A solution, such as a technological invention or the introduction of a new information system, moves the design into the prototype of a new product or process. In the development stage, the innovator attempts to solve problems associated with the production process; this sometimes results in changing the job design. Finally, the solution is used and diffused in the workplace.

In Japan, the innovation process occurs at three levels simultaneously.[103] At the first level, managers and employees look for incremental improvements for existing products, services, or processes. At the second level, they try to make a significant jump between existing and new products, services, or processes by modifying existing ones and then extending these changes further to new ones. At the third level, they attempt true innovation by focusing on primary research. The Japanese hope that success at one of these three levels will result in a new or improved product to replace the existing one. Companies that successfully innovate, such as Sony, also create a culture of innovation and a vision for the company 20 or 30 years from now.[104]

Employees and managers can perform a number of functions critical to the innovation process.[105] Some can generate ideas and test their feasibility; others can champion them by selling them to others in the organization or obtaining resources to support them. Managers or nonmanagerial employees can lead projects, serve as gatekeepers by collecting information and passing it to others, and sponsor the innovations by helping develop people's talents. Finally, managers can buffer the project team from unnecessary organizational constraints. The general management of the organization or division plays a significant role in developing new technology. So do research and development specialists, sometimes under the leadership of the chief technical officer or chief information officer. Organizations must also have people who champion new technology because organizational members and leaders may differ significantly in their commitment to new products and processes. Two roles are particularly critical: the innovation champion and the innovation manager.

An *innovation champion* takes personal responsibility for introducing the innovation and marshalling the resources required to produce it. She plays an essential role in diffusing innovation throughout an organization. A champion builds cross-functional ties, establishes autonomy, deals with the organizational hierarchy, uses informal means of persuasion, and involves all organization members in decision making.[106]

The *innovation manager* creates conditions in which creativity can occur, as well as overseeing the more practical aspects of product or system development. The innovation manager supports the team in identifying the likely users and uses of the product or service. He uses informal rather than formal control and communication systems. The innovation manager collects and evaluates ongoing information about project planning and implementation.[107] An innovation manager

- develops responsibility and commitment;
- develops clarity between all team members about the task at hand;
- enriches the team's jobs by telling team members what to do or what to achieve, but not how to do their work;
- ensures that employees use creative ways of working;
- provides the team with optimal conditions needed to ensure success in working on the task they have accepted; and
- gives support and encouragement when problems arise.[108]

An organization's ability to innovate depends on its resources, its managers' understanding of the technological environment, and innovative strategies used by competitors.[109] Managers and employees must adopt a mind-set that encourages the development and presentation of new ideas. They also must willingly expend resources for innovative activities. They must set unreasonable expectations and stretch their definition of their business. At GE Capital, for example, managers are expected to grow earnings at least 20 percent per year. This unreasonable objective causes managers to think differently about opportunities and how to run their business. Virgin Airways quickly extended their basic air travel business to music retailing, broadcasting, and banking as a way of innovating.[110] Flexible organizational designs (see Chapter 12), as well as collaboration within and between organizations, also facilitate innovation.[111] Innovation adopters who have a broad and influential social network can influence the diffusion of innovation in organizations.[112]

Differentiating Among Intervention Strategies

Intervention strategies differ along a number of dimensions: (1) the target system, (2) the target group, (3) the depth of intervention desired, (4) the nature of the change mechanisms, and (5) the expertise of the change agent. In this section, we offer an overview of these dimensions.

The Target System.   Intervention strategies can focus on an organization's technical, social, administrative, or strategic systems.[113] Low productivity may signal problems with the technical system, which can be solved by providing capital improvements and offering workers additional training.

Inadequate quality of working life may suggest problems with the organization's social system. To address these problems, interventions should alter the reward system, integrate organizational values into change efforts, confront organizational power and politics, and improve communication.

An organization that responds slowly in receiving and distributing information may have an ineffective administrative or communication system. Ensuring that a logical organizational structure exists and communicating the structure to organizational members can improve the effectiveness of the administrative system. So can clarifying policies, procedures, and standards, and maintaining a strong system for collecting and disseminating information.

Management strength and competence reflect the health of the strategic system, which includes top management, long-term planning, and management information systems. Choosing appropriate management styles, systematically evaluating the environment, adapting to changing conditions, building executive succession systems, and encouraging innovation are interventions that strengthen the strategic system.

The Target Group.   The appropriate target for change depends on the diagnosed problem. Interventions can focus on a person, role, pair or trio of employees or managers, team or group, interactions between groups, or the entire organization.[114] Identifying the forces for and against change helps pinpoint the appropriate target. If, for example, one supervisor refuses to adopt a new policy, the intervention should focus on that person. On the other hand, if the organization lacks effective policies for dealing with unions, the intervention should focus on the organization.

Too often, change agents misfocus interventions by addressing the wrong target. Consider the situation in which some employees report late to work. Some organizations try to resolve this problem by instituting earlier official starting times. What is the target of this change? In this situation, the change should focus on the tardy employees, rather than on all employees. The organization instead tries to change the behavior of both the good and the poor-performing employees, which likely results in widespread dissatisfaction and no improvement in the tardiness problem.

Depth of Intervention.   Strategies can range from *deep* (touching more private and central aspects of a person and his relationship with others) to *surface* (dealing with issues external to the person, such as his behavior in public).[115] The deepest-level interventions, which should only be used when surface strategies can't produce enduring change, try to increase a person's knowledge of her own attitudes, values, and conflicts. Somewhat less deep processes attempt to alter individual work style by focusing on feelings, attitudes, and perceptions. Surface-level strategies include modifying reward systems, which affect individual performance and motivation. Best Western uses a surface strategy to increase the quality of its member hotels. Regional service managers visit properties at least yearly and assign as many as 1,000 points to each location. Properties that receive lower scores receive more visits each year.[116]

We can also analyze the depth of intervention by determining the level of the change attempt.[117] First-order changes reinforce present understandings of situations. They include adjustments in structure, reward systems, or other organizational behaviors. Second-order changes modify the present understanding in a particular direction. They involve a change in the schemata (see Chapter 2) used to view the situation and may be a response to major environmental shifts or a crisis experience.[118] For example, a decline in productivity, originally viewed as a technical problem, may instead be handled as a quality-of-working-life issue.

Third-order changes give organizational members the capacity to change their understanding of the situation. The introduction of a business process redesign program could be a third-order change, since it requires employees and managers to think about the organization in a totally new way, with a strong focus on quality, team accountability, and customer satisfaction. Training organizational members to view a situation through new lenses offers more long-term possibilities for change.

Nature of the Change Mechanisms.   The nature of the change mechanisms chosen depends on the problem diagnosis and the forces for and against change that must be altered. The following are a sample of more limited change mechanisms:

- **survey feedback,** use of surveys to gather and provide feedback to organizational members about their or others' attitudes and behaviors;
- **team building,** a variety of activities that help team members work together more collaboratively and productively;
- **sensitivity training,** a structured experience in which individuals learn to handle conflict by confronting and resolving differences and become aware of new norms that emphasize teamwork;
- **process consultation,** the use of an observer to provide feedback to a group about its decision-making, leadership, and communication processes;
- **confrontation meeting,** a structured interaction between two groups that experience conflict in which they air and attempt to resolve their differences;
- **training and development,** the training and education of managers and employees to increase their knowledge and improve their skills;
- **automation of work processes,** the introduction of computerized information systems to improve the efficiency and effectiveness of task performance;
- **human resources policies and programs,** the introduction of new staffing and evaluation systems;
- **reward system,** the alteration of the rewards to encourage new behavior created by a change;
- **job redesign,** the diagnosis and realignment of tasks and job-related activities to improve worker performance and satisfaction; and
- **structural change,** organizational redesign to improve interaction, coordination, and communication.

While some change mechanisms respond best to specific types of problems, people can use more than one intervention to strengthen a change. Diagnosing the strategy that likely will have the greatest impact requires extensive training and experience beyond the scope of this book.

Expertise of the Change Agent.   Of course, the precise change mechanism used depends to some extent on the expertise of the change agent. Managers, employees, and consultants often have training or experience in performing certain types of interventions. Thus, selection of the strategy should complement selection of the change agent.

Finalizing the Action Plan

The action plan specifies each action in the order it will be performed. It should address the following elements:

- actions to enhance forces for change;
- actions to reduce forces against change;
- the feasibility of each action specified;
- a prioritization of actions; and
- a timetable and budget.

A widespread review of the action plan with all people and groups involved in the change increases its likelihood of success. Some companies convene special review groups to monitor plans for organizational changes and ensure their feasibility and completeness. Others rely on senior management to perform the oversight function. Careful scrutiny at this stage often prevents subsequent implementation problems.

▌ ISSUES OF IMPLEMENTATION

The change agent, together with appropriate managers and employees, implements the best change strategy. Those involved need to consider time, cost, responsibility, and ethical issues when implementing change.

Time

Managers and other change agents must realistically assess the time available for change efforts. Employees often complain that they don't have the time to do their regular work, so adding more change-oriented projects becomes problematic. Managers must set clear priorities for change efforts. They must tie rewards to the types of change behavior they want, as well as to normal job performance. Managers leading the changes involved in the creation of BJC Health Systems in St. Louis learned the importance of moving quickly to implement desired changes. The first in a series of changes, the merger of Barnes and Jewish Hospitals, occurred so quickly that managers had to rapidly put in place the desired structures and reporting relationships.[119]

Managers must also evaluate the time required to make the changes. Most managers underestimate the time needed for even the smallest changes. Overcoming resistance to change cannot occur instantly. It typically requires an extensive period of education, communication, or other intervention. Careful project planning can increase the likelihood that managers will allow the appropriate amount of time for either incremental or radical change to have an effect on the workplace.

Cost

Although managers and other change agents generally estimate the costs of a change project during the planning stage, unexpected overruns can occur. Costs may be both direct and indirect—for example, fees paid to consultants and employee time spent on change activities. Careful tracking of expenditures and their impact improves the acceptance of the change effort by top management.

Responsibility

The use of a broad-based steering committee to oversee the change may increase its likelihood of success.[120] Such a group, composed of representatives of top management, first-line supervisors, and rank-and-file employees, can advise on issues related to program budget as well as on organizational policies and priorities. AlliedSignal uses a corporate-wide steering group to oversee its cycle time reduction. It also has senior level managers, who act as process champions, and strategic business unit managers, who act as process leaders. These managers work to improve the core business processes for the company by allocating resources and solving day-to-day problems, respectively.[121]

Increasingly, as noted earlier, employees take responsibility for initiating and implementing changes. Self-managed work teams typically assume significant responsibility for identifying and implementing continuous improvement activities. Top management must willingly relinquish power and control to lower-level managers and employees for successful implementation to occur.

Ethical Issues

The people involved in major change efforts may experience ethical dilemmas in their interactions with managers, employees, and consultants inside and outside the organization. These include misrepresentation and collusion, misuse of data, manipulation and coercion, value and goal conflict, and technical ineptness.[122]

Some managers may implement their personal change agenda at the expense of a solid diagnosis of the organization's needs. Still others may promise more than they can deliver. Some consultants fail to build ways of institutionalizing the change into their process, causing the organization to continue to rely on (and pay) them. Table 14-3 presents the danger signs of unethical behavior.

Those responsible for implementing change should ensure that the change strategies respond to well-documented organizational and individual needs. They must also ensure that the change process respects the rights of individuals in the workplace. Understanding the boundaries of private and public behavior also supports successful change efforts.

▍EVALUATING AND INSTITUTIONALIZING CHANGE

Managers or other change agents need to determine whether the changes they have implemented have accomplished their stated objectives. Comprehensive evaluation also provides information for improving future change efforts. Institutionalizing the changes as a regular part of an organization's function should follow.

▌ TABLE 14-3 ▌

Unethical Behavior Can Adversely Affect Change Efforts.

1. Emphasis on short-term revenues over long-term considerations
2. Routinely ignoring or violating internal or professional codes of ethics
3. Looking for simple solutions to ethical problems; being satisfied with quick fixes
4. Unwillingness to take an ethical stand if there is a financial cost
5. Creation of an internal environment that discourages ethical behavior or encourages unethical behavior
6. Dispatch of ethical problems to the legal department
7. View of ethics solely as a public relations tool
8. Treatment of employees that differs from treatment of customers
9. Unfair or arbitrary performance appraisal standards
10. Lack of procedures or policies for handling ethical problems
11. Lack of mechanisms for internal whistle-blowing
12. Lack of clear lines of communication
13. Sensitivity only to shareholder needs and demands
14. Encouragement of employees to ignore their personal ethical values

Source: Based on R. A. Cooke, Danger signs of unethical behavior: How to determine if your firm is at ethical risk, *Journal of Business Ethics* 10 (1991): 249–253.

Evaluating Change

Both formal and informal evaluation are critical to the success of any organizational change and should occur regularly. Managers, employees, or consultants can collect data about the nature and effectiveness of the change as it occurs. Often the evaluation compares the actual outcomes to the anticipated or expected outcomes, as reflected in goals or effectiveness criteria. The results of the evaluation indicate whether the desired change has occurred and whether the desired outcomes resulted. Unsuccessful changes may call for a return to an earlier stage—for example, reassessing the forces for and against change.

The Four Levels of Change. The effectiveness of a change can be evaluated at four levels, as illustrated in Figure 14-8:

- ▪ **Affective change** refers to participants' attitudes toward the intervention. Questionnaires or interviews can help assess whether organizational members found the intervention useful or effective.
- ▪ **Learning** refers to the participants' knowledge of new ways of acting and their acquisition of new skills as a result of the intervention. Did participants learn how to manage improvement teams? Did they acquire additional information about other cultures or international business as a result of training programs? Analyzing the differences between scores on pre- and post-tests, follow-up interviews, or open-ended survey responses can help determine the extent of learning.

Evaluation of change occurs at four levels.

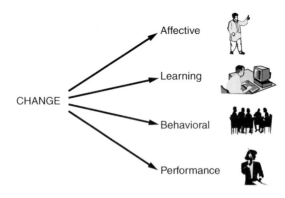

■ **Behavioral changes** include the participants' actions on the job. Do they interact differently with peers and subordinates? Do they use new or different techniques to accomplish their job activities?

■ **Performance changes** are reflected in objective organizational measures, such as productivity and quality rates, sales volume, profit, absenteeism, and turnover, as well as more subjective performance-appraisal ratings. We can assess, for example, whether the introduction of a new reward system increases worker output or whether a new quality-control system improves product quality.

Phoenix Water Services Department reengineered its organization by combining operations and maintenance functions. The organization also established a team-based culture that empowered workers to make decisions and changes. The impact of the program was assessed based on its annual savings, which reached $63.1 million over a six-year period.[123]

Institutionalizing Change

In order for real improvement to result, action must extend beyond short-run changes. Getting the change to "stick" often poses a significant challenge. How, for example, do the changes at Herman Miller become a permanent part of the organization's culture and way of doing business? Certainly, this will be influenced by the way the activities are performed as the organization moves from *prescription* to *action* in the diagnostic approach. Accurately targeting the forces influencing change, followed by carefully selecting change agents and intervention strategies, and concluding with effective action, contribute to long-range improvement. Unsuccessful outcomes may terminate the change process or signal a need for additional or different changes.

Executives must develop and introduce mechanisms for continually monitoring the change. For example, permanent committees or task forces can observe the ongoing implementation and regularly assess the impact of the change. Most of all, commitment to the change by all organizational members will expedite its institutionalization. Managers must build learning organizations, as described earlier, which emphasize ongoing adaptability and personal growth.[124]

MANAGING CHANGE IN THE DOT-COM, GLOBAL WORKPLACE

Making organizational changes in the dot-com environment poses special challenges for managers. The high number of failures of dot-com start-ups offers testimony to the special issues such companies face. Having a quality product with a potential market is only the first step in success. Organizational leaders must be adept at managing the changes that are required as financing options evaporate, competitors appear in the marketplace, timetables suffer, and the organization needs to adapt. Managers and other change agents must pay particular attention to the forces for and against change and continuously evaluate ways to increase drivers and overcome resistance to change. Regularly introducing interventions may be more common in this type of environment as organizations struggle to meet changing environmental demands, the requirements of their funding sources, and a fickle marketplace.

Managers and other change agents must be sensitive to the influence of cultural context on change efforts. For example, change strategy preferences may vary in different countries. In Italy, where managers' and consultants' values do not support dealing with emotionally charged issues in a group context, team building and third-party interventions are common; sensitivity training, confrontation meetings, and process consultation are not common.[125]

The approaches to redesign described here extend to organizations outside the United States. For example, the Dutch use a version of sociotechnical redesign called Integral Organizational Renewal (IOR). They use this approach to transform complex organizations with simple jobs into simple organizations with complex jobs.[126]

Companies in countries other than the United States and Japan have successfully instituted quality improvement and business process redesign programs. 3M successfully introduced continuous improvement to its Aycliffe plant in Ireland, using a program that treats production and maintenance as partners and looks for ways to improve both in their manufacturing plants.[127] The International Relief Organization trained staff members in a health-promoting polyclinic in Tirana, Albania, in the methods of total quality management.[128] Recent research suggests that the attitudes and behaviors related to a continuous improvement change effort may cross national borders, highlighting the commonalities in the change process.[129] Effective diagnosis of the cultural context should increase the effectiveness of an action.

CONCLUSION

In this book, we have looked at the issues related to managing in a wide range of organizations, including those that deal nationally and internationally. We have examined the unique challenges of leading and managing a multicultural workforce. We have considered the special concerns of managing in the dot-com, global workplace.

Managers and other organizational members have significant responsibility for ensuring organizational performance. The leadership style they choose, their ability to communicate with peers, subordinates, and superiors, the quality of their decision making, and their skill in group work contribute to organizational functioning. So does the design of work and the structure of the organization. Understanding and choosing the appropriate individual and group behaviors are essential for employee productivity, satisfaction, adaptability, and other outcomes. Using the diagnostic approach should help managers and other organizational members improve both personal and organizational behavior.

As good diagnosticians, managers must quickly recognize threats to organizational competitiveness. If profits and performance drop dramatically, a major change in the organization's culture, structure, and management style may be required. Remaking the organization—for example, through downsizing, work redesign, or organizational redesign—is another option. Managers must develop new and creative strategies for responding to increasing environmental pressures. The emphasis on teamwork, the movement to a more collaborative culture, and the call for visionary leadership are some of the factors that will ultimately stimulate the development of new organizational forms. The creation of new strategic partnerships, mega-organizations in the service sector due to mergers and acquisitions, and departments within existing organizations that focus on new product and service development, should contribute to increased organizational competitiveness and performance.

▎Summary

1. Organizational change, or action, is the final step of the diagnostic approach, following description, diagnosis, and prescription.
2. Action begins by identifying the forces for and against change.
3. Selection of the people responsible for implementing the change occurs; internal and external change agents differ in their relationship to and knowledge of the organization.
4. Managers, employees, or consultants should choose the appropriate intervention strategy; large-scale strategies include work redesign, virtual employment and alternative work schedules, business process redesign and quality, and learning organizations.
5. Implementation must consider the target system, target group, depth of intervention, prescribed change mechanisms, and expertise of the change agent in selecting the appropriate strategy.
6. Implementation must address issues of time, cost, responsibility, and ethics.
7. Evaluation and institutionalization of changes conclude the process of change.
8. Managing change in a dot-com, global workplace involves a variety of challenges.

A Manager's Diagnostic Review

▢ Increase the forces for change and reduce the forces against change.
  • What forces for and against change exist?
  • How can these forces be increased or decreased?
▢ Select the most appropriate change agent.
  • What types of change agents are possible?
  • Which type of change agent fits best with the situation?

- Implement large-scale change programs.
  - What jobs can be redesigned?
  - In which situations can virtual employment be used?
  - Can the organization implement business process redesign?
  - Is the company a learning organization?
- Implement the most effective intervention strategies.
  - What target system and target group should the strategy address?
  - What depth of intervention is appropriate?
  - What change mechanisms fit best with the objectives of the change and the situation?
- Evaluate organizational changes.
  - Do mechanisms exist for evaluating the change?
  - At what level is change evaluated?
- Institutionalize organizational changes.
  - Do mechanisms exist for institutionalizing the change?
- Manage change in the dot-com, global workplace.
  - What factors affect the change?
  - How should the change be implemented to handle these factors?

Visit the Gordon homepage on the Prentice Hall Web site at

http://www.prenhall.com/gordon

for recommended readings, additional activities, Internet exercises, updated information, and links to related Web sites.

▌Thinking Critically About Organizational Behavior

1. Can forces against change ever be completely reduced?
2. Under what circumstances should companies create departments of internal consultants?
3. Can external consultants be truly objective, or do they merely try to "sell" their favorite solutions?
4. What are the difficulties associated with initiating change from the top? From the bottom?
5. Is job enrichment still a feasible redesign approach?
6. Why don't all companies institute alternative work schedules and virtual employment options?
7. How do you ensure that a company improves its quality?
8. What role do individuals play in learning organizations?

9. What is the most important factor to consider in choosing the appropriate intervention strategy?
10. Under what circumstances should an action plan be revised?
11. Why do organizations skimp on evaluating the impact of change?
12. What new issues does managing change in a dot-com, global workplace present?

ACTIVITY 14-1: BRIDGETON TEMPORARY SERVICES

STEP 1: Your instructor will divide you into groups of four to six people; one group will represent management, and the rest, competing consulting groups.

STEP 2: Read the following description.

Bridgeton Temporary Services provides bookkeeping and accounting services on a contract basis. Employees act as accounts payable clerks, accounts receivable clerks, general bookkeepers, computer programmers, and accountants. The 75 employees are each assigned to a supervisor who decides where each person will work. The supervisor also checks with the client for an evaluation of Bridgeton's employees. Employees report each day to the client, but must notify their supervisor at Bridgeton that they have arrived.

Employees have a variety of education, from high school diplomas to master's degrees. The firm also employs a number of working mothers, certified public accountants who do not want full-time employment. Employees generally stay with Bridgeton 10 to 12 months. Then they secure full-time employment elsewhere, decide they do not wish to be employed at all, or obtain part-time employment with one of Bridgeton's clients. In addition to relatively high turnover, Bridgeton also suffers from high absenteeism. When questioned, the employees say that no one cares about them, their pay is low, their work frequently is uninteresting and below their capabilities, they are moved among jobs too frequently, and they frequently are not notified about their work assignment until 30 minutes before they are expected to be at the workplace. Many add that they feel someone is always looking over their shoulder. The company itself has more requests for temporary help than it can fill, yet it has been unable to secure enough workers. Some clients have complained about poor-quality work from some of the bookkeepers. Also, although revenues are increasing, profits have not kept pace.

STEP 3: The following is a brief description of your roles.

THE MANAGEMENT GROUP

Assume that you are the top management of Bridgeton Temporary Services. You are concerned with the high rate of turnover and absenteeism in your company. You want to hire a group of consultants to diagnose your company's problem and recommend a plan for solving it. The consultants will ask for a preliminary meeting to gather information to use in formulating their proposal. You should be prepared to describe your requirements and timetables, as well as any constraints, financial or otherwise, that you see as relevant to their task. You must then develop guidelines for judging the various proposals presented. You expect, at a minimum, that each will include a diagnosis, change strategy, and plans for implementation, as well as the rationales on which these are based.

THE CONSULTING GROUPS

Your group is interested in being hired as consultants to Bridgeton Temporary Services. The company's president is concerned about the high rate of turnover and absenteeism. The president has asked you to diagnose the company's problems and to recommend a plan for solving them. Specifically, the president wants you to answer the following questions:

1. What do you think the real problem is and why?
2. What solution(s) would you propose and why?
3. How would you implement your plan?
4. What reasons would you give for doing it this way?

You will have the opportunity to meet briefly with the top management of the firm to get answers to your preliminary questions about the company. Then, when directed by your instructor, you will offer your plan. The plan should include diagnosis, change strategy, and implementation.

STEP 4: The management and consulting groups meet independently and then together.

STEP 5: The consulting teams present their proposals one at a time.

STEP 6: The management team selects the consulting team they would like to hire and then describes the criteria for selection.

STEP 7: Discussion. With the entire class, answer the following questions:

1. What group was hired? Why?
2. What symptoms existed?
3. What problems were identified?
4. What intervention strategies were proposed? Would they be effective?
5. What makes an effective consulting proposal?

ACTIVITY 14-2: ELMWOOD CITY

STEP 1: Read the following scenario.

The newly appointed chief administrative officer (CAO) of Elmwood City spends his first week in his new job reviewing a series of management studies that were done for the previous mayor 15 years earlier. He knows that the city operates reasonably effectively, but feels that its operations are not state-of-the-art in most areas. He has been reading a great deal about some cities across the United States that have revamped their accounting systems, human resources policies and practices, and information systems. These same cities changed the way City Hall was structured, who was involved in decision making, and who controlled the budgets for the various departments.

The CAO plans to recommend that the mayor commission a new, comprehensive management study. He expects the people who conduct the study to also lead the implementation of the recommendations. The CAO has asked you to identify the possible change agents to lead this project.

STEP 2: Individually or in small groups, identify all possible change agents for this project. List the pros and cons of each choice. Prepare a brief memorandum summarizing your conclusions.

STEP 3: In small groups or with the entire class, share your memos. What options should the CAO consider? Which type of change agent makes most sense for this project? Who would you choose to conduct the project?

ACTIVITY 14-3: REDESIGNING THE ADMISSIONS PROCESS

STEP 1: Read the following description of an admissions process.

Admission to the doctoral program in the School of Management at State University is highly selective. Members of the admissions staff perform the following steps:

1. Return each telephone call received about the program by answering any questions and mailing a brochure that includes a postcard request for an application.

2. Log each telephone call into a database of potential applicants.

3. Reply to each letter requesting information about the program by mailing a brochure that includes a postcard request for an application.

4. Log each letter request into a database of potential applicants.

5. Process each postcard request for an application received by mailing the applicant a complete admissions packet.

6. Log each complete admissions packet mailed into a database of potential applicants.

7. Create a folder for each individual for whom any of the following is received: application form, letter of recommendation, GMAT or GRE scores, transcript, or other information.

8. Log each application form received into an applicant database.

9. Record on a checklist attached to the folder when each part of the application (application form, three letters of recommendation, GMAT or GRE scores for tests taken within the past five years, transcripts from all colleges or universities attended) is received.

10. Contact individuals by telephone if parts are missing (e.g., recommendations, test scores, etc.) two weeks before March 1 due date.

11. Collect all applications folders into a single pile. Verify that all materials are completed and included within the packet.

12. Circulate the folders to the faculty who serve on the admissions committee.

13. Record on a master form each faculty member's rating (accept, marginal accept, marginal reject, reject) of each candidate.

14. Summarize the ratings and distribute them to the admissions committee for final decisions.

STEP 2: In groups of three to five students, offer a plan for redesigning the admissions process. Be as specific as possible.

STEP 3: Share your plans with the entire class. What are the essential components of a redesign plan for the admissions process? Combine these components into a master plan. How effective will this plan likely be?

ACTIVITY 14-4: THE MEDICINE CABINET CASE

STEP 1: Read the Medicine Cabinet Case.

Jessica and Jeffrey Smith wanted to do some redecorating in their house. The bathroom medicine cabinets were one of the items they decided to replace. The cabinets were about 20 years old, dirty and rusty, and didn't provide enough storage space. After shopping in a number of discount and specialty stores, the Smiths found exactly the cabinets they wanted at a reasonable price in The House Store. They arranged to purchase the mirrors and have an electrician install them.

Three weeks after the mirrors had been installed, Jessica noticed a large crack near the lights in one of them. Because she believed that no one in her family had done anything unusual to cause the crack, she called The House Store to ask how to replace the broken part of the mirror. After 10 rings, the automatic voice mail answered. After listening to the recording, which seemed to last forever, Jessica pressed "5," because she did not know the extension of her party, and was connected to the store operator, who then transferred her call to the customer service department. The person at customer service did not know how to

handle her problem and transferred her call to the kitchen department. After 10 rings, a salesman in the kitchen department answered and told Jessica that she needed to speak with someone in household appliances and that he would transfer her call.

Jessica waited patiently and after a minute realized that she had been disconnected. She called The House Store again, listened to the same voice-mail recording, and asked the operator to transfer her to the home appliance department. A salesman answered the telephone after only three rings, and told Jessica that his department did not handle bathroom cabinets and that Jessica should speak to someone in customer service. Although the salesman also tried to transfer her call, Jessica was again disconnected.

She called The House Store again, listened to the voice mail, was connected to customer service, and told them that she was getting very annoyed. The customer service representative asked his supervisor how to handle this problem. He then connected her to someone in plumbing, who told Jessica to bring in the defective part and they would replace it.

Jeffrey Smith delivered the defective part to the store the next day. He went directly to the customer service desk. A service representative called someone in plumbing, who met Jeffrey and immediately exchanged the part.

STEP 2: In groups of four to six students, identify the quality problems described in the situation. Next, hypothesize the causes of these prob-

lems. Finally, offer a plan for improving quality in the store.

STEP 3: Discussion. Share your plans with the entire class. Then answer the following questions:

1. What types of quality problems exist?
2. What typically causes these problems?
3. How can the problems be corrected?

ACTIVITY 14-5: THE BEAUTIFUL BEAD COMPANY

STEP 1: Your instructor will form you into work teams of The Beautiful Bead Company. Your job is to assemble necklaces precisely to specifications given to you by your instructor. You will be competing with the other teams to obtain bonuses for performance.

STEP 2: Your job is to assemble beaded bracelets to specifications. You will have 10 minutes to make as many bracelets to the specifications as possible. You can organize the work in any way you like. Your team will be judged on the number of complete, saleable bracelets it produces. Spend the next 5 minutes planning for the first production run. Each person must play a role in the production process.

STEP 3: Your instructor will signal when to start production. You will then have 5 to 10 minutes (as determined by your instructor) to make as many bracelets as possible.

STEP 4: Your instructor will appoint a group of two to four "customers" who will evaluate the quality of the bracelets. They will determine the bonus dollars each team will receive based on the number of bracelets produced (10 bonus dollars for each bracelet).

STEP 5: You have 10 minutes to refine your production process. You should review the effectiveness of your team's performance and then reassign roles as appropriate. You may merge with one or more other teams if you feel that a larger group could be more productive. Each team member must have a role. Bonuses will be shared between the two teams.

STEP 6: Your instructor will signal when to start production. You will then have 5 to 10 minutes (as determined by your instructor) to make as many high-quality bracelets as possible.

STEP 7: The customers will again evaluate the bracelets and determine the number of bonus dollars each team should receive. The team with the highest number of bonus dollars wins.

STEP 8: While the output is being evaluated, discuss the effectiveness of your team. What roles did your team create? How effective was each role? What changes did your team make between production runs? Were the changes more or less effective?

STEP 9: Discussion. With the entire group, answer the following questions:

DESCRIPTION

1. What roles did team members assume?
2. Did any teams merge? Why or why not?
3. How satisfied was each team member?
4. What outcomes resulted?

DIAGNOSIS

5. How did your team ensure high-quality output?
6. How specialized were the roles? What was the relationship between specialization and performance?
7. Did you redesign the production processes between runs? If not, could the processes have been redesign?

PRESCRIPTION

8. What changes are needed to improve quality and performance at the Beautiful Bead Company?

ACTIVITY 14-6: REDESIGNING DINING SERVICE JOBS

STEP 1: Individually or in small groups, select a dining hall at your college or university. Spend one to three hours at various times observing the operation of the dining hall. Pay particular attention to the tasks each employee performs.

STEP 2: Describe or list the tasks performed by each employee.

STEP 3: Redesign the dining hall using (1) work simplification and (2) job enrichment. If possible, with the cooperation of the dining services employees and managers, implement one or more aspects of the redesign.

STEP 4: In small groups or with the entire class, share your redesigns. Then answer the following questions:

1. Was it easier to simplify or enrich the jobs in the dining hall?

2. Would simplification or enrichment increase individual performance? Which approach would increase individual satisfaction? Which approach would increase customer satisfaction?

3. If you implemented the redesign, what was its impact?

PART IV CASES

The Kitchen King Company

INTRODUCTION

In November 1985, Billy Sanders, Vice President of the Kitchen King Company, asked a team of consultants to examine his company's inventory and delivery problems. Mr. Sanders was somewhat concerned about the company's lack of ability to forecast inventory needs and to deliver merchandise accurately and promptly.

HISTORY

Kitchen King was started by Tom King in 1949. The company is a wholesaler for the major lines of built-in appliances and cabinets for kitchens and baths. The company maintains a modern showroom floor with their different cabinet styles and sizes as well as various combinations of built-in refrigerators, compactors, ice makers, dishwashers, food processing centers, sinks, bar sinks microwave ovens, warming drawers, built-in or drop-in ovens, cooktops, and hoods arranged in attractive kitchen and bath displays.

The company is divided into two main divisions, as shown in Exhibit 1. The Dealer Sales Division, with its five sales representatives (all men), sells to retail cabinet and appliance dealers in Tennessee, Arkansas, Mississippi, and Kentucky. The salesmen help set up displays in the stores and keep them stocked with literature and current price sheets.

The retail stores call in orders or send them by the salesmen. Orders are delivered by Kitchen King free of charge for large-volume orders. Small shipments and rush orders are sent by local truck lines or UPS, and normally the dealer pays the freight cost. Orders are delivered by Kitchen King in two weeks. They wait until they have enough orders to fill a truck before delivering.

The other division, Builder Sales, has four salesmen who sell to local home builders and contractors within the West Tennessee area. Each salesman has assigned customers. The salesmen visit builders at new home sites and either draw up plans for kitchens and baths or use the builder's blueprints. They write up the order, and the cabinets and appliances are delivered to the job site by Kitchen King. The cabinets and appliances are installed by one of the two Kitchen King installers, by subcontractors, or by the builder's own staff.

ENVIRONMENT

Because the Builder Sales Division only sells to contractors building new homes and offices (no remodeling jobs), their demand for cabinets and appliances depends on the local economy, interest rates, weather conditions, and the percentage of new housing starts in the area. The new home growth in the Memphis and West Tennessee area has been particularly strong, with a more stable economy and a large number of residents moving to the outlying suburbs of Memphis and Germantown, TN. Local business, including Federal Express, International Paper Corporation, and Holiday Corporation, are expanding, and many executives are relocating to the Memphis area.

With the increasing emphasis on gourmet cooking and relaxing innovations in bath fixtures, Kitchen King customers are demanding more of the luxury products. The typical Kitchen King kitchen costs about $10,000. The average sales price of the homes with these products ranges from $125,000 to $500,000.

The Dealer Sales Division sells to retail stores whose customers are homeowners or small remodeling contractors. Demand also depends on interest rates for home improvement loans and advertising. The appliance manufacturers (Kitchen Aid, Thermador, Sub Zero, and Elkay) and the cabinet manufacturer (Merillat) advertise in home improvement and building magazines to stimulate primary demand for the products. The retail stores run ads in local newspapers and radio stations on an individual basis. Kitchen King pays a portion of the retail stores' advertising expenses on a cooperative basis, depending on the stores' purchases.

All the items sold by Kitchen King are high-quality, top-of-the-line goods, and consequently the profit per unit is high. Customers seek out homes

Source: This case was written by Marilyn M. Helms, School of Business Administration University of Tennessee at Chattanooga. It is intended to be used as the basis for class discussion rather than to illustrate either effective or ineffective handling of a management situation. The case was compiled from generalized experience. © 1993 M. M. Helms, University of TN at Chattanooga.

▌ EXHIBIT 1 ▌
Kitchen King Organization Chart

President
Tom King

Secretary/Assistant
Kay Steadman

Vice President and Sales Manager
Billy Sanders

Inventory Clerk
Margie

Manager Dealer Sales
Tommy Malone

Secretary

Manager Builder Sales
John Hughes

Secretary

Design
Mike King

5 Dealer Salesmen

4 Builder Salesmen

Installation Staff

Accounting and Office Manager
Ed Court

— **Billing Clerk**

— **Bookkeeping Clerk**

— **Payroll/ Purchasing Clerk**

Warehouse Manager
Billy Harris

— **Warehouse and Delivery**

Maintenance

— **Printing/Copying**

— **Cleaning/ Maintenance/ Security**

with these products, so builders and retail customers are willing to pay the premium costs to obtain such high-quality appliances and cabinets.

Sales have been increasing steadily since the 1980–1982 recession. Exhibit 2 shows gross sales for Kitchen King since 1978.

Kitchen King, once the only wholesaler for cabinets in the Memphis and surrounding area, was joined by a major competitor in 1988. Kitchen King is still the exclusive distributor for all their appliance and cabinet lines, but other lines are advertising and competing in the area. For their Dealer Sales Division (customer kitchens), Kitchen King has little competition in the high- end market. Their Builder Sales Division also has competition from local cabinet makers and other appliance distributors. Frequently, builders want to save costs and will purchase only cabinets from Kitchen King and buy less expensive appliances from other distributors.

INTERVIEW WITH THE PRESIDENT

To gain insight into the inventory problems at Kitchen King, the consultants first talked to the president, Tom King.

Tom King was a thin, gray-haired main in his early 60s. He began the company as a small distributorship and through the years watched it grow and prosper. His primary duties are to answer correspon-

EXHIBIT 2

Gross Sales (in Million Dollars)

1978	$4.34
1979	4.87
1980	4.68
1981	4.77
1982	4.42
1983	6.15
1984	6.77
1985	6.91
1986	7.20
1987	7.78

dence, sign payroll checks, and order all inventory. The remainder of his time is spent traveling or on the golf course. Frequently, he comes in to fix a major problem or just to let the workers know he is "the boss."

Mr. King described his company to the consultants: "We have over 200 cabinet sizes and types which we use as well as various types of moldings, trims, fillers, and specialty wood parts. We presently stock three styles of cabinets. The Americana line is our most economical line. The doors are laminated and the body of the cabinet is oak. The Homestead Oak line is the same body as Horizon only with solid oak doors. The Omni Line is again the same body with almond-colored doors with oak trim. We can also special-order cherry or walnut lines.

"It's so expensive to carry an entire line of cabinets in inventory plus we must stock the appliances as well. I try to keep cost down to a bare minimum by ordering just what I think we need. I look at our incoming orders each week and just order this amount or a little extra. We frequently have many back orders for items not in stock. It usually takes three weeks to a month to fill the back orders and a week to two weeks to get our regular shipments from the factory. I try to order a full truckload of cabinets each time so I can pay lower shipping costs. The biggest problem is that we never know what we will need."

Work-Flow Patterns

Next the consultants observed the work flow patterns at Kitchen King for a week. They hoped that by examining these patterns they could locate some of the inventory and ordering problems. The following is a summary of their findings. A diagram of the work station arrangement can be seen in Exhibit 3.

Order Processing. A customer, be it a builder or dealer, calls Kitchen King with an order. Their first contact is with the receptionist who is often too busy chewing gum or talking with her friends to connect the caller with the proper department. She sees the customer as an interruption of her day.

The customer finally reaches the proper sales office, and the secretary fills out the order form by hand. She puts the customer on hold while she checks inventory to see if the goods are in stock. With the customer on hold, the inventory clerk checks stock, which is recorded in pencil on cards filed in a large tub-shaped bin. There is a card for each item Kitchen King carries. After she has checked stock and told the secretary, the secretary tells the customer the order's status and terminates the call.

The order is handwritten by the secretary and carried to the order clerk. She files the top copy and then updates her inventory cards as she checks off the items on the order. She writes separate back orders for items not in stock and files these back orders.

The order/inventory clerk then sends the order by pneumatic tube to the credit manager. He checks the customer's account status and then sends the order to the warehouse manager. In the warehouse, the order is pulled from inventory and either scheduled for delivery or shipped out. After the order is delivered or shipped (this may be as much as two weeks later), the warehouse then sends the order form back through the tubes to the inventory clerk. She makes sure all items were sent. (Frequently her cards and the warehouse inventory do not agree and she must make changes on her cards). She adjusts back orders if needed and then gives the order to the proper secretary (either builder sales or dealer sales) for pricing. The secretaries hand-price and total the orders from price sheets. They then give the

EXHIBIT 3
Work Station Arrangement

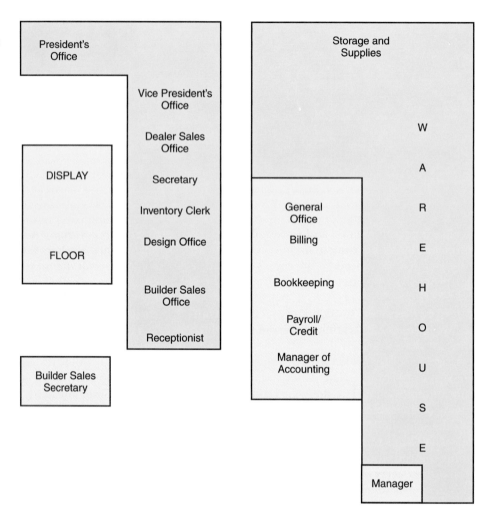

■ EXHIBIT 3 ■
Work Station Arrangement

priced order forms to the president's secretary, Kay Steadman. Kay rechecks the prices and totals. Once Kay approves them, she gives them to the billing clerk. (Kay frequently takes three to four days to check the prices since she must do this in addition to her other work that includes typing correspondence for the company and preparing new price sheets.)

When the billing clerk in the general office receives the checked orders, she then types an invoice from these orders. The invoice contains the same information as the original order only it is now in typewritten form. The billing clerk frequently has to remove the order from the typewriter and correct all the carbon copies with liquid paper if she makes a mistake in her typing.

After she has typed up the orders, she gives them to the office manager, Ed Court, to verify. He checks the totals and returns them to the billing clerk.

The billing clerk now separates the invoices. She mails the top copy to the customer for payment. She sends a green copy to the sales department. This copy is given to the salesman for his records. One copy is stapled to the handwritten order and is filed, and the final copy is sent by Mr. Court to a computer company that processes the information. Kitchen King receives printouts by product lines and customers by the second week of the following month.

The file copy of the invoice is kept by the billing clerk. If the order contains any appliance purchases, she must sign out the appliances by serial number in one of her five product line books. She finds the book for the particular appliance and then finds the correct model number and writes the customer name by the correct serial number. After this time-consuming process is completed, she files the invoices.

Receiving Reports. Incoming goods are also handled in the same jumbled way. Mr. King checks the inventory clerk's cards every Thursday and places an order. The clerk pencils this tentative order in on her cards. When the goods arrive in the warehouse, they are recorded on a receiving form. Appliances with their serial numbers go on one form, and cabinets and goods with no serial numbers go on another receiving report. The receiving forms are sent to Margie, the inventory clerk, who records the items on the same cards. This process usually takes from one to two days. So an item can be in inventory, but her cards will not reflect this until some time later. Margie sends the receiving reports to the billing clerk next. The billing clerk writes the new products and their serial numbers in her books, and she then sends the invoices to the office manager who approves them for payment (to the manufacturer).

Payroll. Each Friday all employees give their time sheets to Mr. King's secretary, Kay. She approves the time sheets and carries them to the payroll clerk, who hand-computes taxes and insurance and then hand-writes the checks. The checks are approved by the office manager and then signed by Mr. King and Mr. Sanders. Paychecks are distributed by the payroll clerk to all the employees by noon on Friday.

EMPLOYEE PROFILE

After a review of the work arrangement, the consultants asked Mr. Sanders, the vice president, to describe the employees in his firm. He replied:

"Ed Court is a good office manager. He has been with the company for over 15 years. He is our only employee with a college degree, and he's been trying to pass the CPA exam too. He keeps the girls in the office straight. He does the best he can with our out dated equipment. He would like to see us get a computer and automate our inventory and billing. But Mr. King keeps telling him that we can't afford it, and besides computers are changing daily so we must just wait until they are perfected.

"Billy Harris is our fourth warehouse manager. He is in his late 50s and he's been sick and the warehouse has not been properly supervised lately. But he's trying to get things back in order. Many of the cabinets are in the wrong place or out of their boxes. We frequently take doors off cabinets to "make" the style we are out of, so the cabinets are scattered everywhere. Harris has a hard time keeping the seven warehouse

workers in line. They often come to work late and get orders messed up. We don't really need that many people—why, one or two people could do that job—but since all the workers don't show up or have problems, Harris just keeps that many to be sure.

"Tommy Malone is a good dealer sales manager. He helps me out with some of the management functions and he has good ideas. I think that he would like to have more responsibility, but Mr. King is the *boss*. So Malone just does his job and that's all.

"John Hughes is the manager of the Builder Sales Division. He has an overconfident attitude. For example, he often goes out to design a kitchen and never makes any notes or measurements. He says he can remember them, but in his office he forgets. Because of this, he sends the wrong cabinets to the job site. He has his favorite salesman and neglects the others. He doesn't give them any training or supervision. He gives a new salesman a catalog and price lists and says 'Go and sell, I know you will because you're paid on a commission.' Turnover in his division is high because he is hard to work with. But Mr. King especially likes him because he has sold more than any other sales manager in the company's history. He's top-notch in King's book.

"Mike King is Mr. King's nephew and he has no official job or job title—he just works where he is needed, which is mostly in builder sales. He designs some kitchen plans and helps with promotions and displays. He has no management responsibility so I wonder if he'll ever be able to prove himself worthy to take over Kitchen King someday."

When asked to describe himself, Mr. Sanders said, "Well, I mostly design displays and plan company-sponsored parties and trips. We have promotions to enhance sales, and I plan the incentive trips and prizes. I don't have a business background so I leave matters to Mr. King. I own a portion of the company, but I'm in my early 50s and I don't know what will happen to Kitchen King after Mr. King and I are no longer around."

INTERVIEWS

Next the consultants interviewed many people at different levels in the organization to try to define the problem at Kitchen King. The interviews were fairly unstructured, but in general the following topics were discussed: the people's feelings, their on-the-job experiences, and what they saw as problem areas in the company.

Mr. King's Secretary, Kay Steadman

"I've been with this company 18 years. I came to Kitchen King straight out of high school. I stay very busy checking prices and typing new price lists. I wish we had a better way to verify prices, but Mr. King won't trust anyone else to do it. He's out frequently so I handle all his business and approve time sheets and sign checks. I'm so busy that I have to take work home with me.

"Most of our help comes to us from high school. We get them trained, and they get married or quit. I like my job but I'm so tired all the time. I don't know if I'll be able to keep up with the job's demands."

Inventory Clerk, Margie Boyer

"Oh, Mr. King thinks that I'm the only one who can keep these inventory cards straight. He hates it when I take a vacation because he worries the cards won't be right. I've kept inventory this way forever both here and at my old job. I have it down to a system. My only problem is that I have to make so many trips back to the warehouse to check on items or see why we're out of something my cards show that we should have. We straighten out the cards every year at inventory time though.

"I see our problem as lack of organization in the warehouse. We often are out of, say, an Omni cabinet so they send a Homestead Oak cabinet with no doors and back-order the doors, or they frequently change doors on the styles to make what we need. All these change-outs are what gets my cards all confused. But we just have to make do with what we have on hand.

"Some of our contractors and dealers just can't wait for cabinets, so we send out whatever we have and correct it later—when we receive the needed cabinets or doors. It's hard to know what we'll need. Some styles and sizes we use more than others, but we are always out of something. The salesmen should use more standard sizes in their designs or not wait till the last minute to check on inventory. They should try to work with their clients and order what they need ahead of time."

Secretary, Dealer Sales

"We add so many new dealers and lose others that I spend most of my time typing up new phone and address lists of the dealers for the salesmen. I also have to spend time pricing orders. Each customer gets a dif-ferent price, and it's hard to know which one to use. If only we had a better system for all of this. I'm glad Kay (Mr. King's secretary) double-checks them. I'm new so I don't know about problems too well. We just have hectic days, with one crisis after another."

Secretary, Builder Sales

"My biggest problem is handling builders who call demanding their orders. They have completion deadlines to meet and need their entire orders on time, but we're often out of something or substituting something else. Part of the problem is that we never know in advance how many kitchens a builder has in progress or what they'll need. You just can't predict it. Always it's up and down.

"I have to handle complaints from the homeowners too. When they move in, they want us to come and fix things. Often it is work that our subcontractors do. We shouldn't have to fix it, but we usually do. Our own installation men stay so busy making service calls or going back to a home to install an item that came in late. I wish we could stay on schedule and keep the builders happy."

Dealer Salesmen's Comments

- "Our best customer in Jonesboro, Arkansas, always complains to me that he never gets what he ordered. The warehouse ships the wrong things or fails to load trucks with his complete order. He then has to wait two weeks or more to get the remainder of his order. This hurts his business and makes him mad at us. I wish the warehouse would shape up."
- "The appliances my customers get are often scratched or bent. The warehouse loads them wrong, and they get damaged in shipping. The warehouse men don't know how to drive the tow-motors or how to properly arrange and stack appliances."
- "The billing process is so slow that orders don't get posted to my credit. I'm paid on a commission. They need a computer to speed up billing. Also, all those back orders cost me a delayed commission."

Builder Salesmen's Comments

- "My boss, John Hughes, is difficult to work for. He's so moody. One day you're his best friend, the next day, you're his worst enemy. He always says that when he takes over Kitchen King, things will be run differently. He plays favorites among the sales staff, and his customer assignments aren't fair."

- "Our builders are always complaining about their orders. They would buy from someone else if we weren't the only one. I don't blame them for being mad. Someone should ask them what they are working on so we could order what they need in advance. Back orders are more expensive than carrying proper inventory. I know we lose sales and customer goodwill. John Hughes also treats the customers badly. They all seem to hate him after they've had to work with him, but they need our cabinets and still buy from us. With new companies around though, this may change."

Warehouse Manager, Billy Harris

"I just can't get my workers to do their jobs. I find them hiding behind boxes and goofing off. Why, just yesterday they made a ball out of wrapping paper and strapping tape and were throwing it around. We frequently have accidents because of their horseplay. The workers just won't act the way they should. They damage things with the forklift. I bet I have to yell at them 10 times a day. 'Just one more time and you're out,' I tell them constantly. Last year I tried to fire a dock worker, but Mr. King gave him his job back. He said not to fire him because they really needed him on the company basketball team. You just can't keep decent help. Of course, we only pay them $4 an hour. King says we have to keep costs down.

"The boys never load an order right. I caution the delivery men when they deliver an order to check it and double-check it. I'm going to have to do something about this."

Warehouse Workers' Comments

- "Mr. Harris treats us like children. He punishes us in front of Mr. King, but when King leaves, he goes in his office and drinks coffee and we do nothing."
- "Really there is nothing to do. We load trucks in the morning and try to look busy in the afternoon."
- "Even Mr. Harris has fun when King's gone. Last week he was cleaning his pocket knife and accidentally cut another employee in the leg. The worker came up behind him and he said it was an accident."

- "Harris doesn't know how to run a warehouse. The place is messed up and unorganized. No one thinks he is effective."
- "We don't feel we have to do much for what we make. No one stays for long. You can't support a family, much less yourself on $140 a week. We do as little as possible. Some even take a few items home to make up for their low salary. The warehouse and inventory are so messed up, they'll never miss a few things."

Delivery Driver's Comments

- "We have to rush to get the stops delivered. We do nothing for a week and then have to speed to get the truck unloaded."
- "No one ever has a chauffeur's license at the warehouse, but Harris never asked. I hope we don't get caught."
- "One driver doesn't even have a regular driver's license. He'll tell you if you ask. He just laughs about it."

Installers' and Subcontractors' Comments

- "I deal with the builders. They are pretty upset about the way John Hughes runs the department; they always have been. They never get their orders on time."
- "We spend all our time correcting doors. If only they would order and send the right thing in the first place."
- "Often when we arrive at the job site, the salesman forgets to leave the plans and we don't know how to set the kitchen."
- "John Hughes also uses us to help him fix up his own house. I've had to fix his closets, install shelves, and even build his kids a tree house on company time. I'm not sure what my duties are. Anything he says, I guess."
- "The salesmen do not work with us on designs. They draw islands and counters that are impossible to install. They should use more standard designs and sizes. They try to get too creative and fancy."
- "No one ever checks our work. We may get a pat on the back from a builder, but Mr. Hughes only talks to us when we've done something wrong."

Office Manager, Ed Court

"Mr. King wants his monthly runs from the computer service center sooner than we can get them back, but he won't buy a company computer. He doesn't understand how it can help us. He looked at one once, but the costs scared him off. He only looks at bottom-line profit. A computer could really help us in payroll; with just a few terminals and some packaged programs, we could eliminate many of our paper problems. We could do ordering and billing and pricing with only one invoice, and our time could be cut in half. But we don't have the personnel to run it anyway. King would want to pay a computer person only $3.35 an hour too.

"I worry about the future of the company when King is gone. The company will be gone too. I spend all my time training new billing clerks. They find out how tedious the job is and stay about six months. A computerized system would change all this, but no one will listen. King has all the money he'll ever need. He will never agree to any changes or improvements that cost him money. I believe you consultants are just wasting your time. King will never agree to anything."

THE CONSULTANTS' REPORT

After these interviews and other data had been collected, the consultants prepared a brief outline of the survey findings. A meeting with Mr. King and Mr. Sanders was scheduled. They listened to these findings and asked, "What do we do to correct these things?" and "How will this program and changes affect our costs and expenses?"

Survey Results

Problematic Aspects—A Summary

Lack of forecasting or planning inventory needs.

No clear goals or objectives for the company, just make more money and keep costs low.

Unwillingness on the part of top management to modernize and automate outdated procedures and machines.

Failure to attract quality, knowledgeable workers and managers because of the low salary structure. (The president's secretary, with 18 years of service, makes only 5.50 per hour.)

No management training or development. Managers treat workers according to Theory X rules.

Workers experience confusion and dissatisfaction with their work, which leads to turnover.

Work load for employees is frantic. Always have to deal with problems and "put out fires."

Customer relations are a problem. Builders and dealers are angry at the company's delivery mistakes and holdups.

Failure of Mr. King to see these problems due to the fact that the company continually makes money despite all the apparent problems.

STEP 1: Read the case.

STEP 2: Prepare the case for class discussion.

STEP 3: Answer the following questions, individually, in small groups, or with the class as a whole, as directed by your instructor.

DESCRIPTION

1. Describe the organization's structure in terms of centralization versus decentralization, chain of command, span of control, division of labor, and coordinating mechanisms.

2. Classify the organization as functional, market-oriented, integrated, or another form.

DIAGNOSIS

3. What problems exist in the company?
4. Evaluate the appropriateness of the structure.
5. What type of structure do the environment, technology, workforce, size, age, and stage of the company call for?

PRESCRIPTION

6. What changes should be made in the structure?

ACTION

7. What activities should the process of redesign include?

STEP 4: Discussion. In small groups, with the entire class, or in written form, share your answers to the preceding questions. Then answer the following questions:

1. Describe the structure of the Kitchen King Company.
2. What problems exist in the company?
3. How could restructuring help solve these problems?
4. How should the new structure look?

Morgan Williams PLC

PART A

Organisation Background

Morgan Williams PLC is a British-owned company,[1] whose sales are largely UK based. Its principal products are the sale and installation of specialist electrical and ground-breaking equipment, mainly to the manufacturing and construction industries.

The company in its present form is the result of a merger of two privately owned British companies. The merger took place in 1992. The logic behind this move was that the joint organisation would benefit from synergy to be obtained by both companies combining their sales networks; in the past Morgan had been based mainly in the south, and Williams in the north. Synergy was also anticipated in a smoothing out of the companies' dependence on cyclical market or environmental circumstances, for example, the weather or construction projects. Sales of Williams' products, for example, tended to be heavily seasonal. Morgan's products had been less dependent on weather, but relied more on the existence of large-scale construction projects. It was also anticipated that customers would benefit from the convenience of both companies being located in depots, which would be able to provide the complete range of both companies' products.

Williams Ltd. had been in existence for over 100 years. Very few new products had been developed in recent years, although staff from the Williams side of the new company claimed that product innovation was rather unnecessary given the unsophisticated nature of their business—ground breaking. However, the situations in which the products were used required technical expertise, and the sales and engi-

neering staff were quite skilled in devising new solutions with what was relatively simple equipment. The company's products were industry standards, and had very strong brand images within their particular marketplace. The company had been heavily unionised and bureaucratic. Rules and regulations abounded, and very little was decided without the agreement of the shop stewards or the union sub-committees. The staff were comparatively well paid, although large overtime payments had been made for very little apparent extra work. The company was widely believed not to have been profitable at the time of the merger, although the published accounts indicated the contrary, and it had probably not been profitable for several years previously.

Morgan Ltd., in contrast, was formed in the 1970s. The entrepreneur who had founded the company had built it up from very small beginnings to a substantial size. He retained full ownership until he sold the company in 1992 and retired. Morgan had been highly profitable for many years. It had been at the forefront of developments of innovative products or product applications, and the company had reaped the benefits of a monopolistic position for a number of years. However, a number of competing firms had entered the marketplace providing similar products at reduced prices, a factor which had started to erode margins. The company had not developed many major new products in the few years before it was sold although a number of product improvements or extensions continued to be developed. As with Williams, the sales and engineering staff were highly specialised in their narrow domain of electrical engineering.

The culture of the company was said to be highly entrepreneurial and unbureaucratic, albeit paternalistic. One description of the company was that the owner allowed his staff to sell anything, even ice cream, as long as it was profitable. He was also said to be involved in all aspects of the company, even going so far as opening post addressed to others. Company outings with the owner and his family were regular occurrences. Salaries in the company were very low. Large cars were often given as substitutes for wages, and promotions, rather gradiose job titles, and new grades were also used as rewards for good performance rather than salary increases. In general, the company was said to be

---

[1]This case study is based on a real company; however, all names and details have been changed, and any resemblance to any real organization or individual is purely coincidental.

Source: This case was written by Dr. Alison Rieple as part of a Ph.D. at Cranfield University. It is intended to be used as the basis for class discussion rather than to illustrate either effective or ineffective handling of a management situation. The case was made possible by the cooperation of an organisation which wishes to remain anonymous. © 1999 Dr. Alison Rieple.

like a large family, with a strong sense of loyalty and commitment to the owner.

Following the owner's sale of Morgan, the company was merged with Williams. This was undertaken by two financiers, who had used a "shell" PLC, cash from a rich investor, to buy and merge the companies. Although their share stakes became comparatively small following the "reversing" of the merged organisation into a listed company, both stayed as executives in Morgan Williams. One, Alistair Finlay, was chairman; the other, Steven Robinson, was finance director.

Morgan Williams, 1992–1994.   Despite the hopes for synergistic benefits, in fact the post-merger period proved exceptionally problematic. Over 800 different staff grades were identified in the combined company. In addition, the range of salaries and "perks" provided was enormous. Two managers from the two merged companies who were doing broadly comparable jobs would find themselves receiving wildly different salaries and perks. As a result, there was considerable dissatisfaction over the unfairness of these discrepancies.

What had seemed likely before the merger to be a potentially beneficial synergy of products had also turned out to be a mistaken assumption. It became apparent that the product and market characteristics were very different, with little commonality between the customers of the two product groups. Although some attempt had been made to integrate the two companies into a combined network of sales depots, the staff from each of the companies in practice had little to do with the others' products. Any potential synergy to be gained by the mix was further blocked by the two organisations' approaches to doing business. The culture of Morgan could have been described as highly entrepreneurial. In contrast, Williams was bureaucratic and old-fashioned and driven by rules. Each company's employees found it hard to understand the others' point of view or way of working. In some areas there was literally no communication, let alone cooperation, between the two camps, and customers had occasionally walked into blazing rows in the offices or sales depots.

A similar problem applied to the senior management group. The senior managers of this time were subsequently heavily criticised by others, not only because of the evident problems resulting from the ill-thought-out merger, but because of what was believed to be inappropriate strategic decisions relating to the company's marketing policies and organisation structure, and because of their failure to begin to tackle the hotchpotch in the company's systems and culture. Other managers also had very poor opinions of some of their colleagues, and the company of the time was described as a hotbed of political activity and extreme ill will. As a result of these evident problems, Alistair Finlay, the chairman and the originator of the merger left the company in 1994, although Steven Robinson, the finance director, remained.

In 1994, a new chief executive, Paul Wilson, was appointed. His previous work experience was as managing director of a national distributor of white goods spare parts, a subsidiary of a large British PLC. He had also had some experience with company rationalisation, restructuring, and the integration of mergers and acquisitions.

PART B

The New Beginnings, 1994–1996

Paul Wilson regarded his brief as to "normalise" the company—"It was going off in all directions. It needed someone to impose some sense onto it, to give it a national identity, and to stamp out the factions which were going off all over the place." In order to help him achieve this, he appointed a new team of directors. These were Donald Boulton, marketing director, who was a new recruit but had been the senior marketing manager in Paul Wilson's former company and was someone with whom he had worked closely previously; Phil Bateman, operations director, who had previously been a sales director in Williams, where he had spent all 25 years of his career; James Horton, operations director, who had been a regional director in the pre-merger Morgan company and again had spent nearly all his working life in the company; Felicity Chambers, human resources director, who was a new appointment brought in because of her previous PLC experience—she had formerly worked in the food industry; and Steven Robinson, who remained as finance director (see Exhibit 1).

Paul Wilson instituted a programme of changes to the staff, systems, and structure of the organisation. The staff salaries, grading, and car policies were rationalised, performance-related pay and share options schemes introduced, and new contracts issued to staff. Other major changes were made to

EXHIBIT 1

Morgan Williams Organization chart, May 1994

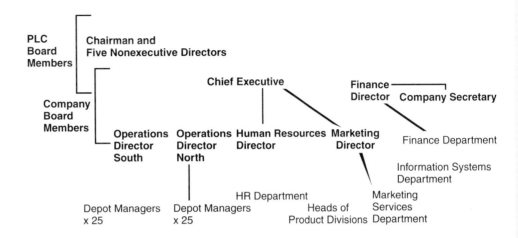

the company. The existing management structure was dismantled. Two sales regions under the direction of two operations directors were set up to replace the six which had existed previously. After a short time, this structure was also disbanded, and Phil Bateman was dismissed. Ten area managers were promoted from depot manager roles to oversee the national network of 30 depots, all of whom reported to James Horton, the remaining operations director. Each of the area managers also retained the responsibility for managing a depot.

Depots were relocated or extended to allow them to sell and service the complete range of the company's products, and to generally improve facilities. A large amount of money was spent on training the depot managers, engineers, and sales staff to deal with the combined product ranges and to encourage commitment to the new direction. New product development was encouraged. Paul Wilson had gone out of his way to encourage projects "which had been on the back burner for many years—no one before had given anyone the slightest encouragement before." New markets were opened up in Eastern Europe, particularly in Russia, Czechoslovakia, and East Germany, in order to capitalize on the fact that their markets lagged behind the UK by about ten years; he believed that products which were obsolete here still had some potential there.

Employees who were unwilling or unable to accept the new terms, or who appeared unlikely to help the company move forward, were made redundant or otherwise dismissed; Paul Wilson regarded the overall standard of the employees within the company that he had inherited to be lower than they needed to be for the company to be successful in the future. A large number of managers at all levels were similarly removed if they appeared unwilling to support the moves that the chief executive was making. They were replaced by new appointments, a large proportion of whom came from Paul Wilson's previous company, A. W. Industries PLC, a company which had grown from very small beginnings to a large and highly successful organisation under Paul Wilson's stewardship. At one point this group comprised 30 percent of the senior managers in Morgan Williams. Paul Wilson had not known all of them personally, although he knew *of* them. They were thus a relatively "known quantity," with successful previous track records and generally higher academic qualifications than the Morgan Williams managers. Some of the most important new managers in Morgan Williams, such as the marketing director and head of one of the product development divisions, which supplied products to the depots, came from this source.

Paul Wilson believed that these changes were essential. The quality of existing staff and the political factions he found in the company on his arrival suggested that he needed to remove those who were backward-looking or whose values were out of lien with his own views. Their replacements, or those who had been allowed to remain, had been chosen for their "fit" into the new company as well as for their generally higher level of academic ability or qualifications. In fact, almost all of the managers within Morgan Williams suggested that they themselves chose new staff on the basis of whether they would be "team players."

However, although this selection for "fit" was accepted by many to be a necessary policy on the part of Paul Wilson, many of his new appointments became a source of considerable friction. Indeed, although many felt that the problems within the company had not begun to be addressed until Paul Wilson's arrival, the sheer number of changes he had instituted, particularly to the staff and management of the company, appeared to cause a considerable degree of stress, resentment, and even fear. Some believed that this had prevented them from concentrating on what they should have been thinking about—how to win more business:

In all these changes, because we've gone through such a horrendous time with the downsizing, with all the redundancies, it's got to have detracted away from the business. It's a classic here, all everyone's talked about over the last 6 months is who is going to be next. And while you're doing that, you're not concentrating on the job on hand.

A considerable proportion of this resentment was directed against the new managers from A. W. Industries. Part of this appeared to be because of their apparently close and privileged relationship with the chief executive, although another related factor concerned the sheer number of newcomers from the same source. Because of this, many of these individuals were seen to pose a significant threat to existing staff:

The trouble is when you bring in people from A. W. Industries PLC, everybody thinks that they are there to find out what is really going on. I'm certainly not going to have anything to do with anybody who I think is some sort of spy at the end of the day.

As a result, this group became an easily targeted "common enemy" against which resistance and resentment could be directed. Indeed, some people described a process of deliberate noncooperation with some of its members and even suggested that some of the new managers' attempts to achieve their objectives were deliberately sabotaged, thus making their acceptance even less likely as any new initiatives met with failure.

One particular problem concerned the newcomers' inherent competence. The performance of Donald Boulton, the marketing director, was a matter for particular concern, and was in time the subject of considerable lobbying by both Steven Robinson and James Horton, who made a determined effort to have him removed. He was in a particularly critical role, given Paul Wilson's stated objectives of product and market development. One of the criticisms made of him was that he had failed to get to grips with marketing in general and the issue of branding specifically. A number of policy decisions, made in close conjunction with Paul Wilson, to do with local advertising, pricing, the product range, and the decision to abandon the two companies' well-known brand names following the merger, were subject to considerable criticism.

Many believed Horton's decisions had been made on the basis of inappropriate assumptions about the company's product and market characteristics. These views were shared by Paul Wilson and were thought to originate from their previous work background. Some of Paul Wilson's other decisions on, for example, the structure and operating policies of the company were also criticised on the same basis (see Exhibit 2). However, a complicating factor concerned both individuals' apparent reluctance to abandon their views. As one manager said, it appeared that they had decided what they were going to do and would do it despite what anyone else might have had to say on the matter.

EXHIBIT 2
Morgan Williams Organization Chart, May 1996

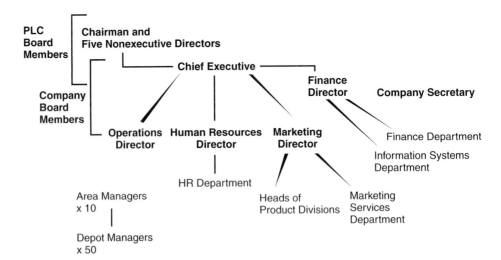

In fact, most thought that both Paul Wilson and Donald Boulton had persisted with mistaken beliefs about the company and its operating characteristics long after they should have done, and both were heavily criticised for being dismissive of dissenting voices elsewhere in the company. They were thus criticised for their communication skills and failure to listen to more experienced voices, and to have made errors of judgement as a result.

Many of these decisions were again subject to a process of lobbying by James Horton in particular:

What happened with Paul, and I'm happy to report that he's now changed his views, when he came here he came from A. W. Industries PLC. I can sympathise with his views, he ran a lot of little outlets, 200 of them all over the country, and these things used to sell little boxes, I'm not demeaning it, that was their business, nothing wrong with it, but they were very much head office driven, because all they did was order twenty more O Rings, or whatever, and these things that were sent out on a lorry that dropped out on a regular day each week, and it was very much driven from the centre. And when he first came, he and I have had many discussions, heated ones about this, but that's how he saw the business, well we're not like that, and I don't want to sound blasé about it, but we need the entrepreneurial flair locally within the depots because we don't just sell things in boxes, we sell concepts.

In time, many of the most criticised decisions were rescinded—and managers spoke of a number of what they described as "U-turns" which returned the organisation to its former ways of operating. These included the type and range of products sold, the companies' original brand names, the local marketing and discounting of products, and the ability of depot managers to advertise and promote their own products. However, these were not rescinded as fast as many (with the benefit of 20/20 hindsight of course) thought should have happened, leading many to blame Paul Wilson and his new recruits for the company's declining financial performance. Even the number of U-turns, rather than being taken as indicators of Paul Wilson's willingness to listen, were used to develop interpretations of indecisiveness (see Exhibit 3).

Paul Wilson was also widely held to have failed to dismiss Donald Boulton as quickly as he should have done, or indeed to deal with the other less competent managers from A. W. Industries PLC as ruthlessly as was warranted. Although he had been responsible for the dismissal or redundancy of a considerable number of other employees, he was now seen to be reluctant to deal with some poorly performing individuals in the same harsh way, leading to further perceptions of indecisiveness or weakness, and to further resentment against Paul Wilson and his former colleagues who were apparently "bullet proof":

That's an example where, I think if you do recognise that you've made the wrong decision you have got to acknowledge it very quickly. I mean we all make wrong decisions, you know, the thing is that once you make that decision and you realise it's wrong, you have to deal with it very quickly.

This perceived failure to take action brought to a head problems between Paul Wilson and Steven Robinson, resulting eventually in their not speaking to one other. In fact, disagreements between the two individuals had already emerged over other aspects of the

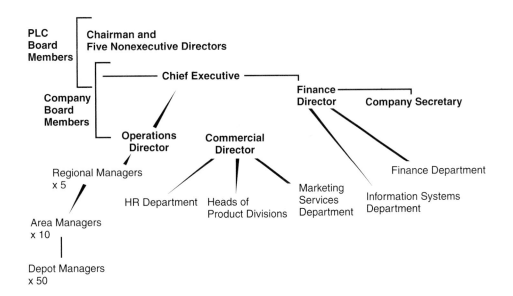

EXHIBIT 3
Morgan Williams Organization Chart, October 1996

EXHIBIT 4

*Morgan Williams
Financial Performance,
1993–1996*

	£000's			
Year ending	30/6/93	30/6/94	30/6/95	30/6/96
Turnover	63,000	57,000	56,000	53,000
Exports	7,000	8,000	6,000	5,000
Pre-tax profit	1,300	1,200	1,100	−1,000
Total assets	50,000	46,000	47,000	46,000
Current assets	25,000	24,000	23,000	20,000
Working capital	−4,000	9,000	4,500	−3000
Return on capital	7%	4%	4%	−6%
Return on assets	3%	3%	2%	−2%
Profit margin	2%	2%	2%	−2%
Current ratio	.8	2	1	.7
Number of employees	1,300	1,000	700	650
Share price	£2.32	£1.64	.76p	.58p

Interim Statement, December 1996

Chairman announces half-year loss of £2.3m (from profits of £700,000 for previous half year). Turnover fell to £25.1 million (£27.7 million). Chairman blames policy decisions in the marketing area as the reason for the poor performance.

Share price falls to 38p. Interim dividend payment is suspended. Paul Wilson resigns.

company's strategic position. Steven's views as to the policy of expansion into Eastern Europe was that it was unwise, and too risky, particularly when there were a number of problems in the UK business still to be resolved. Partly as a result of these disagreements, there appeared to be considerable lack of clarity amongst the company's managers about its strategic position.

During this period, the company's performance did not improve. Turnover steadily declined and profits were similarly poor, and the company reported a serious loss in 1996. There were a number of possible reasons for this which were outside the company's control, for example a decline in the UK's manufacturing base and unseasonal weather. By themselves, these may have caused serious financial difficulties for the company. However, almost all managers within Morgan Williams felt that its performance was worse than it could or should have been even making allowances for these conditions. Comparisons with competitors and internal data indicated that both ROI and turnover were lower than the market average, and profits were similarly at the lower end of the industry range and declining. The share price fell from a high of £2.32p in 1992 to 38p at the end of 1996 (see Exhibit 4).

Paul Wilson's credibility within the organisation was in crisis. After the posting of the loss, several of the managers from A. W. Industries PLC were dismissed, including Donald Boulton. The removal of these managers appeared to symbolise a final critical decline in the chief executive's power within the organisation. Shortly thereafter, an emergency board meeting was convened at which Paul Wilson "resigned."

Brief Details of the Senior Managers

Paul Wilson, aged 47, chief executive 1994–1996. Worked as managing director in two previous companies, both in the supply of electrical or mechanical parts, and had experience with mergers and acquisitions. Prior to that, had worked in strategic planning for an oil company. Committed to the rapid expansion of the company, and great believer in the prospects of Eastern Europe. Said to be swiftly decisive in most things and highly intelligent but not as freely communicative as other board members.

Phil Bateman, aged 58, operations director. Worked all his life for Williams Ltd., latterly as the company's sales and marketing director. Had worked his way up from a position of salesman. Since the merger, had assumed operational responsibility for the south of the country. Dismissed within nine months of Paul Wilson's arrival in the company. Regarded as a highly competent salesman, but was widely believed to have failed to get to grips with the requirements of the operations role. Was also said to have clashed with Paul Wilson, having been outspoken in expressing his criticism of the way the company was going. Is now working for a competitor.

James Horton, aged 48, operations director 1994 onwards. Worked almost his whole career for Morgan Ltd., latterly as one of the company's five regional directors. Since the merger, had been appointed one of two operations directors, initially responsible for the north of the country. Following the dismissal of the southern area director, had assumed responsibility for the whole country. Has the responsibility for managing the whole of the depot network. Regarded without exception as highly competent, experienced, and an extremely fair and honorable man. Combative and well able to stand up for what he believed in. Had been highly critical of Donald Boulton, and had forcibly made his views on this known to Paul Wilson.

Felicity Chambers, aged 35, human resources director 1994–1996. Had worked previously in development and training for two companies, both within the food industry. The only female senior manager within the company. Had implemented some of the major changes to the organisation, for example, the personnel and pay systems in addition to being involved in many of the policy decisions on the removal and appointment of new staff. She had, however, expressed some criticisms of Paul Wilson, particularly what she saw as his appointment of too many staff from his former company and his difficulty in confronting the Donald Boulton problem, but in general shared his values and strategic vision for the company.

Steven Robinson, aged 36, finance director. Accountant by training, has previous experience in finance within a large conglomerate and in merchant banking, where he met Alistair Finlay. Both made their fortunes in the 1980s, and were able to buy Morgan as a result. Retains strong links with other city financiers. Had little or no management experience prior to working in Morgan Williams. Sees things in very black and white terms, and insisted on rigid control of discounts and pruning costs.

Main Dates

Dates

1840	Williams Ltd. founded
1973	Morgan Ltd. founded
1992	Morgan Ltd. sold to Steven Robinson and Alistair Finlay
1992	Morgan and Williams merged
1994	Alistair Finlay removed, and Paul Wilson appointed
1994	New human resources, operations and marketing directors appointed
1996	Paul Wilson resigns

STEP 1: Read the case.

STEP 2: Prepare the case for class discussion.

STEP 3: Answer the following questions, individually, in small groups, or with the class as a whole, as directed by your instructor.

DESCRIPTION

1. What conditions existed that called for change?
2. What changes were made?

DIAGNOSIS

3. What was the culture of the companies before they merged?
4. What was the culture of the merged company?
5. What forces for and against change existed?
6. How did the managers overcome resistance forces?

PRESCRIPTION

7. What additional changes should be made at the end of the case?

ACTION

8. What issues will the company face in making these changes?

STEP 4: Discussion. In small groups, with the entire class, or in written form, share your answers to the preceding questions. Then answer the following questions:

1. What symptoms suggest that problems exist?
2. What problems exist in the case?
3. What theories and concepts help explain the problems?
4. How can the remaining problems be corrected?
5. Are these actions likely to be effective?

Endnotes

CHAPTER 1

[1] S. Rosenbush, Empire builders, *Business Week E.Biz* (May 15, 2000): EB27–EB32; J. Gilbert, AOL's marketing builds service into powerhouse, *Advertising Age* 71(10) (2000): S2, S16; Amazon.com sets sights on overseas marketplace, *Wall Street Journal* (July 20, 2000): C11; R. E. Stross, E-biz cliffhanger: Is Amazon's Jeff Bezos running out of time? *U.S. News & World Report* (July 10, 2000): 44; R. Spector, Manager's journal: Amazon will stand tall, *Wall Street Journal* (July 10, 2000): A34; N. Rand, 25 most influential working mothers, *Working Mother* 23(1) (2000): 76–93; N. Wingfield, E-business: Fledgling online companies flocking to AOL as partner of choice, *Wall Street Journal* (April 3, 2000): B12; D. Roth, Meg muscles eBay uptown, *Fortune* (July 5, 1999): 81–88; P. Sellers, These women rule, *Fortune* (October 25, 1999): 94–126; J. Carlton, EBay gets personal with Wall Street, *Asian Wall Street Journal* (May 23, 2000): 23.

[2] A. Kover, The hot idea of the year, *Fortune* (June 26, 2000): 128–136.

[3] J. Creswell, Cool companies, *Fortune* (June 26, 2000): 98–124.

[4] J. Rossant, The stars of Europe: Leaders at the forefront of change, *Business Week* (June 19, 2000): 162–190.

[5] 2000 agri-marketer of the year: An ear to the ground and one foot in the furrow, *Agri Marketing* 38(6) (2000): I8–I10.

[6] J. A. Byrne, Management by Web, *Business Week* (August 28, 2000): 84–94.

[7] B. B. Wells, At Wachovia, customer focus means information-driven continuous relationship management, *Journal of Retail Banking Services* 21(2) (1999): 33–36.

[8] D. P. Shaffer, Do not interrupt, *Nursing Management* 31(4) (2000): 24D–24F.

[9] J. Neff, The new brand management, *Advertising Age* 70(46) (1999): S2, S19.

[10] W. Royal, Team-centered success, *Industry Week* 248(19) (1999): 56–58.

[11] S. W. Klunk and S. Rose, Building strategic alliances: A case study, *Hospital Material Management Quarterly* 21(4) (2000): 40–46.

[12] Byrne, Management by Web, *op. cit.*

[13] Byrne, Management by Web, *op. cit.*

[14] T. A. Stewart, The search for the organization of tomorrow, *Fortune* (May 18, 1992): 92–98.

[15] R. Sanchez and J. T. Mahoney, Modularity, flexibility, and knowledge management in product and organization design, *Strategic Management Journal* 17 (Winter 1996): 63–76.

[16] J. Coyle and N. Schnarr, The soft-side challenges of the "virtual corporation," *Human Resource Planning* 18(1) (1995): 41–42.

[17] G. G. Dess, A. Rasheed, K. J. McLaughlin, and R. L. Priem, The new corporate architecture, *Academy of Management Executive* 9(3) (1995): 7–20.

[18] N. Chowdhury, The Web is not enough, *Fortune* (June 26, 2000): 248–255.

[19] M. Overfelt, Service on a shoestring, *Fortune* (June 12, 2000): F264T–F264V.

[20] G. MacSweeney, Reinsurance goes virtual at General Life, *Insurance & Technology* 24(13) (1999): 19.

[21] W. R. Pape, Size matters, *Inc.* 21(13): 31–32.

[22] J. M. Folpe, Zara has a made-to-order plan for success, *Fortune* (September 4, 2000): 80.

[23] J. Rossant, The stars of Europe, *op. cit.*

[24] A. Swardson, Workers without borders: In unified Europe, the young go where the jobs are, *Boston Sunday Globe* (April 9, 2000): A10.

[25] M. Hirsh and H. E. Keith, The unraveling of Japan Inc., *Foreign Affairs* 76(2) (1997): 11–16.

[26] S. Van Yoder, Thirst for success, *Industry Week* 249(10) (2000): 35–39.

[27] M. S. Raisinghani, Knowledge management: A cognitive perspective on business and education, *American Business Review* 18(2) (2000): 105–112; J. Hibbard, Knowledge management—Knowing what we know, *Informationweek* (October 20, 1997).

[28] J. Duffy, The KM technology infrastructure, *Information Management Journal* 34(2) (2000): 62–66.

[29] R. Whiting, Myths & realities, *Informationweek* (762) (1999): 42–54.

[30] D. Bonner, Enter the chief knowledge officer, *Training & Development* 54(2) (2000): 36–40.

[31] M. J. Earl and I. A. Scott, Opinion: What is a chief knowledge officer? *Sloan Management Review* 40(2) (1999): 29–38.

[32]K. Moore and J. Birkinshaw, Managing knowledge in global service firms: Centers of Excellence, *Academy of Management Executive* 12(4) (1998): 81–92.

[33]T. Y. Choi and G. H. Varney, Rethinking the knowledge workers: Where have all the workers gone? *Organization Development Journal* 13(2) (1995): 41–50; M. McCrimmon, Bottom-up leadership, *Executive Development* 8(5) (1995): 6–12.

[34]R. Whiting, Myths & realities, *op. cit.*

[35]N. Oxbrow, KM's future in the eworld, *Information World Review* (158) (2000): 18.

[36]P. Warren and G. Davies, Knowledge management at BT Labs, *Research Technology Management* 43(3) (2000): 12–17.

[37]D. A. Andelman, Honest profits, *Management Review* 86(1) (1997): 30–32.

[38]R. B. Schmitt, Little law firm scores big by taking stake in clients—Specializing in Web Start-ups, Venture Law Group turns its back on corporate stars, *Wall Street Journal* (March 22, 2000): B1.

[39]N. Stein, Winning the war to keep top talent, *Fortune* (May 29, 2000): 132–138.

[40]J. Alexander, On the right side, *Worldbusiness* 3(1) (1997): 38–41.

[41]"SIA develops ethics training for institutional brokerages, *Wall Street Letter* 32(5) (2000): 4.

[42]R. M. Snow and A. J. Bloom, A survey-based pedagogical approach to ethics in the workplace, *Journal of Applied Behavioral Science* 32 (March 1996): 89–100.

[43]Does custom equal corruption? *Business Asia* (January 13, 1997): 4.

[44]D. Roberts, China's piracy plague, *Business Week* (June 5, 2000): 44–48.

[45]Alexander, On the right side, *op. cit.*

[46]K. Roberts, E. E. Kossek, and C. Ozeki, Managing the global workforce: Challenges and strategies, *Academy of Management Executive* 12(4) (1998): 93–106.

[47]T. Spencer, Paycheck, health benefits, and a Mercedes, *Fortune* (June 26, 2000): 336.

[48]Roberts, Kossek, and Ozeki, Managing the global workforce, *op. cit.*

[49]D. E. Lewis, Minority women set pace in taking reins of firms, *The Boston Globe* (July 2, 1997): C1, C3.

[50]P. Bartram, Gearing up for the golden age, *Director* 50(6) (1997): 36–39.

[51]R. Ruggless, Arizona Fast Foods, *Nation's Restaurant* 32(4) (1998): 26–27.

[52]S. N. Mehta, What minority employees really want, *Fortune* (July 10, 2000): 181–200.

[53]Mehta, What minority employees really want, *op. cit.*

[54]S. Overman, Managing the diverse workforce, *HR Magazine* 36(4) (April 1991): 32–36.

[55]N. Stein, Winning the war to keep top talent, *Fortune* (May 29, 2000): 132–138.

[56]D. C. Feldman, Managing part-time and temporary employment relationships: Individual needs and organizational demands. In M. London (ed.), *Employees, Careers, and Job Creation: Developing Growth-Oriented Human Resource Strategies and Programs* (San Francisco: Jossey-Bass, 1995): 121–141.

[57]S. Hipple and J. Stewart, Earnings and benefits of contingent and noncontingent workers, *Monthly Labor Review* 119(10) (1996): 22–30.

[58]P. Curry, Help in a hurry, *Industry Week* 249(10) (2000): 69.

[59]P. Curry, Help in a hurry, *op. cit.*

[60]D. E. Lewis, Temporary workers seek equal status to join unions, *The Boston Globe* (March 4, 1997): D12.

[61]P. Brotherton, Staff to suit, *HR Magazine* 40(12) (1995): 50–55.

[62]D. Nye, Not made in heaven, *Across the Board* 33(9) (1996): 41–46.

[63]Adam Smith, *An Inquiry into the Nature and Cause of the Wealth of Nations*, 1776.

[64]F. W. Taylor, *The Principles of Scientific Management* (New York: Harper and Brothers, 1911): 36–37; see also R. Kanigel, *The One Best Way: Frederick Winslow Taylor and the Enigma of Efficiency* (New York: Viking, 1997).

[65]E. A. Locke, The ideas of Frederick Taylor: An evaluation, *Academy of Management Review* 7 (1982): 14–24.

[66]L. Gulick and L. Urwick, eds., *Papers on the Science of Administration* (New York: Columbia University Institute of Public Administration, 1937); and J. D. Mooney and A. C. Reiley, *Onward Industry* (New York: Harper, 1931) offered complementary views of management. F. B. Gilbreth and L. M. Gilbreth, *Applied Motion Study* (New York: Sturgis and Walton, 1917) earlier offered a similar view.

[67]M. Weber, *The Theory of Social and Economic Organization*, trans. and ed. A. M. Henderson and T. Parsons (New York: Oxford University Press, 1947); M. Weber, *Essays on Sociology*, trans. and ed. H. H. Gerth and C. W. Mills (New York: Oxford University Press, 1946): 196–198; R. M. Weiss, Weber on bureaucracy: Management consultant or political theorist? *Academy of Management Review* 8 (1983): 242–248.

[68]C. E. Snow, A discussion of the relation of illumination intensity to productive efficiency, *The Tech Engineering News* (November, 1927). Cited in E. J. Roethlisberger and W. J. Dickson, *Management and the Worker* (Cambridge, MA: Harvard University Press, 1939).

[69]Roethlisberger and Dickson, *op. cit.*

[70]K. Lewin, Forces behind food habits and methods of change, *Bulletin of the National Research Council* 108 (1943): 35–65; M. Radke and D. Klisurich, Experiments in changing food habits, *Journal of the American Dietetics Association* 23 (1947): 403–409.

[71]K. Lewin, Forces behind food habits and methods of change, *op. cit.*

[72]L. Coch and J. R. P. French Jr. Overcoming resistance to change, *Human Relations* 1 (1948): 512–533.

[73]See C. S. Bartlem and E. A. Locke, The Coch and French study: A critique and reinterpretation, *Human Relations* 34 (1981): 555–566, for another view of the significance of research on participation.

[74]H. Simon, *Administrative Behavior,* 2d ed. (New York: Macmillan, 1957); and J. G. March and H. A. Simon, *Organizations* (New York: John Wiley, 1958).

[75]R. F. Bales, Task roles and social roles in problem-solving groups. In *Readings in Social Psychology,* 3d ed., E. Maccoby, T. M. Newcomb, and E. L. Hartley (New York: Holt, Rinehart, and Winston, 1958): 437–447; D. McGregor, *The Human Side of Enterprise* (New York: McGraw-Hill, 1960).

[76]McGregor, *op. cit.;* E. H. Schein, The Hawthorne group studies revisited: A defense of Theory Y (Cambridge, MA: M.I.T. Sloan School of Management Working Paper #756–74, December, 1974).

[77]D. Katz and R. L. Kahn, *The Social Psychology of Organizations,* 2d ed. (New York: John Wiley & Sons, 1978).

[78]T. Burns and G. M. Stalker, *The Management of Innovation* (London: Tavistock, 1961).

[79]J. Woodward, *Industrial Organization: Theory and Practice* (London: Oxford University Press, 1965); P. Lawrence and J. Lorsch, *Organization and Environment* (Boston: Harvard Business School Division of Research, 1967).

Chapter 2

[1]M. Wheatley, ERP disasters; bet the company; and lose, *Financial Director* (March 1, 2000): 35; E. Pasahow, How can you improve the odds for successful ERP implementation? *Digital Systems Report* 22(1) (2000): 24–26; M. Wheatley, ERP training stinks, *CIO* 13(16) (2000): 86–96; J. W. Ross, Clueless execs still keep ERP from delivering value, *Computerworld* 33(38) (1999): 30.

[2]E. J. Gibson, Development of perceiving, acting, and acquiring of knowledge. In E. J. Gibson (ed.), *An Odyssey in Learning and Perception* (Cambridge, MA: MIT Press, 1991).

[3]K. MacArthur, Coke crisis: Equity erodes as brand troubles mount, *Advertising Age* 71(18) (2000): 3, 98.

[4]M. B. Howes, *The Psychology of Human Cognition* (New York: Pergamon, 1990).

[5]J. V. Grimaldi, Hearsay: The lawyer's column, *The Washington Post Online* (May 15, 2000) [at www.washingtonpost.com/wp-dyn/business/industries/legal/A2289–2000May14.html, August 14, 2000].

[6]Food Lion automates checkout, *Chain Store Age* 76(4) (2000): 90–92.

[7]Eckert Seamans' new leadership team commits to long-term branding initiative; retains powerhouse Burson-Marsteller to manage the process, *PR Newswire* (November 18, 1999).

[8]R. L. Solso, Prototypes, schemata and the form of human knowledge: The cognition of abstraction. In C. Izawa (ed.), *Current Issues in Cognitive Processes* (Hillsdale, NJ: Erlbaum, 1989): 345–368.

[9]H. P. Sims Jr. and P. Lorenzi, *The New Leadership Paradigm: Social Learning and Cognition in Organizations* (Newbury Park, CA: Sage, 1992).

[10]D. J. Schneider, Social cognition, *Annual Review of Psychology,* M. R. Rosenzweig and L. W. Porter (eds.), 4(2) (1991): 527–561.

[11]D. A. Gioia and P. P. Poole, Scripts in organizational behavior, *Academy of Management Review* 9 (1984): 449–459; D. A. Gioia and C. C. Manz, Linking cognition and behavior: A script processing interpretation of vicarious learning, *Academy of Management Review* 10 (1985): 527–529.

[12]African women journalists brave stereotyping, sex harassment, *Media Report to Women* 27(4) (1999): 7–8.

[13]G. Keinan and N. Friedland, The effect of stress and self-esteem on social stereotyping, *Journal of Social and Clinical Psychology* 19(2) (2000): 206–219.

[14]Research uncovers ethnic stereotyping, but inability to pay appears to have more impact, *Health Care Strategic Management* 18(4) (2000): 6–7.

[15]N. Zaidman, Stereotypes of international managers: Content and impact on business interactions, *Group & Organization Studies* 25(1) (2000): 45–66.

[16]E. Davis, Women at the top, HR Focus 73 (May 1996): 18; M. K. McGee, Women gaining in IS ranks, *Informationweek* (September 16, 1996): 1.

[17]E. A. Plant, J. S. Hyde, and P. G. Devine, The gender stereotyping of emotions, *Psychology of Women Quarterly* 24(1) (2000): 81–92.

[18]E. P. Kelly, A. O. Young, and L. S. Clark, Sex stereotyping in the workplace: A manager's guide, *Business Horizons* 36(2) (1993): 23–29.

[19]M. E. Heilman and M. H. Stopeck, Being attractive, advantage or disadvantage? Performance evaluations and recommended personnel actions as a function of appearance, sex, and job type, *Organizational Behavior and Human Decision Processes* 35 (1985): 202–215.

[20]B. Roe, A. S. Levy, and B. M. Derby, The impact of health claims on consumer search and product evaluation outcomes: Results from FDA experimental data, *Journal of Public Policy & Marketing* 18(1) (1999): 89–105.

[21]Y2K fears beyond date change for domestic and foreign oil supply fronts, *PR Newswire* (December 20, 1999).

[22]A. Key, Hell (again), Mr. Chips, *Fortune* (April 3, 2000): 298.

[23]D. Eden, Self-fulfilling prophecy as a management tool: Harnessing Pygmalion, *Academy of Management Review* 9(1) (1984): 64–73; T. Dvir, D. Eden, M. L. Banjo, Self-fulfilling prophecy and gender: Can women be Pygmalion and Galatea? *Journal of Applied Psychology* 80(2) (1995): 253–270.

[24]M. K. Kacmar, S. J. Wayne, and P. M. Wright, Subordinate reactions to the use of impression management tactics and feedback by the supervisor, *Journal of Managerial Issues* 8(1) (Spring 1996): 35–53.

[25]A. Montaglianil and R. A. Giacalone, Impression management and cross-cultural adaptation, *The Journal of Social Psychology* 138(5) (1998): 598–608.

[26]L. Chaney and J. Lyden, Impression management: The office environment, *Supervision* 57(4) (1996): 3–5.

[27]M. C. Bolino, Citizenship and impression management: Good soldiers or good actors? *Academy of Management Review* 24(1) (1999): 82–98.

[28]K. Z. Andrews, Impression management, *Harvard Business Review* 73 (July/August 1995): 13–14.

[29]M. R. Leary and R. M. Kowalski, Impression management: A literature review and two-component model, *Psychological Bulletin* 107 (1990): 34–47; M. R. Leary, The interplay of private self processes and interpersonal factors in self-presentation. In J. Suls (ed.), *Psychological Perspectives on the Self: The Self in Social Perspective*, Vol. 4 (Hillsdale, NJ: Lawrence Erlbaum Associates, 1993): 127–155.

[30]P. Rosenfeld, R. A. Giacalone, and C. A. Riordan, *Impression Management in Organizations: Theory, Measurement, Practice* (London: Routledge, 1995).

[31]Rosenfeld et. al., *Impression Management in Organizations, op. cit.;* S. J. Wayne and R. C. Liden, Effects of impression management on performance ratings: A longitudinal study, *Academy of Management Journal* 38(1) (1995): 232–260.

[32]A. Rao, S. M. Schmidt, and L. H. Murray, Upward impression management: Goals, influence strategies, and consequences, *Human Relations* 48(2) (1995): 147–167.

[33]Retailers give an average of $5.8 million to charities, *Fund Raising Management* 31(1) (2000): 4.

[34]M. J. Martinko, Future directions: Toward a model for applying impression management strategies in the workplace. In R. A. Giacalone and P. Rosenfeld (eds.), *Applied Impression Management: How Image-making Affects Managerial Decisions* (Newbury Park, CA: Sage, 1991): 259–277.

[35]J. H. Greenhaus and S. Parasuraman, Job performance attributions and career advancement prospects: An examination of gender and race effects, *Organizational Behavior and Human Decision Processes* 55 (1993): 273–297.

[36]V. L. Barker III and P. W. Patterson Jr. Top management team tenure and top manager causal attributions at declining firms attempting turnarounds, *Group and Organization Management* 21 (September 1996): 304–336.

[37]E. E. Jones, *Interpersonal Perception* (New York: W.H. Freeman, 1990); E. K. Shaver, *An Introduction to Attribution Processes* (Cambridge, MA: Winthrop, 1975).

[38]J. A. Edwards, Effects of causal uncertainty on the dispositional attribution process, *Journal of Experimental Social Psychology* 34(2) (1998): 109–135.

[39]H. H. Kelley, Attribution theory in social psychology, *Nebraska Symposium on Motivation* 14 (1967): 192–241.

[40]E. E. Jones and R. E. Nisbett, *The Actor and the Observer, Divergent Perceptions of the Causes of Behavior* (Morristown, NJ: General Learning Press, 1971).

[41]J. Barry, *Moral Issues in Business* (Belmont, CA: Wadsworth, 1983).

[42]S. L. Payne and R. A. Giacalone, Social psychological approaches to the perception of ethical dilemmas, *Human Relations* 43 (1991): 649–665.

[43]J. Bartunek, Why did you do that? Attribution theory in organizations, *Business Horizons* 24 (1981): 66–71.

[44]H. H. Kelley and J. L. Michela, Attribution theory and research, *Annual Review of Psychology* 31 (1980): 457–501.

[45]A. K. Wiswell and H. V. Lawrence, Intercepting managers' attributional bias through feedback-skills training, *Human Resource Development Quarterly* 5(1) (1994): 41–53.

[46]W. B. Swann Jr. Identity negotiation when two roads meet, *Journal of Personality and Social Psychology* 53 (1987): 1038–1051; Jones, *Interpersonal Perception, op. cit.*

[47]P. Rosenthal, Gender differences in managers' attributions for successful work performance, *Women in Management Review* 10(6) (1995): 26–31.

[48]F. Patterson and J. Silvester, Counter measures, *People Management* 4(9) (1998): 46–48.

[49]J. Cone, How Dell does it, *Training & Development* 54(6) (2000): 58–70.

[50]I. Pavlov, *Conditioned Reflexes: An Investigation of the Physiological Activity of the Cerebral Cortex*, trans. and ed. G. V. Anrep (London: Oxford University Press, 1927). Comparable work was done in the United States by J. B. Watson and is described in *Behaviorism* (New York: Norton, 1924).

[51]B. F. Skinner, *About Behaviorism* (New York: Knopf, 1974); B. F. Skinner, *The Behavior of Organisms* (New York: Appleton-Century-Crofts, 1938).

[52]B. Loafmann, Accelerating safe driving behavior, *Occupational Health & Safety* 68(3) (1999): 66–72.

[53]E. C. Tolman, *Purposive Behavior in Animals and Men* (New York: Appleton-Century-Crofts, 1932).

[54]Want a savvy media relations staff? Train your troops in the trenches, *PR News* 55(31): 1.

[55]F. Luthans and A. D. Stajkovic, Reinforce for performance: The need to go beyond pay and even rewards, *Academy of Management Executive* 13(2) (1999): 49–57.

[56]A. Bandura, *Social Learning Theory* (Englewood Cliffs, NJ: Prentice Hall, 1978).

[57]K. A. D. Stajkovic and F. Luthans, A meta-analysis of the effects of organizational behavior modification on task performance, 1975–1995, *Academy of Management Journal* 40 (1997): 1122–1149.

[58]Luthans and Stajkovic, Reinforce for performance, *op. cit.*

[59]S. Caulkin, Performance! *Management Today* (May 2000): 62–67.

[60]N. J. Lewis and P. Orton, The five attributes of innovative e-learning, *Training & Development*, 54(6): 47–51.

[61]D. Carnevale, Turning traditional courses into distance education, 2000, *The Chronicle of Higher Education* 46(48) (2000): A37–A38.

[62]J. R. Young, Moving the seminar table to the computer screen, *The Chronicle of Higher Education* 46(44) (2000): A33–A34.

[63]J. B. Shaw, A cognitive categorization model for the study of intercultural management, *Academy of Management Review* 15(4) (1990): 626–645.

[64]N. J. Adler, *International Dimensions of Organizational Behavior*, 3d ed. (Boston: Kent, 1997).

[65]J. S. Osland and A. Bird, Beyond sophisticated stereotyping: Cultural sensemaking in context, *Academy of Management Executive* 14(1) (2000): 65–79.

[66]Adler, *International Dimensions, op. cit.*

[67]M. J. Martinko and S. C. Douglas, Culture and expatriate failure: An attributional explication, *International Journal of Organizational Analysis* 7(3) (1999): 265–293.

[68]S. Kumon, Some principles governing the thought and behavior of Japanists (contextuals), *Journal of Japanese Studies* 8 (1984): 5–28.

[69]J. S. Black and M. Mendenhall, Cross-cultural training effectiveness: A review and a theoretical framework for future research, *Academy of Management Review* 15 (1990): 113–136.

CHAPTER 3

[1]G. Colvin, The 50 best companies for Asians, Blacks, and Hispanics, *Fortune* (July 19, 1999): 53–70.

[2]E. Robinson, The trickle up effect, *Fortune* (July 19, 1999): 64.

[3]E. Robinson, Father figure at the front door, *Fortune* (July 19, 1999): 66.

[4]Colvin, The 50 best companies for Asians, Blacks, and Hispanics, *op. cit.*

[5]E. Robinson, Chasing a global edge, *Fortune* (July 19, 1999): 68.

[6]M. Bowler, Women's earnings: An overview, *Monthly Labor Review* 122(12) (1999): 13–21.

[7]C. Higgins, L. Duxbury, and K. L. Johnson, Part-time work for women: Does it really help balance work and family? *Human Resource Management* 39(1) (2000): 17–32.

[8]M. Alverson, Part-time professionals earn full-time satisfaction, *Women in Business* 50(2) (1998): 32–33.

[9]A. M. Morrison, R. P. White, E. Van Velsor, and the Center for Creative Leadership, *Breaking the Glass Ceiling: Can Women Reach the Top of America's Largest Corporations?* (Reading, MA: Addison-Wesley, 1992); S. Barr, Up against the glass, *Management Review* (September 1996):12–17.

[10]M. Jacobs, Women in industry still hit glass ceiling, *Chemical & Engineering News* 78(19) (2000): 36–37.

[11]R. J. Ely, The power in demography: Women's social constructions of gender identity at work, *Academy of Management Journal* 38(3) (1995): 589–634.

[12]M. Halkias, More top exec posts are going to women, *The Arizona Republic* (April 24, 2000): D1.

[13]E. Malkin, Cracks in Mexico's glass ceiling, *Business Week* (July 10, 2000): 166.

[14]P. Dwyer, Out of the typing pool, into career limbo, *Business Week* (April 15, 1996): 92–94.

[15]C. M. Solomon, Women expats: Shattering the myths, *Workforce* 3(3) (1998): 10–12.

[16]C. M. Solomon, How to cultivate female candidates, *Workforce* (May, 1998): 13.

[17]This discussion is drawn from Race in the workplace: Is affirmative action working? *Business Week* (July 8, 1991): 50–63.

[18]D. Leonhardt, The sage of Lloyd Ward, *Business Week* (August 9, 1999): 59–70.

[19]B. L. Betters-Reed and L. L. Moore, The technicolor workplace, *Ms.* 3(3) (1992): 84–85.

[20]D. Lewis, Black women of 'power and influence,' *The Boston Globe* (July 18, 1997): C1, C4.

[21]E. Lesly, Sticking it out at Xerox by sticking together, *Business Week* (November 29, 1993): 77.

[22]J. McCallum and R. O'Brien, MLS takes the offensive, *Sports Illustrated* (October 19, 1998): 28–30.

[23]M. Carvell, Repair job: NASCAR ousts crewmen for racial incident, *The Atlanta Constitution* (August 11, 1999): H1.

[24]C. Cooper, U.K. toolmakers walk off jobs at Ford plant, *Wall Street Journal Europe* (November 10, 1999): 11; C. Cooper, Ford to set up antiracism panels at plants in U.K., *Wall Street Journal Europe* (October 26, 1999): 3; C. Cooper, Ford CEO will seek end to plant's racial incidents, *Wall Street Journal Europe* (October 12, 1999): 5.

[25]K. Labich, No more crude at Texaco, *Fortune* (September 6, 1999): 202–212.

[26]M. Minehan, The aging baby boomers, *HR Magazine* 42(4) (1997): 208.

[27]J. P. Miller, A special news report about life on the job—and trends taking shape there, *Wall Street Journal* (February 29, 2000): A1.

[28]Retailer accused of age bias, *Pittsburgh Post-Gazette* (January 3, 1998): B–6.

[29]P. Barnum, R. C. Liden, and N. DiTomaso, Double jeopardy for women and minorities: Pay differences with age, *Academy of Management Journal* 38(3) (1995): 863–880.

[30]L. Saslow, A touch of gray is no barrier to a job today, *The New York Times* (March 19, 2000): 1.

[31]R. Stodghill, The coming job bottleneck, *Business Week* (March 24, 1997): 184–185.

[32]J. E. Hall and D. Diane Hatch, Supreme Court decisions require ADA revision, *Workforce* 78(8) (1999): 60–67.

[33]Employers are reaching out for disabled workers to fill positions in tight labor market, *Boston Globe* (April 30, 2000): F8.

[34]J. Cleaver, Willing and able, *Home Office Computing* 17(12) (1999): 112.

[35]Employers are reaching out for disabled workers to fill positions in tight labor market, *op. cit.*

[36]T. DeLeire, The unintended consequences of the Americans with Disabilities Act, *Regulation* 23(1) (2000), 21–24.

[37]G. S. Becker, Are we hurting or helping the disabled? *Business Week* (August 2, 1999): 21.

[38]M. F. R. Kets de Vries and D. Miller, Personality, culture, and organization, *Academy of Management Review* 11 (1986): 262–279.

[39]S. D. Moore and M. Waldholz, Frenchman to lead merged Smithkline-Glaxo, *Wall Street Journal* (January 17, 2000): A6.

[40]D. E. Lewis, More firms turning to personality tests for edge, *Boston Globe* (October 13, 1998): D6.

[41]J. B. Hurwitz and M. J. Ippel, Pre-employment testing: The human element, *Risk Management* 46(6) (1999): 35–39.

[42]T. Greene, BellSouth launches telecommuting service, *Network World* 16(36) (1999): 29.

[43]J. B. Rotter, Generalized expectancies for internal versus external control of reinforcement, *Psychological Monographs* 1(609) (1966): 80.

[44]D. A. Riordan and D. L. Street, Type A behavior in the workplace: The good, the bad, and the angry, *Strategic Finance* 81(3) (1999): 28–32; M. Friedman and R. Roseman, *Type A Behavior and Your Heart* (New York: Knopf, 1974); M. T. Matteson and C. Preston, Occupational stress, Type A behavior and physical well-being, *Academy of Management Journal* 25 (1982): 373–391; D. C. Glass, *Behavior Patterns, Stress, and Coronary Disease* (Hillsdale, NJ: Erlbaum, 1977).

[45]See, for example, J. Schaubroeck, G. C. Ganster, and B. E. Kemmerer, Job complexity, 'Type A' behavior, and cardiovascular disorder: A prospective study, *Academy of Management Journal* 37 (1994): 426–439; and P. E. Spector and B. J. O'Connell, The contribution of personality traits, negative affectivity, locus of control and Type A to the subsequent reports of job stressors and job strains, *Journal of Occupational and Organizational Psychology* 67(1) (1994): 1–12.

[46]M. Jamal and V. V. Baba, Type A behavior: Its prevalence and consequences among women nurses: An empirical examination, *Human Relations* 44 (1991): 1213–1228.

[47]T. O'Brien, Which one are you? *Upside* 10(7) (1998): 120.

[48]Riordan and Street, Type A behavior in the workplace, *op. cit.*

[49]R. Zemke, Second thoughts about the MBTI, *Training* 29(4) (April, 1992): 43–47.

[50]The description of types is adapted from W. L. Garner and M. J. Martinko, Using the Myers–Briggs Type Indicator to study managers: A literature review and research agenda, *Journal of Management* 22(1) (1996): 45–83.

[51]Garner and Martinko, Using the Myers-Briggs Type Indicator to study managers, *op. cit.*

[52]D. Shackleton, L. Pitt, and A. S. Marks, Managerial decision styles and Machiavellianism: A comparative study, *Journal of Managerial Psychology* 5(1) (1990): 10–16.

[53]R. Christie and L. G. Geis (eds.), *Studies in Machiavellianism* (New York: Academic Press, 1970).

[54]Christie and Geis, *Studies in Machiavellianism, op. cit.*; J. E. Durkin, Encountering: What low Machs do, in Christie and Geis, *Studies in Machiavellianism, op. cit.*

[55]J. Ricks and J. Fraedrich, The paradox of Machiavellianism: Machiavellianism may make for productive sales but poor management reviews, *Journal of Business Ethics* 20(3) (1999): 197–205.

[56]E. A. Locke, E. Frederick, C. Lee, and P. Bobko, Effect of self-efficacy, goals, and task strategies on task performance, *Journal of Applied Psychology* 69 (1984): 241–25l; R. W. Lent, S. D. Brown, and K. C. Larkin, Comparison of three theoretically derived variables in predicting career and academic behavior: Self-efficacy, interest congruence, and consequence thinking, *Journal of Counseling Psychology* 34 (1987): 293–298; S. A. Stumpf, A. P. Brief, and K. Hartman, Self-efficacy expectations and coping with career-related events, *Journal of Vocational Behavior* 31 (1987): 91–108.

[57]M. E. Gist and T. R. Mitchell, *Self-efficacy: A theoretical analysis of its determinants and malleability,* Academy of Management Review 17(2) (1992): 183–211.

[58]D. G. Gardner and J. L. Pierce, Self-esteem and self-efficacy within the organizational context, *Group and Organization Management* 23(1) (1998): 48–70.

[59]D. Cervone, Thinking about self-efficacy, *Behavior Modification* 24(1) (2000): 30–56.

[60]R. Lachman, Factors influencing workers' orientation: A secondary analysis of Israeli data, *Organization Studies* 9 (1988): 497–510.

[61]S. Oskamp, *Attitudes and Opinions,* 2d ed. (Englewood Cliffs, NJ: Prentice Hall, 1991) offers a good overview of the measurement of attitudes.

[62]See M. Fishbein and I. Ajzen, *Beliefs, Attitude, Intention, and Behavior: An Introduction to Theory and Research* (Reading, MA.: Addison-Wesley, 1975); I. Ajzen, *Attitudes, Personality, and Behavior* (Chicago: Dorsey, 1988).

[63]Fazio, How do attitudes guide behavior? In *Handbook of Motivation and Cognition,* R. M. Sorrentino and E. T. Higgins, eds. (New York: Guilford, 1986), 204–243.

[64]A. R. Pratkanis, The cognitive representation of attitudes. In A. R. Pratkanis, S. J. Breckler, and A. G. Greenwald (eds.), *Attitude, Structure, and Function* (Hillsdale, NJ: Erlbaum, 1989): 71–98.

[65]Fazio, How do attitudes guide behavior? *op. cit.*

[66]D. L. Ronis, J. F. Yates, and J. P. Kirscht, Attitudes, decisions, and habits as determinants of repeated behavior. In Pratkanis et al, *op. cit.,* pp. 213–239.

[67]Originally conceived by L. Festinger, *A Theory of Cognitive Dissonance* (Stanford, CA: Stanford University, 1957); and more recently discussed by H. Marcus and R. B. Zajonc, The cognitive perspective in social psychology. In G. Lindzey and E. Aronson (eds.), *The Handbook of Social Psychology,* 3d ed., Vol. 1 (New York: Random House, 1985), among others.

[68]J. Bullmore, Why yet another relaunch may be just what your brand needs, *Marketing* (May 18, 1999): 22.

[69]S. Draycott and A. Dabbs, Cognitive dissonance 1: An overview of the literature and its integration into theory and practice in clinical psychology, *British Journal of Clinical Psychology* 37(3) (1998): 341–343.

[70]E. A. Locke and G. P. Latham, *A Theory of Goal Setting & Task Performance* (Englewood Cliffs, NJ: Prentice Hall, 1990).

[71]J. Chebbat and P. Kollias, The impact of empowerment on customer contact employees' role in service organizations, *Journal of Service Research* 3(1) (2000): 66–81.

[72]J. Davis and S. M. Wilson, Principals' efforts to empower teachers: Effects on teacher motivation and job satisfaction and stress, *The Clearing House* 73(6) (2000): 349–353.

[73]A. Jackson, Increase job satisfaction without licensing the bottom line, *Workspan* 43(8) (2000): 15; S. Boehle, D. Stamps, and J. Stratton, The increasing value of (flexible) time, *Training* 37(7) (2000): 32.

[74]M. Clugston, The mediating effect of multidimensional commitment on job satisfaction and intent to leave, *Journal of Organizational Behavior* 21(4) (2000): 477–486; J. McLean and T. Andrew, Commitment, satisfaction, stress, and control among social services managers and social workers in the UK, *Administration in Social Work* 23(3/4) (2000): 93–117; L. M. Shore and H. J. Martin, Job satisfaction and organizational commitment in relation to work performance and turnover intentions, *Human Relations* 42(7) (1989): 625–638; M. T. Iaffaldano and P. M. Muchinsky, Job satisfaction and job performance: A meta-analysis, *Psychological Bulletin* 97 (1985): 251–273; C. Ostroff, The relationship between satisfaction, attitudes, and performance: An organizational level analysis, *Journal of Applied Psychology* 77 (December, 1992): 963–974.

[75]This discussion is drawn in large part from D. T. Hall and J. E. Moss, The new protean career contract: Helping organizations and employees adapt, *Organizational Dynamics* 26(3) (1998): 22–37; D. T. Hall, *The Career Is Dead—Long Live the Career: A Relational Approach to Careers* (San Francisco: Jossey-Bass, 1996); M. B. Arthur and D. M. Rousseau (eds.), *The Boundaryless Career: A New Employment Principle for a New Organizational Era* (New York: Oxford University, 1996); and P. Osterman, *Broken Ladders: Managerial Careers in the New Economy* (New York: Oxford University, 1996).

[76]L. A. Burke, Developing high potential employees in the new business reality, *Business Horizons* 40(2) (1997):18–24.

[77]S. Voros, Managing your career: The new realities, *Communication World* 14(3) (February 1997): 28–30.

[78]J. Palmer, Marry me a little, *Barron's* 80(30) (2000): 25–27.

[79]E. W. Morrison, Newcomer information seeking: Exploring types, modes, sources, and outcomes, *Academy of Management Journal* 36(3) (1993): 557–589.

[80]E. W. Morrison, Longitudinal study of the effects of information seeking on newcomer socialization, *Journal of Applied Psychology* 78(2) (1993): 173–183.

[81]D. T. Hall, Breaking career routines, *op. cit.,* p. 133.

[82]J. R. Gordon and K. S. Whelan, Successful professional women at midlife: How organizations can more effectively understand and respond to the challenges, *Academy of Management Executive* 12(1) (1998): 8–24.

[83]J. E. Piercy and J. B. Forbes, The phases of the chief executive's career, *Business Horizons* (May–June, 1991): 22.

[84]P. Nakache, Can you handle the truth about your career? *Fortune* (July 7, 1997): 208.

[85]K. Kram, Mentoring in the workplace. In D. T. Hall and Associates (eds.), *Career Development in Organizations* (San Francisco: Jossey-Bass, 1986): 162.

[86]See K. E. Kram, *Mentoring at Work: Developmental Relationships in Organizational Life* (Glenview, IL.: Scott, Foresman, 1985); R. Rubow and S. Jansen, A corporate survival guide for the baby bust, *Management Review* (July 1990): 50–52; E. A. Fagenson, The mentor advantage: Perceived career/job experiences of proteges versus non-proteges, *Journal*

of Organizational Behavior 10 (1989): 309–320; K. E. Kram, Mentoring in the workplace. In D. T. Hall and Associates, *op. cit.*

[87]D. A. Thomas, Racial dynamics in cross-race developmental relationships, *Administrative Science Quarterly* 38 (1993): 169–194.

[88]G. F. Dreker and R. A. Ash, A comparative study of mentoring among men and women in managerial, professional, and technical positions, *Journal of Applied Psychology* 75(5) (1990): 539–546; W. Whiteley, T. W. Dougherty, and G. F. Dreker, Relationship of career mentoring and socioeconomic origin to managers' and professionals' early career progress, *Academy of Management Journal* 34(2) (1991): 331–351.

[89]D. C. Feldman, W. R. Folks, and W. H. Turnley, Mentor-protégé diversity and its impact on international internship experiences, *Journal of Organizational Behavior* 20(5) (1999): 597–611.

[90]J. A. Wilson and N. S. Elman, Organizational benefits of mentoring, *Academy of Management Executive* 4(4) (1990): 88–94.

[91]M. Conlin, Give me that old-time economy, *Business Week* (April 24, 2000): 99–104.

[92]See K. Little, The baby boom generation: Confronting reduced opportunities, *Employment Relations Today* (Spring 1989): 57–63; and D. C. Feldman and B. A. Weitz, Career plateaus reconsidered, *Journal of Management* 14 (1988): 69–80; B. S. Moskal, Plateaued executives, *Industry Week* (September 20, 1993): 34–36.

[93]L. Bertagnoli, Employees flourish in nonmanagement career tracks, *Marketing News* 34(3) (2000): 13, 16.

[94]M. K. Judiesch and K. S. Lyness, Left behind? The impact of leaves of absence on managers' career success, *The Academy of Management Journal* 42(6) (1999): 641–651.

[95]A. B. Fisher, Japanese working women strike back, *Fortune* (May 3, 1993).

[96]M. Galen, Work & family, *Business Week* (June 28, 1993): 88.

[97]D. Deeprose, When implementing telecommuting, leave nothing to chance, *HR Focus* 76(10) (1999): 13–15.

[98]M. A. Verespej, Balancing act, *Industry Week* 249(10) (2000): 81–85.

[99]C. Fishman, Moving toward a balanced work life, *Workforce* 79(3) (2000): 38–42.

[100]C. Kleiman, More employers now offer 'father-friendly' benefits, *Seattle Times* (February 6, 2000): I1.

[101]S. Caudron, Downshifting yourself, *Industry Week* (May 20, 1996): 126, 130.

[102]P. Dass and B. Parker, Strategies for managing human resource diversity: From resistance to learning, *Academy of Management Executive* 13(2) (1999): 68–80.

[103]M. B. White, Bestfoods: Satisfying a global appetite, *Diversity Factor* 7(4) (1999): 23–28.

[104]B. Leonard, Linking diversity initiatives, *HR Magazine* 44(6) (1999): 60–64.

[105]J. Crockett, Diversity: Winning competitive advantage through a diverse workforce, *HR Focus* 76(5) (1999): 9–10; M. Galen, Diversity: Beyond the numbers game, *Business Week* (August 14, 1995): 60–61.

[106]H. Lippman, Variety is the spice of a great workforce, *Business and Health* 18(5) (2000): 24–29.

[107]Lippman, Variety is the spice of a great workforce, *op. cit.*

[108]O. C. Richard, Racial diversity, business strategy, and firm performance: A resource-based view, *The Academy of Management Journal* 43(2) (2000): 164–177.

[109]L. Feilen, Safety: Converting's number one issue, *Converting Magazine* 16(5) (1998): 62–63.

[110]S. J. Appold, S. Siengthai, and J. D. Kasarda, The employment of women managers and professionals in an emerging economy: Gender inequality as an organizational practice, *Administrative Science Quarterly* 43(3) (1998): 538–565.

[111]S. Moshavi, Japan's women start to resist abuse; more women fight back, but many hold back, *Boston Globe* (January 23, 2000): A 14.

[112]How do you manage a diverse workforce? *Training and Development Journal* (February 1989): 13–21.

[113]B. G. Foster, G. Jackson, W. E. Cross, B. Jackson, and R. Hardiman, Workforce diversity and business, *Training and Development Journal* (April 1988), p. 40.

[114]M. A. Verespej, Zero tolerance, *Industry Week* (January 6, 1997): 24–28.

CHAPTER 4

[1]V. Alonzo, Motivation for a smart and wired world, *Sales and Marketing Management* 152(2) (2000): 34–36; G. G. Marcial, Awards in store at Netcentives? *Business Week* (May 15, 2000): 194; K. Hein, Online awards @ work, *Incentive* 173(7) (1999): 12; A. Postelnicu, NetCentives Inc., *Venture Capital Journal* (December 1, 1999): 1.

[2]A. H. Maslow, *Motivation and Personality*, 3d ed. (New York: Harper & Row, 1987); C. P. Alderfer, *Existence, Relatedness, and Growth: Human Needs in Organizational Settings* (New York: Free Press, 1972).

[3]J. Hamilton, Can we stop having fun yet? *Business Week E.biz* (May 15, 2000): EB125–128.

[4]F. J. Landy, *The Psychology of Work Behavior*, 3d ed. (Homewood, IL: Dorsey, 1985) compares Maslow's and Alderfer's mechanisms of needs satisfaction.

[5]D. McClelland, *The Achieving Society* (Princeton, NJ: D. Van Nostrand, 1961); D. C. McClelland, *Motives, Personality, and Society: Selected Papers* (New York: Praeger, 1984); F. J. Landy, *The Psychology of Work Behavior*, 3d ed. (Homewood, IL: Dorsey, 1985); S. R. Jenkins, Need for achievement and women's careers over 14 years: Evidence for occupational structure effects, *Journal of Personality and Social Psychology* 53 (1987): 922–932.

[6]S. D. Bluen, J. Barling, and W. Burns, Predicting sales performance, job satisfaction, and depression by using the achievement strivings and impatience-irritability dimensions of Type A behavior, *Journal of Applied Psychology* 75 (1990): 212–216.

[7]R. L. Jacobs and D. C. McClelland, Moving up the corporate ladder: A longitudinal study of the leadership motive pattern and managerial success in women and men. *Consulting Psychology Journal of Practice and Research* 46 (Winter 1994): 32–41.

[8]J. F. Langan and S. Roth, Achievement motivation and female entrepreneurs, *Journal of Occupational and Organizational Psychology* 68(3) (1995): 209–218.

[9]F. Herzberg, B. Mausner, and B. B. Snyderman, *The Motivation to Work* (New York: Wiley, 1959); F. Herzberg, *The Managerial Choice: To Be Efficient and To Be Human* (Salt Lake City: Olympus, 1982); J. Phillipchuk and J. Whittaker, An inquiry into the continuing relevance of Herzberg's motivation theory, *Engineering Management Journal* 8(1) (1996): 15–20, more recently validated Herzberg's results.

[10]G. M. Ritzky, Turner Bros. wins safety game with behavioral incentives, *HRMagazine,* 43(7) (1998): 79–83.

[11]See M. A. Wahba and L. G. Bridwell, Maslow reconsidered: A review of research on the need hierarchy theory, *Organizational Behavior and Human Performance* 15 (1976): 212–240; V. F. Mitchell and P. Moudgill, Measurement of Maslow's need hierarchy, *Organizational Behavior and Human Performance* 16 (1976): 334–349; E. E. Lawler III, *Motivation in Work Organizations* (Monterey, CA: Brooks/Cole, 1973).

[12]See B. L. Hinton, An empirical investigation of the Herzberg methodology and two-factor theory, *Organizational Behavior and Human Performance* 3 (1968): 286–309; R. House and L. Wigdor, Herzberg's dual-factor theory of job satisfaction and motivation: A review of the evidence and criticism, *Personnel Psychology* 20 (1968): 369–389; J. Schneider and E. Locke, A critique of Herzberg's classification system and a suggested revision, *Organizational Behavior and Human Performance* 14 (1971): 441–458.

[13]G. R. Salancik and J. Pfeffer, An examination of need-satisfaction models of job attitudes, *Administrative Science Quarterly* 22 (1977): 427–456.

[14]M. L. Williams, Antecedents of employee benefit level satisfaction: A test of a model, *Journal of Management* 21 (1995): 1097–1128.

[15]R. P. Vecchio, Predicting worker performance in inequitable settings, *Academy of Management Review* 7 (1982): 103–110, presents four mathematical models of equity theory.

[16]G. R. Oldham and H. E. Miller, The effect of significant other's job complexity on employee reactions to work, *Human Relations* 32 (1979): 247–260; J.

Greenbert and G. S. Leventhal, Equity and the use of overreward to motivate performance, *Journal of Personality and Social Psychology* 34 (1976): 179–190.

[17]S. Werner and N. P. Nero, Fair or foul: The effects of external, internal, and employee equity on performance changes of Major League baseball players, *Human Relations* 52(10) (1999): 1291–1311.

[18]D. Schwab, Construct validity in organizational behavior. In *Research in Organizational Behavior,* vol. 2, ed. B. Staw (Greenwich, CT: JAI Press, 1980); M. R. Carrell and J. E. Dittrich, Equity theory: The recent literature, methodological considerations, and new directions, *Academy of Management Review* 3 (1978): 202–210.

[19]F. J. Landy and W. S. Becker, Motivation theory reconsidered, *Research in Organizational Behavior* 9 (1987): 1–38.

[20]B. A. Mellers, Equity judgment, A revision of Aristotelian views, *Journal of Experimental Psychology: General* 111 (1982): 242–270; M. H. Birnbaum, Perceived equity in salary policies, *Journal of Applied Psychology* 68 (1983): 49–59.

[21]John E. Dittrich constructed the Organizational Fairness Questionnaire to measure these and other dimensions; see J. Gordon, *A Diagnostic Approach to Organizational Behavior,* 4th edition (Boston: Allyn and Bacon, 1993): 135 for an excerpt.

[22]B. H. Sheppard, R. J. Lewicki, and J. W. Minton, *Organizational Justice: The Search for Fairness in the Workplace* (New York: Lexington, 1992).

[23]S. J. Hartman, A. C. Yrie, and W. P. Galle, Jr., Procedural and distributive justice: Examining equity in a university setting, *Journal of Business Ethics* 20(4) (1999): 337–351.

[24]P. D. Sweeney and D. B. McFarlin, Process and outcome: Gender differences in the assessment of justice, *Journal of Organizational Behavior* 18 (1997): 83–98.

[25]R. A. Posthuma, J. B. Dworkin, and M. S. Swift, Arbitrator acceptability: Does justice matter? *Industrial Relations* 39(2) (2000): 313–335.

[26]R. E. Kopelman, Psychological stages of careers in engineering: An expectancy theory taxonomy, *Journal of Vocational Behavior* 10 (1977): 270–286; M. R. Carrell and J. E. Dittrich, Employee perceptions of fair treatment, *Personnel Journal* 55 (1976): 523–524; R. A. Cosier and D. R. Dalton, Equity theory and time: A reformulation, *Academy of Management Review* 8 (1983): 311–319.

[27]R. C. Huseman, J. D. Hatfield, and E. W. Miles, A new perspective on equity theory: The equity sensitivity construct, *Academy of Management Review* 12 (1987): 232–234.

[28]Cosier and Dalton, Equity theory and time; *op. cit.*

[29]Carrell and Dittrich, Employee perceptions of fair treatment, *op. cit.*

[30]L. Y. Fok, S. J. Hartman, M. F. Villere, and R. C. Freibert, III, A study of the impact of cross cultural differences on perceptions of equity and organizational citizenship behavior, *International Journal of Management* 13(1) (1996): 3–14.

[31]S. Kerr, Rewarding performance, *Executive Excellence,* 17(1) (2000): 4–5.

[32]L. K. Trevino, The social effects of punishment in organizations: A justice perspective, *Academy of Management Review* 17(4) (1992): 647–676.

[33]Roberto Ceniceros, Disney links managers' bonuses: Comp incentive pays off, *Business Insurance* (November 1, 1999): 2.

[34]F. Hansen, Broader range of reward packages helps high-performing companies succeed, *Compensation and Benefits Review* 32(2) (2000): 7.

[35]Joanne Martin and Alan Murray, Distributive justice and unfair exchange. In D. M. Messick and K. S. Cook *Equity Theory: Psychological and Sociological Perspectives* (New York: Praeger, 1983).

[36]See S. Kerr, On the folly of rewarding A while hoping for B, *Academy of Management Journal* 18 (1975): 769–783.

[37]V. H. Vroom, *Work and Motivation* (New York: Wiley, 1964).

[38]R. S. Fudge and J. L. Schlachter, Motivating employees to act ethically: An expectancy theory approach, *Journal of Business Ethics* 18(3) (1999): 295–304.

[39]D. A. Nadler and E. E. Lawler III, Motivation: A diagnostic approach. In *Perspectives on Behavior in Organizations,* ed. J. R. Hackman, E. E. Lawler III, and L. W. Porter (New York: McGraw-Hill, 1977): 26–38.

[40]B. M. Staw, Organizational behavior: A review and reformulation of the field's outcome variables, *Annual Review of Psychology* 35 (1984): 627–666.

[41]N. J. Adler, *International Dimensions of Organizational Behavior,* 3d ed. (Cincinnati: Southwestern, 1996).

[42]See L. E. Miller and J. E. Grush, Improving predictions in expectancy theory research: Effects of personality, expectancies, and norms, *Academy of Management Journal* 31 (1988): 107–122; T. R. Mitchell, Expectancy-value models in organizational psychology. In *Expectation and Actions: Expectancy-Value Models in Psychology,* ed. N. T. Feather (Hillsdale, NJ: Erlbaum): 293–312.

[43]W. Van Eerde and H. Thiery, Vroom's expectancy models and work-related criteria: A meta-analysis, *Journal of Applied Psychology* 81 (1996): 575–586; H. J. Klein, Further evidence on the relationship between goal setting and expectancy theories, *Organizational Behavior and Human Decision Processes* 49 (1991): 230–257.

[44]Hardesty, Greg, Profit sharing an incentive to retain valuable workers in tight market, *The Orange County Register* (April 4, 1999).

[45]E. A. Locke, D. O. Chah, S. Harrison, and N. Lustgarten, Separating the effects of goal specificity from goal level, *Organizational Behavior and Human Decision Processes* 43 (1989): 270–297; E. A. Locke and G. P. Latham, *A Theory of Goal-Setting and Task Performance* (Englewood Cliffs, NJ: Prentice Hall, 1990).

[46]E. A. Locke, G. P. Latham, and M. Erez, The determinants of goal commitment, *Academy of Management Review* 13 (1988): 23–39; M. Erez, P. C. Earley, and C. L. Hulin, The impact of participation on goal acceptance and performance: A two-step model, *Academy of Management Journal* 28 (1985): 50–66; M. G. Evans, Organizational behavior: The central role of motivation, *1986 Yearly Review of Management of the Journal of Management,* ed. J. G. Hunt and J. D. Blair (1986): 203–222.

[47]W. Van Eerde and H. Thiery, Vroom's expectancy models and work-related criteria: A meta-analysis, *Journal of Applied Psychology* 81 (1996): 575–586; H. J. Klein, Further evidence on the relationship between goal setting and expectancy theories, *Organizational Behavior and Human Decision Processes* 49 (1991): 230–257.

[48]Jan O'Neill, SMART goals, SMART schools, *Educational Leadership* 57(5) (2000): 46–50.

[49]E. A. Locke, E. Frederick, E. Buckner, and P. Bobko, Effect of previously assigned goals on self-set goals and performance, *Journal of Applied Psychology* 69 (1984): 694–699.

[50]See B. D. Bannister and D. B. Balkin, Performance evaluation and compensation feedback messages: An integrated model, *Journal of Occupational Psychology* 63 (1990): 97–111 for a model of intervening variables between feedback and motivation; see also J. R. Larson, The performance feedback process: A preliminary model, *Organizational Behavior and Human Performance* 33 (1984): 42–76; R. C. Liden and T. R. Mitchell, Reactions to Feedback: The role of attributions, *Academy of Management Journal* 28 (1985): 291–308.

[51]M. Erez and I. Zidon, Effect of goal acceptance on the relationship of goal difficulty to performance, *Journal of Applied Psychology* 69 (1984): 69–78.

[52]D. Eden, Pygmalion, goal setting, and expectancy: Compatible ways to boost productivity, *Academy of Management Review* 13 (1988): 639–652.

[53]For example, see K. H. Schmidt, U. Kleinbeck, and W. Brockmann, Motivational control of motor performance by goal-setting in a dual-task situation, *Psychological Research* 4 (1984): 129–141.

[54]See, for example, M. Erez and P. C. Earley, Comparative analysis of goal-setting strategies across cultures, *Journal of Applied Psychology* 72 (1987): 658–665.

[55]See E. E. Lawler III, *Strategic Pay: Aligning Organizational Strategies and Pay Systems* (San Francisco: Jossey-Bass, 1990) for extensive discussion of the role of pay.

[56]R. G. LeFauve and A. C. Hax, Managerial and technological innovations at Saturn Corporation, *MIT Management* (Spring 1992): 8–19.

[57]H. Risher, Compensating today's technical professional, *Research Technology Management* 43(1) (2000): 50–56.

[58] R. Schwaneberg, *Job titles in civil service targeted, Whitman vows to cut up to 80 percent of them,* The Star-Ledger, Newark, NJ (November 29,1998): 1

[59]Risher, Compensating today's technical professional, *op. cit.*

[60]K. S. Abosch and B. L. Hmurovic, A traveler's guide to global broadbanding, *ACA Journal* 7(2) (1998): 38–47.

[61]Abosch and Hmurovic, A traveler's guide to global broadbanding, *op. cit.*

[62]G. E. Ledford Jr., Three cases on skill-based pay: An overview, *Compensation and Benefits Review* 23(2) (1991): 11–23; G. E. Ledford Jr. and G. Bergel, Skill-based pay case number 1: General Mills, *Compensation and Benefits Review* 23(2) (1991): 24–38; P. V. LeBlanc, Skill-based pay case number 2: Northern Telecom, *Compensation and Benefits Review* 23(2) (1991): 39–56; G. E. Ledford Jr., W. R. Tyler, and W. B. Dixey, Skill-based pay case number 3: Honeywell Ammunition Assembly Plant, *Compensation and Benefits Review* 23(2) (1991): 57–77.

[63]D. J. Cira and E. R. Benjamin, Competency-based pay: A concept in evolution, *Compensation and Benefits Review* 30(5) (1998): 25–28.

[64]Fred Jesperson, Executive pay, *Business Week* (April 17, 2000): 100–112.

[65]Jesperson, Executive pay, *op. cit.*

[66]R. Trigaux, Sale of Florida bank makes millionaires out of former executives, *St. Petersburg Times* (November 2, 1999).

[67]A. Backover, US West awards executives with bonuses at merger's completion, *Denver Post* (March 14, 2000).

[68]Massachusetts officials strip Harvard Pilgrim officers of $1.3 million in severance pay, *Mealey's Managed Care Liability Report* (January 28, 2000).

[69]S. Allmon, and J. Fahy, Indianapolis hospitals offer incentives to attract nurses, *The Indianapolis Star* (July 14, 1999).

[70]J. Newberg, Cash to cars incentives increasingly innovative, *The Arizona Republic* (February 29, 2000): W11.

[71]E. Schonfeld, The (electronic) personal touch, *Fortune* (March 20, 2000): 214.

[72]M. Ewell and K. O. Ha, Piecework: High-tech jobs done in homes violate laws, *Denver Post* (July 12, 1999): E-07.

[73]S. Reed, Chapter 2 at Pearson, *Business Week* (January 22, 2001): 78–88.

[74]E. E. Lawler III, Gainsharing theory and research: Findings and future directions. In W. A. Pasmore and R. Woodman (eds.), *Research in Organizational Change and Development,* Vol. 2 (Greenwich, Ct.: JAI Press, 1988).

[75]W. Imberman, Pay for performance in a furniture plant, *FDM, Furniture Design & Manufacturing* 71(3) (1999): 150–156.

[76]Kerr, Risky business, *op. cit.*

[77]T. Rollins, Productivity-based group incentive plans: Powerful, but use with caution, *Compensation and Benefits Review* 21(3) (1989): 39–50.

[78]Regina Shanney-Saborsky, ESOP and the employee ownership culture: Balancing compensation and equity issues, *Compensation and Benefits Review* 32(1) (2000): 72–80.

[79]Frank A. Amato, Employee stock ownership, *ACA News* 43(2) (2000): 34–36.

[80]Capital One awards stock options to make all associates owners, *Financial News* (May 12, 1999).

[81]Amato, Employee stock ownership, *op. cit.*

[82]M. Arndt, From milestone to millstone? *Business Week* (March 20, 2000): 120–122.

[83]H. Elliott, Sager enhances employee ownership, *Electronic News* 46(8) (2000): 30.

[84]Amato, Employee stock ownership, *op. cit.*

[85]P. Platten and C. R. Weinberg, Shattering the myths about dot.com employee pay, *Compensation and Benefits Review* 32(1) (2000): 21–27; F. Hansen, Dot.com managers are rewarded with equity, *Compensation and Benefits Review* 32(6): 6.

[86]Such differences do not always exist, as suggested by a comparable level of growth needs among computer programmers in the United States and Singapore, as described by J. D. Conger, Effect of cultural differences on motivation of analysts and programmers: Singapore vs. the United States, *MIS Quarterly* (June 1986): 189–196.

[87]G. Hofstede, Motivation, leadership, and organization: Do American theories apply abroad? *Organizational Dynamics* (Summer, 1980): 42–63.

[88]S. L. Mueller and L. D. Clarke, Political-economic context and sensitivity to equity: Differences between the United States and the transition economies of Central and Eastern Europe, *Academy of Management Journal* 41(3) (1998): 319–329.

CHAPTER 5

[1]Z. Pollon, Federal gaffes fuel N.M. fire, *The Boston Globe* (May 19, 2000): A3; M. Parfit, When good fires go bad, *Denver Post* (May 28, 2000): G-02; R. H. Nelson, Lessons from the western fires Colorado can learn from Los Alamos, *Denver Post* (June 25, 2000): H-02; D. Whitman, An inferno at Los Alamos, a colossal case of oops, *U.S. News & World Report* (May 22, 2000): 34.

[2]C. A. O'Reilly III, Variations in decision makers' use of information sources: The impact of quality and accessibility of information, *Academy of Management*

Journal 25 (1982): 756–771; M. Bazerman, *Judgment in Managerial Decision-Making*, 3d ed. (New York: Wiley, 1994).

[3]T. A. Stewart, How Cisco and Alcoa make real time work, *Fortune* (May 29, 2000): 284–286.

[4]B. D. Cawley, L. M. Keeping, and P. E. Levy, Participation in the performance appraisal process and employee reactions: A meta-analytic review of field investigation, *Journal of Applied Psychology* 83(4) (1998): 615–633.

[5]L. K. Trevino, Ethical decision making in organizations: A person-situation interactionist model, *Academy of Management Review* 11 (1986): 601–617.

[6]K. Biele, Salt Lake faces olympian task, city readies for 2002 in face of world criticism, lengthy report of violations, *Christian Science Monitor* (February 11, 1999): 2.

[7]G. Weiss, Dreyfus deserves more than a slap on the wrist, *Business Week* (May 29, 2000): 210.

[8]D. Beauchamp, The Canadian defense ethics program and the corporate model, *Business and Society Review* (100/101) (1998): 71–74.

[9]W. Royal, Ethical dilemmas, *Industry Week* 249(9) (2000): 8–10.

[10]L. Belsie, Showing workers a way up, companies operating abroad pay closer attention to human rights, *Christian Science Monitor* (April 3, 2000): 11.

[11]J. R. Rest, *Moral Development: Advances in Research and Theory* (New York: Praeger, 1986); T. M. Jones, Ethical decision making by individuals in organizations: An issue-contingent model, *Academy of Management Review* 16(2) (1991): 366–395.

[12]M. Schminke, Gender differences in ethical frameworks and evaluation of others' choices in ethical dilemmas, *Journal of Business Ethics* 16(10) (1997): 55–65; B. Libby and V. Agnello, Ethical decision making and the law, *Journal of Business Ethics* 26(3) (2000): 1.

[13]M. R. Hyman, R. Skipper, and R. Tansey, Ethical codes are not enough, *Business Horizons* (March–April, 1990): 17.

[14]M. France, Ethics for hire, *Business Week* (July 15, 1996): 26–28.

[15]G. R. Chaddock, Big auction houses take closer look at issue of ethics, *Christian Science Monitor* (February 10, 1998): 11.

[16]J. G. March, *A Primer on Decision Making: How Decisions Happen* (New York: The Free Press, 1994).

[17]S. Schroeder, Chapter success, *Risk Management* 46(12) (1999): 45–46.

[18]Hatching a crossborder E-business, *Business Europe* 38(23) (1998): 6.

[19]B. Zerega, Web site supports reader's digest's strengths, *InfoWorld* 20(1) (1998): 74.

[20]A. M. Porter, Team sourcing takes hold, but firms need more practice, *Purchasing* 126(10) (1999): 22–24.

[21]M. Troy, Elevated expectations heighten need for execution excellence, *Dns Retailing Today* 39(11) (2000): 103–107.

[22]A. J. Rose, R. O. Mason, and K. E. Dicken, *Strategic Management: A Methodological Approach* (Reading, MA: Addison-Wesley, 1987).

[23]J. D. Mullen and B. M. Roth, *Decision-Making: Its Logic and Practice* (Savage, MD: Rowman and Littlefield, 1991).

[24]Bazerman, *Judgment in Managerial Decision Making, op. cit.*; J. S. Hammong, R. L. Keeney, and H. Raiffa, The hidden traps in decision making, *Harvard Business Review* 76(5) (1998):47–58.

[25]Bazerman, *Judgment in Managerial Decision Making, op. cit.*

[26]C. Gunsauley, A lot of hot air? *Employee Benefit News* (May 1, 2000).

[27]P. Slovic, B. Fischhoff, and S. Lichtenstein, Behavioral decision theory, *Annual Review of Psychology* 28 (1977): 1–39.

[28]Bazerman, *Judgment in Managerial Decision Making, op. cit.*; March, *A Primer on Decision Making, op. cit.*

[29]D. Kahnemann and A. Tversky, Rational choice and the forming of decisions, *Journal of Business* 59(4) (1986): 5251–5278; A. Tversky and D. Kahnemann, The framing of decisions and the psychology of choice, *Science* 211 (1981): 453–458.

[30]G. Whyte, Escalating commitment in individual and group decision making: A prospect theory approach, *Organizational Behavior and Human Decision Processes* 54(3) (1993): 430–450.

[31]R. Ristelhueber, Silicon Valley standout: Crawford's new challenge is reviving Zilog, *Electronic Business* 24(5) (1998): 36–40.

[32]See J. Bulhart, *Effective Group Discussion* (Dubuque, IA: William C. Brown, 1986); J. T. Wood, G. M. Phillips, and D. J. Pedersen, *Group Discussion: A Practical Guide to Participation and Leadership* (New York: Harper & Row, 1986) for examples.

[33]J. S. Carroll and E. J. Johnson, *Decision Research: A Field Guide* (Newbury Park, CA: Sage, 1990).

[34]P. C. Nutt, Surprising but true: Half the decisions in organizations fail, *Academy of Management Executive* 13(4) (1999): 75–90.

[35]P. C. Nutt, Types of organizational decision process, *Administrative Science Quarterly* 29 (1984): 414–450.

[36]P. van de Braak, Mercuri Urval employs forms processing for efficiency, *Document World* 4(6): 44–45.

[37]G. R. Ungson and D. N. Braunstein (eds.), *Decision Making: An Interdisciplinary Inquiry* (Boston: Kent, 1982).

[38]D. Hogsett, Thomaston bets home can turn mill around, *Home Textiles Today* 20(42) (1999): 1, 21.

[39]D. Dodd-McCue, J. K. Matejka, and D. N. Ashworth, Deep waders in muddy waters: Rescuing

organizational decision makers, *Business Horizons* (September–October, 1987): 54–57.

[40]The last five reasons are drawn from R. C. Snyder, A decision-making approach to the study of political phenomena. In R. Young (ed.), *Approaches to the Study of Politics* (Evanston: Northwestern University, 1985).

[41]H. A. Simon, *The New Science of Management Decision* (New York: Harper, 1960).

[42]O. Behling and N. L. Eckel, Making sense out of intuition, *Academy of Management Executive* 5(1) (1991): 46–54.

[43]T. R. Keen, *Marketing News* (October 21, 1996): 6.

[44]T. R. Mitchell and L. R. Beach, ". . . Do I love thee? Let me count . . ." Toward an understanding of intuitive and automatic decision making, *Organizational Behavior and Human Decision Processes* 47 (1990): 1–20.

[45]Behling and Eckel, Making sense out of intuition, *op. cit.*

[46]P. A. Anderson, Decision making by objection and the Cuban missile crisis, *Administrative Science Quarterly* 28 (1983): 201–222.

[47]D. Barry, C. D. Cramton, and S. J. Carroll, Navigating the garbage can: How agendas help managers cope with job realities, *Academy of Management Executive* 11(2) (1997): 26–42.

[48]J. G. March and J. P. Olsen, Garbage can models of decision making in organizations. In J. G. March and R. Weissinger-Balon (eds.), *Ambiguity and Command* (Marshfield, MA: Pitman, 1986): 11–53; M. D. Cohen, J. G. March, and J. P. Olsen, A garbage can model of organizational choice, *Administrative Science Quarterly* 17 (1972): 1–25.

[49]M. Masuch and P. LaPotin, Beyond garbage cans: An AI model of organizational choice, *Administrative Science Quarterly* 34 (1989): 38–67.

[50]Masuch and LaPotin, Beyond garbage cans, *op. cit.*

[51]Barry et al., Navigating the garbage can, *op. cit.*

[52]T. M. Amabile, How to kill creativity, *Harvard Business Review* 76(5) (1998): 77–87.

[53]E. DeBono, *Lateral Thinking: Creativity Step by Step* (New York: Perennial Library, 1990).

[54]J. L. Adams, *Conceptual Blockbusting: A Guide to Better Ideas,* 2d ed. (New York: W. W. Norton, 1979).

[55]J. L. Adams, *The Care and Feeding of Ideas: A Guide to Encouraging Creativity* (Reading, MA: Addison-Wesley, 1986).

[56]T. M. Amabile, R. Conti, H. Coon, J. Lazenby, and M. Herron, Assessing the work environment for creativity, *Academy of Management Journal* 39(5) (1996): 1154–1184.

[57]J. M. Dorsey, Serbian power crisis fuels demand for wood stoves, *Wall Street Journal* (November 24, 1999): 4.

[58]Adams, *The Care and Feeding of Ideas, op. cit.*

[59]T. Gaynier, Problem-solving software delivers wow! Solutions, *Machine Design* 71(19) (1999): 164.

[60]M. Whitehead, Post modern thinking, *People Management* 5(4): 50–53.

[61]J. B. Thomas, R. R. McDaniel Jr., and M. J. Dooris, Strategic issue analysis: NGT + decision analysis for resolving strategic issues, *Journal of Applied Behavioral Sciences* 25(2) (1989): 189–200; G. P. Huber, *Managerial Decision Making* (Glenview, IL: Scott, Foresman, 1980).

[62]P. N. Prince, N. Demidenko, and G. J. Gerber, Client and staff members' perceptions of assertive community treatment: The nominal group technique, *Psychiatric Rehabilitation Journal* 23(3) (2000): 285–288.

[63]W. M. Fox, The improved nominal group technique (INGT), *Journal of Management Development* 8(1) (1989): 20–27.

[64]A. Van de Ven and A. L. Delbecq, Nominal versus interacting group process for committee decision-making effectiveness, *Academy of Management Journal* 14 (1971): 203–212.

[65]J. G. Mahler, Structured decision making in public organizations, *Public Administration Review* (July/August 1987): 336–342.

[66]H. A. Linstone and M. Turoff (eds.), *The Delphi Method: Techniques and Applications* (Reading, MA: Addison-Wesley, 1975).

[67]G. Rowe and G. Wright, The delphi technique as a forecasting tool: Issues and analysis, *International Journal of Forecasting* 15(4) (1999): 353–375.

[68]B. N. Schwartz and A. L. Gabbin, Constituent feedback in prioritizing the capabilities accounting graduates need, *The Accounting Educators' Journal* 10(1) (1998): 19–32.

[69]A. L. Delbecq, A. Van de Ven, and D. H. Gustafson, *Group Techniques for Program Planning* (Middleton, WI: Greenbrief, 1986).

[70]K. L. Kraemer and A. Pinsonneault, Technology and groups: Assessment of the empirical research. In J. Galegher, R. E. Kraut, and C. Egido (eds.), *Intellectual Teamwork* (Hillsdale, NJ: Erlbaum, 1990): 375–405.

[71]H. A. Linstone and M. Turoff (eds.), *The Delphi Method: Techniques and Applications* (Reading, MA: Addison-Wesley, 1975).

[72]E. F. Harrison, *The Managerial Decision Making Process,* 3d ed. (Boston: Houghton Mifflin, 1987).

[73]Useem, New ethics . . . or no ethics, *Fortune* (March 20, 2000): 83–86; M. Warner, Misadventures in the me-first economy, *Fortune* (March 20, 2000): 100–120.

[74]N. J. Adler, *International Dimensions of Organizational Behavior,* 3d ed. (Cincinnati: Southwestern, 1997).

[75]Adler, *International Dimensions, op. cit.*

[76]Adler, *International Dimensions, op. cit.*

[77]P. R. Harris and G. T. Moran, *Managing Cultural Differences,* 3d ed. (Houston: Gulf, 1991).

CHAPTER 6

[1] Anonymous, Brunswick teams purchasing and IT for competitive edge, *Purchasing* 128(4) (2000): 79–82.

[2] D. Radcliff, Aligning Marriott, (Homewood, IL: Business One Irwin, 1990). *Computerworld* 34(15) (2000): 58–60.

[3] J. D. Orsburn, L. Moran, E. Musselwhite, and J. H. Zenger, *Self-Directed Work Teams: The New American Challenge.* A. G. Dobbelaere and K. H. Goeppinger, The right and the wrong way to set up a self-directed work team, *Human Resources Professional* 5(3) (Winter 1993): 31–35.

[4] M. Moravec, O. J. Johannessen, and T. A. Hjelmas, The well-managed SMT, *Management Review* 87(6) (1998): 56–58.

[5] Moravec, Johannessen, and Hjelmas, The well-managed SMT, *op. cit.*

[6] R. P. Jaleshgari and J. Mateyaschuk, Ready-made management team, *Informationweek* (756) (1999): 135.

[7] T. P. Moses and A. J. Stahelski, A productivity evaluation of teamwork at an aluminum manufacturing plant, *Group & Organization Studies* 24(3) (1999): 391–412.

[8] C. T. Corcoran, ERP implementations raise tricky personnel issues, *InfoWorld* 20(19) (1998): 111.

[9] D. R. Denison, S. L. Hart, and J. A. Kahn, From chimneys to cross-functional teams: Developing and validating a diagnostic model, *Academy of Management Journal* 39 (1996): 1005–1023; R. C. Ford and W. A. Randolph, Cross-functional structures: A review and integration of matrix organization and project management, *Journal of Management* 18 (1992): 267–294; D. G. Ancona, Outward bound: Strategies for team survival in an organization, *Academy of Management Journal* 33 (1990): 334–365; M. A. Hitt, R. E. Hoskisson, and R. D. Nixon, A mid-range theory of interfunctional integration, its antecedents, and outcomes, *Journal of Engineering and Technology Management* 10 (1993): 161–185; J. R. Galbraith, *Competing with Flexible Lateral Organizations* (Reading, MA: Addison-Wesley, 1994).

[10] G. Bernhardt, Goals, teams and letting go, *Textile World* 149(4) (1999): 13.

[11] M. Levinson, Destructive behavior, *CIO* 13(19) (2000): 90–96.

[12] R. W. Napier and M. K. Gershenfeld, *Groups: Theory and Experience,* 4th ed. (Boston: Houghton Mifflin, 1989).

[13] A. V. Carron, L. R. Brawley, and W. N. Widmeyer, The measurement of cohesiveness in sport groups. In J. L. Duda (ed.), *Advances in sport and exercise psychology measurement* (Morgantown, WV: Fitness Information Technology, 1998).

[14] D. Norris and R. Niebuhr, Group variables and gaming success, *Simulation and Games* 11 (1980): 301–312; L. Wheeless, V. Wheeless, and F. Dickson-Markham, A research note: The relations among social and task perceptions in small groups, *Small Group Behavior* 13 (1982): 373–384.

[15] S. M. Gully, D. S. Devine, and D. J. Whitney, A meta-analysis of cohesion and performance: Effects of level of analysis and task interdependence, *Small Group Research* 26(4) (1995): 397–520.

[16] A. V. Carron and L. R. Brawley, Cohesion: Conceptual and measurement issues, *Small Group Research* 31(1) (2000): 89–106.

[17] This discussion is based on J. Moosbruker, Developing a productive team: Making groups at work work. In W. B. Reddy and K. Jamison, *Team Building: Blueprints for Productivity and Satisfaction* (Alexandria, VA: NTL Institute for Applied Behavioral Science, 1988); B. W. Tuchman, Developmental sequences in small groups, *Psychological Bulletin* 63 (1965): 384–399; F. L. Strodtbeck, Phases in group problem solving, *Journal of Abnormal and Social Psychology* 46 (1951): 485–495; B. W. Tuchman and M. C. Jensen, Stages of small group development revisited, *Group and Organization Studies* 2 (1977): 419–427.

[18] J. Lipman-Blumen and H. J. Leavitt, Hot groups "with attitude": A new organizational state of mind, *Organizational Dynamics* 27(4) (1999): 63–72.

[19] Discussion of this model is based on C. J. G. Gersick, Time and transition in work teams: Toward a new model of group development, *Academy of Management Journal* 31 (1988): 9–41.

[20] A. Seers and S. Woodruff, Temporal pacing in task forces: Group development or deadline pressure, *Journal of Management* 23(2) (1997): 169–187.

[21] C. J. G. Gersick and J. R. Hackman, Habitual routines in task-performing groups, *Organizational Behavior and Human Decision Processes* 47 (1990): 65–97.

[22] D. G. Ancona and D. F. Caldwell, Bridging the boundary: External activity and performance in organizational teams, *Administrative Science Quarterly* 37 (1992): 634–665; Information technology and work groups: The case of new product teams. In J. Galegher, R. E. Kraut, and C. Egido, *Intellectual Teamwork: Social and Technological Foundations of Cooperative Work* (Hillsdale, NJ: Erlbaum, 1990).

[23] K. M. Eisenhardt and B. N. Tabrizi, Accelerating adaptive processes: Product innovation in the global computer industry, *Administrative Science Quarterly* 40 (1995): 84–110.

[24] S. B. Knouse and M. R. Dansby, Percentage of work-group diversity and work-group effectiveness, *Journal of Psychology* 133(5) (1999): 486–494.

[25] A. Loudin, Diversity pays, *Warehousing Management* 7(3) (2000): 30–33.

[26] C. E. Larson and F. M. J. LaFasto, *Team Work: What Must Go Right/What Can Go Wrong* (Newbury Park, CA: Sage, 1989).

[27]D. C. Feldman, The development and enforcement of group norms, *Academy of Management Review* 9 (1984): 47–53.

[28]J. Jackson, A conceptual and measurement model for norms and values, *Pacific Sociological Review* 9 (1966): 35–47.

[29]S. G. Cohen, G. E. Ledford, and G. M. Spreitzer, A predictive model of self-managing work team effectiveness, *Human Relations* 49(5) (1996): 643–676.

[30]Jackson, A conceptual and measurement model, *op. cit.*

[31]Napier and Gershenfeld, *Groups, op. cit.*

[32]K. D. Benne and P. Sheats, Functional roles of group members, *Journal of Social Issues* 4 (1948) first introduced this classification.

[33]E. H. Schein, *Process Consultation,* 2d ed. (Reading, MA: Addison-Wesley, 1988).

[34]M. Moravec, Self-managed teams, *Executive Excellence* 16(10) (1999): 18.

[35]J. P. Wanous and M. A. Youtz, Solution diversity and the quality of group decisions, *Academy of Management Journal* 29 (1986): 149–159.

[36]N. J. Adler, *International Dimensions of Organizational Behavior,* 3d ed. (Cincinnati: Southwestern, 1997).

[37]K. Dion, R. Baron, and N. Miller, Why do groups make riskier decisions than individuals? In L. Berkowitz (ed.), *Advances in Experimental Social Psychology,* vol. 5, (New York: Academic, 1970) presents some of the earliest work in this area; see Bazerman, *op. cit.* for recent discussion of this phenomenon.

[38]H. Lamm and D. G. Myers, Group-induced polarization of attitudes and behaviors. In L. Berkowitz, (ed.), *Advances in Experimental Social Psychology,* vol. 11, (New York: Academic, 1978).

[39]P. W. Yetton and P. C. Bottinger, Individual versus group problem solving: An empirical test of a best-member strategy, *Organizational Behavior and Human Performance* 29 (1982): 307–321.

[40]H. J. Einhorn, R. M. Hogarth, and E. Klempner, Quality of group judgment, *Psychological Bulletin* 84 (1977): 158–172.

[41]L. K. Michaelsen, W. E. Watson, and R. H. Black, A realistic test of individual vs. group consensus decision making, *Journal of Applied Psychology* 74(5) (1989): 834–839.

[42]L. N. Jewell and H. J. Reitz, *Group Effectiveness in Organizations* (Glenview, IL: Scott, Foresman, 1981).

[43]See, for example, R. T. Pascale, Communication and decision making across cultures: Japanese and American comparisons, *Administrative Science Quarterly* 23 (1978): 91–110.

[44]I. Janis, Groupthink, *Psychology Today* (June 1971).

[45]Robert Barker, Three contrarians share their secrets, *Business Week* (March 13, 2000): 160.

[46]I. L. Janis and L. Mann, *Decision Making* (New York: Free Press, 1977).

[47]G. Whyte, Recasting Janis's groupthink model: The key role of collective efficacy in decisions, *Organizational Behavior and Human Decision Processes* 73(2,3) (1998): 185–209.

[48]G. Whyte, Groupthink reconsidered, *Academy of Management Review* 14 (1989): 40–56; Lamm and Myers, Group induced polarization, *op. cit.*

[49]R. M. Kramer, Revisiting the Bay of Pigs and Vietnam decisions 25 years later: How well has the groupthink hypothesis stood the test of time? *Organizational Behavior and Human Decision Processes* 73(2,3) (1998): 236–271.

[50]V. Johnson, The groupthink trap, *Successful Meetings* 41(10) (1992): 145–146.

[51]A. B. Hollingshead, The rank-order effect in group decision making, *Organizational Behavior and Human Decision Processes* 68(3) (1996): 181–193.

[52]R. L. Priem, D. A. Harrison, and N. K. Muir, Structured conflict and consensus outcomes in group decision making, *Journal of Management* 21 (1995): 691–710.

[53]P. Farnsworth, Winnipeg School district boosts communications via the Net, *Computer Dealer News* 15(4) (1999): 25.

[54]J. F. Nunamaker Jr., R. O. Briggs, D. D. Mittleman, and D. R. Vogel, Lessons from a dozen years of group support systems research: A discussion of lab and field findings, *Journal of Management Information Systems* 13 (Winter 1996/1997): 163–207.

[55]R. Whiting, Get smart, *Informationweek* 791 (2000): 48–58.

[56]E. M. Bamber, R. T. Watson, and M. C. Hill, The effects of group support system technology on audit group decision making, *Auditing: A Journal of Practice and Theory* 15 (Spring 1996): 122–134.

[57]B. Daily, A. Whatley, S. R. Ash, and R. L. Steiner, The effects of a group decision support system on culturally diverse and culturally homogeneous group decision making, *Information & Management* 30(6) (1996): 281–289.

[58]T. S Bowen, AIC melds outsourcing and internal development, *InfoWorld* 21(43) (1999): 84.

[59]M. Wajsman and G. Lewis, Path to empowerment, *CA Magazine* 132(1) (1999): 45–46.

[60]B. L. Kirkman and B. Rosen, Beyond self-management: Antecedents and consequences of team empowerment, *Academy of Management Journal* 42(1) (1999): 48–74.

[61]J. R. Barker, Tightening the iron cage: Concertive control in self-managing teams, *Administrative Science Quarterly* 38 (1993): 408–437.

[62]B. L. Kirkman and B. Rosen, Powering up teams, *Organizational Dynamics* 28(3) (2000): 48–66; B. L. Kirkman and B. Rosen, A model of work team

empowerment. In R. W. Woodman and W. A. Pasmore (eds.), *Research in Organizational Change and Development* 10 (1996): 131–167. Greenwich, CT: JAI Press.

[63]Orsburn et al., *Self-Directed Work Teams, op. cit*

[64]Moravec, Johannessen, and Hjelmas, The well-managed SMT, *op. cit.*

[65]Barker, Tightening the iron cage, *op. cit.*

[66]W. Royal, Team-centered success, *Industry Week* 248(19) (1999): 56–58.

[67]R. Wageman, Interdependence and group effectiveness, *Administrative Science Quarterly* 40 (1995): 145–189.

[68]S. E. Gross and D. Duncan, Case study: Gainsharing plan spurs record productivity and payouts at AmeriSteel, *Compensation and Benefits Review* 30(6) (1998): 46–50.

[69]E. H. Schein, *Process Consultation*, 2d ed. (Reading, MA: Addison-Wesley, 1988).

[70]P. R. Harris and R. T. Moran, *Managing Cultural Differences*, 2d ed. (Houston: Gulf, 1987): 174–175.

[71]J. R. Hackman, *Groups That Work (And Those That Don't)* (San Francisco: Jossey-Bass, 1989); D. Vinokur-Kaplan, Treatment teams that work (and those that don't): An application of Hackman's group effectiveness model to interdisciplinary teams in psychiatric hospitals, *Journal of Applied Behavioral Science* 31(3) (1995): 303–327.

[72]Larson and LaFasto, *Team Work, op. cit.*

[73]Ancona, Outward bound, *op. cit.*

[74]C. E. Nicholls, H. W. Lane, and M. B. Brechu, Taking self-managed teams to Mexico, *Academy of Management Executive* 13(3) (1999): 15–25.

[75]J. Angus and S. Gallagher, Keep your team in touch, *Informationweek* (681) (1998): 83–93.

[76]A. M. Townsend, S. M. DeMarie, and A. R. Hendrickson, Virtual teams: Technology and the workplace of the future, *Academy of Management Executive* 12(3) (1998): 17–29.

[77]Townsend, DeMarie, and Hendrickson, Virtual teams, *op. cit.*

[78]T. Kayworth and D. Leidner, The global virtual manager: A prescription for success, *European Management Journal* 18(2) (2000): 183–194.

[79]S. L. Jarvenpaa and D. E. Leidner, Communication and trust in global virtual teams, *Organization Science* 10(6) (1999): 791–815.

[80]D. Drucker, Virtual teams light up GE—Customers, suppliers linked in real time with collaboration apps, *Internetweek* (April 10, 2000): 1,16.

[81]J. Cleaver, Let the good times roll, *Home Office Computing* 18(8) (2000): 84.

[82]D. Robey, H. M. Khoo, and C. Powers, Situated learning in cross-functional virtual teams, *Technical Communication* 47(1) (2000): 51–66.

[83]C. Froggatt, Distance makes a difference, *Home Office Computing* 18(8) (2000): 20.

[84]F. J. Milliken and L. L. Martins, Searching for common threads: Understanding the multiple effects of diversity in organizational groups, *Academy of Management Review* 21(2) (1996): 402–433.

[85]J. Couzin, The forest still burns, *U.S. News & World Report* (April 19, 1999): 67.

[86]N. Seppa, Common antibiotic may cure river blindness, *Science News* 157(25) (2000): 389.

[87]N. J. Adler, *International Dimensions, op. cit.*

[88]C. J. Fombrun, Corporate culture and competitive strategy. In C. J. Fombrun, N. M. Tichy, and M. Devanna (eds.), *Strategic Human Resource Management* (New York: Wiley, 1984).

[89]P. R. Harris and R. T. Moran, *Managing Cultural Differences*, 3d ed. (Houston: Gulf, 1991).

[90]W. E. Watson, K. Kumar, and L. K. Michaelsen, Cultural diversity's impact on interaction process and performance: Comparing homogeneous and diverse task groups, *Academy of Management Journal* 36 (1993): 590–602.

[91]*International Consulting News* (April, 1987). Cited in P. R. Harris and R. T. Moran, *Managing Cultural Differences*, 3d ed. (Houston: Gulf, 1991).

CHAPTER 7

[1]M. Hyman, The owner's box gets wired, *Business Week* (May 22, 2000): 89.

[2]This discussion is based on M. Culnan and M. L. Markus, Information technologies. In F. Jablin, L. Putnam, K. Roberts, and L. Porter (eds.), *Handbook of Organizational Communication, An Interdisciplinary Perspective* (Newbury Park, CA: Sage, 1991).

[3]T. Shields, Spinning on the Web, *Editor & Publisher* 133(24) (2000): 118–122.

[4]J. Baljko, SouthTrust launches commercial offering, *Bank Systems & Technology* 36(7) (1999): 37.

[5]S. Rosenbush, Talking Internet, *Business Week* (May 1, 2000): 174–188.

[6]The big picture, *Business Week* (June 12, 2000): 14.

[7]Anonymous, Houston, we have the agenda, *Fortune* Tech Guide (Summer 2000): 95–96.

[8]A. J. Liddle, Information systems, *Nation's Restaurant News* 34(33) (2000): 80.

[9]D. T. Daly, Technology for customer service: Video conferencing at the New York State Teacher's Retirement System, *Government Finance Review* 15(1) (1999): 33–35.

[10]C. D. Marsan, Vendors target e-mail overload, *Network World* 17(35) (2000): 1.

[11]T. A. Stewart, Software preserves knowledge, people pass it on, *Fortune* (September 4, 2000): 390–392.

[12]B. Merrick, Staffing shortages? Hire your friends, *Credit Union Magazine* 66(8) (2000): 18.

[13]Anonymous, Viewer gets center out from under paperwork, *Health Management Technology* 21(4) (2000): 78.

[14]D. E. Léger, Monitoring your online reputation, *Fortune* (May 29, 2000): 172, 174.

[15]M. Conlin, Workers, surf at your own risk, *Business Week* (June 12, 2000): 105–106.

[16]K. J. Gergen and T. J. Thatchenkery, Developing dialogue for discerning differences, *Journal of Applied Behavioral Science* 32(4) (1996): 428–433.

[17]P. Strozniak, The comeback plant, *Industry Week* 248(19) (1999): 42–44.

[18]R. L. Daft and R. H. Lengel, Organizational information requirements, media richness and structural design, *Management Science* 32(1986): 554–571.

[19]R. H. Lengel and R. L. Daft, The selection of communication media as an executive skill, *Academy of Management Executive* 2(1988): 225–232.

[20]Lengel and Daft, The selection of communication media, *op. cit.*

[21]E. W. Morrison and R. J. Bies, Impression management in the feedback-seeking process: A literature review and research agenda, *Academy of Management Review* 16(3) (1991): 522–541.

[22]J. Sullivan, N. Kameda, and T. Nobu, Bypassing in managerial communication, *Business Horizons* 34(1) (1991): 71–80.

[23]C. Harler, Electronic communications may accentuate sex differences, *Communication News* 33 (April 1996): 4.

[24]See M. L. Knapp, *Nonverbal Communication in Human Interaction* (New York: Holt, Rinehart and Winston, 1972); P. Ekman, Communication through nonverbal behavior. In S. S. Tomkins and C. E. Izard (eds.), *Affect, Cognition, and Personality* (New York: Springer, 1965).

[25]C. L. McKenzie and C. J. Qazi, Communication barriers in the workplace, *Business Horizons* 26 (March–April 1983): 70–72.

[26]P. R. Harris and R. T. Moran, *Managing Cultural Differences*, 3d ed. (Houston: Gulf, 1991).

[27]F. Elashmawi and P. R. Harris, *Multicultural Management: New Skills for Global Success* (Houston: Gulf, 1993).

[28]F. Elashmawi and P. R. Harris, *Multicultural Management, op. cit.*

[29]J. W. Gibson and R. M. Hodgetts, *Organizational Communication: A Managerial Perspective*, 2d ed. (New York: HarperCollins, 1991).

[30]C. B. Rogers and R. E. Farson, Active listening. In D. Kolb, I. Rubin, and J. McIntire (eds.), *Organizational Psychology: Readings on Human Behavior in Organizations* (Englewood Cliffs, NJ: Prentice Hall, 1984): 255–267.

[31]L. B. Comer and T. Drollinger, Active empathetic listening and selling success: A conceptual framework, *Journal of Personal Selling & Sales Management* 19(1) (1000): 15–29.

[32]Gibson and Hodgetts, *Organizational Communication, op. cit.*

[33]K. J. Andrews, End e-mail overload, *Target Marketing* 22(6) (1999): 30.

[34]The discussion of load is primarily based on Gibson and Hodgetts, *Organizational Communication, op. cit.*

[35]P. G. Clampitt, *Communicating for Managerial Effectiveness* (Newbury Park, CA: Sage, 1991).

[36]Anonymous, Information architecture practice: An interview with Steen Ritchey Sapient, *American Society for Information Science, Bulletin of the American Society for Information Science* 26(6) (2000): 16–18.

[37]L. Wonnacott, Web site design is a combination of both science and art that satisfies many users, *InfoWorld* 22(5) (2000): 60.

[38]Anonymous, Information architecture practice, *op. cit.*

[39]S. Dinnen, Incentive programs, *Rough Notes* 143(3) (2000): 110–112.

[40]P. V. Lewis, *Organizational Communication: The Essence of Effective Management*, 3d ed. (New York: Wiley, 1987).

[41]J. Brockner, Managing the effects of layoffs on survivors, *California Management Review* (Winter 1992): 9–27.

[42]Anonymous, Case study plant gets drilled on crisis management, *PR News* 54(59) (1998): 1.

[43]E. M. Eisenberg and M. G. Witten, Reconsidering openness in organizational communication, *Academy of Management Review* 12 (1987): 418–426.

[44]D. Fisher, *Communication in Organizations*, 2d ed. (St. Paul, MN: West, 1993).

[45]R. A. Friedman and J. Podolny, Differentiation of boundary spanning roles: Labor negotiations and implications for role conflict, *Administrative Science Quarterly* 37 (1992): 28–47; and S. MacDonald and C. Williams, The survival of the gatekeeper, *Research Policy* 23(2) (March 1994): 123–132 offer examples of this role.

[46]Lewis, *Organizational Communication, op. cit.*

[47]E. Rogers and R. Agarwala-Rogers, *Communication in Organizations* (New York: Free Press, 1976).

[48]P. R. Monge, J. M. Brismier, A. L. Cook, P. D. Day, J. A. Edwards, and K. K. Kriste, Determinants of communication structure in large organizations. Paper presented at the meeting of the International Communication Association, Portland, May, 1976. Cited in G. L. Kreps, *Organizational Communication*, 2d ed. (New York: Longman, 1990).

[49]P. R. Monge and E. M. Eisenberg, Emergent communication networks. In F. Jablin, L. Putnam, K. Roberts, and L. Porter (eds.), *Handbook of Organizational Communication: An Interdisciplinary Perspective* (Newbury Park, CA: Sage, 1991).

[50]T. Gutner, Getting in on the angel game, *Business Week* (May 15, 2000): 190.

[51]J. Green, Calling all car worms, *Brandweek* 41(10) (2000): 22–23.

[52]M. Wilson, Rue 21 rolls out the barrel, *Chain Store Age* 75(10) (1999): 128.

[53]M. B. Goodman, Corporate communications and crisis. In M. B. Goodman (ed.), *Corporate Communication: Theory and Practice* (Albany, NY: State University of New York Press, 1994).

[54]K. R. Woolever, Corporate language and the law: Avoiding liability in corporate communications. In M. B. Goodman (ed.), *Corporate Communication, op. cit.*

[55]L. Moyer, Chase sees 3,000 jobs cut in deal, *American Banker* 165(182) (2000): 1.

[56]D. Dozier, Case study: Employee communications at Kerr-McGee in the aftermath of the Oklahoma City bombing, *Public Relations Quarterly* 43(2) (1998): 13–18.

[57]See, for example, D. Tannen, *You Just Don't Understand: Women and Men in Conversation* (New York: William Morrow, 1990); D. Tannen, *Talking from 9 to 5: How Women's and Men's Conversational Styles Affect Who Gets Heard, Who Gets Credit, and What Gets Done at Work* (New York: William Morrow, 1994).

[58]Tannen, *You Just Don't Understand, op. cit.*

[59]Tannen, *Talking from 9 to 5, op. cit.*

[60]S. S. Case, Cultural differences, not deficiencies: An analysis of managerial women's language. In S. Rose and L. Larwood (eds.), *Women's Careers: Pathways and Pitfalls* (New York: Praeger, 1988).

[61]M. R. Line, The gender impact of temporary virtual work groups, *IEEE Transactions on Professional Communication* 42(4) (1999): 276–285.

[62]G. Wright, Collegial creation, *Building Design & Construction* 41(6) (2000): 58–62.

[63]M. Tahvanainen, Expatriate performance management: The case of Nokia Telecommunications, *Human Resource Management* 39(2,3) (2000): 267–275.

[64]P. McCurry, New angle on 360-degree feedback, *Director* 53(4) (1999): 36.

[65]R. Lepsinger, A. D. Lucia, Creating champions for 360 degree feedback, *Training & Development* 52(2) (1998): 49–52.

[66]A. S. Tsui and B. Barry, Interpersonal affect and rating errors, *Academy of Management Journal* 29 (1986): 586–599.

[67]See, for example, R. Jacobs and S. W. J. Kozlowski, A closer look at halo error in performance ratings, *Academy of Management Journal* 28 (1985): 201–212.

[68]C. M. Vance, S. R. McClaine, D. M. Boje, and H. D. Stage, An examination of the transferability of traditional performance appraisal principles across cultural boundaries, *Management International Review* 32 (1992): 313–326.

[69]W. T. Weaver, When discounting gets in the way, *Training & Development* (July, 1993): 55–61.

[70]J. R. Gibb, Defensive communication, *ETC: A Review of General Semantics* 22 (1965).

[71]J. Hall, Communication revised, *California Management Review* 15 (1973); J. Luft, *Group Processes: An Introduction to Group Dynamics* (Palo Alto, CA: Mayfield Publishing, 1970).

[72]L. Sussman, Managers: On the defensive, *Business Horizons* 34(1) (1991): 81–87.

[73]R. E. Alberti and M. L. Emmons, *Your Perfect Right* (San Luis Obispo, CA: Impact, 1982).

[74]D. K. DuPont, Eureka! Tools for encouraging employee suggestions, *HRMagazine* 44(9) (1999): 134–143.

[75]J. W. Graham, Blowing the whistle, *Administrative Science Quarterly* 38(1993): 683–685.

[76]Whistleblowers at work 1: Contract, confidentiality and the public interest, *IRS Employment Review* (February 1997): I2–I6; K. M. Smith and J. M. Oseth, The whistleblowing era: A management perspective, *Employee Relations Law Journal* 12 (Autumn 1993): 179–192.

[77]C. Yang and M. France, Whistle-blowers on trial, *Business Week* (March 24, 1997): 172–178.

[78]J. A. Benson and D. L. Ross, Sundstrand: A case study in transformation of cultural ethics, *Journal of Business Ethics* 17(14) (1998): 1517–1527.

[79]T. Ewing and P. Waldman, Emulex is victim of Internet hoax—Stock dives 60% on fake news release before recovering most losses—Wild market ride, new economy style, *Asian Wall Street Journal* (August 28, 2000): 19.

[80]R. L. Fink, R. K. Robinson, and D. C. Wyld, English-only work rules: Balancing fair employment considerations in a multicultural and multilingual healthcare workforce, *Hospital and Health Services Administration* 41 (Winter 1996): 473–483.

[81]J. S. McClenahen, How can you possibly say that, *Industry Week* (July 17, 1995): 17–19.

[82]V. Frazee, Establishing relations in Germany, *Workforce* Global Workforce Supplement (April 1997): 16–17.

[83]E. H. Schein, Improving face-to-face relationships, *Sloan Management Review* (Winter 1981): 43–52.

[84]J. H. Simon, U.S.–Japanese management enters a new generation, *Management Review* (February 1991): 42–45.

[85]J. H. Robinson, Professional communication in Korea: Playing things by eye, *IEEE Transactions on Professional Communication* 39 (September 1996): 129–134.

[86]N. Sussman and H. Rosenfeld, Influence of culture, language, and sex on conversational distance, *Journal of Personality and Social Psychology* 42 (1982): 66–74.

[87]W. B. Gudykunst and S. Ting-Toomey, *Culture and Interpersonal Communication* (Newbury Park, CA: Sage, 1988).

[88]N. J. Adler, *International Dimensions of Organizational Behavior,* 3d. ed. (Cincinnati: Southwestern, 1997).

[89]R. C. Maddox and D. Short, The cultural integrator, *Business Horizons* 31 (November–December 1988): 57–59.

CHAPTER 8

[1] P. Sellers, The 50 most powerful women in business: Secrets of the fastest-rising stars, *Fortune* (October 16, 2000): 131–156; D. Clark, H-P awards chairman title to Fiorina, expects to meet profit, revenue targets, *Wall Street Journal* (September 25, 2000): B13; E. Ackerman, Silicon Valley Girl Carly Fiorina gets corner office of her own, *U.S. News and World Report* (August 2, 1999): 44–45; P. Burrows, The boss, *Business Week* (August 2, 1999): 76; R. Charan, How to hire a CEO—Inside or outside? That's question no. 2, *Fortune* (September 6, 1999): 288; K. T. Greenfield, What glass ceiling? *Time Magazine* (August 2, 1999): 72; D. Lewis, In a landmark choice, HP taps Lucent's Fiorina for top post, *The Boston Globe* (July 20, 1999): 1; J. Markoff, HP picks a rising star at Lucent as its chief executive, *New York Times* (July 20, 1999); M. Meyer, In a league of her own, *Newsweek* (August 2, 1999): 56.

[2] B. M. Bass, *Handbook of Leadership: A Survey of Theory and Research* (New York: Praeger, 1981); S. A. Kirkpatrick and E. A. Locke, Leadership: Do traits matter? *Academy of Management Executive* 5(2) (1991): 48–60.

[3] R. M. Stogdill, Personal factors associated with leadership: A survey of the literature, *Journal of Psychology* 25 (1948): 35–71.

[4] S. A. Kirkpatrick and E. A. Locke, Leadership: Do traits matter? *Academy of Management Executive* 5(2) (1991): 49.

[5] Sellers, The 50 most powerful women in business, *op. cit.*

[6] D. Coleman, What makes a leader? *Harvard Business Review* 76(6) (1998): 93–102.

[7] Coleman, What makes a leader? *op. cit.*, p. 95.

[8] M. Warner, Confessions of a control freak, *Fortune* (September 4, 2000): 130–140.

[9] R. M. Stogdill and A. E. Coons (eds.), *Leader Behavior: Its Description and Measurement* (Columbus: Ohio State University Bureau of Business Research, 1957).

[10] E. Fleishman, E. F. Harris, and R. D. Burtt, *Leadership and Supervision in Industry* (Columbus: Ohio State University Press, 1955); E. Fleishman and E. F. Harris, Patterns of leadership behavior related to employee grievances and turnover, *Personnel Psychology* 1 (1959): 45–53.

[11] R. L. Kahn and D. Katz, Leadership practices in relation to productivity and morale. In D. Cartwright and A. Zander (eds.), *Group Dynamics* (Evanston, IL: Row, Peterson, 1953): 585–611.

[12] G. Hamel, Driving grassroots growth, *Fortune* (September 4, 2000): 173–187.

[13] R. Likert, *New Patterns of Management* (New York: McGraw-Hill, 1961).

[14] G. G. Dess and J. C. Picken, Changing roles: Leadership in the 21st century, *Organizational Dynamics* 28(3) (2000): 18–34.

[15] M. Gimein, CEO in motion, *Fortune* (September 4, 2000): 244–250.

[16] S. Wells, *From Sage to Artisan: The Nine Roles of the Value-Driven Leader* (Palo Alto, CA: Davies-Black, 1996).

[17] D. McGregor, *The Human Side of Enterprise* (New York: McGraw-Hill, 1961).

[18] B. Morris, This Ford is different, idealist on board, *Fortune* (April 3, 2000): 123–146.

[19] E. H. Schein, The Hawthorne studies revisited: A defense of Theory Y, Sloan School of Management Working Paper #756-74 (Cambridge: Massachusetts Institute of Technology, 1974).

[20] B. M. Bass, *Bass & Stogdill's Handbook of Leadership: Theory, Research, and Managerial Applications,* 3d ed. (New York: Free Press, 1991).

[21] D. L. Cawthon, Leadership: The great man theory revisited, *Business Horizons* 39 (May/June 1996): 1–4.

[22] C. A. Schriesheim and S. Kerr, Theories and measures of leadership: A critical appraisal. In J. G. Hunt and L. L. Larson (eds.), *Leadership: The Cutting Edge* (Carbondale, IL: Southern Illinois University, 1977); F. Luthans and D. L. Lockwood, Toward an observation system for measuring leader behavior in natural settings. In J. G. Hunt, D. Hosking, C. A. Schriesheim, and R. Stewart (eds.), *Leaders and Managers: International Perspectives on Managerial Behavior and Leadership* (New York: Pergamon, 1984).

[23] B. M. Bass, P. C. Burger, R. Doktor, and G. V. Barrett, *Assessment of Managers: An International Comparison* (New York: Free Press, 1979).

[24] A. J. Ali, A. A. Azim, and K. S. Krishnan, Expatriates and host country nationals: Managerial values and decision styles, *Leadership and Organization Development Journal* 16(6) (1995): 27–34.

[25] R. Hooijberg, A multidirectional approach toward leadership: An extension of the concept of behavioral complexity, *Human Relations* 49 (1996): 917–946, provided empirical support for this observation.

[26] F. E. Fiedler, Engineer the job to fit the manager, *Harvard Business Review* 43 (1965): 115–122; and F. E. Fiedler and M. M. Chemers, *Leadership and Effective Management* (Glenview, IL: Scott, Foresman, 1974) offered the earliest descriptions of this theory. F. E. Fiedler and J. E. Garcia, *New Approaches to Effective Leadership: Cognitive Resources and Organizational Performance* (New York: Wiley, 1987) offers one of the most recent revisions.

[27] L. Willen, Go to the head of the class, *Business Week* (April 3, 2000): 101–104.

[28] F. E. Fiedler, The contribution of cognitive resources to leadership performance, *Journal of Applied Social Psychology* 16 (1986): 532–548; Fiedler and Garcia, *New Approaches to Leadership, op. cit.*

[29]R. J. House, A path-goal theory of leader effectiveness, *Administrative Science Quarterly* 16 (1971): 321–338; R. J. House and T. R. Mitchell, Path-goal theory of leadership, *Journal of Contemporary Business* (Autumn 1974): 81–97; J. Indvik, Path-goal theory of leadership: A meta-analysis, *Proceedings of the Academy of Management* (1986): 189–192; J. Fulk and E. R. Wendler, Dimensionality of leader–subordinate interactions: A path-goal investigation, *Organizational Behavior and Human Performance* 30 (1983): 241–263; G. A. Yukl and J. Clemence, A test of path-goal theory of leadership using questionnaire and diary measures of behavior, *Proceedings of the Twenty-First Annual Meeting of the Eastern Academy of Management* (1984): 174–177.

[30]J. Weber, The mess at Bank One, *Business Week* (May 1, 2000): 162–167.

[31]V. H. Vroom and P. W. Yetton, *Leadership and Decision Making* (Pittsburgh: University of Pittsburgh Press, 1973) presents the original version of the theory; V. H. Vroom and A. G. Jago, *The New Leadership: Managing Participation in Organizations* (Englewood Cliffs, NJ: Prentice Hall, 1988) offers the most recent formulation.

[32]Vroom and Jago, *The New Leadership, op. cit.*

[33]P. Hersey and K. H. Blanchard, *Management of Organizational Behavior: Utilizing Human Resources,* 7th ed. (Englewood Cliffs, NJ: Prentice Hall, 1996); P. Hersey and K. Blanchard, Great ideas revisited: Revisiting the life-cycle theory of leadership, *Training and Development* 50(1) (1996): 42–47.

[34]D. C. Lueder, Don't be mislead by LEAD, *Journal of Applied Behavioral Science* 21 (1985): 143–151; P. Hersey, A letter to the author of "Don't be misled by LEAD," *Journal of Applied Behavioral Science* 21 (1985): 152–153; D. C. Lueder, A rejoinder to Dr. Hersey, *Journal of Applied Behavioral Science* 21 (1985): 154.

[35]D. Brady, Wanted: Eclectic visionary with a sense of humor, *Business Week* (August 28, 2000): 143–144.

[36]J. P. Howell, D. E. Bowen, P. W. Dorfman, S. Kerr, and P. M. Podsakoff, Substitutes for leadership: Effective alternatives to ineffective leadership, *Organizational Dynamics* 19(1) (1990): 21–38.

[37]Howell et al., Substitutes for leadership, *op. cit.*

[38]A. P. Hare, S. E. Hare, H. H. Blumberg, Wishful thinking: Who has the least preferred coworker? *Small Group Research* 29(4) (1998): 419–435; L. H. Peters, D. D. Hartke, and J. T. Pohlman, Fiedler's contingency theory of leadership: An application of the meta-analysis procedures of Schmidt and Hunter, *Psychological Bulletin* 97 (1985): 274–285; J. K. Kennedy Jr., Middle LPC leaders and the contingency model of leadership effectiveness, *Organizational Behavior and Human Performance* 30

(1982): 1–14; Schreisheim and Kerr, *op. cit.*; S. Kerr and A. Harlan, Predicting the effects of leadership training and experience from the contingency model: Some remaining problems, *Journal of Applied Psychology* 57 (1973): 114–117.

[39]Yukl, *Leadership in Organizations, op. cit.*

[40]Yukl, *Leadership in Organizations, op. cit.*

[41]F. E. Fiedler, Research on leadership selection and training: One view of the future, *Administrative Science Quarterly* 41 (1996): 241–250.

[42]J. Cashman, F. Dansereau Jr., G. Graen, and W. J. Haga, Organizational understructure and leadership: A longitudinal investigation of the managerial role-making process, *Organizational Behavior and Human Performance* 15 (1976): 278–296; T. B. Scandura and G. B. Graen, Moderating effects of initial leader-member exchange status on the effects of a leadership intervention, *Journal of Applied Psychology* 69 (1984): 428–436.

[43]H. H. Brower, F. D. Schoorman, and H. H. Tan, A model of relational leadership: The integration of trust and leader–member exchange, *Leadership Quarterly* 11(2) (2000): 227–250.

[44]R. C. Liden and J. M. Maslyn, Multidimensionality of leader–member exchange: An empirical assessment through scale development, *Journal of Management* 24(1) (1998): 43–72.

[45]D. Duchon, S. G. Graen, T. D. Table, Vertical dyad linkage: A longitudinal assessment of antecedents, measures, and consequences, *Journal of Applied Psychology* 71 (1986): 56–60.

[46]R. T. Sparrowe and R. C. Liden, Process and structure in leader–member exchange, *Academy of Management Review* 22 (1997): 522–552.

[47]J. C. McElroy, A typology of attribution leadership research, *Academy of Management Review* 7 (1982): 413–417.

[48]B. Calder, An attribution theory of leadership. In B. H. Staw and G. R. Salancik (eds.), *New Directions in Organizational Behavior* (Chicago: St. Clair Press, 1977).

[49]M. Martinko and W. L. Gardner, The leader/member attribution process, *Academy of Management Review* 12 (1987): 235–240.

[50]T. R. V. Davis and F. Luthans, Leadership reexamined: A behavioral approach, *Academy of Management Review* 4 (1979): 237–248.

[51]C. A. Schriesheim, S. L. Castro, and C. C. Cogliser, Leader–member exchange (LMX) research: A comprehensive review of theory, measurement, and data-analytic practices, *Leadership Quarterly* 10(1) (1999): 63–113.

[52]R. M. Dienesch and R. C. Liden, Leader–member exchange model of leadership: A critique and future

development, *Academy of Management Review* 11 (1986): 618–634; R. P. Vecchio and B. C. Gobdel, The vertical dyad linkage model of leadership: Problems and prospects, *Organizational Behavior and Human Performance* 34 (1984): 5–20.

[53]J. Z. Burns and F. L. Otte, Implications of leader–member exchange theory and research for human resource development research, *Human Resource Development Quarterly* 10(3) (1999): 225–248.

[54]J. C. McElroy and C. B. Shrader, Attribution theories of leadership and network analysis, *Journal of Management* 12 (1986): 351–362.

[55]R. J. House, A 1976 theory of charismatic leadership. In Hunt and Larson (eds.), *Leadership: The Cutting Edge, op. cit.*; J. Conger, *The Charismatic Leader* (San Francisco: Jossey-Bass, 1989); J. Conger and R. N. Kanungo, Toward a behavioral theory of charismatic leadership in organizational settings, *Academy of Management Review* 12 (1987): 637–647.

[56]S. Hamm, Compaq's rockin' boss, *Business Week* (September 4, 2000): 89.

[57]J. Conger and R. N. Kanungo, *Charismatic Leadership in Organizations* (Thousand Oaks, CA: Sage, 1998).

[58]B. M. Bass, *Leadership and Performance Beyond Expectations* (New York: Free Press, 1985).

[59]B. Shamir and J. M. Howell, Organizational and contextual influences in the emergence and effectiveness of charismatic leadership, *Leadership Quarterly* 10(2) (1999): 257–283.

[60]R. J. House, A 1976 theory, *op. cit.*

[61]G. M. Spreitzer, S. C. De Janasz, and R. E. Quinn, Empowered to lead: The role of psychological empowerment in leadership, *Journal of Organizational Behavior* 20(4) (1999): 511–526.

[62]N. D. Nelson, What's in the cards for AMEX? *Fortune* (January 22, 2001): 58–70.

[63]Conger, The charismatic leader, *op. cit.*; J. A. Conger, The dark side of leadership, *Organizational Dynamics* 19(2) (1990): 44–55.

[64]Conger and Kanungo, *Charismatic Leadership in Organizations, op. cit.*

[65]A. Kover, Is Rob Glaser for real? *Fortune* (September 4, 2000): 216–222.

[66]Kover, Is Rob Glaser for real? *op. cit.*

[67]B. M. Bass, Leadership, Good, better, best, *Organizational Dynamics* 13(3) (1985): 26–40.

[68]I. C. MacMillan, New business development: A challenge to transformational leadership, *Human Resource Management* 26 (1987): 439–454.

[69]J. J. Hater and B. M. Bass, Superiors' evaluations and subordinates' perceptions of transformational and transactional leadership, *Journal of Applied Psychology* 73 (1988): 695–702.

[70]B. M. Bass, D. A. Waldman, B. J. Avolio, and M. Bebb, Transformational leadership and the falling dominoes effect, *Group and Organization Studies* 12 (March 1987): 73–87.

[71]J. Barling, T. Weber, and E. K. Kelloway, Effects of transformational leadership training on attitudinal and financial outcomes: A field experiment, *Journal of Applied Psychology* 81 (1996): 827–832.

[72]Conger, The dark side of leadership, *op. cit.*

[73]C. C. Manz and H. P. Sims Jr., Superleadership: Beyond the myth of heroic leadership, *Organizational Dynamics* 19(4) (1991): 18–35; C. C. Manz and H. P. Sims Jr., *Superleadership: Leading Others to Lead Themselves* (Englewood Cliffs, NJ: Prentice Hall, 1989).

[74]Manz and Sims, *Superleadership: Leading Others, op. cit.*; Manz and Sims, Superleadership: Beyond the myth, *op. cit.*

[75]Manz and Sims, Superleadership: Beyond the myth, *op. cit.*

[76]C. P. Neck and C. C. Manz, Thought self-leadership: The impact of mental strategies training on employee cognition, behavior, and affect, *Journal of Organizational Behavior* 17 (1996): 445–467.

[77]Bass, *Leadership and Performance Beyond Expectations, op. cit.*; Bass et al., Transformational leadership and the falling dominoes effect, *op. cit.*; N. M. Tichy and M. A. Devanna, *The Transformational Leader*, 2d ed. (New York: Wiley, 1990); W. G. Bennis and B. Nanus, *Leaders: The Strategies for Taking Charge* (New York: Harper & Row, 1985).

[78]B. S. Pawar and K. K. Eastman, The nature and implications of contextual influences on transformational leadership: A conceptual examination, *Academy of Management Review* 22 (1997): 80–109.

[79]B. M. Bass, Is there universality in the full range model of leadership? *International Journal of Public Administration* 19 (June 1996): 731–761; J. P. Howell and P. W. Dorfman, A comparative study of leadership and its substitutes in a mixed cultural work setting, Unpublished manuscript. Cited in Bass, *Bass & Stogdill's Handbook of Leadership, op. cit.*

[80]K. Tyler, Scoring big in the workplace, *HRMagazine* 45(6) (2000): 96–106.

[81]P. Northouse, *Leadership: Theory and Practice*, 2d ed. (Thousand Oaks, CA: Sage, 2001).

[82]M. Gimein, CEOs who manage too much, *Fortune* (September 4, 2000): 235–242.

[83]Gimein, CEOs who manage too much, *op. cit.*

[84]P. R. Harris and R. T. Moran, *Managing Cultural Differences*, 3d ed. (Houston: Gulf, 1991).

[85]G. Hofstede, Motivation, leadership, and organization: Do American theories apply abroad? *Organizational Dynamics* 9(1) (1980): 42–63.

CHAPTER 9

[1] J. Guyon, The emperor and the investment banks, *Fortune* (May 1, 2000): 134–140; D. Fairlamb, Damage control at Deutsch, *Business Week* (April 17, 2000): 150–151; C. Rhoads and Erik Portanger, American has clout at Deutsch Bank—Investment banker exercised power in abortive merger, *Wall Street Journal* (April 18, 2000): A13.

[2] P. Sellers, The 50 most powerful women in business: Secrets of the fastest-rising stars, *Fortune* (October 16, 2000): 131–160.

[3] H. Mintzberg, *Power in and Around Organizations* (Englewood Cliffs, NJ: Prentice Hall, 1983).

[4] Mintzberg, *Power in and Around Organizations, op. cit.*

[5] W. F. G. Mastenbroek, *Conflict Management and Organization Development* (Chichester, England: Wiley, 1987).

[6] P. P. Fu and G. Yukl, Perceived effectiveness of influence tactics in the United States and China, *Leadership Quarterly* 11(2) (2000): 251–266.

[7] This discussion of dependence is based in large part on J. P. Kotter, Power, dependence, and effective management, *Harvard Business Review* 55(4) (1977): 125–136; and J. P. Kotter, Power, success, and organizational effectiveness, *Organizational Dynamics* 6(3) (1978): 27–40.

[8] A. Toffoletto and L. Toffoletti, Italy: Power and the concept of abuse, *Corporate Finance, Your Guide to Global Competition Law* (July 1999): 25–27.

[9] J. P. Kotter, Power, success, and organizational effectiveness, *op. cit.*

[10] P. M. Blau, *Exchange and Power in Social Life* (New York: John Wiley & Sons, 1964); R. M. Emerson, Power-dependence relations, *American Sociological Review* 27 (1962): 31–41.

[11] B. Markovsky, D. Weller, and T. Patton, Power relations in exchange networks, *American Sociological Review* 53 (1988): 220–236.

[12] R. M. Kanter, The new managerial work, *Harvard Business Review* 67(6) (1989): 85–92.

[13] E. W. K. Tsang, Can *guanxi* be a source of sustained competitive advantage for doing business in China? *Academy of Management Executive* 12(2) (1998): 64–73.

[14] P. Yatsko, The two faces of China, *Fortune* (October 16, 2000): 258–272.

[15] D. H. McClelland and D. H. Burnham, Power driven managers: Good guys make bum bosses, *Psychology Today* (December 1975): 69–71; D. McClelland, *Power: The Inner Experience* (New York: Irvington, 1975).

[16] K. Blanchard, Self-esteem: Taproot of creative expression, *Executive Excellence* 15(1) (1998): 8.

[17] W. C. Grams and R. W. Rogers, Power and personality: Effects of Machiavellianism, need for approval, and motivation on use of tactics, *Journal of General Psychology* 117(1) (1990): 71–82.

[18] See, for example, R. M. Kanter, *The Change Masters* (New York: Simon and Schuster, 1983); and W. W. Burke, Leadership as empowering others. In S. Srivastva and Associates, *Executive Power* (San Francisco: Jossey-Bass, 1986); J. A. Conger and R. N. Kanungo, The empowerment process: Integrating theory and practice, *Academy of Management Review* 13 (1988): 471–482.

[19] G. Hasek, Extraordinary extrusions, *Industry Week* 249 (17) (2000): 79–80.

[20] Conger and Kanungo, Integrating theory and practice, *op. cit.*

[21] J. A. Conger, Leadership: The art of empowering others, *Academy of Management Executive* 3(1) (1989): 17–24.

[22] M. Z. Hackman and C. E. Johnson, *Leadership: A Communication Perspective,* 2d ed. (Prospect Heights, IL: Waveland Press, 1996).

[23] J. Jusko, Turning ideas into action, *Industry Week* 249(17) (2000): 105–106.

[24] T. Mudd, Opening the door to success, *Industry Week* 279(17) (2000): 115–116.

[25] R. Forrester, Empowerment: Rejuvenating a potent idea, *Academy of Management Executive* 14(3) (2000): 67–80.

[26] Forrester, Empowerment, *op. cit.*

[27] T. W. Malone, Is empowerment just a fad? Control, decision making, and IT, *Sloan Management Review* 38(2) (1997): 23–35.

[28] R. Forrester, Empowerment, *op. cit.*

[29] L. E. Atwater and W. J. Wright, Power and transformation and transactional leadership in public and private organizations, *International Journal of Public Administration* 19(6) (1996): 963–989.

[30] L. L. Carli, Gender, interpersonal power, social influence, *Journal of Social Issues* 55(1) (1999): 81–99.

[31] D. Hislop, S. Newell, H. Scarbrough, and J. Swan, Networks, knowledge and power: Decision making, politics and the process of innovation, *Technology Analysis & Strategic Management* 12(3) (2000): 399–411.

[32] See W. G. Astley and P. S. Sachdeva, Structural sources of intraorganizational power: A theoretical synthesis, *Academy of Management Review* 9 (1984): 104–113; I. Cohen and R. Lachman, The generosity of the strategic contingencies approach to sub-unit power within top management teams, *Organization Studies* 9(3) (1984): 104–113, provide recent empirical support for the strategic contingencies theory of organizational behavior originally described in D. J. Hickson, C. R. Hinings, C. A. Lee, R. E. Schneck, and J. M. Pennings, A strategic contingencies' theory of intraorganizational power, *Administrative Science Quarterly* 16 (1971): 216–227.

[33]D. J. Brass and M. E. Burkhardt, Potential power and power use: An investigation of structure and behavior, *Academy of Management Journal* 36 (1993): 441–470.

[34]R. A. Prince and K. M. File, Personal power: Successful client strategy involves three components, *Financial Planning* (July 1, 1999): 157–159.

[35]Sellers, The 50 most powerful women in business, *op. cit.*

[36]J. Conger, Charisma and how to grow it, *Management Today* (December 1999): 78–81.

[37]L. D. Molm, *Coercive Power in Social Exchange* (Cambridge: Cambridge University Press, 1997).

[38]S. J. Pfeffer and G. R. Salancik, *The External Control of Organizations* (New York: Harper & Row, 1978).

[39]D. Farrell and J. C. Petersen, Patterns of political behavior in organizations, *Academy of Management Review* 7 (1982): 403–412.

[40]D. Krackhardt and J. R. Hanson, Informal networks: The company behind the chart, *Harvard Business Review* 71(4) (1993): 104–111.

[41]Sellers, The 50 most powerful women in business, *op. cit.*

[42]S. Kim, Women flex their union muscle, *MS.* 10(3) (2000): 26.

[43]D. Cohen, New Zealand's "new-girl network" at the top: A new governor-general solidifies the cluster of high-ranking women in government, *Christian Science Monitor* (September 8, 2000): 7.

[44]E. Williamson, Linking up: In Poland, the "Ladies of business" change system from inside—Women seek to build on record of gains since fall of the Wall—From loophole to success, *Wall Street Journal Europe* (November 26, 1999): 1.

[45]A. Downs, Women taking steps to gain toehold in political funding, *Boston Globe* (May 17, 1998): 11.

[46]R. E. Kaplan, Trade routes: The manager's network of relationships, *Organizational Dynamics* 12(4) (1984): 37–42.

[47]A. R. Cohen and D. L. Bradford, Influence without authority: The use of alliances, reciprocity, and exchange to accomplish work, *Organizational Dynamics* 17(3) (1989): 4–17.

[48]A. C. Inkpen and P. W. Beamish, Knowledge, bargaining power, and the instability of international joint ventures, *Academy of Management Review* 22 (1997): 177–202.

[49]D. K. Banner and T. E. Gagné, *Designing Effective Organizations: Traditional & Transformational Views* (Thousand Oaks, CA: Sage, 1995).

[50]G. R. Ferris and T. R. King, Politics in human resources decisions: A walk on the dark side, *Organizational Dynamics* 20(2) (1991): 59–70.

[51]L. A. Witt, M. C. Andrews, and K. M. Kacmar, The role of participation in decision-making in the organizational politics–job satisfaction relationship, *Human Relations* 53(3) (2000): 341–358.

[52]G. R. Ferris, D. D. Frink, M. C. Galang, and J. Zhou, Perceptions of organizational politics: Prediction, stress-related implications, and outcomes, *Human Relations* 49 (1996): 233–266.

[53]J. J. Voyer, Coercive organizational politics and organizational outcomes: An interpretive study, *Organization Science* 5(1) (1994): 72–85.

[54]A. Drory, Perceived political climate and job attitudes, *Organization Studies* 14(1) (1993): 59–71.

[55]D. C. Gilmore, G. R. Ferris, J. H. Dulebohn, and G. Harrell-Cook, Organizational politics and employee attendance, *Group and Organization Management* 21 (1996): 481–494.

[56]R. Cropanzano, J. C. Howes, A. A. Grandey, and P. Toth, The relationship of organizational politics and support to work behaviors, attitudes, and stress, *Journal of Organizational Behavior* 18 (1997): 159–180.

[57]K. Neville, *Internal Affairs: The Abuse of Power, Sexual Harassment, and Hypocrisy in the Workplace* (New York: McGraw-Hill, 2000).

[58]J. Weiss, Few women leaders surprised by Army harassment case, *Boston Globe* (April 1, 2000): A1.

[59]J. S. Segal, Sexual harassment prevention: Cement for the glass ceiling? *HRMagazine* 43(12) (1998): 129–136.

[60]M. Horn, Sex & the CEO, *U.S. News & World Report* (July 6, 1998): 32–40.

[61]E. Peirce, C. A. Smolinski, and B. Rosen, Why sexual harassment complaints fall on deaf ears, *Academy of Management Executive* 12(3) (1998): 41–54.

[62]Peirce et al., Why sexual harassment complaints fall on deaf ears, *op. cit.*

[63]L. Martin, A model program against sexual harassment at the Department of Labor, *Employment Relations Today* 18 (1991/1992): 429–432.

[64]M. E. Conway, Sexual harassment abroad, *Workforce* 3(5) (1998): 8–9.

[65]B. Kabanoff, Potential influence structures as sources of interpersonal conflict in groups and organizations, *Organizational Behavior and Human Decision Processes* 36 (1985): 115.

[66]M. Deutsch, Subjective features of conflict resolution: Psychological, social, and cultural influences. In R. Vayrynen, *New Directions in Conflict Theory: Conflict Resolution and Conflict Transformation* (London: Sage, 1991).

[67]D. M. Kolb and L. L. Putnam, The dialectics of disputing. In D. M. Kolb and J. M. Bartunek (eds.), *Hidden Conflict in Organizations* (Newbury Park, CA: Sage, 1992): p. 18; D. M. Kolb and L. L. Putnam,

The multiple faces of conflict in organizations, *Journal of Organizational Behavior* 13 (1992): 311–324.

[68]A. C. Filley, *Interpersonal Conflict Resolution* (Glenview, IL: Scott, Foresman, 1975).

[69]J. A. Wall Jr. and R. R. Callister, Conflict and its management, *Journal of Management* 21 (1995): 515–558.

[70]V. I. Sessa, Using perspective taking to manage conflict and affect in teams, *Journal of Applied Behavioral Science* 32(1) (1996): 101–115; A. Kruse, Third-party roles in conflict management, *Training & Development* 49(5) (1995): 74–76.

[71]R. L. Pinkley and G. B. Northcraft, Conflict frames of reference: Implications for dispute processes and outcomes, *Academy of Management Journal* 37 (1994): 193–205; R. L. Pinkley, Dimensions of conflict frame: Disputant interpretations of conflict, *Journal of Applied Psychology* 75 (1990): 117–126.

[72]See R. L. Kahn, D. M. Wolfe, R. P. Quinn, and J. D. Snoek, *Organizational Stress: Studies in Role Conflict and Ambiguity* (New York: John Wiley, 1964) for the classic discussion, and M. Van Sell, A. P. Brief, and R. S. Schuler, Role conflict and role ambiguity: Integration of the literature and directions for future research, *Human Relations* 34 (1981): 43–71; S. E. Jackson and R. S. Schuler, A meta-analysis and conceptual critique of research on role ambiguity and role conflict in work settings, *Organizational Behavior and Human Decision Processes* 36 (1985): 16–78; K. Klenke-Hamel and J. E. Mathieu, Role strains, tension, and job satisfaction influences on employees' propensity to leave: A multi-sample replication and extension, *Human Relations* 43 (1990): 791–807; E. Kemery, A. G. Bedeian, K. W. Mossholder, and J. Touliatos, Outcomes of role stress: A multisample constructive replication, *Academy of Management Journal* 28 (1985): 363–375; J. Schaubroeck, J. L. Cotten, and K. R. Jennings, Antecedents and consequences of roll stress: A covariance structure analysis, *Journal of Organizational Behavior* 10 (1989): 35–58 for a more recent discussion.

[73]C. D. Fisher and R. Gitelson, A meta-analysis of the correlates of role conflict and ambiguity, *Journal of Applied Psychology* 68 (1983): 320–333; A. G. Bedeian and A. A. Armenakis, A path-analytic study of the consequences of role conflict and ambiguity, *Academy of Management Journal* 24 (1981): 417–424.

[74]D. Whitford, Sammy Sosa's foundation is a major league fiasco, *Fortune* (April 17, 2000): 68–72.

[75]T. J. Hoff, The social organization of physician-managers in a changing HMO, *Work and Occupation* 26(3) (1999): 324–351.

[76]R. A. Baron, Personality and organizational conflict: Effects of the Type A behavior pattern and self-monitoring, *Organizational Behavior and Human Decision Processes* 44 (1989): 281–296.

[77]H. W. Nelson, Injustice and conflict in nursing homes: Toward advocacy and exchange, *Journal of Aging Studies* 14(1) (2000): 39–61.

[78]T. Cox Jr., *Cultural Diversity in Organizations: Theory, Research and Practice* (San Francisco: Berrett-Koehler, 1993).

[79]B. Gilbert, Casting a giant shadow, *Bank Systems & Technology* 37(10) (2000): S9.

[80]J. Pfeffer, Beyond management and the workers: The institutional function of management, *Academy of Management Review* 1 (1976): 26–46; H. Assael, Constructive roles of interorganizational conflict, *Administrative Science Quarterly* 14 (1968): 573–581.

[81]L. R. Pondy, Organizational conflict: Concepts and models, *Administrative Science Quarterly* 12 (1967): 296–320.

[82]M. Egbers and J. Van der Vurst, Interpersonal conflict resolution: The unconscious ally, *Leadership and Organization Development Journal* 7(5) (1986): iii.

[83]This discussion of hidden conflict is based on D. M. Kolb and L. L. Putnam, Introduction: The dialectics of disputing. In D. M. Kolb and J. M. Bartunek (eds.), *Hidden Conflict in Organizations, op cit.* J. M. Bartunek, D. M. Kolb, and R. J. Lewicki, Bringing conflict out from behind the scenes: Private, informal, and nonrational dimensions of conflict in organizations. In Kolb and Bartunek (eds.), *Hidden Conflict in Organizations,* op. cit.

[84]This discussion is drawn from Deutsch, Subjective features, *op. cit.*

[85]K. A. Jehn, A multimethod examination of the benefits and detriments of intragroup conflict, *Administrative Science Quarterly* 40 (1995): 256–282.

[86]Wall and Callister, Conflict and its management, *op. cit.*

[87]L. Greenhalgh, Managing conflict, *Sloan Management Review* 27(4) (1986): 45–51.

[88]Sessa, Using perspective taking, *op. cit.*

[89]Thomas, Conflict and conflict management, *op. cit.*

[90]R. A. Friedman, S. T. Tidd, S. C. Currall, and J. C. Tsai, What goes around comes around: The impact of personal conflict style on work conflict and stress, *International Journal of Conflict Management* 11(1) (2000): 32–55.

[91]This grouping with the exception of arbitration is presented by J. Stockard and D. Lach, Conflict resolution: Sex and gender roles. In J. B. Gittler, *The Annual Review of Conflict Knowledge and Conflict Resolution,* vol. 1 (New York: Garland, 1989): 69–91.

[92]S. Shellenbarger, Companies are finding real payoffs in aiding employee satisfaction, *Wall Street Journal* (October 11, 2000): B1.

[93]P. M. Buhler, The manager's role in preventing sexual harassment, *Supervision* 60(4) (1999): 16–18.

[94]R. S. Slotnick, Resolving arguments by design, *American Scientist* 88(4) (2000): 315.

[95]S. Chaabane and L. H. Mouss, Occupational health and safety in Algeria, *The Safety & Health Practitioner* 16(12) (1998): 23–25.

[96]J. H. Keil, "Hybrid ADR" in the construction industry, *Dispute Resolution Journal* 54(3) (1999): 14–22.

[97]P. L. Perrewe, G. R. Ferris, D. D. Frink, and W. P. Anthony, Political skills: An antidote for workplace stressors, *Academy of Management Executive* 14(3) (2000): 115–123.

[98]S. M. Jex, *Stress and Job Performance* (Thousand Oaks, CA: Sage, 1998).

[99]P. E. Spector and B. J. O'Connell, The contribution of personality traits, negative affectivity, locus of control and Type A to the subsequent reports of job stressors and job strains, *Journal of Occupational and Organizational Psychology* 67(1) (1994): 1–12 illustrates this relationship.

[100]L. Piccoli, J. M. Emig, and K. M. Hiltebeitel, Why is public accounting stressful? Is it especially stressful for women? *The Woman CPA* 50(3) (1988): 8–12.

[101]V. J. Doby and R. D. Caplan, Organizational stress as threat to reputation: Effects on anxiety at work and at home, *Academy of Management Journal* 38 (1995): 1105–1123.

[102]D. R. Frew and N. W. Burning, Perceived organizational characteristics and personality measures as predictors of stress/strain in the workplace, *Journal of Management* 13 (1987): 633–646.

[103]T. H. Holmes, Social readjustment rating scale, *Journal of Psychosomatic Research* 11 (1967).

[104]D. L. Nelson and R. J. Burke, Women executives: Health, stress, and success, *Academy of Management Executive* 14(2) (2000): 107–121.

[105]Cordes and Dougherty, A review and integration, *op. cit.*

[106]V. Culver, Clergy told to watch for signs of burnout, *Denver Post* (October 28, 2000): B–06.

[107]D. Kennedy, Curbing burnout in the 24/7 salesperson, *Realtor Magazine* 33(7) (2000): 33.

[108]C. L. Cordes and T. W. Dougherty, A review and an integration of research on job burnout, *Academy of Management Review* 18 (1993): 621–656; D. Friesen and J. C. Sarros, Sources of burnout among educators, *Journal of Organizational Behavior* 10 (1989): 179–188; W. D. Paine (ed.), *Job Stress and Burnout: Research, Theory, and Intervention Perspectives* (Beverly Hills, CA: Sage, 1982); R. Golembiewski and R. F. Munzenrider, *Phases of Burnout: Developments in Concepts and Applications* (New York: Praeger, 1988).

[109]R. T. Lee and B. E. Ashforth, A further examination of managerial burnout: Toward an integrated model, *Journal of Organizational Behavior* 14 (1993): 3–20.

[110]A. B. Slaby, *60 Ways to Make Stress Work for You* (Summit, NJ: PIA Press, 1988).

[111]R. S. DeFrank and J. M. Ivancevich, Stress on the job: An executive update, *Academy of Management Executive* 12(3) (1998): 55–66.

[112]T. D. Jick and R. Payne, Stress at work, *Exchange: The Organizational Behavior Teaching Journal* 5 (1980): 50–56.

[113]J. R. Terborg, Health promotion at the worksite: A research challenge for personnel and human resources management. In K. H. Rowland and G. R. Ferris (eds.), *Research Personnel and Human Resource Management*, vol. 4 (Greenwich, CT: JAI Press 1986): 225–267; B. D. Steffy, J. W. Jones, and A. W. Noe, The impact of health habits and life-style on the stressor-strain relationship: An evaluation of three industries, *Journal of Occupational Psychology* 63 (1990): 217–229.

[114]A. Milligan, Wellness programs could be the cure, *Business Insurance* 34(4) (2000): 3, 12.

[115]L. McCreary, World wide wellness, *CIO* 11(18) (1998): 55–56.

[116]Milligan, Wellness programs could be the cure, *op. cit.*

[117]C. J. Guico-Pabia and D. Endsley, Lessons from a health promotion victory, *Business and Health* 18(8) (2000): 43–44.

[118]S. Reese, Setting the pace, *Business and Health* 17(8) (1999): 17–18.

[119]Anonymous, Healthy and wise, *Healthcare PR & Marketing News* 9(20) (2000): 1.

[120]S. Reese, Working around the clock, *Business and Health* 18(4) (2000): 71–72.

[121]K. Hawk, Maintaining a winning team, *Catalog Age* 15(11) (1998): 163.

[122]G. Hofstede, Motivation, leadership, and organization: Do American theories apply abroad? *Organizational Dynamics* 9(1) (1980): 42–63; G. Hofstede, *Culture's Consequences: International Differences in Work-Related Values* (Beverly Hills, CA: Sage, 1980).

[123]Cox, *Cultural Diversity, op. cit.*

[124]E. S. Ekhouly and R. Buda, Organizational conflict: A comparative analysis of conflict styles across cultures, *International Journal of Conflict Management* 7(1) (1996): 71–81.

[125]J. S. Black and M. Mendenhall, Resolving conflicts with the Japanese: Mission impossible? *Sloan Management Review* 34(3) (Spring 1993): 49–59; A. Goldman, A

briefing on cultural and communicative sources of Western–Japanese interorganizational conflict, *Journal of Managerial Psychology* 9(1) (1994): 7–12.

[126]S. Ting-Toomey, Managing intercultural conflict effectively. In L. A. Samovar and R. E. Porter (eds.), *Intercultural Communication: A Reader,* 7th ed. (Belmont, CA: Wadsworth, 1994): 360–372.

[127]Ting-Toomey, Managing intercultural conflict effectively, *op. cit.*

[128]J. L. Xie, Karasek's model in the People's Republic of China: Effects of job demands, control, and individual differences, *Academy of Management Journal* 39 (1996): 1594–1618.

[129]V. J. Sutherland and G. L. Cooper, Chief executive lifestyle stress, *Leadership and Organization Development Journal* 16(7) (1995): 18–28.

[130]S. Moshavi, Japanese are falling prey to effects of overwork, *Boston Globe* (April 6, 2000): A12.

CHAPTER 10

[1]S. Carey and W. Bounds, US Air is poised to resume turnaround if attendants ratify tentative contract, *Wall Street Journal* (March 27, 2000):A3; M. Brelis, If talks don't take off, planes may not either despite US Airway's unveiling of new aircraft, plans to expand, labor dispute threatens to ground airline, *Boston Globe* (March 24, 2000):C1; S. Carey, US Air, union progress, but prepare to shut down, *Wall Street Journal* (March 24, 2000):A3; M. Brelis, US Airways, flight attendants agree to continue contract talks, *Boston Globe* (March 26, 2000):A21; B. Adair and S. Carey, United says US Air purchase will result in more routes to benefit consumers, *Wall Street Journal* (June 1, 2000):A4.

[2]K. K. Smith, An intergroup perspective on individual behavior. In H. J. Leavitt, L. R. Pondy, and D. M. Boje (eds.), *Readings in Managerial Psychology,* 4th ed. (Chicago: University of Chicago Press, 1989).

[3]J. D. Thompson, *Organizations in Action* (New York: McGraw-Hill, 1967); A. H. Van de Ven, A. L. Delbecq, and R. Koenig Jr., Determinants of coordination modes within organizations, *American Sociological Review* 41 (1976): 322–338.

[4]D. W. Johnson and F. P. Johnson, *Cooperation and Competition: Theory and Research* (Edina, MN: Interaction, 1989).

[5]N. Chesanow, When a group's expansion divides a town, *Medical Economics* 75(16) (1998): 44–61.

[6]A. W. Gouldner, Cosmopolitans and locals: Toward an analysis of latent social roles, *Administrative Science Quarterly* 2 (1958): 290.

[7]D. Hickson, C. Hinings, C. Lee, R. Schneck, and J. A. Pennings, A strategic contingencies theory of intraorganizational power, *Administrative Science Quarterly* 23 (1978): 65–90.

[8]R. C. Liden, S. J. Wayne, and L. K. Bradway, Task interdependence as a moderator of the relation between group control and performance, *Human Relations* 50(2) (1997): 169–181.

[9]K. A. Ross, Can diversity and community coexist in higher education? *American Behavioral Scientist* 42(6) (1999): 1024–1040.

[10]M. Trombly, Xerox, Sun and iPlanet team up to ease e-billing, *Computerworld* 34(11) (2000): 20.

[11]R. Beckhard, The confrontation meeting, *Harvard Business Review* 45 (1967): 154, presents an early description of this intervention.

[12]W. L. French and C. H. Bell Jr., *Organization Development: Behavioral Science Interventions for Organization Improvement,* 2d ed. (Englewood Cliffs, NJ: Prentice Hall, 1978).

[13]H. Prien, Strategies for third-party intervention, *Human Relations* 40 (1987): 699–720.

[14]R. R. Blake and J. S. Mouton, Overcoming group warfare, *Harvard Business Review* 62(6) (1984): 98–108.

[15]Blake and Mouton, Overcoming group warfare, *op. cit.*

[16]E. Van de Vliert, Escalative intervention in small-group conflicts, *Journal of Applied Behavioral Science* 21 (1985): 19–36.

[17]K. Dunn, Roche chooses health by promoting prevention, *Workforce* 79(4) (2000): 82–84.

[18]G. S. Vasilash, Accelerating product development for diesel engines, *Automotive Manufacturing & Production* 110(10): (1998): 54–56.

[19]C. Stedman, ERP problems plague college, *Computerworld* 33(47) (1999): 4.

[20]G. S. Russ, M. C. Galang, and G. R. Ferris, Power and influence of the human resources function through boundary spanning and information management, *Human Resource Management Review* 8(2) (1998): 125–148.

[21]M. D. Meznar and D. Nigh, Buffer or bridge? Environmental and organizational determinants of public affairs activities in American firms, *Academy of Management Journal* 38 (1995): 975–996.

[22]L. K. Bradshaw, Principals as boundary spanners: Working collaboratively to solve problems, *National Association of Secondary School Principals* 83(611) (1999): 38–47.

[23]J. B. Hornstein, Planning practice, *Planning* 66(9) (2000): 16–19.

[24]C. F. Holm, Building cohesive physician networks, *Healthcare Executive* 14(2) (1999): 48–49.

[25] D. A. Lax and J. K. Sebenius, *The Manager as Negotiator* (New York: Free Press, 1986).

[26] Lax and Sebenius, *The Manager as Negotiator, op. cit.*

[27] R. Fisher and W. Ury, *Getting to Yes: Negotiating without Giving In* (Boston: Houghton Mifflin, 1981) was an early call for this approach.

[28] N. Wreden, Navigating uncharted waters, *Informationweek* (November 15, 1999): 138–140.

[29] K. S. Devine and P. J. Trayner, Labour-management alliances: The case of Albert Power Limited, *Human Resource Planning* 19(1) (1995): 14–25.

[30] See http://www.negotiatorpro.com.

[31] J. S. Pouliot, Eight steps to success in negotiating, *Nation's Business* 87(4) (1999): 40–42.

[32] R. Gourlay, Negotiations and bargaining, *Management Decision* 25(3) (1987): 23.

[33] C. Harris, What's the hub in the U.S.? *Canadian Insurance* 195(3) (2000): 26–27.

[34] J. F. Brett, R. L. Pinkley, and E. F. Jackofsky, Alternatives to having BATNA in dyadic negotiation: The influence of goals, self-efficacy, and alternatives on negotiated outcomes, *International Journal of Conflict Management* 7 (April 1996): 121–138.

[35] D. Ertel, Turning negotiation into a corporate capability, *Harvard Business Review* 77(3) (1999): 55–70.

[36] M. A. Neale and M. H. Bazerman, *Cognition and Rationality in Negotiation* (New York: Free Press, 1991).

[37] W. P. Bottom and A. Studt, Framing effects and the distributive aspect of integrative bargaining, *Organizational Behavior and Human Decision Processes* 56(3) (1993): 459–474.

[38] J. S. Carroll and M. H. Bazerman, Negotiator cognitions: A descriptive approach to negotiators' understanding of their opponents, *Organizational Behavior and Human Decision Processes* 41 (1988): 352–370.

[39] Lax and Sebenius, *The Manager as Negotiator, op. cit.*

[40] L. H. Harrington, Mr. Toad's wild ride, *Industry Week* 248(19) (1999): 109–118.

[41] Neale and Bazerman, *Cognition and Rationality in Negotiation, op. cit.*

[42] P. Nulty, Look what the unions want now, *Fortune* (February 8, 1993): 128–135.

[43] Lax and Sebenius, *The Manager as Negotiator, op. cit.*

[44] B. Kirchheimer, On again, off again, *Modern Healthcare* 30(36) (2000): 36–39.

[45] R. T. Moran and W. G. Stripp, *Dynamics of Successful International Business Negotiations* (Houston: Gulf, 1991).

[46] R. Fisher and S. Brown, *Getting Together* (Boston: Houghton-Mifflin, 1988).

[47] R. W. Johnson, Negotiating strategies: Different strokes for different folks, *Personnel* (March/April 1982).

[48] G. T. Savage, J. D. Blair, and R. L. Sorenson, Consider both relationships and substance when negotiating strategically, *Academy of Management Executive* 3(1) (1989): 37–48.

[49] D. M. Kolb and J. Williams, *The Shadow Negotiation: How Women Can Master the Hidden Agendas That Determine Bargaining Success* (New York: Simon & Schuster, 2000).

[50] J. Nierenberg and I. S. Ross, *Women and the Art of Negotiating* (New York: Simon and Schuster, 1985).

[51] Kolb and Williams, *The Shadow Negotiation, op. cit.*

[52] J. M. Brett, D. L. Shapiro, and A. E. Lytle, Breaking the bonds of reciprocity in negotiations, *Academy of Management Journal* 41(4) (1998): 410–424.

[53] R. J. Lewicki and R. J. Robinson, Ethical and unethical bargaining tactics: An empirical study, *Journal of Business Ethics* 17(6) (1998): 665–682.

[54] M. Schuman and J. L. Lee, North Korea delays summit with the South—Technical problems force postponement of meeting, *Asian Wall Street Journal* (June 12, 2000): 1.

[55] M. C. Jaklevic, What hospitals "see" they get, *Modern Healthcare* 30(10) (2000): 60–62.

[56] Ertel, Turning negotiation into a corporate capability, *op. cit.*

[57] R. Karpinski, GM expands e-biz scope, *Internetweek* (March 15, 1999): PG1.

[58] F. Elashmawi and P. R. Harris, *Multicultural Management: New Skills for Global Success* (Houston: Gulf, 1993): 162.

[59] J. M. Brett and T. Okumura, Inter- and intracultural negotiation: U.S. and Japanese negotiators, *Academy of Management Journal* 41(5) (1998): 495–510.

[60] R. Volkema, Perceptual differences in appropriateness and likelihood of use of negotiation behaviors: A cross-cultural analysis, *International Executive* (May/June 1997): 335–350.

[61] J. A. Reeder, When West meets East: Cultural aspects of doing business in Asia, *Business Horizons* 30 (1) (1987): 263–275.

[62] N. J. Adler, *International Dimensions of Organizational Behavior,* 3d ed. (Cincinnati: Southwestern, 1997).

[63] E. S. Glenn, D. Witmeyer, and K. A. Stevenson, Cultural styles of persuasion, *International Journal of Intercultural Relations,* vol. 1 (New York: Pergamon, 1984).

[64] S. Frank, Global negotiating: Vive les differences! *Sales & Marketing Management* 144(5) (1992): 64–69.

[65] Glenn et al., Cultural styles of persuasion, *op. cit.*

CHAPTER 11

[1] J. Hamilton, Net work, *Business Week E.Biz* (April 2000): EB116–EB129.

[2]R. H. Kilmann, M. J. Saxton, and R. Serpa, Issues in understanding and changing culture, *California Management Review* 28 (1986): 87–94; E. H. Schein, *Organizational Culture and Leadership* (San Francisco: Jossey-Bass, 1985); E. H. Schein, Organizational Culture, *American Psychologist* 45(2) (1990): 109–119.

[3]N. C. Morey and F. Luthans, Refining the displacement of culture and the uses of scenes and themes in organizational studies, *Academy of Management Review* 10 (1985): 219–229; M. R. Louis, Organizations as culture-bearing milieux. In L. R. Pondy et al. (eds.), *Organizational Symbolism* (Greenwich, CT: JAI, 1980); G. Morgan, *Images of Organizations* (Beverly Hills: Sage, 1986).

[4]L. Goff, The top five, *Computerworld* 33(26) (1999): CW4–CW10.

[5]M. Schultz, *On Studying Organizational Cultures: Diagnosis and Understanding* (New York: De Gruyter, 1995).

[6]D. Littlefield, Kerry's heroes, *People Management* 5(9) (1999): 48–50.

[7]J. A. Chatman and K. A. Jehn, Assessing the relationship between industry characteristics and organizational culture: How different can you be? *Academy of Management Journal* 37 (1994): 522–553.

[8]S. G. Harris, Organizational culture and individual sensemaking: A schema-based perspective, *Organization Science* 5(3) (1994): 309–321.

[9]Hamilton, Net work, *op. cit.*

[10]J. P. Kotter and J. C. Heskett, *Corporate Culture and Performance* (New York: Free Press, 1992).

[11]W. E. Fulmer, *Shaping the Adaptive Organization: Landscapes, Learning, and Leadership in Volatile Times* (New York: AMACOM, 2000).

[12]P. Galuszka, Is P&G's makeover only skin-deep? *Business Week* (November 15, 1999): 52.

[13]Schultz, *On Studying Organizational Cultures, op. cit.*

[14]Anonymous, Cultural ambassadors likeliest leaders, *Chain Store Age* 75(13) (1999): 76–77; Anonymous, Attitude becomes the chief export, *Chain Store Age* 75(13) (1999): 82–83.

[15]T. Rollins and D. Roberts, *Work culture, organizational performance, and business success* (Westport, CT: Quorum Books, 1998).

[16]C. Hymowitz, Which corporate culture fits you? *Wall Street Journal* (July 17, 1989): B-1.

[17]J. Martin and D. Myerson, Organizational culture and the denial, channeling, and acknowledgement of ambiguity. In L. R. Pondy, R. J. Boland Jr., and H. Thomas (eds.), *Managing Ambiguity and Change* (New York: Wiley, 1988), and D. Meyerson and J. Martin, Cultural change: An integration of three different views, *Journal of Management Studies* 24 (1987): 623–647 provide the original categorization of perspectives; P. J. Frost, L. F. Moore, M. R. Louis, C. C. Sundberg, and J. Martin (eds.), *Reframing Organizational Culture* (Newbury Park, CA: Sage, 1991) offer additional discussion and examples.

[18]N. Page, Intangible—but with an ever-increasing value: Corporate culture, *Financial Times* (October 1, 1999): 4.

[19]J. Martin, *Cultures in Organizations: Three Perspectives* (New York: Oxford, 1992).

[20]C. O'Reilly, J. Chatman, and D. Caldwell, People and organizational culture: A Q-sort approach to assessing person–organization fit, *Academy of Management Journal* 34 (1991): 487–516.

[21]Chatman and Jehn, Assessing the relationship, *op. cit.*

[22]Chatman and Jehn, Assessing the relationship, *op. cit.*

[23]R. Recardo and J. Jolly, Organizational culture and teams, *SAM Advanced Management Journal* 62(2) (Spring 1997): 4–7.

[24]D. R. Denison and A. K. Mishra, Toward a theory of organizational culture and effectiveness, *Organization Science* 6(2) (1995): 204–223.

[25]See D. R. Denison, *Corporate Culture and Organizational Effectiveness* (New York: Wiley, 1990).

[26]W. Altomonte, W. Mooney, and D. H. Sheldon, Cultural change—empowerment at Sweetheart Cup Company, Inc., bakery division, *Hospital Material Management Quarterly* 21(1) (1999): 53–58.

[27]L. Schein, *A Manager's Guide to Corporate Culture* (New York: The Conference Board, 1989).

[28]W. W. George, Mission driven, values centered, *Executive Excellence* 16(8) (1999): 6–7.

[29]W. Umiker, Organizational culture: The role of management and supervisors, *The Health Care Supervisor* 17(4) (1999): 22–27.

[30]V. Sathe, *Culture and Related Corporate Realities* (Homewood, IL: Irwin, 1985); E. H. Schein, *Organizational Culture and Leadership,* 2d ed. (San Francisco: Jossey-Bass, 1992).

[31]M. Whitehead, Hat trick, *People Management* 5(19) (1999): 38–40.

[32]http://www.accessatlanta.com/community/groups/jdf/, October 9, 2000.

[33]http://www.arrow.ccsd.k12.co.us/HTML/mission.htm, October 9, 2000.

[34]Schein, *Organizational Culture and Leadership, op. cit.*

[35]M. J. Hatch, The dynamics of organizational culture, *Academy of Management Review* 18 (1993): 657–693.

[36]J. Veiga, M. Lubatkin, R. Calori, and P. Very, Measuring organizational culture clashes: A two-nation post-hoc analysis of a cultural compatibility index, *Human Relations* 53(4) (2000): 539–557.

[37]J. Abrahams, *The Mission Statement Book: 301 Mission Statements from America's Top Companies* (Berkeley, CA: Ten Speed Press, 1995).

[38]G. G. Gordon, Industry determinants of organizational culture, *Academy of Management Review* 16(2) (1991): 396–415.

[39]M. Conlin and K. Moore, Dr. Goodnight's company town, *Business Week* (June 19, 2000): 192–202.

[40]T. E. Deal and A. A. Kennedy, *Corporate Cultures* (Reading, MA: Addison-Wesley, 1982).

[41]N. Wood, BMI: Boldt Metronics International, *Incentive* 173(12) (1999): 20–21.

[42]S. L. Solberg, Changing culture through ceremony: An example from GM, *Human Resources Management* 24 (Fall 1985): 329–340.

[43]M. Prewitt, Corporate culture: MRG adopts bigger firms' synergistic precepts, *Nation's Restaurant News* 33(32) (1999): 82, 86.

[44]H. M. Trice and J. M. Beyer, *The Cultures of Work Organizations* (Englewood Cliffs, NJ: Prentice Hall, 1993).

[45]D. Pillsbury, Michigan Millers refocuses on service, *Rough Notes* 142(8) (1999): 30–31.

[46]B. Morris, Can Michael Dell escape the box? *Fortune* (October 16, 2000): 93–110.

[47]L. G. Paul, Work and play, *CIO* 13(5) (1999): 80–87.

[48]E. B. Walker and J. A. Maune, Creating an extraordinary safety culture, *Professional Safety* 45(5) (2000): 33–37.

[49]M. Gunther, Eisner's mouse trap, *Fortune* (September 6, 1999): 106–118.

[50]M. Duff, L. Heller, R. Scalley, and M. Troy, HQ scores top grade with A+ motivation message, *Discount Store News* (April 2000): 44–47.

[51]M. Ritchie, Organizational culture: An examination of its effect on the internalization process and member performance, *Southern Business Review* 25(2) (2000):1–13.

[52]M. Leuchter, DLJ fights its way forward, *USBanker* 110(6) (2000): 52–57.

[53]V. Sathe, How to decipher and change culture. In R. H. Kilmann, M. J. Saxton, R. Serpa, and associates (eds.), *Gaining Control of Corporate Culture* (San Francisco: Jossey-Bass, 1985).

[54]M. Heberling, M. Quinn, and E. L. Tucker, Merging health care systems write a single prescription for core competency, *The Journal for Quality and Participation* 22(6) (1999): 56–68.

[55]J. Van Maanen, People processing: Strategies of organizational socialization *Organizational Dynamics* 7(1) (1978): 19–36.

[56]C. A. King, From lone ranger to team player, *National Underwriter* 103(27) (1999): 29–30.

[57]M. Hickins, Xerox shares its knowledge, *Management Review* 88(8) (1999): 40–45.

[58]Anonymous, Merger brief: The DaimlerChrysler emulsion, *The Economist* 356(8181)(2000): 67–68.

[59]L. C. Harris and E. Ogbonna, Employee responses to culture change efforts, *Human Resource Management Journal* 8(2) (1998): 78–92.

[60]R. L. Allen, Post-buyout Bertucci's places focus on chain's trattoria roots, *Nation's Restaurant News* 33(34) (1999): 4, 125.

[61]A. L. Velocci Jr., Lockheed Martin shaking up company culture in LM21 effort, *Aviation Week & Space Technology* 151(13) (1999): 55–56.

[62]T. Smart, How travelers got moving again, *Business Week* (December 4, 1995): 96.

[63]P. Sellers, "CEO deathmatch! Behind the shootout at Citigroup," *Fortune* (March 20, 2000): 28.

[64]A. L. Wilkins and W. G. Dyer Jr., Toward culturally sensitive theories of cultural change, *Academy of Management Review* 13 (1988): 522–533; E. H. Schein, *Organizational Culture and Leadership, op. cit.*

[65]J. Sheriton and J. Stern, HR's role in culture change, *HR Focus* 74(4) (1997): 27.

[66]R. Carey and C. Meyers, The new breed, *Successful Meetings* 49(2) (2000): 36–42.

[67]L. Estell, Corporate spotlight: Greenfield Online, *Incentive* 174(2) (2000): 26–27.

[68]K. Dunn, Values training spans from Boston to Bangkok, *Workforce* 79(2) (2000): 90–91.

[69]J. Rohwer, GE digs into Asia, *Fortune* (October 2, 2000): 164–178.

[70]N. Bromell, Voulez-vous Yahoo avec moi? *Fortune* (October 16, 2000): 245–254.

[71]C. F. Fey, C. Nordahl, H. Zatterstrom, Organizational culture in Russia: The secret to success, *Business Horizons* 42(6) (1999): 47–55.

CHAPTER 12

[1]A. Kupfer, Don't copy this turnaround strategy: Xerox jam is too much for Thoman, *Fortune* (May 29, 2000): 42–44; W. Zellner, Xerox: Rick Thoman speaks up for himself, *Business Week* (May 29, 2000): 51–52; J. G. Auerbach and J. S. Lublin, Tech stock focus: Xerox struggles to boost morale amid staff cuts— Salespeople are thrown by reorganization, *Asian Wall Street Journal* (May 16, 2000): 17.

[2]P. R. Lawrence and J. W. Lorsch, Differentiation and integration in complex organizations, *Administrative Science Quarterly* 12 (1967): 1–47 offers an early discussion of division of labor.

[3]H. Mintzberg, *Structure in Fives: Designing Effective Organizations* (Englewood Cliffs, NJ: Prentice Hall, 1983).

[4]L. Scism, Despite strides made against churning, Caution is key in purchasing insurance, *Wall Street Journal* (January 21, 1998): C1.

[5]D. Howell, JCPenney making shifts in structure to boost quality, *Discount Store News* 39(3) (2000): 6, 74.

[6]L. H. Kaufman, Centralized or decentralized management? *Railway Age* 201(8) (2000): 47–52.

[7]J. Tata, S. Prasad, and R. Thorn, The influence of organizational structure on the effectiveness of TQM programs, *Journal of Managerial Issues* 11(4) (1999): 440–453.

[8]J. Fulk and B. Boyd, Emerging theories of communication in organizations, *Journal of Management* 17 (1991): 407–446.

[9]M. Slott, Springs reorganizes team into functional structure, *Home Textiles Today* 21(9) (1999): 1.

[10]Mintzberg, *Structure in Fives, op. cit.*

[11]Mintzberg, *Structure in Fives, op. cit.*

[12]Mintzberg, *Structure in Fives, op. cit.*

[13]E. Neuborne and R. Berner, Warm and fuzzy won't save Procter & Gamble, *Business Week* (June 26, 2000): 48.

[14]Mintzberg, *Structure in Fives, op. cit.*

[15]Anonymous, AA revamps outsourcing, *Public Accounting Report* 22(23) (1998): 7.

[16]L. W. Burns and D. R. Wholey, Adoption and abandonment of matrix management programs: Effects of organizational characteristics and interorganizational networks, *Academy of Management Journal* 36 (1993): 106–138.

[17]B. Dyer, A. K. Gupta, and D. Wilemon, What first-to-market companies do differently, *Research Technology Management* 42(2) (1999): 15–21.

[18]F. Ostroff, *The Horizontal Organization* (New York: Oxford, 1999); J. A. Byrne, The horizontal corporation, *Business Week* (December 20, 1993): 76–82; T. A. Stewart, The search for the organization of tomorrow, *Fortune* (May 18, 1992): 92–98; T. Brown, Future organizations, *Industry Week* (November 1, 1993): 20–28.

[19]Ostroff, *The Horizontal Organization, op. cit.*

[20]Ostroff, *The Horizontal Organization, op. cit.;* Byrne, The horizontal corporation, *op. cit.*

[21]Ostroff, *The Horizontal Organization, op. cit.*

[22]This discussion is primarily drawn from G. Hasek, The right chemistry, *Industry Week* 249(9) (2000): 36–39.

[23]R. Whiting, Business intelligence: IBM and SAS team up, *Informationweek* (January 31, 2000): 28.

[24]U. S. Rangan and M. Y. Yoshino, Forging alliances: A guide to top management, *Columbia Journal of World Business* 31(3) (1996): 6–13.

[25]G. Manuel, "CyberWorks and Telstra plan pan-Asian network—Mobile service would be first to cover region—Joint venture could seek IPO next year, *Asian Wall Street Journal* (October 17, 2000): 8.

[26]R. Gulati, Social structure and alliance formation patterns: A longitudinal analysis, *Administrative Science Quarterly* 40 (1995): 443–461.

[27]G. Taninecz, Forging the chain, *Industry Week* 249(10) (2000): 40–46.

[28]W. F. Cascio and M. G. Serapio Jr., Human resources systems in an international alliance: The undoing of a done deal, *Organizational Dynamics* 19(3) (1991): 63–74.

[29]A. S. Miner, T. L. Amburgey, and T. M. Stearns, Interorganizational linkages and population dynamics: Buffering and transformational shields, *Administrative Science Quarterly* 35 (1990): 689–713.

[30]Anonymous, In brief: Fujitsu to supply ATM part for Tidel, *American Banker* 165(198) (2000): 16.

[31]A. C. Inkpen, Learning and knowledge acquisition through international strategic alliances, *Academy of Management Executive* 12(4) (1998): 69–80.

[32]J. M. Liedtka, Collaboration across lines of business for competitive advantage, *Academy of Management Executive* 10 (May 1996): 7–19.

[33]Anonymous, In brief: Mellon buys out joint venture with Chase, *American Banker* 165(199) (2000): 20.

[34]S. Tully, You'll never guess who really makes. . ., *Fortune* (October 3, 1994): 124–128.

[35]J. E. Forrest, Strategic alliances and the small technology-based firm, *Journal of Small Business Management* 28 (3) (1990): 37.

[36]S. Greengard, Design to go, *Industry Week* 249(10) (2000): 89–92.

[37]T. K. Das and B. Teng, Resource and risk management in the strategic alliance making process, *Journal of Management* 24 (1998): 21–42.

[38]T. K. Das and B. Teng, Managing risks in strategic alliances, *Academy of Management Executive* 13(4) (1999): 50–62.

[39]S. D. Moore, Companies: Bayer expands its partnership with Lion—Chemistry experiments will be computerized, *Wall Street Journal Europe* (October 16, 2000): 11.

[40]R. E. Miles and C. C. Snow, Organizations: New concepts for new forms, *California Management Review* 28 (Spring 1986): 62–73.

[41]G. Morgan, *Creative Organization Theory: A Resourcebook* (Newbury Park: Sage, 1989).

[42]G. G. Dess, M. A. Abdul, K. J. McLaughlin, and R. L. Priem, The new corporate architecture, *Academy of Management Executive* 9(3) (1995): 7–20.

[43]S. Tully, The modular corporation, *Fortune* (February 8, 1993): 106–115.

[44]W. W. Powell, Hybrid organizational arrangements: New form or transitional development? *California Management Review* 30 (Fall 1987): 67–87; see also W. W. Powell, Neither market nor hierarchy: Network forms of organization. In B. M. Staw and L. L. Cummings, *Research in Organizational Behavior* 12 (1990): 295–336.

[45]Dess et al., The new corporate architecture, *op. cit.*

[46]Miles and Snow, Organizations, *op. cit.*

[47]C. C. Snow, R. E. Miles, and H. J. Coleman Jr., Managing 21st century network organizations, *Organizational Dynamics* (Winter, 1992): 5–19.

[48]Back to the future, *Industry Week* (October 3, 1994): 61–64; Dess et al., "The new corporate architecture, *op. cit.*

[49]T. A. Stewart, Managing in a wired company, *Fortune* (July 11, 1994): 44–56.

[50]D. E. O'Leary, K. Kuokka, and R. Plant, Artificial intelligence and virtual organization, *Communications of the ACM* 40(1) (1997): 52–59.

[51]W. M. Fitzpatrick and D. R. Burke, Form, functions, and financial performance realities for the virtual organization, *S.A.M. Advanced Management Journal* 65(3) (2000): 13–20.

[52]S. G. Straus, S. P. Weisband, and J. M. Wilson, Human resource management practices in the networked organization: Impacts of electronic communication systems, *Journal of Organizational Behavior* 5(Supplement) (1998): 127–154.

[53]Byrne, The horizontal corporation, *op. cit.*, pp. 98–99.

[54]F. N. Crandall and M. J. Wallace Jr., Inside the virtual workplace: Forging a new deal for work and rewards, *Compensation and Benefits Review* 29(1) (1997): 27–36.

[55]S. Cohen, On becoming virtual, *Training and Development* 51(5) (1997): 30–32.

[56]J.Chutchian-Ferranti, Virtual corporation, *Computerworld* 33(37) (1999): 64.

[57]J. Dash, Coaching to aid IT careers, retention, *Computerworld* 34(12) (2000): 52.

[58]M. Lawlor, Military leaders formulate virtual organization plans, *Signal* 54(7) (2000): 27–29.

[59]G. Edmondson, See the world, erase its borders, *Business Week* (August 28, 2000): 113–114.

[60]Edmondson, See the world, *op. cit.*

[61]M. Kaminski, April 1998—Money & markets— Compounding of interests: Baltic banks team and combine, getting ready to operate in ever-bigger markets, *Wall Street Journal Europe* (March 30, 1998): 25.

[62]Anonymous, Unimate deal aids Need2Buy's global plans, *Electronic Buyers' News* (October 16, 2000): PG10.

[63]H. G. Barkema, O. Shenkar, F. Vermeulen, and J. H. J. Bell, Working abroad, working with others: How firms learn to operate international joint ventures, *Academy of Management Journal* 40 (1997): 426–442.

[64]The mighty keiretsu, *Industry Week* 241(2) (1992): 52–54; C. Rapoport, Why Japan keeps on winning, *Fortune* (July 15, 1991): 76–85.

[65]Anonymous, Finance and economics: The ties that bind, *The Economist* 354(8156) (2000): 71.

[66]B. Bremner, Keiretsu connections, *Business Week* (July 22, 1996): 52–54.

[67]B. Bremner, Mitsubishi: Failed vision, *Business Week* (September 25, 2000): 184.

[68]M. Ihlwan, For the chaebol, A crawl toward reform, *Business Week* (September 4, 2000): 64.

[69]Anonymous, Chaebol still drag down Korea, *Business Week* (September 25, 2000): 96.

[70]J. Larkin, Lessons unlearned, *Far Eastern Economic Review* 163(38) (2000): 64–66.

CHAPTER 13

[1]S. Miller, Ford of Europe's chief gets auto maker's strategy in gear—Striving to revive brand via new models and ads, *Asian Wall Street Journal* (August 14, 2000): 28; S. Miller, Ford names Olsson president of Volvo in strategic move, *Wall Street Journal* (June 7, 2000): B7; K. Kerwin, Remaking Ford, *Business Week* (October 11, 1999): 131–142.

[2]K. E. Brewer III and D. D. Evanoff, Changing financial industry structure and regulation, *Chicago Fed Letter* (157A Special Issue) (2000): 1–4.

[3]C. Power, First Union to test wireless banking services, *American Banker* 165(198) (2000): 1.

[4]G. Inzerilli and A. Laurent, Managerial views of the organization structure in France and the U.S.A., *International Studies of Management and Organization* 13(1–2) (1983): 97–118.

[5]See G. G. Dess and D. W. Beard, Objective measurement of organizational environments, *Academy of Management Proceedings* (1982): 345–349; and D. D. Dess and D. W. Beard, Dimensions of organizational task environments, *Administrative Science Quarterly* 29 (1984): 52–73. See also S. M. Shortell, The role of environment in a configurational theory of organizations, *Human Relations* 30 (1977): 275–302; and R. B. Duncan, Characteristics of organizational environments and perceived environmental uncertainty, *Administrative Science Quarterly* 17 (1972): 313–327. H. Mintzberg, *The Structuring of Organizations* (Englewood Cliffs, NJ: Prentice Hall, 1979); H. Mintzberg, *Structure in Fives: Designing Effective Organizations* (Englewood Cliffs, NJ: Prentice Hall, 1983 specifies five dimensions: complexity, diversity, change, hostility, and uncertainty.

[6]A. M. Zuckerman and R. C. Coile Jr., Creating a vision for the twenty-first century healthcare organization/practitioner application, *Journal of Healthcare Management* 45(5) (2000): 294–306.

[7]B. W. Keats and M. A. Hitt, A causal model of linkages among environmental dimensions, macro-organizational characteristics, and performance, *Academy of Management Journal* 31 (1988): 570–598.

[8]P. H. Dickson and K. M. Weaver, Environmental determinants and individual-level moderators of alliance use, *Academy of Management Journal* 40 (1997): 404–425.

[9]M. S. Kraatz, Learning by association? Interorganizational networks and adaptation to environmental change, *Academy of Management Journal* 41(6) (1998): 621–643.

[10]B. Wimmer, Cool in a crisis, *Asian Business* 35(2) (1999): 17–19.

[11]See the study by M. Yasai-Ardekani, Effects of environmental scarcity and munificence on the relationship of context to organizational structure, *Academy of Management Journal* 32 (1989): 131–156.

[12]V. Hayes, A legacy of confusion: From crisis to credibility, *Ivey Business Quarterly* 63(1) (1998): 42–48.

[13]D. Miller, Environmental fit versus internal fit, *Organization Science* 3(2) (1992): 159.

[14]R. B. Duncan, Multiple decision-making structures in adapting to environmental uncertainty, *Human Relations* 26 (1973): 273–291; H. R. Johnson, Interactions between individual predispositions, environmental factors, and organizational design. In R. H. Kilmann, L. R. Pondy, and D. P. Slevin (eds.), *The Management of Organizational Design*, Vol. 2 (New York: North-Holland, 1976): 31–58.

[15]J. Wechsler, Inside USP, *Pharmaceutical Technology* 24(8) (2000): 12–22.

[16]J. R. Gordon and S. R. Gordon, Structuring the interaction between information technology and business units: Prototypes for service delivery, *Information Systems Management* 17(1) (2000): 7–16.

[17]A. Reinhardt, From gearhead to grand high pooh-bah, *Business Week* (August 28, 2000): 129–130.

[18]J. Woodward, *Industrial Organizations: Theory and Practice* (London: Oxford University Press, 1965); J. Thompson, *Organizations in Action* (New York: McGraw-Hill, 1967).

[19]C. Perrow, A framework for comparative analysis of organizations, *American Sociological Review* 32 (April 1967): 196.

[20]B. Schmitz, Tools of innovation, *Industry Week* (2000): 249(9): 58–66.

[21]J. D. Ford and J. W. Slocum Jr. Size, technology, environment, and the structure of organizations, *Academy of Management Review* 2 (1977): 561–575; L.W. Fry, Technology structure research: Three critical issues, *Academy of Management Journal* 25 (1982): 532–552.

[22]M. Jelinek, Technology, organizations, and contingency, *Academy of Management Review* 2 (1977): 17–26.

[23]M. Liu, H. Denis, H. Kolodny, and B. Stymne, Organization design for technological change. In R. R. Sims, D. D. White, and D. A. Bednar (eds.), *Readings in Organizational Behavior* (Boston: Allyn and Bacon, 1992).

[24]M. Biggs, Tomorrow's workforce, *InfoWorld* (September 18, 2000): S59–S61.

[25]E. Chabrow, Approaches differ by industry, *Informationweek* (September 11, 2000): 385–390.

[26]M. S. Raisingham, Knowledge management: A cognitive perspective on business and education, *American Business Review* 18(2) (2000): 105–112.

[27]S. Thomson, Focus: Keeping pace with knowledge, *Information World Review* (155) (2000): 23–24.

[28]J. B. Quinn, Outsourcing innovation: The new engine of growth, *Sloan Management Review* 41(4) (2000): 13–28.

[29]S. F. Matusik and C. W. L. Hill, The utilization of contingent work, knowledge creation, and competitive advantage, *Academy of Management Review* 23(4) (1998): 680–697.

[30]M. Clifford and M. Kripalani, Different countries, adjoining cubicles, *Business Week* (August 28, 2000): 182–184.

[31]R. M. Steers, *Organizational Effectiveness: A Behavioral View* (Santa Monica, CA: Goodyear, 1977): 21.

[32]R. M. Cyert and J. G. March, *A Behavioral Theory of the Firm* (Englewood Cliffs, NJ: Prentice Hall, 1963).

[33]G. Green, Clinical service lines bring patients into focus, *Nursing Management* 31(3) (2000): 40–43.

[34]H. Simon, *The New Science of Management Decision* (New York: Harper & Row, 1960).

[35]R. E. Miles and C. C. Snow, *Organizational Strategy, Structure, and Process* (New York: McGraw-Hill, 1978).

[36]Kerwin, Rematov Ford, *op. cit.* Miller, Ford of Europe's chief gets automakers strategy in gear, *op. cit.*

[37]See, for example, D. Lavoie and S. A. Culbert, Stages in organization and development, *Human Relations* 31 (1978): 417–438; I. Adizes, Organizational passages: Diagnosing and treating life cycle problems in organizations, *Organizational Dynamics* 8(1) (1979): 3–24; L. Greiner, Evolution and revolution as organizations grow, *Harvard Business Review* 50(4) (1972): 37–46.

[38]These steps parallel the four-stage business cycle: start-up, growth, maturity, and decline.

[39]J. M. Bartunek and B. M. Betters-Reed, The stages of organizational creation, *Journal of Community Psychology* 15(3) (1987): 287–303.

[40]T. R. Schori and M. L. Garee, Like products, companies have life cycle, *Marketing News* 32(13) (1998): 4.

[41]Greiner, Evolution and revolution, *op. cit.*; Adizes, Organizational passages, *op. cit.*

[42]N. C. Churchill and V. L. Lewis, The five stages of small business growth, *Harvard Business Review* (May-June, 1983).

[43]R. Walton, Establishing and maintaining high commitment work systems. In J. R. Kimberly and R. H. Miles (eds.), *The Organizational Life Cycle* (San Francisco: Jossey-Bass, 1980): 208–291.

[44]D. Miller and P. Friesen, Archetypes of organizational transition, *Administrative Science Quarterly* 25 (1980): 269–299; D. Miller and P. Friesen, The longitudinal analysis of organizations: A methodological perspective, *Management Science* 28 (1982): 1013–1034; E. H. Schein, The role of the founder in creating organizational culture, *Organizational Dynamics* 12 (1983): 1–12.

[45] Churchill and Lewis, The five stages, *op. cit.*

[46] Churchill and Lewis, The five stages, *op. cit.*

[47]W. Zellner, Go-go goliaths, *Business Week* (February 13, 1995): 64–70.

[48]See D. A. Whetten, Sources, responses, and effects of organizational decline. In Kimberly and Miles, *The Organizational Life Cycle, op. cit.*

[49]R. Heller, Stop the life cycle in its tracks, *Management Today* (January 1999): 17.

[50]W. Weitzel and E. Johnson, Decline in organizations: A literature integration and extension, *Administrative Science Quarterly* 34 (1989): 91–109.

[51]Weitzel and Johnson, Decline in organizations, *op. cit.*

[52]See J. Child, Organizational structure, environment and performance: The role of strategic choice, *Sociology* 6 (1972): 1–22; D. S. Pugh, D. J. Hickson, C. R. Hinings, and C. Turner, The context of organizational structures, *Administrative Science Quarterly* 14 (1969): 91–114.

[53]D. J. Hickson, D. S. Pugh, and D. Pheysey, Operations technology and organization structure: An empirical reappraisal, *Administrative Science Quarterly* 14 (1969): 378–398.

[54]A. Binkley, In Canada: Shrinking for growth, *Railway Age* 199(2) (1998): 47–48.

[55]Anonymous, Downsizing with decorum, *Business Asia* 30(4) (1998): 1–2; S. Schick, Seagate tries to rise from revenue slump, *Computing Canada* 24(11) (1998): 11–12.

[56]A. Morrall Jr., A human resource rightsizing model for the twenty-first century, *Human Resource Development Quarterly* 9(1) (1998): 81–88.

[57]R. A. Johnson, Antecedents and outcomes of corporate refocusing, *Journal of Management* 22 (1996): 439–483.

[58]S. Taneja, Rightsizing the supermarket, *Chain Store Age* 75(2) (1999): 36–40.

[59]G. W. Dalton, L. T. Perry, J. C. Younger, and W. N. Smallwood, Strategic restructuring, *Human Resource Management* 35 (Winter 1996): 433–452.

[60]D. Wedgeworth, Growth after downsizing, *Business Credit* 101(6) (1999): 22–23.

[61]D. J. McConville, The upside of downsizing, *Industry Week* 242(10) (1993): 12–16.

[62]D. C. Ganster and D. J. Dwyer, The effects of understaffing on individual and group performance in professional and trade occupations, *Journal of Management* 21 (1995): 175–190.

[63]When slimming is not enough, *The Economist* 332(7879) (1994): 59–60; Corporate surveys can't find a productivity revolution, either, *Challenge* 38(6) (1995): 31–34.

[64]Dalton et al., Strategic restructuring, *op. cit.*

[65]Dalton et al., Strategic restructuring, *op. cit.*

[66]M. K. McGee, P&G jump-starts corporate change, *Internetweek* (November 1, 1999): PG30–PG31.

[67]K. Miller, How the merger boom will end, *Fortune* (October 27, 1997): 279–280.

[68]A. Barrett, Coming soon: A feast of mergers, *Business Week* (May 22, 2000): 56.

[69]Anonymous, PYA/Monarch purchase broadens Royal Ahold's distributor holdings, *Restaurants & Institutions* 110(27) (2000): 20.

[70]L. Barrett, Travel sickness, *Marketing Week* 23(27) (2000): 22–25.

[71]Anonymous, Merger brief: First among equals, *The Economist* 356(8185) (2000): 59–60.

[72]E. Williams, Neither a lender nor a dealmaker be, *Forbes* (October 30, 2000): 150–154.

[73]H. W. Lane and J. D. DiStefano, *International Management Behavior: From Policy to Practice* (Boston: PWS-Kent, 1992).

[74]C. A. Bartlett and S. Ghoshal, *Managing Across Borders: The Transnational Solution* (Boston: Harvard Business School Press, 1989); C. A. Bartlett, Y. Doz, and G. Hedlund, *Managing the Global Firm* (London: Routledge & Kegan Paul, 1990).

[75]P. Engardio, The barons of outsourcing, *Business Week* (August 28, 2000): 177–178.

[76]K. J. Fedor and W. B. Werther Jr., The fourth dimensions: Creating culturally responsive international alliances, *Organizational Dynamics* (Autumn 1996): 39–53.

[77]Clifford and Kripalani, Different countries, *op. cit.*

CHAPTER 14

[1]D. Rocks, Reinventing Herman Miller, *Business Week E.Biz* (April 3, 2000): EB87–EB96; D. Bartholomew, E-commerce bullies, *Industry Week* 249(14) (2000): 48–54; M. LaMonica, Life after ERP, *InfoWorld* 21(33) (1999): 34–35.

[2]W. L. French and C. H. Bell Jr., *Organization Development: Behavioral Science Interventions for Organization Improvement*, 3d ed. (Englewood Cliffs, NJ: Prentice Hall, 1984).

[3]M. Stepanek, Clash of the e-consultants, *Business Week Information Technology Annual Report* (June 19, 2000): 123–124.

[4]D. A. Nadler and M. L. Tushman, Types of organizational change: From incremental improvement to discontinuous transformation. In D. A. Nadler, R. B. Shaw, A. E. Walton and Associates, *Discontinuous Change: Leading Organizational Transformation* (San Francisco: Jossey-Bass, 1995).

[5]M. L. Tushman, W. H. Newman, and E. Romanelli, Convergence and upheaval: Managing the unsteady pace of organizational evolution. In K. S. Cameron, R. E. Sutton, and D. A. Whetton (eds.), *Readings in Organizational Decline: Framework, Research, and Prescriptions* (Cambridge, MA: Ballinger, 1988).

[6]T. C. Dubois, The gradual transition to a team-based environment: The success story of a medium-sized manufacturing facility, *Hospital Materiel Management Quarterly* 21(1) (1999): 31–41.

[7]See J. M. Bartunek and M. R. Louis, The interplay of organization development and organizational transformation. In W. A. Pasmore and R. W. Woodman (eds.), *Research in Organizational Change and Development*, vol. 2 (Greenwich, CT: JAI, 1988); J. M. Bartunek, The dynamics of personal and organizational reframing. In R. Quinn and K. Cameron (eds.), *Paradox and Transformation: Towards a Theory of Change in Organizations and Management* (Cambridge, MA: Ballinger, 1989).

[8]See C. J. G. Gersick, Revolutionary change theories: A multilevel exploration of the punctuated equilibrium paradigm, *Academy of Management Review* 16(1) (1991): 10–36; E. Romanelli and M. L. Tushman, Organizational transformation as punctuated equilibrium: An empirical test, *Academy of Management Journal* 37(5) (1994): 1141–1166.

[9]E. Abrahamson, Change without pain, *Harvard Business Review* 78(4) (2000): 75–79.

[10]M. L. Tushman, Winning through innovation, *Planning Review* 25(4) (1997): 14–19.

[11]W. French, Organization development—Objectives, assumptions, and strategies, *California Management Review* 12 (1969): 23–34.

[12]This technique is based on an early work in the field, K. Lewin, *Field Theory in Social Science* (New York: Harper & Row, 1951).

[13]C. M. Pearson and J. A. Clair, Reframing crisis management, *Academy of Management Review* 23(1) (1998): 59–76.

[14]G. Labianca, B. Gray, and D. Brass, A grounded model of organizational schema change during empowerment, *Organization Science* 11(2) (2000): 235–257.

[15]A. B. Fisher, Making change stick, *Fortune* (April 17, 1995): 121–128.

[16]A. Latour, Ericsson chief ousted in dispute over reforms—Nilsson criticized for delays in rolling out products as Swedish firm falters, *Wall Street Journal* (July 8, 1999): A10.

[17]B. Ringhouse and M. Bruggeman, The process-centered organization: How one rural system made the switch, *Health Forum Journal* 42(2) (1999): 33–36.

[18]V. Sathe, Creating change in mindset & behaviour, *Ivey Business Journal* 64(5) (2000): 83–89.

[19]M. London, *Change Agents. New Roles and Innovation Strategies for Human Resource Professionals* (San Francisco: Jossey-Bass, 1988).

[20]Adapted from E. F. Hamilton, An empirical study of factors predicting change agents' effectiveness, *Journal of Applied Behavioral Science* 24 (1) (1988): 37–59.

[21]M. J. Friend and K. H. Steens, Controlling cash in a multiunit environment, *Internal Auditing* 12(4) (1997): 3–12.

[22]L. Davidson, HR turnaround: Tales of a champion, *Workforce* 78(10) (1999): 84–86.

[23]D. K. Carr, K. J. Hard, and W. J. Trahant, *Managing the Change Process: A Field Book for Change Agents, Consultants, Team Leaders, and Reengineering Managers* (New York: McGraw-Hill, 1996):136.

[24]S. Kaham, Putting out fires isn't enough, *The Practical Accountant* 33(7) (2000): 60–62.

[25]N. Shirouzu, Mazda's new president vows more cost cuts—Fields aims to continue Ford-led turnaround that restored profits, *Wall Street Journal* (December 16, 1999): A17.

[26]C. D. Marsan, Remaking Honeywell, *Network World* 26(17) (2000): 1, 18.

[27]W. H. Wagel and H. Z. Levine, HR '90: Challenges and opportunities, *Personnel* (June 1990): 18–42.

[28]F. W. Taylor, *The Principles of Scientific Management* (New York: Harper, 1911).

[29]C. Perrow, The organizational context of human factors engineering, *Administrative Science Quarterly* 28 (1983): 521–541.

[30]D. Maloney, How Pep Boys revs up orderpicking efficiencies, *Modern Materials Handling* 54(7) (1999): 46–48.

[31]J. D. Kilbridge, Reduced costs through job enlargement: A case, *Journal of Business* 33 (1960): 357–362.

[32]D. D. Triggs and P. M. King, Job rotation, *Professional Safety* 45(2) (2000): 32–34; T. Ellis, Implementing job rotation, *Occupational Health & Safety* 68(1) (1999): 82–84.

[33]L. Cheraskin and M. A. Campion, Study clarifies job-rotation benefits, *Personnel Journal* 75(11) (1996): 31–38.

[34]J. Synder and D. Nethersole-Chong, Is cross-training medical/surgical RNs to ICU the answer? *Nursing Management* 30(2) (1999): 58–60.

[35]F. Herzberg and A. Zautra, Orthodox job enrichment: Measuring true quality in job satisfaction, *Personnel* (September–October 1976).

[36]J. R. Hackman and G. Oldham, *Work Design* (Reading, MA: Addison-Wesley, 1980).

[37]R. W. Renn and R. J. Vandenberg, The critical psychological states: An underrepresented component in job characteristics model research, *Journal of Management* 21(2) (1995): 279–303 for more recent research that supports these relationships.

[38]Hackman and Oldham, *Work Design, op. cit.*

[39]Hackman and Oldham, *Work Design, op. cit.*

[40]R. N. Cheser, The effect of Japanese kaizen on employee motivation in U.S. manufacturing, *International Journal of Organizational Analysis* 6(3) (1998): 197–217.

[41]W. M. Fox, Sociotechnical system principles and guidelines: Past and present, *Journal of Applied Behavioral Science* 31(1): 91–105.

[42]J. Woodward, *Industrial Organization: Theory and Practice* (London: Oxford University Press, 1965); E. Trist and K. W. Bamforth, Some social and psychological consequences of the long-wall method of coal getting, *Human Relations* 4 (1951): 3–38; A. K. Rice, *Productivity and Social Organization: The Ahmedabad Experiments* (London: Tavistock, 1958).

[43]T. G. Cummings, Self-regulating work groups: A sociotechnical synthesis, *Academy of Management Review* 3 (1978): 625–634.

[44]M. R. Weisbord, Participative work design: A personal odyssey, *Organizational Dynamics* 13 (Spring 1985).

[45]B. Dankbaar, Lean production: Denial, confirmation or extension of sociotechnical system design, *Human Relations* 50(5) (1997): 567–583; Volvo to close 2 plants and cut 4,500 workers, *The New York Times* (November 5, 1992); S. D. Moore, Volvo planning 2 plant closings at Swedish sites, *The Wall Street Journal* (November 5, 1992).

[46]C. A. L. Pearson, Autonomous workgroups: An evaluation at an industrial site, *Human Relations* 45 (September, 1992): 905–936.

[47]T. D. Wall, N. J. Kemp, P. R. Jackson, and C. W. Clegg, Outcomes of autonomous workgroups: A long-term field experiment, *Academy of Management Journal* 29 (1986): 280–304; J. L. Cordery, W. S. Mueller, and L. M. Smith, Attitudinal and behavioral effects of autonomous group working: A longitudinal field study, *Academy of Management Journal* 34(2) (1991): 464–476.

[48]F. Emery, Participative design: Effective, flexible and successful, now! *Journal for Quality & Participation* 18(1) (1995): 6–9.

[49]T. H. Davenport and K. Pearlson, Two cheers for the virtual office, *Sloan Management Review* 39(4) (1998): 51–65.

[50]M. Mariani, Telecommuters, *Occupational Outlook Quarterly* 44(3) (2000): 10–17.

[51]Mariani, Telecommuters, *op. cit.*

[52]B. Shamir and I. Salomon, Work-at-home and the quality of working life, *Academy of Management Review* 10 (1985): 455–464.

[53]H. Lewis, Exploring the dark side of telecommuting, *Computerworld* (May 12, 1997): 37.

[54]S. T. Posnock, The pros and cons of a virtual office, *Folio: The Magazine for Magazine Management* 29(13) (2000): 112.

[55]I. D. Singer, Work–life benefits can lighten the load, *Business and Health* 17(10) (1999): 25–31.

[56]N. H. Woodward, TGI Thursday, *HRMagazine* 45(7) (2000): 72–76.

[57]B. B. Baltes, T. E. Briggs, J. W. Huff, J. A. Wright, and G. A. Neuman, Flexible and compressed workweek schedules: A meta-analysis of their effects on work-related criteria, *Journal of Applied Psychology* 84(4) (1999): 496–513.

[58]Baltes et al., TGI Thursday, *op. cit.*

[59]S. Reese, Working around the clock, *Business and Health* 18(4) (2000): 71–72.

[60]Anonymous, Flexibility drives hiring of contingent workers, *The Worklife Report* 12(4) (2000): 17.

[61]P. Brotherton, Staff to suit, *HR Magazine* 40(12) (1995): 50–55.

[62]S. Massmann, Temporary workers can leave employers with some long-term liability headaches, *National Underwriter* 103(32) (1999): 6, 31.

[63]A. Bernstein, When is a temp not a temp? *Business Week* (December 7, 1998): 90.

[64]S. L. Schilling, Implementing a successful telework program, *Compensation & Benefits Management* 15(4) (1999): 58–60.

[65]S. G. Schroeder, Alternate workstyles: A solution to productivity problems? *Supervisory Management* 28 (July 1983): 24–30; W. Olsten, Effectively managing alternative work options, *Supervisory Management* 29 (April 1984): 10–15.

[66]B. Olmsted, (Flex)time is money, *Management Review* 76(11) (1987): 47–51; C. Scordato and J. Harris, Workplace flexibility, *HRMagazine* (January 1990): 75–78.

[67]J. W. Newstrom and J. L. Pierce, Alternative work schedules: The state of the art, *Personnel Administration* (1979): 19–23.

[68]J. A. Hollingsworth and F. A. Wrebe, Flextime: An international innovation with limited U.S. acceptance, *Industrial Management* 31(2) (1989): 22–26.

[69]P. Sinclair, Extranet key to support system, *Informationweek* (September 7, 1998): 41–46.

[70]K. M. Kustermann, Reengineering the purchasing function: Identifying the best practices for the city of Chicago, *Government Finance Review* 14(5) (1998): 29–32.

[71]Hammer and Champy, *Reengineering the Corporation, op. cit.*

[72]Hammer and Champy, *Reengineering the Corporation, op. cit.*

[73]P. B. Seybold, Rapid-fire re-engineering, *Chief Executive* 106 (September 1995): 68.

[74]R. E. Yates, Re-engineering guru retools idea, *Chicago Tribune* (February 3, 1995): 1, 2.

[75]B. B. Wells, At Wachovia, customer focus means information-driven continuous relationship management, *Journal of Retail Banking Services* 21(2) (1999): 33–36.

[76]G. MacSweeney, Solutions: Universal Underwriters finds its customer focus, *Insurance & Technology* 25(10) (2000): 26.

[77]J. W. Dean Jr. and J. R. Evans, *Total Quality: Management, Organization, and Strategy* (St. Paul, MN: West, 1994).

[78]J. M. Juran, *Quality Control Handbook* (New York: McGraw-Hill, 1989).

[79]D. Devito and S. Morrison, Benchmarking: A tool for sharing and cooperation, *The Journal for Quality and Participation* 23(4) (2000): 56–61.

[80]M. Gunther, Eisner's mouse trap, *Fortune* (September 6, 1999): 106–118.

[81]Anonymous, Employee boards give staff a stake, *CPA Personnel Report* 19(4) (2000): 1,7.

[82]J. Simmons, Participation provides hope for the new millennium, *The Journal for Quality and Participation* 22(6) (1999): 64.

[83]V. K. Omachonu and J. E. Ross, *Principles of Total Quality* (Delray Beach, FL: St. Lucie, 1994).

[84]E. E. Lawler III, Total quality management and employee involvement: Are they compatible? *Academy of Management Executive* 8(1) (1994): 68–76.

[85]W. M. Lindsay and J. A. Petrick, *Total Quality and Organization Development* (Delray Beach, FL: St. Lucie, 1997).

[86]R. Blackburn and B. Rosen, Total quality and human resources management: Lessons learned from Baldrige Award-winning companies, *Academy of Management Executive* 7(3) (1993): 49–66.

[87]E. C. Nevis, A. J. DiBella, and J. M. Gould, Understanding organizations as learning systems, *Sloan Management Review* 36(2) (1995): 73–85.

[88]J. Redding, Hardwiring the learning organization, *Training & Development* 51(8) (1997): 61–67.

[89]P. M. Senge, *The Fifth Discipline: The Art and Practice of the Learning Organization* (New York: Doubleday, 1990); P. M. Senge, Transforming the practice of management, *Human Resource Development Quarterly* 4(1) (1993); J. K. Bennett and M. J. O'Brien, The building blocks of the learning organization, *Training* 31(6) (1994): 41–49; K. E. Watkins and V. J. Marsick, *Sculpting the Learning Organization: Lessons in the Art and Science of Systemic Change* (San Francisco: Jossey-Bass, 1993): 8; P. West, The concept of the learning organization, *Journal of European Industrial Training* 18(1) (1994): 15–20.

[90]S. Fister, Reinventing training at Rockwell Collins, *Training* 37(4) (2000): 64–70.

[91]P. Senge, Creating learning communities, *Executive Excellence* 14(3) (1997): 17–18.

[92]E. C. Wenger and W. M. Snyder, Communities of practice: The organizational frontier, *Harvard Business Review* 78(1) (2000): 139–145.

[93]J. Storck and P. A. Hill, Knowledge diffusion through "strategic communities," *Sloan Management Review* 41(2) (2000): 63–74.

[94]M. M. Crossan, H. W. Lane, and R. E. White, An organizational learning framework: From intuition to institution, *Academy of Management Review* 24(3) (1999): 538–555.

[95]C. Argyris and D. Schon, *Organizational Learning* (Reading, MA: Addison-Wesley, 1978); C. Argyris, *Overcoming Organizational Defenses* (Boston: Allyn & Bacon, 1990); Senge, *The Fifth Discipline, op. cit.*

[96]F. J. Barrett, Creating appreciative learning cultures, *Organizational Dynamics* 24(2) (1995): 36–49.

[97]Senge, *The Fifth Discipline, op. cit.*; M. E. McGill and J. W. Slocum Jr., Unlearning the organization, *Organizational Dynamics* 22(2) (1993): 67–79.

[98]M. Popper and R. Lipshitz, Organizational learning mechanisms: A structural and cultural approach to organizational learning, *Journal of Applied Behavioral Science* 34(2) (1998): 161–179.

[99]Senge, *The Fifth Discipline, op. cit.*; P. M. Senge, The leader's new work: Building learning organizations, *Sloan Management Review* 32(1) (1990): 7–23; McGill and Slocum, Unlearning the organization, *op. cit.*

[100]D. A. Garvin, Building a learning organization, *Harvard Business Review* 71(4) (1993): 78–91.

[101]D. Q. Mills and B. Friesen, The learning organization, *European Management Journal* 10(2) (1992): 146–156.

[102]A. Rubenstein, *Managing Technology in the Decentralized Firm* (New York: Wiley, 1989).

[103]B. Dumaine, Closing the innovation gap, *Fortune* (December 2, 1991): 56–62.

[104]Dumaine, Closing the innovation gap, *op. cit.*

[105]E. B. Roberts and A. R. Fusfeld, Staffing the innovative technology-based organization, *Sloan Management Review* 22(3) (1981): 19–34.

[106]S. A. Shane, Are champions different from non-champions? *Journal of Business Venturing* 9(5) (1994): 397–421.

[107]J. H. Arleth, New product development projects and the role of the innovation manager. In A. Cozijnsen and W. Vrakking (eds.), *Handbook of Innovation Management* (Oxford: Blackwell Business, 1993): 125.

[108]Arleth, New product development projects, *op. cit.*

[109]R. A. Burgelman, T. J. Kosnik, and M. Van den Poel, Toward an innovative capabilities audit framework. In R. A. Burgelman and M. A. Maidique, *Strategic Management of Technology and Innovation* (Homewood, IL: Irwin, 1988).

[110]G. Hamel, Reinvent your company, *Fortune* (June 12, 2000): 100–118.

[111]J. E. McCann, Design principles for an innovating company, *Academy of Management Executive* 5(2) (1991): 76–93.

[112]R. A. Wolfe, Organizational innovation: Review, critique and suggested research directions, *Journal of Management Studies* 31 (May, 1994): 405–431.

[113]K. Albrecht, *Organization Development: A Total Systems Approach to Positive Change in Any Business Organization* (Englewood Cliffs, NJ: Prentice Hall, 1983).

[114]M. B. Miles and R. A. Schmuck, The nature of organization development. In R. A. Schmuck and M. B. Miles, (eds.), *Organization Development in Schools* (La Jolla, CA: University Associates, 1976).

[115]Miles and Schmuck, The nature of organization development, *op. cit.*

[116]J. Higley, Measuring members, *Hotel and Motel Management* 124(16) (1999): 1103.

[117]J. M. Bartunek and M. Moch, First-order, second-order, and third-order change and organizational development interventions, *Journal of Applied Behavioral Science* 23(4) (1987): 483–500; see also J. M. Bartunek, The multiple cognitions and conflicts associated with second order organizational change. In J. K. Murnigham (ed.), *Social Psychology in Organizations: Advances in Theory and Research* (Englewood Cliffs, NJ: Prentice Hall, 1993): 322–349.

[118]Bartunek, The multiple cognitions and conflicts, *op. cit.*

[119]W. M. Behrendt and W. F. Klein, The spirit of St. Louis, *Health Systems Review* 30(4) (1997): 22–26.

[120]W. L. French, A checklist for organizing and implementing an OD effort. In W. L. French, C. H. Bell Jr., and R. A. Zawacki (eds.), *Organization Development: Theory, Practice, and Research* (Dallas: Business Publications, 1978).

[121]Carr et al., *Managing the Change Process, op. cit.*

[122]L. P. White and K. C. Wooten, Ethical dilemmas in various stages of organizational development, *Academy of Management Review* 8(2) (1983): 690–697.

[123]M. Gritzuk, Water department re-engineering saves money, *The American City & County* 115(11) (2000): 68.

[124]P. M. Senge, The leader's new work: Building learning organizations, *Sloan Management Review* 32(1) (1990): 7–23.

[125]R. W. Bass and M. V. Mariono, Organization development in Italy, *Group and Organization Studies* 12(3) (1987): 245–256.

[126]L. U. de Sitter, J. F. den Hertog, and B. Dankbaar, From complex organizations with simple jobs to simple organizations with complex jobs, *Human Relations* 50(5) (1997): 497–534.

[127]A. Gregory, Prize-winning TPM, *Works Management,* Boardroom Report (Spring 2000): 32–35.

[128]A. M. Mangoud, Establishing a health promoting setting: An experience in an Albanian polyclinic, *International Journal of Public Administration* 23(1) (2000): 1–20.

[129]C. M. Pavett and C. Whitney, Quality values, attitudes, and behavioral predispositions of employees in Mexico, Australia, and the United States, *Thunderbird International Business Review* 40(6) (1998): 605–632.

Glossary

Action research. An approach to change in which the change agent collaborates extensively with the client in gathering and feeding back data.

Active listening. Listening for both the content of and the feelings behind a message.

Adhocracy. A structure that uses temporary liaison devices to encourage mutual adjustment among organizational members.

Affective conflict. Conflict that arises when competing emotions accompany incompatible goals and cause stress.

Affinity diagram technique. A technique for structuring brainstorming that allows groups to organize ideas, show their relationships, and develop action steps via diagrams.

Alternatives. A set of realistic and potentially acceptable solutions to a problem or ways of accomplishing objectives.

Anchoring and adjustment bias. A heuristic whereby individuals make assessments by anchoring onto an initial value and then adjusting it before making a final decision.

Arbitration. A quasi-legal procedure for dispute resolution by an arbitrator acting as a judge.

Attainable-ideal norm. A norm that dictates increasing amounts of a particular behavior until a certain goal is reached and does not advocate exceeding that amount.

Attribution. Specification of the perceived cause of events.

Automation. The use of machinery (computers) to perform tasks previously done by people.

Autonomous work group. A self-regulating worker group in which employees work on interdependent tasks in a single unit, control their own task assignment, and perform many roles traditionally assigned to management.

Availability bias. A heuristic according to which individuals tend to overestimate the likelihood that an event will occur if they can recall past instances.

Bargaining range. The range in which both parties in a dispute would find an agreement acceptable.

BATNA. The best alternative if a negotiated settlement is not reached in a dispute.

Belongingness and love needs. A worker's needs that are focused on the social aspects of work.

Benchmarking. The process of gathering information about how well a company is doing in comparison to a "best-in-class" company in specific areas.

Best-member strategy. A decision-making strategy in which the group relies upon the person who has the most information and ability in this situation.

Bonus. A one-time, lump-sum payment that is tied to exceptional performance.

Boundary spanner. A person who is in a position to interact with individuals or groups in other organizations and, thereby, has significant power potential; a lateral communication specialist at the point where two groups interact.

Bounded rationality. Herbert Simon's decision-making model that reflected the limits of the rational decision-making process by such real-world considerations as a decision maker's inability to obtain the necessary information.

Brainstorming. A technique whereby persons or groups generate large numbers of ideas or suggestions without evaluating their merits.

Broadbanding. A compensation system that places more jobs within the same wage level.

Bureaucracy. Max Weber's basic form of organization, characterized by order, system, rationality, and consistency.

Burnout. The emotional exhaustion that results from being overworked, overwhelmed, or overstressed over a period of time.

Bypassing. The process of missing meaning in communication.

Career. A life-long sequence of related jobs and experiences.

Chaebol. A Korean family of companies joined under various financial agreements with interlocking directorates.

Chain of command. The supervisory relationships in an organization.

Change agent. The person responsible for overseeing a change effort.

Classical conditioning. A process whereby, after repeated pairing of neutral and unconditioned stimuli, the neutral stimulus alone leads to a conditioned response.

Classical school. Henri Fayol's theory of management that described the basic duties and principles of managers.

Clique network. A group of individuals or departments who communicate exclusively with each other.

Codetermination. An organizational structure that gives workers a direct voice in the operation of the companies where they work.

Cognitive conflict. An intellectual discomfort created by trying to achieve incompatible goals.

Cognitive dissonance. A condition that arises when a situation contains contradictions to a person's information, beliefs, or attitudes.

Cohesive groups. Groups that have a strong interpersonal attraction among group members.

Commission. An incentive system that links pay to sales levels.

Communication overload. Too much information contained in a message.

Communication underload. Too little information contained in a message.

Comparison other. The worker that an employee chooses to compare his job situation to and thus feels motivated or unmotivated.

Compatibility test. A test in which a decision maker compares alternatives to a set of standards and chooses the alternative that fits best with the standards.

Conflict. A disagreement, opposition, or struggle between two or more people or groups.

Connotation. An emotional message that affects the meanings of words.

Contingency theory. A theory that calls for an accommodation between organizational processes and the characteristics of the particular situation.

Contingent worker. A worker hired by a company to complete specific projects or tasks.

Coordination. The extent and means by which an organization integrates or holds together its various parts and helps them work together to accomplish a goal or activity.

Core values. Those values that are least susceptible to change in a work situation.

Cultural ethnocentrism. The belief in the preeminence of one's own culture.

Cultural integrator. A person who understands cultural differences and helps an organization adapt to them.

Culture. The set of assumptions, beliefs, and values that organizational members share and use to guide their behavior.

Deep strategy. A change strategy that affects the private and central aspects of a worker's life.

Deep structures. Basic activity patterns of an organization or subsystem that make incremental adjustments to adapt to external changes.

Delegating style. A leadership style in which the leader monitors and observes employees' performance after giving them responsibility for decisions and implementation.

Delphi technique. A structured decision-making technique that uses repeated administration of rating scales to obtain opinions about a decision.

Denotation. The literal meaning of words.

Diagnosis. The application of theories and concepts to explain the reasons for or causes of behavior or attitudes in a real situation.

Diversity training. A series of programs and activities that highlight differences among workers and offer strategies for handling them.

Double-loop organization. A generative organization that uses experience to reevaluate its objectives and values and modify its culture.

Downshifter. A worker who gets off the career ladder for personal or other reasons.

Dynamic network. A structure that combines a variety of subcontractors into a working organization; also known as a modular organization.

Early career stage. The career stage at which a worker is concerned with advancement and establishing a career path.

Entry stage. The career stage at which a worker tries to become an accepted member of the organization as rapidly as possible.

Environment. The factors outside an organization that influence its functioning.

Equity sensitivity. A concept that suggests that people have different preferences for and perceptions of equity.

Equity theory. A theory based on the hypothesis that workers make judgments about job equity based on comparison to another worker in a similar position.

Esteem needs. An individual's needs for mastery, competence, and status.

Exemplars. Person schemas that represent concrete examples rather than general characteristics.

Expectancy. An individual's perception that his or her effort will result in performance.

Extinction. The process of eliminating undesired behavior by withholding positive reinforcement.

Extrinsic rewards. Rewards not linked to the job's content such as pay, job title, or other perks.

Extrovert. An outgoing person who likes variety, enjoys functioning in a social environment, often acts without thinking, and may dominate situations or people.

Feedback. The process of using information about outputs to modify inputs to gain more desirable outcomes.

Feeling type. A person who likes harmony and responds to the values and feelings of others as well as their thoughts.

Fixed reinforcer. A reinforcer that occurs at a predetermined and expected time.

Flat organization. A company that has relatively few levels in the hierarchy.

Flexible benefits plan. A plan in which workers receive a fixed amount of money or points to allocate to various benefit areas as they choose.

Flextime. A discretionary working arrangement that allows workers the choice of starting and ending times to their day so long as they work certain specific hours within a day and meet the requirements of a normal work week.

Flexyear. A discretionary working arrangement that allows workers to agree to the number of hours that they will work in a year but allows them to allocate those hours as desired.

Force-field analysis. An analytical technique that views a problem as the product of forces working in opposite directions.

Formal communication. Transmissions that use formally established or regularly scheduled channels.

Formal goal. A goal that has been specifically stated either orally or in writing.

Frustration. A sense of insecurity and dissatisfaction arising from the inability to satisfy a need or desire.

Full membership stage. The career stage at which a worker is concerned with effective performance, responsibility, management of subordinates, and skill development.

Functional role. A role that is determined by a group's needs for leadership and expertise, the members' abilities and attitudes, and the activities of the group.

Functional structure. A grouping of employees according to major categories of work.

Gainsharing program. An incentive system that allows workers to share in productivity increases by earning bonuses based on group performance.

Garbage can model. A decision-making model that uses the image of a garbage can to describe the serendipitous pairing of seemingly unrelated problems and solutions.

Gatekeeper. A special boundary spanner who screens information and access to a group or individual.

Glass ceiling. The invisible barrier to movement into top management that results from discrimination in the workplace.

Goal. A desired object or future state.

Goal displacement. The process by which individuals or groups divert their energies from the organization's original goals.

Grapevine. The pattern of communication created outside of a formal organization and official channels.

Grievance procedure. A formal process by which a worker can complain to management.

Group attractiveness. The extent to which groups appeal to people and make them want to belong.

Group decision support systems (GDSS). Computer software (such as electronic mail) that helps groups make decisions; also called groupware.

Group process. Activities dealing with the interpersonal interactions within a group.

Groupthink. The mentality that exists when group members avoid critical evaluation so that they can maintain a sense of group unity and consensus.

Groupware. Computer software that helps groups make decisions, for example, electronic mail and electronic meeting capabilities.

Habitual routines. Group routines that affect group performance either positively or negatively.

Halo effect. The tendency to let one key feature or trait dominate the evaluation of a person or thing.

Hawthorne effect. The first dramatic indication that workers' attitudes and feelings could significantly affect productivity.

Heuristics. Simplifying strategies used by decision makers; often a source of error.

Hidden agenda. Goals that individuals conceal from the working group.

Horizontal differentiation. The grouping of jobs at the same organizational level according to their function.

Hostile environment. An organization's environment characterized by conflict, threat, or unexpected or overwhelming competition.

Hourly wages. Wages that are determined by the number of hours worked.

Human relations school. A theory that concentrates on how workers' personalities, emotions, and attitudes affect their work.

Hygiene factors. According to Herzberg's theory, the features of a job's context that affect workers' dissatisfaction.

Hypothesis. A proposed explanation of the relationship between the dependent and independent variables.

Images. The values, morals, beliefs, goals, and plans in a set of standards in a compatibility test.

Impression construction. Selection of the image to be conveyed and the way it will be conveyed.

Impression management. The attempt to influence the perceptions of others by controlling the impression one makes upon them.

Improved nominal group technique. Differs from the nominal group technique in that personal contributions are anonymous; discussion is limited to a single aspect of the problem; evaluation is delayed until all items have been brought forward.

Incentive program. A program that pays workers only for what they produce.

Individual role. A role within a group that tends to be dysfunctional as it puts individual needs above group needs.

Industrial engineer. An engineer who studies the exact series of motions in a job in order to evaluate and improve work processes.

Informal communication. Spontaneous communication that occurs without regard for the formal channels of communication.

Informal goal. A goal that has been implied but never explicitly stated.

Information architect. A person who "cuts through the clutter" and helps deliver important information concisely, often by designing a Web site.

Innovation champion. A manager or employee who takes personal responsibility for introducing an innovation and marshaling the resources to produce it.

Innovation manager. A manager who creates the conditions in which creativity can occur and oversees the more practical aspects of product or system development.

Instrumentality. A person's perception that performance will have certain positive or negative outcomes.

Integrated structure. A hybrid structure that can incorporate both functional and market-oriented structures.

Internet. An international network of computer networks that offers low-cost global communications and access to the World Wide Web.

Interval schedule. A schedule that applies reinforcers after a regular amount of time.

Intragroup conflict. Disagreement among members of a group.

Intrinsic reward. A reward linked to the job itself such as challenge, responsibility, autonomy, etc.

Introvert. A shy and withdrawn person who prefers quiet, dislikes interruptions, and works contentedly alone.

Intuitive decision making. Decision making in which a manager relies on "gut feeling."

Intuitive type. A person who dislikes repetitive actions and enjoys learning new skills.

Job characteristics model. A job enrichment model that specifies the five core characteristics of the job that significantly influence workers' behaviors and attitudes.

Job enlargement. The concept of expanding the scope of a particular job by increasing the number of different but related processes that a worker does.

Job enrichment. The concept of changing a job horizontally by adding tasks and vertically by adding responsibility.

Job extension. A job enlargement program in which a worker does more of the same type of activities.

Job rotation. A form of job enlargement in which the worker performs two or more tasks but alternates them in a predefined way over a period of time.

Job-based pay. Pay that rewards worker for performing certain tasks.

Johari Window. A model that provides an analytical tool to identify information that is available for use in communication; helps diagnose the openness of communication.

Judgment type. A person who likes to finish tasks and works best with a plan.

Kaizen. The Japanese concept that every employee will seek gradual, continuous improvement in performance.

Keiretsu. A Japanese family of companies joined under various financial agreements with interlocking directorates.

Leader-centered team. A team with a strong internal leader as well as a manager.

Leadership Effectiveness and Description (LEAD). An instrument used to measure leadership style.

Learning. The acquisition of skills, knowledge, ability, or attitudes.

Learning organization. An organization that has the ability to fundamentally and regularly revitalize itself.

Life cycle. A series of developmental stages that an organization or an individual moves through from "birth" to "death."

Life-cycle theory. Also known as the situational theory, states that effective leadership results from the fit between a leader's style and the readiness of his or her followers.

LPC (Least-Preferred Coworker) Contingency Theory. A theory that calls for matching managers' preferred styles along the dimensions of task orientation and relations orientation to leader-member relations, task structure, and leader position power.

Machiavellian personality. An individual who demonstrates manipulative and unethical behavior and attitudes; term derived from Machiavelli's *The Prince.*

Maintenance role. A role that helps build and maintain group performance.

Matrix. An integrated structure that combines the best aspects of the functional and product structures.

Mechanistic structure. A pattern of organizational structure characterized by centralized decision making, a unitary chain of command, specialized and standardized work activities, and direct supervision.

Mediation. A third-party intervention in a dispute in which a neutral party helps to resolve disputes.

Mentor. An organization member who helps a younger employee move through the organizational ranks and supports the growth of the younger person's career.

Midcareer. The career stage at which a worker may face a midlife transition that may lead to new choices.

Min-max strategy. A process by which parties in a dispute determine their acceptable alternatives by asking a certain set of questions related to maximum and minimum requirements and goals.

Mission statement. A brief expression of the basic philosophy and goals of an organization.

Modular organization. An organization that combines a variety of subcontractors into a working organization; also known as a dynamic network.

Motivator. According to Herzberg's theory, a feature of a job's content that satisfies higher-order needs.

Munificent environment. An organization's environment that lacks conflict, threat, or unexpected or overwhelming competition.

Mutual adjustment. Informal but direct communication between individuals.

Need for achievement (nach). The need to accomplish and demonstrate mastery.

Need for affiliation (naff). The need for social interaction, love, and affection.

Need for power (npow). The need for control over work or other people.

Negative reinforcement. The process of encouraging a worker to avoid undesirable behavior.

Negotiation. The process by which two or more interdependent parties use bargaining to reconcile their differences.

Network analysis. Analysis of the patterns of interactions; allows managers to analyze the effectiveness of the patterns.

Noise. Interference, psychological or actual, in the communication process.

Nominal group technique (NGT).   A decision-making technique that uses a structured group meeting in which persons brainstorm and then rank order a series of ideas as a way of resolving group conflict.

Norm.   An unwritten and informal expectation that guides behavior.

Normative decision theory.   Suggests that managers select a leadership style according to the amount of participation in decision making that is appropriate for a particular situation.

Operant conditioning.   A process in which the consequence of a behavior determines whether that behavior will recur.

Organic structure.   A pattern of organizational structure that deemphasizes job descriptions and specialization, decentralizes decision making, and has less horizontal and vertical differentiation than personal and spatial differentiation.

Organization chart.   Presents in graphic form all chains of command in an organization; illustrates how workers in an organization are grouped into departments, to whom they report, and how their activities are coordinated.

Organization development (OD).   A behavioral approach that improves communication, group and intergroup behavior, leadership skills, and power relations by changing employees' knowledge, skills, interactions, and attitudes as well as the organizational culture.

Organizational behavior.   The actions and attitudes of people in organizations and the body of knowledge (OB) derived from the study of these actions and attitudes.

Organizational justice.   The fairness with which individuals are treated in the workplace.

Organizational simulation.   A computerized or non-computerized model of an organization that gives researchers the ability to study and control complex behavior.

Orientation to people.   The degree to which a leader addresses the individual needs of his or her workers.

Orientation to task.   The degree to which a leader structures his or her role and the employees' role to accomplish the group's task.

Outcome.   For a worker, the result of labor such as pay or promotion.

Overjustification effect.   The concept that the overpaid worker will work harder to justify his or her pay.

Participating style.   A leadership style in which the leader shifts significant responsibility to the employees.

Participative design.   A method that focuses on ways of democratizing decision making.

Pay compression.   A situation in which newly hired workers earn more than current workers doing the same job.

Perception.   The active process of sensing reality and organizing it into meaningful views or understanding.

Perception type.   A person who adapts well to changing situations; may tend to procrastinate.

Peripheral norm.   A norm that guides behavior that is important but not essential to the organization.

Peripheral value.   A value that is more susceptible to change in a work situation.

Personal differentiation.   Division of labor according to the worker's expertise or training.

Personal network.   A group of individuals who communicate with specific individuals.

Personality.   A set of distinctive personal characteristics, including motives, emotions, values, interests, attitudes, and competencies.

Personality inventory.   A test that presents questions to describe the test-taker's personality.

Physiological needs.   An individual's most basic needs for food, water, shelter, and sex.

Piecework system.   An incentive system that ties compensation to individual performance by paying workers for each item produced.

Pivotal norm.   A norm that guides the behavior that is essential to the organization.

Planned change.   The systematic process of introducing new behaviors, structures, and technologies for addressing problems and challenges organizations face.

Plateaued performer.   A worker who cannot advance because of limited opportunities and whose job responsibilities never change.

Pooled interdependence.   A relationship of groups that rely on each other only because they belong to the same parent organization.

Position power.   The extent to which a leader has the official power to influence others.

Positive reinforcement.   The process of rewarding desired behavior when it occurs.

Power distance.   The extent to which a society accepts the unequal distribution of power.

Preferred-value norm.   A norm that dictates the proper amount of behavior from any worker.

Prepotent need.   A primary or salient need.

Procedures.   The rules and regulations that guide worker behavior.

Process observer.   An individual who gathers information about a team's communication, decision making, and leadership for analysis.

Projective test.   A test that requires the test-taker to describe a picture or a relatively ambiguous stimulus such as an inkblot.

Prototype.   A person schema that represents general characteristics rather than concrete examples.

Punctuated equilibrium model.   A noncontinuous model of group development in which the group's behavior changes over the life of the job or project.

Punctuated equilibrium paradigm.   A paradigm that suggests that organizational change occurs as an alternation of long periods of stability and short periods of revolutionary change.

Punishment.   The process of eliminating an undesirable behavior by causing a negative event to follow that behavior.

Ratio schedule.   A schedule that applies reinforcers after a certain number of behaviors occur.

Rational process.   A step-by-step, systematic decision-making process.

Reciprocal interdependence.   A relationship of two groups whose operations precede and act as prerequisites to each other's.

Reengineering.   Identification of the core processes of an organization's business systems and reorganization of these systems so as to eliminate unnecessary processes and steps.

Reinforcement theory.   A motivational theory that assumes that encouragement of desired behaviors will cause them to be repeated.

Reinforcer.   A reward that encourages desired behavior.

Relations-oriented style.   A permissive, passive, and considerate style of leadership.

Relationship behaviors.   The communication behaviors of a leader—listening, supporting, facilitating, etc.

Relationship constellation.   A group of individuals from various departments in an organization who provide mutual support, friendship, and sponsorship.

Representativeness bias.   A heuristic whereby individuals judge an event in terms of their perception of its absolute frequency, ignoring its relative frequency.

Richness.   The amount of information that media convey and the amount of understanding that is thereby conveyed.

Role.   A prescribed set of activities or potential behavior.

Role ambiguity.   Lack of clarity about the expectations of a role.

Role conflict.   Differing and often incompatible expectations that pressure a role holder to perform in two different ways.

Role overload.   A situation in which a role player finds his or her role requires too much time, effort, or knowledge.

Role set.   Comparable or related roles that interact with each other.

Role-playing exercise.   A testing or training activity that has the test-taker act a role in a prespecified situation.

Safety and security needs.   An individual's desire for security or protection.

Salary.   A fixed yearly wage.

Sanction.   A coercive measure adopted to encourage agreement among group members and compliance with norms.

Satisfice.   To accept satisfactory choices rather than insist on optimal choices.

Schema.   A cognitive framework that includes descriptions of the characteristic features of people, situations, or objects obtained through experience.

Scientific management.   Frederick W. Taylor's theory of management as a science with managers and employees having clearly specified yet different responsibilities.

Script.   A schema about a sequence of events.

Self-actualization needs.   An individual's needs to grow and develop to the fullest possible degree.

Self-efficacy.   A person's perception that he or she can successfully perform a task.

Self-managed team.   A team in which the management responsibility is shared by all the team members.

Selling.   A leadership style in which the leader explains and clarifies decisions and persuades his or her employees to follow directions.

Sensing type.   A person who likes action and focuses on accomplishment.

Sequential interdependence.   A relationship that occurs when one group's operations precede and act as prerequisites for a second group's operations.

Sexual harassment.   A situation in which submitting to unwelcome sexual advances, requests for sexual favors, or other verbal or physical conduct of a sexual nature becomes a condition of a person's employment, is used as the basis for an employment decision, or interferes with a person's work performance by creating a hostile, intimidating, or offensive atmosphere.

Simulation.   A test that asks the test-taker to behave in a prespecified situation.

Single-loop organization.   An adaptive organization that uses routine learning to accomplish its ends without significant changes in its basic assumptions.

Skill-based pay.   Pay that rewards workers for building more competencies and increasing their skills.

Social comparison theory.   A theory based on the hypothesis that workers make judgments about job equity based on comparison to another worker in a similar position.

Social network analysis.   Evaluation of the pattern of interactions among organizational members.

Span of control.   The number of people who report to a manager.

Spatial differentiation.   Grouping of jobs or workers according to their geographical location.

Specialization.   The degree to which a job focuses on a specific and limited set of activities.

Standardization of outputs.   Employer specification of the exact nature of the workers' output.

Standardization of work processes.   Employer specification of the actual steps that employees should follow in performing their jobs.

Strategy.   A statement of an organization's basic mission, purpose, and goals as well as the means for accomplishing them.

Stress.   A psychological and physiological state that results when certain features of the environment cause discomfort, anxiety, or a feeling of being overwhelmed.

Stress interview.   A testing instrument that has the test-taker perform in a prespecified situation to test action under stress.

Stressor.   Environmental features that cause stress.

Structure.   The delineation of jobs and reporting relationships in an organization.

Surface strategy.   A strategy that deals with the external issues of workers.

System.   The representation of an organization as a set of interdependent subsystems in which inputs are transformed into outputs.

Systems theory.   A theory that represents an organization as an open system with such characteristics as openness, interrelatedness, the ability to transform inputs into outputs, the need to maintain equilibrium, multiplicity of goals, and equifinality.

Tactics.   Short-term, focused maneuvers of negotiators in a dispute.

Take-off stage.   The maturation stage of an organization that signals its movement from the entrepreneurial to the professional stage.

Tall organization.   A company with many levels in the hierarchy for its size.

Task activity.   Activities directed at performing the task.

Task behavior.   Actions in which a leader specifies an individual's or group's duties, activities, and responsibilities by goal setting, organizing, scheduling, directing, and controlling.

Task-oriented style.   A controlling, active, and structuring style of leadership.

Task relations.   The activities or processes that interdependent groups perform and the way these activities interrelate.

Task role.   A role that focuses on task or goal accomplishment.

Task structure.   The degree to which a task is clearly defined.

Team.   Work group that emphasizes collaboration in accomplishing the goal.

Team interdependence.   A relationship of multiple groups; a type of interdependence that has the most potential for conflict and the highest requirement for effective communication.

Technology.   The process that converts raw materials into a finished product or service.

Telecommuting.   Workers' use of information technology to perform their jobs at a site away from the organization's physical location.

Telling style.   A leadership style in which the leader guides, directs, establishes guidelines, gives specific instructions, and closely supervises performance.

Thematic Apperception Test (TAT). A test that measures the three needs of McClelland's theory of needs.

Theory X. A theory of leadership that assumes that people have an inherent dislike of work and responsibility.

Theory Y. A theory of leadership that assumes that people find work as natural as rest or play, will work toward their goals without supervision, and can learn to seek responsibility.

Thinking type. A person who excels at logic and responds to ideas more readily than to feelings.

Total Quality Management (TQM). A comprehensive approach to producing high-quality goods and services that meet customers' needs.

Total systems network. The communications patterns throughout an entire organization.

Traditionally managed team. A team with an official leader.

Trait. A personality, social, or physical characteristic.

Transformational change. A change effort by companies that have attempted to reinvent themselves.

Unattainable-ideal norm. A norm that remains always out of reach.

Valence. The value that a person attaches to various outcomes.

Value. A basic principle or tenet that guides a person's beliefs, attitudes, and behaviors.

Variable. The representation of a behavior, attitude, or event under study.

Variable reinforcer. A reinforcer that occurs at unpredictable and various times.

Vertical differentiation. Refers to the number of hierarchical levels in a company.

Virtual corporation. A network of independent suppliers, customers, and competitors usually tied together by computer technology.

Virtual employee. A worker who is connected to his or her office through computer networks.

Wellness program. A health promotion initiative in an organization.

Whisleblower. A worker who voices his or her views of fraudulent or illegal company activities by making them public, often by reporting them to government agencies.

Work group. Two or more people in a work setting with a common goal.

Work simplification. The process of reducing a job to its component parts and reassembling these parts into the most efficient work process.

World Wide Web. A collection of web sites that provides huge quantities of information about diverse topics.

Zero-defect product. A product that has no exceptions or defects.

Name Index

Subject Index